Insights into Child Development

Eighth Edition

by

Stanley K. Fitch

and

Mia Holland

 **CAT PUBLISHING**

ISBN 978-1-56226-646-2 Copyright 2011, 2008, 2007, 2006, 2005, 2004, 2000, 1999, 1998, 1997, 1996, 1995, 1992, CAT Publishing Company, Redding, California

This book is dedicated to my daughters Gina and Debbie, my sons William and Brian, to my wife Teresa, and in memory of my brother Judge Allan Henry Fitch.

Dr. Stanley K. Fitch

"I dedicate this work to the art of perserverance, commitment, and a lifelong passion for learning."

Dr. Mia Holland

About the Authors

Stanley Fitch began his formal schooling in Canada in the traditional one-room school, where one teacher taught all subjects for all eight grades. Dr. Fitch received his Bachelor's degree from United College (now University of Winnipeg) in Canada, where he majored in French, mathematics, and psychology. He received his doctorate in education from the University of Southern California, and has also studied in Belgium and England.

Dr. Fitch's writing career began as a sports writer in professional baseball, and he has also submitted feature stories to several newspapers. Dr. Fitch is also a methodologist and his research has been reported in the *Los Angeles Times*. Dr. Fitch is the author of two previous books, *Insights Into Human Behavior* (Holbrook Press, 1970, 1974) and *The Science of Child Development* (Dorsey Press, 1985). Dr. Fitch has testified numerous times in criminal courts as a legal and psychological expert.

Dr. Fitch has received international recognition for his accomplishments. One such recognition is from New Zealand: A nomination to the World Wide Academy of Scholars; another is "Men of Achievement — 1973" award from England. Recently, Dr. Fitch was selected to participate in the Oxford Round Table, a colloquium for academics, governmental, and business leaders from all over the world, held at Oxford University, England, for the past 800 years.

Dr. Mia Holland earned her Doctorate in Education from Florida's Nova Southeastern University in Child and Youth Studies. Her dissertation resulted in a statewide training for juvenile justice educators in Massachusetts and earned the national honor of Outstanding Applied Dissertation. Dr. Mia Holland's educational credentials also include an M.Ed. in Counseling from Bridgewater State University in Massachusetts, two years of additional graduate training in Clinical/Behavioral Psychology at the University of Massachusetts Dartmouth, and a B.A. in Psychology from the University of Massachusetts Dartmouth. Dr. Holland is Chair of the Studies in Human Behavior programs for Capella University in Minnesota. Dr. Holland is also a Doctoral Dissertation Chairperson and an Adjunct Faculty member for Nova Southeastern University's Fischler School of Education and Human Services. In Massachusetts, she is a Visiting Assistant Professor of Psychology for Bridgewater State University. Since 1990, Dr. Holland has worked with heterogeneous populations of children, adolescents, and adults in a variety of settings including institutions of higher education, state social service and juvenile justice agencies, psychiatric facilities, residential treatment facilities, and public school systems. She has provided consultative services to several state agencies and has managed a Massachusetts Education Opportunity Program grant. As a nationally recognized expert in the field of eating disorders, Dr. Holland has provided expert commentary in published pieces for MSNBC.com, iVillage Health, the "Therapy Times", and the "Baltimore Examiner". She has been an invited speaker at Harvard Medical School on the topic of Eating Disorders. Her specific research interests include eating disorders, identity development, psychological resilience, leadership theory, and curriculum development. Her personal interests include health and nutrition, leisure reading, and travel. She is also a certified personal fitness trainer. She is the developer and proprietor of Certified Nutrition and Wellness Center in New Bedford, Massachusetts. She is also a volunteer member of Habitat for Humanity.

Table of Contents

Chapter 2

PART TWO
Pregnancy And Birth

Chapter 3
Prenatal Development and Birth

PART THREE
Infancy and Toddlerhood -The First Three Years

Chapter 4
Physical Development in Infancy and Toddlerhood (0 to 3 years)

PART FOUR
Early Childhood 177

Chapter 7
Physical Development in Early Childhood (3 to 6 years) 179

Chapter 8
Cognitive Development in Early Childhood (3 to 6 years) **205**

Chapter 12

PART SIX

Chapter 13

Chapter 14

Chapter 15

PREFACE

This text represents a 25-year effort of continuous reading, writing, rewriting, and consultations with experts in child development. During this time, we have endeavored to keep up to date with the latest research, as well as with the trends in thinking in this most interesting field. Insights into Child Development represents our efforts to produce a text which is comprehensive and concise, yet reader friendly. We have relied on experts in the various fields in which child development is rooted in order to keep abreast of updates and growth in the field. In preparing this book, each of these specialists has given his or her approval to the material in this text which represents his or her field of expertise.

This edition of Insights into Child Development includes a significant revision in language and linguistic presentation of content. The major goal is to present language that is clearer and more concise and free of repetition. This seventh edition contains material that has been updated to 2010. For example, current information regarding global concerns, health issues, technological advances, societal influences, and an expansion of drug information (both legal and illicit) have been included in this edition.

Although the text is written for the introductory child psychology student, it is a rigorous portrayal of the science of child development. Throughout the text, there is a search for consistent relationships between the child's environment (causes) and his or her behavior (effects). To this end, the text presents many methods-which have received scientific verification-for studying children from conception until the end of adolescence. Finally, this text presents an in depth discussion of the principles and theories that apply specifically to children.

Orientation of the Book

This text contains several orientations. First, there is a practical orientation. The text includes many discussions of practical problems in child development and how to cope with these difficulties effectively. Using hypothetical child cases, Sarah and Carlos, the reader will be provided with an opportunity to discover how these practical problems are dealt with. Among the various practical issues presented in this text, the reader will learn how to deal with a child's quest for independence, experience with death, peer pressures, societal influences, and nutritional needs.

A second orientation of this text is theoretical. To understand child development better, we must not only become familiar with children's thinking and behavior, but also with theories which allow us to interpret these phenomena. There is no single theory which explains child development and therefore, this text will offer an array of well-researched theories that have been pivotal in the field. Hence, we have presented many competing theories in the hope that you will compare and contrast these theories and come to your own conclusions.

Since no single theory provides a comprehensive and widely accepted view of how children develop, research is needed to lend support, or to refute, any particular theoretical framework. If we have a theory that children become more self-sufficient as adults if they are given considerable independence, we need to conduct research to determine if such is indeed the case. This text provides several instances where research is used to help interpret various theories or to resolve inconsistencies among them.

Since all human beings are biologically evolving creatures, it should not surprise you that one of the orientations in Insights into Child Development is biological. Biological aspects are emphasized throughout the text in an attempt to demonstrate how a child's biological development is interrelated with his or her psychological growth.

Format of the Book

The format of the text captures the strengths of the age-stage (chronological) approach which includes five major stages of child development: Prenatal Development and Birth, Infancy and Toddlerhood, Early Childhood, Middle Childhood, and Adolescence. We have chosen this approach because it gives us an overall view of the child at particular points in development and provides the reader with a natural flow of child development from conception through adolescence. Within these stages, the child develops according to three domains of development: physical, cognitive, and social emotional. Therefore, for the stages of Infancy and Toddlerhood, Early Childhood, Middle Childhood, and Adolescence, this text will offer three separate chapters, each focusing on a specific domain of development.

Although a strong argument can be made for using the chronological approach, we realize that many instructors prefer the topical approach. For those who prefer this method, you may use the text in this order: Chapters 1, 2, and 3 (Basic Foundations of Child Development, Theories of Child Development, and Prenatal Development and Birth); Chapters 4, 7, 10, and 13 (Physical Development); Chapters 5, 8, 11, and 14 (Cognitive Development); and Chapters 6, 9, 12, and 15 (Social Emotional Development).

We are confident that this text will provide introductory child psychology readers with a clear, global, and informative foundation in the science of child development.

Learning Aids

I have provided several basic teaching and learning aids for the student. These include:

- Chapter Overview
- Marginal notations
- End-of-chapter summaries of major points
- End-of-chapter list of important terms, in alphabetical order
- Related readings for each chapter
- Related Website resources for each chapter
- Numerous illustrations and tables
- Material in boxes on special themes
- End-of-text glossary
- Bibliography
- Author and subject index
- Study guide
- Instructor's manual and test booklet

Acknowledgments

It is almost impossible for one person to produce a book of this magnitude. Among those to whom I would like to express my gratitude for their work and interest, in alphabetical order with their specialty in parentheses, are:

Mollie Aby (pediatric dietitian), Gregory Bonomo, M.D. (neurology), Wayne Bramstedt (anthropology), Andrée Brunetti, D.D.S. (dentistry), Judy Brusslan (genetics), Osoba Buki, (pharmacy), Santos Cortez, D.D.S. (pediatric dentistry), Steven Fasteau (student disabilities), Charles Fish, M.D. (medical genetics), Howard Hansen, M.D. (psychiatry), Diane M. Henschel (cognitive processes),William Hoanzl (learning disabilities), Noriko Horgan (history of education),Judith Isbell, R.N. (ultrasound), Thomas Kampwirth (tests and measurements),Vicki Lockridge (testing), Richard Mascolo (statistics),Rocco L. Motto, M.D. (psychoanalysis), Doris Okada (children's disabilities),Mark Sadoff, M.D. (neurology), Danny Shiri, D.D.S. (dentistry),Carl Slawsky (family structures), V. Katherine Townsend (nutrition),Arnold Wachs, M.D. (otorhinolaryngology), Stephan Waterworth (English),Mark Walch (grammar), Katherine White, M.D. (pediatrics), and Alvin S. Yusin, M.D. (pediatrics)

In addition, Dr. Stanley Fitch would like to thank several other people for their assistance: his daughter, Gina Famularo, Emeral W. Price, Gabriel Zamora, Pouya Mirzadeh, Patricia Lecumberry, Susana Puelles, and Jeremy Scott Mericle for their diligent work in editing the manuscript; librarian, Marian Kerr, for her assistance in obtaining information; and Nadine Hata, his dean at El Camino College, for her continual support and encouragement. He would also like to express his appreciation to Leslie Golden and the staff at CAT Publishing.

Stan Fitch

I would like to acknowledge those who have made a significant impression on my life.

To my godchild, Sariya. With her, I am reminded that love is unconditional and full of surprises. Time spent with her is a special gift. Thank you, Sariya, for helping me to become the best Auntie I can be.

To my little sister, McKensie, whose zest for life and fearlessness is inimitable. I am in awe of your perpetual smile, extraordinary sense of humor, and natural ability to love. You are a true spitfire. You are my hero in so many ways.

To my younger brother, Curry. Your sensitivity, insight, and keen observations are extraordinary gifts. Our bond is a unique one and I cherish it more than you will ever know. You have a very big heart and I am grateful to be in it.

To my father, Wayne, who instilled in me the drive, strength, and perseverance needed in a life filled with surprises and speed bumps. Because of you, Dad, I have approached every endeavor in my life with a sense of invincibility and courage. The word "impossible" is not in my vocabulary. Thank you for teaching me that I can do anything.

To my mother, Cindi, who dedicated herself to my early years with love, compassion, and selfless attention. Because of you, I have a caring heart and an innate ability to take care of others. Your "mom-isms" have been invaluable to me and continue to make me giggle when I use them. Thank you for treating me like the most important human being in the universe as a young girl.

To Reno -time spent with you at my feet (and sometimes lying across my laptop) while writing this book was a special gift. I miss you every single day and will never forget you.

To Manual DeSousa - you are the human epitome of love, strength, values, and compassion. Thank you for welcoming me into your life. I am amazed at the amount of love you surround everyone with.

To Paul DeSousa - You will never know how much you mean to me. I am so glad you are alive.

To Susan Boissoneault, Assistant Dean, Bristol Community College - thank you for the extraordinary confidence you had in me during my very first years of teaching at the college level. You were a pivotal contribution to my professional career.

To Dr. David Weintraub, EdD, my doctoral dissertation advisor at Nova Southeastern University. I am grateful for the special friendship we developed as a result of such an important chapter in my life. You will always be a dear friend.

To Dr. Morton Elfenbein, PhD, my undergraduate psychology honors thesis advisor at the University of Massachusetts. You were a fundamental change agent in my growth as a writer and I will forever appreciate your commitment and dedication.

To Miss Duckworth, my fourth grade teacher at historical Rogers School in Fairhaven, Massachusetts. Your support of me as an aspiring "geek", even at age 8, has never been forgotten. Thank you.

To all of the students I have taught in areas of psychology and child development over the years. With each course and each interaction with you, I learned - and for me, learning is a priceless gem.

And, to those who have touched my life in special ways - Isabella Medeiros (you will always be my little Chicken Nugget), Michaela Downey (you have always given me the best hugs), Sarah Downey (I adore you for your love of books and learning), David (thank you for always making me feel special - the birthday calls have always meant a great deal to me), Kathy (I am truly grateful for your support of my love for Sariya), Jocelyn Sherman, Sherri McIntyre, Steven Barthelmeus, Janet Brewer, Tony Bright, MaryEllen, and "Buddy".

To Dr. Stanley Fitch, PhD, whose foundational work on this book has made this edition possible. His contributions to the field of child development are seminal. His passing during this project was heartbreaking. I know his family will be happy to see it finished.

Dr. Mia Holland

PART ONE

INTRODUCTION, THEORIES, AND FOUNDATIONS OF CHILD DEVELOPMENT

Chapter 1

Basic Foundations in Child Development

Chapter Topics	**Learning Objectives**
Case Studies: Sarah and Carlos	Discuss the field of child development and its roots
Introduction: What is Child Development	Discuss the developmental domains and developmental stages of child development
The Three Domains of Child Development	Discuss the important issues and perspectives in development
Developmental Stages of Childhood	Review the research methods and ethical considerations inherent in the study of children
The Scientific Study of Children	
Chapter Summary	

Typical or average child: A composite of all children within the typical range for their gender, at a given age of development.

Atypical child: A child below or above the typical/average child of its gender, at a given age of development.

Case Studies: Sarah and Carlos

Throughout this book, you will be reading stories about Sarah and Carlos. Sarah and Carlos' development will help you to understand the themes, principles, and concepts of child development as they would apply to *typically* and *atypically* developing children.

Sarahs' stories will be based upon a fictional female, Caucasian child who was born in an urban area and is an only child. Carlos' stories will be based upon a fictional male child born into a suburban family of two female siblings, a Caucasian mother and a Latino father.

INTRODUCTION: WHAT IS CHILD DEVELOPMENT?

Child development: A pattern of physical, cognitive, and psychosocial change that involves growth that begins at conception and continues until adulthood is reached at about age 18.

Developmental psychology: A branch of general psychology that is concerned with changes from conception until death.

Child development is a pattern of physical, cognitive, and social emotional change that involves growth beginning at conception and continuing until about age 18. This pattern of development is intricate, interconnected, and can be understood from many perspectives.

To understand the underpinnings of child development, we must first look at *developmental psychology*. Developmental psychology is a branch of general psychology that is concerned with the process of human change from conception until death. More specifically, developmental psychology is concerned with the orderly and sequential changes that occur with the passage of time as an organism (human or lower animal) develops from conception until death. It involves biologically programmed processes that change the organism through interaction with the environment. In essence, developmental psychology is concerned with the physical, cognitive, and social emotional changes that take place across the life span. The more distinct field of child development exists within developmental psychology and focuses on the first 18 years or so of an individual's lifespan.

The Roots of Child Development

Child development is a complex field and draws from a variety of disciplines: biology, sociology, and anthropology. Let's look briefly at each of these fields.

Biology

Biology is the science of life and is concerned with living things and their structure, function, evolution, and relation to the environment. Biology is also concerned with the physical changes that take place as an organism grows to maturity. Sciences concerned with the structure, function, and development of organisms, such as anatomy, physiology, nutrition, and embryology are all part of biology. Also including biology is the science of genetics, which attempts to identify how various characteristics are transmitted from one generation to the next. Of particular interest lately are the biological roots of intelligence and personality characteristics such as worry, creativity, and optimism. In summary, the biological perspective focuses on how bodily events (e.g., electrical impulses that shoot along the intricate pathways of the nervous system or hormones that course through the bloodstream) affect behavior, feelings, and thoughts.

Sociology

Sociology is the scientific study of human relationships, with special emphasis on groups and the environment. A sociologist may study the evolution of the family as it existed at different times, for example in 1900 and then in 2010. Or, the sociologist might study marriage practices, the number of children per family, and child rearing practices in rural and in urban environments. The sociologist may also try to identify the forces that hold families together or weaken them, as well as the conditions that cause families to change with time.

Anthropology

Anthropology (from Greek *anthropos*, "human") integrates the biological, social, and cultural dimensions of humanity from the very beginning to the present. It deals with human evolutionary development, group interactions, and cultural traditions in both primitive and civilized societies. Anthropology helps reveal that many of our beliefs about human behavior derive from, and are limited to, our contemporary society. It also provides a broader perspective with which to view child development.

WHY STUDY CHILD DEVELOPMENT?

Scientists and practitioners study child development for three major reasons: 1) to obtain a profile of the typical child at various ages; 2) to understand why behaviors and events occur at various stages; and, 3) to predict future behaviors and events.

  The first major reason for studying child development is to obtain a profile of the typical child at various ages. In other words, we want to know what is the "normal," or expected, development of children. By studying the normal and expected development of a child, we can also determine what is atypical or abnormal. Normative information answers questions such as, "How early does a child normally begin to walk?" and "How much does a 3-year-old typically weigh?" These overt traits are relatively easy to measure and represent information relative to the physical development of a child. During the past 50 years, there has been increased emphasis on studying "inner" characteristics, or social emotional characteristics, such as anxiety and motivation which can only be assessed indirectly. Questions that inquire about these types of characteristics in child development may be, "When does a child begin to understand that a parent who leaves the room is going to come back?" and "How early does a child begin to feel sad when a parent leaves the room?" Studying these types of questions is important in gaining an understanding of the social emotional development of a child.

  When we are studying the "profile" of typical children at various ages, we often use *norms*. Norms are statistical standards involving averages derived from research of a large, representative sample of a given population. By using norms, we can determine when the average child learns to walk. We can also use norms with superior children—for instance, to determine when the typical bright child learns to read. We can also note serious developmental delays using norms. If an infant is far behind the norm, the parent is alerted to a possible developmental problem. One investigator who relied heavily on norms to

Norm: The standard or average for a specific trait, generally obtained by measuring a large specific group of people.

identify the ages at which different forms of behavior emerge was Arnold Gesell, a child developmentalist.

Second, having described what types of characteristics and behavior occur in children, child developmentalists want to know *why* these behaviors and events occur. Why can most children say a word by 12 months? Why do children differ in IQ? Why are some newborn babies so placid, while others are so irritable?

Finally, the *prediction* of future behaviors and events is also of interest to the field of child development. We can predict that the child who feels good about himself or herself (possesses high self-esteem), does well in school, and has many friends, will likely do well in the future. Conversely, we can predict that the child who has low self-esteem, has few friends, and is doing poorly in school, may become a high school dropout, or even join a delinquent gang. This brings us to the next step in studying child development—modifying behavior.

If a child has low self-esteem, does poorly in school, and cannot make friends because he or she is not receiving enough love and attention at home, we need to take steps to provide the child with these necessities. We might try to encourage the caregiver to be more nurturing or, in some cases, recommend that the child undergo some sort of counseling or therapy.

THE THREE DEVELOPMENTAL DOMAINS OF CHILD DEVELOPMENT

As you study changes in Sarah and Carlos you will see that these developments can be grouped into three specific areas, or domains: Physical, Cognitive, and Social Emotional. These domains overlap and interact with each other throughout life, and an imbalance or dysfunction in one domain affects the others.

Let us review these domains.

- *Physical domain - bodily changes and the acquisition of motor skills.*

- *Cognitive domain - thought, language, and morals.*

- *Social emotional domain - emotions, personality, and social relationships.*

Physical Development
Physical development includes growth and development in height and weight as well as increases in sensory capacities, motor abilities, and brain growth. Toward the end of elementary school, dramatic physical and hormonal changes of puberty have a large impact on the child's self-concept. The physical changes we will see in Sarah and Carlos follow a certain pattern or sequence.

Cognitive Development
Children undergo remarkable changes in their cognitive abilities (e.g. IQ, language, problem solving). These changes are particularly evident when children enter school. From the moment children enter school, they learn vocabulary at an ever-faster pace, they retain more information, and there are changes in the manner in which they learn information and solve problems.

Social Emotional Development

As they develop, Sarah and Carlos begin to differentiate themselves from their mother and father and develop attitudes about themselves (self-concept). From preschool on, peers play an important role in the lives of children, while the home continues to be important. Throughout childhood—as well as adulthood—there is a search for identity, a sense of self and who one is.

You are no doubt aware that the three domains we have just mentioned do not develop separately, nor are they totally distinct. These domains overlap and interact with each other throughout life. An imbalance or dysfunction in one domain affects the others. When Sarah is physically or emotionally upset, her thinking and schoolwork suffer. If she remains upset for any length of time, she may eat less and lose weight. Sarah may then begin to worry about her health, and her relations with her family may deteriorate, causing her to become more upset.

DEVELOPMENTAL STAGES OF CHILDHOOD

Developmental stage: A unique developmental period that occurs during particular times in a child's life, and is qualitatively different from that of earlier and later stages.

A *developmental stage* is a unique developmental period that occurs during a particular time in a child's life. The concept of a developmental stage also implies that a particular capability or behavior pattern predominates during a specific span of time. For instance, in Freud's oral stage (birth to about 1 year of age), babies are particularly sensitive to close interactions with caregivers. In later stages, children become increasingly sensitive to other people. A developmental stage is marked by a period of fairly sudden changes, followed by a period of consolidation. As an example, a child reaches adolescence at about age 12 to 14 after a variety of quick, dramatic changes (in height and weight, for instance), then remains an adolescent for several years. Each developmental stage is distinctly different from any other stage. The six developmental stages of child development are: Prenatal, Infancy and Toddlerhood, Middle, Adolescence, and Emerging Adulthood.

Prenatal Stage (Conception to birth)

The prenatal stage refers to the period from conception until the start of labor. This stage represents the period of greatest physical growth. During this period, the basic body structures and organs are formed. This rapid development enables the unborn baby to use all of its senses and to become capable of learning. A major concern is the various pollutants or teratogens (e.g. radiation, infection, and drugs) which can harm the baby while it is still in the womb.

Infancy and Toddlerhood (Birth to 3 years)

During this period, the baby progresses from an almost totally dependent child to one capable of moving about on its own, using a rudimentary form of language, and developing a sketchy idea of who he or she is (also known as self-concept). During the first 3 years of life, the child forms an attachment to its caregiver, and is able to make many discriminations among things in the environment.

Early Childhood (3 to 6 years)

During this developmental stage, language acquisition is accelerated and becomes more important in a child's life. Children are now able to communicate more effectively with their parents and peers. Their play involves considerable imagination. By about age 3, children become quite independent. Also, by 3 years of age, children begin to reflect many of the influences of their culture—their manner of talking, their walking, and their relations with others are often a duplicate of their parents' or caregivers' behaviors.

Middle Childhood (6 to 12 years)

From age 6 to 12 years, the child's major preoccupation is elementary school. Children can now profit from formal education, and peer interactions become very important, although the family continues to play a major role. Physical agility improves during this period, and children are now much more capable of fine, coordinated movements due to development of the brain.

Adolescence (12 to 18 years)

Puberty: A collection of physical/biological changes, such as the growth of breasts and testes and hormone production, culminating in the ability to reproduce sexually .

The greatest change in early adolescence is *puberty*, a collection of physical/ biological changes, such as the growth of breasts and testes and hormone production, culminating in the ability to reproduce sexually. The physical and emotional changes occurring during adolescence have a profound effect on the adolescent's identity, which is the most important psychological concern during this period.

Cognitive changes in adolescence allow children to engage in abstract thought, enabling them to expand their intellectual horizons to the world of possibilities and to reach new levels of morality. Adolescents are no longer confined to the real world since they can operate logically on symbols. For instance, they can envision a world that is different from, and better than, the one in which they live.

Emerging Adulthood (18 to about 25 years)

Emerging adulthood is a relatively new developmental stage that warrants attention. This is the period of time encompassing the range between age 18 and the first part of the 20s. Adolescence has ended but the full responsibilities and tasks of adulthood have yet to be assumed. For example, the emerging adult may be living away from home at college and not yet financially separate from his/ her parents.

PRINCIPLES AND ISSUES IN CHILD DEVELOPMENT

Throughout this book several themes are repeated. These themes represent issues and principles essential to the understanding of child development. These include: Critical or Sensitive Periods in Development; Continuous vs. Discontinuous Development; and, Nature vs. Nurture.

Critical or Sensitive Periods in Child Development

Critical period: A specific span of time in development when an event will have its greatest impact.

The concept of *critical periods* in child development is borrowed from biology. A critical period is a specific span of time in development when an event will have its greatest impact. The impact can be positive or negative and is often irreversible.

Experts have noted that there is a critical period for learning language in children, particularly grammar. The critical period is from birth to about age 12 years. Children who have been isolated for years, such as in an extreme case of abuse where a child is locked in a closet until age12, are seldom able to master grammar beyond that of a 2-year-old, even with intensive language training and integration into society (Grimshaw *et al.*, 1998; Rymer, 1993).

Sensitive period: A best time for learning a particular task.

The concept of *sensitive periods* is also accepted in the field of child development. The word "sensitive" suggests there is a best time for learning a particular task; but it may also be learned later, although with greater difficulty. Thus, children of 4 or 5 years who are new to a country learn to speak the new language sooner and with less of an accent than their parents who arrived during adulthood.

Continuous vs. Discontinuous Development

Discontinuous development: Changes in amounts like height or weight (the beginning and end of a particular change).

Discontinuous development reflects change that is *"more of the same,"* or a change in amounts such as height, weight, and size of vocabulary. Discontinuous development is fairly straightforward and relatively easy to measure. At birth, for example, the typical baby weighs slightly more than 7 pounds; at 1 year, about 21 pounds; at 2 years, approximately 27 pounds. Similarly, we can measure children's vocabulary expansion using a discontinuous standard: Babies utter their first word at about 12 months; they have a vocabulary of about 250 words at age 2; and their vocabulary is generally in excess of 2,000 words at 5 years of age.

Continuous development: Generally a gradual, continuous process of altering or modifying development where the precise beginning and end is ambiguous.

Continuous development is more difficult to assess, sometimes involving stages or "leaps," but generally it is a gradual, continuous process. Let's take continue with physical development as an example. The child's body changes slowly, with the exception of puberty, and barring accident or disease. There is a continuous difference between the 6-month-old baby who is unable to speak effectively and the 3-year-old who is making her wishes and demands known to all around her. Similarly, the motor abilities of a 7-year-old differ in kind from those of the 2-year-old. The older child is able to perform feats such as skipping that are beyond the capability of the 2-year-old. Even motor abilities, such as walking and throwing an object, differ between any two successive stages of development.

One of the most striking examples of continuous change in child development occurs during the first few weeks after conception when cells that are structurally alike take on specialized forms and functions. One group of cells will develop into the embryo, the term applied during weeks 3 through 8 of prenatal development. By the end of the eighth week of gestation, all of the vital organs (heart, lungs, liver, etc.) will be formed. Thus, what began as a one-celled entity, the zygote, is now a fundamentally different organism than it was a few weeks earlier.

Nature: All of the biological and genetic influences and factors that affect the development of a child, positively and/or negatively.

Nurture: The environmental, social, cultural, and familial influences that affect child development.

Nature vs. Nurture

Nature vs. *nurture* is a long held controversy about the influences on child development. Nature represents all of the biological and genetic influences and factors that affect the development of a child, positively and/or negatively. Nurture, on the other hand, represents all of the environmental, social, cultural, and familial influences that affect child development.

For example, the genetic makeup of a child is known to specifically influence hair color, eye color, and height. These characteristics are determined by the "nature" of the child's genetic code. The child's decision to wear certain types of clothing, on the other hand, is thought to be influenced by social pressures (nurture). The controversy becomes weighted when looking at personality traits. It can be supported by both sides of this debate that personality characteristics, such as aggressiveness or shyness, can be influenced by nature and nurture. While there is no steadfast answer to the nature vs. nurture debate, it is important to consider both as you study the field of child development.

THE SCIENTIFIC STUDY OF CHILDREN

There are several methods of gathering information in the field of child development. Each has its own guidelines and premises and are worthy of discussion. These methods include: systematic observation (naturalistic and structured); case study/clinical method; interview method; experiment; and correlational research (quasi experiment).

Table 1.1 offers a brief description of each method along with strengths and limitations for each.

Systematic Observation

Observation is the most common method of studying children. Observation is employed by parents, psychologists, educators, and researchers. The majority of research on the acquisition of and development of language in children, for instance, uses observation as the source of information (Nippold & Scott, 2010; Corrigan, 1982).

One advantage of observation is that investigators can see the behaviors they hope to explain directly. If our observation of children is to serve a useful purpose, we must first make several decisions. Will we try to observe every movement a child makes, or should we focus on one specific behavior, such as the child's smiling? Should we observe more than one child at a time?

To make observations more accurate, psychologists observe and record data in a systematic manner. For example, all students could be observed for aggressive acts such as hitting, shoving, and name-calling. The data should be gathered objectively so that the observer's prejudices and wishful thinking play a negligible part in the observation.

The first recorded observational studies of children were those of biologist Charles Darwin and the German physiologist Wilhelm Preyer in the nineteenth century. Since these early beginnings, many different types of observation techniques have been employed to study children. Let's look at a two of them: naturalistic and structured.

Table 1.1

Comparison of Major Research Methods

Type	Main Characteristics	Strong Points	Weak Points
Naturalistic Studies	Children observed in normal setting.	Normal setting makes it less likely that the behavior will be distorted.	Does not explain behavior or determine cause and effect.
Biographical Method	Note taking—either casual or incidental—about a child (e.g., when she spoke her first word or sat unassisted).	Observations are continuous, lessening the chances of overlooking significant features of development.	Lack of objectivity. Does not explain cause-and-effect relationships.
Case Studies	In-depth study of a subject with psychological problems to determine background, medical history, or current behavior.	A large amount of material is obtained about one subject.	Because the subject has psychological problems, information must be applied to the general population with caution.
Clinical Method	Combination of observation and individualized questioning developed by Piaget for use with children.	Flexibility allows researcher to tailor questions to each child.	Quality of interview varies with skill of researcher. Difficult to duplicate because of individualized approach.
Interview Method	Subjects questioned in depth about life experiences or opinions on selected topics. Physical exams, intelligence tests, and questionnaires may be used.	Subjects can be questioned on a wide variety of issues.	Subjects may forget certain information or purposely distort it.
Experiment	Manipulation of an environmental condition, process, or event (independent variable) to observe its effect on some behavior, event, or condition (dependent variable).	Establishes cause-and-effect relationship; tight controls make replication possible.	Narrow focus of experiments makes findings difficult to apply to other segments of the population.
Correlational Research: Quasi Experiments	Seeks to establish the degree of relationship, if any, between two characteristics being studied.	Determines if two variables are related, in which direction, and to what degree.	Does not show cause and effect.

Naturalistic observation: Observation of subjects in natural surroundings, often without the subjects being aware of the presence of the investigator.

Normative information: The average age or grade that different forms of behavior can be expected to emerge in normal children.

Structured observation: Observations in a laboratory or clinical settings where the conditions are manipulated and controlled (unlike the "naturalistic" setting).

Naturalistic observation. In the naturalistic approach, children are studied through observation in their natural surroundings, such as the home, school, or playground. No effort is made to manipulate the children or change their environment (Allen, 2000). Usually, the children are not aware that they are being observed. Thus, their normal activities are less likely to change.

Naturalistic observations provide us with *normative information*, for example, the average age at which different forms of behavior can be expected to emerge. Either a single child or a group of children can be observed at the same time. Naturalistic observation is central to a discipline known as ethology, which seeks to understand lower animal behavior through careful observation of species in their natural habitats such as Jane Goodall's research on chimpanzee's social behavior.

Naturalistic observations are also conducted by ecologists studying the relationships between an organism such as the child and environmental systems such as the family and community, as well as the relationships among environmental systems themselves, (e.g., the home, the school). For example, children who have been abused at home will often do poorly in school. Thus, we need to study both systems to obtain a more complete picture of the child's development (Bronfenbrenner & Morris, 1998).

Structured observation. Structured observation is similar to naturalistic observation in terms of the intent to collect a wealth of information regarding a child. However, the significant difference lies in the setting in which the observation occurs. Structured observations occur in laboratory or clinical settings where the conditions are manipulated and controlled (unlike the "naturalistic" setting). For example, a structured observation could occur in a therapist's play room that includes several specific toys and/or props with which the children would play. The observer/researcher would look specifically at how the children played with or interacted with the toys, noting how boys and girls play with gender specific toys (e.g., dump trucks or dolls). The observer/researcher could look at differences in how boys and girls interact with the different gender specific toys to elicit themes and patterns.

Case Study

Case studies usually describe the background and current behavior of a single individual, family, or group with psychological problems (Whitley, 1996). Information about the individual is obtained through observation, interviews, and writings (such as letters). Often psychological tests are administered to determine the child's intellectual and emotional status. Much of Freudian theory—which is rooted in abnormal behavior—is based on case studies.

Case study: A method of obtaining information about an individual through interviews, observations, and writings.

A major strength of the case study is the large amount of material that is obtained about one particular child. This enhances the chances of proper diagnosis and treatment. However, because the subjects are usually severely maladjusted, or *pathological*, any conclusions drawn from their case studies should be applied to the general population with caution (Leary, 2004).

Pathological: related to or caused by disease; disordered in behavior

A major limitation of case studies is their heavy reliance on a person's memories and reconstructions of events; these are frequently distorted or incomplete. Another shortcoming of case studies is the common discrepancy between parent and child reports of negative pediatric life stressors such as divorce, cancer, and death (Johnston *et al.*, 2003).

Piaget's clinical method is considered a type of case study method.

Piaget's clinical method. The *clinical method* is closely associated with Jean Piaget, the Swiss psychologist. This case study method combines observation with careful, individual questioning. The questioning is open-ended and modified throughout the interview. The child's initial response serves as a basis for the next question. Thus, no two subjects are questioned in exactly the same way.

Piaget's clinical method: A type of interview in which the researcher attempts to understand the unique, individual child by using flexible, open-ended questions.

Typically, Piaget would observe what a child said or did in a particular situation and then attempt to understand the reason for the child's response or behavior. Often, Piaget was more interested in the child's incorrect answers, since he believed that these responses provide a clue to the way the child reasons. Below is a sample of the typical questioning Piaget used, in this case to determine whether the child, Gui (aged 4 years, 4 months), believes that items in a row are more plentiful than the same number of items in a pile. Gui has just been asked to exchange six pennies in a row for six flowers in a pile.

Piaget: "What have we done?"
Gui: "We exchanged them," indicating that he recognizes what has happened.
Piaget: "Then is there the same number of flowers and pennies?"
Gui: "No," indicating that Gui does not understand that nothing has been added to, or subtracted from, the pennies or the flowers.
Piaget: "Are there more on one side?"
Gui: "Yes."
Piaget: "Where?"
Gui: "There," pointing to the row of pennies.

On the basis of this questioning, it appears that Gui thinks that there are more items when they are spread out in a row than when the same number of items are stacked in a pile. To be more certain that this confusion exists in Gui's mind, Piaget asks more questions after setting the flowers in a row and the pennies in a pile.

Piaget: "Where are there more?"
Gui: "Here," pointing to the row of flowers.
Piaget: "And here," pointing to the pile of pennies.
Gui: "Less."

An important feature of the clinical method is the use of language that a particular child understands. This often necessitates changing to the language the child uses spontaneously. Each child is asked the same basic questions, but the reply determines the next question. This kind of flexible questioning, tailor-made for each child, often elicits surprising answers that would be difficult to obtain by any other strategy. However, the clinical method is not without its drawbacks.

A major drawback of Piaget's clinical method is the dependence on the skill of the interviewer. The clinical method works best if the interviewer is imaginative and perceptive. Also, the flexibility of the questioning makes it difficult for other investigators to come up with the same results. Any findings obtained about a particular child should be considered tentative, and can be accepted only after they have been corroborated by other researchers.

Interview Method

The interview method: A self-report method for collecting data in which the individual being studied (or assessed) answers questions in an oral dialogue.

This face-to-face method is a "self-report" strategy in which subjects are questioned in depth about their life experiences, attitudes, or opinions about a certain issue. The issue might include the subjects' sexual activity, occupational goals, or work habits in school. The interview technique may be combined with physical examinations, intelligence tests, or personality measures.

A well-known interview of children was conducted by Robert Sorenson (1973). Sorenson contacted 2,042 households, randomly selected from a nationwide sample of 20 city, or suburban neighborhoods and rural locations in 103 areas of the continental United States. The subjects included 411 boys and girls who filled out lengthy questionnaires. An additional 200 adolescents, representing a cross section of 13- to 19-year-olds, were interviewed at length. The purpose of the study was to learn about adolescents' attitudes and behaviors, mostly about their sexuality. Because the study involved sensitive and personal information, parental permission was obtained to interview the subjects.

A problem with the interview method is the high likelihood of inaccuracies. Often, interviewees cannot remember details about a past event. In some instances, interviewees purposely distort their replies to appear more acceptable to the inter-viewers.

Experiment

Manipulation: to manage or influence

Independent variable: A quality or characteristic that is manipulated by the researcher in an experiment by randomly assigning subjects to treatment conditions.

Variable: A quality or characteristic that scientists measure or manipulate in an experiment.

Dependent variable: The quality or characteristic the researcher expects to be influenced by the independent variable in an experiment.

Experimental group: Subjects that undergo some change in their environment and are then measured to determine the effect of the change.

Control group: Subjects similar to those in the experimental group but they are not manipulated by a researcher.

Random sampling: A control technique, such as flipping a coin, to assign subjects to a particular group in an experiment to eliminate bias.

A distinct feature of the experimental method is treatment or *manipulation* of an environmental condition, process, or event (known as the *independent variable*). A *variable* is a concept that can vary in at least two ways. For example, the variable "gender" can be *male* or *female*. Manipulation refers to the ability of the researcher to isolate, control, and systematically vary a particular factor in the environment. The purpose of manipulation is to determine the effect of the independent variable on some behavioral event or response (the *dependent variable*), while holding all other variables constant.

Let's suppose we design an experiment to determine whether infants who receive special handling (picked up more, smiled at more, and massaged) develop faster than those who receive normal care. Our independent variable would be the extra care, and the outcome (babies' development) would be the dependent variable.

The experimental and control groups. Because most babies continue to develop (as long as they survive), we need to devise a way to determine whether the progress made by the babies who receive special handling is due in part to the extra attention given to them. To do this, we need two groups of children. One of the groups, called *experimental*, receives the extra care, while another group, the *control*, receives routine care.

Now suppose that most of the babies who received the special handling (experimental group) show greater gains in development (they weigh more, and are more active, etc.) than the control babies. What conclusions can we draw? Can we say that the extra care is responsible for the greater progress of the experimental babies? The answer is, "We don't know." The experimental babies could have made greater progress because they were healthier. Or, they could have been more mature. To eliminate such confusion, we need *controls*. One type of control is random sampling.

Random sampling. Randomness means that each subject has an *equal chance* of being included in either the control or in the experimental group (Shaughnessy, Zechmeister, & Zechmeister, 2003). One way to do this is to put all the names of the participants in a hat and then place all the even-numbered draws (second, fourth, sixth, etc.) in one pile and the odd-numbered draws (first, third, fifth, etc.) in another pile, and then arbitrarily call one pile "experimental" and the other pile "control," or vice versa. Using the technique of *random sampling*, we can be reasonably certain that the control and experimental groups are approximately the same with regard to weight, health, and other relevant factors. Because the two groups of babies are approximately the same at the beginning of our experiment, we can then say that any difference in the babies' development at the end of the experiment is *likely* due to the independent variable—the extra care.

An advantage of experimental studies is that they allow us to make assumptions about cause-and-effect relationships. Furthermore, the findings of an experimental study can be verified by replicating the original study.

Despite their strengths, experimental studies have limitations for use with children. A major drawback involves the nature of the information we are seeking. Very often, we want to find out the effects of unpleasant or stressful experiences on children—malnutrition, parental fighting, or rejection by peers.

For ethical reasons, we cannot assign children arbitrarily to an experimental group for the purpose of under-feeding them or subjecting them to some other form of deprivation and then study their progress.

CORRELATIONAL RESEARCH QUASI EXPERIMENT

Correlational research: A quasi form of experiment to determine the strength of a relationship and the direction between two conditions.

In *correlational research*, the main purpose is to determine the degree, or strength, of a relationship and the direction (positive or negative) between two variables. For instance, we might want to find out if children who receive more attention from their parents do better in school. If we found such a relationship, we could say that there is a positive correlation (but not necessarily cause and effect) between the additional attention the children received from their parents and their school performance.

A correlation tells us that two factors or events seem to be related in a systematic way. As tempting as it is, we cannot assume causality when two events or characteristics are correlated. However, the more strongly two events are correlated (or associated), the more effectively we can predict one event from the other (Whitley, 2002).

Correlations also tell us the extent or degree to which two measures are related to one another. The degree of a systematic relationship (correlation) between two variables is measured numerically and can vary from +1.00 through 0.00 to −1.00. A correlation of +1.00 indicates a perfect positive relationship when we compare two sets of variables, such as height and weight. If the correlation is +1.00, then the tallest person weighs the most, the next tallest the next most, until we get to the shortest person, who weighs the least. A correlation of -1.00 would mean exactly the opposite. The tallest person would weigh the least, the next tallest the next least, with the shortest person weighing the most. A correlation of 0.00 means that there is no relationship, such as between the color of a person's eyes and his or her height or weight.

Significate: A term used by Piaget for the actual object or event represented by a signifier.

Very few correlations are perfect (either +1.00 or −1.00). Most relationships studied in child development are between 0.00 and ±1.00. We usually look for *significant* correlations or associations. A significant association of say +.80 or +.90 means that the same results would be highly likely if the study were repeated, technically called replication.

The statistic (+ 1.00, -1.00, etc.) that measures the direction and strength of the relation between two variables is called a correlation coefficient.

The most serious drawback of correlational research is its failure to indicate the cause of a relationship. We cannot assume that a correlation of +.80 between parental fighting and children's aggression means that the parents' bickering has resulted in their children's aggression. Nor can we say that if a correlation exists between the stress and illness of a person, that the stress causes the illness. Both the stress and the illness could be the result of another factor such as poor general health, racial discrimination, or poverty. Correlational studies cannot generate the kinds of conclusions that controlled experimental studies produce. Although researchers can examine relationships (correlations) among factors being studied, they cannot draw conclusions about causes and effects.

Choosing a Method to Study Children

You have just reviewed some of the methods to studying children. You may wonder how researchers decide which method to use. Here are some guidelines. First, regardless of which method is used, the results will be of little value if the data are not collected and recorded carefully. Second, each method has certain strengths and weaknesses. All results must be regarded as tentative. They should be verified by duplicate studies—the more the better.

RESEARCH PERSPECTIVES

One of the considerations in studying children is the way in which data are collected. Should the same children be measured more than once so that researchers can see changes in their development with age? Should children of different ages be measured once on a dependent variable? Should both methods be combined? We can gain some insight if we study the *longitudinal, cross-sectional*, and *mixed* designs.

Longitudinal Design: Follow the Children

Longitudinal design: A research technique that involves repeated observations of the same group of subjects over an extended period.

Sarah's mother is beside herself. She wants to place her six-month-old daughter in day care but is concerned about the effects such placement might have later. One way to make such an assessment is a longitudinal study which involves repeated observations of the same group of subjects over an extended period. To study the effects of day care, researchers might use two groups of children—experimental and control. The experimental children are those placed in day care; the control children are raised by their parents at home.

The families of experimental and control children should be similar on such characteristics as socioeconomic level (education, income, and occupation), current marital status, attitudes toward child rearing, and ethnicity. The major difference between the two groups of children would be day care versus home care by parents. As the study progresses—for four, five, or ten years—researchers would interview the parents and assess the children's emotional adjustment, social skills, and cognitive development. Each assessment would allow the researchers to assess how the two groups are developing.

One of the most ambitious and best-known longitudinal studies was conducted by Lewis Terman (1877 – 1956) of Stanford University. Terman's classic study (begun in 1921 and still in progress) was designed to explore the characteristics of gifted children. Giftedness was defined in terms of academic talent (the top 2 percent) and measured by the score on an intelligence test, called an intelligence quotient, or IQ. The IQs ranged from about 140 to more than 190. Without a doubt, these children ("Termites" as they called themselves) were an elite group. Terman's study involved 857 boys and 671 girls from the larger public school systems in California, with an average age of 11 years at the time of identification (Terman, 1925).

Using the longitudinal approach, Terman was able to disprove many misperceptions about highly intelligent individuals. For instance, Terman discovered that his intellectual subjects not only excelled academically (as expected), but were also more mature emotionally and socially than their less gifted peers, and were superior physically. Terman disproved the popular myth, "early ripe, early rot," meaning that highly intelligent children are subject to later physical, psychological, and social problems both as children and as adults. A major advantage of the longitudinal method is that it gives a truer reflection of the process of development. A disadvantage is the long period of time that must pass—often several years—before the results are available. Another disadvantage is the monetary consideration. It is usually quite expensive to carry on a study for several years. There is also the problem of subject loss due to death or change of residence.

Cross-Sectional Design

.**Cross-sectional design:** A research method that examines subjects of different ages at one point in time.

Most studies of children are conducted one time by comparing groups of children of different ages who share important characteristics such as education, socio-economic status and ethnicity. This method, called *cross-sectional*, has generated most of our normative, descriptive data on age-related growth patterns in children. Many studies of memory development in children (as well as in adults) have been carried out using cross-sectional designs. This research technique consists of observing the participants (subjects) during a limited time span, or only once.

To study the development of memory, using chronological age as an independent variable, one might first test how samples of 4-year-olds, 10-year-olds, and 16-year-olds (known as cohorts) remember a list of familiar words. By comparing how children of different ages go about remembering their tasks and what the results of their efforts are, we can arrive at an explanation of developmental changes in memory.

Some of the advantages of the cross-sectional design are readily apparent. The design takes less time and is less expensive than the longitudinal approach because several age levels can be sampled at the same time. The limited time commitment makes it less likely that participants will drop out of the study. Also, it is easier to recruit subjects for the study because of its limited duration.

Cohort: A group of persons of approximately the same age who have had similar major life experiences, such as cultural training, economic conditions, and education.

Despite these attractive features, cross-sectional designs have drawbacks. The most serious limitation is that subjects in a particular group may differ in more than just age. Suppose we want to compare the memories of 8-year-olds with 18-year-olds about their first year in school. We would likely find a difference between the two groups. But are these differences due to age alone or to different life experiences as well? If the older group entered the first grade when there were a series of mass murders in their neighborhood, their memories of first grade could be quite different than those of the *cohort* (children of roughly the same age) that was not affected by such tragedy.

Cohort effect: The effect on people of a given age by historical forces unique to the time in which they lived.

Typically, if the age difference between cohorts is not great (2 or 3 years), different life experiences do not pose a problem, known as *cohort effect*, as in cohorts with age differences of 15 or 20 years who grew up in quite different worlds. Cross-sectional studies should be used only to the extent that the subjects are equivalent, except for the factor of age.

Mixed design: The same individuals are tested more than once.

Mixed Design

Mixed design is repetitive testing of the same individuals over a short period of time (weeks or months) and includes an experimental component. Longitudinal design consists of repetitive testing over several or many years. In an attempt to overcome the drawbacks of both the longitudinal and the cross-sectional designs, the *mixed* design is used. In the mixed method, the same individuals are tested more than once. The differences that arise over a period of time for different groups of subjects (cohorts) are then measured. The mixed design also has its drawbacks. It is quite complicated and expensive. A greater criticism is the possibility of over-looking major influences in development between testings.

ETHICAL CONSIDERATIONS IN STUDYING CHILDREN

Suppose that a friend of yours, a developmental psychologist, tells you that he would like to study your 9-month-old baby. Would you give your approval? Would you want some guidelines for the study? Certainly most parents would want to place some restrictions for fear of possible harm to the baby. Most educational institutions and various psychological organizations, such as the American Psychological Association (APA) have established ethical standards that investigators must follow to conduct research with children. However, these controls have not always been in place. In 1955, children were deliberately infected with hepatitis at the Willowbrook State Hospital in New York City, without the children's knowledge, to develop a vaccine.

Child development researchers are obligated to abide by ethical guidelines developed to protect the rights of humans who participate in research studies. The American Psychological Association and the Society for Research in Child Development are examples of professional organizations that publish such guidelines. Regardless of the research method employed, ethical guidelines must be adhered to.

Ethical standards for research involving children (human participants) include the following:

- Protection from harm: Research that may cause the participants permanent psychological or physical harm is unethical. For example, if a particular study would include talking to children about uncomfortable experiences such as abuse, the researchers conducting the study must provide the children with counseling.
- Informed consent: Informed consent is a detailed form informing the participant of any potential harm or risk that might result from participating in the study. Parents are required to sign an informed consent for their children who participate in any study, even if the risks are minimal or nonexistent. Children who are 7 years old or older are required to sign in addition to their parents.
- Confidentiality: All study participants have the right to confidentiality. Researchers must keep the names and identities of study participants confidential so that participants can not be identified

as having been part of the study. However, when working with children, researchers and other child care workers and/or educators are required to report any instances where a child has revealed that they have been abused.

- Knowledge of results (debriefing): In any setting where research takes place, the participants, their parents, and the setting administrators have the right to view a written summary and explanation of the study's results. (Deception: If deception has been a necessary part of any study, the participants also have the right to be informed of the deception immediately after the study has finished.)

SUMMARY

Child development is a specific branch of developmental psychology that focuses on the study of how children change over time. These changes are defined by three developmental domains, or areas of development: physical, cognitive, and social emotional development. All three domains develop over time and can be understood by viewing childhood in five developmental stages: prenatal, infancy and toddlerhood, middle childhood, adolescence, and emerging adulthood. The field of child development contains influences from the areas of biology, sociology, and anthropology. There are three reasons to study child development: 1) to obtain a profile of the typical child at various ages; 2) to understand why behaviors and events occur at various stages; and, 3) to predict future behaviors and events.

Several principles and issues in child development provide a basis for understanding the discipline. First, critical or sensitive periods in development guide researchers and psychologists in understanding how and when children experience the greatest impact from a particular event. There may be a specific time frame or time where an event might create the most effective or strongest impact on a child. Second, development occurs both continuously (a gradual, continual process) and discontinuously (an incremental change process) as a child grows. Finally, the nature versus nurture debate is considered a major principle in child development and possesses support for both sides of the question.

The field of child development uses several methods of gathering information and each has its strengths and weaknesses. These methods include: systematic observation (naturalistic and structured); case study/clinical method; interview method; experiment; and, correlational research (quasi experiment). All of these methods have a purpose in studying child development. Ethical considerations are mandated in the study of child development to protect a child's privacy and safety. Confidentiality is a major ethical consideration in the field of child development.

IMPORTANT TERMS

Atypical child

Average child

Case studies

Child development

Cognitive domain

Cohort effect

Continuous development

Control group

Correlational research

Critical period

Cross-sectional design

Dependent variable

Developmental psychology

Developmental stages

Discontinuous development

Experimental group

Independent variable

Informed consent

Intelligence quotient (IQ)

Interview method

Longitudinal design

Mixed design

Naturalistic observation

Norm

Physical domain

Piaget's clinical method

Puberty

Random sampling

Replicability

Sensitive period

Social emotional domain

Structured observation

Variable

RELATED RESOURCES

Readings

Agin, D. P. (2010). *More than Genes: What Science can Tell Us about Toxic Chemicals, Development, and the Risk to Our Children.* Oxford; New York: Oxford University Press.

Blumberg, M. (2005). *Basic Instinct: The Genesis of Behavior.* New York: Thunder's Mouth Press, Avalon Publishing.
ISBN: 1560256591
This books discusses such questions as: What makes us who we are? Do our genes really predestine us not only to be effective humans, but to be a farmer or a soldier, scholar, or thief? Or do we go through a minievolution, as it were, developing our instincts as we grow, adapting to the environments we encounter?

Firthel, Richard A.,editor (2007). *Focus on Medical Genetics and Down's Syndrome Research.* New York: Nova Biomedical Books.

Hurley, J. C., & Underwood, M. K. (2002). Children's understanding of their research rights before and after debriefing: Informed assent, confidentiality, and stopping participation. *Child Development,* 73, 132-143.

Hoagwood, K., Jensen, P. S., & Fisher, C. B. (1996). *Ethical Issues in Mental Health Research with Children and Adolescents.* Mahwah, NJ: Lawrence Erlbaum.

Jones, S. (2008). Nature and nurture in the development of social smiling. *Philosophical Psychology*, 21(3), 349-357.
Research on the origins of human social smiling is presented as a case study of how a species-specific, species-typical behavior may emerge from thousands of momentary events in which a continuously changing biological organism acts to make, respond to, and learn from its experience.

Leakey, R. & Lewin, R. (1992). *Origins Reconsidered: In Search of What Makes Us Human.* New York: Doubleday.
This book is a personal account of the authors' fossil hunting at Lake Turkana and the reassessment of human prehistory based on new evidence. The authors incorporate ideas from a variety of subject fields: molecular biology, philosophy, anthropology, and linguistics. The authors investigate not only how humans evolved anatomically, but how they acquired consciousness and humanity.

Nippold, Marilyn A. & Scott, Cheryl M., editors (2010). *Expository Discourse in Children, Adolescents, and Adults: Development and Disorders.* New York: Psychology Press.

Shurkin, J. N. (1993). *Terman's Kids: The Groundbreaking Study of How the Gifted Grow Up.* Boston: Little, Brown.
Shurkin, a journalist, identifies a handful of Termites (subjects in Lewis B. Terman's longitudinal studies of gifted children) and describes their later years in some detail. One category consists of the successful gifted in Terman's group; another category consists of Terman's gifted children who failed to live up to their promises.
Soby, Jeanette M. (2006). *Prenatal Exposure to Drugs/Alcohol: Characteristics and Educational Implications of Fetal Alcohol Syndrome and Cocaine/Polydrug Effects.* Springfield, Ill.: Charles C Thomas.

Turner, M. (1967). *Philosophy and the Science of Behavior.* New York: Appleton-Century-Crofts.
This book provides an excellent overview of the relationship between philosophy and science. The book also discusses the basis of the scientific method of inquiry.

Websites

American Psychological Association. http://www.apa.org/research/responsible/human/index.aspx Human Research Protections

Society for Research in Child Development http://www.srcd.org/
The Society for Research in Child Development (SRCD) was established in 1933 by the National Research Council of the National Academies of Science. The history of the Society's origin and evolution parallels that of the academic specialty of child development.

Chapter 2

Theories of Child Development

Chapter Topics	**Learning Objectives**
What is a Child Development Theory?	Understand what a child development theory is
Learning Theories	Understand learning theories: classical conditioning, operant conditioning, social cognitive theory
Psychoanalytic Theories	Understand psychoanalytic theories: psychosexual theory, psychosocial theory
Cognitive Theories	Understand cognitive theories: cognitive development theory, sociocultural theory, information processing theory
Biological and Ecological Theories	Understand biological and ecological theories: ontogenetic theory, ethology, bioecological theory
Chapter Summary	

Four-year-old Carlos' parents are beside themselves. Their son is making "sexual advances" toward his mother. He puts his hands on his mother's breasts repeatedly and watches her intently as she undresses. He often asks the mother to lie down with him, and, when she does, he snuggles up to her in a "provocative" manner. What is the cause of this behavior and how can it be remedied? Is this behavior normal for a 4-year-old? In order to solve problems like this, parents, psychologists, teachers, etc...need theories.

WHAT IS A CHILD DEVELOPMENT THEORY?

Child development theory: Sets of statements that propose general principles of child development.

A theory is a broad framework or body of principles that can be used to understand the relationships among an organized set of facts or principles (Thomas, 1996). A child development theory is a set of statements that propose general principles of child development. The first goal of a theory is to integrate data to explain and predict behavior. In the case of Carlos' "sexual advances," we are interested in developing a theory of the cause of his behavior and whether his advances will continue.

One theory might be that Carlos' sexual advances are imitations of his father's more amorous moments; another might be that he is going through a stage of sexual development that all boys go through. If we believe that Carlos' behavior is simply an imitation of his father's actions, then we might suggest that the father show more discretion in front of Carlos. If we believe that Carlos is typical of 4-year-olds who show fleeting interest in their mother's sexuality, we would wait for the stage to resolve itself without any intervention.

After we have discovered a theory for Carlos' behavior, we can apply it to similar behavior by other children. Thus, a theory takes us from one isolated incident to a general framework for similar problems. We will revisit Carlos' behavior later in the chapter.

In this chapter, we will discuss the three major categories of theories of child development: *learning, cognitive,* and *biological and ecological.* These theories will also be referred to throughout the book as we study the development of Sarah and Carlos.

LEARNING THEORIES OF CHILD DEVELOPMENT

Learning theory: A theory that views child development as a result of an accumulation of experiences.

Learning theories view child development as a direct result of an accumulation of experiences. Each learning theory has its own distinctive approach for explaining how experience shapes child development.

The following learning theories will be discussed here: *classical conditioning, operant conditioning,* and *social cognitive theory* (formerly known as social cognitive learning theory).

Classical conditioning: A type of learning in which a subject learns to associate a neutral stimulus (such as a tone) with a meaningful stimulus (such as food) so that the neutral stimulus elicits a reflexive response originally made only to the meaningful stimulus.

Ivan Pavlov's Classical Conditioning: Learning by Association

Russian physiologist Ivan Pavlov (1849–1936), a pioneer learning theorist, was awarded the Nobel Prize for devising a technique revealing how saliva and other secretions contribute to a dog's digestion of food. Pavlov discovered that a relatively simple involuntary and unlearned, unconditioned response, known as a reflex, can be modified continually through forms of learning, called *classical conditioning*, to create more complex behaviors.

Pavlov's basic discovery was that a dog can be taught to salivate upon presentation of a neutral stimulus such as a bell. In his experiment, a bell was paired repeatedly with a natural stimulus such as food (Pavlov, 1927). Pavlov's experiments stemmed from his work in the 1890s on the digestive processes of dogs. He would place powdered meat on the dog's tongue and observe its physiological reactions, including salivation, which occur naturally without training when food is placed in the mouth.

Pavlov noted, to his annoyance, that quite often the dog did not wait for the meat to be placed in its mouth before salivating. The dog would sometimes salivate as soon as it heard Pavlov's footsteps. Pavlov reasoned that the dog had learned to *associate* the sound of his footsteps, or some other signal, with meat and thus began to salivate in anticipation. Pavlov speculated that the dog could learn to associate other stimuli, such as the sound of a bell, with the meat. In time, as soon as Pavlov struck the bell, the dog would salivate. The dog had now been *conditioned* to salivate to a formerly *neutral* stimulus: the bell. This method of learning is called *classical conditioning*.

Figure 2.1
The Pavlov Frame

An illustration of Pavlov's original apparatus for classically conditioning salivation in the dog. A tube is attached to the dog's salivary gland collects saliva secreted by the gland, and the number of drops from the tube is recorded on a revolving drum outside the chamber. The experimenter can watch the dog through a one-way mirror and deliver food by remote control. The chamber is soundproof so that nothing except the desired stimulus, such as the sound of the bell, distracts the dog.

Source: Yerkes, R. N., & Morulis, S. The Methods of Pavlov in Animal Psychology. *The Psychological Bulletin*, 1909, 6, 257-273.

Application of Classical Conditioning. Instances of classical conditioning with children are found everywhere. Psychologist John B. Watson (1878-1958) conditioned 11-month-old Albert to fear a white rat by striking a steel bar with a hammer as the boy reached for the animal. Initially, Albert had no fear of the rat but eventually began to cry at the site of the rat. Similarly, 4-year-old Carlos cries every time he is in the family car as it passes a white building where he received inoculations from his pediatrician. Sarah experiences unpleasant emotions when she looks at the cookie jar because her mother scolded her the other day for helping herself to the cookies in the jar. A key concept in classical conditioning is generalization, or spreading, of the conditioned response. Eleven-month-old Albert became afraid not only of the rat, but of many other furry objects, including rabbits, dogs, and Santa Claus masks. Many phobias can be traced back to experiences that involved classical conditioning.

Watson's experiment with little Albert receives much criticism today because the experiment itself did not abide by any ethical guidelines. As we learned in Chapter 1, ethical guidelines are required for any work with children. However, these guidelines were not yet in place during Watson's experiments. Today, the little Albert experiment would not be allowed since it would violate the "protection from harm" ethical code.

Limitations of Pavlov's Classical Conditioning. In classical conditioning, a reflex (such as salivating to food or blinking to a puff of air) is transferred to another stimulus (such as the sound of a bell) that would not normally produce the (conditioned) response. In this type of learning, the animal is passive: The dog simply waits for food to be delivered to its mouth and salivates to the sight or sound of the bell after it begins to associate the bell with food.

Most behavior is voluntary, rather than passive as in Pavlov's classical conditioning of the dog. Dogs do not usually sit still until food is placed in their mouths. They may beg for food even when they are not hungry. Why? Because of signals we give before the dog comes to us. If I whistle every time I throw the dog some food, in time the dog may come to me every time I whistle, whether I have food or not.

The notion that environment (reward or punishment) determines an organism's directly observed behavior formed the basis for a new approach to psychology known as *behaviorism*. Watson coined the term behaviorism as a result of his belief that children could be "trained" to be or do anything as a result of environmental manipulation.

Behaviorism: An approach to psychology that emphasizes the study of observable behavior and the role of environment as a determinant of behavior.

Skinner's Operant Conditioning: Radical Behaviorism

Behaviorism is based on a learning theory that emphasizes that most of the behavior of children is learned. Appropriate behavior may be positively reinforced by pleasant, rewarding experiences; undesirable behavior may be weakened or eliminated by lack of reinforcement or punishment. The form of behaviorism that has become most popular is *operant* (or *instrumental*) *conditioning*.

Operant conditioning: A form of learning in which a voluntary response is strengthened or weakened, depending on its association with reward or punishment.

The operant conditioning model of learning was demonstrated by Burrhus Frederic Skinner (1904-1990) in experiments with lower animals. Skinner coined the phrase *operant conditioning* to describe a type of learning in which an organism "operates" on the environment instead of passively reacting to it as in Pavlov's classical conditioning experiment. Skinner experimented with rats, and later with pigeons, by rewarding them with food each time they responded correctly. In experiments where pigeons were rewarded (reinforced) if they pecked on a green bar, they soon learned to distinguish colors. A favorite Skinnerian experiment was training pigeons to make a 180° turn (or even a complete circle). The desired behavior was accomplished by *rewarding* each *correct response* as the bird continued toward its goal. Skinner called this type of learning *shaping through the method of approximations*. Let's discuss this method of learning in more detail.

Box 2.1
Biography of the Foremost Mechanistic Theorist

Burrhus Frederic Skinner (1904-1990)

B.F. Skinner, the most prominent and perhaps the most controversial psychologist today, was born in Susquehanna, Pennsylvania. He was the elder son of Grace Burrhus, an amateur musician, and William Skinner, a lawyer. He had a strong moral upbringing, and was taught to fear God, the police, and what people would think.

From an early age, Skinner demonstrated superior mechanical ability. Among his more notable creations was a steam cannon made from a discarded water boiler. He also created a flotation system to separate green and ripe elderberries, which he sold door to door, and made kazoos from combs and toilet paper. In high school, young Skinner played in a jazz band and also demonstrated a flair for writing. During his college days, Skinner became known as a troublemaker. Antics such as covering the walls of Class Day exercises with bitter caricatures of the faculty almost prevented him from graduating.

After receiving his bachelor's degree, Skinner turned his attention to one of his boyhood interests: animal behavior. He had become fascinated with Pavlov's work with reflexes and with John B. Watson's experiments on conditioning and the notion that behavior is totally predictable and controllable. He had also become greatly interested in Thomas Hobbes and Julien de La Mettrie, 17th- and 18th-century philosophers who viewed people and animals as machines. Skinner was now ready to pursue a doctorate in psychology. He entered Harvard University, from which he earned a Ph.D. in psychology, and where he taught from 1948 until his retirement in 1974.

*Skinner published many books, his best-known being **Beyond Freedom and Dignity**. In it, Skinner argues that people are not responsible for their conduct. Hence, people should not be given credit for desirable behavior or blamed for undesirable behavior—environment is the master. Skinner also wrote a novel, **Walden Two** (1948), a nonfiction examination of his utopian society in which he examines the importance of understanding how to control behavior in everyday life. In 1969, Skinner received the prestigious Medal of Science award. Today, Skinner is considered a leading authority on behaviorism, an approach that concerns itself with directly observable behavior rather than with unobservable concepts such as thought and feelings.*

Method of approximations: Skinner's method of shaping behavior by rewarding each correct response until the goal is reached.

Shaping behavior through the method of approximations. If Skinner wants to make a pigeon turn 180°, he first waits for the bird, which has been deprived of food, to make a movement toward the right or left. As soon as the hungry pigeon finishes its movement in the desired direction, a buzzer sounds and a reward, such as a pellet of food, is given. Skinner then waits until the pigeon makes another move slightly farther in the desired direction. Again, a sound is made and the pigeon is rewarded. The pigeon's behavior is shaped gradually until it reaches its goal (180° turn) without hesitation. What a pigeon will do for a pellet of food: climb stairs, play ping pong, and peck a key 10,000 times!

Reinforcement (reward): In operant conditioning, the consequences of a behavior that makes the response either more or less likely to be repeated.

In operant conditioning, the consequences of a behavior produce changes in the probability of the behavior's occurrence. A behavior followed by a *reward* is more likely to recur; a behavior followed by pain is less likely to recur.

Operant conditioning does not always rely on reinforcement,[1] or reward. In some instances, punishment is used to decrease the likelihood of a certain form of behavior. A rat may avoid a series of electric shocks if it presses a bar as soon as a light flashes, signalling an impending shock. The deliberate avoidance of the shock is called *negative reinforcement.*

Negative reinforcement: The strengthening of a response if it is followed by the removal of an aversive (unpleasant) stimulus.

Using operant conditioning with children. Although Skinner's research was conducted primarily with animals, child development researchers are convinced that operant conditioning is applicable to the study of children.

Even young babies can change (operate on) their environment when positive or negative reinforcement—two key elements of operant conditioning—is used.

Studies have demonstrated that newborn babies quickly learn to turn their heads clockwise or counterclockwise when the correct response is followed by a sugar water (positive) reinforcer. Also, newborns will suck faster to see visual designs or to hear music and human voices. Young babies also respond to negative reinforcement. For example, they will often stop crying when they notice that the caregiver is about to pick them up.

Operant behavior is particularly noticeable in the classroom where positive reinforcement is used in the form of verbal approval, systematic praise of appropriate behavior, ignoring disruptive behavior, and rewarding children with tokens for good behavior. Occasionally, teachers use negative reinforcement such as refusing to dismiss the class until everyone is quiet. We can also see a demonstration of negative reinforcement when a driver slams on his or her brakes to avoid an accident or when a couple uses a condom to avoid pregnancy.

Bandura's Social Cognitive Theory

Observational learning: A process in which an individual learns new responses by observing the behavior of another (a model) rather than through direct experience.

Model: A person who engages in (usually new) behavior that is observed and imitated by another person.

Social cognitive theory: Albert Bandura's behavioristic theory of child development that stresses observation, imitation, and modeling.

Prior to the 1940s, most researchers believed that learning could be explained by conditioning theories such as those proposed by Pavlov and Skinner. By the 1960s, however, the predominant belief was that learning occurs by observing. In *observational learning,* the individual learns new responses by observing the behavior of another (a *model*) rather than through direct experience. The key proponent of the idea that human learning is acquired by observing other people in a social context is Albert Bandura (1925-), who relies heavily on the principles of classical and operant conditioning.

Albert Bandura's *social cognitive theory* (formerly called social-cognitive learning theory) has several assertions which make his theory particularly appealing to child developmentalists:

- *Learning can occur without punishment or reward.*

- *Learning occurs through observation and imitation of other people (role models), such as parents, teachers, and siblings. Observation is one of the most important tools for the child who is learning something (Bandura, 1999).*

- *A child can learn something through imitation of a role model by observation, even though he or she has not had a chance to have personal experience.*

- *Cognitive factors (e.g., thoughts, expectations, memory, and motivation) play an important role in learning, particularly in the more complex forms of learning. We can think about what is happening, evaluate it, and act accordingly (Mischel, 2004).*

- *Reinforcement is not always necessary for learning to occur; children often learn highly complex behaviors without identifiable sources of reinforcement.*

---

1. Reinforcement can be *positive* or *negative*. Positive reinforcement consists of a reward such as food, praise, or a hug. Negative reinforcement is something that the subject wants to avoid, such as the warning buzzer in a car if you don't fasten the seat belt.

- *The child plays an important (active) role in the learning process. For instance, Sarah selects problems to solve, and decides among solutions to a problem.*

According to Albert Bandura, this preschooler is modeling the attire she has observed on an older model such as her teenage sister or mother.

According to Bandura (1977; 1982; 1986; 1989; 1999; 2000), children do not naturally imitate every type of behavior they see. Sarah will imitate a model if she was paying attention, if she was able to retain what was observed, and if she had the incentive to do so. This means that cognitive factors are an important feature of Bandura's theory. For instance, the child chooses the models she wants to imitate. Usually, children imitate models of high status who reflect their own personality, or models who children find attractive, talented, intelligent, powerful, or popular. According to Bandura, younger children tend to choose models who they perceive as kind. For older children, it is very important that their model be of the same gender. A critical feature of Bandura's theory is *self-efficacy*, the extent to which a person believes that he or she can perform behaviors that are necessary to bring about a desired outcome. Self-efficacy influences a student's choice of subjects (difficult or challenging versus easy) in school (Zimmerman & Schunk, 2004). People experience a sense of self-efficacy when they have high aspiration and experience notable achievements (Bandura *et al.*, 2001).

Self-efficacy: The belief that one can master a particular situation and bring about a favorable outcome.

Box 2.2
Biography Of A Prominent Social Cognitive Theorist

Albert Bandura (1925-)

Albert Bandura was born in Alberta, Canada. As a young man, he worked at a variety of jobs, including repairing the Alaskan Highway. After graduating from the University of British Columbia, Bandura attended the University of Iowa, from which he received a Ph.D. in clinical psychology. Bandura has been teaching at Stanford University since 1964, where he is David Starr Jordon, Professor of Psychology.

Bandura's social cognitive theory has been expanded to include imitation and identification, behavior change through modeling, and social reinforcement. For Bandura, imitation plays a key role in learning many kinds of behavior. Bandura believes that human beings have choices and that they can direct the course of their lives. Bandura believes that behavior, environment, and cognition are the key factors in child development.

Today, Bandura is regarded as one of the most influential active psychologists in the United States. In 1980, he received The Award for Distinguished Scientific Contributions.

Intrinsic reinforcement:
Behavior which is rewarding for its own sake and there is no external reward or consequence.

Vicarious reinforcement:
Learning (second-hand) by watching the consequences to others of their behavior.

Extrinsic reinforcement:
External rewards such as praise, grades, and money.

While Bandura believes that reinforcement is not always necessary for learning, he does describe different types of reinforcement that might play a role in learning. For instance, reinforcement may be *intrinsic*, an internalized sense of satisfaction, as when the child is elated upon learning how to solve a puzzle without receiving an external reward such as praise or money. Or, reinforcement can be *vicarious,* as in the case where a child sees his friend receiving candy for behaving properly or being punished for misbehaving. Bandura minimizes the role of external rewards such as praise, grades, or money called *extrinsic reinforcement.*

Bandura argues that children may learn many different types of behavior, including proper morals, through observation of others (models). In one practical application of Bandura's social cognitive theory, a 2-year-old was toilet trained with a model, using a doll and a container for water. The child first watched the doll "wet," then helped reward the doll for good behavior by refilling the reservoir with juice, enabling the doll to wet again. Conversely, there are just as many examples of children who learn immoral behaviors and actions through the observation of others as well.

Critique of Learning Theories

Learning theories have always been recognized for their emphasis on precise research methods, a clear definition of goals, and a clear-cut method of defining progress and development. A major criticism of learning theories is their description of the important role of environment. Adherents, such as B. F. Skinner, believe that *all* behavior can be understood in terms of the environment. Albert Bandura's social cognitive theory, in particular, pays little attention to hereditary influences and focuses on observation and processing of external events as the mode of learning. Subsequently, he has made an important contribution to learning theory through his incorporation of cognitive aspects of development.

PSYCHOANALYTIC THEORIES OF CHILD DEVELOPMENT

Stage theories: Theories that are characterized by distinct stages

Qualitative: Described or defined by fluid words (as opposed to quantitative - described by numbers)

Discontinuous: Stage-like (not fluid); characterized by distinct change

Psychoanalytic theories are considered stage theories. *Stage theories* focus on different levels of development that are *qualitatively* different from other levels. Each successive developmental level or stage represents a structural reorganization in which new information, feelings, and behavior are integrated with previous information and behavior. Although Sarah uses arm and leg movements in walking, just as she did in crawling, these movements are different and result in a different behavior/action. For example, in walking, Sarah uses her arm movements to balance herself, rather than for locomotion and support, as she did when she was crawling.

Stage theorists maintain that progression from stage to stage is *discontinuous*. Development from stage to stage is a fixed, irreversible sequence, and is therefore invariant. The advances from one stage to the next follow an apparently preordained course, regardless of the child's culture, education, or maturity. Although teaching and experience can speed up or slow development, they do not change the basic sequence.

The following psychoanalytic stage theories will be covered here: psychosexual theory and psychosocial theory.

FREUD'S PSYCHOSEXUAL THEORY OF CHILD DEVELOPMENT

Psychosexual theory: According to Sigmund Freud, the theory which guides child development through different stages to satisfy the sexual drive, known as the libido.

Even though there are vast differences among different children (like Sarah and Carlos), each child's development can be explained by Sigmund Freud's (1856 - 1939) psychosexual theory (Freud, 1963). Here is a preview of four of the concepts of Freud's theory:

- *Levels of awareness or consciousness (conscious, preconscious, unconscious).*

- *Functional divisions of the personality or psyche (id, ego, superego).*

- *Stages of psychosexual development (oral, anal, phallic, latency, genital).*

- *Defense mechanisms (e.g., repression, rationalization, and regression).*

Freud's Levels of Awareness

Conscious: Awareness of our thoughts, feelings, and beliefs which reside in the mind.

Preconscious (foreconscious): Part of the mind just beneath the surface of awareness, which can be easily brought to consciousness.

Unconscious: Part of the mind outside awareness where painful memories (anxiety, guilt, and fears) are submerged.

According to Sigmund Freud, an Austrian physician who treated patients suffering from mental illness, there are three levels of awareness: conscious, preconscious, and unconscious. *Conscious* functioning includes all that we are aware of through our various sense organs. The *preconscious* (sometimes called the foreconscious) includes those functions that have been suppressed but can be recalled to awareness. Finally, there is the *unconscious*, which contains painful memories that are submerged. Hence, a person is never directly aware of his or her unconscious memories, since they can never be recovered and brought to consciousness.

According to Freud, all humans have an *unconscious* from which vigorous sexual and aggressive drives struggle to emerge. Occasionally, these sexual and aggressive forces emerge when we take part in self-defeating behavior or commit a "Freudian slip," for example, using the word "promiscuous" rather than "permissive" or "attacker" rather than "attractive" (Reason, 2000). Usually, unconscious forces are repressed by defense mechanisms—unconscious mental devices for coping with anxiety-producing situations. This repression, says Freud, often leads to psychological problems. To clarify the nature of unconscious memories, which often produce conflicts, Freud proposed a three-part classification of our personality.

Freud's Three-Part Structure of Personality

Freud divided personality, or the psyche (all that constitutes the mind and its processes), into three mental components: the *id*, the *ego*, and the *superego* which interact with one another. The id is impulsive, the ego is rational, and the superego is moral.

Id: Freudian personality structure that deals with the basic instincts of sex and aggression; the seat of psychic energy.

For Freud, the *id* (the innate reservoir of sexual and aggressive impulses) is the most primitive and fundamental feature of the psyche. Present at birth, it is the keeper of all instinctual drives and is completely unconscious. The id is guided by the pleasure principle (seeking immediate gratification of its biological urges and avoidance of pain) and is both primitive and illogical.

Ego: The practical, rational component of personality which evolves out of the id.

The *ego* evolves out of the id during the second year of life. It is the practical, rational component of personality. Basically an organizing or mediating force, the ego attempts to strike a balance between the raw impulses of the id and the reality of the child's environment. If a child is driven by the id to touch a hot stove, the task of the ego is to inform the child of the possibility of getting burned.

Superego: The child's conscience and the reservoir of personality.

Ego Ideal: The superego's idealized sense of how a person should behave.

According to Freud's classical model of personality, the *superego*, or "voice within," is the child's conscience and the reservoir of morality. It embodies such moral precepts as, "Thou shalt not…" and "This type of behavior is wrong." The superego also includes the *ego ideal* meaning how a moral person ought to behave, such as, "I must help…." or "I should go…." The superego is acquired from about the third to the sixth year by adopting (internalizing) the parents' (and later, significant members' of the community as well) rules, restrictions, and moral teachings as his or her own. The superego places restrictions on both the id and the ego.

Freud viewed all psychological disorders as resulting mainly from unresolved unconscious conflicts between the raw impulses of the id and the limits placed on these impulses by the superego. Freud also believed that these impulses originate in early childhood.

Psychosexual development: According to Sigmund Freud, development which goes through different stages to satisfy the sexual drive, known as the libido.

Stages of Psychosexual Development

According to Sigmund Freud, psychosexual development includes successive stages which serve to satisfy the sexual drive, known as the libido. Freud proposed that Sarah and Carlos go through several different stages in satisfying their innate sexual drive, called the *libido*. The libido was considered the master motive of human behavior and is the psychological term for the physical and emotional energy associated with instinctual drives. As Sarah and Carlos continue to develop and reach new stages, different parts of the body—called erogenous zones—are used to satisfy their sexual drives. These stages occur in sequence: *oral, anal, phallic, latency,* and *genital.*

Libido: The driving force or sexual energy in Freud's psychoanalytic theory of personality development which provides the motivation for human thought and behavior.

Oral stage: In Freudian theory, the first psychosexual stage of infancy when the child's attention is focused on the mouth.

Anal stage: The second stage of Freud's psychosexual development, when there is a preoccupation with toilet training.

Phallic stage: In Freudian theory, a period from about age 3 to 6 years, in which a child receives gratification in the genital area.

Oedipus (Oedipal) complex: In Freudian theory, a girl's or boy's sexual attraction to a parent of the opposite gender.

Electra complex. In Freudian theory, a universal conflict in females during the phallic stage of psychosexual development, at about age 4 or 5, when the girl becomes attracted to her father and is hostile toward the mother.

Latency stage: In Freudian theory, the fourth stage of psychosexual development when there is an absence of sexual strivings.

Genital stage: In Freudian theory, a period from about 11 years on, when mature sexuality occurs.

Defense mechanism: An unconscious mental devise used by the ego to defend itself when anxiety is too great.

The Oral Stage. In the oral stage, which lasts approximately through the first year, a child is particularly concerned about feeding. The mouth is used to examine objects, and the child gains satisfaction from activities such as sucking the thumb or a pacifier.

The Anal Stage. Freud's second stage is called the anal stage and lasts from about 1 to 3 years of age. In this stage, Sarah and Carlos are preoccupied with toilet training and may experience pleasure from elimination.

The Phallic Stage. In the phallic stage, which lasts from about 3 to 6 years of age, the child is concerned primarily with his or her genitals. Sarah and Carlos are now curious about their anatomical features, the origin of babies, and the sexual activities of his parents. Carlos may discover that manipulating his genitals provides a pleasurable sensation. An important subphase is the *Oedipus (or Oedipal) complex*, in which Carlos becomes sexually attracted to his mother and dislikes his father (which would be a potential explanatory theory for Carlos's behavior described at the beginning of this chapter). According to Freud, Sarah would be similarly attracted to her father and resentful of her mother during this stage—called the *Electra complex.*

The Latency Stage. In the latency stage, which lasts from about age 6 to 11 years, there is an absence of sexual strivings according to Freud. Freud thought that sexual conflicts from earlier stages are only temporarily submerged, to burst forth again at puberty during the genital stage.

The Genital Stage. In this stage, which lasts from about 11 years on, mature sexuality occurs. The genital zones reactivated as an area of sensual pleasure.

In each of these stages, Freud proposed that the child has a conflict between innate drives, such as sex and aggression, and the constraints of society. The child will grow up to be a normal person if its caregivers strike a proper balance between the two opposing forces. Should the child have difficulty with any of these stages, he or she will not be able to adapt successfully in times of stress. Moreover, severe psychopathology may result, says Freud. According to Freud, how children experience and resolve their conflicts in the different stages will determine how they turn out as adults (Salkind, 2004). For example, a child whose oral needs are not met during infancy may become an overeater in later life. Or, a child whose toilet training is characterized by severe parental pressure and expectation might experience obsessive compulsive issues as an adult.

Defense Mechanisms: Unconscious Deception of Oneself

Freud noticed that many of his patients who experienced considerable turmoil or conflict ended up struggling with anxiety. Freud proposed that this conflict was the result of a struggle between the id (which wants to satisfy all human urges) and the superego (the person's conscience). According to Freud, it is the job of the ego to maintain a proper balance between the excessive demands of the id and the harsh judgments of the superego. If the ego is unsuccessful in maintaining a proper balance between the id and the superego, Freud invented the concept of *defense mechanisms*, a series of mental devices that distort reality and protect and insulate the individual from psychic pain such as anxiety. Defense mechanisms are automatic and typically unconscious in nature. They are used in normal functioning to reduce anxiety and are abnormal when their use is habitual or impedes effective solutions to a problem.

Repression: In Freudian theory, a defense mechanism of forgetting painful or threatening material by blocking it off in the unconscious and preventing it from reaching consciousness.

Rationalization: In Freudian theory, a defense mechanism in which a person may give a "good" reason for unacceptable behavior.

Regression: In Freudian Theory, a defense mechanism in which a person returns to an earlier form of behavior, such as wetting one's underwear instead of using the toilet.

Neoanalysts: Psychoanalysts who focus less on the unconscious and more on conscious choice and self-direction.

While there are about a dozen identifiable defense mechanisms, we will discuss the three most common here: repression, rationalization, and regression.

One of the most common defense mechanisms is *repression*. Individuals who have had painful experiences will often repress these events by banishing them from consciousness and thrusting them into the unconscious. These unpleasant ideas, experiences, or feelings are hidden deep in the person's psyche. The teenage girl severely mistreated by her stepmother may be totally unaware that she harbors (represses) considerable hostility toward the woman who took her mother's place. Freud proposed that repression occurs when emotional experiences in childhood are so traumatic that allowing them to enter consciousness would later cause the individual to be totally overwhelmed by guilt and anxiety. Freud said that repression is the cornerstone of psychoanalysis and that mental illness results when repression fails.

In *rationalization*, another defense mechanism, the individual may resort to giving "good" reasons for behavior that is unacceptable. The college student failing in her psychology class may rationalize that her poor grade is the fault of the professor or the fault of her noisy roommate. A person who rationalizes places responsibility for their behavior onto someone or something else.

Regression, a return to an earlier form of behavior, such as wetting one's underwear instead of using the toilet, is also a common defense mechanism. A less serious example than toilet training reversal would be a child who stops tying his or her shoes asserting that he/she "does not know how."

Freud Today

During the first half of the 1900s, Freud's psychosexual theory dominated explanations of how the human mind works, however, it has lost considerable popularity during the last three or four decades (Cairns, 1998). Instead of attempting to solve a person's problems by delving into his or her unconscious, which presumably shapes behavior and thinking as Freud suggested, today's psychologists and therapists rely more on psychopharmacological drugs and psychotherapy that focuses on present patient issues and future goals. Currently, only a small number (about 1,000) of men and women in the United States are fully qualified classical psychoanalysts. Some of them call themselves *neoanalysts*, rather than psychoanalysts, because they focus less on unconscious processes and sexual instincts than Freud did and more on conscious choice and self-direction (Eagle, 2000).

One reason for the loss in popularity for psychoanalysis is the difficulty of verifying the many broad assumptions of classical psychoanalysis. How does one prove that experiences in early childhood are as important as Freud claims? How does one prove that an individual has the proper balance among the id, ego, and superego when there are no measurement techniques for these mental structures? Today's researchers also downplay Freud's emphasis on the importance of instinctual urges in shaping a child's development and rely more on the importance of attachment and other early interpersonal relationships (Schultz & Schultz, 2001). Yet, Freud has made many contributions to child development.

Gender identity: The psychological sense of being masculine or feminine.

Erikson's psychosocial theory: A theory consisting of eight developmental stages when the self and society interact to resolve conflicts, contradictions, and periods of disharmony.

Freud's ideas about children are original and creative. One of his major contributions is an explanation of the nature of children's sexuality—they are sexual creatures from birth. Among other contributions by Freud is the nature of our unconscious thoughts and emotions (Emde, 1992) and our defense mechanisms. A fundamental discovery of Freud's that remains valid today is that some aspects of mental functioning are not subject to conscious recall, yet they may influence a person's behavior, emotions, and thinking (Friedman & Downey, 2000).

Those who continue to follow psychoanalytic thinking often revise some of its basic framework (Eagle, 2000). A major change is seeing infantile sexuality in the broader perspective of *gender identity*, the psychological sense of being masculine or feminine. One popular revisionist of Freud's theories is Erik Erikson.

Box 2.3
Biography of a Psychosexual Theorist

Sigmund Freud (1856-1939)

Sigmund Freud was born in 1856 in Freiberg, Moravia (now Príbor, the Czech Republic), but lived most of his life in Vienna. Freud's father was a wood merchant and a gentle man known for both his humor and his skepticism. Sigmund was the first child born to his father's second wife. Young Sigmund had a devoted mother and there was a close mother-son relationship. The mother continually referred to Sigmund as her "goldener Sigi" until her death at the age of 95.

The family moved to Vienna when Sigmund was 4 years old. His first teachers were his parents. At the age of 9, Freud entered Sperl Gymnasium (equivalent to an American high school) in Vienna. Young Freud was an outstanding student, but he found that as a Jew in an anti-Semitic society, his career choices were limited. Reluctantly, he chose medicine.

Sigmund Freud entered the University of Vienna at the age of 17, specializing in physiology. After earning his M.D. degree, Freud became an intern at the General Hospital in Vienna, serving in the psychiatric clinic. He was chosen lecturer in neural pathology and early in his career distinguished himself by his research on the human nervous system. To this day, some of Freud's contributions to scientific literature remain classic descriptions of neurological disease.

In 1885, Freud won a grant to study in Paris with the most famous neurologist of his time, Jean-Martin Charcot, a master of the art of hypnosis. Upon Freud's return to Vienna, he was joined by another physician, Josef Breuer, in a practice involving hypnosis in the treatment of hysteria, where a person has signs of a physical disease, but there is no physical damage. As a result of his work with Charcot and Breuer, Freud developed many ideas that are the foundations of psychoanalysis, a psychodynamic model in which people's behavior is considered to be determined by unconscious processes.

Freud's accomplishments are staggering. In addition to maintaining a full-time clinical practice for most of his career, Freud published hundreds of essays and books, lectured regularly at universities, served as chief editor of a number of psychoanalytic journals, and maintained a large regular correspondence with many friends and colleagues. Freud died in London in 1939 from cancer, which is believed to have been caused by his heavy smoking.

ERIKSON'S PSYCHOSOCIAL THEORY OF HUMAN DEVELOPMENT

Stage theory: The belief that growth and development involve different levels which are qualitatively different from one another.

Erik Erikson's (1902-1994) psychosocial theory is the most comprehensive *stage theory* of personality development as it described the entire life span. Basically, Erikson was interested in describing the personality and emotional structure of individuals, as well as their usual ways of interacting with other people who play a prominent role in one's life. Erikson identified eight such stages, each being involved in a critical period of development he calls a *crisis,* or conflict, which the child must work out or resolve for satisfactory development. Contrary to Freud's psychosexual theory, Erikson's psychosocial theory places more emphasis on the role of environment in development.

Crisis: According to Erikson, a critical period in a child's (or in an adult's) development.

For Erikson, a neo-Freudian, each *crisis* is a turning point in either a positive (healthy) or in a negative (unhealthy) direction. If a person adjusts satisfactorily to the demands of each crisis, a healthy ego (that part of personality that organizes, plans, and keeps the person in touch with reality) will emerge and the individual will move toward the next crisis. If the crisis is not resolved satisfactorily, the person will continue to struggle with it and an unhealthy ego will develop. Erikson reminds us that development is an ongoing process throughout life.

Box 2.4
Biography of a Psychosocial Theorist

Erik Erikson (1902-1994)

Erik H. Erikson was born in 1902 near Frankfurt, Germany, of Danish parents. His father died when Erikson was quite young, and his widowed mother married a prominent pediatrician. Although the stepfather wanted Erikson to become a doctor, young Erik chose to be an artist instead. Early in his career as an artist and teacher in Vienna, Erikson met Sigmund Freud and undertook psychoanalytic training. After his analytic training, Erikson met and married a young American artist and moved to the United States in 1933.

After immigrating to the United States, Erikson was a training analyst at the Austen Riggs Center, a private residential treatment institution for disturbed young people in Stockbridge, Massachusetts. He also participated in research at the Harvard Psychological Clinic, the Yale Institute of Human Relations, the Institute of Child Welfare at the University of California, Berkeley, and the Western Psychiatric Institute in Pittsburgh. Erikson was professor of human development and a lecturer in psychiatry at Harvard University. He was also affiliated with the Menninger Foundation. Erikson accomplished all this with a "Ph.D. in nothing," as a colleague noted. He did not possess a Ph.D. or M.D. degree. In fact, he didn't even have a bachelor's degree.

In addition to his work at colleges and universities, Erikson did considerable fieldwork. He initiated early fieldwork on American Indians by observing the Oglala Sioux of Pine Ridge, South Dakota, and the salmon-fishing Yurok Indians of Northern California.

Erikson coined the term "identity crisis," so common in adolescence when a teenager asks himself or herself questions such as, "Who am I?" and "Where do I belong?" Erikson also wrote extensively on the concept of personal identity. One of his books, Ghandhi's Truth *(1969), won a Pulitzer Prize and the National Book Award. In this book and in others such as* Young Man Luther, *Erikson encourages the psychoanalytic study of historical figures. He also wrote biographies of Jesus, Albert Einstein, William James, and Charles Darwin. Little wonder Erikson has been called "the most widely known and read psychoanalyst in America", even though he did not follow traditional psychoanalytic teachings expounded by its founder, Sigmund Freud. While Freud believed that sexual needs were the key to growing up, Erikson believed that social relationships were the key "identity crises" to describe adolescence.*

Erikson's Eight Stages or Crises.

Basic trust versus mistrust:
Erikson's theory of
psychosocial development, in
which infants develop a sense
of how reliable people are.

Autonomy: The ability to
govern oneself, to choose
one's actions freely, and to
regulate oneself willingly.

Initiative versus guilt: This
stage, which corresponds to
Freud's phallic stage, is
concerned with the child's
desire to explore and initiate
activities such as running and
climbing.

Industry versus inferiority:
This stage corresponds to
Freud's latency stage. It
revolves around the child's
desire to produce things and
to succeed at self-accepted
tasks.

Identity: An individual's
sense of uniqueness and
belonging.

Identity versus confusion: A
critical period in a person's
development when there is a
search for answers to
questions such as, "Who am
I?" and "Where am I going?"

Intimacy versus Isolation:
This crisis involves the extent
of disclosure of one's "real
self" to another person to
achieve true and satisfying
intimacy.

Basic Trust Versus Mistrust (Birth to about 1 year). Erikson believed that a sense of trust and hope is the cornerstone of a healthy personality. If a child's world is predictable and supportive, a healthy trust is likely to develop, and the first crisis is likely to be resolved satisfactorily. An unhealthy resolution results in the child being distrustful of others. The quality of care determines the outcome of this stage, which corresponds to Freud's oral stage. A key concern: Is the child's world predictable and supportive? In other words, Erickson's theory of basic trust versus mistrust provides infants with a sense of how reliable people are. Are the child's basic needs met? Food, clothing, care - are these things provided in a timely, caring fashion free from stress?

Autonomy versus shame and doubt (About 1 to 3 years). This crisis centers around the child's motor and mental abilities and corresponds to Freud's anal stage. A major problem is how to handle the child's increasing demands to do things for himself or herself while at the same time ensuring that someone is present in case he/she needs help. The child needs to be gently protected from excesses while being granted autonomy in simple matters. *Autonomy* is the ability to govern oneself, to choose one's actions freely, and to regulate oneself willingly (Rodgers, 1998). The child's concern is whether he/she is capable of doing something by himself or herself or must he/she rely on others. If a child's struggle for autonomy is disapproved of or if he/she is criticized when exploring his/her abilities, the child will experience rage, shame and self-doubt and feel helpless.

Initiative versus guilt (About 3 to 6 years). This stage, which corresponds to Freud's phallic stage, is concerned with the child's desire to explore and initiate activities such as running and climbing. Another concern is hand and finger control for taking things apart, molding clay, and handling balls. Sooner or later, the child makes a mess or breaks things. The caregiver's reactions help the child answer the questions: "Are my actions acceptable?" and "Am I good or bad?" The lack acceptance of a child's initiative during this phase will result in guilt. Parental reactions to initiative and "mistakes" should be positive and supportive; punishment and criticism during this phase will yield guilt.

Industry versus inferiority (About 6 years to puberty). This stage corresponds to Freud's latency stage. It revolves around the child's desire to produce things and to succeed at self-accepted tasks. To resolve this crisis satisfactorily, the child must be provided with challenging tasks that can be mastered and that the child finds interesting. The crucial question for the child is: "Am I successful or worthless?"

Identity versus Role Confusion (Adolescence–about 12 to 18 years). This crisis involves questions such as: "Who am I?" "Where am I going?" and "Where do I belong?" If a satisfactory answer is found, the child has achieved an *identity*. Identity refers to an individual's sense of uniqueness and belonging. If the answer is unclear, and the child is not accepted by his or her peers or is not able to reconcile the contradictions of society, he/she may continue to experiment with various goals and lifestyles—a state of roleconfusion.This period corresponds to Freud's genital stage.

Intimacy versus Isolation (About 18 to 30 years). This crisis involves the extent of disclosure of one's "real self" to another person to achieve true and satisfying intimacy. The goal is to develop relationships beyond adolescent

Generativity versus Stagnation: This stage involves generativity, being productive and creative versus being stagnant or filled with absorption of personal needs.

Ego Integrity versus Despair: This stage is characterized by a personal life review, self-acceptance, and an integration of earlier stages.

superficial love. During this stage, most people become parents and build bonds with offspring as well.

Generativity versus Stagnation (About 30 years to late adulthood)

This stage involves *generativity*, being productive and creative versus being *stagnant* or filled with absorption of personal needs. The focus during this stage is occupational achievement or creativity and an intent to rear the next generation. The goal is to turn oneself outward instead of focusing inward.

Ego Integrity versus Despair (Late adulthood and beyond)

This stage is characterized by a personal life review, self-acceptance, and an integration of earlier stages. One may reflect on life with satisfaction or become despondent.

Table 2.1

Two Psychoanalytic Perspectives of Child Development: Psychosexual (Freud) and Psychosocial (Erikson)

Approximate Age	Psychosexual Theory (Freud)	Psychosocial Theory (Erikson)
Birth to 1 year	*Oral Stage:* The mouth is the focus of the baby's pleasurable sensation; gratification is obtained from sucking, biting, eating, and mouthing.	*Basic Trust vs. Mistrust:* Trust is the chief crisis resolved in the first year. The direction of trust depends on the type of care received. The direction may be positive (healthy) or negative (unhealthy).
1 to 3 years	*Anal Stage:* Pleasurable sensations are derived from the anus as the baby learns to control elimination.	*Autonomy vs. Shame and Doubt:* The child is confronted with dual problems of exercising his or her will versus learning control; an unhealthy balance results in shame (rage) and doubt.
3 to 6 years	*Phallic Stage:* Pleasure is derived from manipulating the genitals. The children are sexually attracted to the opposite-gender parent.	*Initiative vs. Guilt:* Children want to explore and initiate their own activities. Restriction of freedom to be independent produces guilt.
6 to Puberty (ages 10 to 12 for girls; 12 to 14 for boys)	*Latency Stage:* Absence of sexual strivings. Focus on mastering skills is valued by adults.	*Industry vs. Inferiority:* Children want to be productive or they feel inferior. Need to acquire social and academic skills. Chief social agents are teachers and peers.
Adolescence (about ages 12 to 18)	*Genital Period:* Period of mature sexuality. There is strong sexual interest in other people and in the establishment of mature sexual relationships.	*Identity vs. Role Confusion:* Need to resolve identity problems such as who one is, where one is going, and who one will be in the future. Failure to resolve identity problem results in confusion.
Young Adulthood (late teens and the 20s)		*Intimacy vs. Isolation:* "Shall I share my life with another person or live alone?" is the major question.
30 through retirement		*Generativity vs. Stagnation and Absorption:* "Will I be useful or will my life dwindle?"
After retirement		*Ego Integrity vs. Despair:* "Have I lived a full life or have I failed?"

CRITIQUE OF PSYCHOANALYTIC THEORIES

Table 2.1 presents the key aspects of Freud's psychosexual theory and Erickson's psychosocial theory. Psychoanalytic theories such as these have gained support for their emphasis on early relationships between children and caregivers as well as the inherent changes in children's needs within these relationships. Hence, there is an importance placed on the dynamic and changing parenting approaches for growing children. For example, an infant's needs are very different from an adolescent's needs. Sarah, at age 6 months is reliant on her parents for food, bathing, and physical comfort and assistance. Sarah's needs at age 17 years are very different - she can make her own food, bathe herself, and needs much less physical comfort and assistance from her parents.

Many researchers find that Erikson's theory is easy to relate to because of its relevance to child development. Everyone knows, for instance, that social and cultural factors, which are stressed by Erikson, influence human development. Researchers can also relate easily to the crises that characterize each stage. Erikson's theory also provides guidelines for the future since it covers the entire life span instead of just the short span of childhood.

Those who criticize psychoanalytic theories point out that some of the concepts are difficult to verify objectively or to use as a basis for research. For example, how does one quantify or measure the concepts of id, ego, and superego. Also, it has been noted that Erikson is imprecise about the causes of psychosocial development. For example, he has never clearly outlined what kinds of experiences resolve various psychosocial conflicts or crises. Others question whether an individual progresses through the different stages as Erikson suggests. Ciaccio (1971), for instance, found that Erikson's first five crises reflect different expressions of the same underlying crisis: The establishment of autonomy. Another major criticism of psychoanalytic theory points to Freud's heavy emphasis on sexual urges and aggressiveness as the rot of psychological discomfort. Many opponents of this paradigm hesitate to rely on this as the basis for all psychological issues and would like to have a broader pool of reasons for mental angst.

Freud's personality constructs and defense mechanisms have been and continue to be helpful in working with psychological issues such as anxiety and depression. While there are supporters and opponents to the views of unconscious urges purported by Freud's theory, personality constructs and defense mechanisms are important in understanding human angst.

COGNITIVE THEORIES OF CHILD DEVELOPMENT

Cognition: Activity of knowing, or the mental processes by which knowledge is acquired, elaborated, retrieved, and used to solve problems.

Cognitive theories of child development focus on the workings of the brain and its activities (mental processes). Three cognitive theories will be discussed here: cognitive developmental, sociocultural, and information processing theory.

PIAGET'S COGNITIVE DEVELOPMENTAL THEORY

Whereas Freud and Erikson were primarily interested in personality and emotional development, Piaget (1896 - 1980) concentrated on the individual's *cognitive* development. Cognition refers to the activity of knowing or to the mental processes by which knowledge is acquired, elaborated, stored, retrieved, and used to solve problems. Cognition includes a wide variety of activities, such as thinking, remembering, paying attention, perceiving, and learning—in short, everything that goes on in the human mind (Flavell, 1985). Piaget viewed cognitive development as the product of children's efforts to actively construct their understanding of the world and then to act on their world.

Box 2.5
Biography of the Foremost Cognitive Theorist

Jean Piaget (1896-1980)

Piaget was born in the small university town of Neuchâtel, Switzerland. His father was a professor of history who specialized in medieval literature. Young Piaget's main interest was the observation of animals in their natural surroundings. By age 11, Piaget had published his first professional paper, which was about an albino sparrow he had seen in a park.

In school, Piaget concentrated on biological sciences, and his genius was soon recognized. At age 15, he was offered the post of curator of the mollusk collection in a natural history museum, a job he turned down.

After graduating from high school, Piaget entered the University of Neuchâtel and earned undergraduate and graduate degrees, including a Ph.D., in natural science. Shortly after he received his doctorate, Piaget traveled to Zurich, where he served a brief internship at Eugen Bleuler's psychiatric clinic. It was here that Piaget was introduced to psychology. He studied Freudian theory and wrote a paper relating psychoanalysis to child psychology. He next studied abnormal psychology in Paris.

Shortly after his arrival in Paris, Piaget obtained a position at the Binet Laboratory constructing a standardized French version of reasoning tests developed in England. After administering the tests to his students, Piaget found that the children's incorrect answers were often more intriguing than the correct ones. He began to attend to those childish remarks and questions that adults usually find interesting or nonsensical. Piaget became convinced that children's "cute" sayings indicate the existence of a thinking process different from adults. Upon further questioning, Piaget found that many children believe that the sun and moon follow them when they are out for a walk; that anything that moves is alive; and that the names of objects reside in the objects themselves.

Piaget accepted an appointment as director of research at the Jean-Jacques Rousseau Institute in Geneva. There, he was able to devote all his energies and time to children's thinking. It was at the Rousseau Institute that Piaget developed his now famous clinical interview method that we discussed in Chapter 1.

Piaget viewed children as actively constructing their own cognitive worlds. Children are not passive creatures like machines that simply have information "poured" into them. Piaget believed that children act like scientists from the day that they are born. Like scientists, infants create integrative theories of their physical and social worlds as they try to adapt to their surroundings. As children interact with their surroundings, their view of the world keeps changing. In Piagetian terms, children continually acquire new *schemes* or *schemata* (Sing. scheme or schema), or patterns of behavior and thinking. For example, 2-year-old Sarah who lives next to a dairy farm and is familiar with cows has a cow scheme which consists of large, four-legged animals found near her house. Then, if she sees a horse for the first time and notices how it differs from cows, Sarah now has two different schemes, one for

Scheme: Basic mental structure which enables a child to coordinate and organize a systematic pattern of action or ways of reasoning.

cows and another for horses. She must now think differently about cows than about horses. For Piaget, the points at which Sarah's thinking undergoes major reorganizations are considered the beginnings of different stages in cognition.

Piaget's Four Stages of Cognitive Development

Piaget's cognitive developmental theory, like Freud's psychosexual theory and Erikson's psychosocial theory, is a stage theory. Piaget divided cognitive development into four major stages that he believed children go through according to their chronological age. Each cognitive stage is increasingly complex and qualitatively different from other stages. Furthermore, Piaget claimed that all children progress through the stages in exactly the same order. There is no skipping of stages because each successive stage builds on previous ones; there is an accumulation of skills and knowledge that depends upon the earlier stage. For instance, a child who has not mastered walking will not be able to run. Piaget believed that Sarah and Carlos actively construct their understanding of the world as they go through the four stages of cognitive development.

Table 2.2 summarizes Piaget's four cognitive stages as presented here.

Sensorimotor stage: The first of Piaget's cognitive stages, when learning occurs through sensing and manipulating objects.

- *Sensorimotor Stage*—Birth to 2 years. Initial knowledge is acquired through sensory perception (touching, hearing, and seeing) and through reflexes such as grasping and sucking.

Preoperational stage: The second period of Piaget's cognitive theory when there is increasing use of symbols and prelogical thought processes.

- *Preoperational Stage*—Ages 2 to 7 years. Symbols are used to represent the world cognitively, such as a 3-year-old "riding" a broom as if it were a horse or using a hair brush to "dust" the table. The preoperational child has not yet mastered the logical qualities of the next two stages.

Concrete-operational stage: In Piaget's theory, the third stage of cognitive development from about age 7 to 11 years when the children begin to think logically about concrete objects and situations.

- *Concrete-Operational Stage*—Ages 7 to 11 years. Children can now perform mental operations (addition, subtraction, multiplication, and division) that permit a kind of problem solving. Concrete-operational children know that the amount of play dough in front of them remains the same regardless of its appearance, such as in the form of a snake or a ball. For example, if Carlos were given two balls of play dough that were exactly the same size and each ball was then made into a different shape, Carlos would still recognize that they are the same size. Children still in the preoperational stage would not have this ability.

However, children's thinking in the concrete-operational stage falls short of adult intelligence, a hallmark of the formal-operational stage.

Formal-operational stage: In Piaget's theory, the fourth stage of cognitive development, which begins at about age 11 and when the individual can think logically about abstract principles and hypothetical situations.

- *The Formal-Operational Stage*—Ages 11 years and beyond, or never. This stage consists of higher-level abstract operations, including those that do not exist (e.g., total peace in the world) but are possible, as opposed to those that exist. Formal-operational children can now solve problems using abstract symbols such as the following:

Problem: Using X for boys, and Y for girls, how many boys and girls are there if there is a total of 45 children and there are 25 more boys than girls?

Solution: $x + y = 45$

$x - y = 25$

$$2x = 70$$

$x = 35; y = 10$

Answer: There are 35 boys and 10 girls

Operation

Operation: A mental routine for separating, combining, and transforming information mentally in a logical manner.

An important aspect of Piaget's stages of cognitive development is *operation*. For Piaget, an operation is a systematic, rational cognitive framework applied to concrete objects and to a world of possibilities where one operates logically on symbols and information that do not necessarily have counterparts in the real world. A key feature of an operation is its *reversibility,* a logical process or action that a child can do and undo. A child is capable of reversing his actions if he knows he can get back home from his friend's place if he retraces his steps in the opposite direction from which he came.

Reversibility: In Piaget's theory, the notion that something that has been changed can be retuned to its original state by undoing (reversing) the process that led to the change.

According to Piaget, a child is first able to operate at about age 7 years, the beginning of the concrete-operational stage. However, concrete-operational thinking falls short of adult intelligences in that it is not yet abstract. Concrete-operational thinking is focused on real, tangible objects and events. Formal-operational children (from age 11 on) are able to deal with events or relations that are possible but do not exist, as opposed to those that actually exist.

For Piaget, the ability to progress from one cognitive stage to another is based on two overriding assumptions about intelligence: *organization* and *adaptation*.

Organization

Organization: Piaget's term for the process of synthesizing and analyzing perceptions and thoughts.

An important feature of Piaget's view of cognitive development is the constant internal integration and rearrangement or *organization* of schemes. Once children form new cognitive structures (schemes), they start to rearrange them, linking them with other schemes so that they form a part of a strongly interconnected system. For example, Sarah may discover that the schemes of "trees," "children," and "parents" all move. She may next organize this new scheme of "moving objects" into "people" and "nonpeople." The process of organizing schemes into a strongly interconnected system enables Sarah to apply them jointly to the environment. By acquiring new schemes, Sarah is able to move from sucking on the mother's breast to doing complicated algebra problems. According to Piaget, Sarah would not be able to make the progression from one scheme to another if she could not adjust her thinking to accept new ideas or information, a cognitive process Piaget calls *adaptation*.

Table 2.2
Piaget's Stages of Cognitive Development

Approximate Age	Stage	Primary Schemata for Representing Experience	Developmental Milestones
Birth to 2 years	Sensorimotor	Development occurs through an infant's use of sensory and motor capabilities. At birth, an infant's intelligence consists of reflexes. By the end of the sensorimotor period, schemata are more complex, enabling babies to perform difficult sensorimotor coordination.	Primitive sense of "self" and "others." Object permanence: Child learns that an object continues to exist even when it is out of sight. Representational thought: Ability to imagine objects not present.
2 to 7 years	Preoperational	Use of symbolism in images and language to represent and understand environment. Children center on single, salient aspect of object or feature. Egocentric thought.	Children become imaginative in their play. Children realize that others may not see the world as they do. Capable of intermediate classification.
7 to 11 years	Concrete operations	Children use cognitive operations to reach a logical conclusion. Operations underlie logical problem solving and are also a system of internal (mental) actions.	Children are no longer fooled by appearances. Children can: • Classify • Conserve • Decenter • Reverse • Understand cause and effect.
11 years and beyond	Formal operations	Children now use systematic and abstract thought. Can think about thinking. Adult-type thinking is employed.	Use of hypotheses. Systematic deductive reasoning that permits consideration of several possible solutions and selection of correct answer.

Adaptation

Adaptation: Piaget's term for the inborn tendency to adjust one's thinking to become more attuned to the conditions imposed by the environment; takes place through assimilation and accommodation.

Piaget's concept of *adaptation* is rooted in his training as a biologist. He believed that a child is born with rudimentary cognition, or intelligence, in the form of reflexes such as sucking, grasping, and breathing. For Piaget, a reflex is a form of intelligence because it enables the baby to *adapt* to its environment and learn a new operation. An operation is a mental routine for separating, combining, and transforming information in a logical manner such as that involved in addition and subtraction.

In many instances, the child may find that new information does not match his current schemes. Such a conflict may occur if Carlos gets bitten when he tries to lay his head on the family dog just like he does on his pillow. If Carlos realizes that he must treat the dog differently than his pillow, the process of adaptation has occurred. For Piaget, the highest form of adaptation is cognition (or knowing). Piaget proposed that adaptation is reached when children revise and reorganize their schemes through two complementary processes: *assimilation* and *accommodation*.

Assimilation and accommodation. According to Piaget, when an individual is faced with a new situation, two types of responses are possible. One way of responding is to make some modifications in existing schemata, the other is to use a new set of schemata. When various experiences are taken in by the organism and are transferred to existing schemata, the adaptation process is called *assimilation*. For example, Carlos' ability to suck on his mother's breast enables him to suck on a bottle after he has made some minor adjustments, which Piaget calls assimilation. When new experiences cannot be assimilated by

Assimilation: The transfer of various experiences by the organism to existing schemata.

Accommodation:
Modifications in behavior and thinking that take place when the old ways of understanding something, the old schemes, no longer fit.

Equilibration: In Piagetian theory, an innate self-regulatory process that begins with the discovery of a conflict between the child's cognitive structures or schemes and results in equilibrium.

the child, existing schemata must be modified considerably in a process Piaget calls *accommodation*.

To illustrate *accommodation*, let's suppose that you have just bought a new car. You would likely find that you have little difficulty switching from your old car to the new one, although you might have to make some minor adjustments (do not press the brake so hard, use less force to turn the steering wheel). These slight adjustments are *assimilations*, to use Piaget's term. Now suppose that you want to learn how to fly an airplane. Airplanes and cars are so different that slight adjustments (assimilations) will not suffice. You must now learn a new set of responses (accommodation). The process by which assimilation and accommodation bring about more organized and powerful schemes for thinking is called *equilibration*. Equilibration refers to the movement from equilibrium to disequilibrium and back to equilibrium, in an attempt to adapt to a new situation.

Equilibration occurs when Carlos is unable to resolve a situation. He now exchanges ideas with others, argues with them, and tries new things. He realizes that others have a different point of view than he does and that there may be other ways of solving the problem. Such conflict, according to Piaget, promotes more complex forms of thought, action, and knowledge and results in the acquisition of new schemes.

Critique of Piaget

Piaget is regarded as one of the key figures in influencing our understanding of cognitive development (Zigler & Gilman, 1998). One contribution is that children may find a familiar event is uninteresting since it requires no changes in schemes. On the other hand, a child may not be interested in tasks or events that are totally incomprehensible because he cannot assimilate them.

One of the most frequent criticisms of Piaget is his claim that children's learning cannot be accelerated. For instance, Piaget says that children under 7 years of age cannot categorize objects into consistent, exhaustive, hierarchical categories. It appears that not only can children perform some operations before Piaget thought they were capable of such functions, but that children can be in different stages simultaneously (Flavell, Miller & Miller, 2002).

One theorist who disagreed sharply with Piaget's views on cognitive development was Russian psychologist Lev Vygotsky, discussed next. One point of disagreement was Piaget's contention that direct teaching by adults is not as important as Vygotsky claimed. Instead, Piaget emphasized children's active, *independent* efforts to make sense of the world. Also, Vygotsky did not think that all children move through the same sequence of stages as Piaget claimed. For Vygotsky, language was the key to continuous changes in thought and behavior that can vary greatly from culture to culture.

VYGOTSKY'S SOCIOCULTURAL THEORY

Sociocultural theory:
Vygotsky's approach that emphasizes how cognitive development proceeds as a result of social interactions among members of a culture.

It has only been fairly recently that the theory of Lev Vygotsky (1896-1934) on the child development has become widely available in the West. Vygotsky's cognitive based *sociocultural theory* recognizes both the cultural and social aspects of a child's development. He also stressed that the child's play is an integral part of constructing his or her own knowledge base according to his or her own individual genetic or biological makeup and experiences.

Natural Development

Vygotsky first recognized that children have a natural pattern of biological development which he called the "natural line" (Vygotsky, 1978). Maturation and growth form the basis of this development. Society and culture add to the experiences by giving input through the senses to facilitate cognitive development. The child has an inborn structure within the brain, which may be characterized as a scaffold. The scaffold is not static and changes over time through a process of social collaboration.

Box 2.6
Biography of a Sociocultural Theorist:

Lev Semenovich Vygotsky (1896 - 1934)*: A Major Contextualist*

Born in czarist Byelorussia of middle class Jewish parents, Vygotsky was the second of eight children. His mother, a licensed teacher, was devoted to raising the family and his father was a bank manager. His early education consisted of a combination of public and private schools as the family moved from the country to Gomel, a small yet culturally developed city. Thus, he was widely educated in the liberal arts tradition. A gifted student at a very young age, he was described as a brilliant man, an excellent scholar and a highly productive theorist.

His search for a formal education was difficult because of his Jewish heritage. Only a small percentage of students of Jewish heritage were allowed to enter higher education institutions. When the time came to apply to college the situation became more difficult as the few Jews who met the high standards were put into a lottery for admission. Luckily, Vygotsky was among the very few whose names were drawn.

His choice of subject areas to study was also limited due to his background. He could not study anything that might lead to public school teaching, as Jews were not allowed to teach in the state-run schools. He chose law, and at the same time he joined an unofficial group of scholars outside of the University. With these professors he pursued the fields of art and literature and later psychology.

The rest of his life was devoted to reading and studying in the field of psychology while translating the work of Freud, Piaget, Kohler, Stern, Gesell, and others for the Russians. He focused on developing a theory of child development that would fit well with the Marxist philosophy of cultural and social change that was redefining Russia.

After the Russian revolution of 1917 he became more active in the field of psychology. Being literate in eight languages he was able to read widely in his many fields of interest. Unfortunately, just as these areas of study were exploding across Europe, he became ill with tuberculosis. He died as a result of this illness at the age of thirty seven.

Vygotsky lived in the turbulent and violent times of the Russian Revolution. His work was banned by the politicians of the time and did not really surface in the west until after the death of Stalin in 1953. Even then, the popularity of the Behaviorists and the Constructivists kept Vygotsky from being well known. Only in the last few decades have scholars continued to research and extend his ideas. We are starting to see and hear more of Vygotsky's theories as researchers and educators see the benefit of looking at the child's cognitive development within a societal framework.

Scaffolding

Scaffolding: Vygotsky's term for an instructional process in which the teacher continually adjusts the amount and type of support he or she offers as the child continues to develop more sophisticated skills.

Scaffolding Vygotsky's term for an instructional process in which the teacher continually adjusts the amount and type of support he or she offers as the child continues to develop more sophisticated skills. Each area influences the other right from the beginning. Scaffolding helps the individual adapt mental processes to the needs of his or her particular culture. For example, if you lived in a hot hunter-gatherer society which incorporated much subtle knowledge about the natural environment, then your mental structure would exhibit the language, tools and abilities that would make you successful in that environment. However, if you grew up in the inner city, low income, mechanized society, your mental structures would conform to the abilities that would make you successful on the streets of a metropolis.

Vygotsky suggested that mental functions appear first as shared cultural experiences and then become part of each individual's cognitive-psychological functioning (Vygotsky, 1993).

Language

Vygotsky believed that the kinds of changes that occur for any particular child are the result of the interaction between the child's unique mental and physical constructs and his society and culture. Language is the primary tool for human interaction. Vygotsky also believed that private speech (self-talk) helps children become more socially competent (Santiago-Delefosse & Delefosse, 2002). Language (both self-talk and the talk of others) is also an important mediator in a cognitive process. Language allows a child to master signs, symbols, and communication with others in his or her society. This is one reason Vygotsky hypothesized that there is such a wide variance and breadth of human cognitive ability. It also suggests that people from very different cultures literally cannot "speak the same language." They don't have enough common experiences to fully understand each other. Language functions help mental functions move from inter-personal to intra-personal or internal mechanism (Vygotsky, 1993).

Zone of Proximal Development (ZPD)

Zone of Proximal Development: The area between what a child can do by himself or herself and what the child can achieve with the help of a competent adult or peer.

Vygotsky's concept of the *Zone of Proximal Development* is perhaps the most useful to educators. This zone is the area between what the child can do entirely by himself or herself and what the child can achieve with the help of an adult or a competent peer. The adult's language and actions become the bridge for furthering the child's cognitive development. The adult needs to exhibit warmth, acceptance and responsiveness which helps to keep the child in the ZPD where most learning takes place. Tasks below the ZPD are too simple and of little value; those above the zone are too difficult to be very useful.

Figure 2.2

Vygotsky's Collaboration and the Zone of Proximal Development

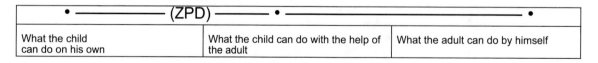

What the child can do on his own	What the child can do with the help of the adult	What the adult can do by himself

Figure2.2 indicates the ZPD for a child as he or she collaborates with an adult or competent peer who is a tutor or mentor. The ZPD is influenced by what the child already knows and moves as the child becomes more competent

and attains a higher level of functioning. Let's use Vygotsky's ZPD to illustrate how 9-year-old Carlos' cognitive development can be "moved" forward (with his father's help) to determine the size of his bedroom in the new home the family has just purchased.

Carlos' understanding of room size can be pushed further ahead by using age-appropriate, but cognitively demanding, speech such as describing the size of his new bedroom in more complex terms (for Carlos) such as "square feet," rather than in simpler terms such as "big" or "small".

To teach Carlos how to calculate the size of his new bedroom, his dad (a skilled adult) could have Carlos measure the size of the linoleum tiles (which are 1 square foot each) and counting the number of tiles on the floor. After figuring that each title is 1 square foot and that 300 tiles cover the floor, Carlos discovers that the floor is 300 square feet.

Carlos can also discover the size of the floor by multiplying the length of the room by the width (20 feet by 15 feet) and obtain the figure of 300 again. Carlos' ZPD could be moved still further ahead by calculating the dimensions of an area that contains fractions such as $10^{1}/2$ by $15^{1}/4$. With each new task the father adjusts the amount and type of support he offers as Carlos develops more sophisticated skills, an instructional process Vygotsky calls scaffolding.

Vygotsky's View on the Importance of Play

Vygotsky argued that learning leads to cognitive development rather than development leading to learning as in the Piagetian paradigm (Vygotsky, 1967). Nowhere is this more evident than in the play of children. In play, the biological aspects of development come together with the sociocultural aspects to make sense and create meaning for children in a shared context.

Interaction in a play setting with peers or even with things by himself or herself would lead a child to internalize and learn from that experience. Language becomes a tool in the play setting that facilitates learning through speech, social interaction, and cooperative play. A child is an active participant in the interpsychological exchange of play. As he or she internalizes the experiences, he or she changes his or her intrapsychological perspective. He or she becomes able to move to a higher level of understanding. Each layer of learning substantially changes the layer beneath and transforms the previous learning (Vygotsky, 1993).

Critique of Vygotsky's Sociocultural Theory

Lev Vygotsky's concept of sociocultural constructivism makes him right for our times. As the world and our society changes, we are left with troubling questions about child development. How could our children have become so violent? So self-involved? So uncaring about the effect of their negative actions upon themselves and others? Vygotsky's model helps us understand how our societies mold the way children think and act.

The strength of Vygotsky's approach lies in the expanded definition of the thinking-learning process and the emphasis on language as a transmitter and a storage system for knowledge. The inclusion of the sociological component into the idea of cognitive development broadens the perspective in a logical way. Many other theories recognize the role of society in shaping behavior. Vygotsky has us thinking about society's impact on thinking itself. The theory demands that we look at the rapidly changing world in which we live and realize that now is the time to give children the abilities to live in such a diverse world.

Despite all that Vygotsky has to tell us and all the ways in which he stimulates our imaginations and our thinking processes, it is best to remember a number of weaknesses in his work. The first is only knowing his theoretical perspective from translations where the essence may have been altered. In fact, his own theory warns us of such a possibility.

Vygotsky's theories have a strong link with other theoreticians in the U.S. and Europe (e.g. John Dewey and Jean Piaget). It is helpful to read his work in light of these other men and in the light of the historical perspective of his times.

A major controversy about Vygotsky's theory is the role of language. Vygotsky claims that language and thought are socially based even in their earliest forms. He also says that when young children talk to themselves, they are using language to govern their behavior and to guide themselves. Piaget says that when young children talk to themselves (known as self-talk), they are reflecting their immaturity.

Omissions in his theory are the questions that Vygotsky did not discuss, perhaps due in part to his untimely death at the age of 37 years. He did not focus on the individual's development from the perspective of the child. Certainly these basic individual differences would create various outcomes from the interaction of adult and child. Vygotsky always presented the adult's role in a positive supportive light. What would it be if purposeful harm or ignorance were presented? Finally, there are assumptions that we are not able to test. For example, do people in different cultures really process information differently? What would happen to those that have limited or no language?

Undoubtedly, a major reason for the multitude of questions concerning Vygotsky's theory of child development is his inability to spend more time on his theory due to his untimely death. It is an exciting time in which we live. We are again asking fundamental questions that engage us in debate. Certainly, Vygotsky has given us much to talk and think about.

INFORMATION-PROCESSING THEORY

Information processing:
The application of mental operations that we use in completing intellectual tasks in a step-by-step fashion.

Information-processing theory emerged in the 1970s and is another cognitive-based theoretical perspective that explains how the mind manages information and tackles intellectual tasks. The underlying paradigm of *information processing* theory is that the brain and its actions are similar to that of a computer. Analogies are drawn between computer hardware and the brain, and computer software and cognitions. Therefore, while no specific human founder of this theory can be identified, it is often said that computers themselves are the creators of this theory.

Unlike Piagetian stage theory and similar to Vygotsky's continuous sociocultural theory, informational processing theory does not describe development in stages like fashion. Instead, cognitive development is a continuous process in which information processing abilities increase over time.

The central foundation of information processing theory focuses on memory processes and how the mind processes, stores, and retrieves information. Memory is a major cognitive function composed of several components: sensory memory, short term memory, and long term memory.

Figure 2.3 shows how these three components work together. Sensory memory notices all sensory information - spoken word, tactile sensations, visual pictures. The sensory memory selects the information that will be further processed and sends it to short term memory. Short term memory is said to have the capacity to store 7 chunks of information at one time. This memory store is where we repeat and remember a phone number given to us by calling information. We simply need that number for a short amount of time, enough time to dial the number we are calling. Short term memory selects and processes information to be sent and permanently stored in our long term memory bank for future use and retrieval.

The process of understanding a known spoken word can be understood well under the information processing theory. The word is first heard when the sounds enter the sensory memory. The sound patterns of the word are recognized and the word moves into the short term memory store for purposes of being processed. Because information is processed in the short term memory, it is also known as working memory.The word's meaning is retrieved from long term memory and placed in short term memory so that the word and its meaning can be linked for understanding and use. Let's use the word "no" as an example. As a two-year-old, Sarah hears the word "no" often from her parents. They use it to warn her of danger and to teach her appropriate behaviors. When Sarah asks for a third cookie and hears the word "no" from her mother, her short term memory matches the word "no" with its meaning from long term memory. The meaning has been stored from previous experience with the word. Sarah now understands that she will not get the third cookie that she wanted.

Critique of Information Processing Theory

Information processing theory is seen as a mostly positive contributor to the field of child development. Proponents value the stance that children are active in seeking and manipulating information as opposed to the inactivity of some learning theories. This theory also provides very detailed explanations and descriptions of cognitive processes that prove useful in studying child development. While there is considerable worth in this theory, opponents purport that it does not contain enough description of the actual developmental changes in cognition over time.

Figure 2.3
Information Processing Theory Model

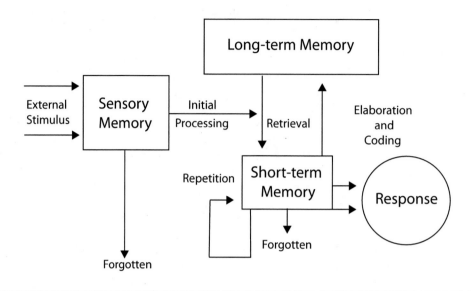

Source: Citation: Huitt, W. (2003). The information processing approach to cognition. Educational Psychology Interactive. Valdosta, GA: Valdosta State University. Website: www.chiron.valdosta.edu/whuitt/col/cogsys/infoproc.html

BIOLOGICAL AND ECOLOGICAL THEORIES OF CHILD DEVELOPMENT

While some "environmental" theorists, such as Pavlov, Skinner, and Bandura claim that factors that are not inherited (reward, punishment, and past experiences) form the basis for child development, other theorists subscribe to a biological origin.

Biological theory: A model of development that views all organisms as having a basic set of material characteristics such as survival, metabolism, and regulation.

A cornerstone of *biological theories* of development is that every species has its own distinctive form of physical organization and pattern of behavioral traits. These tendencies are programmed in the genes or influenced by physiological processes, such as hormonal changes. Of particular interest to biological theorists are innate responses (a child smiling at its mother and one child pushing another) that are instrumental in the individual's development. The cry of an infant may be biologically programmed because such behavior usually results in the caregiver rushing to the infant. Biological theorists further believe that the caregiver's quick response to the cry is caused by biological factors (Bowlby, 1973). We should not forget that despite the heavy emphasis on biological factors, environment also plays a (minor) role in the child's development according to biological theorists. Among those who place considerable emphasis on the role of biology in a child's development is Arnold Gesell.

Gesell's Ontogenetic Theory

Gesell's ontogenetic theory: A biological theory that stresses that a child's development is genetically prescribed (hereditary) and controlled by maturation.

Arnold Gesell's (1880-1961) biological theory of child development, called *ontogenetic*, was prominent in America during the first half of the twentieth century. Gesell's major thesis is that a child's development is genetically prescribed, and unfolds according to a particular hereditary blueprint known as *maturation* (Gesell & Ilg, 1943-46). Maturation is the orderly sequence of changes dictated by our genetic blueprint. According to Gesell, maturation plays an almost exclusive role in the early development of Sarah and Carlos. Environment plays a slightly more important role later.

Maturation: The orderly sequence of changes dictated by our genetic blueprint.

Box 2.7
Biography of a Maturation Theorist

Arnold Gesell (1880-1961)

Arnold Gesell was born in Alma, Wisconsin. When he graduated from high school, he was already committed to science and teaching. Gesell earned his Ph.D. in 1906 at Clark University, where he came under the influence of G. Stanley Hall, one of the pioneers in child psychology.

Following graduation, Gesell spent several years as a teacher and principal in a public school and as a university professor. He founded the Gesell Institute of Human Development in 1911 at Yale University and remained its director until his formal retirement in 1948. While at Yale, Gesell obtained a degree in medicine, hoping that medical training would give him greater depth as a researcher.

Gesell combined clinical work with scientific observation of children. His photographic and one-way mirror studies of infants brought new exactitude to the study of young children. Gesell also wrote books for parents with advice such as feeding babies only when they display signs of hunger, and allowing the children to sleep, play, or explore according to their own schedules. Gesell will probably be best remembered for his development of statistical norms–a type of developmental timetables–for various behaviors in children.

Gesell believed it is possible to predict different stages of a child's behavior as a result of controls exercised by maturation, the natural unfolding of a person's potential at a sequence of change governed by a genetic hereditary blueprint that is relatively independent of environmental events. A particular process, such as walking, cannot be hurried since we must wait until the child is ready. By readiness, Gesell meant completion of necessary physical and neurological development (e.g. leg strength and balance). As a result of his emphasis on the importance of maturation in the developmental process, Gesell popularized the idea that children cannot learn new behaviors until they reach the appropriate level of physical and neurological readiness.

Developmental norms: Standards developed by Arnold Gesell to identify the ages at which different forms of behavior emerge.

Gesell developed standards, or *developmental norms*, to identify the ages at which different forms of behavior (crawling, sitting) could be expected to emerge. In a 1938 publication, Gesell and Thompson provided 40 tables of information containing norms (group averages) for children's activities such as waking and sleeping patterns, vocalizing, playing, feeding habits, standing, and walking (Gesell & Thompson, 1938; Gallahue & Ozmun, 2002). Developmental norms are useful benchmarks for parents as long as they don't expect their children to develop precisely according to the norms. However, if the deviation from the norm is considerable, professional help should be sought.

Critique of Gesell

There is some question whether Gesell's findings apply to all children. For instance, the upper-middle-class children Gesell studied might become ready for school without special training. But children from disadvantaged homes appear to need extra stimulation (compensatory education) before they are ready for school. Gesell has also been criticized for the minor role he attributes to environment.

Gesell's work is important because of the systematic and objective methods he used to collect information. His method of compiling norms on children's development has been extended to other areas of study, adulthood and aging.

Ethology

Ethology: The study of lower animals in their natural habitats.

Much of the knowledge about the biological origin of children's behavior comes from ethology. *Ethology* is the study of lower animals in their natural habitats with emphasis on the interaction of genes and the environment. This relatively new field of study became prominent during the 1950s when several European zoologists argued that many theorists had overlooked or ignored important biological contributions to human and lower animal behavior. Ethologists claim such application is warranted because lower animals are quite similar to human beings. In short, ethology stresses that behavior is strongly influenced by biology (Rosenzweig, 2000). Indeed, lower animals and humans share about 98 percent of DNA (the chemical basis of heredity).

Although ethologists, like other biologically oriented theorists, spend considerable time delving into the innate features of animal behaviors, they do not ignore the role of environment. However, ethologists insist there are certain behavioral elements, such as an infant's attachment to its mother, that must be regarded as innate and therefore are relatively unchangeable.

The principles of ethology are based largely on inborn or biologically inherited influences such as *instinct*, *critical periods*, and *imprinting*.

Instinct: Behavior whose underlying biological pattern has been produced by maturation, rather than by learning.

Instinct. Instinct is a behavior whose underlying biological pattern has been produced by maturation (an inherited biological plan), rather than by learning, and is consistent throughout a species. Ethologists consider certain behaviors to be biologically determined (instinctual) in the same way as physical structures of the body.

Critical period: A limited time frame during which child is biologically able to acquire new information and skills.

Examples of instinctual behavior abound. Konrad Lorenz (1903–1989), a zoologist who won the Nobel Prize for his discoveries in ethology, demonstrated how young geese begin to follow their mothers from birth as part of their instinct for survival. If hatched in an incubator, the goslings follow the first moving object they see, a form of attachment Lorenz called *imprinting*.

Imprinting: A newborn's innate attachment behavior to the first moving object it sees, usually its mother.

Critical periods and imprinting. Lorenz noticed that there was a critical period—usually during the first 2 or 3 days after hatching—when goslings could be imprinted to their mother. For ethologists, imprinting refers to a sudden biologically primed form of bonding during a critical period in development when animals, including humans, are biologically programmed so that certain experiences, such as seeing a moving object, are particularly influential.

While a form of imprinting, or bonding, appears to take place in humans, the timing of the critical period is less certain than in lower animals. According to some investigators, the critical period for human babies is from about 6 months to about the end of the first year of life. For other investigators, the critical period for bonding between a human mother and her infant is during the first few hours of life. According to this view, if bonding (imprinting) does not take place during the first few critical hours after birth, the baby will feel harmful effects that may last indefinitely (Klaus & Kennel, 1982).

Biological Bases of Temperament and Other Traits

While most biological theorists focus on shared patterns of behavior, one group has focused on the influence of biological factors which make us unique. For instance, a major focus of this group of researchers has been the individual's emotionality (the tendency to get distressed or upset easily), activity (the tendency toward vigorous, rapid behavior), and sociability (the preference of being with others rather than alone) (Buss & Plomin, 1984; 1986). These basic styles with which an individual responds to the environment, and which can be observed during the first months of life, are collectively called *temperament*. According to ethologists, the traits which compose temperament are inherited and persist throughout life (Plomin, 2002; Plomin & DeFries, 1985).

Temperament: Basic innate behavioral style and characteristic emotional response to one's environment.

In addition to possible biological origins of temperament, researchers have studied inherited components of specific traits such as intelligence and language acquisition (Piatelli-Palmerini, 1980). The ability to use language appears to mature at a fixed pace inherited by all human beings even though environment plays a role in "triggering" the realization of linguistic potential.

Critique of Biological Theories

One of the major arguments against the biological origin of behavior is the lack of evidence for genetic control of specific human social behavior (Edelman, 1982). For instance, no one has yet found a gene which controls aggressiveness or shyness.

Despite the lack of direct evidence of genetic control of social behavior, biological theorists continue to build their case. Psychologists who adopt the biological perspective have recently presented considerable evidence indicating that psychological development of traits such as temperament is a progression of stagelike advances caused by changes in the biological structure of the organism.

BRONFENBRENNER'S BIOECOLOGICAL THEORY OF CHILD DEVELOPMENT

Bioecological theory of child development: Bronfenbrenner's term for the environmental effects on a child's development within a larger family context that includes brothers and sisters, grandparents, the parents' jobs, and the neighborhood.

In the past couple of decades, there has been a strong push to consider the context, known as ecology, in which the child lives. The *bioecological theory of child development* stresses the importance of understanding not only the relationship between organisms and the various environmental systems, but also the relations between such systems themselves. A major proponent of the *bioecology of child development* is Urie Bronfenbrenner (1917–1999).

Bronfenbrenner (1979a, 1979b, 1986, 1989, 1995, 2000) proposed a model of child development with levels of a child's physical and social environment that simultaneously influence individuals. Bronfenbrenner argues that we cannot fully understand human development without considering how a person is influenced by each system or level, such as his family or peers, *as* well as by broad cultural factors such as society's views on premarital sex and on homosexuality. Bronfendbrenner stresses that all relationships are bidirectional. That is, adults affect children's behavior, but the children also affect the parents' behavior. A father who is more than six feet tall is likely to have a different effect on his children than if he were five feet tall. On the other hand, the children are likely to react differently to a taller father than to a shorter one. If these reciprocal reactions occur often over time, they have a lasting impact on children's development (Collins *et al.*, 2000).

Bronfenbrenner's Five Environmental Systems

In Bronfenbrenner's view, Sarah and Carlos' developments are influenced by five environmental systems, ranking from the contexts of direct interactions with people such as the immediate family to the broad-based contexts of culture such as religion and politics.

Microsystem: In Bronfenbrenner's ecological systems theory, the activities and interaction patterns in the child's immediate surroundings.

1. *The microsystem.* The most central system or level in Bronfenbrenner's ecological theory of development is the *microsystem*, the immediate environment in which the child lives. This context includes the child's family, peers, school, and neighborhood. As the child develops, he or she is increasingly able to shape his or her microsystem. For instance, the older a child is, the more he or she can influence the behavior of his or her peers by being nice to them, cooperative, critical, and so on.

Mesosystem: In Bronfenbrenner's ecological systems theory, the activities which involve the reciprocal relationships between microsystems.

2. *The mesosystem.* The next system or level is the mesosystem, which involves the reciprocal relationships between microsystems. For example, what happens at home (divorce, death, etc.) influences what happens at school, such as a decline in the child's school performance. The mesosystem is like links in a chain that bind children to parents, students to teachers, and the family to its school.

Exosystem: In Bronfenbrenner's ecological systems theory, the activities which includes social settings that do not contain the children but inherently affect their experiences in their immediate settings.

3. *The exosystem.* The third level of Bronfenbrenner's ecological theory of development is called the exosystem. The exosystem represents the broader influences including societal institutions such as the city government, recreational facilities, churches, and the police. Usually children are not directly involved as active participants in the exosystem, but are affected by it. For example, the happenings in the parent's workplace do not directly include the children (they are not present there). However, the child's life, home life, will be directly affected by parental workplace satisfaction or financial constraints.

Macrosystem: In Bronfenbrenner's ecological system theory, the cultural values, laws, customs, and resources that influence experiences and interactions at inner levels of the environment.

4. *The macrosystem.* The fourth level of Bronfenbrenner's ecological theory is called the macrosystem that includes the ideologies, values, laws, and customs of a particular culture. For example, a major reason for my receiving a good education was the high regard for education in the community (Ukrainian-Polish) in which I grew up.

Chronosystem: In Bronfenbrenner's ecological system theory, the interconnectedness of environmental influences on child development.

5. *The chronosystem.* The fifth level or system of Bronfenbrenner's ecological theory of child development is called *chronosystem*, the patterning of life events and transitions over the life course, as well as sociocultural circumstances. For example, the negative effects of divorce on children peak in the first year after the parental breakup. The effects are more traumatic for sons than for daughters.

Bronfenbrenner's ecological approach emphasizes the interconnectedness of environmental influences on child development. A parent's loss of a job may affect the child's relationship with his peers. Conversely, a change in one system may have little impact if the other systems or levels remain unchanged. For instance, the introduction of the most sophisticated computers in school may have little effect on the child's school performance if the family continues to downplay the value of education.

As children get older, they consistently modify, select, and create their own settings and experiences. According to ecological theory, children are both the products and producers of their environments which create a network of independent effects. For example, a child may turn a deaf ear to his parents when they downplay the value of an education but listen attentively to a neighbor who extols the value of an education. The neighbor's encouragement may motivate the child to study harder and get better grades. Earning higher grades may lead to friendships with the better students in class.

Since a child's heredity joins with environmental forces to mold a child's development, Bronfenbrenner recently characterized his perspective as a bioecological model, adding biological influences to his theory, but still insisting that environmental contexts predominate in child development.

Critique of Bronfenbrenner's Bioecological Theory

Bronfenbrenner's bioecological theory of child development has gained considerable prominence among scientists during the last couple of decades. It provides the most differentiated and complete account of contextual influences on children's development. Contextual influences means that development is the product of both immediate and distant environments (e.g., family divorce and the war in Iraq), which influence each other. Further, contrary to most theories of child development which emphasize development during the first 15 or 20 years of life, Bronfenbrenner stresses influences on development over the entire life span. He also presents a systematic examination of macro and micro dimensions of environmental systems and pays considerable attention to connections between environmental settings (mesosystem).

A recurring criticism of Bronfenbrenner' theory is it pays too little attention to the biological foundations of child development. Also, it has been pointed out that inadequate attention is given to cognitive processes.

Figure 2.1

Bronfenbrenner's bioecological mode

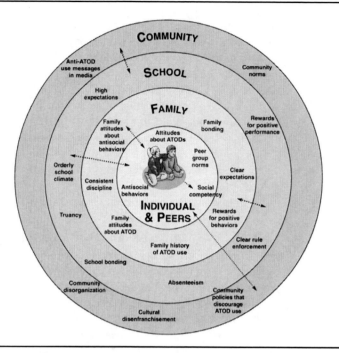

Source: The Virginia Department of Behavioral Health and Developmental Services website; www.dbhds.virginia.gov

Box 2.8

Biography of a Bioecological Theorist

Urie Bronfenbrenner (1917- 2005)

Upon his death, Urie Bronfenbrenner was the Jacob Gould Sherman Professor of Human Development and Family Studies and of Psychology at Cornell University. Born in Moscow, Russia in 1917, he came to the United States at the age of 6. After graduating from high school in Haverstraw, N.Y., he received a bachelors degree from Cornell University in 1938, where he completed a double major in Psychology and Music. He then went on to graduate work in Developmental Psychology, completing an M.A. at Harvard followed by a Doctorate from the University of Michigan in 1942. The day after receiving his degree, he was inducted into the Army. From Ph.D. to Pvt in 24 hours!

During World War II, he served as a psychologist in a variety of assignments in the Air Corps, the Office of Strategic Services, and, after completing officer training, in the U.S. Army Medical Corps. Following demobilization, and a two-year stint as an Assistant Professor of Psychology at the University of Michigan, he moved in 1948 to his present location at Cornell.

From the very beginning of his scholarly work, Bronfenbrenner pursued three mutually reinforcing themes: 1) developing theory and corresponding research designs at the frontiers of developmental science; 2) laying out the implications and applications of developmental theory and research for policy and practice; and 3) communicating - through articles, lectures, and discussions - the findings of the private and public sector. Bronfenbrenner also played an active role in the design of developmental programs in the United States and elsewhere, including being one of the founders of Head Start.

His widely-published contributions won him honors and distinguished awards both at home and abroad. He held six honorary degrees, three of them from European universities. The most recent American award (1996), henceforth to be given annually in his name, is for "Lifetime Contribution to Developmental Psychology in the service of Science and Society."

Description of Bronfenbrenner obtained at Bronfenbrenner's BioPage (Cornell U.)

Comparison of Theories

When comparing the theories presented in this chapter, it is important to remember that no single theory offers a complete framework for interpreting child development (Vancouver, 2005). Each theory attempts to tell us something about Sarah and Carlos' development. Each theory, in its own way, sees Sarah and Carlos' development as the result of interaction between innate and environmental forces. Also, different theories focus on different aspects of development. For example, Piaget's theory focuses on cognitive development, whereas Erikson's theory focuses on social and emotional development.

The various theories differ in their emphasis on scientific experimentation. Psychoanalysts have generally spurned scientific experiments; behaviorists have a fetish for them. All other theories are between these two extremes. Regardless of the position of a theory on this continuum, most theorists agree that we need new theories. Here is a chance for you to test your own ideas since many people believe that every individual possesses naive or intuitive theories about the world (Springer, 1990). One theorist (Thomas, 2000) has developed 25 theories of human development, each theory delineating a particular aspect of culture that shapes people.

Table 2.3
Comparison of Major Theories of Child Development

Perspective	Main Characteristics	Strengths	Weaknesses
Learning Theories	*B.F. Skinner's Operant Conditioning:* • Behavior is predictable and controllable. • Environment controls our behavior. Development involves behavior changes that are shaped by reinforcement and punishment.	Precise research (scientific) methods. Clear definition of goals.	Failure to define appropriate reinforcement.
	Pavlov's Classical Conditioning: • Unconditioned responses can be conditioned when paired with neutral stimuli. Learning occurs when neutral stimuli become so strongly associated with natural stimuli that they elicit the same response.	Provides a solid foundation for understanding the development of phobias.	Cognition, emotion, social factors, and heredity are ignored.
	Bandura's Social-Cognitive Learning Theory: • Individual plays an active role as a learner; environment affects the child. • Learning occurs by observing model. • Reinforcement is not necessary for learning.	Cognitive elements in learning are emphasized. Wide variety of learning is possible.	Little attention is paid to biological factors. Ignores qualitative changes in cognition.
Psychoanalytic Theories	*Freud's Psychosexual Theory:* • Behavior is controlled by unconscious forces which are usually sexual and/or aggressive in nature. Childhood trauma and experiences provide foundation for adult behavior and problems.	Demonstrates importance of unconscious behavior.	Based largely on assumptions that are untestable. Findings are based on studies of abnormal people.
	Erikson's Psychosocial Theory: • Personality development proceeds throughout life in 8 stages (crises). • Lifelong search for identity.	Emphasis on social and cultural influence on development. Easy to relate to crises.	Difficult to verify concepts. Imprecise causes of psychosocial development.
Cognitive Theories	*Piaget's Cognitive Development Theory:* • Intellectual development proceeds in qualitatively different stages. • Intellectual growth is the result of interplay between biological and environmental factors. • Individual is an active organism, constantly seeking to adapt. • Learning occurs through assimilation and accommodation. • Cognition is represented by schemata.	Demonstrates that children's thinking undergoes qualitative changes. Indicates similarity in learning for all children.	Maintains that children's learning cannot be accelerated. Ignores unconscious motivation. Too preoccupied with biological processes.

Table 2.3

Comparison of Major Theories of Child Development

Perspective	Main Characteristics	Strengths	Weaknesses
	Vygotsky's Sociocultural Theory: • Social interaction is the source of cognitive development. • Learning leads to cognitive development rather than development leading to learning. • Child's play is an integral part of constructing his own knowledge base.	The expanded definition of the thinking-learning process and the emphasis on language as a transmitter and a storage system for knowledge. The inclusion of the sociological component into the idea of cognitive development broadens the perspective in a logical way.	Lack of focus upon the individual's development from the perspective of the child. Lack of further theoretical explanation due to Vygotsky's early death.
	Information Processing Theory: • The brain and its actions are similar to that of a computer; analogies are drawn between computer hardware and the brain, and computer software and cognitions. • Focused on memory processes and how the mind processes, stores, and retrieves information.	Children are active in seeking and manipulating information as opposed to the inactivity of some learning theories. Provides very detailed explanations and descriptions of cognitive processes that prove useful in studying child development.	Does not contain enough description of the actual developmental changes in cognition over time.
Biological and Ecological Theories	*Gesell's Ontogenetic Theory:* • Child develops through maturation process (but not through stages).	Systematic and objective methods are used to collect information.	Findings are based on upper-middle class children—may not apply to all children.
	Ethology: • Major influence on children is nature, which is similar in both lower animals and humans. • Lower animals are studied in natural habitats.	Reminds us that children are inherently biological creatures whose inborn characteristics affect their development.	No evidence for genetic control of specific human social behavior. Many claims are untestable (e.g., cannot prove that certain behaviors are inborn). Role of environment is de-emphasized.
Perspective	Main Characteristics	Strengths	Weaknesses
	Bronfenbrenner's Bioecological Theory: • Development is the individual's growing ability to understand and influence his or her ecological environment.It unfolds like a set of nested structures, each inside the next, like a set of Russian dolls. • The child and environment continually influence one another. • Focus is on the context in which development occurs. • Development is influenced by immediate and more distant environments which typically influence each other.	Stresses the importance of understanding the relationships between the organisms and various environmental systems such as the family. Expanded view of children's environment by going beyond conditions immediately surrounding the child.	Continuity and change are emphasized at the expense of stability. Individual differences are not emphasized.

SUMMARY

The major theories that describe child development are *learning, psychoanalytic, cognitive, and biological and ecological.* Table 2.3 presents a comparison of the major child development theories.

Learning theories encompass those of Pavlov, Skinner, and Bandura and focus on the environment as playing a pivotal role in development. Psychoanalytic theories are less scientific than learning theories and include Freud's psychoanalytic theory and Erikson's psychosocial theory. Freud emphasized the power of the unconscious while Erikson focused on cultural and social influences in identity development.

Cognitive theories included cognitive development, sociocultural, and information processing. These theories are characterized by cognitions and the development of intellectual activities. Jean Piaget's cognitive development theory is a famous stage theory characterized by active interaction between a child and his/her environment. Vygotsky's cognitive based *sociocultural theory* recognizes both the cultural and social aspects of a child's development. He also stressed that the child's play is an integral part of constructing his own knowledge base according to his own individual genetic or biological makeup and experiences. Information processing theory is known for its link between human cognitive development and computer processing.

Biological theories, Gesell's ontogenetic theory and the theory of ethology, provided an understanding of development as it relates to hereditary and genetic factors. Bronfenbrenner's bioecological theory is known for highlighting the importance of understanding the relationships between the organisms and various environmental systems such as the family.

Each of the these theories have strengths and weaknesses and each have contributed to the field of child development. While no theory is a perfect interpretation for any and all child development questions, they each can provide an important perspective. For example, we saw an example of Carlos' behavior described at the beginning of this chapter be potentially explained by Freud's psychosexual theory. We could also apply behaviorism to Carlos' behavior with recognition that perhaps this behavior is simply an imitation of what Carlos has observed of his father.

IMPORTANT TERMS

Accommodation
Adaptation
Anal stage
Assimilation
Autonomy
Basic trust versus mistrust,
    Erikson's
Behaviorism
Bioecological theory of child
    development, Bronfenbrenner's
Biological theory
Chronosystem
Classical conditioning
Cognition
Sociocultural theory, Vygotsky's
Concrete-operational stage
Conscious
Conservation
Crisis
Defense mechanism
Developmental norms
Ego
Ego ideal
Electra complex
Equilibration
Equilibrium
Erikson's basic trust
Ethology
Extrinsic reinforcement
Formal-operational stage
Gender identity
Genital stage
Gesell's ontogenetic theory
Id
Identity
Identity crisis
Imprinting
Instinct
Intrinsic reinforcement
Latency stage
Learning theory
Libido

Maturation
Method of approximations
Microsystem
Model
Negative reinforcement
Neoanalysis
Observational learning
Oedipus (Oedipal) complex
Ontogenetic theory, Gesell's
Operant conditioning
Operation
Oral stage
Organismic theory
Organization
Phallic stage
Preconscious (foreconscious)
Preoperational stage
Psychoanalysis
Psychosexual development
Psychosocial theory, Erickson's
Rationalization
Repression
Reversibility
Role confusion, Erikson's
Scaffolding
Schema (scheme)
Self-efficacy
Sensorimotor stage
Shaping
Social cognitive theory, Bandura's
Sociocultural theory, Vygotsky's
Stage theories
Superego
Temperament
Theory
Unconscious
Variable
Vicarious reinforcement
Zone of proximal development,
    Vygotsky's

RELATED RESOURCES

Readings

Bjork, D.W. (1993). *B.F. Skinner: A Life.* New York: Basic.

Skinner, the founder of "radical behaviorism," is vividly portrayed as having a normal childhood. We get a glimpse of him inventing a steam cannon to shoot plugs of potatoes and carrots over the houses of neighbors and attending dances given by families of eligible girls, only to discover that couples had paired off at pre-dance dinner parties.

Bjork presents a persuasive defense of Skinner's ideas, among these, that there is no individual freedom and that a human being is little more than a set of memories reacting to his or her environment.

Chamberlain, L. (2000). *The Secret Artist: A Close Reading of Sigmund Freud.* London: Seven Stories Press.

A key point in this book is attempting to address the simple but fundamental question, "Why can't there be more *real* and *fulfilled* love?" The answer? We don't have more real and fulfilled love because we make ourselves miserable and have created a society that is very good at making us even more miserable.

Dennett, D. (1993). *Consciousness Explained.* Boston: Little Brown.

This book revolves around the concept of consciousness. Rather than thinking of consciousness as Freud did, a thought process (the ego) that mediates between the superego and id, Dennett offers his own theory. For him, consciousness is a fluid process in which one set of neurons responds by activating another group of neurons, thus creating feelings and ideas. Dennett also sees a close link between humans and lower animals.

Erikson, E. H. (1963). *Childhood and Society.* 2nd ed. New York: W. W. Norton. This beautifully written classic presents the main concepts of Erikson's psychosocial theory. He describes how studying American Indians and observing patients in treatment led to the development of his "Eight Ages of Man." Erikson also analyzes several American subcultures, as well as the childhoods of Hitler and Maxim Gorky.

Freud, S. (1963). *The Sexual Enlightenment of Children.* New York: Collier Books.

This book contains several essays in which Freud analyzes the sexual implications of some of the fantasies children have and the lies they tell. In one essay, Freud advocates that children be told the truth about sexual matters. The book also contains the complete history of Hans, the little boy whose phobia, initially directed toward horses, was actually directed toward his father.

Websites

Institute for Psychoanalytic Training and Research
http://iptar.org/

Nobelprize.org
http://nobelprize.org/educational_games/medicine/pavlov/readmore.html
This website describes Pavlov's experiments in classical conditioning.

Jean Piaget Society: Society for the Study of Knowledge and Development
http://www.piaget.org/index.html

PART TWO

PREGNANCY AND BIRTH

Chapter 3

Prenatal Development and Birth

Chapter Topics		Learning Objectives
How does a baby develop from conception to birth?		Understand the science of conception and fetal development.
What is the science of genetics?		Recognize some potential genetic and chromosal disorders (e.g. Down Syndrome).
What are some potential genetic and chromosomal disorders?		Understand the three stages of pregnancy: germinal, embryonic, and fetal stages.
What are the three stages of prenatal development?		Recognize the important issues in prenatal development: teratogens, maternal infections, maternal drug use, and, maternal factors.
What are the important issues in prenatal development?		Know the various birthing options (traditional and alternative).
What are parents' choices for birthing methods?		Understand the three stages of labor: dilation, birth of the baby, expulsion of the placenta.
What are the three stages of labor?		

No doubt you have noticed that your friends resemble their parents in a variety of ways: physical features (size, color of skin, and bone structure), personality, intelligence, and in some cases, mental disorders. How do we explain these similarities and differences?

The beginning of an explanation for any resemblance or difference between parents and children is *biological* inheritance. Sarah looks more like her father than her mother because more of her father's genes have been expressed than her mother's.

Environment also plays an important role in development. The role of *environment* in child development is evident when the baby is still in the mother's womb. Drugs (an environmental factor) taken by the mother during pregnancy affect the baby before and after birth (Agin, 2010; Soby, 2006; Rugh & Shettles, 1971; Webster & Freeman, 2003). Also, children show delayed growth during periods of malnutrition. If malnutrition is severe and chronic, the result is permanent damage to the child, including deleterious effects on the central nervous system. From this brief account, you can see that heredity and environment seldom—if ever—act alone.

If someone were to ask you to name the nine most important months of your life, what would your answer be? If you said the nine months you spent in your mother's womb, you would be right. At no time in your life was development more dramatic or precarious.

On the first day of prenatal life you were a one-celled organism (the zygote), no bigger than the period at the end of this sentence. Just 266 days later, you were approximatley20 inches long and weighed roughly 7 pounds. Furthermore, you could breathe, eat, react to stimuli (such as sounds or lights), and cause your mother to run to your side at breakneck speed by crying. In this chapter, we will look at the three stages of prenatal development. Next, we will examine the hazards a baby may face before it is born.

CONCEPTION (FERTILIZATION)

Conception (fertilization): The penetration of an ovum by a sperm.

Ovulation: The process in which a female gamete is released into the fallopian tube.

Sperm: Amature male reproductive cell

Ovum: A mature female reproductive cell (egg)

Fertilization: The creation of a zygote through the penetration of a sperm into an ovum

Sarah and Carlos began their lives with conception. To understand *conception*, we need to begin with puberty, the process that leads to sexual maturity, and the ability to reproduce for the first time. At puberty, or shortly thereafter, the sexually mature woman or girl undergoes a process known as *ovulation*, which normally occurs about once every 28 days. Ovulation involves the release of an egg (ovum) through the wall of the ovary into the fallopian tube (Figure 3.1). If the woman has sexual intercourse with a fertile male a few days prior to or after ovulation, and one of the *sperm* penetrates the *ovum*, we have the beginning of Sarah or Carlos. The penetration of the ovum by the sperm, called *fertilization*, usually takes place in the fallopian tube, or oviduct.

Figure 3.1
Female Reproductive System

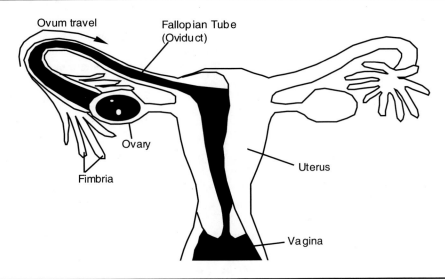

Conception usually occurs in the fallopian tube where a ripened ovum is penetrated by a sperm.

Chromosomes: Rod-shaped portions of DNA that form 23 pairs.

Gene: A basic unit of heredityconsisting of an ordered sequence of chemicals that are the building blocks of DNA, the blueprint of genetic material.

Zygote: A newly fertilized cell formed by the union of sperm and ovum at conception.

Within a few hours after fertilization, the sperm and ovum begin to disintegrate, each releasing 23 *chromosomes* (which look like long, thin strands of colored beads when seen through a microscope). Chromosomes are chemical, threadlike structures made up of *genes*.[1] The genes carry the hereditary blueprint (DNA) for each individual. The result of the disintegration of the sperm and the ovum is the formation of a single cell called a *zygote*. Although only about $1/20$th the size of the head of a pin, the zygote contains about 15,000 identical (homozygous) or similar (heterozygous) pairs of genes on the 46 chromosomes, contrary to the 50,000 pairs of genes formerly thought to exist. One member of each pair of genes comes from each parent (Mader, 1993). If even one gene is defective or missing, the developing human being may be doomed to catastrophe such as cancer, deformity, or early death. Although Sarah begins her development with the formation of the one-celled zygote, this soon changes through the production (duplication) of body (somatic) cells, a process known as mitosis.

---

1.   A gene (a segment of DNA) is the basic unit of heredity and consists of an ordered sequence of chemical building blocks called nucleotides, designated by their chemical initials A, T, C or G. Traits (e.g., blue eyes versus brown eyes) are determined by the *sequence* of the nucleotides. The entire packet of genetic instructions (code) for producing a living organism is called the genome. Each person (except monozygotic twins) has a slightly different code, but the human genome is 99.9 percent the same for any two persons except for monozygotic twins. An international effort, called the Human Genome Effort, completed mapping the entire human genetic code in 2001.

Sex chromosomes: In both males and females, the 23rd pair of chromosomes which determine an individual's gender and are responsible for sex-related characteristics.

Will it be a Boy or a Girl?

Gender assignment is made by the 23rd pair of chromosomes, often called *sex chromosomes*, or sex cells, which consist of either the sperm or the unfertilized egg. In a normal male, the 23rd pair of chromosomes consists of one Y and one X chromosome; in the female both sex chromosomes are Xs. The presence of two X chromosomes in one's hereditary blueprint means that the offspring is a genetic female, while the presence of one Y and one X chromosome defines a genetic male. Hence, the father plays a key role in determining the gender of the offspring—depending on whether he contributes an X or a Y chromosome.

THE SCIENCE OF GENETICS

Why are Sarah and Carlos of average height while another child is quite short? Why does Carlos have his mother's nose and his father's chin? Why are some children more outgoing than others? Are children born "easy-going?" To help us answer these questions, we begin with our biological inheritance and the principles of heredity known as genetics. Genetics is the study of the transfer of characteristics from one generation to the next.

The field of genetics began in the last half of the 19th century with the work of an Austrian monk named Gregor Mendel. Working with various plants, including garden peas and snapdragons, Mendel wanted to know how tall pea plants were able to produce short offspring in the second generation of their descendants. He discovered that the offspring are produced according to certain principles or laws.

Figure 3.2
Gregor Mendel (1822-1884)

Gregor Mendel, the Austrian monk whose work with garden peas in the mid-1800s forms much of the basis of our present-day knowledge of genetics. Mendel's greatest contribution was his discovery of how genes determine genetic dominance and recessiveness by breeding, counting, and sorting generations of peas and then relating characteristics to parent plants as well as to offspring.

Mendel's Principles of Inheritance

Although Mendel's principles of the transmission of traits from "parent" (plants) to offspring were subsequently shown not to apply universally, his work has helped researchers determine how traits are passed from parents to offspring in both plants and human beings.

Dominant trait: The expression of a physical characteristic by one gene in preference to another gene of the same type

.

Recessive trait: The expression of a trait only if two genes of the same type (alleles) are present in an individual.

Allele: A member of a gene pair that is located at a specific point on a chromosome.

Homozygous: A gene pair in which the genes are identical.

Heterozygous: Pertaining to a gene pair in which each allele contains different chemical instructions for the composition of a trait.

Phenotype: Observable physical and psychological characteristics due to inheritance.

Genotype: A person's hereditary makeup.

Incomplete dominance: A condition in which a stronger (dominant) allele fails to mask all the effects of a weaker (recessive) allele.

Mendel explained the preponderance of one trait over another by his law of dominance. Genes for contradictory traits (like tallness and shortness) will result in only one of the traits being expressed. This trait is called *dominant* because it overrides the subordinate trait called *recessive*.

We can see Mendel's law of dominance expressed in eye color. If a child inherits one gene for brown eyes and the other for blue eyes, he or she will have brown eyes because brown is dominant to blue. Blue eye color is expressed only if the child possesses two genes for blue eyes since genes for blue eyes are recessive.

Mendel also devised the Law of Recessive Inheritance to explain "skipped" generations for a particular trait, such as red hair and double-jointedness. Because two *genes (alleles)* are necessary for recessive traits to be expressed, several generations of a particular family may not have red hair even though they may carry one gene for this trait. This means that both the mother and the father must have a recessive gene for red hair before they can have a red-headed child.

Homozygous and heterozygous alleles. For a recessive trait, such as blue eye color to appear, the individual must possess two identical genes or alleles (a pair of genes affecting a trait). When the alleles are similar, they are said to be *homozygous*. (Note that alleles can be homozygous for recessiveness as well as for dominance.) When the alleles are different, they are called *heterozygous*.

Phenotypes and genotypes. Mendel discovered that when a purebred tall plant (contains two genes for tallness) is crossed with a purebred short plant (contains two genes for shortness), the first offspring are all tall. When this first generation is crossbred, the ratio of tallness to shortness in the second generation is 3:1. In the description of the parent trees and their offspring in Figure 3.3, the observable trait of height is called *phenotype*. Phenotype can often be observed directly (color of a person's hair, for example). But why do some children have red hair and others have brown or black hair? The answer is the interaction of the environment with a person's *genotype*.

A genotype is a person's particular set of genes inherited from the parents. With the exception of identical twins, no two individuals have identical genotypes.

Postmendelian Principles of Inheritance

Using molecular genetics, investigators have discovered that the boundaries between dominant and recessive alleles are not always as distinct as Mendel had purported (Plomin & DeFries, 1998). Some single-gene disorders have common traits that were not identified by Mendel and include: incomplete dominance, codominance, mutation, sex-linked inheritance, and the fragile X syndrome.

Incomplete dominance. In *incomplete dominance*, neither member of a pair of genes (alleles) is entirely dominant, nor entirely recessive. Incomplete dominance is seen when purebred red- and white-flowered snapdragons are crossed, and the result is pink, an intermediate color.

Figure 3.3
The Phenotype (Observed) Expression of a Trait

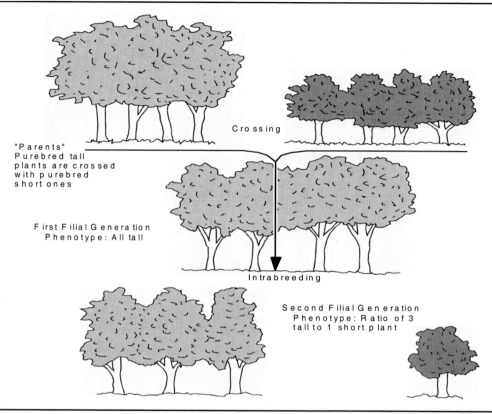

The phenotype is concerned only with the visible (outward) expression of a trait. A counterpart to phenotype is genotype, the underlying combination of genetic material present (but not outwardly visible) in an organism. In Figure 3.3, in the first filial generation, each plant is heterozygous for height, which means that each plant contains one gene for tallness and one for shortness. In the second filial generation, on the average, one plant is homozygous for tallness, another plant is homozygous for shortness, and two plants are heterozygous for tallness.

Codominance: A trait resulting from the full expression of both alleles of a pair

Polygenic inheritance: The genetic influence on a trait by several genes, rather than by a single (dominant) gene or by a pair of (recessive) genes.

Multifactorial inheritance: In genetics, means that traits are affected by many influences, both genetic and environmental.

Codominance. In codominance, the phenotype of the heterozygous individual represents an exact compromise of the two genes for a particular trait or characteristic that the person inherited, since both genes are equally strong or expressive. This means that neither form of the gene (allele) is able to dominate the other. A heterozygous person who inherits an allele for blood type A from one parent, and an allele for blood type B from the other parent will exhibit a codominant outcome—type AB blood that represents an exact compromise between blood types A and B, and is qualitatively different from either type.

Polygenic (multifactorial) inheritance. Modern geneticists have discovered that the combined activity of many separate genes can produce a trait.

Genetic inheritance in which multiple genes determine a particular characteristic is called *polygenic inheritance*. Notable examples of polygenic inheritance are height, weight, intelligence, skin color, and temperament. Hence, although traits like the color of a flower are determined by a single gene according to Mendel's textbook model of inheritance, such is seldom the case with humans.

Although polygenic inheritance is often used interchangeably with *multifactorial inheritance,* technically the two terms are different. While polygenic inheritance means genetic inheritance in which several genes determine a particular trait, multifactorial inheritance means that both environment *and* genes determine a trait.

GENETIC AND CHROMOSOMAL DISORDERS

Genetic Disorders [2]

More than 6 percent of children are born with diseases caused by an abnormality of a gene or by an incorrect number of genes. Let's see how some disorders are transmitted genetically.

Inherited Abnormalities

Autosomes: The 22 matching chromosome pairs in each human cell.

Disorders of *autosomal inheritance* can involve dominant or recessive genes. About 20 percent of birth defects are inherited, the other 80 percent are caused by a faulty environment such as birth injuries.

Autosomal inheritance: A trait that is determined by genes on any chromosome other than the sex (X or Y) chromosomes.

In most cases, normal genes prevail over those carrying abnormal traits. Occasionally, this is not true and an abnormal trait is transmitted by a single dominant gene. If one parent has a single faulty dominant gene for the disorder, and a normal counterpart gene, each offspring has a 50 percent chance of developing the affliction, providing the possibility of a large pool of afflicted individuals within a short period of time.

When both parents are heterozygous and each parent carries one abnormal recessive gene (each parent is a carrier), each child has a 50-50 chance of being a carrier for the defect. In such instances, the disease may be passed on to the offspring, even though the carrier does not suffer from the defect. Furthermore, each child has a 25 percent chance of having the disorder and a 25 percent chance of being unaffected.

Phenylketonuria: An inherited disorder in which babies are born lacking a liver enzyme.

This pattern of autosomal recessive inheritance applies to diseases such as *phenylketonuria* (PKU). The IQ of children with untreated phenylketonuria is often below 50 (Plomin *et al.,* 1997). Fortunately, the disease can be prevented if the pregnant woman with PKU changes her eating habit to a phenylalanine-restricted diet (low-protein, avoidance of meat, fish, and dairy products) before or shortly after conception (Levy & Ghavemi, 1996). Here is an instance in which environment (restricted diet) can prevent or cure a genetic disorder (phenylketonuria). Currently, all 50 states require PKU screening with a blood or urine test for all newborns.

Sex-linked inheritance: The gene(s) for a particular trait are on either the X or Y chromosome

Inherited sex-linked disorders. Sex-linked traits—both normal and defective—are transmitted by genes on the sex (usually X) chromosome. Hemophilia is an example of a sex-linked recessive disorder resulting in improper clotting of the blood that is caused by lack of a vital protein either factor VIII or IX. This disorder is normally passed from a carrier mother to a son through the X chromosome.

---

2. For more information on genetic disorders, write to: Alliance of Genetic Support Groups, 1001 22nd Street, N.W., Suite 800, Washington, D.C., 20037, or call 1-800-336-GENE.

If the mother has one normal (dominant) gene and one abnormal (recessive) gene for hemophilia, the son has a 50 percent chance of inheriting the disorder. An affected father can never pass the gene to his son, since he contributes a Y chromosome to his male offspring; however, an affected father can pass the defective gene to his daughter, who then becomes a carrier.

Chromosomal Abnormalities[3]

Average children like Sarah and Carlos have 23 pairs of chromosomes. Each pair of chromosomes has a characteristic size and shape (see Figure 3.4). Some chromosomes are defective in number, shape, or part of the chromosome is missing, or is attached to another chromosome. Most chromosomal abnormalities are the result of errors during meiosis when the ovum and sperm are formed. The vast majority of these chromosomal abnormalities are lethal to the fetus. Let's look at three instances involving an incorrect number of chromosomes: Down syndrome, Klinefelter syndrome, and Turner syndrome.

Figure 3.4
The Chromosomes of the Human Male (Male Karyotype)

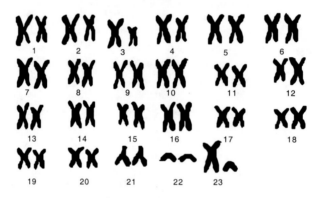

Each pair of chromosomes is characterized by the size and proportion of the arms on each side of the junction. The 23rd pair is the sex chromosomes.

---

3. For more information on chromosomal abnormalities write to: Klinefelter Syndrome and Associates, P.O. Box 119, Roseville, CA, 95661-0119. (Enclose stamped, self-addressed envelope.)

Table 3.1
Some Common Birth Defects in the U.S.A.

Disease or Condition	Causes and Effects	How Common and Who is at Risk?	Treatment
Alpha antitrypsin deficiency	Enzyme deficiency often causes cirrhosis of the liver in early infancy and severe lung problems in old age.	1 in 1,000 Caucasians.	None.
Thalassemia minor	A shortage of production of hemoglobin, a pigment that gives red blood cells their color, causing a shortage of oxygen. Usually there are no symptoms, but the individual is a carrier of the disease.	Babies of African, Malaysian or Southeast descent are affected most often.	No treatment is required.
Thalassemia major (Cooley's anemia)	A shortage of production of hemoglobin. Victims inherit the hemoglobin defect from both parents. Victims usually die by early adulthood.	Families of Mediterranean descent are usual victims.	Frequent blood transfusions. (Danger of iron overload)
Cystic fibrosis	Lack of enzyme (hereditary) causes body to make too much mucus which obstructs lungs and digestive tract, drowning the victims. Death usually results by age 30, but longevity is increasing.	1 in 1,000 births. Most common inherited deadly disease among young Americans, next to AIDS. It is the most commonly occurring life-threatening disorder of Caucasian children (McMullen, 2000).	Antibiotics; physical therapy to loosen mucus. Lung transplantation has about a 40% 5-year survival rate.
Diabetes mellitus (certain forms) Type 1	Failure of body to produce enough insulin results in elevated blood sugar, excessive sugar in urine, and excessive urine output. Fatal if untreated.	1 in 25 to 40 of all diabetics.	Low sugar diet, oral medication, exercise, insulin injections.
Down syndrome	An extra 21st chromosome causes minor to severe physical and intellectual retardation as well as eye, ear, and heart problems.	1 in 700 births; more common in mothers over age 35.	Programs of intellectual stimulation are helpful.
Fragile X syndrome	Affected males usually have mild to severe mental retardation, delayed speech and motor development. Believed to be main cause of autism. X chromosome is compressed in places and sometimes separated into two or more pieces.	Affects 1 in 1,250 male births; 1 in 2,000 females. (In girls, the "good" X chromosome usually cancels out the "bad"); the most common hereditary cause of mental retardation.	None.
Hemophilia (bleeding disease)	Excessive bleeding due to a deficiency of a clotting ingredient known as factor VIII or IX; may cause swelling of joints; hereditary.	1 in 21,500 live births of males; females are not affected as often.	Emergency treatment consists of transfusions of fresh blood.
Muscular dystrophy (Duchenne)	Wasting away (atrophy) of muscles leading to loss of all motor capabilities; hereditary.	1 in 4,000 males.	Physical therapy.

Table 3.1
Some Common Birth Defects in the U.S.A.

Disease or Condition	Causes and Effects	How Common and Who is at Risk?	Treatment
Neural tube defects; anencephaly and spina bifida	Absence of central brain lobes and parts of skull are missing in anencephaly. Condition is not survivable. In spina bifida, part of spine is not closed; victims live from one year to near normal. Cause of either condition is not known, although a vitamin deficiency is suspected.	1 out of 1,000 fetuses have anencephaly; 3 out of 1,000 have spina bifida.	None for anencephaly; surgery to close spinal cord in spina bifida. Folic acid may prevent spina bifida if taken early in pregnancy (400 mcg daily).
Phenylketonuria	Lack of enzyme to digest certain food (hereditary); causes severe mental retardation and hyperactivity.	1 in 10,000 Caucasian births.	Diet low in phenylalanine.
Sickle-cell anemia	Disintegration of red blood cells (hereditary); causes blood vessels to clog, resulting in shortage of oxygen. Symptoms include pain, frequent infections, shortage of breath, and stroke. Milder form is sickle-cell trait.	1 in 500 African-Americans; much less common among other ethnic groups.	Pain killers, transfusions; antibiotics for infections.
Tay-Sachs disease	Deterioration of brain leads to death before age 5. Disease is inherited. Lack of an enzyme causes waste build-up in the brain.	1 in 3,000 Eastern European Jews.	Supportive treatment includes tube feedings of nutritional supplements and mild laxatives to relieve constipation.

Source: Adapted from Tisdale, 1988; McKusick, 1986; Cahill, 1998.

Note: All these disorders are genetic, except neural tube defects.

Down Syndrome (Trisomy 21)[4]

Down syndrome: A disorder caused by an extra chromosome resulting in mental retardation and in a distinctive appearance.

First discovered in 1866 by Dr. Langdon Down, a British physician, *Down syndrome* was termed Mongolism because the victims were thought to have an Asian look, owing to features such as small head; short, broad hands; cardiac abnormalities; and epicanthal folds at the inner corners of the eyes (Down, 1866). The disorder affects 1 in 800 live births (Firthel, 2007). Down syndrome is the most common chromosome disorder and is a leading cause of irreversible mental retardation (Firthel, 2007; Yang, Rasmussen, & Friedman, 2002).

The average IQ of a Down child is between 50 and 60. The speech of many Down children is delayed; often it is unintelligible. A common problem is hypotonia, or low muscle tone, which is likely to affect learning and development (Appl, 1998). Often the Down child is susceptible to upper respiratory infection and many have a heart defect (Freeman *et al.*, 1998). Hearing loss is common. Even Down children who are near normal, lag behind agemates in behavior such as smiling and laughing and in development of eye contact. The life expectancy for people with Down is only around 50 years (Firthel, 2007; Irons, 1995; Tolmie, 1997).

---

4. Information about Down syndrome and local support services is available from the National Down Syndrome Congress, 1640 West Roosevelt Road, Chicago, IL, 60608, or call 1-800-221-NDSC.

Box 3.1
Diagnosis of Defects in the Unborn Baby

Amniocentesis

In amniocentesis, a sample of amniotic fluid (which contains fetal cells) is withdrawn and tested for any chromosome or metabolic disorders (Pinette et al., 2004) The procedure is usually done between the sixteenth and eighteenth week of pregnancy. The doctor first determines the position of the baby and placenta by means of ultrasound which transforms high frequency sound waves into a detailed picture of the baby. A long, hollow needle is then inserted into the pregnant woman's abdomen and amniotic fluid is withdrawn from the amniotic sac and analyzed for chromosomal or developmental problems. About 95 percent of amniocentesis results are normal.

Although most doctors will tell you they are certain that amniocentesis is perfectly safe, such certainty does not seem to be warranted. Among the negative side effects is miscarriage (about 1 in 200). Since there appears to be some risk involved, the best advice is to use the procedure sparingly. Certainly, amniocentesis should not be used to determine the child's gender, which is one capability of this procedure. Hence, amniocentesis is recommended only in certain instances: When the expectant mother is over 35; or when both parents are carriers of Tay-Sachs disease or sickle-cell anemia, or have a history of Down syndrome, spina bifida, or muscular dystrophy. Another point to keep in mind: Amniocentesis is not always accurate (about 97 percent). Warning: Amniocentesis is a complicated, costly, and invasive procedure with risk to the fetus and the mother. It should be employed primarily when high risk of birth defects is suspected.

Fortunately, amniocentesis is no longer used routinely in pregnancies as it was only a decade ago. The role of amniocentesis has now been relegated to potential problems in pregnancy. Ultrasound is now used routinely in two-thirds of normal pregnancies.

Chorionic Villus Sampling (CVS)

Introduced in 1983, this relatively new procedure, which tests for the same abnormalities as amniocentesis, consists of taking fetal cells from the chorion, a tissue that forms the placenta, by means of a catheter or a needle inserted through the mother's cervix into the uterus. Two advantages of CVS are immediacy of results (within a few days) and ability to obtain a sample early in the pregnancy (between about the tenth and twelfth weeks of pregnancy). The procedure should be done only after age 35. CVS allows for an earlier, safer abortion, should the mother make that choice. Among the risks are fluid leakage and maternal cramping (Goldsmith, 1988). There is also a higher risk (5 percent) of miscarriage and neonatal death than in amniocentesis. Further, CVS is only about 80 percent accurate.

Maternal Alphafetoprotein Test

This procedure is a blood test of the pregnant woman that is used primarily to detect defects in the neural tube, which forms the spinal column and brain. High levels of alphafetoprotein may indicate an incomplete closure of the baby's spine or skull, and the possibility of spina bifida or anencephaly (defects in the brain and/or spinal cord). Low levels of alphafetoprotein may be linked to Down syndrome and other chromosomal abnormalities. Ultrasound and/or amniocentesis are generally used to confirm or deny a problem.

Update: The alphafetoprotein test is now called the triple screen because it currently measures three substances in the mother's blood: alphafetoprotein, estriol, and human gonadotropin. The test can yield a false negative, suggesting no problem when there is actually a defect.

Ultrasound

Ultrasound (sonar)–the most common form of prenatal testing–is a method of scanning the womb with sound waves. The high frequency sound waves are "bounced" off the fetus to produce a picture, known as a sonogram, of the uterus, fetus, or placenta. A wealth of information is provided by ultrasound: Length of pregnancy, when the baby is due, welfare of the fetus, gender, position of the fetus, and abnormalities. The procedure carries some risks, such as false-positive readings: An indication of a problem when none exists. Ultrasound is often used in conjunction with amniocentesis to determine the precise location of the fetus in the mother's abdomen.

Fetal Fibronectin Test (FBT)

FBT is a biochemical "Carloser" that identifies women at high risk for preterm delivery. The test, comparable to a Pap smear, analyzes a woman's vaginal and cervical secretions. In case of damage to fetal membranes, a protein called fetal fibronectin is released.

Box 3.1
Diagnosis of Defects in the Unborn Baby

Other Diagnostic Techniques

Two other methods of diagnosing the unborn baby are umbilical cord assessment *and* fetoscopy. *Umbilical cord assessment is a new technique which involves taking samples of fetal blood by threading a needle into tiny blood vessels of the umbilical cord under the guidance of ultrasound. This procedure enables the doctor to obtain a blood count and assess other bodily functions. Umbilical cord assessment can determine the presence of infection, anemia, and heart failure. A key advantage of this technique is its ability to diagnose potential problems that are unobtainable through either amniocentesis or CVS. But there are some major problems, the most serious being infection.*

Fetoscopy is another new form of fetal monitoring. In this method, a tiny spaghetti-thin periscope, called a fetoscope, is inserted through the mother's vagina into the uterus so that the baby can be looked at directly. Like all forms of fetal monitoring, this procedure carries some risk.

A relatively new procedure for detecting unusual defects in the unborn baby earlier than previously is called sonoembryology. Sonoembryology involves high frequency transvaginal probes and digital image processing. This technique can detect more than half of all malformations during the first trimester of pregnancy. When sonoembryology is used in connection with ultrasound more than four out of five of all malformations can be detected accurately during the second trimester.

In the near future, the testing of the genetics of the fetus will be done by a blood test in which fetal cells are isolated from the blood of the mother-to-be.

A Postscript on Prenatal Diagnosis of Birth Defects

Since science never stands still, it's almost a foregone conclusion that more prenatal diagnostic methods will be available in the future. Undoubtedly, these new procedures will enable doctors to identify more problems sooner than ever before. With these new advances, there will likely be an increase in the number of abortions. On the other hand, advances in prenatal surgery and medication will make it possible to treat babies when they are still in the mother's womb, thus making it possible for them to enter this world as healthy, normal babies.

Trisomy 21: An extra chromosome in a pair of number 21 chromosomes resulting in Down syndrome.

Approximately 95 percent of Down syndrome cases are due to an autosomal accident known as *trisomy 21* (Firthel, 2007; Yoon *et al.*, 1996). The chromosomes fail to split during meiosis; the new cell receives three number 21 chromosomes (Capone, 2001). An unexplained feature of Down syndrome is the relationship between the mother's age and incidence: The older the mother at the time of birth of her child, the greater the likelihood of Down syndrome in her child. The incidence of the disorder increases from 1 in 1,667 births for mothers aged 20, to 1 Down child in 952 births for mothers 30 years old, to 1 Down child per 375 births for mothers aged 35, to 1 Down child in 106 births for mothers who are 40 years old.

Klinefelter Syndrome (XXY)

Klinefelter syndrome: A disorder resulting in genetically male individuals who have an extra X chromosome.

Although Klinefelter victims have an extra X chromosome, they are genetically male. The most obvious symptoms of this disorder are sexual underdevelopment, small genitalia, scant pubic hair, sterility, and feminine physical characteristics such as rounded hips and large breasts, and trouble with language. This disorder is of unknown origin and occurs in about 1 of every 900 males born in the United States (Smyth & Bremmer, 1998). Treatment for Klinefelter syndrome consists of administering the male sex hormone, testosterone, to promote male physical characteristics. There is no treatment for the sterility accompanying the disorder (Hagenas & Arver, 1998).

Turner syndrome: A disorder resulting in a genetically female individual with 45 (only one X) chromosomes.

Turner Syndrome (XO)

Individuals with *Turner syndrome* are genetically female. A key genetic characteristic is 45 (instead of the usual 46) chromosomes. The missing chromosome is the X, making the person XO instead of XX, or the second chromosome is partially deleted (Frias & Davenport, 2003). Females with Turner syndrome are sterile, underdeveloped sexually (genital parts such as ovaries or the vagina may be missing), and short in stature. The girls never menstruate because their ovaries never function properly. Other physical anomalies include webbing of the neck, and cardiac and renal disorders. Typically, victims are of normal intelligence and no neurological defects have been found.

Turner victims are prone to various autoimmune disorders (an abnormal condition in which the body injures its own healthy tissue) such as diabetes and juvenile arthritis. The incidence of this syndrome is about 1 in 2,000 live female births.

PRENATAL DEVELOPMENT AND PREGNANCY

The Three Stages of Prenatal Development

The 9 months of pregnancy (about 266 days) can be divided into three well-defined stages with distinctive features. Let's look at each stage briefly.

The Germinal Stage (Fertilization to 2 Weeks)

Germinal stage: The first phase of the prenatal period which takes place during the first 2 weeks following conception.

The *germinal stage* begins with the fertilization of the ovum by the sperm and the formation of the zygote. You may recall that a zygote normally contains 46 chromosomes, 23 from each parent.

Approximately 36 hours after fertilization, the zygote begins to divide in a process called mitosis. Mitosis causes the fertilized cell to gradually pinch together in the middle, and then to divide into two separate cells. Sometimes the first two cells separate *completely,* creating two *separate* one-celled organisms. Since the genetic material is identical in both cells (basic principle of mitosis), we have the beginnings of two identical persons called identical, or *monozygotic,* twins. They should not be confused with dizygotic twins, who are the product of two separate eggs fertilized by two sperm. *Dizygotic twins*—who occur in two-thirds of twin pregnancies—are no more alike than any two children in the same family. About 3.5 per 100 newborns are identical; about 8.5 are dizygotic[5].

Monozygotic (identical) twins: Twins who develop from a single fertilized egg.

Dizygotic (fraternal) twins: Two-egg twins that can be of different genders.

Morula: A cluster of cells which develop from a single-cell zygote.

In a single fetus pregnancy, the division process continues, and by about the fourth day, the zygote consists of about 36 cells (Insel & Roth, 1977). Now called a *morula* (a roundish mass of cells that looks somewhat like a mulberry), it begins to move down the fallopian tube toward the uterine cavity. It is now a hollow, fluid-filled sphere resembling a balloon, and is called a

---

5. **Additional facts on twins**: More black than white mothers have twins; the most recorded sets of twins by one woman is 15. Since 1980, there has been a 40 percent increase in the number of twins born, largely as a result of fertility drugs.
    Still more facts on twins: Fraternal twins can be of either gender and differ Carlosedly in appearance, stature, and in skin color (e.g., one baby is white and the other is black). The reason for the difference in twins? The mother was impregnated by two different men (one black; the other white) at approximately the same time.

Blastocyst: A tiny mass of cells that form a hollow, fluid ball.

Embryonic stem cells: A group of cells inside the blastocyst that give rise to tissue or organs such as the heart and lungs.

Placenta: A structure that allows oxygen and nutrients to pass into the fetus from the mother's bloodstream and bodily wastes to pass out to the mother.

blastocyst. The blastocyst floats in the uterus for a few days until it becomes attached to the wall of the uterus some 2 weeks after fertilization.

A key feature of the *blastocyst* is an inner cell mass consisting of about 30 cells, known as *embryonic stem cells,* which are created when a fertilized egg first begins to grow. Embryonic stem cells give rise to the multiple specialized cell types that make up the lungs, skin, and other tissues.

The other event that occurs while the cells of the blastocyst are being organized and differentiated is the development of supporting structures that will nurture and protect Sarah during her intrauterine life. These supporting organs include the *placenta*, which lies next to and is attached to the uterus and to the umbilical cord. The placenta is a multipurpose system that serves essentially as the liver, lungs, and kidneys for the developing baby. The placenta is also an endocrine gland that secretes hormones to preserve the pregnancy and to regulate the baby's development. It serves as a filter through which foodstuffs and oxygen, obtained from the mother's blood, pass on their way to (and through) the umbilical cord and then to the baby. In a reverse process, metabolic wastes and carbon dioxide pass through the placenta into the mother's blood to be excreted from the body.

The umbilical cord—about 2 feet long and $1/2$ inch thick—serves as a passageway between the baby and the placenta. It is the baby's lifeline. The umbilical cord connects the embryo to the placenta. The umbilical cord contains no nerves, so cutting it does not hurt the mother or the baby. The amniotic sac is the inner fluid-filled membrane that encases Sarah, cushions her, and maintains a steady temperature.

The Embryonic Stage (2 to 8 Weeks)

Embryonic stage: A period in pregnancy from 2 through 8 weeks when the unborn baby's structures develop rapidly.

The *embryonic stage* (or period) begins once the zygote is completely embedded in the uterine wall, and is called an embryo. This new stage typically begins during the third week after conception and lasts until the end of the eighth week.

A significant feature of the embryonic stage is the rapid development of supporting structures. After only 8 weeks of gestation, most of the organs found in the baby (liver, kidneys, and lungs) are in place in some form, even though the embryo is only about 1 inch long and weighs only a fraction of an ounce. Almost all developmental birth defects, such as cleft palate (narrow opening in the roof of the mouth), blindness, heart defects, and deafness occur during the first trimester (3-month-period) of pregnancy.

Spontaneous Abortion (Miscarriage)

Spontaneous abortion (miscarriage): Accidental expulsion of the embryo before it is able to survive outside the mother's womb.

Spontaneous abortion, or miscarriage, is the accidental expulsion of the embryo from the uterus before it is viable, or able to survive outside the mother's womb. In medical circles, this is before 20 weeks of gestation. About three out of four spontaneous abortions occur during the first trimester. Many women miscarry without knowing that they were pregnant.

Spontaneous abortions may be triggered by a variety of factors. Among these are chromosomal abnormalities, a malformed or immature uterus, an unfavorable location for implantation, an inadequate supply of oxygen or nourishment (the most common problem in pregnancies), cigarette smoking, and cocaine use (Ness *et al.*, 1999). Diseases, such as (genital) herpes, can result in a miscarriage. Mothers with a history of babies with neural tube defects, such as spina bifida, are likely candidates for spontaneous abortion.

The age and health of the mother also seem to be factors in a miscarriage. Heavy caffeine and alcohol use, and poor maternal nutrition also play a role in spontaneous abortion as does a deficiency of folic acid (George *et al.*, 2002).

The Fetal Stage (8 Weeks to Birth)

During the third and final period, called the *fetal stage*, structural development continues to completion. Fingers and toes are formed; hair and nails appear. All body systems (heart, lungs, and liver) begin to function.

A significant development during the fetal stage is *viability*, the baby's ability to survive outside the womb. Usually, this momentous event occurs after about 7 months of gestation.

During the eighth and ninth months of pregnancy the "finishing touches" occur. The wrinkled skin of the fetus begins to fill out due to newly deposited fat under the skin, and the major organs (heart, liver, and kidneys) begin to function more efficiently.

Fetal Evaluation Through Ultrasound

Ultrasound is used increasingly to determine the status of the mother and her unborn baby.

Ultrasound, a small instrument, called a transducer, is moved over the mother's abdomen, causing high-frequency, low-power sounds. These sounds produce an electronic image (sonogram) of the baby (or of the mother's body) on a monitor. An ultrasound can also be done internally in high-risk and emergency situations. In internal fetal monitoring, one end of a wire is attached to an ultrasound monitor that is placed on the mother's abdomen and the other end of the wire is inserted through the vagina and screwed into the fetus's scalp.

Ultrasound helps confirm the baby's due date, helps the physician make sure that the baby is developing normally, and confirms the diagnosis of twins. Ultrasound also helps to determine if there are any complications such as fetal cardiac malformations, cleft lip, cleft palate, or neural tube defects. This technique is also invaluable in diagnosing placenta previa, a high-risk condition when the placenta covers the cervix. Ultrasound can also detect disorders such as microencephaly, a form of mental retardation involving an abnormally small brain (Bahado-Singh *et al.*, 2003).

Fetal stage: The third and final period of prenatal development.

Viability: The baby's ability to survive outside the womb.

Ultrasound: A form of fetal monitoring which helps to confirm the baby's due date, the diagnosis of twins, and the presence of fetal complications.

Table 3.2

Development of Structure and Function of the Embryo and Fetus

Month	Structure	Function
First Month	During the first month, growth is more rapid than at any other time in prenatal or postnatal life. The beginnings of several major organs are evident. Limb buds are visible, the eyes and ears are forming, vertebrae are present in primitive form, and nerves begin to take shape. A digestive system with an esophagus, stomach, liver, and gall bladder are quite evident, as is a two-chamber heart, a brain, and kidneys. Gender cannot yet be determined. The baby measures $1/4$ to $1/2$ inch. The brain's physical structure, or "hard wiring", begins by the third week after conception.	The lifeline to the mother, the umbilical cord, is functioning toward the end of the first month of gestation. The first "behavior" — a heartbeat — appears when the embryo is only about one-sixth of an inch long and about 3 weeks old. Neurons, or nerve cells, begin to differentiate by the end of the first month of prenatal development.
Second Month	By the end of the second month, the baby reaches the fetal stage and is human in appearance. It is about 2 inches long and weighs about $1/3$ ounce. The limbs, including hands and feet, are formed; fingers and toes are still webbed together. The head is still unusually large, making up about half the total length of the fetus. Bone cells appear. Teeth begin to form at about 6 weeks in utero.	There is some reflex movement, possibly due to primitive muscular development. The heartbeat is steady; although faint, the baby's heart is pumping blood to the embryo by the seventh week. The stomach produces digestive juice; the kidneys remove uric acid from the body.
Third Month	The placenta and embryo are linked together by the umbilical cord. Other supporting structures, such as the amnion, a thin, tough transparent membrane that holds the amniotic fluids and surrounds the embryo, have taken shape, as has the chorion which surrounds the amnion. Facial parts are clearly developed. The baby has eyes, a mouth that opens and closes, a tongue, and teeth buds. The baby also has a thin covering of skin and a spinal cord. Lungs become gland-like. The external, middle, and inner ear assume their final form. Sex organs clearly indicate the gender of the baby. Muscles develop more extensively, and blood forms in the bone marrow. Finer details, such as fingernails, toenails, and vocal cords are now present. The baby has fingerprints. By the end of the third month, the fetus weighs 1 ounce and measures about 3 inches in length.	The brain is functioning and coordinates the workings of the various organs. The fetus can move its legs and arms. There is some kidney and liver function. The stomach produces digestive juices and the liver produces blood cells. The skin is sensitive to tactile stimulation. The fetus can now breathe, and urinate (directly into the amniotic fluid). If the lips are touched, the fetus will suck; if the sole of the foot is stroked, the toes spread out. In some cases, the baby can even perform somersaults. The sense of hearing develops about this time. The baby can hear the mother's voice, the rumblings of her stomach, and the sounds of eating. The fetus begins to make gross breathing movements.

Table 3.2
Development of Structure and Function of the Embryo and Fetus

Month	Structure	Function
Fourth Month	By the end of the fourth month, the baby looks human. She now measures from 8 to 10 inches and weighs about 6 ounces. Body proportions have changed so that the head is about $1/4$ of the total body length. The kidney attains its final shape; the uterus and vagina are recognizable in females. The scrotum and testes (although not yet descended) are present in males. Two divisions of the brain are visible. Bones begin to form (the first one is the breast-bone) and collect calcium which makes them harder and denser. Because there is no subcutaneous fat and the skin is thin, the blood vessels of the scalp are visible; eyes and ears are well developed.	The baby is capable of quickening. This is movement in the mother's womb, and consists of the baby kicking, stretching, squirming, and occasionally hiccoughing. The mother can feel these movements. The fetus can sense changes in the mother's posture due to development in the vestibular system of the middle ear, which controls the sense of balance, and is sensitive to light through the lids. Digestion is fair. The fetus also makes mouthing and sucking movements and respiratory movements have begun.
Fifth Month	The fetus now weighs about 12 ounces and measures about 12 inches. The bones contain enough calcium for X rays to reveal a skeleton of 222 bones. (Due to rapid bone growth, mothers need more than the ordinary amount of calcium.) The baby has coarse eyebrows and eyelashes; fine hair on the head; and hair, known as lanugo, covers the body. Brown fat, which will help the newborn baby stay warm, begins to form. By the end of the fifth month, the baby has all the nerve cells (about 100 billion) it will have as an adult. The respiratory organs (the last major system to develop) are too immature to enable the fetus to survive outside the womb.	There is a Carlosed decrease in fetal activity due to development of the higher regions of the brain that makes more complex control of activity possible (Hofer, 1981); the fetus is now less responsive to stimulation. The fetal heartbeat is strong enough to be heard by placing an ear to the mother's abdomen. The sweat and sebaceous glands are functioning. The baby now responds to external sounds. For example, she may jump and kick when the mother raises her voice. The fetus reacts to temperature change and begins to swallow amniotic fluid. Although the baby can survive if born at this time, there is an 80 percent chance that it will have some disability such as cerebral palsy or mental retardation (Marlow *et al.*, 2005).
Sixth Month	By the end of the sixth month, the baby is about 14 inches long and weighs about 1 $1/2$ pounds. The eyes are complete and fat has been deposited under the skin. The air sacs of the lungs are still incomplete, making breathing difficult. Scalp hair emerges and unique fingerprints and footprints have formed.	The fetus has a well-developed grasp reflex and is capable of thin crying. The lungs are not sufficiently developed and the fetus has difficulty maintaining the alkaline-acidity balance of the blood. The fetus is active, moving its limbs, changing position, and sucking its finger. The visual and auditory senses appear to be functional (Allen and Capute, 1986). The baby has a 70 percent chance of survival.

Table 3.2
Development of Structure and Function of the Embryo and Fetus

Month	Structure	Function
Seventh Month	By the end of the seventh month, the fetus is about 16 inches long and weighs 3 to 5 pounds. From this point in time, the fetus gains up to $1/2$ pound per week. The lanugo begins to disappear and the head continues to grow. The fetus looks red and is covered with wrinkles which will eventually be erased by fat. The internal organs are maturing in preparation for life outside the uterus. The baby is not yet sensitive to pain. The bones are hardening, though the skull remains soft. The lungs are mature enough so that the fetus can survive on its own—outside the womb. The eyes are open and taste buds form. The boy's testes begin to descend to the scrotum.	The major development during this period is viability. More than half the babies born at this time survive with good care. Fetal brain activity can now be recorded (Altman, 1975). The endocrine system is regulating body chemistry, enabling the fetus to digest food, retain salt, burn calories, and gain extra strength. The pituitary gland, which sends hormones that activate other glands, releases the growth hormone. The nervous system's pathways and necessary chemicals are present. The baby sleeps and wakes, and occasionally coughs. The lungs are capable of breathing, and the central nervous system is sufficiently developed to direct rhythmic breathing movements. If born at this time, the baby may need to be kept in an isolette until it reaches 5 pounds.
Eighth Month	By the end of the eighth month, the fetus has grown to about 18 inches and weighs 5 or 6 pounds. Much of the weight gain is due to deposit of fat directly under the skin. The fetus' skin is smooth, and the legs and arms have a chubby appearance. The baby is now sensitive to pain. The bones continue to harden, but the head remains soft and flexible for delivery. The baby looks much the same as she will at birth, but her body still needs some filling out.	The movement of the fetus is curtailed due to the cramped quarters as a result of the increase in the baby's size. Due to the deposit of fat, the fetus is able to adjust to varying temperatures outside the womb. The breathing is regular and strong, and the sucking reflex is more pronounced. The immunological system is not fully developed, making the fetus highly susceptible to infection.
Ninth Month	At 9 months, the fetus weighs an average of $7 1/4$ pounds if a girl and $7 1/2$ if a boy. Its length is about 20 inches. Its skin has a creamy coating. The fine, downy hair (lanugo) has largely disappeared. The fingernails of the fetus may protrude beyond the ends of the fingers. The baby gains about $1/2$ pound per week until birth. The fetal head is about 60 percent of its adult size; the brain is about $1/4$ of the adult human brain; other organs are about $1/20$ of the size and weight of adult organs. At 9 months, 25 percent of body length is accounted for by the head, 42 percent by the trunk, and 33 percent by the legs. The head is more fully developed than other parts of the body; the baby appears "top heavy."	By the end of the ninth month, the fetus is usually ready to be born and can now function outside the uterus. The placenta begins to disintegrate; antibodies against various diseases pass from the mother's blood to the baby's, providing the baby with some immunity to diseases. The fetus secretes a chemical to trigger the birth process. The baby has smooth skin and the bones of the head are soft and flexible for delivery.

ISSUES IN PRENATAL DEVELOPMENT

Teratogens in the Prenatal Environment

Teratogens are hazards in the environment that interfere with normal prenatal development and can cause birth defects. We can classify teratogenic agents into five broad areas: *Radiation, maternal infections, drugs,* and *environmental chemicals* (Agin, 2010; Shepard & Smith, 1977).

Teratogens: Environmental agents that cause deviations from normal development during the prenatal period and lead to abnormalities or death.

Radiation

In today's world, we are exposed to many types of damaging high-energy particles, called *radiation*. One form of radiation that might occur during pregnancy is diagnostic X rays.[6] Exposure to X rays early in the pregnancy—8 through 15 weeks after fertilization—is the most dangerous period (Barnett & Maulik, 2001). Even small degrees of exposure to radiation can produce brain damage and childhood cancer, particularly leukemia.

Radiation: High-energy particles such as solar radiation and diagnostic X rays which can damage the unborn baby.

Maternal Infections

An unborn baby may be exposed to a variety of infections that can cause it damage. The critical period is the first 3 months of pregnancy, when the principal organs, such as the heart and liver are being formed. Most infections spread from the mother to the unborn baby by crossing the placental barrier. In a few instances, the baby may be infected while it is passing through the birth canal. Infectious diseases include rubella, and various sexually transmitted diseases such as AIDS and Herpes simplex, Type 2.

Rubella (German Measles)

Rubella, or "German measles," is a benign disease if it is contracted by a child or adult, however it can cause severe birth defects (the most common consequence is deafness) in about one-half of all babies born to mothers who suffer from the disease during the first 12 weeks of pregnancy when the baby's eyes, ears, heart, and the nervous system are beginning to form. If a pregnant woman contracts German measles before the eleventh week of gestation, deafness, heart defects, low birth weight, growth retardation, pneumonia, mental retardation, or blindness are almost certain to occur in her baby. Infant death is also possible. Fortunately, with the discovery of the rubella vaccine in 1969, the disease is not the problem that it used to be.

Rubella: A usually benign disease which can cause severe birth defects to an unborn baby.

Acquired Immune Deficiency Syndrome (AIDS)

The most serious maternal infection affecting newborns is *Acquired Immune Deficiency Syndrome (AIDS)*[7], a sexually transmitted disease that was first identified in the United States in the early 1980s. The AIDS virus may be transmitted to the unborn baby by crossing the placental barrier during delivery when the baby is exposed to the mother's infected blood or through breast feeding (UNAIDS, 2002).

AIDS is an autoimmune disease in which the cells of the immune system--the body's first line of defense against invading substances and

AIDS: A sexually transmitted disease produced by the HIV virus and ultimately results in death.

---

6. The primary site of radiation damage is the cell's genetic apparatus. Symptoms of radiation include a fall in white blood count, nausea, vomiting, and loss of hair.
7. For information about AIDS call: National AIDS Hotline, 1-800-342-AIDS.

microorganisms--attack and destroy normal body cells. AIDS is caused by an infection with HIV (human immunodeficiency virus).

The first sign of HIV infection is usually a failure to grow normally, followed by serious, repeated infections. Brain development is often affected, resulting in impaired motor and cognitive development (Wachsler-Felder & Golden, 2002). Abnormalities in AIDS babies also include small heads (microcephaly); big, slanting eyes, and boxlike foreheads. AIDS is the fastest growing cause of mental retardation among children.

Herpes Simplex, Type 2 (Genital Herpes)

Herpes Simplex, Type 2: A disease with two stages which causes damage to a baby if it is delivered during the active phase of the illness.

Herpes simplex, Type 2 – a form of genital herpes – is the most common sexually transmitted disease. A baby delivered during the active phase of this disease faces a risk of periodic skin sores and serious inflammation of the brain and spinal cord. Other possible damages include blindness and death. To prevent damage, the baby is usually delivered by cesarean section. There is no cure for the disease, although a tablet, Zovirax (acyclovir), decreases duration, severity, and frequency of symptoms.

Maternal Drug Use

Anything a mother puts in her body reaches the growing fetus through the bloodstream. Hence, the drugs a mother takes (prescription or nonprescription) can damage the fetus (Agin, 2010; Free *et al.,* 1990). Many drugs cross the placenta and enter the unborn baby's bloodstream, slowing fetal breathing and heart rate. Since the effects of drugs can be serious, pregnant women should not take any medication without first consulting their obstetricians.

Caffeine

Massive doses of caffeine in lower animals appear to cause birth defects, such as limb and skeletal malformations (Holt, Sears, & Sears, 1997); however, the effect on the human fetus is uncertain. There appears to be some evidence of a link between a mother's excessive coffee drinking (3 cups a day, or more) and birth defects such as miscarriage, low birth weight, and withdrawal symptoms (Eskenazi, 1993). In 1980, scientists on the staff of the Food and Drug Administration issued a warning to pregnant women, advising them to avoid, or use sparingly, foods and drugs containing caffeine.[8]

Tobacco (Nicotine)

Statistically, the smoking mother is twice as likely to deliver a baby that is about one-half pound lighter than the average newborn. Much of this decreased weight comes from a smaller brain. Low-birth-weight infants experience physical, emotional, and intellectual impairments in childhood, and many are born preterm. Smoking also causes stillbirths, miscarriage, and deaths at birth (DiFranza & Lew, 1995), an accelerated heart beat, and convulsions. A major reason for these problems is constriction of placental blood vessels, reducing uterine blood flow as it carries nutrients and oxygen from the mother to her baby.

---

8. The American College of Obstetricians and Gynecologists warns pregnant women to drink fewer than 4 cups of coffee a day and to eat something when they have a caffeine drink.

Alcohol

The scientific community is in agreement that alcohol causes birth defects.[9] Research indicates that children of alcoholic parents are also at greater risk of becoming alcoholics than children of nonalcoholic parents. Most authorities (e.g., Niebyl, 1991; Papalia & Olds, 1990; Soby, 2006) agree that any amount of alcohol is harmful to the fetus.

Fetal alcohol syndrome: A constellation of many defects in children born to heavy-drinking mothers.

Fetal alcohol syndrome (FAS). In 1973, investigators recognized a pattern of physical and mental birth defects in some children born to heavy drinking mothers (8 or more drinks per day). This constellation of some 20 defects is called the *Fetal Alcohol Syndrome*, or FAS (Steinmetz, 1992). FAS is Carlosed by facial disfigurement (*e.g.,* short, broad nose, and thin upper lip), smaller head and body size, and mild to moderate mental retardation (National Institute on Alcohol Abuse and Alcoholism, 1987). FAS is also a primary predisposing factor of behavioral disorders in children, including attention-deficit-hyperactivity disorder and learning disabilities (Autti-Raemoe, 2000; Soby, 2006), and is the third leading cause of mental retardation (after Down syndrome and neural tube defects). Adolescents and adults who were born to heavy-drinking mothers tend to remain cognitively impaired and to have a higher-than- usual rate of psychological problems (Kelly, Day, & Stressguth, 2000).

Marijuana

Marijuana can cause chromosomal damage in pregnant rats and other lower animals. The major active ingredient of marijuana, tetrahydrocannabinol (THC), crosses the placenta with little difficulty in lower animals such as mice. Information has been mounting about the damage of marijuana to human babies before they are born. There is also suggestive evidence of increased risk of cancer to the children if their mothers used marijuana during their pregnancies (Grufferman *et al.*, 1993). One study has found that pregnant women who used marijuana during pregnancy are five times more likely to deliver infants with features similar to FAS (Hingson *et al.*, 1982). In another study (Fried, 1982) of 583 pregnant marijuana users (more than five cigarettes per week), a relationship was found between the mothers' marijuana use and abnormalities of the nervous system in their newborn babies and earlier deliveries.

Cocaine

We know that the damage to the fetus from cocaine is considerable. There is risk of miscarriage or preterm (historically called premature) delivery, and cocaine babies tend to be smaller than normal at birth (Smith *et al.*, 2001). Babies exposed to cocaine before birth are at greater risk of developing neurological problems, malformed genital and urinary organs, and brain-damaging strokes (Bingol *et al.*, 1987; Konkol & Olsen, 1996; Soby, 2006). A smokable form of cocaine, known as "crack" or "rock", has become an even greater menace than cocaine in its more familiar powdered form.[10] Although the negative effects of

---

9. For further information on birth defects write to: March of Dimes Birth Defects Foundation, P.O. Box 2000, White Plains, NY, 10602, or call 1-888-4-BABIES, or check your phone book for local chapters.
10. Efforts have been made to prosecute women who use drugs during pregnancy. In 1989, a 23-year-old Florida mother became the first woman in the country to be convicted of "delivering" drugs (cocaine) to her unborn baby.

prenatal exposure to cocaine are similar to the damage caused by other drugs such as tobacco and alcohol, there is a belief that the damage is much worse.

Environmental Chemicals

In the United States, poisoning by mercury is a problem. When contaminated fish are eaten by pregnant women, mercury is easily transferred across the placenta. The result can be birth defects involving the unborn baby's brain and nervous system (Castoldi, Coccini, & Manzo, 2003).

In the United States and elsewhere, we see the effects of air pollution (often called smog). One investigator who has done considerable research on the effect of smog on fetuses and infants is Dr. Beate Ritz, an epidemiologist at the University of California at Los Angeles (UCLA). In her most recent study, she found that women who are exposed to high levels of ozone and carbon monoxide (components of smog) are three times more likely than others to have babies with cleft palates, cleft lips, and defective heart valves (Ritz *et al.*, 2002).

Another pollutant of major concern for young children in is lead-based paint found in their toys. The children often develop lead poisoning by sucking, gnawing, or licking the toys. The effects from lead poisoning are cumulative, increasing with continued exposure. Often lead poisoning occurs with no obvious symptoms and the effects can be irreversible. Children can be tested for lead in their blood.

Babies also absorb considerable amounts of formaldehyde found in carpets, especially new carpets, because of the closeness of their skin to the carpet as they crawl around the house.

OTHER MATERNAL FACTORS THAT CAN HARM AN UNBORN BABY

In addition to the many ways mentioned above that an unborn child can be damaged (X rays, diseases, and drugs), maternal factors such as stress, advanced age during pregnancy, and malnutrition are also harmful to the unborn baby.

The Mother's Emotional State and Stress

Maternal anxiety and stress have often been associated with the infant's cleft palate, infant apathy, neuroses, and alteration in the maternal-fetal blood flow. Some investigators have associated maternal stress with a baby's sleeping and digestive disorders.

Parental Age

The link between a mother's age and her child's health has been noted for centuries. Women who are over 40 when they have their first baby are twice as likely to have a cesarean than women in their 20s (Gilbert, Nesbitt, & Danielson, 1999).

Hydrocephalus: A condition involving increased accumulation of cerebrospinal fluid in the brain.

Risks of chromosomal birth defects rise steadily each year past the birth mother's age of 40. Other possible problems for the baby if the mother gets pregnant after age 40 are *hydrocephalus* (water on the brain) and Down syndrome (McCarthy, 1998). Babies born to mothers in their 40s are also likely to be smaller, premature, and stillborn (Cnattingius, Berondes, & Forman, 1993).

Table 3.3

Recommended Daily Dietary Allowances for Pregnant Women

Type of Nutrient and Sources	Function	Recommended number of servings/ dosage per day
Breads, cereals, pasta, or rice	Provide fiber, minerals, and energy. Help heart and nervous system function properly.	9
Fruits (orange slices, citrus fruits, or strawberries)	Essential for sound bones and teeth.	Four $\frac{1}{2}$ cups
Vegetables (dark-green, leafy vegetables such as spinach, kale, or chard)	Helps maintain the skin, eyes, urinary tract, and digestive system.	3-4 vegetables
Milk, yogurt, or cheese	Helps develop the red blood cells; helps in the proper functioning of the nervous system.	3
Protein foods (poultry, fish, eggs, dried beans, or nuts)	Provides necessary building blocks (amino acids) for growth, and repairs body tissues such as muscles, heart, lungs, eyes, and skin.	3
Water	Builds new tissue, aids in digestion, and dissolves the food the mother eats; carries waste products away from both the baby and the mother.	At least eight, 8-ounce glasses
Iron (Iron sources include poultry, red meat, legumes, dried fruit, and dark, leafy vegetables)	Circulates oxygen in the body, assists the immune system, and produces energy.	Approximately 30 mg.
Folate (folic acid), a B vitamin contained in liver and leafy green vegetables such as spinach.	Ensures proper development of the nervous system and helps avoid anemia and birth defects such as spina bifida, a disorder in which the embryo's neural tube does not close properly.	0.4 mg. (amount in most prenatal vitamins)

Maternal Nutrition During Pregnancy

A pregnant woman's diet can have important consequences on the baby's health and performance. For instance, a proper amount of folic acid (folate), found in green, leafy vegetables, dried beans, and liver is particularly important in the first trimester of pregnancy to help prevent spina bifida and spontaneous abortion. Despite the importance of a proper diet during pregnancy, many women do not eat adequately. One reason is our cultural obsession with thinness and dieting, but failure to eat properly during pregnancy causes a variety of problems.

Improper maternal nutrition during pregnancy has been linked to a variety of deficits in the baby which are often evident before birth. Researchers Myron Winich, Jo Ann Brasel, and Pedro Rosso (1972) discovered that the brains of fetuses who were aborted to protect the health of the malnourished mothers contained as few as 60 percent of the normal number of brain cells. Malnutrition during pregnancy has also been associated with stillbirth, prematurity, low birth weight, neonatal deaths, rickets, epilepsy, mental retardation, and susceptibility to disease (Barker, 1995; Godfrey, 1998). The malnutrition does not have to be severe to increase the risk to the fetus of low birth weight and miscarriage (Jones, 1997).

FETAL EVALUATION

Ultrasound

Ultrasound is used increasingly to determine the status of the mother and her unborn baby.

Ultrasound: A form of fetal monitoring which helps to confirm the baby's due date, the diagnosis of twins, and the presence of fetal complications.

Ultrasound, a small instrument, called a transducer, is moved over the mother's abdomen, causing high-frequency, low-power sounds. These sounds produce an electronic image (sonogram) of the baby (or of the mother's body) on a monitor. An ultrasound can also be done internally in high-risk and emergency situations. In internal fetal monitoring, one end of a wire is attached to an ultrasound monitor that is placed on the mother's abdomen and the other end of the wire is inserted through the vagina and screwed into the fetus's scalp.

Ultrasound helps confirm the baby's due date, helps the physician make sure that the baby is developing normally, and confirms the diagnosis of twins. Ultrasound also helps to determine if there are any complications such as fetal cardiac malformations, cleft lip, cleft palate, or neural tube defects. This technique is also invaluable in diagnosing placenta previa, a high-risk condition when the placenta covers the cervix. Ultrasound can also detect disorders such as microencephaly, a form of mental retardation involving an abnormally small brain (Bahado-Singh *et al.*, 2003).

BIRTH AND THE NEWBORN BABY

Conventional Birthing Choices

The Lamaze Method of Childbirth

Lamaze method of childbirth: A method for minimizing pain during childbirth by teaching women proper breathing and minimal use of drugs.

Fernand Lamaze (1891-1957), believed that childbirth involves some considerable pain and that this pain could be minimized if the woman is taught breathing and relaxation techniques designed to occupy the brain. The Lamaze method advocates minimal use of drugs and as natural a childbirth experience as possible. An important feature of the Lamaze method of childbirth is attendance by a support person (often the husband). Each year, more than 1 million women give birth in the United States by the Lamaze-coached method.

Obstetric Medication: Drugs During Childbirth

Obstetric medication: The use of drugs during childbirth.

Currently, the use of drugs in childbirth, known as *obstetric medication*, is widespread. Slightly more than 18 percent of all childbirths in the United States are assisted by drugs. There are three basic kinds of drugs that are used for labor or childbirth: analgesics, oxytocics, and anesthetics:

- *Analgesics* include narcotic drugs such as morphine and Demerol—synthetic painkillers. Analgesics also include tranquilizers and barbiturates.

• *Oxytocics* are synthetic hormones that are used in very early labor to stimulate uterine contractions, thus speeding up the birth process, such as exciting the breast to produce milk (lactation).

• *Anesthetics* are used in late first-stage labor during expulsion of the baby and is injected into the space around the spinal cord to numb the lower body (from the waist down), lessening the transmission of pain messages from the abdomen and legs to the brain. Epidurals do diminish the mother's ability to push the baby, prolonging labor.

Cesarean Delivery ("Surgical" Birth)

Cesarean delivery (C-section)—the most common major operation in the U.S.—is a surgical procedure often used in removing the baby through incision in the mother's abdomen and uterus (Hamilton *et al.*, 2004). More than 20 percent of all babies in the United States are born by cesarean (Centers for Disease Control and Prevention, 2000; Martin, Park, & Sutton, 2002).

One of the most common reasons for cesarean birth is an abnormal or difficult labor. Often, the baby is in the *breech position* (the buttocks or legs emerge before the head). Another reason for a cesarean is *placenta previa,* a condition in which the placenta separates and lies in an abnormally low position in the uterus and may block the cervix completely.

ALTERNATIVES BIRTH CHOICES

Although established childbirth practice is in a hospital setting where a physician delivers a baby—using medication and surgical procedures "if necessary"—there are exceptions.

Home Birth

Although most babies (about 97 percent) are born in a hospital, one alternative to hospital delivery is home birth.

Home births appear to be at least as safe as hospital deliveries (Remez, 1997). As a rule, support for childbirth at home is provided by people who are not physicians like a *certified nurse-midwife* (CNM). A CNM has special training in obstetrics and provides labor support. More than 10,000 midwives in the United States have been certified through the ACNM Certification Council (Shah, 2002). The World Health Organization (WHO) and maternal-fetal medicine specialists believe that 70 to 80 percent of pregnancies and births should be cared for by midwives (e.g., Strong, 2000)

Birthing Rooms in Hospitals

In response to the growing criticism of traditional childbirth practices, many hospitals have developed *birthing rooms*. A birthing room is a combination of the labor, delivery, and recovery room. Many birthing rooms in hospitals now have a homelike atmosphere, including curtains and rocking chairs. The mother remains in one room throughout her hospitalization and the healthy newborn remains continuously at the mother's bedside.

Cesarean delivery: A birth process in which the baby is surgically removed from the mother's body by means of an incision into the uterus, usually by way of the abdominal wall, rather than by travelling through the birth canal.

Breech position: The buttocks or legs emerge before the head during childbirth.

Placenta previa: An abnormal pregnancy condition in which the placenta is implanted in the lower uterine segment.

Certified nurse-midwife: A nurse with special training in obstetrics.

Birthing room: A combination of labor, delivery, and recovery room.

Free-Standing Birth Centers

Free-standing birth center:
A facility for delivering
babies that is a compromise
between home birth and
hospital birth.

The *free-standing* (without attachment or added support) *birth center* is a compromise between home birth and traditional hospital birth. Care in free-standing birth centers is usually provided by certified nurse-midwives, although one or more physicians may be on staff or on call. These centers strive for a warm, homelike atmosphere, with birthing rooms similar to typical bedrooms. After the baby is born, there is usually postpartum care provided by the birth center, including home visits.

THE THREE STAGES OF LABOR OR CHILDBIRTH

Labor: The process of
uterine muscular contractions
that literally push the baby
out of the uterus.

Oxytocin: A hormone that
stimulates contractions of the
uterus during childbirth.

Labor, the first stage of the birth process, is the rhythmic, physiological process by which the fetus and the placenta are separated and expelled from the mother's body. Labor begins when the pituitary gland and uterus release a hormone called *oxytocin* that stimulates contractions of the muscles of the uterus (Mittendorf *et al.*, 1990). On average, active labor lasts for 12 hours for first births and seven hours for subsequent births (More & Persaud, 2003).

When Sarah was born, her mother went through three overlapping stages of labor: *Dilation, baby expulsion*, and *placental expulsion*.

First Stage: Dilation (Dilatation)

Dilation: The first stage of
labor accompanied by uterine
contractions.

Dilation is the longest period (from 1 to 24 hours) in first deliveries, and lasts about 6 to 12 hours in later deliveries. Its name refers to the expansion (stretching) of the cervix. Since the cervix is the entrance from the uterus to the vagina, through which the baby will be expelled, it must dilate from 0 to 10 centimeters (about 4 inches). The dilation is accomplished by uterine contractions.

About halfway through the dilation stage, the contractions increase in frequency and intensity. The contractions may now occur about 2 minutes apart and last for more than a minute. The mother may also feel chills and experience shaking.

Second Stage: Baby Expulsion—The Birth of a Baby

Expulsion: The birth of a
baby.

This stage is the one that we most often associate with childbirth and lasts about 1 1/2 hours. It begins when the cervix is fully dilated and the baby's head starts to move through the cervix and vaginal canal, and ends when the baby emerges completely from the mother's body.

Most babies are delivered head-first, attached by the umbilical cord to the placenta (which is still inside the mother's body). About 3 percent of babies are born feet first or bottom first (called breech position). Such deliveries pose additional difficulties, and the doctor or nurse often uses medical instruments to aid in the delivery. In many instances, the breech baby is delivered by cesarean section.

Third Stage: Placental Expulsion

This stage ends with the expulsion of the remainder of the afterbirth (umbilical cord, placenta, and amniotic sac) 8 to 10 minutes after delivery of the baby, followed by a certain amount of bleeding from the uterus. The expulsion occurs as a result of uterine contractions that also control uterine bleeding by constricting the large blood vessels that recently supplied blood to the placenta.

SUMMARY

Heredity: The transmission of mental and physical qualities from parents to their children.

Ovulation takes place prior to conception. The mother and father each contributes 23 chromosomes to their offspring. Also, prior to conception, germ cells divide in a process called meiosis. Soon after conception, cells begin to divide in a process called mitosis. An X Y combination of chromosomes produces a boy; an X X combination produces a girl.

Genetics is the study of the principles of *heredity*. A prominent pioneer geneticist was Gregor Mendel. Among Mendel's laws of genetics are the Law of Dominance and the Law of Independent Assortment.

Types of inheritance include dominant and recessive, incomplete, codominance, polygenic, and sex-linked. Alleles (members of a gene pair) may be homozygous or heterozygous. The expressed trait is known as the phenotype, the genetic pattern is called the genotype. Both heredity and environment influence an individual's attributes, although in varying amounts.

Genetic disorders include inherited genetic abnormalities and chromosomal defects. A common chromosomal disorder is Down syndrome.

Labor consists of three stages: dilation, the birth of the baby, and expulsion of the afterbirth. Several methods are used in assisting the birth process. Traditional and alternative birthing choices are available for parents to choose from. Traditional choices include: the Lamaze method, obstetrical medications, and Cesarean delivery. Prospective parents often prepare for the birth of their baby by participating in childbirth classes, such as Lamaze. These classes are designed to make delivery less stressful through specific breathing techniques and to have both the mother and father involved. Alternative birthing choices include: home birth, hospital birthing room, or in a free-standing birth center.

IMPORTANT TERMS

Acquired Immune Deficiency Syndrome (AIDS)
Birthing room
Blastocyst
Breech position
Certified Nurse-Midwife (CNM)
Cesarean birth (delivery)
Dilation
Dizygotic twins
Embryo
Embryonic disc
Embryonic stage
Embryonic stem cells
Expulsion
Fetal alcohol syndrome (FAS)
Free-standing birth center
Fetal stage
Gene therapy
Genital herpes
Germinal stage
Herpes simplex (Type 2)
Hydrocephalus
Identical twins
Labor
Lamaze method of childbirth
Lanugo
Low-birth-weight baby
Monozygotic twins
Morula
Obstetric medicine
Opiate
Oxytocin
Placenta
Placenta previa
Radiation
Rubella (German measles)
Spontaneous abortion (miscarriage)
Stem cells
Stillborn
Synthetic drugs
Syphilis
Teratogen
Teratology
Ultrasound
Viability

RELATED RESOURCES

Readings

Agin, D. P. (2010). *More than genes: what science can tell us about toxic chemicals, development, and the risk to our children.* (New York: Oxford University Press).

Elder, Kay (2005). *Infections, infertility, and assisted reproduction.* (Cambridge, UK: Cambridge University Press).

Faúndes, Aníbal (2006). T*he human drama of abortion: a global search for consensus.* (Nashville, Tenn.: Vanderbilt University Press).

Hrdy, S.B. (1989). *Mother nature: Maternal Nature and How They Shape the human Species.* (New York: Ballantine).
This is a brilliant book on the profound subject of motherhood. Hrdy's perspective on motherhood is based on decades of research and her own experience as a mother. Hrdy views motherhood from a combination of a Darwinian and cultural approach. Hrdy also discusses a crucial problem for many women today: the clash between career and motherhood.

Jain, Lucky & Wapner, Ronald (2008). *Cesarean delivery: its impacts on the mother and newborn.* (Philadelphia, Pa.: Saunders).

Kaplan, A. (1996). *Am I My Brother's Keeper?*, (Bloomington, Ill.: University of Indiana Press).
The author takes a strong position against cloning human beings. Kaplan says that people like Dr. Arthur Seed, the Chicago physicist who wants to be the first person to clone humans, is no different than Dr. Kevorkian, the pathologist who has defied the law to help people die. According to Kaplan, scientists interested in cloning human beings are "out on the fringe" of society.

Moore, Keith L. (2008). *Before we are born: essentials of embryology and birth defects.* (Philadelphia: Saunders/Elsevier).

Powers, R. (1993). *The Gold Bug Variations.* (New York: Morrow).
This book deals with James Watson's and Francis Crick's discovery of the double-helix structure of the DNA molecule in 1953. Powers asserts that most of us have failed to recognize its significance, even though at present scientists are on the verge of cracking the genetic code that has shaped all behavior from the beginning. Although the genetic code is being discovered, we may find that we tampered with it beyond the point of recovery, says Powers.

Peate, Ian & Hamilton, Cathy (2008). *Becoming a midwife in the 21st century.* (Chichester, England: John Wiley & Sons).

Rosene-Montella, Karen (2008). *Medical care of the pregnant patient.* (Philadelphia, PA: ACP Press/American College of Physicians).

Smith, Moyra editor. (2009). *The year in human and medical genetics.* (Boston, Mass: Blackwell Pub.).

Soby, Jeanette M. (2006). *Prenatal exposure to drugs/alcohol: characteristics and educational implications of fetal alcohol syndrome and cocaine/polydrug effects.* (Springfield, Ill.: Charles C Thomas).

Watson, J. D. (1968). *The Double Helix.* (New York: Signet).
A fascinating description of the discovery of DNA, the molecule that carries genetic information in cells. This book also contains a description of the mundane aspects of this great scientific discovery, such as interpersonal jealousy.

Nippold, Marilyn A. & Scott, Cheryl M. editors (2010). Expository discourse in children, adolescents, and adults: development and disorders (New York: Psychology Press).

Soby, Jeanette M. (2006). Prenatal exposure to drugs/alcohol: characteristics and educational implications of fetal alcohol syndrome and cocaine/polydrug effects (Springfield, Ill.: Charles C Thomas).

Agin, D. P. (2010). More than genes: what science can tell us about toxic chemicals, Development, and the risk to our children (Oxford; New York: Oxford University Press).

Firthel, Richard A. editor (2007). Focus on medical genetics and Down's syndrome research (New York: Nova Biomedical Books).

Websites

Human Genome Project

http://www.ornl.gov/sci/techresources/Human_Genome/home.shtml

Completed in 2003, the Human Genome Project (HGP) was a 13-year project coordinated by the U.S. Department of Energy and the National Institutes of Health. During the early years of the HGP, the WellcomeTrust (U.K.) became a major partner; additional contributions came from Japan, France, Germany, China, and others. See our history page for more information.

Project goals were to identify all the approximately 20,000-25,000 genes in human DNA, determine the sequences of the 3 billion chemical base pairs that make up human DNA, store this information in databases,

improve tools for data analysis, transfer related technologies to the private sector, and address the ethical, legal, and social issues (ELSI) that may arise from the project.

Though the HGP is finished, analyses of the data will continue for many years. Follow this ongoing research on our Milestones page. An important feature of the HGP project was the federal government's long-standing dedication to the transfer of technology to the private sector. By licensing technologies to private companies and awarding grants for innovative research, the project catalyzed the multibillion-dollar U.S. biotechnology industry and fostered the development of new medical applications.

World Health Organization

http://www.who.int/en/

WHO is the directing and coordinating authority for health within the United Nations system. It is responsible for providing leadership on global health matters, shaping the health research agenda, setting norms and standards, articulating evidence-based policy options, providing technical support to countries and monitoring and assessing health trends. In the 21st century, health is a shared responsibility, involving equitable access to essential care and collective defence against transnational threats.

PART THREE

INFANCY AND TODDLERHOOD -THE FIRST THREE YEARS

Chapter 4

Physical Development in Infancy and Toddlerhood (0 to 3 years)

Chapter Topics		Learning Objectives
Why do we study physical development?		Know the importance of studying physical development and its relation to other areas of development.
Principles in physical development.		Understand the principles of physical development: cephalocuadal and proximodistal.
What is the newborn baby like?		Recognize the characteristics of a newborn baby.
Assessing a newborn's health.		Review the standard assessments for determining newborn health.
Individual differences among newborns.		Understand the differences between male and female infant's physical development.
What does physical development look like from infancy through toddlerhood?		Understand the various areas of physical development for newborns through toddlerhood: height, weight, skeleton, brain, senses, and motor development.
		Understand the physical illnesses and fatal conditions that effect newborn babies and toddlers.
Chapter summary		

THE FIRST THREE YEARS: THE NEWBORN BABY THROUGH TODDLERHOOD

Neonatal period: The first four weeks after a baby is born.

Toddlerhood: The period in a child's development from about 18 months until about age 3 years.

In this chapter, we will study the child's physical development during the first 3 years. The first four weeks after birth is called the *neonatal period* and infancy then lasts for the first 1½ to 2 years. *Toddlerhood* lasts from about 18 months until the child is 3 years of age.

One of our tasks in this chapter is to discuss the reasons for studying physical development. We will then learn about the newborn baby. We will also look at the various areas of physical development during the first 3 years, including a child's early brain and sensory development.

When discussing physical development, early motor development in which environment plays a crucial role is of particular importance. We will conclude the chapter by studying illnesses and death in infancy and toddlerhood.

WHY DO WE STUDY PHYSICAL DEVELOPMENT?

It is essential for you as a psychology student study physical development. This is because each of the three domains of child development that you learned about in chapter 1 (physical, cognitive, and social emotional) are interconnected with one another. An infant who is not yet able to crawl cannot interact fully with his/her environment and therefore, cannot learn as much as one who is mobile. The child's physical development also influences the way people respond to him or her. An 18-month-old who cannot walk and sits practically motionless for hours, is treated quite differently than one who is able to walk and is constantly running into things.In terms of a cognitive and social emotional development, a child whose language skills are well developed will have the ability to establish strong social relationships.

Directions of Physical Development: Down and Out[1]

The most casual observer can see that a child's head is much larger at birth in relation to its total body size than in the adult. When the child is fully grown, its head is the same proportion to his or her body as in other adults. This is one of two acknowledged principles of development known as the *cephalocaudal principle*. The second principle is *proximodistal* which states that physical growth occurs from the middle of the body outward. These two principles are complementary in males and females in physical growth and motor development.

---

1. You may obtain a brochure, which lists developmental milestones up to six years by sending a stamped, self-addressed, business envelope to: Developmental Milestones, Dept. C.P.O. Box 297, Elk Grove, IL, 60009-0927.

Figure 4.1
Growth Chart for Boys: Birth to 36 Months*

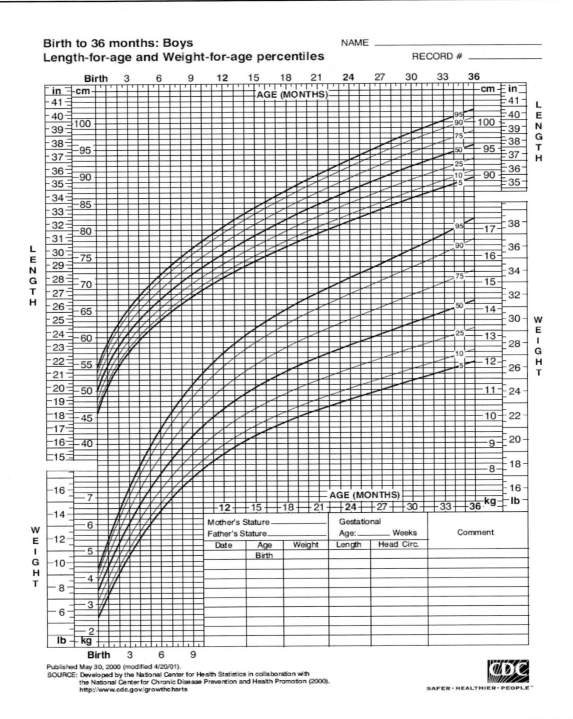

Percentiles tell us the percentage of individuals whose height or weight lies below a particular score. Thus, a child whose weight is at the 50th percentile is heavier than 50 percent of all individuals of the same age group. (Doctors use percentiles as a way of determining whether a child's growth is likely to be within normal limits. Weight should be about the same percentile as height.)

Figure 4.2
Growth Chart for Girls: Birth to 36 Months

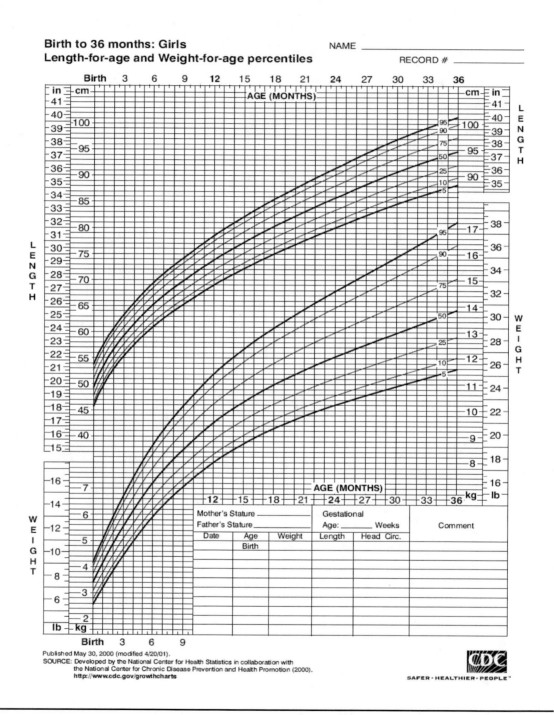

Percentiles tell us the percentage of individuals whose height or weight lies below a particular score. Thus, a child whose weight is at the 50th percentile is heavier than 50 percent of all individuals of the same age group. (Doctors use percentiles as a way of determining whether a child's growth is likely to be within normal limits. Weight should be about the same percentile as height.)

Cephalocaudal Development

Cephalocaudal development: The principle that growth proceeds from the head down.

The *cephalocaudal* ("head-to-toe") principle states that development proceeds from the head (top) down to the lower parts of the body. This principle is evident before the baby is born; the brain and central nervous system develop first, followed by developmental changes in the lower parts of the body.

There is also a general tendency for the muscles near the head and neck to develop earlier than the muscles of the arms, legs, and torso. Hence, Sarah can sit before she can stand; stand before she can walk. More specifically, by about 3 months, most infants can support their own heads while being carried around, they can turn their heads while lying on their backs, and lift their heads while lying on their stomachs. By 6 months, as strength and control move downward, babies can keep their entire backs straight when being held in a sitting position. By 9 months, babies have enough strength and control in their knees and feet so that they can stand on their own.

Proximodistal Development

Proximodistal development: The principle that development proceeds from the center of the body to the periphery.

The *proximodistal* (Latin: near-to-far) principle states that growth proceeds from the center of the body (axis) to the periphery. This principle is also evident in prenatal development. Arm buds develop before hands; hands develop before fingers. During postnatal development, the baby first acquires the ability to use its hands and feet before its fingers and toes. Also, infants reach for things while twisting their entire bodies, before they extend just their arms.

WHAT IS THE NEWBORN BABY LIKE?

Now let's look at Sarah and Carlos' physical characteristics and then at specific functional changes that occurred when they were born.

Physical Characteristics of the Newborn

Like about 95 percent of all full-term babies, Sarah and Carlos each weighed between 5½ and 10 pounds and measured between 18 and 22 inches at birth. Carlos was a little heavier than Sarah—7½ pounds to Sarah's 7 pounds—and a little longer—20 inches to Sarah's 19½ inches; Sarah had a bit more fat than Carlos. Figures 4.1 and 4.2 show growth charts for boys and girls respectively through 36 months.

A distinctive feature of the newborn is variation in physical proportions from those of the adult. Newborns appear top heavy because their head is about a fourth of their total length, compared with about one-eighth in the adult. The newborn's eyes are set low, the nose is small and flat, and the legs are quite skinny and very short.

At birth, the baby's bones are composed mostly of soft cartilage, making them more reactive to pressure and sudden movements.

Fontanels: Soft openings in an infant's skull bones that are covered with soft tissue.

A newborn's underdeveloped bones are quite noticeable in the soft spots, or *fontanel*s. The fontanels are six separate gaps between the bones in the skull. They are covered with tough membranes under the scalp that turn into bones by the middle of the second year (Schmidt & Segalowitz, 2008; Young, 1990). In a way, this late development is fortunate because the underdeveloped bones make it possible for the head to "mold" during the birth process, easing the baby's passage through the mother's pelvis. Bone underdevelopment is also evident in the newborn's nose, which is somewhat flat.

Myelin: A fatty substance that helps insulate neurons and speeds the transmission of nerve impulses

Physiologic jaundice: A condition characterized by yellowness of the skin due to bile deposited by a malfunctioning liver.

Vernix caseosa: A cheesy varnish on a newborn that serves as a protection for the neonate against infection and drops off shortly after birth.

Lanugo: Fine hair on a newborn which drops off shortly after birth.

Meconium: Fetal waste matter.

At birth, the newborn's brain weighs close to a pound, about 25 percent of its adult weight, and contains about 100 billion nerve cells (neurons) which are the pathways of the brain's subtle and efficient communication.

Some of the newborn's neurons are insulated with *myelin*, a white fatty, or lipid, substance that sheathes the nerves (Schmidt & Segalowitz, 2008; Spitzer & White, 2008). Since the insulation is incomplete, the newborn baby's responses to stimulation are slow and imprecise. Large areas of the newborn's brain are still not functional. The newborn's brain activity is concentrated in the brain stem which controls automatic physiological functions such as breathing, digestion, and reflexes.

When Sarah was born, her head was misshapen from the molding as it passed through the birth canal, her nose was flat, and she had a bluish tinge to her skin from anoxia (temporary lack of oxygen during birth). (Sometimes infants are a fiery red, due to temporary allergic reactions.) A few days after birth, some babies develop a yellowish tinge to their skin and eyes, a condition known as *physiologic jaundice*, caused by a rise in bilirubin, a pigment produced in the bloodstream by the liver. This condition disappears after about 2 weeks when the liver matures enough to process the bilirubin.

At birth, Sarah was covered with an oily substance, called *vernix caseosa*, or cheesy varnish, that serves as protection against infection and dries within a few days. She had some fine body hair, called *lanugo*, which dropped off shortly after birth. Furthermore, she excreted *meconium*, a stringy, greenish-black waste (feces) that formed in the fetal intestinal tract. Meconium consists mainly of bile and cell debris that Sarah ingested while in her mother's womb. This was a temporary condition and disappeared within a day or two after birth.

Alert parents usually notice several interesting features in their newborns. For instance, most light-skinned infants have blue eyes at birth, even though their genetic destiny is brown eyes. Also, the bottom half of a baby's body is darker than the top half for about the first 6 months due to an immature circulatory system, which causes the blood to pool in the lower limbs (Young, 1990).

Transition from Fetal to Newborn Vital Functions

Metabolism: The complex chemical reactions that provide and use energy in an organism.

Almost immediately after Sarah entered this world, she started breathing automatically; she could now rely on her own heart—even though it was only about $1/16$ the size of an adult's heart. Prior to birth, Sarah's oxygen source was the umbilical-borne blood. For the first few days after birth, Sarah's breathing rate was very high (40 breaths per minute compared with 14 to 20 for an adult). The respiration rate then subsided to 25 breaths per minute, but was erratic (Young, 1990). Sarah was able to ingest food from the moment of birth (mainly through sucking) and to absorb the nutrients in a complex cycle of energy transference and molecular breakdown called *metabolism*. Furthermore, since Sarah had developed layers of fat during the last couple of months before birth, she could now control her temperature to some extent. Prior to birth, these functions were performed by the mother's body.

As Sarah matures, her reflexive movements become better organized, voluntary, and controlled. This change is the result of brain development so that movement control switches from the brain stem, which controls more basic responses, into higher regions such as the cortex.

Reflexes: Our Inborn Physical Skills

Reflex: A primitive, unlearned, involuntary action that can be elicited by specific forms of stimulation.

How does a newborn "know" that it must breathe to survive? The answer: If the newborn "forgets" to breathe, carbon dioxide accumulates in the blood and triggers a reaction that forces the baby to breathe. This type of "prewiring" is called a *reflex*.

A reflex is a primitive, unlearned and involuntary action that can be elicited by specific forms of stimulation. Remember in chapter 2 we learned about Pavlov's dogs and their innate salivatory reflex. All primitive reflexes appear at or near birth. Many reflexes disappear within 2 to 4 months after birth; others remain for some time.

Reflexes serve a variety of purposes. Some reflexes, such as the one which "jump starts" the baby to breathe, help the infant's survival. Reflexes are also important determinants of healthy development.

A well-known reflex that is present at birth is the rooting reflex, which can be elicited by stroking the corner of a baby's mouth or cheek, causing it to turn its head toward the stimulated side. The rooting reflex is particularly prominent in breast-fed babies who will turn quickly in the direction of stimulation to reach the nipple Table 4.1 presents some typical newborn reflexes.

Table 4.1

Some Newborn Reflexes

Type of Reflex	Stimulus	Behavior	Significance
Rooting	Baby's cheek is touched or stroked with finger or nipple.	The head turns in the direction of stimulation; mouth opens; sucking movements begin (normally absent by 4 months).	Survival value because reflex enables baby to locate food (Absent in depressed infants).
Swallowing	An object touching the lips; usually follows sucking.	Often swallowing is coordinated with sucking (permanent).	If weak or absent, may indicate a prematurity or neurological defect.
Sucking	Placing finger or some other object in baby's mouth.	Infant sucks finger or object rhythmically (replaced by voluntary sucking after 4 months)	If weak or absent, may indicate a prematurity or neurological defect.
Palmar grasp (also called Darwinian grasping)	Placing finger or some other object against baby's palm.	Infant's grasp may be strong enough to be raised to a standing position (absent between 3 and 12 months).	Absence may indicate neurological problem. Fades by 3 to 4 months.
Moro or Startle	Dropping a baby unexpectedly, loud noise, or sudden change of position.	Arms go out with hands open, back is arched, head held back, legs extended (absent by 5 to 8 months).	If reflex is weak or absent, there may be a central nervous system problem. Fades by about 6 months.
Babinski	Stimulation of the sole of the foot toward the heel.	The toes curl and fan out; foot twists inward (absent by 8 to 12 months).	Decline in reflex and then disappearance from 8 to 12 months indicates normal neurological functioning.
Stepping or "walking"	Holding infant upright and allowing one foot to touch a surface.	Infant will imitate walking. Normally present in infants 3 to 4 weeks old. (absent by 3 months).	Significance disputed; may be kicking, not walking motion. Fades by about 8 weeks.
Tonic Neck	The baby is laid on its back with head turned to one side.	Infant stretches out arm or leg on the side that he is facing and flexes the other arm and leg (absent by 4 months).	If not gone by 4 months, there may be brain malfunction. Paves way for eye-hand coordination.

DETERMINING A NEWBORN'S HEALTH WITH NEONATAL SCALES

Physicians have discovered that a newborn with problems must be identified and treated immediately, or the child may suffer irreparable damage, or even die (Nugent, Petrauskas, & Brazelton, 2009). To minimize the possibility of such occurrences, doctors use standardized assessment methods: the *Apgar Scale*, designed by anesthesiologist Virginia Apgar; and, the *Brazelton Neonatal Behavioral Assessment Scale*, developed by pediatrician T. Berry Brazelton.

The Apgar Scale

Apgar scale: Standard medical assessment of a newborn that uses criteria such as the baby's appearance, pulse, and grimace.

The *Apgar scale* utilizes five vital signs of neonatal activity: Pulse (heart rate), breathing (respiratory effort), activity (muscle tone), grimace (reflex irritability, obtained by such means as a pinch or by placing a finger in the baby's mouth), and appearance (color). The Apgar scale (see Table 4.2) is a quick and simple method of diagnosing the newborn's physical status and is administered at 1 and 5 minutes after delivery (Apgar, 1953).

Each infant characteristic is rated on a 3-point scale (0, 1, 2). A total of 10 points (2 for each dimension) is "perfect"; scores of 7 to 10 (obtained by 90 percent of normal infants), indicate that the infant's condition is good. Apgar scores from 4 to 7 indicate that the infant is in fair condition, but may have some problems, such as breathing difficulty, which usually requires supplemental oxygen. Babies with an Apgar score of 0 to 3 obtained at 10, 15 and 20 minutes after birth often suffer from nerve and muscle damage, a neurological condition known as cerebral palsy. These children are in extremely poor condition and need life-saving treatment, including resuscitation.[2] Children with low Apgar scores are more vulnerable in a compromising environment (e.g. unclean home, insufficient heat and clothing).

Table 4.2

The Apgar Scale Showing the Scoring System for a Newborn's Physical Condition

Vital Sign	Ratings		
	0	1	2
Heart rate	Absent	Slow (below 100 beats/minute)	Over 100 beats/minute
Respiratory effort	Absent	Slow or irregular breathing	Good crying, strong breathing
Muscle tone	Flaccid or limp	Weak; some flexion of extremities	Active motion, strong flexion of extremities
Reflex irritability	No response	Grimace, weak cry, cough or sneeze	Vigorous cry, cough or sneeze
Color	Blue, pale	Body pink, extremities blue	Completely pink

Source: Apgar

---

2. Note: The Apgar is not a completely reliable prognostic instrument. Except for very low readings, the Apgar score does not predict the eventual health of the baby.

The Brazelton Neonatal Behavioral Assessment Scale

Brazelton Neonatal Behavioral Assessment Scale: Measure of a newborn's neurological condition.

Another test used to evaluate the newborn's condition 24 to 36 hours after birth is the *Brazelton Neonatal Behavioral Assessment Scale.* One of the major purposes of this scale is to assess the baby's neurological condition (Feldman & Eidelman, 2003; Nugent, Petrauskas, & Brazelton, 2009). The scale is also used to determine the progress of preterm infants, to compare newborns of different cultures, and to evaluate programs designed to alleviate developmental difficulties (Brazelton & Cramer, 1990; Feldman & Eidelman, 2003).

The Brazelton scale tests characteristics such as reflexes, motor capacities, muscle tone, and attention span. The equipment required to conduct the test is simple: A rattle, a bell, a flashlight, and a pin. The test takes 30 minutes to administer. Typical test items include the examiner repeatedly calling the baby's name in a high-pitched voice while the examiner moves her head up and down and from side to side. Another item includes a test of the baby's cuddliness, with the examiner holding the baby against his or her chest or shoulder.

STATES OF AROUSAL

State of arousal: The degree of sleep and wakefulness.

Even a casual observer can see that newborns go through cycles or daily rhythms in their sleep and wakefulness, similar to adults. A newborn's cycle lasts about 1½ to 2 hours. A cycle is a *state,* which is "a behavioral condition that (1) remains stable over a period of time, (2) occurs repeatedly in an individual infant, and (3) can be encountered in very similar forms in other individuals" (Hutt, Lenard, & Prechtl, 1969). States of arousal are caused by "information" from the various senses—hunger, pain, physical distress (Wolff, 1966; 1996) — and are quite prominent by the fifth day of life. Several states of arousal or degrees of sleep and wakefulness have been identified in the newborn baby.

Regular Sleep

During regular sleep, Carlos sleeps soundly and is hardest to wake. His eyes are closed; his breathing is regular and slow. He lies motionless, except when there is strong stimulation, such as a loud noise. The baby's reflexes (primitive and unlearned responses to specific forms of stimulation) are almost totally absent. On an arousal continuum, this state is the low point.

Irregular Sleep

Although Carlos' eyes are closed in this state, his breathing is irregular, and occasionally he is restless. He is also more sensitive to sounds than in regular sleep. Noises or sounds that would not normally arouse Carlos now awaken him, bringing responses such as smiles, grimaces, and pouts. His heart and respiration are irregular and fast, and his muscles twitch from time to time. The newborn spends some 75 percent of its sleep in this state, with each period lasting from 20 to 45 minutes (Hutt, Lenard, & Prechtl, 1969; Lu Rang, 1981; Nugent, Petrauskas, & Brazelton, 2009).

Drowsiness

Drowsiness occurs both before and after sleep, and resembles it. In this state, the eyes may be open and body movement is somewhat more active than in regular sleep. Breathing is usually irregular, and reflexes, such as the patellar (knee jerk following a blow to the leg immediately below the knee), are usually weak.

Alert Inactivity

Alert inactivity occurs after the baby has been fed, diapered, and burped. The newborn may move his or her arms and head while remaining generally quiet and inactive. In this state, Carlos spends much time fixating on objects. His eyes are open and have a bright, shining quality.

Many researchers believe that parents should take advantage of the child's attentiveness to its surroundings during the alert state by providing the child with learning experiences. Experts suggest that family members should talk to the infant, and provide it with a better view of its surroundings by propping the infant up during this state.

Waking Activity and Crying

Babies are most difficult to take care of in this state, which may begin quietly, then turn to crying and fussing. The cause may be internal stimulation, such as hunger or pain, or external, such as removing the baby's bottle. Respiration is the fastest and most irregular in this state (Hutt, Lenard, & Prechtl, 1969; Marcus, 2008). Reflexes are strongest.

Many investigators have noticed that the nature of a baby's crying signifies a particular form of distress (Barr, Hopkins, & Green, 2000; Hopkins, 2000). For instance, brain-damaged infants often have a weaker cry than normal babies. An angry cry is loud and long; a pain cry is like a wail.

Investigators have noticed that the various behavioral states change as infants develop. First, states become more distinct with age. Second, the amount of time babies spend in each state changes with time. Such information provides physicians with a tool for comparing the maturity of one infant with another.

INDIVIDUAL DIFFERENCES AMONG NEWBORNS

If you look at any group of newborns casually, you will notice physical differences among them such as size, color, and general build. There are also physical differences between males and females. Boys usually weigh more than girls at birth; girls have a bit more fat. At birth, the girl's nervous system and bones are about 2 weeks more mature than the boy's.

There are also behavioral differences among newborns. Some newborns are startled easily when asleep. Others are more irritable. Babies have different temperaments. One group of researchers (Chess & Thomas, 1982) have classified infant temperaments into three broad categories: The easy child, the difficult child, and the slow-to-warm-up child.

Although the different states are common to most newborns, the patterns vary from one infant to the next (Schmidt & Segalowitz, 2008). Whereas Sarah sleeps 20 hours a day, Carlos sleeps only 13 (the average is 16 to 18 hours).

GROWTH IN HEIGHT AND WEIGHT

Physical development is particularly rapid during the first year. The baby's length increases by 10 to 12 inches in the first 12 months, its birth weight doubles at 5 months, and nearly triples by the end of the first year. Carlos measured about 20 inches and weighed 7½ pounds at birth. At the end of the first year, he measured about 30 inches and weighed about 21 pounds. Sarah grew slightly less.

This dramatic physical growth during the first year slows down considerably in the second year. Children generally gain about twice as much in height and weight during their first than during their second year. For instance, while Carlos's length increased by about 10 to 12 inches during the first year, his length (or height) increased by only about 4½ inches during the second year. Similarly, whereas Carlos gained approximately 14 pounds in the first year, in the second year, he gained only about 7 pounds.

By the end of the second year, Carlos measured 34 inches in height and weighed 28 pounds; Sarah's gains were slightly less. Both children roughly quadrupled their birth weights by 2 years; both were roughly half of their adult heights on their second birthdays.

Growth slows still further in the third year. The height gain is 3 to 4 inches; weight increase is 4 to 5 pounds. On his third birthday, Carlos was 39 inches tall and weighed 32 pounds; Sarah's gains were slightly less.

One way that Carlos's and Sarah's parents can determine if their child's growth is within normal limits is to use the 4- or 5-to-1 formula. That is, from about the first year until puberty, the weight gain should be approximately 4 to 5 pounds per inch of increase in height. Of course, with the onset of puberty, there will be a marked increase in both height and weight for both Carlos and Sarah (Puckett, 2007; Williams & Bollela, 1993).

Nonorganic Failure-to-Thrive Syndrome

Although most children experience normal weight gain as they grow older, some children gain very little weight even when there appears to be no organic basis, such as illness, or obvious nutritional deficiency. This condition is called *nonorganic failure-to-thrive syndrome*, a label that is applied to any child below the third percentile (97 percent of the children are taller and heavier) when compared with other children of the same age and gender (Dykman *et al.*, 2001). The child stops growing or may even lose weight, despite apparently normal health and adequate nutrition.

The nonorganic failure-to-thrive syndrome is present in the majority of cases by 18 months of age (Puckett, 2007). The most obvious feature is a substantial loss in weight, which makes the child look wasted and emaciated. The behavior of the infants includes passivity, little smiling or vocalization, and a lack of cuddliness when picked up. Also, infants with the nonorganic failure-to-thrive syndrome display very little facial expression when compared with other infants (Abramson, 1991; Kessler, & Dawson, 1999) and tend to be very irritable. Some nonorganic failure-to-thrive children have neurological disorders such as epilepsy, migraine, cerebral hemorrhage, and convulsions.

Physical development is rapid in the first year. At birth a baby's head is much larger in proportion to its body than at any other time.

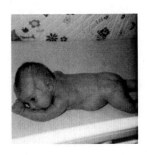

Nonorganic failure-to-thrive syndrome: Growth retardation in young children when there appears to be no organic condition for the disorder.

Deprivation dwarfism: A condition in older children similar to failure-to-thrive syndrome in younger children.

The nonorganic failure-to-thrive syndrome is believed to be caused by factors such as inadequate caregiving, including abuse and neglect. This syndrome points to the importance of the environment—particularly the quality of the mother-infant interaction—for proper physical development. In older children, the disorder is called *deprivation dwarfism*.

CHANGES IN SHAPE

With age, a child's body increasingly resembles that of his or her same-gender parent (Puckett, 2007). If we compare Carlos's body at birth, then again at 1, 2, and 3 years of age with that of his father's, we see it resembling the father's body more and more as Carlos gets older. At birth, the baby's head is much larger in proportion to its body (one-fourth of total body length) compared with an adult (one-eighth of total body length). With time, differences in body proportions become less.

To enable children to reach their adult physical proportions by about age 20, children's smaller and shorter lower body parts grow faster in elementary school than their heads, illustrating the cephalocaudal principle. From birth to maturity, the head doubles in size, the trunk triples, and the arms and legs quadruple. Since growth proceeds in a head-to-toe fashion, different parts of the body have their own periods of rapid and slow growth, each reaching its mature size at its own time. However, growth in all parts of the body is continuous and concurrent.

Another factor that helps to change body shape is distribution of fat under the skin, or subcutaneous fat known as baby fat. Subcutaneous fat is first deposited about 2 months before birth and peaks at about 9 months after birth. This results in the chubby baby look (particularly in females), familiar in advertisements. At about 1 year, the child becomes more active, losing some of its appetite, and the layer of fat under the skin declines. This decline in fat continues until about age 6 or 7, then rises until adolescence.

CHANGES IN SKELETAL STRUCTURE

Ossification: Conversion of cartilage into bone.

Calcification: The hardening of bones by the deposit of lime salts, including calcium.

A major change in a young child's skeletal structure is the conversion of cartilage, a soft flexible tissue, into bone, a process known as *ossification*. Ossification begins before birth through *calcification*, the deposit of lime salts, including calcium. With maturity, the bones harden, and become longer and denser, usually at predictable rates. Ossification continues throughout childhood into late adolescence.

The eruption of teeth is a major part of the ossification process. While the first tooth, usually a lower front one, erupts at about 7 months, teeth begin to form under the gums from the third prenatal month. By 9 months, the average baby has three teeth; the first temporary molars (4 of them) erupt by about 15 months. By the end of the third year, the child usually has a complete set of 20 deciduous (primary or "baby") teeth. Dental maturity is about the same in boys as in girls.

THE GROWTH OF THE BRAIN

"Look how she has grown!" is frequently heard about a young child's development. Such comments are usually made about the child's height. However, equally important—if not more so—is the child's brain development.

Figure 4.3
Changes in Form and Proportion of the Human Body during Fetal and Postnatal Life

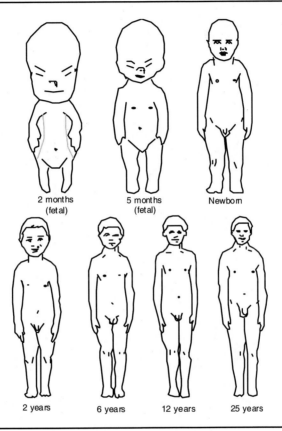

2 months (fetal)	5 months (fetal)	Newborn

2 years	6 years	12 years	25 years

Changes in form and proportion occur in physical development throughout childhood. Notice the size of the head in relation to the rest of the body in the 5-month-old fetus as compared with the 12-year-old. Also note the relative length of legs and arms.

Source: *C.M. Jackson, 1929.*

Neurons: Specialized cells which receive and transmit information to other cells in the body.

Sarah's brain develops at a faster rate during the first 2 years than at any other time. At birth, a newborn's brain is about 25 percent of its adult weight, at 2 years about 75 percent (Schmidt & Segalowitz, 2008; Tanner, 1990). Also, at birth, the female brain is more mature than the male brain. Before birth and shortly after birth, Sarah's brain shows a spurt in the growth of brain cells. The brain's growth spurt also consists of a branching out of the *neurons* (the pathways to the brain's subtle and efficient communication system) to form new connections with neighboring cells (Johnson *et al.*, 1996) enabling the brain to send and receive electrical impulses more efficiently. By about 7 months after conception, all six layers of the mature brain are in place, beginning with the deepest layer, followed by neurons in the second layer, and so on (Rakic, 1995).

Glial "glue" cells: Cells which surround neurons and hold them in place.

In infancy, the brain also undergoes a growth spurt in supporting cells called the *glia*. Glial cells surround neurons and hold them in place. They also buffer neurons physically and chemically from the rest of the body and act as "housekeepers" by destroying and removing neurons that are killed by injury or die from old age. Another function of glial cells is to prevent toxic substances in the blood from reaching the delicate cells in the brain (Schmidt & Segalowitz, 2008).

The rapid growth of the infant's brain enables it to perform a variety of functions. One function is sorting out cells, another is myelination. Another brain function includes cerebral lateralization.

Myelination

Myelination: The process of covering nerve fibers by a sheath of white, fatty substance called myelin.

Another physical change in the brain and nervous system that contributes to the newborn's intellectual development is *myelination*, the covering of nerve fibers with a sheath of a white, fatty substance known as myelin. Myelin insulates nerve fibers from "outside" interference, speeding the transmission of messages between nerve cells within the brain and between the brain and other parts of the body (Casper, 1993; Sampaio & Truwit, 2001; Schmidt & Segalowitz, 2008).

At birth, nerves in the upper portion of the body have more myelin than those in the lower portion of the body, which is the reason that babies are less able to control the lower trunk and legs than older children. This is in accordance with the cephalocaudal ("head-to-toe") principle of development. Myelination is most noticeable shortly after birth in nerves leading to and from the brain.

Synaptic Pruning

Synaptic pruning: The process of weeding out unnecessary cells.

One reason why the brain functions more efficiently in older children than in babies is a process called *synaptic pruning*. Synaptic pruning is downsizing, in which unnecessary cells are weeded out or eliminated (Greenough & Black, 1992; Spitzer & White, 2008). Only those cells that are reinforced by experience survive, creating a more efficient system for transmitting impulses (Healy, 1994). Synaptic pruning begins shortly after birth and continues throughout childhood and adolescence (Casper, 1993; Huttenlocher, 2003).

Cerebral (Dominance) Lateralization: Brain Specialization

Cerebral lateralization: The dominance of one hemisphere of the brain in the performance of a certain function.

As soon as the brain begins to function, various duties are "assigned" to specific areas of the brain (Schmidt & Segalowitz, 2008). Beginning early in life, the right side of the body is controlled mainly by the left hemisphere, the left side mainly by the right hemisphere. This domination by one hemisphere of the brain over a particular function is known as *cerebral lateralization*. The left hemisphere controls functions (although not exclusively) such as speech, hearing, verbal memory, decision making, mathematics, and processing of language. The right hemisphere processes visual-spatial information and nonlinguistic sounds such as music, touch, and emotional expression (Nelson & Bosquet, 2000). In shorthand terminology, we can think of the left hemisphere as being a verbal specialist and the right hemisphere being concerned mostly with visual-spatial information. Cerebral lateralization is a gradual process and continues throughout childhood.

Cerebral lateralization does not mean that the hemispheres work in isolation and are totally dominant over a particular function. For example, although the left hemisphere generally controls the production of speech, the right hemisphere gives speech its appropriate emotional intonation (the particular distribution of stress or pitch) (Snow, 2000). Hence, in most situations, the two hemispheres cooperate naturally, with each one making a valuable contribution.

During the last few decades, scientists have noticed that cerebral lateralization is not as complete as once thought. For instance, the left hemisphere does not control the language function in all people. Rather, it controls language functions in most right-handed people and in about two out of three left-handed individuals (Pinker, 1994). The brain is plastic or changeable until about age 14, so the children who lose the left hemisphere of the brain through surgery to control epilepsy are usually able to talk because their right hemisphere assumes the speech function.

Effect of Brain Development

With brain development, comes more efficient motor behavior: better balance and better control of movement. Brain development has important psychological consequences as well, such as giving the child confidence. Sarah's brain development enables her to remember better, to attach meaning to people and to objects, and to reason better. Also, with brain development, Sarah is able to make better social adjustments.

The Role of Plasticity in Brain Development

Until 40 or 50 years ago, it was thought that brain development was genetically determined and that environment played no part. Researchers now tell us that experience—particularly early in life—can influence brain development. This molding by the environment is called *plasticity* (Ono, Squire & Marcus, 1993; Sptizer & White, 2008). Plasticity is the degree to which a developing structure is capable of being molded and modified by experience, regardless of the genetic codes at work.

Plasticity: The degree to which a developing structure is capable of being molded and modified by experience, regardless of the genetic codes at work.

Studies of plasticity have shown that environment can affect a baby's brain adversely or favorably. Early detrimental experiences such as malnutrition or maternal intake of alcohol during pregnancy can hinder a baby's ability to learn and to store information. An enriched environment can improve brain efficiency. Rats and other animals raised in enriched environments, with wheels to run on, rocks to climb and stand on, and levers to manipulate, have heavier brains, thicker layers of cortex, and more cells in the visual cortex than rats raised in standard cages, or in isolation. Similarly, as a result of neural plasticity, the left hand is larger in pianists than in nonpianists, and pianists have increased left-hand dexterity (Amunts *et al.*, 1997).

In young children, the plasticity of the brain can be seen in the size of their vocabulary. Children's vocabulary size is related to the brain's activity and complexity of neural structures, which are incomplete at birth, and continue to develop during childhood. Studies show that vocabulary size and the growth of the brain are correlated with the child's environment. The more hugs, coos, songs, and toys Carlos receives, the larger the size of his vocabulary. Similarly, the more talkative the household, the greater the size of Carlos's vocabulary and the more complex his neural network. The brain's development can be verified through powerful research tools like imaging devices that provide moving pictures of neural development in the brain (D'Antonio, 1997).

The brain's plasticity can be seen by using imaging techniques when a person loses his or her sight. Other senses such as touch and hearing become sharpened. This type of cross-modality is also seen when the left cerebral hemisphere suffers severe damage and the right hemisphere--over time--can recover language-related abilities (Miller, Gordon, & Buddie, 1999). However, the brain is not infinitely plastic, even for children. Children who appear to have recovered from traumatic brain injury often exhibit subtle neurological deficits when they reach puberty.

NUTRITION

There is considerable controversy over proper nutrition in early childhood. To complicate matters, food available to children is often governed by economic status and culture (McGuire & Beerman, 2010). A baby seems to thrive best if the basic nutritional needs are met. The newborn needs about 450 calories a day, divided among protein, carbohydrates, and fat. Protein is needed for rapid cellular growth and maintenance; carbohydrates and fat are needed for energy. Nutrient and fluid needs should be increased during illness. The infant and toddler also need plenty of minerals and vitamins (Fox *et al.*, 2004; Goday & Sentongo, 2009).

Adequate minerals and vitamins are needed to prevent deficiencies like scurvy (hemorrhaging and abnormal bone formation due to deficiency of vitamin C) and rickets (inadequate bone formation due to lack of vitamin D and calcium) (Eckstein, 1980; Goday & Sentongo, 2009). Sometimes, babies do not receive enough fat. Because they fear heart trouble in their children when they get older, many mothers mistakenly feed skim milk or 2% low fat milk to their babies. There is no evidence that this is beneficial, and in fact it is known to be harmful. The Committee on Nutrition of the American Academy of Pediatrics recommends against feeding reduced-fat milk to infants less than 2 years old because such milk contains too few calories. Another danger is feeding the baby cow's milk before it is 1 year old, which increases the risk of iron deficiency anemia. Cow's milk is low in iron, and the iron in cow's milk is poorly absorbed; cow's milk in the infant's diet also decreases the absorption of iron from other dietary sources (McGuire & Beerman, 2010). Ancommon iron supplement for infants is ferrous sulfate drops.

Sugar intake in the infant's diet should be at a minimum—no more than six ounces per day.

Bottle-Feeding Versus Breast-Feeding

In 1979, the American Academy of Pediatrics (AAP) announced that one of its major goals would be to urge all mothers to breast-feed their babies, a position long advocated by the La Lèche League[3], a breast-feeding advocacy and support organization. In the United States, slightly more than one out of two mothers

---

3. In addition to the La Lèche League as a source of information on breast-feeding, information is available from local chapters of the Nursing-Mothers Council. To obtain information from the La Lèche League, write to: La Lèche League International, P.O. Box 1209, Franklin Park, IL, 60131-8209. Or call 1-800-525-3243.

(about 60 percent) breast-feed their babies, although most do so for only a few months (US Department of Health and Human Services, 2000).

Proponents of breast-feeding point out many advantages over formula or cow's milk: Breast-fed babies thrive better even in underdeveloped countries (Cadwell, 2009). The mother's milk provides short-term immunity for some diseases, including respiratory infections and intestinal illnesses. The illnesses are usually prevented by the white blood cells which flow directly from the mother's milk into the infant's intestine, where they create immunity against many organisms that can cause gastrointestinal infections (Cadwell, 2009; Reynolds, 2001). Breast milk is easier to digest and to absorb than infant formulas; it contains all needed nutrients, with the correct balance of protein, sugars, and fat in adequate amounts which vary with the infant's changing needs. And it's free.

The mother's milk may be especially helpful for the preterm baby. Breast-feeding is also one of the most effective preventive measures against asthma. There is also some evidence (Cadwell, 2009; Elliot, Kjolhede, & Rasmussen, 1997) that breast-feeding decreases the risk of the child becoming an obese adult. The American Academy of Pediatrics cites the following benefits of breast-feeding for infants: Greater chance of survival, decreased risk of Sudden Infant Death Syndrome, reduced risk of diabetes, cancer and obesity, and a slightly higher IQ.

Studies of maternal-infant bonding show that there is much more going on during breast-feeding than simply the provision of nutrition. Sarah not only satisfies her need for food, but also receives warmth, security, and love while being breast-fed. Within 24 hours of birth, studies show that a bond has been forged between the mother and her breast-fed baby that will last a lifetime. The American Academy of Pediatrics recommends that infants be breast-fed exclusively for 6 months and that breast feeding continue for at least the first year.

Breast-feeding is not advisable for every newborn baby. Some mothers are unable to nurse for reasons such as inverted nipples and extreme discomfort. Other mothers do not produce enough milk. One indicationof possible difficulty is the mother's breasts not swelling sufficiently during early pregnancy; another is the baby not wetting it's diaper enough timeseach day (about six). Breast-feeding is not in the best interest of the baby if the mother is HIV positive. The mother should not breast-feed her baby if she uses alcoholic beverages, because alcohol concentrates in breast milk and can inhibit milk production (American Academy of Pediatrics, 2005). Bottle-fed babies may have early dental problems (e.g., teeth discoloration and decay) from taking a bottle containing liquid and sugar to bed (Skolnick, 1990). To avoid this problem, known as "nursing-bottle mouth," mothers are advised to give their babies liquid from a cup as soon as possible and a bottle filled *only* with water at bedtime or naptime.

EARLY SENSORY CAPABILITIES

At birth, Sarah and Carlos possess the same sensory equipment as their parents for receiving, locating, and reacting to stimuli such as light and sound. Yet, their sensory capabilities are quite immature. Let's look at vision first.

Vision

Vision is the least developed of the newborn's senses. A newborn's eyes are smaller than those of adults; the retinal structures are incomplete, and the optic nerve is underdeveloped. The lens is also immature—the image is focused behind the retina instead of on it, as it should, causing the image to be blurred.

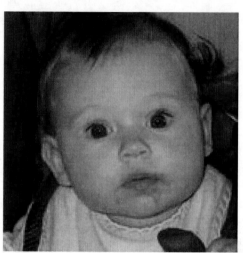

Although the infant in the photo appears to be staring into empty space, she may be looking at something specific like a human face. Further, she may be looking at specific features of the human face, depending on her age. For example, a 1-month-old baby tends to direct its gaze to the outer or external regions of the facial stimulus such as the hair and chin while a 2-month-old child tends to direct its gaze to inner features such as the eyes and mouth.

Visual acuity: The sharpness of the visual image at the retina.

Pupillary reflex: A reaction to the amount of light entering the eye by constricting or expanding the pupils.

Tracking (pursuit) ability: Following a moving object visually.

Fixation: Visual direction and focus on a particular stimulus for a period of time.

Visual acuity, the ability to detect and recognize the separation in parts of a visual stimulus, such as the large "E" on the Snellen (eye) chart, is not completely developed at birth (Bushnell & Boudreau, 1993; Puckett, 2007). At birth, a baby's visual acuity can range from 20/300 to 20/800 (Cole & Cole, 1993), meaning that the newborn needs to be within 20 feet to see what the average adult can see at 300 to 800 feet. The newborn's limited visual acuity appears to be due to the immaturity of the retina, the connections between the retina and the brain, and the areas of the brain involved in vision (Maurer & Lewis, 2001). By 6 months to a year, Sarah's visual acuity approximates normal adult vision. By 2 years, most children have 20/60 vision.

Pupillary reflex. When her nurse dimmed the lights in the nursery where 1-hour-old Sarah had been placed, Sarah's pupils began to dilate; conversely, if the nurse made the lights brighter, Sarah's pupils constricted. This sensitivity to differences in the brightness or intensity of light is called the *pupillary reflex*. Although sluggish at birth, the newborn's sensitivity to light becomes livelier within a few days.

Tracking (pursuit) ability and fixation. Within about 4 days after birth, Sarah can follow a moving object visually, an ability known as *tracking,* or *pursuit*. At birth, infants can also scan their surroundings in the dark. Newborns can also *fixate*, direct and focus on a particular point for a period of time.

Figure 4.4
Visual Preferences in the Newborn

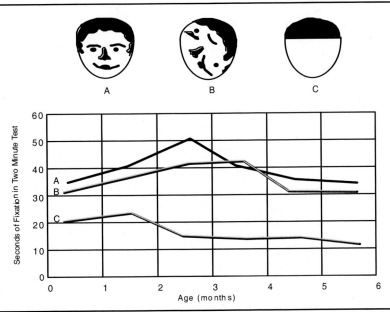

The newborn prefers to look at complex figures rather than simple ones and at realistic rather than abstract depictions of the human face.

Source: Fantz, 1961

Depth perception: The ability to judge the distance of objects from themselves and from one another. The capacity to perceive the dimensions of height, width, and distance.

The visual cliff: A glass covered platform that appears to have a shallow side and a "deep" side that is used to study an infant's depth perception.

Visual preferences. Some types of visual patterns gain and hold an infant's attention more than others. (See Figure 4.4 above) This pattern in newborns was tested by Robert Fantz (1961; 1965; 1967). Fantz devised a looking chamber, an apparatus that enabled the babies to look at the ceiling of an apparatus covered with visual patterns. Fantz watched the babies' eyes through a hole in the top of the looking chamber to determine which patterns the infants looked at and how much time they spent looking at a particular design. He discovered that babies as young as two days of age favored patterned designs such as newsprint over plain stimuli such as colored circles. Infants only a couple of days old preferred to look at a human face rather than at newsprint, a bull's-eye pattern, or at unpatterned red, white, and yellow disks.

Other researchers have discovered that newborns prefer clear images to blurred ones, and curved over straight lines (Legerstee & Schaffer, 1998); newborns prefer red and blue colors over yellow or green, just as adults do. Also, infants prefer to look at part of a stimulus, rather than at all of it; they prefer contrasts of light and dark over a single color, and they prefer circles over squares.

The Visual-Cliff Experiment: A Test of Depth Perception
Some time around 6 months, of age, babies can judge the distance of objects from themselves, and from one another. This ability is called *depth perception*. Evidence indicates that depth perception may be associated with crawling (Campos *et al.*, 2000). This was the finding in a classic experiment by Eleanor Gibson and Richard Walk (1960). Their experiment is known as the *visual cliff*. (See Figure 4.5 below.)

Figure 4.5
The "Visual-Cliff" Experiment

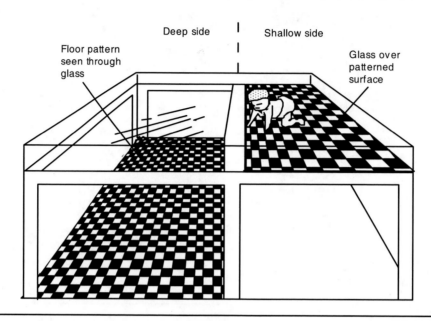

In this experiment, infants are placed on the centerboard, facing the clear portion of glass. Looking down, they have the illusion of being on a cliff. Even with coaxing from their mothers, they are not likely to cross the "deep" side; most young children will cross the "shallow" side, which indicates that they can perceive depth.

Source: Gibson and Walk, 1960.

In the visual-cliff experiment, Gibson and Walk place a clear sheet of glass on a frame supported by legs. Patterned or checkered linoleum is then placed directly under one-half of the glass, and another sheet of the same material is placed several feet below the other half of the glass. A centerboard divides the two halves. When one looks down on the glass from above, the half with the patterned linoleum which is attached directly underneath the glass appears to be a solid surface. The other half appears to be a sheer drop, as if the viewer is looking down from the edge of a cliff.

Gibson and Walk tested 36 infants aged 6½ to 14 months, with their mothers attempting to coax them to crawl onto the clear portion of the glass and into the "chasm." Few infants traversed the apparent chasm, while most crossed the side that appeared to be shallow. This demonstrates that infants perceive depth at about 6 months, perhaps as early as 3 or 4 months, an ability that may be an inherited predisposition. The realization that it is possible to fall off the cliff occurs when the children begin to crawl.

Size and Shape Constancy

Carlos, 18 months old, is watching his father leave home in his car. As the car recedes into the distance, it appears to get smaller and smaller. So does Carlos's retinal image of the car. Yet, Carlos knows that the car is not shrinking; it remains the same size regardless of the distance. Carlos "knows" that he cannot trust his retinal image; he is aware of the car's true size at all times because he has reached a milestone in perception known as *size constancy*: An object's

Size constancy: The realization that an object's actual size remains the same despite changes in the size of its retinal image.

perceived size remains relatively constant regardless of its distance from the viewer (Bower, 2002).

Later, Carlos is going outside to play. As he approaches the door, he notices that it is half open. Although he perceives the image of a trapezoid on his retina (the edge of the door closer to him appears taller than the hinge edge farther away), Carlos is not disturbed by the distortion since he "knows" that the door is rectangular in shape. He has now achieved *shape constancy*, an ability that begins when babies are as young as 4½ months (Needham, 1998). Shape constancy means that a person knows that an object remains the same even when it looks as if its form has changed (Slater, Field, & Hernandez-Reif, 2002). Hence, for the child who has achieved perceptual constancy in both size and shape, his or her perception of the physical world remains constant, even though the sensory stimulation is changing (Bower, 2002).

Shape constancy: The realization that an object's shape remains the same (e.g., rectangular or triangular) despite changes in the shape of its retinal image.

Hearing (Audition)

The relative maturity of a newborn's hearing has been noted by a number of investigators (Puckett, 2007). Newborns respond to sound by an increase in heart rate, blinking, head movement, and crying, or interruption of crying. Heart rate and movements increase as the intensity (loudness) of the sound increases. Very early, infants can make subtle discriminations between sounds of different pitch and duration. Even in their first hours, newborns are particularly sensitive to speech directed at them that is spoken with the high pitch and slow, exaggerated pronunciation known as "baby talk."

The most impressive aspect of a newborn's auditory competence is its ability to distinguish the phonemes (unique sounds that can be used to create words) in its language. For instance, a newborn can distinguish the sound of the word "it" in English from "eu" in French. By 2 to 3 months, Sarah can distinguish the source of a sound and follow it. Young babies also respond differently to the sounds of vowels than of consonants. By 4½ months, Sarah and Carlos can recognize their own names (Jusczyk, 1995). Further, in the second half of the first year of life, infants become "native listeners," and are especially attuned to the sounds of their native language (Jusczyk, 2002). By 1 year of age, infants lose the ability to hear sounds that are not present in the language they hear every day. If the children become attuned to the sounds of their native language by the time they are one year old, is it any wonder that many non-native English speakers, like one of your authors (Ukrainian-Polish), never lose the accent of their native language completely?

Smell

Studies have demonstrated that newborns can distinguish between odors, and also show a preference for certain smells in the same manner as adults. A newborn can also distinguish its mother's fragrance from all others. This sensitivity to smell increases during the first few weeks after birth (Porter *et al.*, 1992). Newborns seem to like the smell of bananas, vanilla, and strawberries, and dislike the smell of ammonia, rotten eggs, and fish. If a new mother washes one breast and not the other, most newborns will grasp at the unwashed breast, indicating that they are guided by smell (Porter & Winberg, 1999).

Indications of smell in newborns are seen by their abilities to recognize the smell of their mother's milk and bodies. Infants only a few weeks old are more attracted to a breast pad worn by its nursing mother than toward a pad worn by another nursing mother (Porter *et al.*, 1992). This holds true only for breast-fed babies.

Taste

The newborn's sense of taste, like smell, is quite acute. Some newborns reject their mothers' breast milk after she has eaten a heaping plate of broccoli. Taste buds on the tongue enable a newborn to detect four basic flavors: sweet, sour, bitter, and salty. Judging by their facial expressions, infants prefer a sweet taste to a sour one. If given bitter fluids, they will pucker their lips up, turn the edges of their mouths down, stick out their tongues, and occasionally spit out the substance. Sweet tastes result in relaxed expressions and apparent enjoyment. Also, newborns will suck on a bottle longer and pause for shorter periods when fed sweet substances compared with reactions to water. If sugar is added to the water, babies will suck on it longer; the greater the concentration of sugar, the stronger the sucking response.

Touch

The ability to detect touch develops early in the prenatal period. Many reflexes demonstrate a response to tactile stimulation. For instance, a touch on the cheek will activate the rooting and sucking reflexes. A touch on the sole of the foot triggers the Babinski reflex, the toes fan out and the foot twists in when the sole of the foot is stroked.

If the mother touches the newborn, it helps her to establish a bond with her baby. The baby responds to the mother's touch in much the same way that it does when she smiles or talks to it. Touching also serves intellectual functions for the baby. By touching things, the child can explore the world. It learns very early in life that some objects have one shape (*e.g.*, round) while other objects have a different shape (*e.g.*, square); some things are cold, while others are warm. Touching a baby also heightens its immune responses. Low-birth-weight infants appear to benefit the most from being touched (Field, 2001).

EARLY MOTOR DEVELOPMENT

Motor development refers to the complex changes in the child's body, activities, and movements. If we compare the activities of 16-month-old Sarah with her 5-week-old cousin Emma, we see that Sarah has a larger array of motor skills. Whereas Emma's arm movements are limited to waving and a few other gestures, Sarah can direct her waving toward a target and grasp it as well. Sarah can also place blocks where she wants them, and is able to let go of a block once she gets it in place. Let's look at some major milestones in motor development. Table 4.3 below shows some milestones in motor development in the first two years. Figure 4.6 shows the infant's progression in learning to walk.

Table 4.3
Motor Development in the First Two Years

Skill	Age in Months
Lifts head at shoulder	0.1
Dorsal suspension—lifts head	1.7
Sits with support	2.7
Sits alone momentarily	5.4
Walks with help	9.9
Stands alone	11.3
Walks alone	11.8
Walks upstairs with help	18.7
Walks upstairs alone, Carloss time	22.7
Walks downstairs alone, Carloss time	22.9

Source: N. Bayley, 1965.

Figure 4.6
Progression in the Baby's Walking Sequence

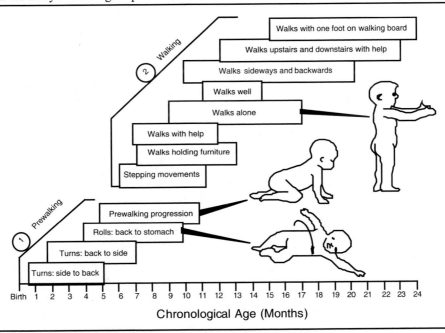

The baby learns several walking-related skills before she or he can walk.

Some Milestones in Motor Development

Quickening: Fetal movements that can be felt by the mother.

Sarah made her first movements long before she entered this world. Her first movements, known as *quickening*, were made in the womb after about 4 months of gestation. These initial movements consisted of kicking, stretching, and squirming. The movements were simple, generalized activities with little conscious control. In fact, it would be more accurate to say that fetal movements are under subcortical control.

Sarah made her first major purposeful movements by turning from her stomach to her back at 3 months of age. A couple of weeks later, she was able to reverse this procedure—roll from back to stomach. At about 4 months of age, Sarah could lift her head and push up on her arms. Her movements became more deliberate, being directed by the cortex. The next motor task Sarah mastered was sitting alone without support. At 5 months of age, she could sit on her own by raising herself from a lying position or sit down (usually quickly) from a standing position. At 6 months, Sarah could sit up in a high chair.

Sarah reached the major milestone of getting about on her own (by crawling) at about 6 months (6 to 9 months is normal). Sarah's first attempts at locomotion were rather awkward: She would draw one leg up underneath her body and lunge awkwardly ahead. Later, she would pull herself along with her legs dragging behind aimlessly. At 8 months, Sarah's arm and leg movements became more coordinated, enabling her to crawl. Shortly after Sarah learned to crawl, she practiced standing by pulling herself up, holding on to furniture. This practice came in handy when she took her first three steps on her first birthday.

By age 14 months, Sarah was a "handful." She would climb on anything (chairs, tables, and counters) to reach for an object; she would push chairs and toys against walls, windows, and doors to get at things. If restrained, she would scream, bite, and try her best to break free. By age 1½ years, Sarah was walking upstairs quite efficiently (although she was hesitant to walk downstairs). She soon learned that her legs could be used for means other than walking, such as kicking a ball. By age 2 years, Sarah could run and jump, and by age 3, she could balance herself on one foot and even hop, although somewhat awkwardly.

When Sarah first began to walk, her steps were short and rapid, with feet wide apart, the toes pointed slightly outward. (Toes pointed out, or in, severely, or in different directions, indicates a problem.) By age 2½, Sarah's steps were less rapid, with the feet closer together (more like an adult walking).

By 3 years of age, Sarah had also made progress in gross motor skills such as jumping and hopping. She could jump down from a step and hop 1 to 3 times on the same foot, with a stiff upper body and the non hopping leg held still. By age 3, Sarah could also push a riding toy with her feet.

Hand Control

Hand control begins early. Newborn babies are capable of grasping objects with their palms. However, this is not intentional and is actually a spontaneous, reflexive movement known as the Palmar,or Darwinian grasp. By 3 to 4 months, infants begin using the *ulnar grasp*, where they awkwardly hold objects between their fingers and their palm. At 5 months, Sarah grasps objects with good aim and may transfer an object from hand to hand.

Eye-hand coordination improves markedly by 9 months of age. Most babies can now guide their hand movements with a single glance (Ashmead *et al.*, 1993), and can use their thumbs in opposition to their fingers when picking up objects. This is called the *pincer grasp*, the use of the opposing thumb to grasp objects between the thumb and the fingers. With the ability to move about from one place to another, (*locomotion*) and the ability to reach and grasp, it is not at all uncommon for 10-month-old Sarah move from one area of the house to another.and make her presence known by turning dials, pulling things off the coffee table, or pulling on the lamp cord.

At about 16 months of age, Carlos puts his hands to new use; he can scribble with a crayon. By the end of the second year, he can copy simple figures

Ulnar grasp: The awkward ability for an infant to hold an object between their fingers and their palms

Pincer grasp: The use of the opposing thumb to grasp objects between the thumb and the fingers

Locomotion: The ability to move from one place to another.

composed of horizontal and vertical lines. This proficiency is due to ever-greater control over simple movements, which are integrated into increasingly complex, coordinated actions (Fentress & McLeod, 1986; Puckett, 2007).

By 2 years of age, children usually show a preference for one hand or the other, a specialization of brain function, called cerebral dominance or lateralization. Not only is *cerebral dominance* (lateralization) involved in hand preference, but other parts of the body also play a role. In right-handers, the right ear and the right eye are correlated with the left-hemisphere; however, cerebral dominance seems less clear in left-handers. Attempting to get children to switch hands is a complex issue involving many body parts, and it may cause problems later on (Dean & Anderson, 1997).

In the third year, Sarah is capable of fine motor activities which often require finger dexterity such as unscrewing lids, turning knobs, and unwrapping paper. The 2½-year-old can hold a pencil in a writing position, draw with chalk and crayons, draw vertical and horizontal strokes, and use scissors with parental supervision. By age 3 years, the child usually has enough muscle coordination to play a simple musical instrument. These abilities increase with age as Sarah becomes more coordinated, develops cognitively, and makes better use of her vision.

Cerebral dominance (lateralization): The process by which each of the two sides of the brain performs different functions and controls different areas of the body. For example, the left cerebral hemisphere controls speech and hearing; the right side controls the left side of the body and music ability.

INFLUENCES ON MOTOR DEVELOPMENT

Children learn to perform activities such as sitting, standing, and walking in a fairly consistent sequence. Is this because of genetic programming, a blueprint for the regular, largely predetermined progression of motor skills? Or, is motor development the result of environmental factors such as practice and nutrition (Von Hofsten & Ronnquist, 1993)? Research shows that both factors are involved.

The Influence of Genetics on Motor Development

Comparison of lower animals such as birds, fish, and monkeys with human infants suggests that motor development is similar in all members of a species and is therefore an innate or inherited skill. A particular skill unfolds for an individual according to his or her genetic blueprint. A person's genetically determined pattern of change that occurs as a person ages is called maturation and is relatively independent of the individual's environment.

Arnold Gesell and Henry Thompson (1929) demonstrated the inflexibility of the maturation process on motor development by testing identical twins. One twin, identified as T for training, was given 6 weeks of daily practice in stair-climbing, beginning at 46 weeks. The other twin, identified as C for control, indicating that he received no special training, had an opportunity to climb stairs for 2 weeks beginning at 53 weeks of age, 7 weeks after Twin T had started climbing the stairs.

Although Twin C received only 2 weeks of practice, it climbed the stairs more rapidly and more efficiently than Twin T, who received the extra practice. This study shows the limited effect of training or practice when the nervous system and muscles, called neuromuscular apparatus, are not mature enough for training. However, some studies demonstrate that it is possible to speed up motor development, suggesting the influence of environment.

Figure 4.7
Sequence of Motor Development and Locomotion in Infants

Source: Shirley, M. M. (1933). *The First Two Years*: Vol. 2. *Intellectual Development*. Minneapolis: University of Minnesota Press. Copyright renewed 1961.

The Influence of Environment on Motor Development

The influence of environment on motor development has been demonstrated many times. For example, it has been argued that African babies tend to be more advanced than U.S. and European infants in sitting, walking, and running because of the special training African children receive in various motor skills such as stepping exercises to strengthen the muscles. Many cultures actively encourage early development of motor skills (Gardiner & Komitzki, 2005). In the Zambian culture, where mothers are noted for the stimulation they give to their children, Zambian babies far surpass their European counterparts from the first day after birth in the development of a variety of activities, including walking. Before weaning the children, Zambian mothers sleep with them, breast-feed on demand (feeding the baby whenever it is hungry), and continually talk to their babies. One researcher, Thomas Bower (1982), demonstrated that babies who practiced reaching for an object during the first 4 weeks of life (babies normally reach for an object at 10 weeks) were better at seizing dangling objects than babies who did not have this practice.

The influence of environment on motor development has been demonstrated with institutions, such as orphanages. In a classic study, Wayne Dennis (1960) showed that environment affects motor development in children by comparing children in three different Iranian institutions: I, II, and III.

In Institution I, most of the children were under 3 years of age and spent most of their time on their backs in cribs. They drank from propped bottles and were seldom handled by the overworked staff, being removed from their cribs only on alternate days for a bath. After the children could sit unsupported—often not until they were 2 years of age compared with 7 months for the average child—they had no toys or child-sized furniture. When these children began to move around, they scooted by pushing their bodies forward with their arms and legs, rather than creeping on their hands and knees. This inability to creep was apparently due to the children's lack of practice in raising their heads or pulling their arms and legs beneath their bodies—practice they would have received if they had been placed on their stomachs. None of the children could walk before 2 years of age.

In Institution II, the children were more than 3 years of age and were drawn mainly from Institution I. Child care was similar to that in Institution I, but sanitation, cleanliness, and nutrition were poorer, as was the health of the children.

Institution III was established primarily to demonstrate improved methods of institutional care. This facility consisted of the more retarded children from Institution I, who were transferred in the early months of life. The number of children per attendant was 3 or 4. The children were held in the attendant's arms while being fed. They were propped in a sitting position at times, and numerous toys were provided.

Differences in motor abilities among the children in the three institutions were significant. Whereas fewer than 15 percent of the children in Institutions I and II could walk by age 3, almost every child in Institution III was able to do so. What was the reason for this difference? Undoubtedly, malnutrition was one cause, but it did not appear to be the sole factor. Inadequate personal attention and handling in Institutions I and II—due to a large child-to-caretaker ratio of 10 children to 1 adult—seemed to be crucial factors, indicating that motor development is not based solely on maturation.

Surprisingly, the children's retardation appeared to be largely temporary. By the time the children in all three institutions reached school age, they worked and played within the normal range. However, some residues of retardation remained, even among children in Institution III. This indicates that good institutional care seldom approaches the early nurturing of a warm, accepting home.

ILLNESSES AND DEATH IN INFANCY

Fortunately, many illnesses that were prevalent quite a few years ago (mumps, whooping cough, diphtheria, and typhoid fever) are not nearly as common today. Smallpox is another example of a childhood disease that has been virtually eliminated within the last couple of decades. However, several illnesses continue to complicate the lives of newborns and small children.

Infant Illnesses

Among illnesses found in young children today are *colic, otitis media, asthma,* and even *heart disease* (Wheeler, Wong, & Shanley, 2007).

Colic: A sudden abdominal discomfort and distended stomach.

Colic involves a sudden abdominal discomfort. The colicky child will cry vigorously, draw its arms and legs up to its body, clench its fists, and its stomach will appear distended or inflated. This condition may be caused by food allergy, by swallowing excessive air during feeding (the nipple does not fit the mouth), or by environmental stress. In some instances, colic may be caused by immaturity of the digestive system which prevents food from moving smoothly through the system. Fortunately, most infants outgrow this condition by 3 or 4 months (McDonough, 1990).

Otitis media: A middle ear infection.

A problem that continues to plague young children is infection of the middle ear, known as *otitis media,* the most common reason for doctor visits by young children (Chartrand & Pong, 1998; Wheeler, Wong, & Shanley, 2007) The incidence of otitis media is as high as 50 percent in the first year. The cause of otitis media is congestion of the eustachian tube—the tube through which fluid in the middle ear drains. Since otitis media often results in fluid build-up in the middle ear, causing temporary hearing loss, the children's speech and language may be delayed because children learn to speak by listening to others. The first line of treatment for otitis media is amoxicillin, an antibiotic. If otitis media is left untreated, complications can arise such as a ruptured eardrum and infection of the brain.

Asthma: A lung disease that periodically inflames and narrows air passages, making it difficult to breathe.

An illness among young children that is reaching epidemic proportions is *asthma* – a chronic lung disease that periodically inflames and narrows air passages, making it difficult to breathe. Asthma is the leading chronic illness and the primary cause of hospitalizations among children younger than 15 years of age. Nearly 5 million children now suffer from the disease – a number that has more than doubled in the past 20 years. Most of the victims are 0-to 4-year-olds.

Some experts believe that the explanation for the rapid increase in children's asthma is the hygiene hypothesis, the idea that today's children are overprotected from dirt and bacteria which reduces some infections and childhood diseases that could strengthen the immune system and reduce asthma attacks (Busse & Lemanske, 2005). Preventive measures include breast-feeding the baby exclusively for 6 months or more (Oddy, 2004; Cadwell, 2009), banning second-hand tobacco smoke (Wong *et al.*, 2004; Wheeler, Wong, & Shanley, 2007), and sealing mattresses and pillows in air-tight covers to get rid of dust mites. The medical cornerstone of treatment for asthma is inhaled corticosteroids. Asthma is also easier to deal with if the affected child and the parents learn that they can control the disease and that the child can do almost everything that his or her friends do.

Infant Death

Fortunately, infant death has decreased due in large part to expensive neonatal equipment that saves smaller and sicker newborns, and to immunizations (Wheeler, Wong, & Shanley, 2007). Infant mortality is generally calculated by counting the number of babies who die within the first year. At present, the infant mortality (death) rate in the United States is about 9 deaths per 1,000 live births. (It has gone up slightly recently.)[4] However, when we categorize infant mortality according to race, a disturbing difference is seen. Black babies are more than twice as likely to die in the first year as White babies.

Since 1970, there has been a dramatic increase in heart defects in newborns. Cardiac difficulties include "blue" spells (a condition resulting in breathlessness), failure to grow normally, and rapid breathing. Often surgeons perform delicate operations on these babies. However, congenital (present at birth) heart defects continue to be responsible for many deaths of newborns, despite recent improvements in pediatric cardiac surgery.

Sudden Infant Death Syndrome (SIDS)

Sudden Infant Death Syndrome: The sudden unexplained death of a seemingly healthy baby.

Each year about 6 thousand apparently healthy American infants—1 out of every 500—dies mysteriously and apparently without cause (Andolsek, 1997; Gurbutt, 2007). They are the victims of *Sudden Infant Death Syndrome* (SIDS), also known as crib death. SIDS[5] is defined as the sudden death of an infant under 1 year of age that remains unexplained after a thorough investigation (Kinney *et al.*, 1995; Sears, 1995). In most cases, the babies seem normal when put to bed, but die sometime during the night, apparently painlessly and with no sign of a struggle.

Risk factors for SIDS. Victims of SIDS fall into patterns or categories. The disease strikes more boys than girls, and is more prevalent in preterm than in full-term infants. Breast-fed babies are less likely to be victims than bottle-fed babies. Afflicted babies are most likely to be Black males whose birth weight was low. Maternal characteristics include the young, unmarried, and poor who received little or no prenatal care, and who use drugs or smoke.

Sleep apnea: Abnormal breathing and heart rate while asleep.

Cause. The cause of SIDS is unknown (Gurbutt, 2007). However, a potential precipitating condition mentioned most often in medical literature is *sleep apnea*, abnormal breathing and heart rate while asleep (Gurbutt, 2007; Schoendort & Kiley, 1992).[6] Some research suggests that the mother's smoking is a cause (Mendelowitz, 1998). Other investigators suspect that drugs that are used to treat the baby's respiratory problems or elevated body temperature cause SIDS. Another theory is that infections and toxins passed from the mother to the fetus might be a cause.

Some studies have indicated that there are behavioral differences between SIDS infants and control infants (Riese, 2003). For instance, SIDS victims have been found to be more irritable, more resistant to soothing, and to make fewer movements during sleep. Researchers have also suggested that the differences in temperament and behavior between SIDS victims and control infants are the result of deficiencies in the central nervous system. If autopsy and careful investigation find no apparent cause of death, the diagnosis is SIDS (Byard, 2004).

Prevention. The most promising preventive technique for SIDS to date is changing the baby's sleeping position from sleeping on the stomach to sleeping on the back (Gurbutt, 2007; Stephenson, 1997). However, when the

---

4. United States Department of Health and Human Services http://www.dhhs.gov/
5. To find out more about SIDS, write to: the National Sudden Infant Death Syndrome Alliance, 1314 Bedford Ave., Suite 210, Baltimore, MD, 21208, or call 1-800-221-SIDS.
6. In sleep apnea, the child stops breathing while asleep, then awakens, takes a few breaths, and falls asleep again. This cycle may be repeated hundreds of times per night. This is normal. Sometimes, however, the child stops breathing for a longer-than-normal period of time and can't recover. The result is SIDS.

baby does sleep on its back, its head should be rotated to one side and then to the other to avoid a misshapen head, known medically as plagiocephaly. Also, there should be no smoking around the infant and the baby should be dressed in light clothing to prevent overheating. There should be no pillows or toys in the crib when the baby is sleeping. Finally, breast-feeding appears to lower the incidence of SIDS (Horne *et al.*, 2004).

SUMMARY

The newborn baby is a complex being whose characteristics and vital functions are interesting and important to assess. The Apgar Scale and the Brazelton Neonatal Assessment Scale are two common standardized assessments used with newborn babies to determine their health status.

Studying physical development is important to the field of child development because it is connected to cognitive development and social emotional development in ways that might not be readily apparent. For example, increased physical mobility allows a child to explore his/her environment and gain valuable cognitive skills. A child's physical development also has psychological consequences. One of these is shaping the child's image; successful physical interaction with the environment can directly effect a child's sense of self and feelings of accomplishment.

Physical development is guided by two complimentary principles: cephalocaudal and proximodistal development. Cephalocaudal development defines development as occuring from the head down and reflects the reason that an infant's head is much larger in proportion to the rest of its body. The proximodistal principle states that growth proceeds from the center of the body (axis) to the periphery.

Understanding the characteristics of a newborn baby is important. Newborns follow a rhythm of several cycles known as states of arousal and each state has a distinct set of characteristics. Newborns are most difficult to care for in the waking activity and crying state. Individual differences and differences between males and females are apparent among babies from the moment they are born.

Physical development from infancy through toddlerhood includes: height and weight increases, sensory development (e.g. vision, hearing), brain development, and motor development.

Growth in height and weight are quite rapid at first, then slow down a bit at the end of toddlerhood. There are also changes in body shape (e.g. reduction in baby fat) and skeletal structure.

The growth of the brain involves myelination, synaptic pruning, and cerebral lateralization. Environment plays a role in the development of the brain. We also begin to see hand preferences in toddlerhood.

An infant's motor development progresses in a definite sequence. Although regulated by a genetic blueprint, motor development can be slowed or accelerated by the environment.

Illness and death are of particular concern in infancy. One enigma is Sudden Infant Death Syndrome, which strikes babies without warning.

IMPORTANT TERMS

Anoxia

Apgar scale

Asthma

Brazelton Neonatal Behavioral
  Assessment Scale

Calcification

Cephalocaudal principle

Cerebral cortex

Cerebral lateralization

Colic

Deprivation dwarfism

Depth perception

Fixation

Fontanel

Glial cells

Lanugo

Locomotion

Maturation

Meconium

Metabolism

Myelin

Myelination

Neonatal period

Neuron

Non organic failure-to-thrive syndrome

Ossification

Otitis media

Palmar (Darwinian) grasp

Physiologic jaundice

Pincer grasp

Plasticity

Proximodistal principle

Pupillary reflex

Quickening

Reflex

Shape constancy

Size constancy

Sleep apnea

Sudden Infant Death Syndrome (SIDS)

State of arousal

Synaptic pruning

Toddlerhood

Tracking (pursuit) ability

Ulnar Grasp

Vernix caseosa

Visual acuity

Visual-cliff experiment

RELATED RESOURCES

Readings

Gurbutt, Dawne (2007). *Sudden infant death syndrome: learning from stories about SIDS, motherhood and loss.* (Oxford: Radcliffe Pub.).

Puckett, Margaret (2007). *Understanding infant development.* (St. Paul, MN: Redleaf Press).

Nugent, J. Kevin & Petrauskas, Bonnie J. & Brazelton, T. Berry (2009). *The newborn as a person: enabling healthy infant development worldwide.* (Hoboken, N.J.: Wiley).

Coch, Donna & Fischer, Kurt W. & Dawson, Geraldine (2007). *Human behavior, learning, and the developing brain. Typical development.* (New York: Guilford Press).

Riordan, Jan & Wambach, Karen (2010). Breastfeeding and human lactation. (Sudbury, Mass.: Jones and Bartlett Publishers).

Koren, Gideon (2007). Medication safety in pregnancy and breastfeeding: the evidence-based, A-to-Z clinician's pocket guide. (New York: McGraw-Hill Medical).

Websites

American Academy of Pediatrics
http://www.aap.org/
Dedication to the health of all children. Committed to the attainment of optimal physical, mental, and social health, and well being for all infants, children, adolescents, and young adults.

American Sudden Infant Death Syndrome Institute
http://www.sids.org/
Founded in 1983, the American SIDS Institute, a national nonprofit health care organization, is dedicated to the prevention of sudden infant death and the promotion of infant health through an aggressive, comprehensive nationwide program of: research, clinical services, education, and family support.

Chapter 5

Cognitive Development in Infancy and Toddlerhood (0 to 3 years)

Chapter Topics		Learning Objectives
How do the different types of learning differ from one another?		Understand the types of learning that apply to infancy and toddlerhood: habituation, dishabituation, classical conditioning, and operant conditioning.
How are the three views of intellectual development different?		Understand the three views of intellectual development: Calculating IQ, Piaget's Cognitive Development Theory, and Information Processing Theory.
What are the major characteristics of the six substages of Piaget's Sensorimotor Stage of Cognitive Development?		Understand the six substages of Piaget's Sensorimotor Stage of Cognitive Development.
What are the three theories of language development?		Know the three theories of language development: behaviorist view, nativist view, and interactionist view.
How does language develop in infants and toddlers?		Understand the beginnings of language development in infants and toddlers.
Chapter Summary		

Cognition: Knowing, learning, thinking, and related concepts.

In an earlier chapter, we discovered that most infants, $6\frac{1}{2}$ to 14 months of age, are aware of depth. In the visual-cliff experiment, most infants would not cross the center board from the "shallow" side to the "deep" side. Is this apparent fear of heights inherited or learned? Is fear of heights attained after learning to crawl and falling off something a few times? What goes on in a baby's mind when confronted with heights? Is any problem solving involved? How does a child know that "deepness" or "height" is unsafe? Knowing, learning, thinking, and related concepts are called *cognition.*

In this chapter, we will begin our study of an infant's and toddler's cognitive development by first looking at the different types of learning. Next, we will examine three major ways of studying intellectual development in infants and toddlers: Calculating intelligence (IQ), Piaget's cognitive-developmental theory, and the Information-Processing model. We will also examine three views of language development: behaviorist, nativist, and interactionist. We will conclude this chapter with a review of the characteristics of language development and acquisition in the infant and toddler.

LEARNING

Learning: A relatively permanent change in behavior as a result of experiences such as exploration, observation, and practice.

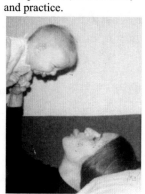

Imitation is a type of learning.

Learning seems like a simple concept, but it is complex and difficult to define. Psychologists generally believe that learning involves a change in behavior and in brain chemistry which meets three basic criteria:

1. The individual thinks, perceives, and reacts to the environment in a *new* way.

2. The change is the result of repetition, study, practice, and observations (experience), but not heredity, maturation, or injury.

3. The change is relatively permanent.

TYPES OF LEARNING IN INFANCY AND TODDLERHOOD

During the period of infancy and toddlerhood, psychologists are particularly interested in learning by habituation, and its counterpart, dishabituation. They are also interested in learning by classical and operant conditioning.

Habituation

Habituation: A decrease in the response to a familiar stimulus after repeated presentations.

Habituation is a simple physiological form of learning by which an organism gets used to a particular stimulus and ceases to respond to it after repeated exposures. For example, suppose that you move into an apartment and you discover that the couple next door is very loud. You can hear virtually every word they say. However, after a week or two when a visitor asked you how noisy this couple is, you say that it used to bother you, but doesn't any more. In psychological terms you have become habituated to your neighbors' conversations.

The capacity to habituate to repeated sights, sounds, smells, and touch is present in newborns (Rovee-Collier, 2002) and increases during the first 10 weeks of life. Investigators make use of the infant's ability to habituate in assessing its sensory and perceptual abilities, such as hearing, eye movement, heart rate, and brain activity. Infants can be presented with sights, sounds, odors, tastes, and tactile experiences (other than those that are painful) to determine when babies respond to these stimuli as different or as similar. If an infant fails to respond to a familiar stimulus, it means that it has habituated or gotten used to it (Rovee-Collier, 2002).

A classic experiment on habituation was conducted by Bronstein & Petrova (1952), who repeatedly presented sounds to neonates from 2 hours to 8 days old. The object of this study was to determine whether the babies could discriminate among sounds, which included the playing of organ pipes, a harmonica, whistles, and tapping of pencils.

The first time the babies heard a sound, they usually stopped sucking on their pacifiers and did not begin sucking again until the sound stopped. After several repetitions, the babies ceased to pay attention to the sound and continued to suck on their pacifiers, showing that they could hear the difference between that sound and others. Habituation had occurred.

Habituation has a predictive value. Newborns who are slow to habituate, are slow intellectually later (McCall & Carriger, 1993). Habituation prevents babies from focusing on past experiences and allows them to seek out new experiences. Reviews of habituation studies have shown that infants who habituate rapidly during the first 6 months of life outscore their slower-habituating agemates significantly on standardized intelligence tests and on measures of language ability later in childhood. In fact, some researchers claim that habituation is a better predictor of intellectual competencies than traditional infant intelligence tests (Fagan, 1985).

Why does habituation occur? One common explanation is the recognition of a familiar experience, event, or stimulus. But, before the child can recognize something, he or she must build a mental model, storing information about a particular event or stimulus. When the mental model matches the new event or stimulus, the child stops responding, or habituates. Each time the infant habituates to a stimulus, it means that he or she has encoded that stimulus into his or her memory; further repetition is "old hat" and not worth repeating. The baby will usually respond to a familiar stimulus only if it changes in some way, a form of behavior called *dishabituation*. It seems that the brain is prewired to pay more attention to changes in the environment than to stimuli that do not change.

Dishabituation:
Reinstatement of the intensity, frequency, or duration of a response to a familiar stimulus that has been changed in some way.

Dishabituation: The concept of *dishabituation* can be illustrated by dangling a teddy bear repeatedly in front of 1-year-old Sarah and then removing it. During the initial presentations, Sarah will stare at the teddy bear for a considerable length of time. However, with repeated presentations, Sarah appears to get bored. She spends less and less time looking at the object dangled in front of her. If her mother lays the teddy bear down and dangles a toy dog in front of Sarah, she will show renewed interest. The renewed interest, or dishabituation, shows that Sarah can distinguish between the teddy bear and the dog. Sarah is able to make this distinction between the two stimuli because she can remember the object (the teddy bear) she was shown a short time ago and can distinguish it from the new stimulus (the dog).

Classical Conditioning

Classical conditioning: A form of learning that involves a neutral stimulus with a stimulus that leads to a reflexive response.

Can 2-day-old Sarah learn to suck at the sound of a buzzer if the sound is presented repeatedly each time when she is about to suck on her bottle? In other words, can Sarah learn to respond to a neutral stimulus (the sound of the buzzer) if it has been paired repeatedly with a natural response (sucking) and a natural stimulus (the mother's breast nipple)? Sucking the nipple is the unconditioned response, and the nipple is the unconditioned stimulus. Sucking only to the sound of the buzzer (after it has been repeatedly presented with the bottle) is called a conditioned response (Morra, 2008). This entire process is called *classical conditioning*, described in Chapter 2.

For many years, researchers doubted that classical conditioning could occur in newborns. Yet, a classic experiment by Dorothy Marquis (1931) shows that newborns are capable of such learning. In her experiment, Marquis divided a group of 1-day-old infants into experimental and control groups. Members of the experimental group heard a buzzer 5 seconds before they were fed, while control group heard the buzzer but did not receive food immediately.

By the fifth day, 8 out of 10 experimental infants made sucking movements and opened their mouths as soon as they heard the buzzer. They also tended to stop crying and moved their bodies when the buzzer was sounded. The control babies showed no reaction to the buzzer. Classical conditioning had been achieved with the experimental group.

Operant Conditioning

Operant conditioning: A form of learning in which a spontaneous behavior is followed by a stimulus that influences the probability that the behavior will occur again.

By the time Carlos was 2 months old he smiled more because smiling would get his parent's attention. He was beginning to manipulate his environment and the world around him, a form of learned behavior known as *operant conditioning* (Morra, 2008). Jerome Bruner (1968) employed operant conditioning when he demonstrated that newborns could learn to suck faster or slower to bring a picture into sharper focus, indicating that infants desire clarity from birth.

While operant conditioning of the newborn consists of relatively simple behaviors, such as smiling if it gets the parent's attention, the slightly older baby can learn more complex behaviors. For instance, through exposure to the grasp-and-reward method, 6-month-old Carlos has learned to use to establish an association between the choice of a red block and the presentation of a sweet substance. He has learned to produce a specific environmental result by acting (operating) on a particular stimulus—an example of operant conditioning.

THREE VIEWS OF INTELLECTUAL DEVELOPMENT

There are three views on evaluating intellectual development:
   1. Calculating IQ: The Mental-Age Concept
   2. Piaget's Cognitive Behavioral Approach
   3. Information Processing Approach

Calculating IQ: The Mental-Age Concept

If asked whether some children are brighter than others, you would undoubtedly answer, "Yes." We can anticipate your answer because of the incontrovertible fact that people differ in their intellectual skills. Some can remember names better than others, solve problems more quickly, have larger vocabularies, or analyze a situations faster. We say that these people are more intelligent than those who are not quite so proficient. It was precisely this type of thinking that led to the development of intelligence tests, which measure individual differences in *intelligence quotient* (IQ). These differences are quantified by numbers, and they tell us the relative standing of a child compared with his or her peers (Sattler, 2008).

Intelligence quotient (IQ): The ratio of mental age divided by the chronological age, multiplied by 100.

To determine a child's IQ, we must first calculate his or her *mental age*. Mental age is the average age at which normal (average) individuals achieve a particular intelligence score. The concept of mental age is a diagnostic strategy derived by Alfred Binet and Theodore Simon in 1904 to ensure the benefits of instruction for "defective" children.

Mental age: Assessment of a child's intellectual abilities and knowledge by comparing his or her score with the average chronological age of children who have scored similarly.

A child's mental age is calculated by adding the number of items answered correctly and matching this total with the average age of those who have scored similarly. IQ expresses intelligence as a ratio of mental age (MA) to chronological age (CA), multiplied by 100 to eliminate decimals:

$$IQ = MA/CA \times 100$$

The figure of 100 is used as a multiplier so that the IQ score will have a value of 100 when MA is equal to CA. When the mental age is greater than chronological age, the IQ is over 100; when the mental age is less than chronological age, the IQ is under 100. Here are some examples:

- **An 8-year-old (CA = 8) with a mental age of 8 (MA = 8) has an IQ of 100, or average for her age group (scores from 90 to 110 are usually considered within the average range).**

- **An 8-year-old (CA = 8) with a mental age of 12 (MA = 12) has an IQ of 150 (in the top 1 percent of all children her age).**

- **An 8-year-old (CA = 8) with a mental age of 6 (MA = 6) has an IQ of 75 (may need special instruction in school).**

Tests of Infant Development and Intelligence

Sarah has just celebrated her first birthday. Her mother thinks that Sarah is very bright. How bright is she? To find out, Sarah's mother proudly takes her young daughter to a psychologist. The psychologist tests Sarah's ability to play pat-a-cake, use a cup or spoon, grasp a rattle, turn toward a voice, and imitate sounds. The psychologist also tests Sarah's ability to hold her head up, stand, and walk. Sarah's achievement is assessed in terms of norms—the average ages at which children can perform various test items (Sattler, 2008).

Developmental quotient: A comparison of a person's developmental age (score on motor, language, and adaptive behavior, excluding intelligence) with the person's chronological age.

Developmental Quotient. The psychologist determines that Sarah's performance is at the norm for her age group, or average. But instead of receiving her score as an IQ, she is given a *developmental quotient*, or DQ, which compares a child's *performance* on a series of tasks with norms established on the basis of observation of what large numbers of infants and toddlers perform at particular ages. Developmental quotient (DQ) is a score developed by Arnold Gesell to evaluate an infant's skills *other than intelligence* (*e.g.*, motor, language, adaptive, personal, and social).

When measuring a child's DQ, we want to know, for instance, if a child of 4 years shows typical 4-year-old's speech and curiosity. The rationale for determining an infant's DQ is the same as that for figuring out a child's IQ. A DQ of 100 is average, that is, the child has passed all problems listed as appropriate for his or her age group and none for the next higher age group; less than 100 is below average; above 100 is better than average for his or her group.

Bayley Scales of Infant Development. Another developmental test is the Bayley Scales of Infant Development. Although the *Bayley Scales of Infant Development (BSID-II)* is often used to test infant intelligence, the test was not designed for this purpose (Sattler, 2008). A major purpose of the BSID-II is to classify the risk status of children aged 2 to 42 months due to neurological or developmental delays and the necessity of placement in early intervention services (Gauthier *et al.*, 1999). The test consists of three developmental areas:

Bayley Scales of Infant Development: A measure that evaluates an infant's development from 2 months to 42 months.

1. The *Motor Scale* assesses motor coordination and manipulatory skills such as sitting, walking, and the ability to grasp objects of various sizes. The 1-month-old is tested on its ability to make a fisted hand; at 26 to 42 months, the task is to copy a circle.

2. The *Mental Scale* measures memory, learning, language ability, and habituation. The 1-month-old is measured on its ability to habituate to a rattle; the 12-16-month-old is expected to find a toy under a reversed cup.

3. The Infant Behavior Profile assesses the child's attention span, goal directedness, persistence, and social and emotional development. The behavior record is based on the examiner's observation of the child during the test.

A major criticism of the Baley Scales of Infant Development is its failure to predict intelligence on later tests. A major reason for this lack of consistency of test scores is a difference in the content of the tests. The Bayley Scales stress things such as manual dexterity and visual and auditory alertness. The intelligence tests designed for older children emphasize symbolic abilities such as language ("What is a "horse"?) and problem solving ("How many nickels are there in one dollar"?).

Fagan Test of Infant Intelligence: A nonverbal, individual intelligence test used with infants, which is useful for screening infants at risk for mental retardation.

Fagan Test of Infant Intelligence. A well-known test of infant intelligence is the *Fagan Test of Infant Intelligence*, a nonverbal, individual test which is used to assess habituation through means such as having very young infants first look at two pictures, then having one of the pictures replaced with another picture. Normal babies usually spend more time looking at the new picture than at the picture they saw previously (dishabituation). The Fagan test is also used for screening infants at risk for mental retardation.

Calculating IQ or DQ cannot measure *changes* in intelligence with time. For example, a 10-year-old boy can remember much more than he could at age 5 because at age 10, the mental strategies are different than those used earlier. Given a list of things to do, a 5-year-old may try to recall them. A 10-year-old may organize the duties according to location (things to do in the kitchen and in the bathroom) or priority ("First I do this, then this..."). While intelligence tests cannot measure these types of changes in intelligence, these various strategies and abilities can be tested best by cognitive developmentalists

Piaget's Cognitive-Developmental Approach to Intellectual Development

Piaget is interested in patterns of intellectual development that are common to all children (Morra, 2008). Unlike the intelligence testing approach, little attention is given to individual differences in the cognitive-developmental approach. The cognitive-developmental approach focuses on the nature of cognitive structures (strategies used and types of logic applied). The main proponent of this view is Jean Piaget.

For Jean Piaget, intellectual development can be measured by revolutionary changes in thought which occurs three times over the life span. As we discussed in Chapter 2, Piaget divides intellectual development into four stages: Sensorimotor (birth to 2 years), preoperational thought (2 to 7 years), concrete-operational thought (7 to 11 years), and formal-operational thought (adolescence and beyond). According to Piaget, each of these stages is marked by a distinctive way of thinking.

The Sensorimotor Stage (0-24 months)

Imagery: The ability to associate words with the objects or ideas to which they refer.

Jean Piaget compared infant intelligence during the first 1½ years (the first five substages of the sensorimotor stage) to a slow motion film that shows one static frame after another but gives no simultaneous, all-encompassing view. This is because infants have not yet developed *imagery*, the ability to associate words with the objects or ideas to which they refer. If someone says "mother" when the parent is absent, Sarah is not able to visualize her mother. She does not possess the language to connect the word "mother" with the concept. According to Piaget, it is not until Sarah is 18 months old that she can mentally represent the world in images or symbols, such as words. For Piaget, mental representation is the ability to envision objects or events that are not present. Table 5.1 shows the six substages of Piaget's Sensorimotor Stages.

Table 5.1
Substages of Piaget's Sensorimotor Stage

Substage	Characteristics of Substage
Substage 1 (Birth to 1 month): Use of Reflexes	Infants' behaviors consists almost entirely of inborn reflexes, such as sucking and looking. Infants consolidate their reflexes through accommodation as a result of experience. They have not developed object permanence.
Substage 2 (1 to 4 months): Primary Circular Reactions	Infants repeat a variety of pleasurable motions, such as waving their hands or kicking their feet for their own sake. Actions are called primary because they focus on the baby's own body; also, infants cannot distinguish between their own bodies and outside objects or events. Infants display newly acquired adaptations, such as sucking different objects differently. They have not yet developed object permanence.
Substage 3 (4 to 8 months): Secondary Circular Reactions	Infants understand that their actions can have external results; behaviors are more deliberate and purposeful—they may move a mobile by hitting it. Although actions are intentional, they are not initially goal-directed. Infants can now coordinate information from two senses, and partially develops the concept of object permanence. Infants will search for a partially hidden object, showing that they have some idea of object permanence.
Substage 4 (8 to 12 months): Coordination of Secondary Schemes to Achieve a Goal	Infants now understand causality and begins to combine actions to get things they want. An infant at this stage may push a pillow away to get a toy under it. Behaviors are now more deliberate and purposeful and infants use familiar strategies to attain goals. Infants can anticipate events. Object permanence is quite advanced, although infants will look for objects in first hiding places, even after seeing it moved to a second hiding place.
Substage 5 (12 to 18 months): Tertiary Circular Reactions	Children are now "scientific experimenters" as they purposefully vary their actions to see results. Infants do considerable exploring and manipulating objects, demonstrating improved motor skills. Infants cannot fully understand events outside themselves, and will not search for an object they have not observed being hidden; they will follow a series of object displacements. Infants cannot yet think.
Substage 6 (18 to 24 months): Mental Combinations (Beginning of Thought)	Children can now use internal representations such as words and images to stand for objects. The symbol system allows children to think about events and anticipate them and not be confined to trial and error to solve problems as was the case previously. Action is minimized and object permanence is complete.

The sensorimotor stage lasts from birth until about 2 years. For Piaget, intelligence during the sensorimotor stage is physical in nature, not mental. Physical intelligence means behaviors such as manipulating objects, knowing how to locomote, and knowing what things look and sound like. For Piaget, a child's sensorimotor intelligence begins with reflexive behavior and ends with symbolic processing, which improves gradually during the preoperational stage when the child is 2 to 7 years old. Piaget divides sensorimotor intelligence into six substages. Substage One: The Use of Reflexes (Birth to about 1 month) According to Piaget, at birth, infants have intelligence mostly in the form of reflexes that enable them to adapt to their environment. The most important reflex is sucking behavior. Babies suck in order to eat, to elude hunger, and to prolong the excitation of the meal (Piaget, 1952). Adaptations are also seen in infants' babbling. If babbling results in parental attention, the babies' babbling increases, indicating that they are already active seekers of stimulation. For Piaget, these initial behaviors are the starting points, or building blocks, from which all future cognitive development proceeds. A highlight of Piaget's Substage One is an infant's ability to use his reflexes to adapt to his environment, as in sucking the breast when he is hungry.

Substage Two: Primary Circular Reactions (1 to about 4 months)

At about 1 month of age, Sarah begins to coordinate various facets of her behavior. She no longer sucks reflexively. When she is hungry, she brings her arms closer to her mouth, rather than flailing about as she did earlier. In fact, when Sarah's hands brush against her face, her mouth opens, though the hands may never reach her mouth. These actions indicate the beginning of goal-directed behavior. With practice and maturation, Sarah is soon able to put her thumb in her mouth almost at will, thus developing a new schema (Flavell, 1963). According to Piaget, Sarah continues to put her thumb in her mouth because it is pleasurable. She also sucks her thumb differently than the bottle, indicating that she has acquired rudimentary adaptations, or changes in behavior to accommodate new situations.

Lack of object permanence. How many times have you said something like, "I know that my keys are somewhere in this house." You know that the keys have not ceased to exist because you have achieved *object permanence*, an awareness that an object continues to exist even when it is not present to the senses.

Object permanence: The realization that an object continues to exist even when it is not being looked at, touched, or heard.

Object permanence is attained by degrees, but it is completely lacking during the first two substages of Piaget's sensorimotor stage. During this time, Sarah constantly encounters objects such as her bottle or rattle, loses contact, and then re-encounters them. If the bottle is taken away, Sarah does not search for it. Something ceases to exist for Sarah if it cannot be seen, felt, heard, smelled, or tasted. Sarah has not yet achieved object permanence.

Substage Three: Secondary Circular Reactions (4 to 8 months)

One day, when Sarah is 6 months old, her mother hears squeals of joy. Upon investigating, the mother realizes that Sarah has discovered that she can produce music from a mobile above her head by swiping at it repeatedly, indicating the beginning of intentional actions. Instead of merely repeating random movements, Sarah can now perform an act because of its consequences. She will now shake a toy to hear it rattle. Sarah is beginning to realize that objects are more than extensions of her actions. Yet, in this substage, Sarah has very elementary notions of objects and space.

The beginnings of object permanence. When Sarah is about 6 months old, her father decides to test her intelligence by showing her a bottle but hiding it when she extends her hand to take it. Purposely, the father lets Sarah see one end of the bottle, whereupon she starts kicking and screaming, indicating that she wants it. She has achieved *partial* object permanence—still only partial because if the entire bottle had been hidden, Sarah would have stopped crying and acted as if the bottle no longer existed even if she saw it being hidden (Piaget, 1963). Some researchers (e.g., Baillargeon, 1992) say that the beginnings of object permanence occur sooner than 6 months, as Piaget claims.

Substage Four: Coordination of Secondary Schemes to Achieve a Goal (8 to 12 months)

During this substage, infants become increasingly goal-directed, as in the following example described by Piaget. Piaget tested his daughter, Jacqueline, by having her overcome the obstacle of his hand by moving it when she tried to obtain a toy duck:

"At 0;8(9)[1] Jacqueline tries to grasp her celluloid duck, but I also grasp it at the same time she does. Then she firmly holds the toy in her right hand and pushes my hand away with her left. I repeat the experiment by grasping only the end of the duck's tail; she again pushes my hand away" (Piaget, 1952, p. 219).

According to Piaget, a child of 9 months is capable of invisible imitation. That is, infants can imitate actions such as protruding the tongue, which is relatively invisible to them. Before 1 year of age, Sarah can reach a goal by coordinating two separate cognitive categories, or schemes. If she sees her mother put a bottle under a pillow directly in front of her, Sarah pushes the pillow aside with one hand while retrieving the bottle with the other. Piaget believed that such behavior is the earliest form of true problem solving — because several schemes are employed to achieve the desired effect.

Further attainment of object permanence. Sarah's ability to retrieve the hidden bottle in Substage Four indicates another step toward object permanence. At about 9 or 10 months, Sarah looks for an object behind a screen if she saw it being hidden there. If an object is moved from the original hiding place to another location while Sarah watches, she looks for it in the *original* hiding place because she has not yet attained complete object permanence (Bremmer, 1982).

Substage Five: Tertiary Circular Reactions (12 to 18 months)

At 1 year of age, Sarah is a "scientific experimenter." She now attempts to solve problems. If one approach does not work, she will try another. She acts intentionally to find new solutions to problems. Even if a particular action produces the desired results, Sarah will not repeat her actions in exactly the same way. Variation will produce new results, leading to completely new intelligent acts (Piaget, 1952).

Deferred imitation: Piaget's term for the child's ability to imitate an action that the child observed earlier.

According to Piaget, a baby is capable of *deferred imitation* when it is approximately 18 months of age. Deferred imitation means the ability to imitate past actions of a model such as the mother. For instance, 18-month-old Sarah may push the buttons on the remote control of the television just as she saw her mother do the previous day.

Although Sarah's intelligence advances considerably toward the end of this substage, she still lacks all the schemata needed for complete sensorimotor knowledge. Children cannot fully understand events outside themselves or learn

---

1. These numbers refer to the year, month, and day of life.

to manipulate symbols in this substage. In short, Sarah and Carlos have *not* yet begun to think.

Almost complete object permanence. At approximately 12 to 18 months, the child has developed a schema of the permanent object. If an object is hidden in one place within Sarah's full view and then moved to another place within her view, she looks for it where it was seen last (Piaget, 1963). She is able to follow a sequence of visible displacements. If Sarah cannot find the object in one place, she will look for it elsewhere. However, she cannot imagine such displacements; hence, the attainment of object permanence is not yet complete.

Substage Six: Devising New Means Through Mental Combinations (18 to 24 months)

Sarah can now *think*. She pictures events in her mind and solves problems by devising mental combinations. She can consider various possible actions, locations, and uses of an object in her head. She tries out solutions in her mind and discards those that she thinks will not work. She no longer has to go through the laborious process of trial and error every time she attempts to solve a problem.

Mental representation: Cognitive portrayal of the world that is not present including ideas, images, concepts, and principles, that are the foundations of thinking and problem solving.

Sarah's thinking enables her to use *mental representation*, in which one thing stands for another. For example, using a Popsicle stick for a prop, Sarah pretends she is brushing her teeth. Sarah also recognizes her mother's voice as a symbol of her mother. Sarah's symbolic processing is revealed in her language, gestures, and pretend play. Finally, Sarah is capable of deferred imitation, mocking an action that she saw earlier. For instance, she may chase the neighbor's dog from her front yard just like she had seen her father do an hour earlier. For Piaget, mental representation marks the beginning of true thought when a child is able to envision objects and events that are not present.

Piaget also says that children begin to understand mental representation of number concepts at about age 2. According to Piaget, the concept of counting appears at about the same time that a child begins to use symbols, such as words. These symbols are derived by integrating information from initially disconnected sights, sounds, and tactile sensations.

Complete object permanence. When Carlos is in Piaget's sixth substage of the sensorimotor stage, he can understand invisible displacements. If an object is concealed in a variety of places while he looks on, he seeks for the object in the most recent hiding place, and will search for objects he has not seen being hidden. The schema of the permanent object is now complete. Carlos now realizes that objects continue to exist (have permanence) even if they are out of sight or touch.Critique of Piaget's Sensorimotor Stage

Piaget's theory of sensorimotor development has aroused considerable controversy. Most researchers agree that the sequence of cognitive development Piaget outlined is found in children under 2 years of age. This means that ambitious mothers (and educators) wishing to start educating their children early have some guidelines. Babies can be given practice in representational thought (naming objects, for instance) as early as 18 months of age. Critics agree with Piaget that the child's thinking changes in quality. For instance, a baby in Substage Six does more thinking and less trial and error than in Substage Four or Five.

Researchers generally disagree with Piaget on the timing of behaviors (Morra, 2008). One disagreement is over the appearance of deferred imitation— the ability to reproduce the behavior of an absent model. Piaget claimed that babies are incapable of deferred imitation before 18 months because they are unable to construct images of the behavior which can be used in reconstruction later.

Research indicates, however, that infants who are as young as 9 months are able to reproduce adult behavior. In two separate experiments, Andrew Meltzoff (1985; 1988; 2002) found that most infants aged 14 months, and some 9-month-olds, pulled a two-piece wooden toy apart or shook a plastic rattle just as they had seen an adult do 24 hours earlier. This task requires the infant to transform the perception of the blocks being pulled apart by someone else into the child's behavioral imitation. As expected, the older babies were more likely to reproduce the behavior, presumably because of their superior ability to store and recall mental images.

Researchers also disagree with Piaget on the appearance of invisible imitation—using unseen parts of the body, such as the tongue or mouth, to reproduce behavior (Morra, 2008). Piaget said that invisible imitation does not begin until the baby is about 9 months of age. Andrew Meltzoff and M. Keith Moore (1998) found that newborns imitate gestures such as mouth opening and tongue protrusion, actions and parts of their bodies which they cannot see, from the moment of birth.

One reason why researchers disagree with Piaget on the appearance of invisible imitation is the finding of sensitive technology that was not available to Piaget. It is now possible to measure activity changes anywhere in the brain, not just in the outer layers, by using fMRI (functional magnetic resonance imaging) which indicates that preverbal infants have memories, goals, and even mental combination in advance of Piaget's stages (Thomas & Casey, 2003).

The Information-processing Approach

Information processing: A theoretical explanation of cognitive development based on an analogy with the workings of a digital computer.

At 8 months, Sarah is shown a ball by her father who then hides it from her view. Three seconds later, Sarah begins to search for the ball and is successful. Why is Sarah able to find the ball? What is going on in her mind? This is the task of a relatively new field known as *information processing* (Bauer, 2007; Hunt, 1985). Information processing sees people as manipulators of perceptions and symbols. In other words, the goal of information processing is to discover what people do with information from the time they perceive it until the time they use it. The information processing approach was introduced in Chapter 2.

Encoding: The conversion of information into a form that can be stored in memory.

Information processing offers a detailed, step-by-step description of the child's thinking (Siegler, 1998; Siegler & Booth, 2004)[2]. Information from the environment is *encoded*, or taken in by the organism and retained in symbolic form. For example, a 5-year-old might remember (encode) the digit 6 as a curved line. Encoding can be semantic, which includes the meaning of words; it can be acoustic, which involves the sound of words; or visual, which deals with pictures or images. After the information is encoded, it can be placed into relatively permanent *storage*. Research indicates that information is stored in different parts of the brain (Rolls, 2000). The information that is stored (our memories) apparently consists of synaptic connections among neural cells. Our memories are recorded in the brain in the form of changes in size, shape, chemical functioning, and connectedness of neurons (Squire & Kandel, 1999).

Storage: The retention of information in memory.

The storage of memory can be enhanced in a number of ways. One way is through association, such as thinking of Mr. Skinner as being thin and tall. It

Retrieval: The recovery of information from memory.

is also easier to store memory through rehearsal, saying something over and over again.

The *retrieval* or recovery of information can be enhanced in many ways. One way is to follow a certain routine. For example, it is easier to remember where you laid your car keys if you always put them in the same place. It is easier to remember Mr. Glass' name if you visualize him holding a glass of wine at a party.

The model of memory developed by Richard Atkinson and Richard Shiffrin (1968) states that information is processed in three successive stages: sensory memory, which lasts for about 1 second; short-term memory, which lasts for about 20 seconds; and, long-term memory, which can be stored for a lifetime.

A basic assumption of the information-processing model is that all forms of cognition can be understood by organizing them into component parts (Bauer, 2007). It assumes that cognitive growth is typified more by quantitative change than by qualitative change (Siegler, 1991). More specifically, information processing asks the following questions.:

- How is information stored mentally and processed? In other words, how is information acquired, stored, and retrieved in ways that allow a person to think, reason, and solve problems?

- What mental processes are involved in the various intelligence tests?

- How quickly and accurately are these mental processes carried out?

- What is the nature of mental representations of information that these processes act upon?

- Does a person become more efficient in a task, such as reducing response time in pressing a button when he hears a buzzer because of a physiological change (change in hardware), or is the increased efficiency due to experience such as learning new ways of responding (change in software)?

Information processing views the human mind much like a digital computer. The mind is a symbol-manipulating system through which information flows. The goal is to identify the mental processes that underlie intelligent behavior. Investigators who employ the analogy of the child-as-information-processor, view cognitive development as the result of changes in both children's neural *hardware* and their *software*.

The hardware of cognition consists of "wiring," such as nerves and synapses; the software consists of the *program* that uses the basic hardware. One way to understand the thinking process is to learn how the hardware is constructed (the capacity of the system). We must also know the programs that

2. The way that the brain processes information in sequential steps, much the same way as a computer performs serial processing- that is one step at a time - can help us understand why some people are able to figure things out in an extremely short time. Information processing explains why it takes Jimmy three minutes to figure out the answers to 11 x 43-, 11 x 62-, and 11 x 72+, whereas Brian can figure out the answers in 15 seconds. The "trick" is the use of information processing. Using information processing, Brian first visualizes the two figures in the multiplicand, 43, 62, and 72, then spreads the figures, thus 4-3; 6-2; and 7-2, then adds each set, obtaining sums of 7, 8, and 9, then inserts these numbers in the blank space between the digits of the multiplicand. And voila! we have the answers, 473, 682, and 792, respectively.

have to be *run* to perform a particular task: the input (facts or data), the encoding, decoding, remembering, and analyzing that is required. We need to know whether children use new strategies to learn as they grow older, or do they apply the same procedures (basic programs) to new material.

A persistent question confronting information-processing theory is why older children can process more information than younger ones. While an 8-month-old is able to retrieve a ball up to 3 seconds after it disappears from sight, her 10-month-old cousin will search for the ball if the delay is 7 seconds or more (Kagan, 1979). Is the greater cognitive ability due to changes in cognitive hardware such as maturation of the brain and nervous system (Kail & Hall, 1994; Klahr & Wallace, 1976)? Those who attempt to study the child's cognitive development by utilizing the information-processing approach often follow Piagetian thinking. That is, they believe that cognitive development is composed of qualitatively changing sequences. However, the notion of stages is rejected (Morra, 2008; Siegler, 1981).

According to cognitive-developmental theorists such as Piaget, information can be processed (learned) if the children rehearse it. Children as young as 2 or 3 years show signs of rehearsal (saying something over and over again). In one study (DeLoache, 1986), 2-year-olds often talked about the location of a toy they had seen hidden earlier. When instructed to start looking for the toy 4 minutes after the toy was hidden, the children seemed to profit from the rehearsal.

One shortcoming of Piaget's approach to information processing is his failure to describe how the various forms of development (schemes, assimilation, accommodation, and operations) work internally. Piaget simply looks at the child's output. Cognitive developmentalists such as Piaget tell us that children become better at processing information as they get older because they learn more effective strategies (improvements in software). Two- and three-year-olds may be unable to solve a problem because they cannot sustain attention, not because the problem is too difficult. As children get older, their strategies become more sustained and systematic, enabling them to solve more problems.

Children may improve their performance of a task because of improvements in recall (retrieval of a piece of information that is not presented currently). Recall first appears in infants by 2 or 3 months of age. Babies taught to kick an overhead mobile will spontaneously repeat this act up to 18 days later, if they are reminded by seeing the mobile move (Adler, Gerhardstein, & Rovee-Collier, 1998).

Metacognition: The knowledge that people have about their own thinking processes, and their ability to monitor their cognition.

Thinking also seems to be aided by *metacognition* (an awareness of one's thinking process, for example, knowing that you think differently in math than in history). Metacognition is associated with strong academic achievement (Landine & Stewart, 1998). Students who are strong in metacognition notice when a passage in a textbook is especially difficult and they spend more time on it or seek help. An aspect of metacognition is *metamemory*, an awareness of one's memory processes, which appears at about 2 years of age.

Metamemory: An awareness of one's memory processes.

Controversy over metacognition. There appears to be little doubt that we can be aware of our thinking process (metacognition). For instance, Lev Vygotsky (1934), noted that human beings can control thought deliberately. Other scientists, primarily Sigmund Freud, believed that we are not entirely in control of our thoughts and behavior.

THEORIES OF LANGUAGE DEVELOPMENT

There are three theories of language development:
- The Behaviorist View
- The Nativist View
- The Interactionist View

Table 5.2 How do children learn to speak a language? Is it the product of maturation (heredity), environment, or both? Since children are unable to speak by the age of 2 or 3 months, maturation is a factor. However, environment is also influential: children in France speak French; those in Russia speak Russian. Those who believe that environment plays a strong role in language acquisition are called *behavior theorists*; those who believe that the capacity for learning language is inborn are called *nativists,* and those who believe in the interaction between environment and the inborn ability for language are call *interactionists* (Shulman & Capone, 2010). Table 5.2 summarizes the three major theories of language acquisition.

Theories of Language Development: A Comparison

Language Development Theory	Theory Supporter/ Developer	Major Premise
Behaviorism	B.F. Skinner Albert Bandura	- Environment plays the sole role in language development. - Children acquire verbal behavior when their relatively unpatterned vocalizations, which have generally been reinforced, gradually assume forms that produce the desired consequences. - Imitation provides the basis for language development.
Nativism	Noam Chomsky	- Heredity plays the sole role in language development. - Language Acquisition Device (LAD): a biological neurostructural predisposition for language acquisition. - People learn to talk as naturally as they learn to walk.
Interactionism	Melissa Bowermann	- Environment and heredity play an interrelated role in the development of language (neither the environment or heredity are the sole factor in language development). - Language development depends upon both internal and external factors. - This theory is a combination of Behaviorism and Nativism.

Behaviorist Theory

Speaking for behavior theorists, B.F. Skinner explains language acquisition purely in terms of operant conditioning such as reinforcement, observation, and imitation. Skinner states that children acquire verbal behavior when their relatively unpatterned vocalizations, which have generally been reinforced, gradually assume forms that produce the desired consequences. As her mother walks into the room, little Sarah babbles her favorite string of phonemes (the minimal units of sound that convey a meaning in a particular language), for example, "ma-ma-ma." The mother beams saying, "You want to talk to me?" and picks Sarah up gently (Skinner, 1957). For behavior theorists, innate factors play no role in language acquisition.

Overregularization:
Applying rules of grammar too broadly, such as saying "mices," instead of "mice."

According to social cognitive theorists such as Albert Bandura, imitation provides a basis for language development. Two people participate, a role model and an observer. The model produces a word; the observer produces a replica of the model's statement, presumably with the idea of being rewarded (Bandura, 1997).

Critique of learning theory. Bandura's social cognitive theory—that language is the product of factors such as observation, imitation, and, reinforcement—has been largely discredited for a number of reasons. If we listen to the language of young children, we often hear quite creative grammar—regular grammatical patterns are extended to irregular words: "He ran*ned* home," and, "She fall*ed* down." Certainly most parents don't use this type of "creativity"—applying rules to words that are exceptions—called *overregularization*. Most theorists believe that children's use of overregularization demonstrates that they are working actively to master the rules of a language.

Normally, parents do not correct their children's grammar. In fact, parents often comment on the cuteness or cleverness of their children's sayings. Most parents respond to the truth value" of the child's utterances. Some studies have found that when mothers engage in systematic correction of poor pronunciation and reward proper pronunciation, the children have smaller vocabularies than those whose mothers correct them less.

Chomsky says we are programmed to learn to talk.

Nativism: A theory that children have an innate, or biological, predisposition for certain types of behavior such as learning a language.

Language Acquisition Device: Noam Chomsky's view that the brain contains certain structures and neural wiring that enable individuals to learn a language naturally in the same way that children learn to walk without special training

Imitation appears to play a part in language development as Albert Bandura claims. Children tend to pronounce words like their parents. However, imitation is not the sole explanation of language development. Children may overregularize their words (apply the rules of the language too rigidly) because many languages, like English, have exceptions to their grammatical rules (Maratsos, 2000). Let's look at Noam Chomsky's explanation of language development called nativism, which has a strong biological, hereditary foundation.

Nativism: A Biological Predisposition to Language Development

Followers of linguist Noam Chomsky (1968; 1972; 1986) hold the view that human beings have an inborn capacity for language that facilitates the comprehension and production of speech. Presumably, this capacity, or predisposition, is due to brain structures and neural wiring that enables humans to discriminate among the various sounds of a language and to acquire rules of syntax. According to nativists, people learn to talk as naturally as they learn to walk. The experiences children have (hearing parents speak French or Spanish, for instance) activate their innate capacity for language, according to Chomsky. He calls this innate capacity for languages the *Language Acquisition Device*, a form of *nativism*, which views human beings as having an inborn capacity for acquiring certain skills. Hence, Chomsky takes the epigenitic (genes-plus-environment) approach to infants learning a language (Bradford, 2009).

One way to think of this innate capacity for language acquisition is to view the child's brain as a computer with a prewired (inborn) *Language Acquisition Device* (LAD) containing all the universal rules of language behavior. Chomsky argues that the universal rules of language (LAD) consists of specialized cognitive structures that are hard-wired into the brain as a product of evolution. The LAD enables Sarah not only to understand language but also to extract grammatical rules easily from what she hears. The LAD enables the child to scan, detect, sift out, and tie pertinent features or properties of a language together and to listen attentively to speech sounds throughout infancy. At about 6 months, the LAD triggers babbling (kaka, lala, and mama); the first word follows 6 months later, indicating a biological component to the acquisition of speech.

Critique of nativism. There are several studies which support Chomsky's claim that human beings have a universal instinct for rules to master the building blocks of language. One study (Marcus *et al.,* 1999), researchers determined that 7-month-old infants can make sense of speech by figuring out simple rules about the patterns of language structure and grammar on their own.

Human beings have some unique, inborn capacity for language. However, there is no solid evidence that children are biologically programmed for language learning, as nativists claim. If that were the case, all languages would be similar from one community to the next. Hence, in any language we would use the same sequence of words, or syntax, to express the same thought. But we say "I love you" in English and "Je vous aime" (I you love) in French.

The most controversial aspect of Chomsky's view of language development is the small role he ascribes to environment. Environment does play an important role in language development. One way of studying this is to consider *motherese* (the scientific term is infant-directed speech), the language adults generally use with young children. Motherese is often spoken in a slow, high-pitched voice; the sentences are short, simple (*e.g.,* "go bye-bye, night-night"), and highly repetitive (*e.g.,* choo-choo, bye-bye). Often "y" endings (doggy, mommy) are used. In using motherese, the articulation is clearer, and there is greater emphatic stress on certain words.

Motherese: Infant-directed speech which adults generally use with young children.

Investigators have found that when parents use many repetitions or partial repetitions (a characteristic of motherese), their children's language develops rapidly. Apparently children learn a language more efficiently if they hear motherese because of its frequencies. Researchers have also found that a child is motivated to the next level of language skill if her mother prods her just beyond the range of his or her current competence (Bradford, 2009; Hoff-Ginsberg, 1997; Sénéchal, Thomas, & Monder, 1995). In support of Chomsky's LAD, children seem to have a "built-in" preference for the high-pitched voice of motherese, rather than lower-pitched, faster speech (Werker, 1987). However, the high pitch of depressed mothers often seems to hinder a child's language development, perhaps because depressed mothers tend to be less attuned to their babies (Reissland, Shepherd, & Herrera, 2003).

One investigator who believes that environment plays a crucial role in the acquisition of language is Lev Vygotsky (1896-1934), a Russian psychologist. Vygotsky sees the development of language as an apprenticeship in which children advance their language when they collaborate with other people (teachers, parents, and older siblings) (Tudge & Scrimsher, 2003). Vygotsky claims that a newborn attends to all sounds and can discriminate among them. He also claims that with continuing exposure to culture, such as the speech of adults, the child's elementary use of language is transformed into an ever-higher form.

Interactionism: Environment and Heredity in Language Development

Interactionism: the view that language development results from both environmental and hereditary factors.

The *interactionism* view of language development is, just as its name reveals, defined as an interaction or combination of environmental and hereditary factors that contribute to language development (Bradford, 2009). The idea behind interactionism is that both internal and external factors are responsible for language development and acquisition. There are two common themes that underlie this view. First, interactionists believe that newborn babies have an innate propensity to pay more attention to language than to any other type of information they might be exposed to. Second, they believe that infants do not possess a present module that is specific to language development (i.e. the LAD coined by Chomksy). Instead, they purport that the infant brain has a generalized set of tools that they use in all areas of cognitive development (not solely for language). Interactionists disagree with any strict view of language development, such as the behavioral view or the nativist view.

THE BEGINNINGS OF LANGUAGE DEVELOPMENT

Sarah, aged 1½ years, has an important tool at her disposal: *Language*. She can express her wants and thoughts, and she can label objects. Building on the one-word-vocabulary she had at age 1 year, Sarah now has an arsenal of more than 50 words. She has also made dramatic improvement in her ability to understand simple words that refer primarily to objects and secondarily to actions. Sarah recognizes that names often refer to general classes of objects or events (Oviatt, 1982).

Pivot words: The speech of young children at the two-word stage when one word functions in a fixed position, and other words fill in the empty slot.

By the time Sarah is 2 years old, her recognition vocabulary (words children understand but may not use regularly in their speech) will contain about 300 words. Also, Sarah will begin to tackle the third and final major task of learning to speak: Sentences. To form sentences, 2-year-olds use *pivot words*, such as "my" and "doggie." These are key words employed in two-word phrases. Once Sarah has learned the concept of pivot words, she will be able to construct chains of many related phrases such as "my doggie," "my mommy," "doggie go," and "doggie eat." By the age of 3, Sarah will compose three- and four-word sentences.

During the third year, Sarah makes considerable gain in pronunciation and vocabulary. During this year, children more than triple their recognition vocabulary size, going from about 300 words at age 2, to about 900 words at age 3. Sarah learns pronunciation by   imitation, picking it up from people with whom she associates. Children with bilingual parents tend to pronounce words with the same accent as their parents, a fact that may follow the children throughout life. Regardless of surroundings, a child's accent and pronunciationusually become clear by the age of 2 or 3 years.

Sarah's ability to use language is a clear indication of her developing cognitive ability, including mental representation, in which a word stands for (represents) an array of people, objects, or events. Unfortunately, not all children are able to talk when they are 2 or 3 years old. They may suffer from a hearing impairment or language disorder that requires immediate treatment (Ratner, 2001). Let's go back and see how language development begins.

Understanding Language

Not only must children learn to understand a language before they can speak it, they must do so in a particular sequence. Kaplan and Kaplan (1971) propose the following sequence of five stages:

1. Infants can determine the source of sounds only a few minutes after birth and can also distinguish between sounds based on frequency, intensity, duration, and tempo.

2. At 2 weeks, infants recognize the difference between voices and other sounds.

3. At about 2 months, babies can pick up emotional cues, withdrawing from angry voices and smiling and cooing at friendly ones. They can also differentiate between familiar and unfamiliar voices as well as between male and female voices.

4. At about 6 months of age, babies become conscious of intonation and rhythm, responding intelligently to phrases in a strange language that have a familiar overall intonation pattern.

5. Toward the end of the first year, children can distinguish among individual sounds, or phonemes, of their language and can also distinguish between pairs of words that differ only in initial sounds, like *"cat"* and *"bat."*

Many language authorities claim that the baby understands much more language during the first year than Kaplan and Kaplan indicate. These authorities point out that by about 4 months, infants can recognize the sound of their names. By 5 months of age, infants can discriminate between their native language and that of another language that differs in rhythm and familiarity (Nazzi, Juczyk, & Johnson, 2000). The 8-month-old infant may use a grunt or a whine to get his mother's attention. At 9 or 10 months of age, the infant may communicate by pointing. The 1-year-old can carry out commands, such as, "Put the dog on the chair" and "Show me your eyes," which indicates that words are more than sounds to children at this age. By 2 years of age, the typical child's vocabulary is several hundred words (Anglin, 1993). Also, in the second year, babies often make gestures to describe objects (e.g., blowing at a stove to indicate "hot"), suggesting that words and gestures are related to the development of language. We should also remember that according to Lev Vygotsky, verbalization contributes to more competent performance.

Prelinguistic vocalization: An infant's verbal communication which progresses from cooing to babbling.

In addition to Sarah's ever-increasing understanding of language during the first year of life, she is also making progress toward meaningful utterances. This first step toward talking is known as *prelinguistic vocalization*.

Prelinguistic Vocalization: Sound Without Words

Cooing: A form of prelinguistic vocalization consisting mostly of repeated vowel sounds such as "Oh, oh, oh" and "oo, oo, oo."

Language authorities agree that a rudimentary form of prelinguistic speech begins at about 2 months when the baby begins to *coo*. Cooing is vocalization without meaning and consists mostly of vowel sounds repeated over and over, for example, "Oh, oh, oh...." or "Oo, oo, oo...." At around 6 to 10 months, the child's prelinguistic vocalization progresses to *babbling,* consisting of vowel-consonant combinations, such as "ababab" or "nanananana," which may last until around 18 months, and even continue after Sarah has uttered her first word at around one year of age.

Babbling: Speechlike sounds that have no meaning, such as "dah," "bah," "guh."

At first, babbling consists of sounds used in many languages. Soon it begins to reflect the sounds and intonation (pattern of rising or falling pitch) that babies are most likely to hear. Sounds that Sarah does not hear drop out of her babbling (Jusczyk, 2002). Between 9 and 10 months, the baby's babbling begins to mimic the rhythm and intonation of the language spoken at home. For example, Michelle's French babble stresses the second syllable (Stanley, 2000). While all babies start babbling at around 2 months, even the hearing impaired, in deaf children, the more advanced forms of babbling are absent (Oller, 2000).

Many parents think that babbling is evidence that the baby is using words. However, research suggests that babbling sounds have no symbolic value. Babbling is analogous to putting a puzzle together repeatedly and helps babies to learn how to manipulate the pieces of the sound that make up language (Golinkoff & Hirsch-Pasek, 1999). The baby who is babbling is not yet using meaningful utterances, an ability known as linguistic speech.

Linguistic Speech

Linguistic speech: The use of meaningful communication which progresses from the one-word stage to telegraphic speech to the use of grammar.

The development of communication through *linguistic speech* proceeds according to a particular sequence, similar to prelinguistic vocalization (Bradford, 2009). Carlos said his first word "mama" on his first birthday; about 8 months later, he said his first two-word sentence. A few months later, his use of grammar became quite noticeable.

The one-word stage. Sarah and Carlos both spoke their first word at 12 months, with the ages for the first word of individual children ranging from 10 to 17 months (Dale & Goodman, 2004). Most one-word utterances name objects in the visual field; *e.g.,* "cat," "dog," and "mother." Another group of words used in early speech is action words (bye-bye, go, and fall). There appears to be a close relationship between language acquisition and cognitive development (Woodward & Markman, 1998). For instance, babies tend to learn words connoting disappearance within a few weeks of learning object permanence. Parents often find that their child's first words are quite confusing. "Mama" may mean, "I want my mother," "Mother is here," or "Where is mother?"

It is important that the caregiver talk to his or her children before they are a year old, even though they do not understand the conversation. The caregiver's sounds and silences teach babies the joys of verbal communication indirectly. Talking with a young baby paves the way for learning a host of abilities like storytelling and reading, skills that will not emerge for years (Golinkoff & Hirsh-Pasek, 1999).

Holophrase: The use of a single word to express a complete thought.

Single-word utterances designed to express a number of ideas are called *holophrases,* from *holos,* a Greek word meaning "whole." Holophrastic speech refers to the use of a single word to express a complete thought, even though listeners may not always be able to identify the meaning.

Telegraphic speech: Verbal communication that is stripped to its essentials.

Telegraphic speech. This form of speech is referred to as telegraphicbecause it resembles a telegram (Hoff-Ginsberg, 1997). Whereas a child of 15 months might say "Doggie," at about 18 or 20 months he may use two words—"See doggie"—to convey a thought. Although parts of speech such as articles (e.g., *the* and *a*) and prepositions (e.g., *at* and *by*) are omitted, the utterance is now longer and more complex. Such communication is called *telegraphic speech* and consists of nouns without plurals, verbs without tense endings, and speech stripped to its essentials. Once the child acquires the ability to use telegraphic speech, he or she may also use rising intonation to indicate a question ("Me go?") and word stress to indicate location ("Play *yard*?").

Grammar: The structure of language made up of morphology and syntax.

Morphology: Refers to word formation and is the smallest unit of sound with meaning.

Morpheme: The smallest unit with meaning in a language.

Phoneme: The smallest sound unit with distinctive features.

Syntax: Refers to the form, or structure, of a language, or to the way that language arranges words into meaningful phrases, clauses, and sentences.

The use of grammar. Toward the end of the second year, when children use two-word phrases and sentences efficiently, they begin to use *grammar*. Grammar includes two main facets: *morphology* and *syntax*. Morphology refers to word formation and is the smallest unit of sound that has meaning, called morphemes. *Morphemes* are constructed from more basic sounds called phonemes. A *phoneme* is the smallest sound unit with distinctive features that can signal a difference in meaning. For example, it takes two different phonemes to make up the morpheme "*it.*"The word *cups* is also composed of two morphemes: *cup*, which refers to an object, and *-s*, which indicates the plural of the word. Morphemes also include suffixes such as *-ed* for past tense and prefixes such as *un-* and *dis-*, which modify the meaning of the words to which they are added.

Syntax refers to the form, or structure, of a language, or the way that a language arranges words into meaningful phrases, clauses, and sentences. Hence, the same words can have different meanings if the word order (syntax) is changed as in the following illustration:

1. Mike hit Bob.
2. Bob hit Mike.

Young children have considerable difficulty learning syntax. Often, their sentence construction (syntax) differs considerably from those around them. For instance, a two-year-old child may say, "We goed to store," or "He gived me candy," two instances that appear to contradict the popularly held belief that children imitate the language they hear.

SUMMARY

Learning is a relatively permanent change in behavior that occurs as a result of experience. Heredity (maturation) and environment both produce changes in the child's cognitive abilities, which enable learning to take place.

Very young infants are capable of several types of learning, including habituation (reduced response to a stimulus), dishabituation, and classical and operant conditioning.

There are several approaches to studying intelligence: Intelligence Quotient (IQ) testing, Piaget's cognitive-developmental theory, and information processing. IQ tests, which measure individual intellectual differences result in quantifiable scores. These scores tell us the relative standing of a child compared with his or her peers. The Piagetian approach is concerned with qualitative changes in cognitive development that begins with reflexes at birth. Information processing compares the human mind to a computer, and is concerned with the processes underlying cognitive development. Among other things, information processing is concerned with how people manipulate symbols, and what they do with the information that they receive.

Three major theories of language acquisition are: behaviorism (which emphasizes the role of environment); nativism (which holds that people have an inborn capacity to learn language); and, interactionism (which supports the combination or interaction between environment and heredity in the development of language).

Language development is an important part of a child's development. It proceeds in a definite sequence: understanding language, prelinguistic vocalization, and linguistic speech.

IMPORTANT TERMS

Babbling
Bayley Scales of Infant Development
   (Second Edition) (BSID-II)
Causality
Chronological age

Cognition
Cooing
Deferred imitation
Denver II test
Developmental quotient (DQ)
Deviation IQ
Dishabituation
Encoding
Fagan Test of Infant Intelligence, The
Goal-directed behavior
Grammar
Habituation
Holophrase
Imagery
Information processing
Intellectual power
Intelligence quotient (IQ)
Language Acquisition Device (LAD)
Learning theory
Linguistic speech

Mental age
Mental representation
Metacognition
Metamemory
Morpheme
Morphology
Motherese
Nativism
Object permanence
Overregularization
Phoneme
Pivot word
Prelinguistic vocalization
Psychometry
Radical behaviorist
Reliability
Retrieval
Sensorimotor stage
Stage
Standardization
Storage
Syntax
Telegraphic speech
Validity

RELATED RESOURCES

Readings

Bickerton, D. (2009). *Adam's Tongue: How Humans Made Language, How Language Made Humans* (New York: Hill and Wang, 2009).

Chomsky, N. (2006). *Language and Mind* 3rd ed. (Cambridge; New York: Cambridge University Press, 2006).

Gardner, H. (1985). *Frames of Mind* (New York: Basic Books).

Kaufman, J. editor (2009). *Intelligent Testing: Integrating Psychological Theory and Clinical Practice* (Cambridge [England]; New York: Cambridge University Press).

Nisbett, R. (2009). *Intelligence And How To Get It: Why Schools And Cultures Count* (New York: W.W. Norton & Co.).

Shulman, B. and Capone, N. editors (2010). *Language Development: Foundations, Processes, and Clinical Applications* (Sudbury Mass.: Jones and Bartlett Publishers).

VanTassel-Baska, J. editor (2008). *Alternative Assessments with Gifted and Talented Students* (Waco, Tex.: Prufrock Press).

Websites

The Noam Chomsky Website
www.chomsky.info/
chomsky.info was originally created by Pablo Stafforini, with the purpose of celebrating Chomsky's work and encouraging activism worldwide. In December 2003, it became Noam Chomsky's official website.

Child Development Institute
www.childdevelopmentinfo.com/development/language_development.shtml

This website is designed to provide the information and tools parents need to understand their unique child/children and to enable them to help each child develop into the successful human being they were meant to be.

The philosophy is built on years of child development research which shows that while each child is "pre-wired" with certain traits, temperament and abilities, it's the interaction with their environment, especially their parents, which ultimately determines how these characteristics are manifested as they grow and develop into competent adults.

Development is the result of "transactions" between the child and his/her environment. Each transaction results in new learning which results in the development of skills and traits. The right frequency, quality and intensity of interactions between children and their environment will result in each child reaching his or her full potential.

Chapter 6

Social Emotional Development in Infancy and Toddlerhood (0 to 3 years)

Chapter Topics		Learning Objectives
What are the two major theories of personality development in infancy?		Be familiar with Freud's Psychosexual Theory and Erikson's Psychosocial Theory relative to social emotional development in infancy.
What are the three expressions of emotions?		Understand the emergence of emotions and their expressions in infancy.
What is infant temperament?		Know the types of temperament evident in infancy: easy child, difficult child, and slow-to-warm-up child.
What role does the family play in the psychosocial development of infants?		Understand the role of the family (mother, father, caregiver) in infant psychosocial development.
How do disruptions in the parent-child relationship effect psychosocial development in infancy?		Understand the potential effects of situational disruptions in the parent-child relationship (i.e. orphanages, foster homes, hospitalizations, institutionalizations).
What are the characteristics of social development in infancy?		understand social behavior, empathy, and individual differences in infant social development.
Chapter summary		

Sarah, now 2½ years of age, is upset with her dog who just ate the steak off her plate. She tells Buster that he is bad; asks the dog why he took her steak, and warns him not to repeat his meat-stealing act. The other day, Carlos, who is also 2½, patted Buster when he helped himself to Carlos' dinner. Despite differences between Sarah's and Carlos' behavior, there are many similarities. Both children say "No" often. Both children have become increasingly aware of themselves (developing a sense of self), and both seem to become increasingly attached to their parents. Sarah and Carlos react similarly when confronted with a stranger and when they are separated from their parents. Finally, both children are increasingly able to exercise self-control.

These brief descriptions indicate various aspects of young children's development. Sarah is upset with her dog, and she is capable of expressing her emotions. Carlos' tolerance shows that his temperament is different from Sarah's. Repeated "No's" indicate that the children are moving from a dependent to an independent stage. They are becoming increasingly aware of themselves as distinct persons with different personalities. Let's first look at two theories that may help us to understand the development of the personalities of infants and toddlers: Freud's psychosexual theory and Erikson's psychosocial theory.

TWO THEORIES OF EARLY PERSONALITY DEVELOPMENT

Personality: A relatively stable, but unique, pattern of thoughts, feelings, and actions.

If we study children, we will notice that their patterns of thoughts, feelings, and actions are similar from one day to the next. Furthermore, each child's behavior is unique. This relatively stable, but unique, pattern of thoughts, feelings, and actions is called *personality*. Two recognized models of personality development are Freud's psychosexual theory and Erikson's psychosocial theory. You might remember the introduction of these theories in chapter 2, Theories of Child Development.

Freud's Psychosexual Theory

You may recall that Freud believed that personality is formed as a result of conflicts between an individual's early biological instincts and the requirements of society, particularly by the parents. These conflicts can be identified by five stages (oral, anal, phallic, latency, and genital). The first two stages occur during infancy and toddlerhood.

Oral Stage (Birth to about 1 year)

"Look at her, she is all mouth," Maureen's mother would say, referring to her newborn daughter. The mother was expressing Freud's view that a newborn's mouth—or, more specifically, its mouth, lips, gums, and other parts of the oral region—forms the focal point of an infant's personality.

Fixation: In psychosexual theory, the likelihood that earlier experiences will be reflected in behavior later in life.

Freud maintained that a child's personality begins during the oral stage and that it is essential that babies receive the proper amount of oral gratification. Otherwise, *fixation* will result, meaning that the children will attempt to resolve this "locked" stage later in ways such as nail biting or "bitingly" critical personalities. Babies who do not receive continual oral satisfaction may become compulsive eaters or smokers (Freud himself smoked), as well as "gullible" adults. The child's personality begins to form during the oral stage which builds the foundation for the anal stage.

Anal Stage (12 months to about 3 years)

The anal stage is normally concerned with toilet training. For Freud, it is one of the most important periods of development in the socialization process. The anal stage also influences future behavior. In Sarah's case, her parents seldom become upset when she has an accident, and they allow her to examine her feces and show normal curiosity. The effect seems to be positive because Sarah does not become anxious about having a bowel movement and is seldom constipated. According to Frued's theory, this freedom to explore has affected her social behavior so that she now relates easily to others.

Maureen has a different "anal" personality: *Anal-retentive*. As an adult, she is overly concerned with minute details and is obsessively precise and compulsive about routines (everything must be done on time in a certain way). Maureen's mother was very strict in toilet training. The mother would become upset and punish Maureen if she played with her feces or had a toileting accident. Maureen's younger sister has an *anal-aggressive personality*. She has difficulty controlling her angry and aggressive feelings and impulses. She often takes temper tantrums.

Erikson's Psychosocial Theory

Like Freud, Erikson believed that a child's early experiences form his personality, which develops in eight stages. If the child's experiences are negative, ego development (e.g., logical thought, adaptation, problem-solving, and control over the instinctual demands of the id) and mastery of subsequent stages may be prevented.

Crisis I: Basic Trust Versus Mistrust
(Birth to about 12 months)

Carlos received good care from the moment he was born—important in Erikson's view because quality is more important than quantity. Carlos' mother picked him up frequently, hugged, kissed, smiled at him often, and fed him regularly. Consequently, Carlos is a trusting baby and, like most trusting infants, Carlos sleeps deeply, eats well, and enjoys bowel relaxation. The warm bond between Carlos and his mother conveys a feeling of security and comfort. Carlos does not become anxious when his mother leaves his sight "because she has become an inner certainty as well as outer predictability" (Erikson, 1950, p. 217). For Erikson, basic trust is the "cornerstone of a vital personality." If Carlos has trust, he knows that he can depend on his caregiver to meet his needs for sustenance, protection, comfort, and affection.

Unlike Carlos, Joan is a mistrusting child. According to Erikson, Joan is mistrusting because her caregiver seldom fed her when she was hungry, was unduly harsh, seldom paid attention to her, and usually did not respond to her cries for attention or help.

Anal-retentive personality: According to Freud, a person who is obsessively precise and compulsive.

Anal-aggressive personality: According to Freud, difficulty controlling one's anger and aggressive feelings.

Basic trust versus mistrust: According to Erikson, the period when an infant develops a sense of trust or mistrust depending on how well the child's needs have been met by his or her caregivers.

Crisis: According to Erikson, a turning point in an individual's development that is resolved in either a positive or a negative direction.

Autonomy versus shame and doubt: According to Erikson, a period during which a child develops a sense of independence or doubt and rage.

Crisis II: Autonomy Versus Shame and Doubt (12 months to about 3 years)

In the second year, a baby enters Erikson's crisis of *autonomy versus shame and doubt* (which corresponds to Freud's anal stage). This crisis evolves largely as a result of maturation and the basic sense of trust developed in the sensorimotor stage. Sarah's developing muscles enable her to walk, to feed herself, and to dress herself. Her developing language allows her wishes and needs to be known, enabling her to become increasingly autonomous. According to Erikson, shame and doubt are created mostly in the context of harsh toilet training.

Sarah's struggle for autonomy is most evident in her negativism, often called the "terrible two's." Sarah may say "No" to everything. She can be very demanding and insist on doing things her way. Or, Sarah may aggravate her parents by dumping out the underwear drawer, banging pots and pans, or tinkering with her parents' computer.

The parents' job is to allow Sarah freedom to express herself. On the other hand, parents need to provide Sarah with a safe environment. According to Lev Vygotsky, the Russian psychologist known for sociocultural theory, Sarah will begin to guide her own behavior safely when she incorporates adult standards into her speech and uses it to instruct herself, such as, "No burn" and "Yes, go." This self-directed form of language is called private speech.

If Carlos is ridiculed or criticized constantly, he will fail to develop a sense of mastery or autonomy. Instead, he will develop shame and doubt about himself and be uncertain about his capabilities. Again, Erikson states that shame and doubt are created mostly in the context of harsh toilet training and can last a lifetime.

Critique of Freud's and Erikson's Theories

Both Freud's and Erikson's theories are difficult to verify objectively. How does one prove that early childhood experiences are as important as Freud claims? How does one prove that personality develops through crises as Erikson claims? Both Freud and Erikson seem to place extraordinary emphasis on the immediately caregiver's role in personality development. It is important to note that non-immediate family members, other children, aunts, and uncles also influence personality development. The child's *temperament* (individual personality attributes that have a hereditary basis) is also a factor of considerable attention.

Temperament: Individual personality traits that have a hereditary basis.

Yet, Freud's and Erikson's theories have helped us tremendously to understand how personalities develop. In particular, Erikson's psychosocial theory helps us to understand how dependent infants become independent toddlers, as well as autonomous older children and adults.

EMOTIONAL DEVELOPMENT

Carlos, aged 2½ years, looked surprised when his grandmother appeared. His surprise was soon replaced by joy when the grandmother gave him some candy. The next day, Carlos panicked when the neighbor's big dog ran toward him. Carlos showed anger and disgust when the dog knocked him down. Like Carlos, infants and toddlers are capable of a broad range of emotions. Emotion means a complex pattern of bodily and mental changes that include physiological arousal, feelings, cognition, and behavioral reactions made in response to something that an individual perceives as significant.

The Emergence of Emotions

How early do children's emotions begin? At 5 months of age? At 2 months? At birth? Are children's emotions different from those of adults? One pioneer researcher (Bridges, 1932) believed that infants are born with only one emotion—an undifferentiated excitement called distress. John B. Watson (1920), the behaviorist, claimed that babies are born with three emotions: Fear, anger, and love. More recent research suggests that, judging by facial expressions, babies have a wide range of emotions in the first few months of life. For instance, Paul Ekman, a developmental psychologist, believes that we have a set of core, primary emotions that are present at birth which are revealed through our facial expressions (Ekman, 1997).Table 6.1 presents the approximate time of emergence of fundamental emotions. .

Table 6.1
The Emergence of Infant Emotions:

Expression of Fundamental Emotions	Approximate Time of Emergence
Interest	Present at birth
Neonatal smile (a sort of half smile that appears spontaneously for no apparent reason)	Present at birth
Startle response	Present at birth
Distress (In response to pain)	Present at birth
Disgust (In response to unpleasant taste or smell)	Present at birth
Social smile	4-6 weeks
Anger	3-4 months
Surprise	3-4 months
Sadness	3-4 months
Fear	5-7 months
Shame, shyness, self-awareness	6-8 months
Contempt	Second year of life
Guilt	Second year of life

*From Trotter, 1983.

There are different patterns of crying.

Three Expressions of Emotions: Crying, Smiling, and Laughing

An infant's first cries are heard the moment it enters the world. About a month after the baby is born, the parents notice that their baby is smiling; a few months later, the infant is capable of laughter.

Patterns of Crying in Infancy

As a newborn, Sarah cries about 2 hours a day; Carlos cries considerably more. Both babies are normal and vary in the amount of crying they do from day to day. Peter Wolff (1969) discovered four patterns of crying in neonates:

1. **Basic rhythmic cry** starts with a whimper and becomes louder and more sustained. Periodically, the rhythmic cry is followed by a brief silence, then by a short inhalation whistle, and then by another brief silence. It is sometimes associated with hunger.

2. **Mad or angry cry** is a variation of the rhythmic cry in which excess air is forced through the vocal cords. It is more intense than the hunger cry.
3. **Pain cry** begins with a long shriek followed by seconds of silence (as the baby takes a deep breath), and then more vigorous crying.
4. **Cry of frustration** begins with two or three long drawn-out cries with the breath held for short periods.

The sound quality of an infant's cry may be a useful diagnostic tool. Some listeners can distinguish the cries of infants who are at risk for developmental difficulties from the cries of normal infants. Underdeveloped babies, preterm infants, and babies born with complications such as brain damage, cry differently (more piercing, grating, and unpleasant) than normal-weight, full-term babies with normal deliveries (Boukydis & Lester, 1998).

Colic: Pertaining to gastrointestinal (stomach or intestinal) pain.

Functions of crying. The main reason a baby cries is to signal distress. The baby may cry because it is hungry, in pain, or frustrated. One common reason for crying shortly after birth is *colic* (gastrointestinal pain).

Cries may be useful in making long-term predictions about the babies' development. The cries of preterm and full-term babies can be used to predict their scores on developmental tests at 18 months and at 5 years of age.

Soothing a crying baby. Soothing a crying baby means eliminating the source of the distress: A hungry baby should be fed; an unclothed baby, who flails about, should be clothed or held close to the body, and a baby with a wet or soiled diaper should be changed. If the baby has colic, it may need to be taken to an allergist. If the colic is due to the bottle being held horizontally during feeding, then holding the bottle upright may alleviate the condition.

Swaddling: Wrapping a child snugly in a blanket or clothes to prevent free movement and to help a baby sleep peacefully.

A number of researchers have discovered that rocking, humming, or continuous, rhythmic stimulation may quiet a restless baby. *Swaddling* (wrapping the child snugly in a blanket) may also satisfy a restless baby, possibly because the wraps provide continuous tactile sensation. Another successful technique is picking the baby up and holding it to the shoulder. This provides the baby with new visual stimulation. If the caregiver does not intervene until the baby is extremely upset, brain structures that buffer stress may fail to develop properly, resulting in an anxious, reactive temperament (Nelson & Bosquet, 2000).

One way to soothe a baby who objects to a new babysitter (the baby cries excessively, stiffens its body, and avoids eye contact) is to take advantage of the baby's (natural) bonding to its mother's body odor. This can be done by having the babysitter wear the mother's bathrobe without washing it after the mother wore it last.

How much attention should a crying baby get? One question mothers ask is whether they will harm their babies if they respond to their cries immediately. While it is possible to spoil a crying baby by picking it up (particularly if it is over 18 months of age), usually this does not seem to be the case. In fact, it is practically impossible to harm a baby by responding to each cry swiftly when the baby is less than 3 months old (Karlsrud & Schultz, 1993). Ignoring an infant's cries by letting him "cry it out," teaches the child that his plea for help (the crying) has no value (Sears and Sears, 1997).

A crying baby usually needs attention.

Mary Ainsworth and her colleagues (1972) found that mothers who are quick to respond to their infants' cries have babies who cry very little. Why is this so? It appears that mothers who respond to their babies' cries quickly and with regularity are also responsive to other attempts at communication their babies make, such as smiles, babbles, and arm movements. A baby may also cry less if it is given immediate attention because repeated parental responses build a sense of trust in the infant who thinks something like, "I don't need to cry, I know that my mother will be here soon, she has always taken care of me in the past." However, while the mother should generally be responsive, she does not need to panic every time her baby cries.

Smiling

At 2 weeks, Carlos begins to curl up the corners of his mouth and to "smile" in response to changes in his internal sleep state. Since this first smile occurs when Carlos is very drowsy or asleep, his parents usually do not notice the smile.

The second stage of smiling occurs when Carlos is 4 to 6 weeks of age. Carlos now smiles at any human face, and he now has reached the stage of social smiling. Following the emergence of social smiling, Carlos becomes more discriminant. By the fourth month, Carlos enters another stage of smiling. He is more sober toward the faces of unfamiliar people. For example, whereas 4-month-old Carlos may start a "conversation" with his parents by aiming his broad smile at them, he may react to his babysitter with a hesitant smile. At about 6 months of age, Carlos begins to develop a reaction known as *stranger anxiety*, an uneasiness about strange people and places which causes him to smile less. Carlos is less anxious if he meets a stranger in his home and is also less anxious if the stranger approaches Carlos slowly.

Stranger anxiety: An uneasiness about strange people and places.

The progression of smiling is due to cognitive and perceptual changes in the brain and nervous system. These changes also improve the baby's ability to focus the eyes, to see more detail (visual acuity), and to scan objects systematically. Reinforcement also plays a part in smiling. Parents usually smile in response to the baby's smile, causing the baby to smile more (a form of operant conditioning); strangers are less likely to smile at the baby. In time, the baby is more likely to smile at familiar faces than at strange ones.

Laughing

Sarah's mother is delighted because her 2-month-old daughter is exhibiting a new form of behavior: laughter (Walden & Garber, 1994). Young babies laugh only when the stimulus is vigorous and intrusive (such as forceful kissing of the stomach) or auditory ("I'm gonna get you" game). From the fourth to the sixth month, laughter results from less intense, but more interesting tactile and auditory stimulation. For instance, a baby may laugh uproariously at a "funny" face while being gently touched on the stomach.

By the time Carlos is 7 months of age, he laughs at social and visual stimulation. He now laughs at games of peek-a-boo and hide-and-seek. By 1½ years, Carlos laughs at events he creates himself, for instance, getting a thrill at seeing the family cat scamper when he chases it. By 2 years of age, laughter is often accompanied by comments such as "You funny," or "Look, kitty run".

Infant Temperament: A Genetic Origin?

Carlos' mother knew that her son had the *temperament* (an inborn style of approaching events and people) of a *difficult* baby the moment he was born. Carlos cried more than other newborns, he was more irritable, and more irregular in his biological functions. As he grew older, Carlos became more obstinate and had temper tantrums at least once a day. He could resist change and was slow to adapt to new situations.

Sarah was a joy to raise. She was typically quiet and would adapt easily to new situations. Her temperament was that of an *easy* child. Joan was still different. She was withdrawn, her responses were mild, and she required considerable time to adapt to change. Joan had a *slow-to-warm-up* temperament. Most babies (about two-thirds) can be grouped into these three broad temperamental categories: *difficult*, *easy*, and *slow-to-warm-up* (Kagan & Snidman, 2004). About one-third of the infants are classified as average because they do not fit neatly into one of these three types of temperament proposed by pediatricians Alexander Thomas and Stella Chess and their associates, in their classic study called The New York Longitudinal Study (NYLS), (Thomas & Chess, 1977; 1984; Thomas et al., 1963).

The New York Longitudinal Study (NYLS)

A Study of the Stability of Temperament and its Biological Roots

The New York Longitudinal Study: A study identifying three different types of temperament in newborn children: easy, difficult, and slow-to-warm-up.

The Thomas and Chess study, also called the *New York Longitudinal Study* (NYLS), was begun in 1956 and concluded in 1988 with 141 middle- and upper-class children who were followed from their first few months of life over a period that extended into adulthood. As the study progressed, other children were added, including 95 children from working-class Puerto Rican backgrounds, as well as children suffering from neurological impairment and mental retardation.

Beginning shortly after the birth of their child, the parents in the NYLS were asked to fill out questionnaires. The questionnaires included questions about how the children reacted to their baths, to wet diapers, and to their first taste of solid food. Later, the children were administered tests, their teachers were interviewed, and the parents were interviewed many times and administered more questionnaires. A major purpose of the Thomas and Chess study was to determine how individual differences in temperament influence a child's personality and behavior later in life.

Easy baby: A child that is easygoing, even tempered, adaptable to new experiences, and regular and predictable.

Difficult baby: A child who is active, irritable, irregular in habits, resists changes in routine, and has difficulty in adapting to new situations

Slow-to-warm-up baby: A child that is inactive, moody, resists new routines, and adapts to new situations slowly.

The Thomas and Chess data revealed that there are nine aspects of behavior which composed their definition of temperament (*see* Table 6.2). Thomas and Chess also noticed that certain temperament attributes tended to cluster, enabling them to identify three general types: *Easy (about 40 percent)* (easygoing and even tempered, adaptable to new experiences, regular and predictable); *difficult (about 10 percent)* (active, irritable, irregular in habits, resists changes in routine vigorously, has difficulty adapting to new situations); and *slow-to-warm-up (about 15 percent)* (inactive, moody, resists new routines, and adapts to new situations slowly). Many studies (e.g., Seifer *et al.*, 1996) have confirmed Thomas's and Chess's findings of temperamental differences at birth. These temperaments are well established by the time infants are 2 or 3 months old, according to Thomas and Chess, and they are fair predictors of children's temperament at 10 years of age. Other studies (e.g., Rothbart, Ahadi, & Evans, 2000) indicate that the quality of temperament in early childhood remains constant until adulthood (Rothbart, Ahad, & Evans, 2000).

Table 6.2

Thomas' and Chess' Basic Categories of Temperament

Trait	Definition
Activity level	The motor component present in a child's functioning, and the proportion of inactive and active periods in daily situations.
Rhythmicity (Regularity)	The degree of predictability of biological functions such as eating, sleeping, and toilet functions.
Approach or withdrawal	The nature of the initial response to a new stimulus, such as food, a toy, or a person.
Adaptability	The ease with which initial responses to a situation are modified.
Threshold of responsiveness	The intensity level of a stimulus that is needed to evoke a response.
Intensity of reaction	The energy level of a response.
Quality of mood	The amount of joyful, pleasant, and friendly behaviors relative to unpleasant and unfriendly behaviors.
Distractibility threshold	The effectiveness of extraneous stimuli in disrupting or altering the direction of ongoing behaviors.
Intention span and persistence	Two related indicators of the length of time an activity is pursued, particularly with obstacles or distractions present.

Source: Chess and Thomas, 1982.

An intriguing aspect of the Thomas and Chess study is that about one-third of the children did not fit neatly into one of these three groups. Rather, they showed unique blends of temperamental characteristics. For example, some children displayed difficult temperament in one situation and easy temperament in another situation. A few children fit into all three temperamental styles.

Implications of the New York Longitudinal Study

The New York Longitudinal Study has had great influence because it shows that there may be a genetic component to temperament. It may be possible to identify infants who are likely to develop behavior disorders on the basis of temperament types. Temperament may predict general school performance and health status.

Goodness-of-fit model:
Thomas' and Chess' model which states that an effective match or "good fit" between child-rearing and the child's temperament leads to favorable development and psychological adjustment.

According to Thomas and Chess, an important dimension of child development is the *goodness-of-fit* between a child's temperament and the demands placed on it by the environment, such as the parents, caregivers, teachers, and peers. For instance, reserved, inactive children need caregivers who are highly involved with them, question them continually, instruct the children frequently, and keep pointing out objects. However, too much intervention may dampen the natural curiosity of very active children. A "good fit" between a child's temperament and its child-rearing practices leads to favorable development and psychological adjustment; a "poor fit" results in distorted development and maladjustment.

The implication of infant temperament for parents and teachers is clear; they must accept the child as he or she is and work within that framework. The difficult child needs to set his or her own schedule (including feeding) as much as possible. We also need to remember that a certain amount of noncompliance in young children is healthy. Direct defiance and passive noncompliance by a 2- or 3-year-old may be an indication of the child's growing autonomy. As for the easy child, parents can place him or her on a more rigid feeding schedule. Also, the easy child needs high levels of stimulation. The slow-to-warm-up child needs time to adjust to a new situation. Finally, parents who have tried to do their very best but are disappointed with the results should not feel quite so guilty. Much of the way their child turned out could be due to temperament, which may be inherited (Rothbart & Putnam, 2002).

Since the seminal (highly original) work of Thomas and Chess on temperament, interest and research in this area has expanded considerably. The majority of recent research has focused on social phobia, withdrawal from unfamiliar settings, people, or objects; irritability, introversion, and extreme caution.

A key question on temperament is its stability over time. For example, does a difficult newborn become a difficult adult? Predictions from temperament in early years to preschool and beyond have not been very reliable. However, by the age of 12 months, the prediction about a child's temperament seems to be quite similar to the child's behavior in later years (Woodward et al., 2001).

THE FAMILY AND PSYCHOSOCIAL DEVELOPMENT

The family environment is the single largest influence on Sarah's and Carlos' psychosocial development. Before we look at the ways a family affects the child's psychosocial development, let's overview today's family. Certainly, it is different from that of a century ago. First, many more of today's families are broken. Whereas 100 years ago, the divorce rate was 1 out of 1,000 marriages, today the figure is nearly one-half of all marriages. Family breakup has resulted in many more single-parent families and stepfamilies ("blended" families).

Currently, there are more one-parent families and stepfamilies than biologically intact families. Another change is the ever-increasing trend for mothers to work outside the home. With both the father and the mother working, young children are often left unsupervised with potential for harm or delinquency. A phenomenon of skyrocketing proportions lately (1 out of 4 of all mothers) is the never-married mother, seldom heard of in our grandparents' generation. Another family structure which has received increased attention is one involving a gay/lesbian partner.

The Role of the Mother

Most child developmentalists agree with a Chinese proverb that one may give up a father, even if he is a magistrate, but not a mother, even if she is a beggar. Despite changes in the family structure (divorce, working mothers, and stepfamilies), the mother continues to play a central role in her child's development. Development is enhanced if there is a strong mother-infant bond (a strong and almost exclusive social-emotional attachment).

Imprinting. The mother-infant bond has often been studied in lower animals. Offspring follow their mother almost from the moment of birth, just as human babies crawl after their mother, ducklings follow the mother duck, and baby geese trail the mother goose. This action appears to be the result of instincts, innate biological determinants of behavior. However, if we separate an infant, such as a baby chick, from its mother immediately after hatching and arbitrarily substitute a moving object such as a block of wood, the chick will follow the block of wood. If the block of wood is presented at a critical period, the chick will continue to follow it even after the mother is returned to the chick. This type of bonding, or attachment, is called *imprinting.*

Imprinting: A learning mechanism specific to some social species that occurs in the life of an individual within a limited critical period that results in the formation of an attachment or a bond.

Bonding: The process by which a mother becomes attached to her baby immediately after it is born.

Controversy over the mother-infant bond.[1] When Sarah was about to be born, her mother requested the attending physician to have both she and her new baby transferred to a rooming-in ward until Sarah was ready to go home to ensure a process called *bonding*. Bonding refers to a type of attachment or emotional tie. Like Sarah's mother, some investigators believe that bonding is much more likely to take place if there is close physical contact between a mother and her newborn baby.

Research does not support the critical importance of early bonding. One of the severest critics, Stella Chess (1983) writes that, "By now the whole 'critical period concept' has been generally discredited in human development theory." Critics point out that the child's early experiences, including bonding, are unreliable predictors of later behavior. They claim that no single factor is all-important. Many factors, including the child's temperament and sociocultural background, interact to influence development at each age level. In fact, some investigators (e.g., Rowe, 1990) believe that parents play a far less crucial role in a child's development than is generally recognized. These investigators claim that parents should be given less credit for children who turn out well, and should take less blame for children who turn out poorly.

Contact comfort: Harry Harlow's term for a pleasant and reassuring feeling an infant derives from touching or clinging to someone close, usually the mother.

The baby's need for "contact comfort." Studies of lower animals suggest that physical proximity with a caregiver—known as *contact comfort,* is just as important for a baby as food. The importance of contact comfort for babies was first demonstrated in a series of classic studies with rhesus monkeys by Harry Harlow. For Harlow, contact comfort is derived from stimuli that satisfy the infant's tactile needs, helping it form an attachment to its mother.

Harlow created two kinds of surrogate (or substitute) mothers (Harlow, 1958). One, called the "cloth mother," consisted of a cylinder of wood covered with a sheath of terry cloth; the second, the "wire mother," consisted simply of a wire cylinder. Inside each "mother" was a bottle containing nourishment. Both surrogate mothers were placed in the same area with eight baby monkeys. All eight baby monkeys preferred the terry-cloth mother.

The baby monkey's preference for the terry-cloth mother was no surprise to Harlow. However, he was amazed that the infants spent most of their time (17–18 hours a day) with the cloth mother even when nourishment was supplied *only* from the wire mother. Harlow demonstrated a revolutionary idea: Baby primates become more attached to a source of warmth (or contact comfort) than to a source of food. The effects persisted after separation of the cloth "mother" and the baby monkeys.

After a year's separation, the "cloth-raised" monkeys eagerly embraced their terry-cloth "mothers" when reunited. The "wire-raised" monkeys showed no interest in their wire "mothers." Also, the babies "raised" by cloth surrogates explored their surroundings more. However, neither "wire-raised" nor "cloth-raised" monkeys grew up normally (Harlow & Harlow, 1962). Both sets of monkeys were more aggressive and fearful than normally raised monkeys; they were unable to engage in normal sexual relations, and most of the females were unable to nurse their own young.

---

1.   The word "bond" is often used interchangeably with attachment. However, "bond" normally relates to the mother's early attachment to her baby; "attachment" refers to an emotional tie between the baby and the caregiver later.

Figure 6.1
The Importance of Contact Comfort

Although the infant monkey is fed by the wire "mother," it becomes attached to the terry-cloth "mother," who has no food, as judged by the amount of time it spends on each "mother." Apparently touch or contact comfort is a more powerful determinant of development in infant monkeys than food.

Implications of Harlow's studies. Harlow's studies of contact comfort have pointed out the importance of touch for the proper development of babies. In fact, Harlow's studies demonstrated that holding babies is as important as feeding them. Studies show that human mothers who hold their newborns for at least an hour a day after birth bond more quickly with their babies. Such babies are also less fussy (Rubenstein, 1990).

Human mothers are now urged to spend more time in physical contact with their babies, not only by holding them for a longer period, but also by spending more time breast-feeding, bathing, and diaper-changing. Recent studies (*e.g.*, Carlson & Earls, 1997) show that if children are raised without being hugged regularly, caressed or stroked, they have abnormally high levels of stress hormones which destroy their brain cells. The result is serious long-range effects on learning and memory.

Attachment: The Emotional Tie That Binds

As 1-year-old Sarah sits in her crib with her mother nearby, she smiles at her mother, makes eye contact from time to time, and occasionally holds a "conversation" with her mother. At times, Sarah will cling to the mother while crying. These patterns of behavior are forms of *attachment*, the bond that young children form with their primary caregivers, usually their parents. The word attachment has been used particularly in the theoretical work of John Bowlby

Attachment: An emotional tie between a child and its caregiver.

(1907-1990), a British psychiatrist, and Mary Ainsworth and her colleagues (1972; 1978; 1979; 1993). For Bowlby, "attachment" describes an infant's biologically based ties to its mother and is an important emotional link, or "affectional bond," between two people. Bowlby also says that children who form an attachment to an adult are more likely to survive.

According to Bowlby, attachment is based on the child's experiences with its caregiver. As a result, the child forms expectations (a) of his or her own role in relationships (e.g., worthy versus unworthy) and of (b) others' role in relationships (e.g., caring versus uncaring and accessible versus inaccessible).

The child who is attached to his or her mother uses the parent as a "safe base" from which to explore, for encouragement, and as a source of comfort when distressed or frightened. Remember that one cannot always tell the quality of attachment by studying the child's behavior. A child who is attached to his or her mother may at one time cling to the mother while crying, and at another time play by himself or herself, glancing at the parent occasionally. It is not the frequency of contact between child and caregiver that determines the quality of attachment. Rather, it is the pattern of behaviors. Several methods or models have been used to investigate the quality of a child's attachment to its caregiver. The most common method is Mary Ainsworth's *Strange Situation,* which exposes children to a series of separations and reunions with their mothers (Ainsworth, 1993; Ainsworth *et al.,* 1978; Bretherton & Main, 2000).

Ainsworth's Strange Situation: A study of a baby's reaction to a series of eight episodes to determine the quality of the child's attachment to its caregiver.

Ainsworth's Strange Situation: Measuring Strength and Quality of Attachment

The test of a baby's attachment developed by Ainsworth (1913-1999) and her associates provides a series of eight episodes, during which the baby (typically about 12 months of age) is exposed to various events which might cause it distress. The strength and quality of the baby's attachment to its caregiver are determined by whether the baby reunites easily with the caregiver, then returns to comfortable exploration of the surroundings (secure attachment), or resists or avoids the caregiver during reunions (ambivalent, avoidant.) Here is a list of the eight episodes—each 3 minutes long—to which the baby is exposed sequentially in Ainsworth's test:

1. The mother and baby enter an empty, unfamiliar room that is full of toys.
2. The mother sits down, leaving the baby free to explore.
3. A stranger enters the room, and after 1 minute of silence, begins a conversation with the mother, then offers the baby a toy and attempts to engage the baby in play.
4. The mother leaves the baby alone with the unfamiliar adult for 3 minutes. If the baby becomes distressed, the stranger tries to comfort her or him.
5. The mother returns, greeting and comforting the baby, and the stranger leaves the room.
6. The mother leaves the baby alone in the room for a few minutes. (The baby's reaction provides some of the most useful information for researchers.)
7. The stranger returns instead of the mother.

8. The stranger leaves the room as the mother comes back. The mother encourages the baby to explore and play again, comforting the baby if needed.

Ainsworth's patterns of attachment. The Strange Situation has enabled Ainsworth and her associates to identify three patterns of attachment between the child and the parent or caregiver. One pattern or type is *secure attachment*, and the other two are forms of insecure attachment—ambivalent and avoidant. Let's look at these patterns of attachment in a little more detail.

Secure attachment: A relationship in which an infant has come to trust and depend on its mother or other caregiver as a secure base from which to explore.

- **Secure attachment** – At this form of attachment, the baby shows a distinct preference for his or her mother over the stranger. The baby uses the mother as a base from which to explore. A secure infant has little difficulty in separating from the mother to assess its surroundings, so long as it can get back to its mother or caregiver from time to time to test for reassurance. The infant may cry when his or her mother leaves, but stops as soon as she returns. The securely attached infant is usually cooperative and exhibits relatively little anger.

  About 60 to 65 percent of American babies have secure attachment relationships. This positive relationship provides a solid base for later social development with the quality of attachment generally remaining stable from infancy into adulthood (Waters et al., 2000). According to Ainsworth, the basis for a baby's security lies primarily in the way a mother treats her baby in the first year. The key ingredients, according to Ainsworth, are the mother's sensitivity and responsiveness to her baby's needs (Seifer *et al.*, 2004).

Ambivalent attachment: A baby's type of insecure emotional bond before the mother leaves and shows both approach and avoidant behaviors when she returns.

- **Ambivalent (resistant) attachment** – A baby with this type of insecure attachment has trouble in the strange situation, even before the mother leaves. The baby stays close to the mother and is extremely upset when she leaves. When the mother returns, the baby shows both approach and avoidant behaviors. The baby may cry to be picked up and then squirm angrily to get down. Or, the baby may cry for a while when the mother returns, but pushes her away. Furthermore, an ambivalent baby does not resume playing when its mother returns. instead, the baby keeps a wary eye on the mother. About 10 to 15 percent of American children are in this group.

Avoidant attachment: A type of insecure relationship between an infant and caregiver in which the baby does not cry when left alone and is just as likely to be comforted by a stranger as by its mother.

- **Avoidant attachment** – Children with this type of insecure relationship do not cry when left alone, nor do they pay much attention to the mother when she is present. When the mother returns, the child may approach her tentatively, turn, or look away. If the child does cry, he or she is just as likely to be comforted by a stranger as by its mother, tending not to cuddle or to cling when picked up. About 20 percent of American children fall into this group.

Disorganized/disoriented attachment: A form of attachment in which the child is confused and exhibits contradictory behavior.

- **Disorganized/disoriented attachment** Some investigators have suggested other forms of attachment in addition to those mentioned by Ainsworth. For example, another form of insecure attachment that has been proposed is *disorganized/disoriented* (Main & Solomon, 1990). In this form of attachment, the child exhibits dazed behavior, he or she is confused, and may show inconsistent, contradictory behavior patterns simultaneously, such as moving toward the mother while keeping the gaze averted.

Factors determining the quality of attachment. Ainsworth and her colleagues concluded that all babies become attached to their mothers by 1 year. However, the quality of attachment varies depending on the mother's responsiveness. Mothers of securely attached infants are more responsive to their infants' needs. They provide more social stimulation (talk to and play with the infants), and show more affection (Isabella, 1993). The mothers of securely attached infants also tend to hold their babies closer, providing a sense of security, and adjust more easily to their babies' moods and temperaments.

Insecure attachment (ambivalent and avoidant) is associated with insensitive or unresponsive mothering during the first year. The mother tends to respond more to her own wishes or moods than to her baby's. The mother will respond to the baby's cries for attention only when she feels like cuddling the baby. Children who belong to the disorganized/disoriented group are often abused.

The infant's temperament also plays a role in the mother-child relationship. For instance, newborns who become extremely distressed when their feeding is interrupted, are more likely to be evaluated as insecurely attached 1 year later. This suggests that infant temperament influences attachment (van den Boom, 1997). In general, ambivalent babies have more difficulty in forming a good attachment than those who are more flexible (Ainsworth *et al.,* 1978).

Long-term effects of different types of attachment. Do babies who are securely attached to their mothers remain secure when they are older? In general, the quality of early attachment has long-lasting effects on the child's development (Atkinson & Goldberg, 2004).

In one study (Jacobson & Willie, 1984), children who were securely attached in infancy played more and cried less when separated from their mothers at age 1½ years than their anxiously attached peers. Alan Sroufe (1982) found that 2-year-olds who were securely attached as infants were more likely to approach problems with enthusiasm, were more persistent, and often used their mother's help. Peers who were insecurely attached were more likely to throw temper tantrums, act aggressively, and ignore their mothers' suggestions.

Differences between attachments in infancy are still evident at age 5. Children who were securely attached as infants are at lower risk of becoming school bullies or the victims of school bullies. These children are also less likely to develop attention-deficit disorder (hyperactivity) in kindergarten.

There are other benefits of secure attachment in infancy. An early secure attachment helps children develop a positive self-concept, and to think of themselves as competent individuals (Ainsworth, 1979; Ladd & LeSieur, 1995). They have less need for physical contact with their mothers. Instead, secure children spend more time with their peers, and explore their environments more (Clarke-Stewart & Hevey, 1981). As early as 3½ years of age, securely attached children are often described as "peer leaders."

Unfortunately, not all securely attached infants are secure when they are older (Seifer *et al.,* 2004, Thompson, 2000). The stability of attachment depends on the permanence of the child's life circumstances. If the family is going through a difficult period due to poverty, illness, divorce, unemployment, or conflict between parents, there is a greater chance that the securely attached infant will become less secure when he or she grows up.

Many investigators are hesitant about associating the quality of attachment in infancy with the quality of the mother-child relationship later on. No single factor determines the pattern of attachment. The innate characteristics of the child (easy, difficult, or slow-to-warm-up), the interrelationship between caregiver and baby, and life circumstances all help to create attachment patterns; however, it appears that the type of attachment bonds established early in life (secure, ambivalent, avoidant, or disorganized) provides a window into future behavior as to how one processes information, how one sees the world, and the nature of one's social experiences (Elicker, Englund, & Sroufe, 1992; Johnson & Marano, 1994).

Maternal Employment

More mothers are working outside the home today than ever before. By 2001 there were over 10 million American mothers with children under 6 years of age in the workforce (U.S. Census Bureau, 2002). Over half the mothers in the United States with children under 1 year of age are employed, and the number is increasing; 75 percent of all school-aged children live in families in which both parents work outside the home.

Effects of a mother's employment. Considerable evidence shows that maternal employment is not harmful and may be helpful for the children. Lois Hoffman (2000) says maternal employment may benefit children because the mother's working presents a pattern better suited to preparing children for adult life than the traditional stay-at-home-mom pattern. In particular, several studies point to the benefits derived by girls when their mothers work. Daughters of employed mothers perceive women as having more freedom of choice, greater satisfaction, and being more achievement/career-oriented (Hoffman, 2000). However, many researchers claim that if the mother is employed, the child's development is affected adversely, particularly if the child is less than a year old (Brooks-Gunn, Han, & Waldfogel, 2002).

Some researchers (Gottfried, Gottfried, & Bathurst, 2002; Hoffman and Youngblade, 1999) claim that if a relationship exists between a mother's employment and her child's attachment, it is a weak one. A critical factor seems to be the mother's attitude toward employment. Since many women feel better about themselves if they are employed outside the home, they are able to assume their mothering duties with a more positive attitude. Furthermore, the efficiency of today's household (e.g., washing dishes by machine, rather than by hand) may result in children of today's working mothers receiving more attention than the children of full-time homemakers in the past.

Despite the advantages of a mother working outside the home, there appear to be some disadvantages. For instance, there is some evidence that infants of full-time working mothers tend to be less securely attached than babies of full-time mothers. The duration of breast-feeding is considerably shorter for mothers who are employed full-time than for full-time mothers (16.5 weeks versus 24.4 weeks). Some researchers suggest that the working mother tends to compensate for extended absences by spending more time with her child when she is not working. Time-use research studies have found that mothers who work outside the home spend almost as much time playing with their babies (14.5 hours per week) as do mothers without jobs (16 hours per week) (Huston & Aronson, 2005).

Day Care

Day care: All facilities that provide care for children until formal grade school.

The term *day care* is used broadly to include all facilities that provide care for children prior to formal grade school. Every day, about 13 million American children spend part or all of their day in nonparental care. Many of these children are as young as 11 weeks of age.

Overall, research shows no significant deleterious effects from day care (Hoffman, 2000). In fact, some studies show that children who are in day care are superior to those who stay at home with their mothers. Some studies have found that the benefits of day care last into adulthood. These studies suggest that children in day care benefit because they learn to be independent, they make marked gains in language and cognitive development, and they become friendlier with other infants and toddlers.

Despite this optimistic picture, not all evidence is positive. Most research on day care has been conducted at university-affiliated centers of high quality. These centers have highly trained personnel in charge of small groups of children, good equipment, and educationally stimulating activities. These day-care centers also provide emotional support for the children. Such day-care centers are not representative of the experiences of day-care children as a whole. For most parents, the quality of day-care is unpredictable. A major deficiency of many day-care centers is the child's inability to become attached to an adult.

One of the first studies to document a difference in attachment between babies reared at home and those reared in full-time day care was conducted by Mary Curtis Blehar (1974). In this study, more children in the day-care group were judged to be anxiously attached to their mothers. Children are more likely to be insecurely attached to their caregivers if they spend more than 30 hours per week in day care when they are less than 1 year of age.

In a study of more than 1,300 toddlers by the National Institute of Child Health and Human Development (NICHHD) (Garrision, 2001), the length of time the toddlers spent in day care was found to be linked to behavior problems such as aggression, disobedience, and defiance in kindergarten. This finding held true regardless of the quality or type of child care (nannies, relatives, or the children's fathers). The more time the children spent in day care, the more severe their behavior problems were.

The NICHHD study also found benefits for toddlers if they attend high-quality day-care centers. The children performed better on tests of language, knowledge, and memory than children who spent more time at home with their mothers or in a low-quality day-care center.

During the past two decades a major concern has been the effect of day care on children less than 1 year of age. In about 60 percent of the cases, the mothers are in the labor force. Studies indicate that if children are placed in day-care during their first year of life, they are at developmental risk for social and emotional problems such as acting out more, they have less ability to tolerate frustration, and are meaner. Age, temperament, and gender make a difference. Infants under 1 year of age experience more stress in day care than older children, as measured by their secretion of the stress hormone cortisol. Also, boys are more vulnerable to stress in child care than girls (Crockenberg, 2003). Some of the negative effects of day care on children less than 1 year of age are due to the poor quality of many day-care facilities. Another negative effect of day care is the instability of the care, with many of the children being moved from one day-care facility to another within a short period of time. The adverse effects of day care are most noticeable when other risk factors (e.g., neglect, punishment, and rejection) are also present (Belsky, 2001). Despite differences in the length of time the child spends in day care, the main determinant of child development is the mother's warmth and responsiveness (NICHD, 2005).

THE CHANGING ROLE OF FATHER

In Tolstoy's *Anna Karenina*, set in 19th century preindustrial Russia, an expectant father paces the floor and wrings his hands as he listens to the terrifying and inexplicable sounds coming from a bedroom upstairs where his wife is giving birth to their baby. In the past, fathers did not involve themselves in the birthing process or in the care of their newborn children. Also, fathers generally spent less time with their children than mothers, even when both parents were at home. The father's role was mostly that of the strong, responsible and punitive force in the family. Fathers were seldom seen as warm, caring, and nurturing parents—that was the mother's role. But the father's role is changing from that of the determined authoritarian provider to an active, loving nurturer (Silverstein & Auerbach, 1999).

The father can be a good "mother"

Nothing changed the father's role in the family in the twentieth century more than the mother's participation in the work force. The 1979 film, *Kramer vs. Kramer*, also had a hand in the change. In this movie, the workaholic father becomes the primary parent after being awarded custody of his child following a divorce. Child care expert, Dr. Benjamin Spock, also played a role in the father's greater involvement with his children. In the 1968 edition of Spock's classic book, *Baby and Child Care*, the father's role was depicted as a "warm father and a real man," who "occasionally" fed the baby or diapered him or her. Just eight years later, in the 1976 edition of his book, Spock wrote that the father should have equal responsibility for the care of the child.

Many of today's fathers form close attachments to their children soon after birth and demonstrate responsive and nurturant behavior (Parke, 2004). Studies of the fathers' attachments show that they look at their babies, kiss them, and give them bottles. Fathers can become more attached to their infants and young children than mothers. Fathers have the most difficult time as caregivers when the children are very young and the mother is working (Grych & Clark, 1999), particularly if the fathers are over the age of 35 (Heath, 1994).

Although fathers can form close attachments to their children, they interact differently than mothers (Kosterman *et al.*, 2004). While playing with their children, fathers toss the infants up in the air and wrestle with the toddlers, whereas mothers tend to play gentler games, sing, and read to their children. Despite these differences, fathers are often just as sensitive to their babies' needs as the mothers. In addition to the fathers affecting their babies directly, such as wrestling with them, they also play an indirect role. For instance, father-mother harmony is associated with good child adjustment (Cowan & Cowan, 2000).

Stranger Anxiety

Grandmother is about to meet her 8-month-old granddaughter, Sarah, for the first time. How exciting! But just as granny bends over to swoop her grandchild into her arms, Sarah cries hysterically. What a disappointment! What an embarrassment! This "unreasonable" behavior is a social development known as *stranger anxiety*, a stage marked by cognitive growth. The development of stranger anxiety at about seven months of age signifies that an infant has established a true object or person relationship with her mother or primary caregiver and has become wary of strangers.

The greatest degree of stranger anxiety occurs when the family is going through major changes, such as the birth of a baby, a family move, or a parent changing his or her job. Also, children show more fear of strangers if they are generally more fearful. The least amount of stranger anxiety occurs when the mother holds the child, providing him or her with a "secure" base. Also, infants who are exposed regularly to large numbers of adults show less stranger anxiety than other babies (Colin, 1996).

The cause of stranger anxiety appears to be the child's new ability to distinguish between familiar and unfamiliar people. Before children can make this kind of discrimination, they must first develop some pattern (schema) of a face against which all others are measured (Schaeffer, 1973). Therefore, an unfamiliar face may be experienced as an inconsistent or fearful event.

Several studies have indicated that sociability with strangers is related to the quality of the caregiving environment (Shaffer, 2000). Securely attached infants generalize the trust and confidence they experience at home to initial encounters with strangers. Conversely, insecurely attached infants are likely to respond more negatively to strangers because of inconsistent, unsatisfying, and unhelpful relationships with their caregivers.

Separation Anxiety (Protest)

When babies are somewhere between 8 and 10 months of age, they are often distressed when they are separated from their parents or concerned that they will be separated. The children cry, then stop crying, and cling or try to follow. This type of behavior is known as *separation anxiety*. In the more extreme cases it is called separation anxiety disorder. When the child is in the toddler stage and can talk, separation anxiety may include words of protest: "Mommy stay," "I go," or "Wait here."

Some evidence suggests that separation anxiety does not occur until the child has achieved object permanence: The child must first understand that the caregiver exists permanently before the child can realize that the missing adult is somewhere else. Separation anxiety varies according to the children's temperament, age, and situation. Sarah may react quite differently when her mother leaves her with a caregiver at home to go shopping than when she is left in a day-care center. Separation anxiety can often be seen in older children when they learn about parental illness. First graders may resist going to school even though they adjusted well when they first started school.

Separation anxiety appears to be closely related to stranger anxiety. Both are rare before the age of 5 or 6 months; both rise in frequency until about 12 to 16 months, then decline. Both appear to be related to some basic cognitive or other age-related developmental time table. Many investigators believe that stranger anxiety and separation anxiety are two signs of the child's normal growing attachment to its caregiver. However, if the anxiety is pronounced, the behavior may be an early sign of excessive distrust.

Stranger anxiety and separation anxiety can be reduced by having familiar people and objects with the child at the time of separation or introduction of a stranger. Another way is by choosing sensitive substitute caregivers (Shaffer, 2000).

Social Referencing

Social referencing: Relying on another person's emotional reaction to appraise an uncertain situation.

As 8-month-old Sarah moves about the room, she continually glances at her mother as if to ask, "Is it okay for me to do this?" If the mother's face shows concern, Sarah may hesitate before continuing or try something else. This type of communication, in which babies keep a watchful eye on the caregiver to monitor the acceptability of their behavior, is called *social referencing* and marks a new emotional relationship between infants and their caregivers (Walden, 1991). Social referencing is also a crucial precursor of language acquisition.

Social referencing tells a child if a situation or object is to be feared, delightful, or neutral. It also provides the child with feedback about his or her behavior. While babies generally use their mothers as a social reference, fathers may also fulfill this function.

DISRUPTIONS IN PARENT-CHILD RELATIONSHIPS

Most children are raised by their biological parents (or parent), but there are many instances (death, desertion, divorce, or child abuse) when the children are raised by someone else. One common method of raising these children in the past was the orphanage. What happens to these children? Historically, placing a young child in an orphanage has been viewed as a death sentence for the child (Johnson, 2002). Do institutionalized children suffer irreversible mental and emotional damage?

René Spitz's Studies of Orphanages

Anaclitic depression: Spitz's term for a syndrome developed by most children reared in an orphanage due to lack of social stimulation.

One researcher who attempted to illustrate the devastating effects of orphanages was René Spitz (1888-1974), an Austrian physician (1945; 1946). Spitz noticed that between 31.7 and 90 percent of babies reared in orphanages died in their first year of life. Spitz also noticed that most children reared in orphanages developed a syndrome called *anaclitic depression* due to lack of social stimulation. In the initial stages of the syndrome, the babies would often respond to separation with violent crying, screaming, and constant agitation. As the syndrome worsened, the babies became increasingly unresponsive to other people, they withdrew from their environment, and appeared to be very depressed. The withdrawal and depression often prompted mental and physical deterioration, and even death. Spitz claimed that if children are to grow up normally, there must be an emotional interchange between mother and child, particularly during the child's second 6 months of life.

Foundling home: An institution for abandoned children.

Spitz based his conclusions on a study of 135 children in a *foundling home* (an institution for infants found after their unknown parents have abandoned them). The children were less than 1 year old and came from a variety of backgrounds. Spitz used a control group in another institution, which he labeled the nursery. In the nursery, the mothers were emotionally disturbed, but gave their babies full-time care. At the end of the first year, children in the foundling home had "spectacularly deteriorated," according to Spitz. He found them retarded in height and weight and much more susceptible to diseases than the control group. By the end of the second year, the physical condition of the children in the foundling home had deteriorated further and their development had worsened considerably, whereas the control children had developed normally.

For Spitz, the emotional interchange between mother and child is the most important psychosocial element in an infant's life. According to Spitz, this emotional interchange has a particularly pronounced effect on the child's mental and physical health during the second 6 months of life.

Bowlby's Studies of Hospitalized Children

At about the same time that Spitz was conducting his studies in orphanages and nurseries, psychiatrist John Bowlby (1907-1990) of Great Britain was conducting similar studies and reaching similar conclusions. Bowlby discovered that many institutionalized children had difficulty forming close, lasting relationships. Most significantly, Bowlby's work delineated the stages of separation anxiety babies experience if they are placed in an institution when they are between 15 and 30 months of age (Bowlby, 1958; 1969; 1973; 1980; 1988).

These distinct, sequential stages are protest, despair, and increased emotional distance. During the protest stage babies cry, rattle their cribs, and avoid new people, or even members of their family. They are alert for any signs of their mothers' return, looking eagerly for any sight or sound of the missing parents and fretting over their loss. The closer the mother-child relationship, the longer the children protest.

In the despair stage, children accept care, food, and gifts from nurses and other attendants but remain quiet, listless, and apathetic, and appear uninterested in their surroundings. If the mothers return during this period, the babies are indifferent to them and appear unperturbed when the mothers leave. It is often assumed *incorrectly* that babies in this stage have accepted the despair stage.

In the final stage—increased emotional distance—children are no longer eager for their mother's comfort or for contact with any person. Moreover, the children do not become upset when there is a change in nurses; they are aloof and superficial in their social behavior. Like Spitz, Bowlby believed that the reason that these children fared so badly was a disturbed mother-child relationship (Bowlby, 1969; 1973; 1980). According to Bowlby, the mother-child relationship involves a biological underpinning which develops during a sensitive period. After this time, it may be impossible for the child to form a truly intimate emotional relationship with anyone (Bowlby, 1988).

Variable Effects of Institutional Care

Whereas Spitz and Bowlby claimed that children in institutions suffer because of their mother's absence, there is no evidence that infants need to be cared for or "mothered" by a single caregiver or by their biological mother. Some research claims that it is the depressed conditions in institutions that cause the children's retardation. Often, children living in institutions do not receive adequate social stimulation and physical contact, such as being held, patted, and caressed.

Should these deficiencies be alleviated, children can thrive in institutions, as researchers such as Harriet Rheingold (1956) have demonstrated.

Rheingold separated 16 6-month-old institutionalized infants into experimental and control groups. During an 8-week period, Rheingold "mothered" the experimental group 7½ hours each day for 5 days each week. The control group was routinely cared for by hospital staff and volunteer workers. Also, while the experimental group was exposed to only one "mother," the control group had contact with 17 different caregivers during the experimental period.

Following the "mothering" period, the experimental group showed dramatic differences compared with the control group. The "mothered" children became more responsive socially (they smiled more and babbled more) not only to Rheingold but to other people as well. They showed no signs of emotional shock or anaclitic depression noticed by Spitz. A year and a half later, the experimental group still vocalized more than the control group, although no other differences were evident. Another study which showed the positive effect of an enriched environment in an institution was the study by Harold Skeels in the 1930s (1966).

Skeels' study of institutionalized children. Skeels studied 13 children who were transferred from an orphanage to an institution for the mentally retarded. These (experimental) children were considered to be too severely retarded for adoption. Skeels believed that tender, loving care—more typical of institutions for the mentally retarded than of orphanages—could be beneficial for the quiet, slow, unresponsive children. The 13 children were studied throughout their childhood, and were compared with a similar (control) group of 12 children who remained in the orphanage.

At the time of transfer, the 13 (experimental) children, approximately 18 months old, had an average IQ of 64, with a range from 35 to 89. The control group had an average IQ of 87. One and a half years later, the average IQ of the 13 transferred children (the experimental group) was 91.8; that of the control group had fallen to 60.5.

A follow-up study of the children as adults 21 years later—when they were between 25 and 35 years old—revealed that 12 of the 13 transferred (experimental) children were quite productive; of the 12 control children, only one became self-sufficient. The follow-up study also discovered that the control children had a median (half above this figure; half below) of third-grade education; the experimental group had a median of 12th-grade education.

Why was there such a dramatic increase in the IQs and performances of the transferred children and a decline in the control children? The answer is that the children in the orphanage received very little personal care or attention, but those who were transferred (experimental children) were the center of attention. As soon as they arrived at the institution for the mentally retarded, the children were "adopted" by an older female inmate. Other inmates became "aunts." Attendants and nurses took the children on excursions and bought them gifts.

Studies such as the one by Skeels indicate that even when children suffer negative effects of institutionalization, the damage is seldom irreversible. It is also clear that the presence of a mother figure — even if she is mentally retarded with a mental maturity of 5 years—can make a positive difference in children. Children *can* recover if they are placed in environments that include opportunities for locomotion, objects to use in spontaneous activity, and a parent figure with whom they can develop close relationships. The extent of the children's recovery also depends on the type and level of care (Jackson, 2000), the degree of impairment, and on the expectations that are communicated to the children. In some instances, an institutional stay (such as in a hospital) may be made more tolerable for a child if the parents are allowed to sleep overnight, or if the child is left with his grandparents overnight before the hospital stay.

SOCIAL DEVELOPMENT

As two 6-month-old babies sit on the floor, they look at each other, touch one another, imitate each other's actions, vocalize, and smile at one another (Hay, Pedersen & Nash, 1982). Despite these behaviors, there is very little reciprocal response. At most, a child's response to another child's behavior at this early age might be a glance at the other child. This pair of children is involved in a rudimentary form of *social behavior.*

Social behavior: The ways in which people interact with one another, including negative attitudes such as prejudice, and the way they attempt to influence one another.

Social behavior begins at about 6 months and is more evident by about 10 months. By 14 months, children not only spend part of their time playing with other children, but they also show consistent preference for some children. By the time children are 2 years old, they occasionally interact with another child for a sustained period of time if the activity involves taking turns, such as spinning a wheel or competing in throwing a ball at a target. Up until the age of 2, children are basically loners.

Development of empathy. Toward the end of the first year, infants develop the ability to identify and to understand how another person is feeling and to respond. Carlos can now match his own feelings with those of another, a form of social behavior known as *empathy.* Empathy is the first moral virtue that sensitizes children to different points of view and increases their awareness to the ideas and opinions of other people.

Empathy: Putting oneself in another's place and vicariously experiencing that person's emotions.

According to Martin Hoffman (2002), empathy emerges in four broad stages. The first stage occurs during the first year when the infant matches someone else's emotions. For example, a 1-year-old will usually cry upon hearing the cries of other infants. The second stage occurs at about 12 to 18 months when the child responds to another's problem with some distress of his or her own. Sarah may show sadness or call her mother for help when another child is hurt. In the third stage of empathy, which occurs at 2 to 3 years, children notice others' feelings and respond to their distress in nonegocentric ways (they consider another person's point of view). A child may offer her brother food if he is crying while she is eating. In Hoffman's fourth stage of the development of empathy which occurs in late childhood or adolescence, the empathic response is general. The child may be more concerned about another person's chronic depression than if the problem is more transient, such as the mother's disgust at not being able to find her car keys.

Much of the difference in children's social development depends on the mother. Mothers who are warm, positive, and responsive tend to have children who are socially competent with their peers. Mothers who are harsh, rejecting, and hostile tend to have children who are hostile and are rejected by their peers (Appelbaum, 2001).

Individual Differences in Social Development

Children as young as 1 year of age show differences in their social behavior. These differences may be partly due to the mother's degree of sociability. Also, children who have plenty of contact with other children, such as those in day care, play with other children sooner than those who are raised alone. Furthermore, toddlers who are securely attached as infants, seem to be more positive toward other children than those with histories of anxious attachments. Finally, parents who are helpful, show more empathy, and are more thoughtful of others, have children who are more altruistic (unselfish).

There are also gender differences in social development. From about 2 years of age, boys seem to be more aggressive, assertive, and dominant than girls. Some of these differences may be hormonal or biological. Gender differences in social development can also be environmental. Boys as young as 1 year tend to be punished more than girls for aggressive behavior because they tend to act out their aggressive feelings more than girls who tend to use indirect aggression such as gossip or excluding peers from a social group.

SUMMARY

Two important theories of early personality development are Freud's psychosexual theory and Erikson's psychosocial theory, first introduced in chapter 2. Freud stresses biological and maturational factors; Erikson stresses cultural influences. Freud emphasizes the role of oral and anal factors in the child's early development, while Erikson accents the importance of crises in shaping the child's psychosocial development.

There is considerable controversy over when a child's emotions appear, and the nature of these emotions. Three expressions of emotions which appear in infancy are crying, smiling, and laughing.

The New York Longitudinal Study identified three clusters of temperament. Most children can be classified as *easy, difficult,* or *slow-to-warm-up.* Temperament can be influenced by the child's environment.

The mother plays a central role in the child's psychosocial development. An important relationship between the child and the mother is bonding or attachment. The baby needs "contact comfort," which is often missing if the baby is in day care, or if the mother works outside the home. Occasionally the father assumes the maternal role with considerable effectiveness. More information and research is emerging on the role of the father.

Two emotions that develop at about 6 months are stranger anxiety and separation anxiety. Often the child uses social referencing to receive feedback on its behavior.

A persistent controversy is the impact of nonmaternal care facilities such as the orphanage and hospitals. The effect seems to be influenced by the quality of care in the institution.

Social behavior begins at about 6 months of age. By the end of 2 years, the child is capable of aggression and social behaviors such as playing with another child, understanding how another child is feeling, and reacting to these feelings.

IMPORTANT TERMS

Ambivalent attachment
Ainsworth's Strange Situation
Anaclitic depression
Attachment
Anal-retentive personality
Anal-aggressive personality
Autonomy versus shame and doubt
Avoidant attachment
Basic trust versus mistrust
Bond
Colic
Contact comfort
Crisis
Day care
Difficult baby
Disorganized/disoriented attachment
Easy baby
Empathy

Fixation
Foundling home
Goodness-of-fit model
Imprinting
New York Longitudinal Study
   (NYLS)
Personality
Secure attachment
Separation anxiety (disorder)
Slow-to-warm-up baby
Social behavior
Social development
Social referencing
Strange situation
Stranger anxiety
Swaddling
Temperament

RELATED RESOURCES

Readings

Evans, Richard (1981). *Dialogue with Erik Erikson* (New York, N.Y.: Praeger).

Cassidy, Jude & Shaver, Phillip (1991). *Handbook of attachment: theory, research, and clinical applications* (New York: Guilford Press).

Leach, Penelope (2009). *Child Care Today: Getting it Right for Everyone* (New York: Alfred A. Knopf).

Zigler, Edward (2009). *The Tragedy of Child Care in America* (New Haven, Conn: Yale University Press).

Greenberg, Cathy (2009). *What Happy Working Mothers Know: How New Findings in Positive Psychology can Lead to a Healthy and Happy Work/Life Balance* (Hoboken, N.J.: John Wiley & Sons).

Morgan, Kimberly (2006). *Working Mothers and the Welfare State: Religion and the Politics of Work-Family Policies in Western Europe and the United States* (Stanford, Calif.: Stanford University Press).

Websites

Child Development Institute

http://www.childdevelopmentinfo.com/index.shtml

A website designed to provide the information and tools parents need to understand their unique child/children and to enable them to help each child develop into the successful human being they were meant to be.

Understanding Behavioral Individuality

http://www.temperament.com/parenting.html

Why are children so different? Because each has his or her own temperament! This accounts for why infants and children need to be raised in different ways. Parenting methods and techniques must be compatible with their personalities.

Baby Talk

http://www.babytalk.org/materials/topics/essay-attachment.htm

Baby TALK's mission is to positively impact child development and nurture healthy parent-child relationships during the critical early years. Baby TALK collaborates with hospitals, schools, libraries, health clinics and literacy programs to reach every young family living in a Baby TALK community.

Child Development Media

http://www.childdevelopmentmedia.com/mary-ainsworth-and-attachment-theory.html

Mary Ainsworth and attachment theory are discussed.

Classics in the History of Psychology

http://psychclassics.asu.edu/Harlow/love.htm

Harlow's classic rhesus monkey study is described.

PART FOUR

EARLY CHILDHOOD
(3 TO 6 YEARS)

Chapter 7

Physical Development in Early Childhood (3 to 6 years)

Chapter Topics		Learning Objectives
What physical changes are visible in the early childhood years?		Distinguish the physical changes that occur during early childhood (i.e. height, weight).
How does the brain develop and change during early childhood?		Understand brain development in early childhood (i.e. myelination, cerebral lateralization).
How do boys and girls differ in their motor development from ages 3-6?		Recognize the differences in motor development between boys and girls from 3-6 years.
How does nutrition effect physical development in early childhood?		Explain the differences between healthy and unhealthy eating in early childhood.
What minor and major illnesses are evident in early childhood?		Identify the risks for minor and major illnesses in early childhood.
What role does poverty play in the physical development of preschoolers?		Identify the poverty related issues in early childhood.
Why is dental health important to the physical health of preschoolers?		Understand the importance of dental health in relation to physical development of preschoolers.
What is the difference between normal and abnormal sleep patterns during early childhood?		Recognize the characteristics normal sleep and discuss sleep problems.
how does child abuse effect the physical development of preschoolers?		Understand the implications of child abuse on the physical development of preschoolers.
Chapter Summary		

Early childhood: The preschool years from age 3 to 6.

Three-year-old Carlos is getting bigger and stronger by the day, even though his growth rate has slowed considerably during the last year. He also continues to make height and weight gains throughout the preschool years (ages 3 to 6), commonly known as *early childhood*. There are other physical developments as well. For instance, motor skills improve considerably during early childhood, which is sometimes called the play years.

Motor development in early childhood builds on activities learned in infancy and toddlerhood. For example, climbing evolves from crawling. Jumping, hopping, and walking on a line are based on walking. By age 6, the child can learn almost any motor skill to some level of effectiveness.

Although, or possibly because, the preschooler's appetite has decreased, it continues to be of concern to parents. A major problem is providing the child with the proper type of food. This problem is aggravated by the proliferation of fast-food restaurants, overly processed foods, and the economic stress associated with buying and preparing healthy foods.

While most children sleep normally, some have disturbances. Two sleep problems are enuresis and night terrors. A major problem in early childhood is child abuse. Various studies have been conducted to determine the causes of child abuse, and how to deal with the problem. Many abusers repeat the pattern of violence in which they grew up.

PHYSICAL APPEARANCE AND GROWTH CHANGES

Changes in Appearance

Children undergo considerable change in appearance during the preschool years (Nurse, 2009). They develop a longer, thinner look due to loss of "baby fat," and faster growth of the arms, hips, and legs in relation to the growth of the head.[1] By age 5, Carlos and Sarah resemble the appearance of an adult much more than they did in toddlerhood. Their bodies are now more proportionate with the size of their heads.

Growth in Height and Weight

Carlos will not undergo as many dramatic changes in height and weight during early childhood as he did during the first three years. His height of 38 inches at 3 years will increase to about 46 inches by age 6, and his current weight of 32 pounds will increase to about 48 pounds. Sarah's height and weight increases will be slightly less than those of Carlos' (National Center for Health Statistics, 2000). Much of the weight gain is due to large muscle development as children run, jump, and climb. These activities become increasingly directed toward more specialized motor and muscular skills such as riding a bicycle and climbing stairs. Figure 7.1 and Figure 7.2 belowshow normal growth for males and females 2-20 years of age respectively. Figure 7.3 compares the growth of various parts of the body over time.

---

1. Exceptions are the earbones (the anvil, the hammer, and the stirrup), which stop growing at about age 5 years of age.

Figure 7.1
Normal Growth Charts: Height-for-age and Weight-for age Percentiles* for Males 2-20 years of age.

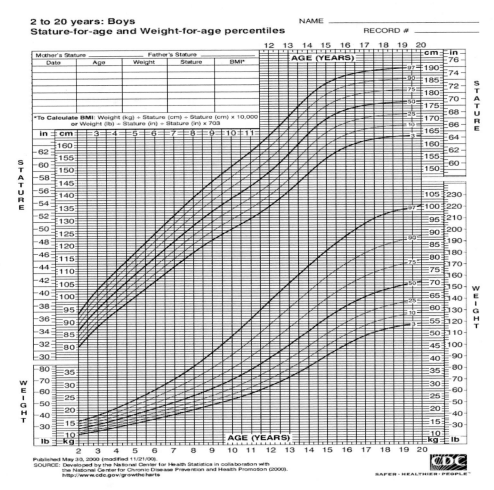

* A percentile score is a way of telling us what percentage of scores in a data set falls at or below a certain score. For instance, a child whose weight is at the 50th percentile is heavier than 50 percent of all children of the same age group. Weight should be the same percentile as height. (Doctors generally use percentiles to determine whether a child's growth is within normal limits.)

Figure 7.2

Normal Growth Charts: Height-for-Age and Weight-for-Age Percentiles for Females 2-20 Years of Age.

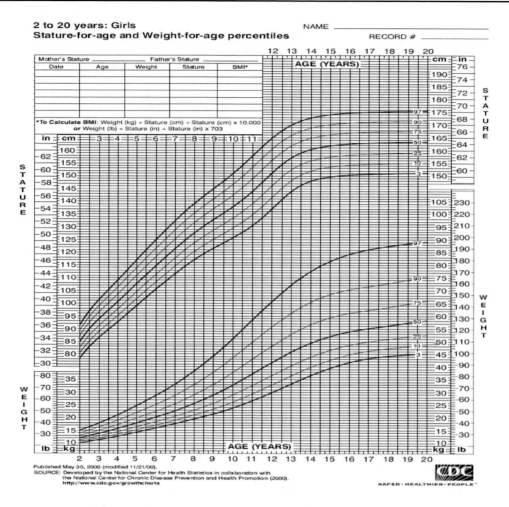

Brain Development

Important developments occur within the brain during early childhood (Schmidt & Segalowitz, 2008). Whereas at 3 years, the brain and head are about 50 percent complete, by age 6, they are about 90 percent complete. The brain doubles in size in the first 5 years and is the fastest growing body part in early childhood (See Figure 7.3).

Myelination: The coating of neural fibers with myelin (a white fatty substance) resulting in an increase in the speed of neural impulses.

Myelination. One important brain development is *myelination* of neural fibers. This means that certain neural fibers become coated with a white, fatty substance called myelin that increases the speed of neural impulses along appropriate fibers resulting in quicker motor responses. Another result of myelination is smoother performance of voluntary movements, such as those involved in writing.

Figure 7.3
Growth of Body Parts at Different Ages

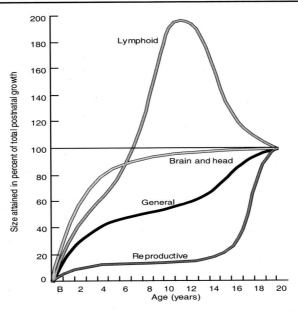

Growth curves of different parts of the body, showing the four chief types. The timing of the fastest growth varies for each of the body parts.

Source: Tanner, J. M. Growth in Adolescence (2nd ed.). Oxford: Blackwell Scientific Publications: Philadelphia: Davis, 1962.

Cerebral lateralization:
Preference for one side of the body or the other in performing a particular task.

Cerebral lateralization. Another important brain development that occurs during early childhood is increased *cerebral lateralization* —a general preference for one side of the body over the others in performing particular tasks. You may remember that cerebral lateralization is controlled by the brain, with the right cerebral hemisphere controlling the left side of the body and the left hemisphere controlling the right side. Cerebral lateralization is seen in handedness—the preference of one hand over the other for performing tasks. Although handedness is apparently well established by age 3, the child's preference for one hand or the other becomes stronger over time. The brain's right hemisphere demonstrates clear superiority when the left hand (not the right) is used in visuospatial skills such as copying figures and solving jugsawlike puzzles.

The importance of cerebral lateralization can be seen in children who have not established a dominance in preschool (Schmidt & Segalowitz, 2008). In one study (Tan, 1985), 4-year-olds who had not yet established cerebral dominance, were uncoordinated and delayed in motor development.

Development of the Lymphatic System

Lymphatic system: A group of tissues through which an alkaline fluid, called lymph, passes and provides immunity against infections.

One type of physical development in early childhood that has received little attention in the medical community is the *lymphatic system.*The lymphatic system is an accessory circulatory group of tissues, including glands, vessels, and sinuses through which an alkaline fluid, called lymph, passes. The single most important function of the lymphatic system is to return proteins to circulation after they leak out of the capillaries. Failure to return the proteins results in death within one day. Another function of the lymphatic system is to provide the body with immunity by filtering out foreign cells and bacteria. The lymphatic system does not develop fully until middle childhood which is a major reason why preschoolers contract more communicable diseases than older children.

The lymphatic system develops more rapidly than any other system, other than the head and brain, during the preschool period. It is approximately 50 percent complete by age 3 and 90 percent complete by age 6. This rapid development provides more immunity against infections than was possible in infancy and toddlerhood.

MOTOR DEVELOPMENT

By their third birthdays, Carlos and Sarah have mastered three major movement skills: *Locomotor* (walking, running, and jumping); *manipulative* (throwing, catching, and kicking); and *stability* (bending, stretching, and turning). By age 6, Carlos is capable of performing complex motor skills. Some reasons for the great strides in motor development are greater lung power, rapid development of the major muscles, and increased strength and stamina. (The 6-year-old is about twice as strong as the 2-year-old.) Table 7.1 below summarized the development of large motor skills in preschool.

The lower center of gravity, due partially to the loss of baby fat (and the protruding stomach), provides for more fluid movement and coordination when Carlos and Sarah enter early childhood (Pelligrino, 2009). Increased intersensory functioning—the ability to interrelate information received from the different sensory systems (hearing, sight, touch, etc.)—allows the child to make more precise judgments and movements. In preparing to catch a ball, the 3- year old is better able to react (move to one side or the other and to raise or lower his hand) to the ball coming toward him than he was earlier. Much of this progress is due to neurological development.

Environment also plays a role in advancing motor skills in early childhood, since motor activities develop best if children have opportunities to practice their skills (Pelligrino, 2009; Schickedanz et al., 2000). Children need materials and activities such as climbing ladders and jungle gyms, throwing balls, and running to exercise their large muscles. Children also need to exercise their small muscles, with activities such as using pencils, crayons, blocks, and toys. Studies show a positive link between exercise and brain function such as improved attention and memory.

While many preschool activities may seem insignificant to caregivers, they usually have value for the child. Repeatedly dropping the spoon at the breakfast table provides the child with an opportunity to develop manual dexterity (which involves the voluntary release of an object), as well as to learn about the laws of gravity. Usually, considerable imagination accompanies preschoolers' motor activities. A preschooler may pretend that he is a lion or some predator while running after another child (Steen & Owens, 2000).

Motor Development at Age Three
On her third birthday, Sarah can walk or run in a straight line, jump off the floor with both feet, and climb a ladder. These activities require the use of the large muscles found in the back, legs, and arms.

Sarah still has difficulty with small-muscle skills, such as tying her shoes or buttoning her coat. Nor is she very good at catching and throwing a ball, eating with a spoon or fork, or drawing within the lines of a coloring book. A 3-year-old does not possess the balance or motor coordination to change direction or to stop quickly while running but is capable of drawing recognizable forms with a little help from adults.

Table 7.1
Large Motor Skills in Preschool

Age	Walking	Running	Jumping	Pedaling	Climbing	Throwing
8 mos.-1 year	Walks in a wide stance like a waddle				Climbs onto furniture and up stairs as an progression from creeping	
1-2 years	Walks in a toddle and uses arms for balance (does not swing arms)	Moves rapidly in a hurried walk in contact with surface; may begin to run awkwardly	Uses bouncing steps off bottom step of stairs with one foot	Sits on riding toy and pushes with feet slowly	Tries climbing up anything climbable	Throws items, such as food, in a jerky sidearm movement
2-3 years	Walks upstairs, two feet on a step	Runs stiffly; has difficulty turning corners and stopping quickly	Jumps off bottom step with both feet	Sits on riding toy and pushes with feet more quickly	Tries climbing to top of equipment, although cannot climb down	Throws ball by facing target and using both forearms to push; uses little or no footwork or body rotation
3-4 years	Walks with arms swinging; walks up stairs, alternating feet; walks downstairs, two feet on step	Runs more smoothly; has more control over starting and stopping	Springs up off floor with both feet in some cases; jumps over object, leading one foot	Pedals and steers tricycle	Climbs up and down ladders, jungle gyms, slides, and trees	Throws overhand with one arm; uses body rotation; does not lose balance
4-5 years	Walks up and down stairs, alternating feet; walks circular line; skips with one foot	Displays strong, speedy running; turns corners; starts and stops easily	Jumps up, down, and forward	Rides tricycle rapidly and smoothly	Climbs up and down ladders, jungle gyms, slides and trees	Uses more mature overhand motions and control, but throws from elbow
5-6 years	Walks as an adult, skips alternating feet	Shows mature running, falls seldom, displays increased speed and control	Jumps long, high, and far; jumps rope	Rides small bicycle	Displays mature climbing in an adult manner	Steps forward on throwing arm side as he throws

Source: Adapted from Beaty, Janice J. (1986). *Observing Development of the Young Child*, Columbus, OH: Merrill p. 148.

Motor Development at Age Four

Four-year-old Carlos can skip, hop on one foot, catch a large ball with both hands, and run much faster than 3-year olds. He has less difficulty turning a corner while running than he did at 3 years of age because he is capable of shifting his weight by leaning to one side or to the other. Carlos can now walk downstairs by alternating his feet, which is more difficult (requiring a more complex shift in balance) than walking upstairs. He is capable of two other fine-motor tasks that are first evident at about the same time—brusing his teeth and tieing his shoes.

Motor Development at Age Five

By age 5, a child's locomotor skills begin to approach those of an adult (Pelligrino, 2009). Whereas the toddler may jump off a low height while moving his arms forward and up at take-off (winging), the 5-year-old leans forward like adults. About 81 percent of children are proficient jumpers by age 5. They are also more graceful while riding a bicycle and running, and possess greater balance than younger children. Five-year-olds can walk a curved line and a balance beam (a board raised off the ground), which requires placing one foot in front of the other. Five-year-old Carlos can skip smoothly and broad jump up to 3 feet.

Fine motor skills: Small body movements, especially those of the hands and fingers.

Five-year-olds can perform a variety of *fine-motor skills* (Brachlow, Jordan, & Tervo, 2001; Pelligrino, 2009). They can copy letters or numbers, copy a square (which is more difficult than copying a circle), cut on a line with scissors, and put pegs on a pegboard. One reason for this improvement is greater ability to use the fingers.

Gender Differences in Motor Development

Gross motor skills: Physical abilities that involve large body movements such as walking, running, and jumping.

We can see many motor differences between boys and girls by age 3. Carlos is better than Sarah in *gross motor skills* such as throwing a ball, jumping, and going up and down ladders. Sarah is better than Carlos in small-motor coordination, such as that required in threading a needle and in writing. Sarah is also superior in hopping, rhythmic movement, and balance (Pelligrino, 2009; Tanner, 1990).

Hand preference is usually evident by age 3 when children are grasping for objects and holding crayons or writing objects. Left-handedness tends to occur more in boys than girls.

NUTRITION

Although Sarah is 3¹/₂ years old, she seems to eat very little. Her appetite is less than it was a year ago. The reason for the smaller appetite is due to her slower growth. She now needs fewer calories per pound of body weight. However, once in a while, Sarah will go on an eating "binge." These bursts of increased appetite are due to corresponding bursts of faster growth. Sarah's mother need not worry about her daughter's appetite; Sarah's body will "tell" her how much to eat. A greater problem is what *types* of food are good for young children.

Children's need for food can be satisfied by following simple nutritional rules (Goday & Sentongo, 2009). First, preschoolers need about 1,800 calories per day. Second, there should be a proper balance from among the food groups: dairy, protein, fruits and vegetables, grains, fats, and sugar. Dairy products include milk, yogurt, and cheese (McGuire & Beerman, 2010). The protein group includes fish, poultry, eggs, dried beans, and peas. Examples of fruits include apples, oranges, and strawberries. Examples of vegetables include carrots and broccoli. The grain group includes bread, cereal, and pasta. Fats should be consumed in the form of olive oils and nuts. The food pyramid below illustrates current nutritional recommendation from the U.S. Department of Agriculture.

Source: http://www.mypyramid.gov/

A proper diet for young children should consist of about 55 percent carbohydrates, particularly complex carbohydrates (vegetables, cereals, and fruits); 30 percent fat to provide energy; no more than 10 percent saturated fatty acids (butter and cream cheese); and 300 milligrams of cholesterol (1 medium egg has about 225 mg. of cholesterol).

Fast-Food Restaurants

Four-year-old Carlos wants his mother to take him to the local fast-food restaurant where he can eat and play with his friend Jimmy. What's a mother to do? Carlos' mother knows that there are significant nutritional deficiencies as well as a large amount of unhealthy ingredients in fast-food menus for children. Fast-food menus are high in fat and sodium and contain little to no dietary fiber which is necessary for removing cholesterol and toxins from the body, but let's not keep Carlos in suspense. No, Carlos should not go to the fast-food restaurant.

If Carlos' mother lets her young son of one or two years eat fast foods such as French fries, sugary drinks, and snacks such as potato chips, he can be hooked on fast foods by the time he is three years old, setting him up for a lifetime of health problems such as obesity and diabetes. When children are exposed to salty, fatty, sugary foods at a young age, their taste and brain receptors will become accustomed to those types of food, only to want more (Goday & Sentongo, 2009; McGuire & Beerman, 2010).

Marketing Unhealthy Foods to Children

A major concern about young children's diet is selective targeting of children by promoting unhealthy foods through commercial messages on television, radio, internet, comics, magazines, and even at school. About 95 percent of food advertisements designed for children promote foods with an excessive amount of saturated fat, sugar, and salt. Fruit and vegetables are hardly ever mentioned.

The advertising of unhealthy foods is linked to a variety of health problems for children. First, a diet high in fatty, sugary and/or salty foods, increases the risk of developing coronary heart disease, cancer, hypertension, and diabetes. Furthermore, a link has been established between low consumption of fruit and vegetables and asthma, which is on the increase.

Why do young children consume so much of the junk food they see advertised? One reason is that they believe that the advertising is a reliable source of information. Usually, they do not grasp the motives behind the advertising. This means that young children need special protection against advertisements for unhealthy foods. Although there are some restraints against selectively targeting children with promotions of unhealthy foods, the controls are usually voluntary and are often ignored. Another reason for the unfortunate consumption of unhealthy fast food is a direct result of society's fast pace and economic strains. Families have little time and energy to shop for and prepare healthy meals. Also, healthy food is more expensive than unhealthy food, making it economically challenging to provide nutritious food to children and families.

HEALTH

Illness is a major problem in early childhood. Some illnesses, like the common cold or middle ear infections, are fleeting and not too serious. Other illnesses, like diabetes and asthma, are of a more permanent or chronic nature. Illness is often related to poverty and in today's economy can also impact the middle class as well. Another major health problem is stress. Given the societal and global events that impact families and children on a daily basis, stress has become a significant impediment to good health.

Attention needs to be paid also to the child's dental development. Correct care of teeth is important. Dental issues include improper care resulting in decay and misaligned teeth due to thumbsucking.

Brian, aged 4, has just returned from the doctor with his mother. He has a middle ear infection, known as otitis media, the most frequently diagnosed illness in young children (Chartrand & Pong, 1998). Preschoolers are susceptible to otitis media because of the anatomy of their faces. The eustachian tubes, which connect the middle ears to the throat, are in a nearly horizontal position during preschool since the lower part of the face develops later than the upper part. Fluid gathers in the middle ear during a cold, but it doesn't drain as easily as in adolescents or adults. The trapped fluid becomes infected, leading to an ear infection. Otitis media often occurs suddenly after a cold or a respiratory infection during the winter months. It is often treated with an antibiotic such as Zithromax.

Major Illnesses

About 1 in 10 preschool children has a serious illness that may last weeks to months or a lifetime. Among these serious illnesses are diabetes mellitus, asthma, and ulcers (Wheeler, Wong, & Shanley, 2007). Some major illnesses are of relatively short duration. One such group is communicable diseases: measles, rubella (German measles), mumps, whooping cough, and chicken pox, known in medical circles as varicella.

One reason why communicable diseases are so common among preschoolers is their high degree of sociability. Preschool children share toys, touch one another frequently, and occasionally talk to one another while only a few inches apart. When they sneeze and cough, they usually fail to cover their mouths and noses and rarely w.ill wash their hands unless prompted.

Fortunately, during the past century there has been a remarkable reduction in children's—as well as in adults'—illnesses (Wheeler, Wong, & Shanley, 2007). Diphtheria has been virtually nonexistent in recent years due to immunization. Smallpox has been eliminated throughout the world as a result of global vaccination programs. Tetanus and tuberculosis are declining rapidly (Hull, 1993). Polio (shortened form for poliomyelitis), the world's great crippler of children, will likely be erased from the Earth shortly. Deaths from lymphoma, including Hodgkin's disease, have declined by approximately 50 percent in the last four decades. Mortality from leukemia (cancer of the tissues which make blood cells) has declined due to better treatment methods, such as drugs (*e.g.*, Taxol or Paclitatel), better surgical and radiotherapy techniques, better blood products, and improved bone marrow handling.

Before 1970, young children with cancer had little chance of survival, whereas today, three quarters survive past the critical five-year remission mark. There is also some good news about human immunodeficiency virus (HIV). With the introduction of antiretroviral therapy, the progression from receiving diagnosis of HIV infection to having acquired immunodeficiency syndrome (AIDS), has slowed substantially. Other children's illnesses which have declined dramatically lately are measles, smallpox, and scarlet fever. Fortunately, since 1990, public health workers have helped to save more than 1 million lives in developing countries by teaching families how to administer the cure for diarrhea (Bellamy, 2000). But the news about children's illnesses is not all good.

The incidence of childhood leukemia (cancer of the bone marrow) is on the rise, even though its mortality has declined (Wheeler, Wong, & Shanley, 2007). Cancer is the second leading cause of death in children, after accidents. Although the survival rate for children with cancer has improved dramatically, the treatment often causes considerable damage. For example, chemotherapy can damage the cells in the cardiac muscle, causing heart failure years after the child's cancer has been cured. Since the side effects of treatment can be so drastic, doctors are now concentrating on ways of minimizing the damage caused by treatment such as reducing the dosage of toxic chemotherapy and in some cases eliminating radiation without affecting survival.

Recently, tuberculosis has resurfaced in the United States and, despite its decline worldwide, tuberculosis still kills more than 2 million people annually.The bacteria that causes the disease now infects one-third of the world's population.

Respiratory disorders and diarrhea continue to be the biggest killers of children in the third world, in spite of the fact that diarrhea is easily treated with a solution of glucose, salt and water that quickly replaces the loss of body fluids. Finally, pneumonia remains a leading cause of death among children throughout the world, although the mortality rate for children is decreasing in developed countries (Dowell, 2000). Although the Americas have been free of polio since 1991, the disease is still rampant in 23 countries throughout the world, particularly in parts of sub-Saharan Africa and the Indian subcontinent.

H1N1 flue virus: The swine flu, similar in nature to the seasonal flu, is spread through human-to-human contact (Center for Disease Control, 2010).

In 2009, the World Health Organization declared a pandemic of the H1N1 flu virus, known as the Swine Flu. The swine flu, similar in nature to the seasonal flu, is spread through human-to-human contact (Center for Disease Control, 2010). Swine flu symptoms include fever, cough, sore throat, runny or stuffy nose, body aches, chills, headache, and fatigue. Since August 2009, the CDC has reported 30 deaths in children ages 2-4 years and 102 deaths in children ages 5-11 as a result of the swine flu. A swine flu vaccination was developed and made available to the public in late 2009. As with any vaccination, especially a new one for a relatively unknown disease, significant controversy exists regarding its effectiveness and safety.

Dental Health

By age 3, a child has all 20 of his or her primary, or deciduous, teeth. They are white, translucent, and uniform in color. By the end of preschool, young children begin to lose these primary, or baby teeth. American children get their first secondary, or permanent tooth at about 6½ years (Burns, 2000). Dental maturity is about the same in boys as in girls.

Proper care of teeth is important for many reasons.

Dental Care

Proper early care of teeth is important, not only for chewing, but for other reasons as well. Good dental care is linked to proper speech habits, to preparing proper space for the permanent teeth, and to proper formation of the jaws, which grow forward and become more prominent in adolescence.

The teeth should be cleaned as soon as they appear by brushing (at least twice a day) with a soft toothbrush. The teeth should then be wiped off with a piece of damp gauze to prevent plaque buildup, a sticky decay-causing substance. By age 3, children should be brushing their own teeth with adult supervision, using a pea-sized dot of toothpaste. The widespread use of fluoride in recent years has helped to reduce the incidence of tooth decay by as much as 50 to 70 percent; so has the use of dental sealants, a clear plastic similar to superstrength adhesive applied to the chewing surfaces of the back teeth (Ismail, 1998).

A source of cavities in teeth is sweet and starchy foods. These foods should be kept to a minimum. The most damaging form of sugar is found in sticky form.[2] Among the culprits are chewable candy, cake frosting, and chewing gum. Sucking on a lollipop is particularly conducive to tooth decay. The baby also risks severe tooth decay when it nurses continuously from the breast or bottle during naps or at night. Tooth decay of the primary teeth is a strong predictor of decay in permanent teeth. Since the greatest threat of cavities occurs shortly after eating, children should brush their teeth immediately after eating or chewing candy or other sweet stuff. The first dental visit should occur when the child is around 1 year of age.

Remineralization: A process to reduce tooth decay by delivering calcium and phosphate to replace lost minerals.

A new technology to help strengthen teeth and reduce children's cavities is *remineralization*. This process delivers extra doses of calcium and phosphate to replace minerals that are lost as a result of daily assaults by food and bacteria in the mouth. If the cavities are detected early, remineralization will

---

2. We must remember that other forms of food can be just as damaging to teeth as sugar. Snacks like crackers and potato chips contain cooked starches that turn to sugar in the mouth. The sugar is then turned to acid by bacteria that live on teeth.

enable teeth to strengthen and repair themselves. A discovery on the horizon is a vaccine which will eliminate dental cavities.

Despite the best precautions, young children usually have some tooth decay. Almost half of all children have caries (decay of teeth) by age 3. Hence, children should have regular dental check-ups after about age 3 and avoid snacks that contain sugars (Ismail, 1998).

Sleep: Normal and Abnormal

Before 4-year-old Sarah goes to bed, she follows a certain routine. First, she listens to a bedtime story. Next, she uses the bathroom, makes a trip to the kitchen for a drink, then hesitates while looking at her mother as if to say, "I don't really want to go to bed." She asks for another story. Finally, with her head bowed, Sarah picks up her doll and heads slowly toward her bedroom. While at her bedroom door, Sarah asks her mother to sleep with her for a while. About 30 minutes after getting in bed, Sarah is asleep for 11 or 12 hours.

Transitional object: An object such as a toy or teddy bear that a child focuses attention and affection on while in transition between high parental dependency and greater independence.

Sarah's behavior is normal. Most children follow a bedtime routine which takes about 30 minutes. It is also normal for Sarah to ask for a drink before going to bed, and to take a teddy bear or some other *transitional object* to bed. Transitional objects help a child separate from his or her parents at bedtime. However, while the use of a transitional object by young children is normal and even helpful, such use by after childhood (18 years and up) may be a sign of an emotional disturbance such as separation anxiety (disorder), the fear and distress of being left behind by the caregiver.

Types of Sleep Problems

Night terrors: A sleep disorder in which a child awakes suddenly from a deep sleep in a state of panic.

One sleep disorder, which is common between 3 and 8 years of age, is *night terror*s (Marcus, 2008). In night terrors, the child awakes suddenly from a deep sleep in a state of panic. The child may wake up screaming with wide-open, glassy eyes and make thrashing movements for 2 or 3 minutes. He or she may breathe quickly, and be in a total state of fright. The face and body are dripping with perspiration and parental comforting has little effect. Within a few minutes, the attack passes, and the child returns to sleep. In the morning, there is little recollection of the previous night's trauma.

Sleepwalking: Walking in one's sleep or moving about aimlessly and not remembering the incident after waking up.

A sleep problem that is related to night terror is *sleepwalking*, where the child sits up suddenly from his or her sleep with eyes open, then moves about aimlessly, usually needing protection from trying to leave the house or from hurting himself or herself accidentally. Once the episode ends, usually within a few minutes, the child goes back to bed peacefully, remembering nothing of the incident the next morning.

Enuresis: Bed-wetting after about age 5 years.

Enuresis, or repeated urination during the day or night in clothing or in bed, after about age 5 (American Psychiatric Association, 1994), can be upsetting to parents. Research shows about three times as many boys as girls are enuretic at age 5.

If enuresis (bed-wetting) persists beyond age 5, there may be a psychological cause which may require therapy. Or, the cause could be physical such as a structural defect in the urinary tract, that has been present since birth. Other physical causes could be diabetes mellitus or a disorder of the nerves that serve the urinary system. At no time should the child be punished or scolded.

What Can Be Done About Sleep Problems?[3]

Fortunately, most children's sleep problems are not very serious and do not need professional help. If the sleep problems are minor, home management can often result in normal sleep habits.

Home management for children's minor sleep problems. Parents or other caregivers can often alleviate children's sleep problems such as night terrors by giving them coping strategies. For instance, caregivers can ask Carlos to come up with a way of dealing with the dragon he sees in his sleep. Carlos can also be asked who he wants to call on in his dreams for help. Sarah can draw a picture of her bad dream. Caregivers should validate a child's fears and say something like, "My goodness, that does sound scary."

If a child is sleepwalking, caregivers should take measures to prevent the child from hurting himself or herself. Hazardous objects such as sharp furniture should be removed from the child's room, stairs should be blocked with a gate, and the front door should be bolted at night. If Carlos begins to sleepwalk, he should be guided gently to his bed without waking him up.

Caregivers can help an enuretic child by explaining that it is not his or her fault for wetting the bed. The child can also be helped by allowing him or her to drink only one or two ounces of liquid after 6 p.m. Another suggestion is to have the child use the bathroom just before going to sleep. Some investigators (e.g., Butler, Forsythe, & Redfern, 1990) suggest that children will stop wetting the bed when they understand what it means to be dry.

Professional help for sleep problems. If sleep problems are severe and chronic (last for a long time), professional help should be sought. The type of treatment that is used depends on the nature of the problem.

Professional help for night terrors often consists of systematic desensitization where an attempt is made to have the child approach the feared object gradually. Many therapists also attempt to have the child resolve the underlying conflict, such as the youngster's concern over her father not visiting her after the parents' divorce, by having the father pay more attention to his daughter. Although psychoanalysts generally believe that night terrors can be a symptom of deep underlying conflicts, many therapists believe that night terrors are usually not a serious problem (Thiedke, 2001). However, if the problem persists for more than two or three months, the child should be taken to a therapist.

If sleepwalking is a persistent problem, medication is now the favored form of treatment. One drug that is commonly used is Klonopin (clonazepam) which calms the central nervous system and assists in sound sleep. When psychotherapy is used, an attempt is usually made to discover the underlying conflict.

Enuretic children seem to benefit more from psychological treatments than from psychopharmacological (drug) treatments (Houts, Berman, & Abramson, 1994). Regardless of which technique is used, it is important to explain to the child that it is not his or her fault for wetting the bed and that you will help him or her find a solution.

A rather common professional technique to combat enuresis is *aversive conditioning*. In this procedure, an undesirable or maladaptive response, such as enuresis, is paired with an unpleasant outcome, such as electric shock. One

Aversive conditioning: Pairing punishment with an undesirable response in the hope that the pain associated with punishment will prevent recurrence of the undesirable response.

---

3. For further information on sleep disorders, write to: National Sleep Foundation, 1367 Connecticut Ave., N.W., Dept. N, Washington, D.C. 20036.

procedure is to have the child sleep on a sheet containing electrical wires. When the sheet is wet, a buzzer rings, thus waking the child up. This technique has become one of the most effective methods of treating nocturnal enuresis (Mellon & McGrath, 2000).

Accidents

In the United States, accidents are now the leading cause of death in preschool children. Accidents account for more than one-third of all preschool deaths, surpassing the total number of fatalities due to cancers, birth defects, influenza, and pneumonia combined. Automobile accidents are the most common cause of fatalities.

Many accidents occur in and around the home (Delgado *et al.,* 2002). Children may drown in bathtubs, drink poisonous substances, swallow medicine, or be accidentally burned. While house fires cause many deaths, hot water causes the most serious nonfatal burns. Children are also at greater risk for accidents when their parents are under stress and are less cautious about dealing with hazardous situations.

Accidents also happen on playgrounds. Four- and five-year-olds like to experiment with their physical skills as part of normal physical development. Since climbing is a common pastime, preschoolers often sustain injuries from falls. The most serious injuries (and deaths) are caused by children falling off of something that is high off the ground (Greensher & Mofenson, 1985). Many playground injuries are also caused by swings and other playground equipment (Haupt, 1998). Notably, most playgrounds have removed merry-go-rounds and see-saws because of their tendency to cause injuries.

Effects of accidents. The effects of accidents are both physical and psychological. Children can become cognitively impaired as a result of a blow to the head in a car accident or from ingesting toxic substances. A severe concussion can result in permanent brain damage. An accident can also result in a social emotional effect such as a phobia. A child involved in a car accident may develop an intense fear of cars and driving for the rest of his or her life, a phenomenon called *posttraumatic stress disorder* (PTSD). The diagnosis of PTSD is generally made when the symptoms persist for at least 1 month following a traumatic event (American Psychiatric Association, 1994). Children with PTSD may become depressed, isolated, have mood swings, socialize less, and have nightmares.

Accident prevention. Although some people believe that most accidents cannot be prevented because they are unpredictable and without deliberate cause, scientists believe that most accidents can be linked to specific events. For instance, various life events, including marriage, divorce, relocation of the family, the birth of a child, and death are associated with an increased number of accidents.

Once we know that there are certain conditions that usually lead to accidents, the next step is to take steps to prevent accidents. The most obvious way to prevent automobile accidents is safe, defensive driving. The use of regulated infant car seats and safety belts, now a law in all 50 states and the District of Columbia, should be practiced at all times. The importance of safety belts has been demonstrated by a number of studies. One study (Decker *et al.,* 1984) found that children not in restraints are 11 times more likely to be killed in car accidents than those restrained.

Posttraumatic stress disorder: A disorder in which a very stressful event such as a car accident results in later emotional symptoms such as nightmares.

In a recent study (Taft, Mickalide, & Taft, 1999) of car restraints for children, the investigators found that the risk of death in car accidents could be reduced by 71 percent if the babies' car seats were installed correctly and used properly. Unfortunately, the study also found that 85 percent of the car seats were not used properly. The most common misuses were: "Safety belt not holding seat tightly" (63 percent) and "Harness straps not snug enough" (33 percent).

Another way to prevent accidents is through proper construction of playground facilities. For example, the playground can be made safer by placing protective impact-absorbing surfacing such as sand, soft wood chips, or rubber mats (rather than concrete, asphalt, or brick) under play equipment. There should be safety zones around moving equipment, such as swings, and the height of equipment should be limited. Preschoolers are just as happy climbing to a height of five feet as ten. Finally, even when playgrounds are relatively safe, young children need continuous supervision.

Stress

Preschool children are often subjected to a variety of stresses: parental discord, death, child abuse, and lack of affection. Let's look at how children react to stress.

Effects of stress. One of the more dramatic effects of stress on children is its inhibition of physical growth, even though the child is otherwise healthy. As many as 3 percent of preschool children in the United States may be admitted to a pediatric hospital for this type of physical retardation, known as failure-to-thrive syndrome. Current thinking is that the stress inhibits the production of the *human growth hormone*, a chemical substance, that is secreted by the pituitary gland to stimulate the body to grow. If the stress is relieved and the child receives attention, secretion of the growth hormone usually resumes, enabling the child to catch up in growth (Underwood, 1991). The absence or deficiency of the human growth hormone may occur in infancy or in later childhood (Hintz, 2003).

The effects of stress on physical development were illustrated in a study by Elsie Widdowson (1951). In this study, children who lived in a German orphanage with a punitive matron grew more slowly than children living in another orphanage where the matron was kinder, but the food had fewer calories.

In addition to causing physical problems, stress can cause behavioral problems. A preschooler under stress may not be able to sleep or may have nightmares. The child may become aggressive with playmates or become an isolate: that is, he or she may lack in social skills, avoid the company of others, and have no friends within his or her group.

Individual differences in response to stress. Not all children react to stress in the same way. Whereas one child may become aggressive after a divorce, another child may sit in a corner and cry for days. Still another child may cling more to his mother. Securely attached children are better able to cope with stress than those who are less secure (Wallerstein, 1984; 1987).

The way that children are treated is also a factor in their response to stress in others (Gurwitch *et al.,* 2001). For example, abused children often react to their peer's distress with disturbed behavior, such as physical attacks or displays of anger or fear. Nonabused children from the same socioeconomically

Human growth hormone: A chemical substance produced by the pituitary gland to stimulate the body to grow.

disadvantaged backgrounds are more likely to respond to the distress of another child by touching, talking, or providing some form of assistance.

Death of a Family member

While 4-year-old Carlos was being tucked in bed by his grandmother, she suddenly clutched her chest and fell to the floor. After a few minutes, Carlos tried to wake her up, but was unsuccessful. Carlos' grandmother had just had a fatal heart attack. Carlos had just witnessed a traumatic event—death.

The next morning, Carlos' parents tried to explain the phenomenon of death. Despite their efforts, Carlos was more concerned when his grandmother would wake up. Then, he suddenly bolted toward the door. When asked where he was going, he replied casually, "Out to play." Although most children do not experience death first hand, they do hear family members and their friends talk about death.

Effect of Death

Although preschool children are seldom able to understand death, they are still affected by it. They may feel betrayed by their parent's death, thinking that he or she died on purpose. Some preschoolers blame themselves. Children often feel vulnerable and depressed. Youngsters who have lost someone close to them through death may have sleep disturbances, loss of appetite, extreme fatigue, or depression. Other symptoms may be moodiness, sleeplessness, and poor performance in school. The children may adopt the mannerisms or symptoms of the deceased person which is viewed by therapists as a symptom of a very serious problem. Other signs of an unhealthy grief include prolonged fear of being alone, acting much younger than usual for a long time, and withdrawal from friends.

POVERTY

Poverty: In 2005, an annual income of $19,350, or less, for a family of four, was considered poverty.

Although most children in the United States appear to be well nourished, approximately 15 million children—higher than in any other industrialized country in the world—suffer from malnutrition (Children's Defense Fund, 1996). They are innocent victims of poverty. In 2005, the U.S. Department of Health and Human Services defined poverty as an annual income of $19,350 or less for a family of four. Approximately 25 percent of all children in the United States under 6 years of age live in families below the poverty line (McWhirter *et al.*, 1998). Each year an increasing number of families with children are finding themselves below the poverty line (National Center for Children in Poverty, 2010). This increase is partly due to a greater inequality of incomes between for people from the upper and lower socioeconomic groups the than during the 1970sand to a change in the political climate leading to drastic cuts in aid to the poor in 1981.

The 1990s showed a marked increase in the number of children in poverty,[4] with the number of poor American children increasing from 13 to 15 million between 1990 and 1995 (Nelson, 1996). In addition, Public Law 104—

---

4.   Children under 18 years of age account for 40 percent of the poor in America.

193, The Personal Responsibility and Work Opportunity Reconciliation Act of 1996, restricted welfare for many families (PL 104-193, 1996). This new law, replaces—and is more restrictive than—the 61-year-old program of Aid to Families with Dependent Children (AFDC). This new welfare reform bill requires recipients to get jobs within 2 years after applying for benefits which have a 5-year cap over a lifetime.

According to the National Center for Children in Poverty (2010), statistics reveal that the national percentage of children under the age of 18 who live in "low-income" situations is 41 percent. Low income is defined by the federal government as those who family income is less than twice the federal poverty threshold. The federal poverty threshold for a family of four with two children was $22,050 in 2009. "Poor" families are those who live below this threshold.[5]

Effects of Poverty

The effects of poverty on children were highlighted in a monumental survey of more than 44,000 families (Weil, 1999). Among the findings of this survey:

- **Nearly one-half of lower-income families worried about or had difficulty affording food.**

- **Twelve percent of the children lacked health insurance at the time of the survey.**

- **Children in poor families had more behavioral problems (lying, cheating, and not getting along with other children) and emotional difficulties (sadness, depression, and feelings of worthlessness).**

- **Children from low-income families were more likely to lack a regular medical provider and to be disengaged from homework and classes.**

For most poor children, their problems began before they were born. Their mothers did not eat properly during pregnancy and received poor prenatal care. The relationship between maternal nutrition, prenatal development, and postnatal health is well documented (Goday & Sentongo, 2009). If the mother does not get enough food during her pregnancy, there are increased risks to the fetus. The babies are more likely to be born with defects and to be sick more often. By the time the children reach school age, they are at risk for a cascade of health and other problems. The earlier that poverty begins and the longer it lasts, the more devastating are its effects on the child's physical and mental health and on school achievement.

Families experiencing poverty are subjected to many other factors inhibiting the child's development. More than half of all families below the poverty level have only one parent or caregiver. In addition to coping with not enough money, the single parent/caregiver is usually exhausted due to trying to do what is a demanding job for two adults. Then, there is loneliness. Often the single parent has little energy left for the children. Children who grow up in poverty-stricken, fatherless homes are more likely to become unmarried parents themselves, transmitting poverty and fatherlessness across generations in a cycle of dysfunction, despair, and hopelessness.

---

5. In Bangladesh, 9 out of 10 families are living in poverty.

Among the physical problems of poor preschoolers are ear infections, hearing loss, vision problems, and iron-deficiency anemia which results in chronic fatigue (Carley, 2003). There are also displays of temper, depression, and aggression.

Children from poverty-stricken families are at a disadvantage in school (Cooter, 2004). They often enter school with limited exposure to books and with limited language skills. Their ability to study effectively is diminished by poor health, hunger, and lack of sleep. Often, they are ignored by the teachers and receive little encouragement from their parents to do well in school (Garbarino, Kostelny, & Dubrow, 1991). Many times, they are wrongly perceived as having behavioral problems. Furthermore, the poor diets, unsafe housing, and high levels of community violence and unemployment that are so common in impoverished areas may all contribute to a child's inadequate cognitive functioning (Bronfenbrenner *et al.,* 1996). Usually, the schools in the poorer areas are inadequate and have difficulty attracting the best teachers. Available funds often have to be spent to repair the damage done by vandals rather than for educational items such as textbooks and maps.

Poor families frequently live in impoverished environments where sanitation and medical care are inadequate (Children's Defense Fund, 2000). Almost 2 million poor children are living in homes containing lead-based paint which was outlawed in 1978. Consequently, many of these children suffer from lead poisoning which contributes to reading disabilities and juvenile delinquency (Coontz, 1997). Recently, the plight of those living in poverty has worsened because of increased violence in poor areas, the spread of AIDS, and the explosiveness of gangs. These pervasive features indicate that being poor involves more than having little money, a poor education, and unemployed parents.

Mothers who live in poverty-stricken homes are often young and lack sufficient knowledge or experience to respond to their children appropriately. They face stress creating factors, such as lack of resources. Stressed single mothers may resort to substance abuse which can have a negative influence on the way they respond to their children.

Despite the somber picture of poor families, many of them provide a strong environment for raising their children (Luthar, 1999). Many poor parents read to their children, engage in religious and volunteer activities, and make sure that their children's physical needs are met.

Thumb Sucking

A common worry of parents is thumb sucking. If the sucking persists, the upper teeth can be pushed forward and the lower front teeth pushed back. Parents have little to worry about if the habit stops by the age of 5 or 6 years.

One cause of continued thumb sucking appears to be emotional instability. Parents need to provide their child with an emotionally secure and intellectually stimulating environment. When the child feels secure and accepted, thumb or finger sucking often disappears. In some instances, the child's thumb sucking will disappear if he or she is given a pacifier. In other cases, ignoring the practice is effective.

Thumb sucking needs attention if it goes beyond 5 or 6 years.

CHILD ABUSE [6]

Child abuse is a prevalent[7] concern that occurs in various forms. When we think of child abuse we normally think of physical assault (spanking) that leads to injuries. Another form of child mistreatment is sexual abuse involving fondling, sexual intercourse, or sexual suggestions. Still another form of child abuse is neglect involving depriving children of adequate food, clothing, or medical aid. Finally, there is psychological or emotional abuse involving ridicule, rejection, humiliation, or lack of attention.

According to the latest data report available from the National Abuse and Neglect Data System (2010), approximately 772,000 children were found to be victims of child abuse and neglect in 2008, revealing a 10.3 per 1,000 maltreatment rate. Eighty percent of the children who die from child abuse are younger than 5 years of age; 40 percent are younger than 1 year of age. As alarming as these statistics are, there is overwhelming evidence that the number of abused children is much higher due to under reporting (Findelhor, 1994; Smithey & Ramirez, 2004). A major concern is the increase in child abuse (which may be due in part to better reporting). For instance, a total of 3.1 million cases of child abuse were reported in 1998, an increase of 132 percent over the previous decade (U.S. Department of Health and Human Services, 2000).

Historically, *child abuse* meant physical assault or sexual abuse of a child by a parent or caregiver. Today, child neglect, such as failure by parents or other caregivers to provide the child with adequate food, shelter, safety, health care, or emotional care is also considered to be child abuse. Recently, additional forms of psychological maltreatment, such as constantly berating or humiliating a child, is also considered to be a form of child abuse.

Physical Abuse

Physical abuse is the second leading cause of death of infants 1 to 6 months old following Sudden Infant Death Syndrome. After the first year, physical abuse ranks second to accidents as a cause of death. In 2008, 16.1 percent of the reported abuse and neglect cases in the United States were cases of physical abuse of children (National Abuse and Neglect Data System, 2010). Physical abuse can be in the form of a severe beating, stabbing, whipping, or scalding. A classic type of fatal child abuse occurs in families with single mothers. The abuse is usually inflicted by the mother's boyfriend who baby sits while the mother is out. About 9 out of 10 parents use physical punishment, commonly known as spanking, to discipline their children. Most parents believe that they are doing the right thing and think that spanking will develop children properly. Unfortunately, the opposite is usually true (Gunnoe & Mariner, 1992; Smith & Brook-Gunn, 1997; 2004). Some authorities view any kind of physical punishment—even a mild slap—as a form of child abuse. It is also widely thought by psychologists and other child development specialists that spanking teaches and promotes violence.

---

6. Information on child abuse may be obtained by calling 1-(800) 55-NCPCA or by
        writing to: the National Committee to Prevent Child Abuse, Box 2866, Chicago, IL,
        60690, or by calling Parents Anonymous (call local operator for your 800 number).
7. Children's Defense Fund: http://www.childrensdefense.org/

Spanking also conveys messages to a child such as: (1) "My dad does not respect me;" (2) "I'm bigger than you, so I can use punishment and get away with it;" and (3) "Violence is the way to settle disputes."

Effects of physical punishment (spanking). There are many disadvantages to physical punishment. Physical punishment can increase children's aggression toward others (Anderson, 2002). Often the spanked child becomes the school bully. Also, children who are physically punished often engage in social disruption (Parke, 1977; 2004), and are less able to get along with others (Trickett, 1993). Although punishment may be effective in the short term, its long-term effectiveness is questionable (Kazdin, 2000).

Spanked children often avoid both the person who punishes them and the situation in which the punishment occurred. Children who are spanked are also likely to have poor motivation and to do poorly in school—an outcome which lessens their chances of success in life (Margolin & Godis, 2000). Spanking also sets up a model of violence for the child. In later years, he or she is more likely to be physically aggressive when he or she is unable to cope with a problem. A major problem with spanking is the child's resentment for being spanked. Many investigators believe that any adult who relies on physical discipline is at serious risk of becoming a child abuser. In 1998, the American Academy of Pediatrics took an official position against spanking, stating that it has negative consequences, and is no more effective than other approaches.

Symptoms of physical abuse. Symptoms of physical child abuse are not always as obvious as a broken leg or profuse bleeding. Consequently, investigators have learned to look for subtle signs. Members of certain professions have characteristic ways of spotting physical abuse in children.

Abused children may have serious burns, untreated diaper rash, and dirt under the fingernails. The physician can often spot child abuse by X ray photography when there is a swollen periosteum, or covering of the bone. This swelling may occur when an adult twists a child's arms or legs. X rays can also detect periosteal bleeding, often caused by a severe blow. Computerized tomography can detect whiplash, whereas ultrasound can document the extent of pelvic and abdominal injury more accurately. Physicians can also recognize physical abuse by the presence of untreated broken bones, bruises (particularly to the cheek), hemorrhage of the retina, and brain damage which can result from slapping, shaking, or blows to the head. The term "shaken baby syndrome" was coined in the late 1990s as a result of a nanny who was convicted for violently shaking a baby in her care to death. Autopsy results revealed severe brain bruising from the thrashing he endured.

Teachers can identify child abuse by the child's unusual behavior at school. Abused children often spend more time at school, arriving very early, and staying late because of fear at home. Abused children may also have difficulty in school, showing learning disabilities and limited attention span. Teachers may also suspect child abuse if they see extreme anger in children, who often take out their hostility on others. Lack of self-esteem is also very common. Psychologists notice symptoms of child abuse such as fear of being alone, fear of new situations, and chronic depression. Also, abused children may distrust others and show little response to praise. The psychologist may also notice avoidance, resistance, and noncompliance by abused children.

Sexual Abuse of Children

Incest: Sexual intercourse between two family members.

Although society has laws against sexual molestation of children and against *incest* (sexual intercourse between two family members), sexual abuse of children occurs far too frequently. Sexual abuse may consist of sexual intercourse, exhibitionism, suggestive language, or fondling. About 22 percent of women and 9 percent of men were sexually abused as children (Gorey & Leslie, 1997). Younger children are more likely to be sexually assaulted (in 9 out of 10 cases) by a member of the family or by an acquaintance than by a stranger (DeJong, Emmett, & Hervada, 1982). In 2007, there were approximately 150,000 substantiated cases of child sexual abuse in the United States, although the actual figure is believed to be about 500,000 because many cases remain unreported or unnoticed. In 2008, 9.1percent of abuse and neglect cases were sexual in nature (National Abuse and Neglect Data System, 2010).

Symptoms of sexual abuse. Because only about 6 percent of child sexual abuse cases are reported to authorities, it is important to identify signs of possible sexual abuse. Physical symptoms of sexual abuse may include injury to the genital area, vaginal or penile discharge, preteen pregnancy, venereal disease in a young child, and nightmares. (Briere & Elliott, 1994).

Psychological signs of sexual abuse are evident when a parent treats a child in a significantly different way from other children in the family. Such children will often appear nervous, aggressive, hostile, and unable to make friends. Many older victims will regress to bed-wetting; some will change their sleeping patterns. They may also turn to alcohol or drugs. Often sexually abused children hit, harass, threaten, and avoid adult caregivers, especially when the adults approach them in a friendly way. The two most prevalent and pervasive effects of childhood incest appear to be an inability to trust others and the existence of depression (Mullen *et al.*, 1995). Two other common problems with adolescents who have been sexually abused are binge drinking and suicidal ideation (Lester & Small, 1997).

Who is the Abused Child?

Although any child can become the target of child abuse, some are more vulnerable than others. For example, children under 3 years of age and members of a large family are more likely to be abused. Also, abused children tend to be more irritable, to cry more, to be sick more often, and to be more demanding. Abused children tend to be physically unattractive, hyperactive, and disobedient, and to have a greater-than-average need for affection. Often they are desperate for affection (hugging, kissing, and patting), making them easy prey for child abusers and predators (Tsai & Wagner, 1979).

Treatment for Abused Children

Treatment for abused children varies. In some instances, the abused child needs to be removed from the home immediately to prevent further abuse. In most instances, children who have been abused need psychotherapy. Among the objectives of therapy is the development of a healthy trust in people. It is particularly important to establish trust in a child who has been abused sexually (Greenfeld, 1990). Trust can be fostered by being nonjudgmental, by listening, and by accepting what the child says.

Most importantly, children also need to be told that it is not their fault that they were abused. In some instances, children need to be given alternative ways of seeking love or attention. An important understanding that sexually abused children need to have is the privacy of their bodies. They should be told that no one has the right to make them feel uncomfortable by talking intimately about sexual things, touching, or molesting them.   It is important to train parents to be more sensitive to their children's behavioral and emotional indicators (*e.g.*, extreme avoidance of certain people and excessive crying) of possible sexual abuse (Ligezinska *et al.*, 1996).

With the passage of the Child Abuse and Treatment Act of 1974, all professionals (teachers, psychologists, and doctors) must report suspected child abuse to civil authorities. The informers are usually granted immunity if their suspicion is unfounded.

Treatment for the abused child has had limited success. Hence, efforts have been made recently on primary intervention that prevents child abuse.[8] This approach consists of social strategies such as increasing economic self-sufficiency of poor families, discouraging corporal punishment, and providing affordable child care (Bethea, 1999).

SUMMARY

Preschool children continue to grow and develop physically between the ages of 3 and 6, but more slowly than during infancy and toddlerhood. On the average, boys are slightly taller and heavier than girls at this developmental stage.

An important physical development during early childhood is myelination, the sheathing of neural fibers in the brain. Another brain oriented development is cerebral lateralization, preference for one side of the body over the other.

There is considerable development in gross motor skills during the early childhood years. Some of this progress is due to neurological development. Environment also plays a role in advancing motor skills. Gender differences are noticeable at this time. For example, boys tend to engage in rough and tumble play more than girls.

Nutrition is important for proper growth and health. Children need a balanced diet of essential nutrients in order to support proper physical growth and development.

The preschool child is susceptible to a variety of illnesses—both minor and major. Two sources of serious illness are accidents and stress. Unforeseen illnesses can also arise and effect children (i.e. 2009 H1N1 flu virus). Accidents can occur in automobiles, in the home, or on the playground. Stress can result from family discord, poverty, or abuse.

Poverty and hunger continue to plague many young children and are compounded by other problems such as illnesses, depression, and aggression. The impact of poverty has been affected by reduction of welfare programs over the last three decades.

All of the primary teeth have erupted by age 3. Proper care is important for many reasons, including prevention of cavities, decay, and proper jaw

---

8.   For information on preventing child abuse, call: National Committee to Prevent Child Abuse. Telephone: 1-800-CHILDREN.

formation. Thumb or finger sucking after the age of 5 or 6 can cause lasting damage in the positioning of the teeth.

Bedtime rituals, such as getting a drink of water before going to bed, are usually normal. Sleep problems include night terrors and sleepwalking. Another problem is enuresis, urination in bed or clothing after the age of 5 or 6 years.

Death of a family member is psychologically and emotionally stressful fora preschool child, even though he or she lacks the cognitive capacity to grasp its entire significance and meaning. The child should have his questions answered truthfully and be allowed a period of mourning.

A serious problem in early childhood is child abuse and includes spanking, emotional neglect, ridicule, and sexual abuse.Most cases of abuse go unreported. Professionals should watch for signs of abuse. Both the child and the abuser usually need treatment. The prognosis (chances of recovery) for the child abuser is quite unfavorable.

IMPORTANT TERMS

Aversive conditioning	Lymphatic system
Cerebral lateralization	Multiple sclerosis
Child abuse	Myelination
Dominance	Night terror
Early childhood	Postpartum stress disorder
Enuresis	Poverty
Fine motor skills	Posttraumatic stress disorder (PTSD)
Gross motor skills	Remineralization
H1N1 Flu Virus (Swine Flu)	Sleepwalking
Human growth hormone	Transitional object
Incest	

RELATED RESOURCES

Readings

Koplan, Jeffrey, Liverman, Catharyn and Kraak, Vivica editors (2005). *Preventing Childhood Obesity: Health in the Balance.* Washington, D.C.: National Academies Press.

Nurse, Angela (2009). *Physical Development in the Early Years Foundation Stage.* London; New York: Routledge.

Evans, Gary and Wachs, Theodore editors (2010). *Chaos and ItsInfluence on Children's Development: an Ecological Perspective.* Washington, DC: American Psychological Association.

Sirotnak, Andrew (2009). *Child Abuse and Neglect: Advancements and Challenges in the 21st century.* Philadelphia, Pa: Saunders.

Websites

United Stated Department of Agriculture
http://www.mypyramid.gov/

Children's Defense Fund
http://www.childrensdefense.org/

United States Department of Health and Human Services
http://www.dhhs.gov/

Prevent Child Abuse America
http://www.preventchildabuse.org/index.shtml

United States Census Bureau
http://www.census.gov/

WebMD - Night Terrors
http://children.webmd.com/guide/night-terrors

Whole Family - Early Childhood Physical Development
http://www.wholefamily.com/aboutyourkids/child/normal/
physical_development.html

Centers for Disease Control and Prevention - 2009 Swine Flu
http://www.cdc.gov/h1n1flu/qa.htm
30 deaths in children 2-4 years old, 102 deaths in children 5-11 years old

Chapter 8

Cognitive Development in Early Childhood (3 to 6 years)

Chapter Topics		Learning Objectives
What are the major theoretical approaches to cognitive development in early childhood?		Know the major theoretical approaches to cognitive development in early childhood: Piaget's Cognitive Development Theory, Psychometric Approach, Information Processing Approach, Vygotsky's Sociocultural Theory.
What are the factors that influence children's intellectual development?		Recognize the factors that influence intellectual development in early childhood: parenting, socioeconomic status.
What are the characteristics and effects of different day care programs?		Know day care characteristics and the effects of various day care programs: preschool, Montessori preschool, contemporary preschool education, Project Head Start, Kindergarten.
How does language develop in early childhood?		Understand Vygotsky's Sociocultural Theory as it applies to language development in early childhood.
Chapter Summary		

When my grandson, Kenny, pounded his chest on his third birthday and said, "I big and strong," I replied, "Yes, and I think you are bigger and stronger than your daddy." Kenny looked at me with a slight smile and said, "No joking, grandpa." How did Kenny know that I was joking? Answer: His cognitive development, including his greater familiarity with language, enabled him to realize the incongruity between reality (Kenny was not as big and strong as his father) and what I said. Incongruity, of course, is the basis of humor. Kenny also knew that I was joking because of his ability to use *representational thought*—the skill to use images, such as recalling the past and imagining the future, and his knowledge of arbitrary symbols such as words to represent actions or things (Sullivan & Winner, 1993).

Representational thought: Capacity to think about properties of things when they are not present.

In this chapter we will look at the cognitive development of preschoolers (ages 3 to 6 years) through three theoretical approaches: Piaget's preoperational stage, the psychometric approach, with its emphasis on intelligence testing, and the information-processing approach.

Another mission of this chapter is to study the role of various forces in cognitive development. Most importantly, we will study the role of the family. We will then look at how socioeconomic status and day care influence cognitive development, and the role of school, including compensatory education. We will also study the influence of television and technology. Finally, this chapter will address the young child's emerging language skills.

PIAGET'S PREOPERATIONAL STAGE (AGES 2 TO 7)

According to Piaget's Cognitive Development Theory, after the first 2 years of life, Carlos makes the transition from the sensorimotor stage to the preoperational stage. He is now capable of more complex cognitive functioning.

When Sarah was in the sensorimotor stage, she acquired her knowledge through her senses and motor activities. She made considerable progress in her cognitive functions in the sixth (and last) sensorimotor substage by being able to *think* for the first time. By thinking, Piaget means the ability to work with ideas and to solve problems using *symbolic (mental) representation*, which consists of images, words, and pictures, or other configurations to represent real objects.

The Use of Symbols: Mental Representation

On the morning of her third birthday, Sarah bursts into her parents' bedroom holding her birthday present, a teddy bear that had been placed in her bed during the night. Sarah hugs the teddy bear and begins talking to it, but the expression on her face shows that she knows that the teddy bear cannot say anything. Later that morning, Sarah again plays with her teddy bear, treating it like a living person. Sarah is now capable of a form of symbolic thinking known as *mental representation,* where symbols such as images, words, numbers, pictures, and other configurations represent real objects (Morra, 2008). Sarah's symbolic thinking enables her to *pretend* that an inanimate object (the teddy bear) is a living human being with whom she can interact and care for (Harris & Kavanough, 1993; Lillard, 1993). The belief that inanimate objects have lifelike qualities and are capable of action and feeling is called *animism*. In one of Piaget's classic examples of animism, when a 6-year-old boy was asked why a boat floats on water but a little stone sinks, the boy answered, "The boat is more intelligent than the stone" (Piaget, 1929).

Symbolic (mental) representation: The use of images, words, pictures, and other configurations to represent real objects.

Animism: Belief that inanimate objects possess lifelike qualities and are capable of action and feeling.

Deferred imitation:
In Piagetian theory, a person's ability to imitate an action that the person had observed earlier.

Signifier:
A mental image of an object.

Significate:
Piaget's term for an object.

Identity constancy:
The perception that an object remains the same although it may undergo changes in appearance.

That afternoon, while alone in the kitchen, Sarah attempted to clean up a mess she made, just as she saw her mother do earlier that morning. In this instance, Sarah demonstrated another kind of symbolic representation, known as deferred imitation, which is performing a particular act some time after learning or observing it. In *deferred imitation*, children form a mental image or representation of an act or object, and later, when they can no longer see the original stimulus, they imitate the activity or object.

Preoperational children are capable of yet a third kind of mental or symbolic representation: The ability to evoke a symbol without any external cues. This type of thinking occurs when Sarah is involved in symbolic play such as moving her body from side to side and extending her arms, pretending to be driving the family car. Piaget called symbols used in pretend play (e.g., mental image of the car) *signifiers*; the object represented (the car), is called the *significate*. The ability to use symbols to represent something else forms the foundation for the development of reading and writing.

Understanding Identity Constancy

Carlos, aged 5 years, knows that he is the same person when he is outside playing, when he is in bed, or in the bathtub. Carlos also recognizes his father when he is dressed, and when he is in the bathroom wearing his pajamas and has shaving cream on his face. Carlos has achieved a milestone in cognitive development: The understanding of *identity constancy*, a significant component of Piaget's concept of conservation.

Identity constancy was illustrated by Rheta De Vries (1969) by using a trained black cat named Maynard. Masks resembling a dog's, or a rabbit's head, were placed on Maynard, and children between 3 and 6 years of age were asked what they thought the animal was. Then Maynard was unmasked, and the youngsters were questioned again. The youngest children had no knowledge of identity constancy. They thought that Maynard had changed species when he wore the mask. Children 5 and 6 years of age knew that Maynard's identity was always the same despite changes in his appearance. These children had achieved identity constancy. Children at an intermediate age believed that Maynard's name changed when he wore a mask, but not his species, indicating that identity constancy develops gradually.

Understanding Relationships

Piaget assumed that preschoolers are consistently primitive in their logic. Despite this immaturity, Piaget believed that preoperational children are able to understand the relationship between events. For example, although Sarah may not understand why the light comes on when the switch is flicked, she knows that there is a functional relationship between the two events. This ability to predict makes the world more orderly. A predictable and orderly world allows children to make sense out of life (Flavell, 1977).

Limitations of Preoperational Thought

Although 5- and 6-year-olds often impress us with their vocabulary, they are far from being like adults according to Piaget. For instance, the preoperational child's self-centeredness, or egocentrism, is particularly noticeable. Other shortcomings at this developmental stage include centration, irreversibility, and difficulties in classification, seriation, reasoning, and focusing on states (Morra, 2008).

Egocentrism: Difficulty in seeing the world from another person's point of view, typical of children in Piaget's preoperational stage.

Egocentrism

Sarah is waiting for the rain to stop. She wonders why it continues to rain when *she* wants it to stop, a characteristic Piaget called *egocentrism*. Sarah's thinking is focused on herself as the center of the universe and she is unable to understand things from any viewpoint other than her own. Because of their egocentrism, children fail to understand why dinner is not ready when they are hungry, or that anyone has a life that differs from theirs. Furthermore, preoperational children tend to assume that everyone else sees things just as they do.

Piaget demonstrated preoperational children's egocentrism by using a doll and three papier-mâché mountains. Each mountain was distinctively marked, and each had a different size and shape. The children in the study were first familiarized with all vantage points by walking around the display. Next, the children stood on one side of the display while Piaget placed the doll at various vantage points, and then asked the children which of the three mountains the doll could "see." Piaget discovered that children must be at least 7 years of age before they can identify the vantage point of the doll correctly, or imagine what another person is thinking (Piaget & Inhelder, 1967).

However, children are not always egocentric. Vygotsky was the first leading developmentalist to emphasize that young children can think about the world from another person's point of view. They can also be very responsive to the wishes and emotions of others. Further, young children often learn and repeat adult language they hear from their parents or other adults. These premises are part of Vygostsky's sociocultural theory, first introduced in chapter 2.

Centration: A narrow approach to a situation that is characteristic of Piaget's preoperational stage.

Conservation: Piaget's term for a child's ability to realize that some aspects of an object or substance remain unchanged no matter how its form may be altered.

Centration: A Drawback to Conservation

For Piaget, a key feature of preoperational thinking is that children focus their attention on only one salient aspect, or dimension, of a situation to the exclusion of all other features. A 3-year-old will say, "Daddy is older than mommy because daddy is taller than mommy." Such a child reaches this conclusion by *centering* on height and equating it with age.

Piaget illustrated centration in a classic experiment using the concept of *conservation*, the idea that objects remain the same even when there are external changes in shape or arrangement. Children were first shown two identical glasses holding the same amount of liquid, then asked if both glasses held the same amount. Children 4 years of age and older generally answered that both glasses held the same amount. However, Piaget discovered that if he emptied the contents of one glass into a shorter, wider container in full view of the children, then asked the same question, the answer varied according to the age of the children (see Figure 8.1).

Figure 8.1
Conservation of Liquid Quantity *

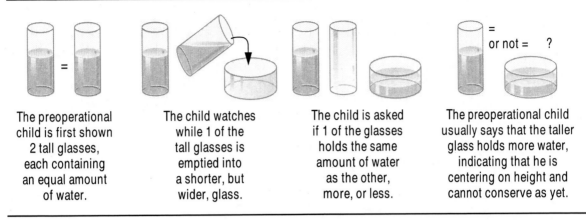

| The preoperational child is first shown 2 tall glasses, each containing an equal amount of water. | The child watches while 1 of the tall glasses is emptied into a shorter, but wider, glass. | The child is asked if 1 of the glasses holds the same amount of water as the other, more, or less. | The preoperational child usually says that the taller glass holds more water, indicating that he is centering on height and cannot conserve as yet. |

* The preoperational child is unable to recognize that quantity—in this case water—remains the same when it is rearranged.

Children younger than 7 would usually insist that one glass held more water than the other. Their identification of the "bigger" glass depended on whether they centered on width or on height, since they were unable to consider both dimensions at once (Piaget, 1972). Most 3- and 4-year-olds centered (focused) their attention on the height of the glasses. This inability to decenter (to take two or more dimensions of a stimulus into account simultaneously) is a major reason why preoperational children are not able to conserve.

Irreversibility

Irreversibility: Piaget's term for the inability to think about how one arrived at the state in which he finds himself; the inability to reverse a particular sequence mentally.

Another reason why preoperational children are unable to conserve is their inability to *reverse* a process mentally. The preoperational child thinks that there is more material when a clay ball is made into a snake because he or she does not understand that if the snake were made into a ball again, he or she would still have the same amount of material that he or she started with. Another example of *irreversibility* is seen when 5-year-old preoperational Carlos says that he has a sister, but denies that his sister has a brother. In Piaget's conservation experiment with two identical glasses and the shorter and wider glass container mentioned above, children who have learned to conserve realize that if the liquid in the short, broad container were poured back into the tall, narrow glass, the original height and width of liquid would be restored. Children who have not mastered conservation cannot perform this mental reversal.

Difficulty in Classification

Classification: Jean Piaget's term for the tendency to group objects into categories or classes on the basis of particular sets of characteristics.

When Jean Piaget and Barbel Inhelder (1959) gave plastic objects of different colors and shapes to children aged about 2½ to 4½ years and told them to "put together those that are alike," the results differed. The younger children made figural collections according to whether the objects appeared to be lines, or circles. However, they failed to sort out the pieces by shape and color. They could not make one pile of red triangles, another of yellow squares, and so on. These children had not yet learned to *classify*, or put things in categories on the basis of one or more common elements such as size, shape, and color. Children of about 4½ years could make partial classifications, that were tentative and inconsistent, skipping capriciously from one type of classification to another.

Typically, they would make one pile of red triangles and circles and another pile of red, blue, and yellow squares.

Difficulty in Seriation (Ordering) Tasks

Seriation: The hierarchy or levels within a classification.

Suppose that we build a staircase pattern with 10 sticks of varying sizes by arranging them according to some dimension such as length, a concept known as *seriation*, shown in . Then, we destroy the arrangement and ask 4-year-old Sarah and her 5-year-old friend, Anna, to reproduce the staircase. What is the result of the girls' efforts? Not too successful. The girls can reproduce the staircase effect only on the side of the longer sticks, not on the shorter side, as shown in Figure 8.3.

This failure indicated to Piaget that most children of 4 and 5 years center on only one end of the staircase at a time. Children of 6 years can reproduce the entire staircase, although with some difficulty. However, if six-year-olds are given extra sticks of varying length to insert in their proper places, they are not able to do so.

The ability to make inserts in a seriation problem requires an understanding of the concept, "bigger than…but smaller than…". As in most other kinds of cognitive development, seriation is a step-by-step process; we must wait for children to mature cognitively before expecting them to proceed to the next step. The ability to make inserts, as shown in Figure 8.4, is not reached until the age of about 7 or 8 years.

Figure 8.2
Piaget's Serial Arrangement of Sticks

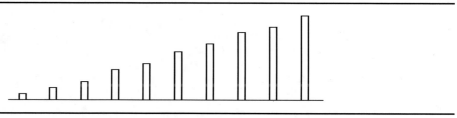

An illustration of the serial arrangement of sticks used by Piaget to determine if children of various ages are able to reproduce this particular order.   Source: Papalia and Olds, 1982.

Figure 8.3
Serial Arrangement Made by 4- and 5-year-olds

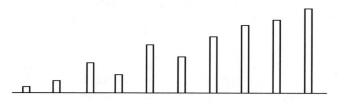

Typical arrangement made by 4- and 5-year-olds when asked to reproduce Figure 8.2. Children of this age are able to make the correct arrangement only on the longer end, showing that they center their attention on only one aspect of the problem.
Source: Papalia and Olds, 1982.

Figure 8.4
Serial Task Requiring Insertion

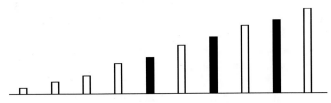

Children are able not only to seriate by the age of 7 or 8 years, they are also able to make insertions (shown in bold black color), a task beyond the ability of the preoperational child. Four- and 5-year-olds are not able to make proper insertions of sticks according to length.   Source: Papalia and Olds, 1982.

Artificialism: The belief that environmental events like snow and rain are human inventions.

Immanent Justice: The belief that breaking a rule always leads to punishment.

Transductive reasoning: A type of reasoning in which connections are made between two specifics where none may exist.

Deductive reasoning: A form of logical reasoning which proceeds from the general to the specific.

Inability to Understand Causality

It has already been mentioned that the preoperational child is able to understand that there is a relationship between flicking the light switch and the light coming on. Preoperational children may also understand that the mother burned her hand when she touched the stove, but they do not know the precise connection (causality) between flicking the light switch and the light coming on, or what caused the injury to their mother's hand. To understand causality, children must be aware that one's actions can be the cause of an effect. According to Piaget (1955; 1962), children begin to master the concept of causality at about 8 years of age. To pinpoint a cause, preoperational children often resort to *artificialism*. For example, a child may believe that leaves fall off trees to keep us warm. Or, the sun shines to make us happy. Another example of artificialism is the preoperational child's thinking that babies are made in factories. In other instances, preoperational children use the concept of *immanent justice* to explain cause, believing that suffering stems from evil behavior. This form of thinking is called *transductive*, which we will discuss next.

Transductive Reasoning

Any adult who has ever tried to reason or argue with a preschool child knows that such efforts are usually fruitless. Why? Because the preoperational child does not use the same logic as the adult. The preoperational child reasons *transductively*, making a connection between two specifics where none may exist. Thus, Carlos might assume that his grandfather's grey hair is causing his grandmother's hair to turn the same color. Or, Carlos might reason that his mother is not home because he is hungry. In another type of transductive reasoning, the child may reason backward from effects to causes, answering the question, "Why is it raining?" by replying, "For me to play in." Or, the child who reasons transductively may draw an inference about a relationship based on a single attribute. For instance, Brian may say that his father will bring a baby home when he returns from the hospital because that is what happened when his mother came home from the hospital with his new baby sister. A preschool child does not reason logically.

Logical reasoning is of two basic types: Deductive and inductive. *Deductive reasoning* proceeds from the general to the specific; "All humans are persons. I am a human. Therefore, I am a person." In deductive reasoning, the person is required to make appropriate conclusions from the information given. Suppose we tell a child the following facts and ask her to make a conclusion:

1. If Carlos hits Sarah, she will cry.
2. Carlos hit Sarah.

The correct conclusion is that Sarah cried. Formal-operational children are able to reach this conclusion. Concrete-operational children will occasionally reach the correct conclusion, not because of their logical thinking, but because of their experience. Preoperational children are not able to reach the correct conclusion. Hence, they are not able to perform mental tasks which require deductive thinking or reasoning which forms the basis for formal mathematics and logic.

Inductive reasoning: A form of logical reasoning that proceeds from the particular to the general.

Inductive reasoning proceeds from the particular to the general, as in this syllogism, "Investigation has shown that marijuana, alcohol, tobacco, and other drugs are harmful to the unborn baby. Therefore we can assume that all drugs are harmful to a baby." Since inductive reasoning is based on assumptions, it does not permit us to draw absolute conclusions. We cannot be certain, for instance, that all people (some 6 billion plus in the world) would get sick if they ate a particular food if everyone in the sample studied (some 200 or 300 people) got sick from eating that food.

Focus on States

Preoperational thought is disconnected, somewhat like static frames on a Power Point presentation. Since preoperational children focus on individual positions, they are not able to explain how a bar, that was originally in an upright position, is now in a horizontal position, even though they saw the bar fall. Preoperational children focus on the initial and final positions only. Similarly, preoperational children are not able to grasp that a car moving toward them will soon be occupying the space they are in. This limitation may be one reason why so many automobile/pedestrian accidents involve young children.

Inability to Distinguish Between Appearance and Reality

One limitation of preoperational children is their inability to see beyond the obvious. For instance, in one study (Friend & Davis, 1993), in which 4-year-olds were presented with a picture of a smiling school-aged girl, the youngsters stated that the girl in the picture was happy, even though they were told that she was sad. Apparently the 4-year-olds were not able to differentiate between the girl's appearance (smiling) and her true feelings (sadness). Most 7-year-olds (typically in the concrete-operational stage) were able to distinguish between the girl's appearance and her feelings. Since cognitive development is quite limited in early childhood, it is no wonder that preoperational children have difficulty in understanding concepts such as death.

Theory of mind: An individual's thoughts about how mental processes work.

A major reason why the 4-year-olds were not able to distinguish between the girl's outward expression (smiling) and her true feelings (sadness) in the example above is an immature theory of mind. *Theory of mind* refers to a person's understanding of the mental world—what a person thinks about phenomena such as thoughts, beliefs, desires, and intentions (Doherty, 2009). Theory of mind has emerged within the last decade as one of the most researched areas in cognitive development. Another area of study of theory of mind is false beliefs. For instance, a 5-year-old thinking that he can touch his thoughts.

Inability to Understand Death

Recall the scenario given in Chapter 7 illustrating a preschooler's response to death: while 4-year-old Carlos was being tucked in bed by his grandmother, she suddenly clutched her chest and fell to the floor. After a few minutes, Carlos tried to wake the grandmother up, but was unsuccessful. Carlos' grandmother had just had a fatal heart attack. Carlos had just witnessed an event which few children now experience, since most people die in a convalescent home or in a hospital.

The next morning, Carlos' parents tried to explain the phenomenon of death. Despite their efforts, Carlos was more concerned about when his grandmother would wake up. Then, he suddenly bolted toward the door. When asked where he was going, he replied casually, "Out to play."

Why was Carlos so nonchalant about his grandmother's death? The answer is that he was unable to comprehend the abstract concept of death. Also, his cognitive development was not sufficiently advanced to understand the irreversibility of death (*i.e.,* that it was not possible to bring the grandmother back to life) (Johnson, 2001). This is why he asked when his grandmother would wake up. Being egocentric, Carlos was unable to understand that death is universal and will eventually happen to him. Hence, Carlos was unable to empathize with his parents, or to think of death as a tragedy. As a preoperational child (Piaget's second cognitive stage), Carlos was also unable to understand two essential attributes of death: That it has a specific cause and that it involves a cessation of bodily functions.

Carlos' 6-year-old cousin, now in the transitional period between preoperational and concrete-operational thinking, has a much better understanding of death. At about 11 years of age, children view death as an adult does—as irreversible and final, and that they too will die some day (Speece & Brent, 1992).

Jessica tells her grandmother, "Don't see me!"

Evaluation of Piaget's Preoperational Stage

Piaget's preoperational stage has many applications, particularly to preschool education. Teachers realize that children can learn only as fast as they can adapt and organize. Pushing children does not work. Unless the children can sort out material and accommodate information (restructure one's cognitive organization to take new information into account), they will learn by rote (repetition without attention to meaning), and will not understand what they have learned.

Are preschoolers capable of causal reasoning? According to Piaget, preschoolers are incapable of understanding cause-and-effect relationships. Piaget believed that this ability appears at about 8 years of age. However, there is considerable evidence that, when the task is sufficiently simplified, preschoolers understand causal relationships to an extent far beyond what Piaget thought typical. For instance, 3-year-old Calros knows that his parent is angry at him because he did something that he wasn't supposed to do. Although this example represents very simple kinds of causal relationships, it clearly indicates that preschoolers have some understanding of causality.

THE PSYCHOMETRIC APPROACH TO MEASURING INTELLIGENCE

As 4-year-old Sarah sits in a room with a strange woman, she is asked to differentiate among a square, a circle, and a triangle, to define words such as "*ball*" and "*bat*", to count up to four objects, and to solve problems such as, "In the daytime it is light; at night it is___."Sarah is also asked to string beads, to build with blocks, and to identify the missing parts of a picture.[1] When Sarah is finished, after about 30 or 40 minutes, the stranger does some calculating and comes up with a number of 100, which represents Sarah's score on the intelligence test she has just taken. Sarah's score of 100 is average, meaning that 50 percent of the children Sarah's age earned lower scores. Stated another way, Sarah performed at the mental age (average age at which normal individuals achieve a particular score on a measure of intelligence) that is equivalent to her chronological age.

The Stanford-Binet Intelligence Scales

Stanford-Binet Intelligence Scale: An individual intelligence test that assesses verbal, nonverbal, quantitative, and memory items of children 2 years old through adult.

Psychometrist: A specialist in administrating tests of mental ability.

Individual ability test: A test that is administered to one individual at a time.

Sarah has just taken the *Stanford-Binet Intelligence Scale*, now in its fifth edition and one of the most popular intelligence tests administered to children (Kaufman, 2009). The "stranger," who administered the test is a psychometrist, a specialist in administering and interpreting tests of mental ability and is typically well-trained in mathematics, statistics, technology, and computer programming. Using the psychometric approach to evaluate Sarah's intelligence, the *pychometrist* assumes that intelligence has several factors that can be measured by standardized tests using existing norms.

An *individual ability test,* The Stanford-Binet Intelligence Scale is organized into two levels extending from 2 years of age through adult. The Stanford-Binet taps four broad areas of mental ability: verbal reasoning, quantitative reasoning, abstract/visual reasoning, and short-term memory. There are also motor tasks such as stringing beads and folding paper into various shapes. The Stanford-Binet Intelligence Scale is widely used for assessment of preschool children's cognitive ability (Kaufman, 2009; Saylor *et al.,* 2000; Sattler, 2008). The assessment can be made when the child is 18 months of age, which makes it possible for the child to receive proper intervention before starting school (Sattler, 2008; Kaufman, 2009; Dezoete, MacArthur, & Tuck, 2003).

Not every individual is given the same problem when taking the Stanford-Binet. Whereas 2-year-olds may be asked to name pictures of familiar objects and answer questions about everyday life, older children may be asked to define words, to solve an abstract problem, and to decipher an unfamiliar code. The examiner determines the appropriate starting place for each child who then proceeds progressively to more difficult questions until he or she fails all the questions. A deviation IQ is assigned according to how many questions the child passed compared with the average number passed by children of the same age.

The Wechsler Preschool and Primary Scale of Intelligence—Revised (WPPSI-III)

The *Wechsler Preschool and Primary Scale of Intelligence—Revised (WPPSI-III)* has two separate levels for ages 2½ to 4 years and 4 to 7 years. Like the Stanford Binet, the WPPSI-III is an individual test given to one child at a time, and takes between 30 minutes to one hour to administer. The WPPSI-III consists of verbal and performance scores as well as a combined score and has been

---

1. The questions and tasks described are paraphrased versions of those on the Stanford-Binet test.

validated for special American preschool children such as those who are autistic or have language disorders.

The verbal subtests of the WPPSI-III are designed to measure a child's vocabulary (e.g., "Tell me what an airplane is."), arithmetic reasoning ("Joan had six donuts. She ate two of her donuts. How many does she have left?"), and word similarities ("Tell me how an *apple* and an *orange* are alike."). The performance tests assess nonverbal skills such as completing pictures, solving mazes, and reproducing geometric designs. The separate verbal and performance scales are useful when testing non English-speaking children. Like the Stanford-Binet, a child's score is calculated on the basis of deviation IQ, an intelligence score obtained by comparing a child's performance with that of other children of his or her age.

Wechsler Preschool and Primary Scale of Intelligence—III: An individual test of the mental development of children from age 2½ years through 7 years.

The McCarthy Scales for Children's Abilities (MSCA)

A test that holds considerable promise as a nondiscriminatory tool is the *McCarthy Scales for Children's Abilities (MSCA)*. The MSCA appears to be particularly suited for the assessment of intelligence of ethnic minority-group children, particularly preschoolers and kindergartners (Kaufman, 1982). A special feature of the test is its apparent nondiscriminatory assessment of Mexican-American children (Mishra, 1981; Valencia, 1983), who comprise a large percentage of minority children in Southwestern United States. The MSCA is a standardized test and measures children's abilities in five areas: verbal, perceptual, memory, motor abilities., and quantitative (Sattler, 2008).

The McCarthy Scales for Children's Abilities: An intelligence test that is apparently nondiscriminatory toward Latino-American children.

The Kaufman Assessment Battery for Children (K-ABC-II)

Another test designed for minority and learning-disabled children is the *Kaufman Assessment Battery for Children (K-ABC-II)*. The test measures several types of information-processing skills as well as achievement in academic subjects. The authors claim that the K-ABC-II is more fair to minority and handicapped children than either the Stanford-Binet or the Wechsler Scales (Kaufman, 2009; Kaufman & Kaufman, 2003). The test attempts to measure how children, 2½ to 12½ years of age solve problems and process information, rather than how much information they have already acquired. For instance, one scale on the K-ABC-II measures simultaneous processing, that is, how well the child integrates various types of information at the same time. An example is forming a cohesive picture—such as deriving meaning from the sequence of words: "You like Jim and Nora," is different from, "Jim and Nora like you." The norms (standardizations) for the test are based on the 2001 census data and include representative proportions of Whites, Blacks, Latinos, Asians, Native Americans, and exceptional children. Figure 8.5 presents additional sample questions from the K-ABC_II.

Kaufman Assessment Battery for Children (K-ABC-II): A culturally fair intelligence test for children, including the learning disabled.

Many psychologists are calling the K-ABC-II a revolutionary IQ test which assesses the intelligence of minority and majority children more realistically. The K-ABC-II is the first major intelligence test to be grounded in information-processing theory. This test reduces IQ differences between Blacks and Whites by about half (to about 7 points) and eliminates any differences in IQs between Latinos and Whites. Hence, the K-ABC-II test attempts to answer a long-standing criticism of traditional intelligence tests—namely, that they discriminate against children who are from poor and/or minority families.

Figure 8.5
Some Questions from the Sampler Set of the K-ABC-II

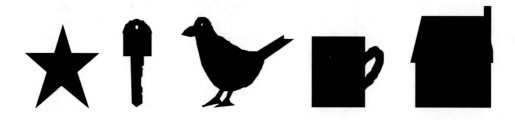

Instructions for all ages: ***Say****, See these pictures? (****Point to pictures****.) I want you to name them.* ***For each picture, ask****, What is this?* ***Correct the child as necessary and repeat until the child associates the appropriate term with each picture. Then proceed to the next sample item.*** *Some sample items from the "revolutionary" IQ test known as the K-ABC-II. This test is designed to be fair to students from all cultures.*

Source: Kaufman and Kaufman, 1983.

Dynamic tests: Tests based on Vygotsky's theories which emphasize potential rather than present achievement. The tests seek to capture the dynamic nature of intelligence.

Zone of proximal development: the range of tasks that are too difficult for children to accomplish alone but they can manage with guidance.

There is an ongoing controversy concerning the use of intelligence tests. Should a single score be used to describe how individuals perform? Are traditional intelligence tests capable of measuring important dimensions of intelligence such as "street smarts," the ability to get along with people? One class of tests that have tried to answer some of these controversies are the *dynamic tests*.

Dynamic tests, which are based on Vygotsky's theories, emphasize a child's capability rather than present achievement. Dynamic tests attempt to demonstrate the dynamic nature of intelligence as an alternative to traditional "static" tests that are up to two years above a child's current level of competence.

A key feature of dynamic tests is the help that the children receive from examiners when they are taking the test. Thus the test provides a learning situation for the child. The difference between the items Sarah can answer alone and the items she can answer with the help from the examiners is called the *zone of proximal development* (ZPD). The ZPD provides an indication of the child's potential rather than his or her current level of competence.

THE INFORMATION-PROCESSING APPROACH TO MEMORY

Although they are only 3 years old, Sarah and Carlos have amazing memories (Bauer, 2007). Carlos repeats things that he heard his father say several days ago, and both children are able to recall considerable information about places that they have visited. How can children remember so much? In other words, what is the nature of their memory? No one knows. However, there are many theoretical models of memory.

Sensory memory: The retention of information that is received through the senses for a brief instant.

Working (short-term) memory: The storage of information for about 30 seconds.

Long-term memory: Permanent memory from past experience.

One theoretical design of memory has been proposed by Richard Atkinson and Richard Shiffrin (1968), which envisions human memory as similar to a computer information-processing system. According to Atkinson and Shiffrin, there are three memory stores through which information must pass to be firmly embedded: *Sensory memory*, *working* (or short-term) *memory*, and *long-term memory.*

Sensory memory receives information through the senses, and is retained for a brief instant. Although the images and sensations disappear quickly, there is usually an awareness of this "input." Working (short-term) memory is the main workplace of the mind. Among other things, it is the seat of conscious thought and reasoning. Usually information is retained in the working-memory store for a period of about 30 seconds, although it can be held slightly longer. Since working memory performs mental computations, it can be thought of as a blackboard on which the mind does its calculations. Long-term memory preserves information for long periods (often throughout life).

In addition to the stores, Atkinson's and Shiffrin's model of memory focuses on control mechanisms which govern the processing of information within the three stores, and the movement of information from one store to another. Three of these control processes are *encoding*, *retention* (storage), and *retrieval.*

Encoding is the process by which sensory input is converted to a mental representation that is remembered more easily. Sometimes, we encode information visually, such as remembering a man's name, Mr. Short, because of his short stature. Or, we might encode information by using an acronym, such as remembering the names of the great lakes of North America (Huron, Ontario, Michigan, Erie, and Superior) by condensing the initial letters to HOMES. This is similar to storing information on a disk and retrieving it when we need to use it. A computer encodes information by translating input (keystrokes) into an electronic language.

Retention: The process of retaining information in memory so that it can be used at a later date.

Retrieval: The process of recovering information stored in memory so that we can be consciously aware of it.

The second step of memory is *retention*, or storage of information. This is similar to a computer storing information on a computer hard drive. However, human memory is much more fragile and less literal than the memory in a computer. For instance, we tend to forget details more easily, and to distort information unlike a computer.

The third step in memory processing, according to Atkinson and Shiffrin, is *retrieval* or remembering. Retrieval is the mental process by which long-term memories are brought into working memory where they become part of the flow of thought.

Now, let's consider the information-processing approach to help us understand two aspects of memory that are of special concern in early childhood: *Recognition* and *recall*. We will also look at a few factors that enhance memory in early childhood, as well as *metamemory*, an individual's knowledge about his or her memory processes.

Metamemory: An individual's knowledge about his or her memory process.

Recognition

Recognition is the ability to realize that you have seen or experienced something before. By age 5, Sarah can recognize meaningful words, people's faces, and places that the family has visited. Recognition ability in preschool children may be measured by showing them a number of objects, putting them away, and showing them again along with new items to determine how many of the original items the children can remember.

Recognition: A retrieval method in which one must identify present stimuli which were presented previously.

Recall: Bringing forth an image or stimulus from memory.

Recall

Recall requires us to get the memory out of storage, such as reproducing a name or a number independently, without any cues. While recognition requires that the item be stored in memory, recall requires both storage and retrieval. A common way of testing recall is to show the child a number of objects, put them away, and then ask the child to name as many of the objects as he or she can.

Most children can recognize better than they can recall. Two-year-old children average about 80 percent correct on nine recognition items, but average about 23 percent on recall. Four-year-olds average about 90 percent correct on recognition, but recall only about 35 percent of the items.

Metamemory. Many investigators believe that a major reason why preschool children can remember better than younger children is the development of metamemory. Metamemory is an individual's knowledge about his or her own memory process. Metamemory begins to develop when the child is about 4 or 5 years of age. An example of metamemory is the child's realization that it is easier to remember something that happened yesterday than an event that occurred last month. Metamemory helps a child to become aware that if instructions for homework are unclear, he or she needs to ask for a clarification, leading to better recall.

Memory Development in Early Childhood

Both recognition and recall improve considerably in early childhood. One possible reason for this progress is that the physical capacity of short-term memory increases. Another possibility is that neurological development enables the child to become more proficient at recognizing items, and at performing operations on them (Bauer, 2007).

There are other reasons that memory improves in early childhood. There is a definite link between memory and attention span, which improves in preschool. Children are most likely to learn things that they pay attention to. The knowledge base is also a factor. It is easier to learn and remember new information if it is related to ideas or information that is already known. If preschoolers are shown a group of items that include a computer, the child who has seen a computer before is more likely to remember it.

Factors that Influence Intellectual Development

Ever since Brian can remember, his parents spent part of every evening reading. There was a library in the home crammed with books, and Brian would continually see his parents going to the public library. When Brian recalls his preschool years, he can remember his mother and father trying to impress him with the importance of a good education. Despite their emphasis on academics, Brian's parents usually had time for him, and they were warm and gentle in their treatment. Could Brian's superior IQ be the result of the high quality of parenting he received?

Relationship of Parenting Style to Children's Intellectual Development

Numerous studies during the past 30 years have indicated a strong link between a child's cognitive development and parenting styles. Young children who score high on intelligence tests and whose IQs increase during the preschool period, tend to have sensitive, warm, encouraging, and loving parents. The parents usually accept their children's behavior, letting them explore and express themselves freely. These parents use reasoning or appeal to their children's feelings, rather than employ harsh, rigid rules to enforce discipline. Recently, worldwide studies have demonstrated that children with higher IQs tend not to be spanked (Strauss, 2001).

Parents contribute to their children's intellectual development by providing stimulating toys and books. Valuing intellectual activities and being a good role model are also important (McCall, 1983). Also, high-quality interaction between parents and children (e.g., the mother and child "connect" with one another by being responsive to each other's cues) can enhance children's cognitive development (Crandell & Hobson, 1999). Children should be given more independence in preschool when they become more competent and are better able to express their needs and interests due to increased language ability (Landry *et al.,* 2000).

There is a close link between Carlos' scores on an intelligence test and his language development in which parents play an important role. If the parents' language is rich and complex, it will stimulate their children's verbal skills. However, the complexity of the parents' speech should be only slightly ahead of their children's current language skill. Language development is enhanced if parents talk about their youngsters' immediate, day-to-day concerns, and if they answer their children's questions elaborately and informatively.

Since women still assume primary responsibility for child care despite recent changes in family structure, it is not surprising that the mother plays a more crucial role in the child's cognitive development than the father. A child's development of object permanence is largely dependent on the extent to which the mother communicates with her baby. The level of a mother's security is also strongly related to her child's intellectual development and language ability. Studies (e.g., Crandall & Hobson, 1999) also show that children of secure mothers demonstrate superior intellectual functioning when compared with children of insecure mothers.

The impact of the father on the preschooler's intellectual development is not clear. There is some evidence that the father can enhance the child's intellectual development if he is warm and loving. There is also some evidence that a child's intellectual development is related to the degree to which the father is attached to his child (Cabrera *et al.,* 2000). The father can have a deleterious effect if he is strict, dogmatic, and authoritarian. The negative influence seems to be greater on daughters than on sons.

One way to look at the relative influence of the mother and father on their child's cognition is to study the child's school achievement when the parents are separated. Children from broken homes tend to show no loss in school achievement following the family breakup if they spend considerable time with both parents (Bisnaire, Firestone, & Ryard, 1990). However, there is a a significant amount of research to indicate that the children are at a higher risk for school failure, drug abuse, teenage pregnancy, delinquency, dropping out of school, and suicide if the absent fathers are not involved with their children.

Socioeconomic status: The grouping of people on the basis of income, occupation, and education.

Socioeconomic Status and Children's Cognitive Development

Socioeconomic status is the grouping of people within a society on the basis of income, occupation, and education. The family's *socioeconomic status* appears to have little effect on intellectual development when the children are very young. For the first few months of life, genes appear to be important determinants of cognitive development (Bayley, 1965). As children grow older, the home's socioeconomic status takes on increasing importance, as underscored in a study by Rosalyn Rubin and Bruce Balow (1979). These researchers used the Bayley Scales of Infant Development to measure the IQs of 1,382 eight-month-old babies from a spectrum of socioeconomic levels. A follow-up study of these children at ages 4 through 9 years found that socioeconomic status was more accurate in predicting later intelligence than early test scores.

The relationship between socioeconomic status and level of intelligence is graphically illustrated in children with mental retardation. Mental retardation is generally defined as an IQ below about 70 to 75 and an impairment in adaptive ability (e.g., self-care, social skills, and personal-social responsibility, such as getting to school or to a job on time), which originated before the age of 18 years. Mental retardation is found more frequently among children from poor families than among children from wealthy families. Furthermore, there has been a proportionate rise in mental retardation among children from poor families during the last couple of decades as the number of families at the poverty level has risen (Wehman, 1997).

The effect of the family's socioeconomic status was also demonstrated by Hilda Knobloch and Benjamin Pasamanick (1963). These investigators found that the IQs of children in middle-class and superior working-class homes increase after infancy. The IQs remain relatively stable for children from average working-class homes, but decline for children from deprived working-class homes.

DAY CARE AND PRESCHOOL IN EARLY CHILDHOOD

Every day, hundreds of thousands of children across America are escorted by their parents (usually the mothers) to a day-care facility or preschool. Children who attend day care usually receive physical care and supervision for the entire day while their parents work. Those who attend preschool receive some form of instruction. Some of these children are enrolled in a special type of preschool known as Montessori, a school where children study in a "prepared environment" by making use of their senses.

When the children are about 5 years old, they usually make a transition from preschool to kindergarten. Many disadvantaged children are enrolled in a compensatory program throughout their preschool years.

Day Care for Preschoolers

Day care: A wide range of facilities for caring for young children, ranging from informal family day care to day-care centers.

Informal family day care: An arrangement in which a group of children is cared for in the home of a nonrelative.

At present, about two-thirds of U.S. mothers with children younger than 6 years are working and have placed their children in some form of *day care* (U.S. Bureau of the Census, 2000). There is a wide range in what is called "day care." The most popular arrangement is *informal family day care,* an arrangement in which a group of children is cared for in the home of a nonrelative. About one quarter of the children enter child care during the first 5 months after birth and about half begin regular child care before they turn 3 years of age (Singer *et al.,* 1998). There are strong arguments on both sides as to whether infants should be placed in day care when they are under a year old (Belsky, 2001).

Usually, day-care centers have at least one trained caregiver and the centers are often licensed and receive public funding. Day-care centers typically offer a wide variety of learning experiences, and the discipline can be strict with a school-like atmosphere. Other day-care facilities do little more than provide custodial service, making certain that the children get their meals and do not get hurt. Regardless of the center's quality, there is usually a long waiting list, with the demand far exceeding available places.

How to Select a Quality Day-Care Center

The first consideration in selecting a day-care center is the physical features which affect the child's safety. Is there adequate fire protection? Is a nurse or doctor available at all times? Another consideration is meals. Are there regular mealtimes? There should also be plenty of toys, and a climbing/crawling area with ramps, tunnels, and swings. The center should be licensed and amenable to the parents staying with their children or visiting unannounced.

The number of children in a day-care center is important. In fact, some authorities claim that the size of the day-care group is the single most important factor. The recommended maximum number of preschool children per staff member is eighteen (Howes, Hillips, & Whitebrook, 1992).

Day-care centers need a highly trained staff who have a warm and attentive relationship with the children. The most effective teachers at day-care centers speak to the children at a level that they can understand. It is also important that day-care providers structure the children's activities by giving them things to do (Stith & Davis, 1984). However, there should be a balance between structured activities and freedom for the children to explore on their own.

Effects of Day Care

During the 1970s, many studies found that placing a child in day care had no harmful effects, and some studies found that there were many benefits.

Benefits of day care. Most investigators have concluded that as long as the day-care center is of high quality it can enhance children's intellectual and social development. Children can be taught positive ways to interact with peers and learn constructive ways to resolve disagreements. If the day-care centers are adequately staffed, children from low-income homes, with poorly educated parents, can make marked gains in language and cognitive development (Lamb, 1998). Other researchers claim that children who derive most benefits from good day care come from disadvantaged, stressed, and dysfunctional homes (Scarr & Eisenberg, 1993).

Negative effects of day care. One concern about day-care is the possibility of children contracting infectious diseases. Large day-care centers have more diseases than smaller ones because the children come in contact with larger numbers of children. Centers that are more prone to infectious diseases include those that allow drop-in children (youngsters who attend occasionally because they are sick) and facilities that employ immigrants from certain countries. Children younger than 3 years of age are especially vulnerable to disease because their immune systems are not fully developed.

Another concern about daycare relates to social development. Children aged 2 to 4 years who are in day care have shown very low rates of response to other children's distress. Although children are capable of empathic response before the age of 2, at one day-care center the children responded to only 26 percent of crying incidents (Phinney, Feshbach, & Farver, 1986). Some researchers (e.g., Lamb, 1998) have indicated that day-care children may be more aggressive, argumentative, and less compliant later.

A consistent criticism of day care is a lack of quality. Too many children spend their days in unsafe facilities under the supervision of inadequately trained caregivers. One study (Galinsky *et al.,* 1994) indicates that the quality of day care—in this case, informal family day care, where children are cared for in someone else's home—is seldom good. This five-year study ranked only 9 percent of informal family day care as good; 56 percent were ranked as adequate, meaning the children are basically safe "but nothing is happening to enhance their growth;" and 35 percent were ranked as inadequate, meaning "a place where we worry about our children being physically harmed."

Preschool

Preschool: A school or nursery designed to give children (usually 3, 4, and 5 years of age) a good start academically before they attend formal school.

Preschool is a school or nursery designed to give children a good start academically before they start formal school. Although the first preschools were established in Europe in the 1700s, public preschools were not established in the United States until 1919. Since these early beginnings, the number of preschools in the United States has increased dramatically. The enrollment has doubled in the last decade despite a 22 percent decline in population of this age group, with an increasing proportion of African-Americans being enrolled. In 2007, approximately 11 million 3-, 4-, and 5-year olds were enrolled in preschools in the United States.

Curriculum. The curriculum offered in preschools is designed to improve social, intellectual, emotional, and motor skills, as well as personal hygiene. Some preschools attempt to meet these goals through a child-centered approach where the teacher provides the children with a variety of activities from which the children select and spend most of the day in free play. Other preschools emphasize academic skills and are teacher-directed. The program is structured and the children are taught academic skills such as numbers, letters, and shapes. A major feature of most preschools is a lack of competition. Preschool programs concentrate on individual improvement rather than on comparison with the performance of other children.

Recently, there has been an increased emphasis on cognitive development in preschool. In particular, preschools that subscribe to the theories of Jean Piaget and Maria Montessori have a strong cognitive orientation (Follari, 2007). Cognitive development is enhanced by providing materials for children to play with, by teaching academic subjects, and by telling stories.

Montessori school: A school where children study in a "prepared environment" by making use of their senses.

Sensitive period: Montessori's term for a period in early childhood when children are able to acquire a great deal of knowledge and skill with very little effort.

Montessori: A child-centered approach. The Montessori method of teaching preschoolers was originally designed for retarded and poor Italian children (Follari, 2007). Today, there are approximately 5,000 Montessori schools in the United States. One reason for this popularity may be the realization that young children are capable of learning more than previously thought, a point emphasized by Dr. Maria Montessori (1870-1952), an Italian physician.

The Montessori method is based on the theory that children under 6 years of age have "a universal, once-in-a-lifetime ability to absorb knowledge from their surroundings just by living" (Follari, 2007; Kahn, 1995). According to Montessori, during preschool, the child's "absorbent mind" enters various sensitive periods when learning is at its maximum. For example, by about 2½ years, the child enters a *sensitive period* for language development which lasts until age 5 or 6. During this period, children extend their vocabularies and improve their grammar. There are also sensitive periods for social and moral development and for rational thinking, according to Montessori.

To take maximum advantage of sensitive periods, close observation is necessary to determine a child's readiness for a particular experience. The Montessori classroom is carefully structured to provide proper equipment and materials so that the children can realize their potential.

An important feature of the Montessori school is sensorial teaching aids, such as rods to teach lengths, cubes to teach size, and bells to teach musical pitch (Follari, 2007). There are also materials to teach history, art, and music. Montessori also tries to foster moral development by emphasizing positive traits such as cooperation, self-control, and patience. The children are allowed to proceed along a mostly individual course, moving at their own pace. The teachers observe the children closely, providing emotional and intellectual help. There is very little direction, and the children can move freely from one activity to another, with the teachers serving mostly as facilitators of learning (Humphryes, 1998). Montessori teachers provide materials for exploration, they usually answer questions, rather than ask them, and they support learning rather than forcing it through direct teaching. The Montessori model is in accord with current developmental research and remains popular in many nations (Lillard, 2005). One of the authors of this book attended a Montessori preschool as a child in Massachusetts.

Evaluation of Preschool

The value of attending preschool has been verified by a number of studies. Early educational intervention is an effective way to prevent learning difficulties and to promote healthy development (Reynolds *et al.*, 2001). Preschool attendance also appears to help prevent delinquency.

Children with preschool education are much more likely to graduate from high school, to enroll in a vocational training program, and to have a job as adults. There are other benefits as well. Children who have been in preschool, perform better on competence tests, and are less likely to be arrested. The young women are less likely to become pregnant.

One study (Schweinhart, Weikart, & Larner, 1986), found that the benefits of preschool depend on the types of programs that are offered. Children who attended a preschool which emphasized learning numbers, letters, and words did better in elementary school than children who attended preschool with a social-emotional emphasis, or a program which fell between the two. However, children who attended preschool with a heavy academic emphasis had the most behavioral problems by the time they were 15 years old. They had lost much of their interest in school and displayed serious social and emotional problems, including vandalism and juvenile delinquency.

Compensatory Preschool Education

Kindergarten resembles real school.

Compensatory preschool education programs: An education program that attempts to make up for early disadvantages of some children. An example of such a program is Project Head Start.

Project Head Start: A compensatory preschool education program funded by the federal government.

Let's consider Sarah's preparation for school. Her mother not only talks to her about school, but also engages Sarah in many of the same activities that are a part of school routine: Holding a conversation, learning nursery rhymes, learning the meaning of words and names of familiar items, and expressing herself with drawing materials, water colors, and toys. Since school routine is already somewhat familiar to Sarah, she looks forward to her new experience of attending school.

Marlene's story is different. Marlene is bilingual with a minimal command of English. Not only will Marlene have difficulty understanding many words, she will also have difficulty relating to situations that the words describe. Furthermore, even if Marlene were to ask for explanations, she would have difficulty understanding what is said because of her deficient listening skills.

For preschool children like Marlene—who often have problems such as poverty, an absent father, and a mother with a pessimistic outlook on the world—concentration is difficult. Most educators and psychologists agree that assistance designed to remedy Marlene's deficiencies should start long before she starts school. To achieve this goal, *compensatory preschool programs* such as Project Head Start have been designed (Follari, 2007; Vinovskis, 2005).

Project Head Start: The War on Poverty

Project Head Start[2] is one of the best known national compensatory preschool education programs for poor children (Vinovskis, 2005). It was initiated by the U.S. Office of Education in 1965 and continues to the present. Head Start—as this program is usually called—is a blanket term covering most federally funded programs and is aimed at preparing children from disadvantaged socioeconomic backgrounds for school. Two basic assumptions of Head Start are that the optimal time for improvement is early in a child's life, and that intelligence is malleable. Currently, about one million poor children, 3 to 5 years of age, are enrolled in Project Head Start programs (Head Start Bureau, 2000) at an annual cost of more than $6 billion dollars.

Goals of Head Start. The initial goals of Head Start are staggering: (1) To provide preschool-aged children from disadvantaged homes enrichment in language and cognitive skills, (2) to help children overcome shyness, and to help them speak and listen effectively, (3) to assist in the development of the children's motor skills and self-image, and (4) to involve parents and the community in these goals, including social services, medical care, and health education for the parents (Vinovskis, 2005). Originally, the children were to receive medical and nutritional assistance. Beginning in the 1970s, many changes were made in Head Start.

First, funding cuts eliminated many of the parent services, and many eligible children cannot be accommodated in the preschool component. Head

---

2.   For more information on Project Head Start, contact Head Start Bureau Chief, Education Service Branch, P.O. Box 1182, Washington, D.C., 20013.

Start still provides disadvantaged young children with preschool experience, social services, and medical and nutritional assistance.

Another change in Head Start since the 1970s is a deemphasis on children's social competence, emotional development, and cultural diversity (Raver & Zigler, 2004). Recently, Head Start has begun to emphasize basic academic skills such as pre-algebra and reading to prepare disadvantaged children to do well in kindergarten (Vinovskis, 2005; Cooper, 1999). Because not all Head Start programs have initiated these changes, there are different offerings at various locations of the program.

Since the goals of Head Start are so varied, most Head Start centers concentrate on a few goals. For example, some programs concentrate on teaching the children how to stay healthy and to socialize with others effectively. Recently, Head Start has emphasized basic academic skills such as reading in order to prepare disadvantaged children to do well in kindergarten (Cooper, 1999). Another type of Head Start program emphasizes academic preparation such as teaching children to connect sounds with letters of the alphabet and written numbers with quantities. This model emphasizes better training for teachers and less emphasis on play and creativity.

Evaluation of Head Start. Although evaluations of Head Start programs have generally been encouraging, about 40 percent of the programs are of poor quality. Another criticism of Head Start is that the gains are usually of short duration, disappearing by about the third grade.

One of the more encouraging early assessments of Head Start was the Head Start Synthesis, Evaluation and Utilization Project, conducted by CSR, a private research firm (Collins & Deloria, 1983). The most promising, consistent, and clear-cut finding to emerge from this study was evidence of substantial gains in children's cognitive and language development. Equally encouraging was the finding that children from the most disadvantaged backgrounds appeared to benefit most. The Head Start Analysis Project, as the CSR study came to be called, also found favorable effects on children's social-emotional development, including curiosity and task orientation. Other studies have also discovered positive results for Head Start. One 20-year study (Lee *et al.*, 1990) showed benefits of Head Start similar to the value of preschool in general. Still other studies show that in Head Start programs that target infants who are "at risk" due to low birth weight, low income, or low parental IQ, the children's intelligence-test scores show increases by as much as nine points by age three and the initial gains in reading and math persist into adulthood (Campbell *et al.*, 2001).

Another positive evaluation of Head Start is the series of follow-up studies conducted by Grover Whitehurst and his colleagues (Whitehurst & Lonigan, 1998; Whitehurst *et al.*, 1999). These investigators found that if children are taught the prerequisites to reading and writing (vocabulary, the letters of the alphabet, the knowledge that the word *bat* begins with the sound "b," for example) in Head Start, their reading and writing skills benefit when they enter regular school.

According to some researchers, the early gains from Head Start are deceptive. Results of a study by the Westinghouse Corporation and Ohio University (Williams & Evans. 1969). indicated that the gains in cognitive skills disappeared by third grade, and students who had not participated in Project Head Start performed at equivalent levels.

The Carolina Abecedarian Project

The Carolina Abecedarian Project: An intensive, highly qualified program designed to test whether early quality intervention can prevent mental retardation and improve academic performance for children from impoverished families.

Recent studies indicate that intervention programs are more effective if they are begun in infancy and last for several years. This was the finding of the *Carolina Abecedarian Project*, an experiment designed to test whether early, intensive, high-quality preschool programs can prevent mental retardation and improve academic performance in children born to impoverished families (Campbell & Ramey, 1994; Ramey & Ramey, 1992).

The Carolina Abecedarian Project identified over 100 African-American infants in families at risk for producing mildly mentally retarded children. All of the families were on welfare, and most were headed by a single parent, the mother, whose IQ was considerably below normal. The project began in the early 1970s when the children were between 3 weeks and 3 months of age. The infants were randomly assigned to an experimental (day-care) group or to a control group. Both groups received the same dietary supplements, social services, and pediatric care.

A unique feature of the experimental group was attendance in a specially constructed child-care center for 8 hours a day, 50 weeks a year, for at least 5 years. The center was of very high quality with a curriculum designed to promote cognitive, language, and social skills. As children grew older there was increased emphasis on language and academic skills. Finally, the mothers received instruction in principles of child development. Children in the control group received no day care.

When the Carolina Abecedarian children entered elementary school, half of the experimental and half of the control children received special intervention for three years until they were 8 years old to compare the impact of early and late intervention. Children in this second experiment were provided with a special resource teacher who introduced supplementary activities which were specially designed for the children's specific needs.

The high-risk experimental children began to outperform the control children by 18 months of age. The average IQ score of the experimental children was at or slightly above the national average from age 3 onward. Children in the control group scored 6 to 17 points below the national average. At age 15, the experimental (early intervention) group maintained a test advantage of five points over their peers in the control group; they were performing better on math and reading achievement tests, and were less likely to repeat a school grade (Ramey & Ramey, 1998). Although the superiority of the experimental group decreased across the school years, some of the positive effects of the intervention were still evident when the subjects were 21 years of age.

The Carolina Abecedarian Project clearly shows that many children who are born into economically disadvantaged families can reach their potential if they receive intensive intervention early. Unfortunately, there are not nearly enough available programs such as The Carolina Abecedarian Project to meet the needs of all children (Children's Defense Fund, 2000).

Kindergarten (A Garden for Children)

Kindergarten: A school or class which serves as a transition between nursery school and first grade.

Kindergarten is a school or class which serves as a transition between nursery school, such as Project Head Start and Montessori schools, and first grade. Yet, kindergarten is considered a part of the elementary school rather than of the preschool system. One reason is that kindergarten teachers are usually certified by the state, while nursery school teachers may not be. Also, the nursery school

Child-centered kindergarten: Education that involves the student's needs and considers the student's physical, cognitive, and social development as well as the children's individual interests and learning styles.

may be located far from the children's homes. Kindergarten, however, is usually located in a neighborhood public school and offers training for the first grade. Over 4 million youngsters are now enrolled in kindergarten; the greater proportion of the children are Caucasian.

Types of kindergarten programs. One type of kindergarten program which has become quite popular is called *child-centered*. Many child-centered programs use Piaget's model that allows children to discover ideas at their own pace and in their own way. The curriculum in the child-centered program involves the whole child and includes activities that develop children's physical, emotional, intellectual, and social powers. Each child follows a program that is tailor-made for him or her. The children's activities include exploring, restructuring, and speaking.

Another type of kindergarten program emphasizes reading. Unfortunately, many of these programs are unsatisfactory because they place too much emphasis on achievement, success, and competition. This tends to stifle the child's curiosity, critical thinking, and creative expression. Children should not only associate reading with fun, they should also associate reading with feelings of success and pride. One way to make reading enjoyable is to refrain from constantly pointing out errors that the child makes.

Some kindergarten programs have a social orientation (Estes, 2004). There is a heavy emphasis on children developing new friends, on helping one another, and on protecting children from physical harm. There is also an emphasis on helping maladjusted children such as those who appear very anxious, who avoid the classroom, and who are overly dependent on teachers, clinging to them and asking for help even when they do not need it.

Guidelines for kindergarten readiness. It is important for children to be ready to enter kindergarten. Children often appear deceptively ready if they are able to use and understand complex sentences and show interest in words, letters, and numbers, but there are other factors to consider.

Children entering kindergarten should possess sufficient visual-motor integration to perform writing activities with considerable ease. They should also have sufficient conceptual development to perform skills such as recognizing colors and coins, counting, and classifying. Impulse control is also important. It may be necessary to delay a child's entry into kindergarten if his or her vision is immature. Preschool children are often farsighted and are not able to see up close as well as they can far away. This problem usually disappears by the time the child enters first grade (Dutton, 2003).

Some studies indicate that one critical guideline for entering kindergaren is the child's age. Studies have found that children who entered school at 6 years of age, instead of at age 5, have superior test scores in reading, language, and mathematics when they reached the first, fourth, and eighth grades. However, other studies (e.g., Graue & DiPerna, 2000) indicate that the younger children make just as much academic progress as older children in the same grade. Nor does delaying a child's entrance into kindergarten appear to enhance his or her self-esteem, peer acceptance, or teacher ratings (Spitzer, Cupp & Parker, 1995).

Television and Technology

Four-year-old Sarah watches television or DVDs an average of 3 hours a day. By the time she is 18 years old, she will have spent more than 3 years watching television (Plowman, Stephen, McPake, 2010; Linn, 2008; Huston, 1992). Sarah often watches educational television or DVDs featuring Sesame Street. She also watches cartoons that have the highest amounts of violence. What effect does television viewing have on children's cognitive and social development? Before we answer this question, let's first look at *Sesame Street*, the most popular educational show for preschoolers and viewed by 85 percent of 3- to 5-year-olds.

Apparently, preschoolers like *Sesame Street's* leisurely episodes with a clear story line (Truglio, 2000). Evaluations of *Sesame Street* during the first and second years of broadcasting showed that children who watched the program the most showed the biggest improvements in cognitive skills such as reciting the letters of the alphabet and in writing their names. The children were better prepared for school and were more interested in its activities. Several studies indicate that the amount that children learn from television depends primarily on the content of the programs that are viewed. For example, children learn more from watching *Sesame Street* than from watching general cartoons. Several studies have found that the academic gains made by preschoolers from watching *Sesame Street* persist into high school (Anderson *et al.,* 2001).

Two other television programs with considerable educational value are *Blue's Clues* and *Mickey Mouse Clubhouse*. These programs are created for a target audience of 2- 5-year olds. *Blue's Clues* presents a live-action host who lives with his animated puppy Blue in an animated house. In each program, Blue presents the host with a problem to be solved by collecting three clues, each marked with Blue's paw print. The audience is invited to participate in the problem-solving with animated characters presenting additional problems to be solved.

One effect of watching *Blue's Clues* is viewers pay closer attention to understand the nature of the problem presented and to work out a solution, when compared with watching entertainment content. Another benefit is the transfer of techniques learned when watching *Blue's Clues* to different television programs.

Preschoolers who view educational television programs such as *Sesame Street* can learn prosocial behavior such as helping others and sharing. Another benefit is extending the horizons of imagination. Children who watch educational television are exposed to hundreds of events that they are unable to experience personally. Research has consistently found that children's development (academic, social, and intellectual) is most likely to be enhanced if the television programs are child-oriented. For instance, in a 3-year study of two cohorts of children (ages 2-5 and 4-7 years), children who viewed child-oriented TV programs performed better on tests of reading, math, vocabulary, and school readiness than children who watched general-audience programs.

Educational television (as well as television in general) has been criticized because the distinction between reality and appearance is not clear enough. This confusion is particularly prevalent among preschoolers. The 4-year-old seldom realizes that the world is not divided into good guys and bad guys, as is often portrayed on television.

A word of caution. More sophisticated research since the 1980s has shown that the effects of viewing television and DVDs are quite uncertain (Plowman, Stephen, McPake, 2010; Linn, 2008). In most recent years, this uncertainty has increased exponentially, especially since the world of technology has exploded in recent decades. We do not know if watching

"Educational TV" enhances academic achievement. Nor can we tell its effects on narrow academic skills such as reading (Reinking & Wu, 1990). While children spend more time with TV, DVDs, and computers, there is concern that their social skills and reading abilities are compromised (Plowman, Stephen, McPake, 2010; Linn, 2008). TV and technology have become baby sitters for children whose parents and caregivers are busy with other tasks. Children are increasingly kept busy with the isolated activity of watching television and DVDs.

A recurring criticism of television is the effect of violence—a criticism of educational programs such as *Sesame Street* as well. Those who oppose violence on TV claim that children imitate what they see. The majority of studies establish a link between children's viewing violence and their aggression (Plowman, Stephen, McPake, 2010; Linn, 2008; Singer & Singer, 2005; Slaby *et al.,* 1995).

The link between the amount of violence children watch on TV and their aggression is reflected in U.S. crime reports. For example, U.S. crime rates have been increasing most rapidly among youth who were in their formative years when children's TV was deregulated in the 1980's and violent programs flooded childhood culture, supporting Albert Bandura's social cognitive theory that children act out what they see (Simmons, Stalsworth, and Wentzel, 1999). As a result of such criticism, Sesame Street has curtailed much of its violence, as well as gender stereotyping (showing more males than females and depicting females as passive, for instance).

The effect of watching violence on television on preschool children was forcefully demonstrated in a series of classic experiments by Albert Bandura and his co-workers (1963). In these experiments, several groups of children watched an adult yell at a large, inflatable "Bobo" doll, hit it on the head with a mallet, throw it across the room, punch it, and abuse the doll in other ways. When the children were given an opportunity to play with the doll, they were much more likely to behave aggressively than other children who had not been exposed to the aggressive model abusing the Bobo doll.

According to Bandura's social cognitive theory, children tend to imitate what they see, regardless whether the phenomenon is real or televised. Bandura's study also demonstrates that parents may inadvertently teach their children to behave aggressively if they punish their children for misbehaving.

Although most studies have concluded that there is a cause-and-effect relationship between watching violence on TV, as well as on other media such as videos, psychoanalysts claim that if children view violence they can release their aggressive instincts in an acceptable manner. This acceptable release of negative emotional energy is related to unconscious conflicts and is called *catharsis*. However, many investigators believe that aggression cannot be curbed through catharsis. In fact, researchers have shown that if children watch televised aggression, their aggressive behavior increases.

Catharsis: The psychoanalytic notion that the acceptable release of some negative tendencies can serve a purging function.

LANGUAGE IN EARLY CHILDHOOD

Three-year-old Sarah is frantically trying to get her mother's attention. Over and over again she says, "Dylan hitted me, Dylan hitted me." Brian, also aged 3 years, is carrying on a conversation with his father. He seldom interrupts his father and seems to understand that his father does not agree with him. Here are two illustrations of children's language ability in preschool: Sarah shows us that she can construct her own grammatical rules—even though they are wrong; Brian demonstrates that preschoolers are able to carry on a conversation while taking another person's perspective. Let's look at language development in early childhood a little closer.

Vocabulary Development

By age 3, Sarah has a vocabulary of about 900 words. By her fifth birthday, Sarah will have amassed a vocabulary of more than 2,000 words. By her sixth birthday, her vocabulary will have grown to 10,000 words (Anglin, 1993).

Although preschoolers make large gains in vocabulary, they still become confused, particularly if the words express different dimensions of a particular phenomenon (Shulman & Capone, 2010). Three-year-olds will often confuse simple relationship words such as "less" and "more." By about 3½ years of age, children begin to realize that "more" refers to the greater of two amounts. They can readily understand "more" when it refers to countable objects (pennies, blocks), but have difficulties when it refers to uncountable quantities (clay and sand) (Gathercole, 1985). By about age 4½, children can use "more" accurately with both countable and mass quantities. Similarly, children master other adjective pairs little by little. In some instances, even when children can use an adjective pair such as "big-small" correctly, they may still use it in place of more specific adjective pairs such as "long-short," "thick-thin," and "high-low." By about age 6, many of these confusions disappear. This progress is due largely to the child's cognitive development.

Children are more likely to learn new words if they are asked questions about a story that is read to them than if the story is simply read to them and no questions are asked (Shulman & Capone, 2010). Children should be questioned about the names in a story and asked to describe pictures in a book that is read to them. Also, the more time preschool children spend watching educational programs such as *Sesame Street*, the more their vocabulary improves.

Pronunciation

We can gauge a preschooler's language development by his or her word pronunciation. Children learn pronunciation by imitation, picking it up from people with whom they associate. Regardless of their surroundings and their accent, children's pronunciation becomes quite clear in their "mother" tongue by about age 3. Preschoolers also learn that some letters have more than one pronunciation. For example, the letter "a" is pronounced differently in "cat" than in "table" (McGee & Richgels, 2000). By age 5, children pronounce about 90 percent of their words correctly. The remaining 10 percent are not mastered until later childhood or adolescence—in some cases never. For instance, some adults never pronounce the "l" in the word "polka."

Formation of Phrases

Pivot word: A word that can be combined with a variety of other words to produce simple two-word phrases.

We can approximate a child's age by the phrases he or she constructs. At age 3, Carlos uses many *pivot words*, such as "my" and "doggie", key words that children employ to construct two-word phrases. Once Carlos has learned the concept of pivot words, he can construct chains of many related phrases, using utterances such as "*my* doggie," "*my* mommy," "*doggie* go," "*doggie* eat," and so on.

Sentence Formation and Grammar

Shortly after Carlos learns to use *pivot words,* he begins to compose three- and four-word sentences, including subjects and verbs, in his speech, "Where mommy is going?" and "I no go." By age 4, Carlos can rearrange words within a sentence. Rather than saying, "Where mommy is going?," he says, "Where is mommy going?" By this time, Carlos has become adept at expressing himself in more than one way. For instance, on his fourth birthday, Carlos used three different expressions to get one point across: "Get off my blocks!" "Why don't you stay away from my blocks?" and "You're standing on my blocks."

By age 5, Carlos can not only construct sentences of eight to ten words, he also knows which part of a verb to change to indicate tense. When the father is putting his new bicycle together, Carlos might say, "Where does this go?" rather than, "Where do this goes?" (Bradford, 2009; Galambos & Goldin-Meadow, 1990).

Overregularize: An inappropriate extension of the general rules of language to irregular instances, for example, saying, "camed" instead of "came."

An interesting feature of early gains in language is an *increase* in grammatical errors! Two-year-olds make fewer grammatical errors than 4-year-olds. Why? Because the toddler simply repeats what he hears. The 4-year-old makes his own sentences, following certain basic principles of grammar that he has heard. The 4-year-old will often apply the rules too broadly; a phenomenon called *overregularization.* For instance, 4-year-old Sarah says "My teeth hurts" and "I broked my toy," words that she has not heard (Fenson *et al.,* 1994). Sarah doesn't realize that some verbs are irregular and that their past tense is formed by using a different word altogether (e.g., "I am *going...,*" but, "I *went* yesterday"). As the preschool years draw to a close, children use most of the grammatical constructions of their language correctly (Tager-Flusberg, 2000).

Private Speech

Private speech: A person speaking to him- or herself privately either aloud, in a whisper, or silently.

You might have heard children carrying on "conversations" with themselves. *Private speech,* as this form of language is called, helps Sarah to control or monitor her behavior. Thus, the 3-year-old, while shoveling sand, may give herself directions by saying, "No, not there," "Put it there," or "I put that there."

Private speech seems to peak at about ages 5 to 7 years. According to Lev Vygotsky (1934), the Russian psychologist, private speech is a positive form of communication which helps children integrate language with thought and helps them to control their actions. For Vygotsky, thought and speech are independent in early development but join together around the second year of life, when Carlos and Sarah begin to use words to label objects. Private speech is particularly helpful in solving difficult problems. Even adults use private speech from time to time when faced with a seemingly insurmountable task.

Questions about private speech. Although private speech is used universally by young children, there is considerable controversy about its role in child development. This controversy is most forcefully demonstrated by two cognitive developmental giants: Lev Vygotsky and Jean Piaget. For example, whereas Vygotsky argues that private speech is an indicator of a child's cognitive development, Piaget claims that private speech reflects a child's immaturity.

Another disagreement between Vygotsky and Piaget is the source of the drive toward cognitive development. Piaget says that the drive comes from within the child. Vygotsky says that cognitive development is the result of spoken interaction between a child and his or her teacher, parent, or peer which results in private speech, an intermediate step in cognitive development. Piaget says that spoken interaction between a child and an adult or more knowledgeable peer hinders a child's cognitive development. He says that, "Every time we teach a child something, we prevent him from discovering it on his own." Research tends to support Vygotsky (Berk, 1994).

From Private, Egocentric Speech to Social Speech

If we listen to 22-month-old Sarah's speech, we note that it is self-centered, or egocentric. Being egocentric, Sarah is aware only of her own feelings and has little knowledge of the world outside her needs and thoughts. She centers her universe on herself, so that her language consists mainly of personal pronouns ("*me* too," "*I* like you," and "give *me*"). Despite this self-centeredness, there are a few attempts to engage others in a conversation called *social speech*, where language is intended to be understood by a listener.

Social speech: Language that is intended to be understood by a listener.

By about age 4, children's speech becomes more social. Youngsters this age take turns listening and talking and refraining from interrupting the conversational partner. Many 3- and 4-year-olds realize that others may have a point of view different from theirs. This is in contrast to Piaget's claim that egocentric speech is not replaced by socialized speech until age 6 or 7 years (Piaget, 1926).

Caregivers can encourage their children's language development in a variety of ways. The children can be provided with language-rich play in which they are required to follow verbal directions. Storybook reading also helps the child with his or her language, particularly if the adults engage the preschoolers in discussions and interpretations of the story content. In low socioeconomic homes of a low socioeconomic status, the parents often need training in how to get their youngsters to interact with books. Often, these parents need to be provided with children's books as well (High *et al.,* 2000).

Individual Differences in Language Development

One reason for language differences is gender (Bradford, 2009). Girls mature at a faster rate than boys which promotes earlier development of the left cerebral hemisphere that is largely responsible for language development. Also, a girl's language may advance more quickly because mothers talk more to toddler-aged girls than to boys. Socioeconomic status—which is often related to the level of the parents' education—is another factor in the child's language development. Children from lower socioeconomic homes tend to have smaller vocabularies than those from more affluent homes. Part of this difference is the result of the type of vocabulary that is used in the two types of homes. Families in lower socioeconomic homes tend to use shorter words which are often discipline-oriented such as, "Be quiet" and "Go to bed."

SUMMARY

According to Piaget, children are in the preoperational stage of cognitive development from the age of about 2 to 7. Children are now able to represent objects or events symbolically or through mental representations. Children in the preoperational stage are capable of deferred imitation; they understand identity constancy, and have some understanding of relationships between events. Preoperational children have many limitations. They tend to be egocentric and they are unable to decenter, conserve, reverse, or seriate.

One way of assessing intelligence in early childhood is by using psychometric tests. These include the Stanford-Binet Intelligence Scale and the Wechsler Preschool and Primary Scale of Intelligence—III. Another approach to understanding intellectual development is information processing. This method is useful in understanding recognition and recall.

There are many factors which influence intellectual development. Among these are quality of parenting, socioeconomic status of the family, and language in the home.

Day care is a critical issue in early childhood, since many mothers work. There is considerable controversy about the effects of day care. The best results are obtained from high quality facilities.

There are many types of preschools. Recently, preschools have placed greater emphasis on cognitive skills. A unique type of preschool is Montessori. Compensatory programs, such as Project Head Start, have received mixed reviews. Some studies have indicated both short-term and long-term benefits.

Kindergarten is a transitional stage in the education process. Some guidelines are needed to ensure that children are ready for kindergarten.

Educational television enhances children's cognitive development but there is considerable controversy around watching television and DVDs with regard to social skill development and reading abilities. While some research supports the positive and long lasting effects of watching educational television programming like *Sesame Street*, recent decades have brought increased concern about the violence that is observed in TV and DVDs.

Preschool children make considerable gains in their language development. They make dramatic gains in vocabulary, pronunciation, sentence formation, and grammar. Private speech and egocentric speech diminish, while social speech increases.

IMPORTANT TERMS

Animism
Artificialism
Carolina Abecedarian Project
Catharsis
Centration
Child-centered kindergarten
Classification
Compensatory preschool education
Conservation
Day care
Deductive reasoning
Deferred imitation
Dynamic tests
Early childhood
Egocentrism
Encoding
Identity constancy
Immanent justice
Individual ability test
Inductive reasoning
Infant-directed speech
Informal family day care
Irreversibility
Kaufman Assessment Battery for
    Children (K-ABC-II)
Kindergarten
Logical reasoning
Long-term memory
McCarthy Scales for Children's
    Abilities (MSCA)
Metamemory
Montessori school

Montessori's sensitive period
Neuroscience
Overregularize
Pivot word
Preschool
Preoperational stage
Private speech
Project Head Start
Psychometrist
Recall
Recognition
Representational thought
Retention
Retrieval
Sensitive period
Sensory memory
Seriation
Sesame Street
Significate
Signifier
Social behavior
Social speech
Socioeconomic status
Stanford-Binet Intelligence Scale
Symbolic (mental) representation
Theory of mind
Transductive reasoning
Wechsler Preschool and Primary
    Scale of Intelligence-Revised
    (WPPSI-III)
Working (short-term) memory
Zone of Proximal Development

RELATED RESOURCES

Readings

Anderson, Daniel R. (2001). *Early Childhood Television Viewing and Adolescent Behavior: the Recontact.* Boston: Blackwell Publishers.

Becker, Nettie (2009). *Developing Quality Care for Young Children: How to Turn Early Care Settings into Magical.* Thousand Oaks, Calif.: Corwin Press.

Bers, Marina (2008). *Blocks to Robots: Learning with Technology in the Early Childhood Classroom.* New York: Teachers College Press.
Follari, Lissanna M. (2007). *Foundations and Best practices in Early Childhood education: History, Theories and Approaches to Learning.* Upper Saddle River, N.J.: Pearson/Merrill Prentice Hall.

Leach, Penelope (2009). *Child Care Today: Getting it Right for Everyone* New York: Alfred A. Knopf.

Lillard, Angeline Stoll (2007). *Montessori: The Science Behind the Genius* Oxford; New York: Oxford University Press.

Marsh, Jackie editor (2005). *Popular Culture, New Media and Digital Literacy in Early Childhood.* London; New York: Routledge Falmer.

Zigler, E. & Muenchow, S., (1992). *Head Start: The Inside Story of America's Most Successful Educational Experiment.* New York: Basic Books.

Websites

Pearson - WPPSI-III
http://www.pearsonassessments.com/HAIWEB/Cultures/en-us/
Productdetail.htm?Pid=015-8989-317

Jean Piaget Society: Society for the Study of Knowledge and Development
http://www.piaget.org/index.html

Child Development Institute
http://www.childdevelopmentinfo.com/development/
language_development.shtml

The Noam Chomsky Website
http://www.chomsky.info/

Pearson - Kaufman Assessment Battery for Children
http://psychcorp.pearsonassessments.com/HAIWEB/Cultures/en-us/
Productdetail.htm?Pid=PAa21000&Mode=summary

Pearson - McCarthy's Scales of Children's Abilities
http://www.pearsonassessments.com/HAIWEB/Cultures/en-us/
Productdetail.htm?Pid=015-8188-608&Mode=summary

Early Childhood News - The Role of Technology in Early Childhood Programs
http://www.earlychildhoodnews.com/earlychildhood/
article_view.aspx?ArticleID=302

Chapter 9

Social Emotional Development in Early Childhood (3 to 6 years)

Chapter Topics		Learning Objectives
How do Freud and Erikson explain social emotional development in early childhood?		Understand Freud's and Erikson's theories in the context of social emotional development in early childhood.
What are the terms related to gender role development?		Know the terms related to gender role development: gender, gender concept (or constancy), gender identity, gender typing, gender role stereotyping.
Why do boys have a different gender identity than girls?		Recognize the theories that explain differences in gender identity: psychoanalytic, cognitive developmental, and gender-schema.
How do children develop phobias and aggression?		Understand the developmental process of fear, phobias, and aggression in early childhood.
What factors play a role in a child's social emotional development?		Know the factors that play a role in social emotional development in early childhood: family, culture, television.
What is the role of play and peer relationships in a child's social emotional development?		Be familiar with the theories that describe the role of play and peer relationships in a child's social emotional development.
Chapter summary		

Although Carlos and Sarah are only 5 years old, already there are indications of the kinds of adults they will be. Carlos watches his father closely and tries to be like him, a process Freud called identification. Like his father, Carlos has already shown several signs of aggression.

Sarah identifies more with her mother, rather than with her father. She plays "house" and is often seen feeding her "baby." Compared with Carlos, Sarah tends to excel in verbal ability.

Our goal in this chapter is to study Sarah's and Carlos' psychosocial development. We will first look at Freud's psychosexual theory and then at Erikson's psychosocial theory to learn their perspectives on early childhood. We will also study the development of emotions, fears, and aggression. We will look at various theories to learn how gender roles are developed, including the role played family, culture, and television. Since children's play provides a window into their social emotional development, we will look at various theories of play as well.

FREUD'S PHALLIC STAGE (3 TO 6 YEARS)

Why did 3-year-old Sarah laugh when she saw Carlos run out of the bathroom nude chasing the family cat? The answer? Sarah was intrigued with how Carlos' genitalia differed from hers. For Freud, this is a display of normal interest in the genital area—a curiosity typical of children during the phallic stage, which consists of the Oedipus and Electra complexes, and the development of the superego.

The Oedipus Complex

In chapter 2, we introduced Freud's belief that human beings inherit the predisposition (are biologically programmed) to be erotically attracted to their opposite-gender parents. He believed that this biological heritage increases in intensity when the child is between 4 and 5 years of age (Friedman & Downey, 2000).

You will recall that in Freud's Oedipus complex, boys feel a rivalry with their father for the mother's affection. A boy also develops considerable hostility toward his father out of a desire to have a sexual relationship with his mother. The boy becomes jealous of his father and wants to take the father's place. This rivalry produces a conflict because, on the one hand, the boy has a genuine affection for his father, but on the other hand, he feels hostility and fear.

According to the Oedipus complex, a child of this age is old enough to know that his desire to have his father die is considered bad. He also thinks that his parents know every thought he possesses. He feels guilty about his thoughts and is in constant fear of being punished. The boy's greatest fear is that he will be castrated by his father, an emotion called *castration anxiety*.

In this model, castration anxiety causes a male child to repress his sexual feelings for his mother and his hostility toward his father. Consequently, he stops trying to rival his father and "incorporates" the image of his father. He now attempts to match his behavior to the image of his father, a defense mechanism process called *identification*. Freud also believed that by identifying with his father, a boy is developing a sense of empathy, or the ability to participate in the feelings of another person and to respond accordingly.

Castration anxiety: In Freudian theory, a boy's unconscious fear of losing his genitals as punishment by the father for the boy's sexual attraction to the mother.

Identification: Taking society's standards and values as one's own.

Once a boy begins to take on his father's characteristics, he reduces the chances of being punished by his father and simultaneously takes on some of his father's power. The father's values and moral judgments form the core of the boy's conscience, or superego, and he is able to develop into a healthy, mature adult. This entire process occurs unconsciously according to Freud and is usually completed, or resolved, by the time the child is about 5½ years old.

The Electra Complex

Electra complex: In Freudian theory, a universal conflict in females during the phallic stage when the girl becomes attracted to her father and hostile toward her mother.

Freud says that a process parallel to the Oedipus complex, known as the *Electra complex*, takes place in girls during early childhood. In the Electra complex, a girl sees her mother as a rival for her father's sexual attention. She also resents her mother for for sending her out into the world "ill-equipped" because she lacks a penis. These behaviors, thoughts, and emotions cause fear of losing her mother's love. This conflict is resolved when the girl compromises by having sexual relations (vicariously) *indirectly* with the father by identifying with the mother. This identification also helps the girl to learn about her mother's value system and assists her in the development of a healthy superego.

Development of the Superego

According to Freud, the superego, the child's conscience, controls moral scruples ("Is this right or wrong?"). In other words, the superego is the internal representation of social and traditional values to which the child has been exposed. It is developed primarily by incorporating, or identifying with, the values and ideals held by the parents and other people who have played an important role in the child's early life. The superego is formed primarily when the child is between 3 and 6 years of age. It is unconscious, and controls the child's behavior from within, without the child realizing why he or she thinks or behaves in a particular way.

Ego ideal: The superego's idealized sense of how a person should behave.

Conscience: The part of the superego containing the individual's standards for morally bad behavior, established through punishment.

According to Freud, the superego has two parts: (1) The *ego ideal*, which contains desirable behavior, or "shoulds" (derived from parental identification) against which the worth of the self is measured, and (2) the *conscience*, which contains the "should nots," and for which one is punished or may feel guilty or ashamed. Once children have incorporated the superego, they can control their own behavior without having to rely on other people, particularly their parents.

An Evaluation of Freud's Phallic Stage

Phallocentric bias: A belief that men are superior to women.

Some authorities believe that Freud's greatest weakness was his *phallocentric (masculine) bias* and tremendous emphasis on sex. Freud adopted himself as the norm and then judged women according to this masculine standard. Recently, many psychoanalysts have withdrawn from this emphasis on male superiority and are now valuing the feminine and masculine perspectives.

Many investigators strongly disagree with Freud that the child models his or her behavior after the same-gender parent out of fear, guilt, or anxiety as the Oedipus and Electra complexes suggest. Rather, Freud's critics believe that children imitate "gender-appropriate" behavior because of incentives such as reinforcement and punishment and because of the model's status or value, not because of sexually driven complexes. Boys show a stronger identification with their fathers and display more masculinity when the fathers are warm and

Gender typing: Interests, personality attributes, and behaviors that are classified as "feminine" or "masculine."

nurturant, rather than overlypunitive or threatening. Despite this harsh critique of Freud's phallic stage, we should not overlook his contributions.

Most researchers agree with Freud that the child's *gender typing,* or gender role (interests, personality attributes, and behaviors which are classified as feminine or masculine), occurs largely during the phallic stage. There is also agreement with Freud's view that the father plays an important role in the child's development of "gender-appropriate" behaviors and attitudes. Boys, whose fathers are absent during the phallic stage are often less masculine than boys from father-present homes.

ERIKSON'S CRISIS III: INITIATIVE VERSUS GUILT (AGES 3 TO 6)

Initiative: In Erikson's theory, the child's urge to explore his or her social and physical world.

Although Erikson accepts Freudian concepts such as the Oedipus complex and the central role of the father in a child's gender typing, he is more concerned with the effect of social forces. Erikson believes that social forces play a crucial role in early childhood as children strive to make things happen, set goals, and take leadership, behavior which Erikson calls *initiative*. Initiative involves the child's natural urge to explore his or her social and physical world. Some exploration focuses on the child's gender or color of skin. For example, 5-year-old Carlos may dress up in women's clothing and wear high-heeled shoes. Sarah may base her exploration on ethnicity by painting her face black.

Preschoolers attempt to gain initiative by changing their relationship with their parents. Instead of being totally attached to their parents, as they had been earlier, preschoolers now identify with them. Carlos adopts many of his father's characteristics, (including beliefs, values, and attitudes), an emotional level of learning that goes beyond simple observation and imitation of a model. This change occurs mostly from a "spirit of equality experienced in doing things together" (Erikson, 1950, p. 258).

Preschoolers express initiative in a number of ways, according to Erikson,. They may explore their bodies or play "doctor," taking turns at being a doctor or a patient. The children may create "magic potions" by mixing mud and soap, or they may show initiative by asking questions or asserting their presence.

According to Erikson, the alternative to initiative is guilt. Guilt is the emotion associated with a sense that one has been responsible for an unacceptable thought, fantasy, or action. Guilt occurs when parents make too many demands on the child for self-control. The result is a feeling of helplessness, self-blame, and remorse. According to Erikson, the primary way in which parents risk disrupting their child's resolution of the initiative-versus-guilt complex is by being too controlling and critical.

Evaluation of Erikson's Theory

As a classical psychoanalyst like Freud, Erikson has received some of the same criticisms. One of these criticisms is directed toward Erikson's phallocentric belief that the male is the norm and the ideal by which both genders are judged. Some researchers have questioned whether Erikson's crises reflect different aspects of personality development. Ciaccio (1971), for instance, found that Erikson's first five crises reflect different expressions of the same underlying crisis—the establishment of autonomy—even though traits such as initiative and industry develop in an orderly progression with age. Another criticism of Erikson's theory is its broad scope, making it almost impossible to verify its validity.

On the positive side, Erikson's theory seems to contribute a general outline for healthy socialization and personality development. One major contribution is a demonstration of how the stages of development (eight in all) require the individual to adapt to the social environment by changes in the ego or self. According to Erikson, the ego develops as new demands are continually being placed on it by the social environment.

GENDER-ROLE DEVELOPMENT

The day Sarah was born, her father bought her a wardrobe: A white dress, socks, a pink bonnet, and pink hair bows. When questioned by the shop owner about the recipient of the clothes, her father answered that he was now the proud daddy of a cute baby girl. When Carlos was born, his father reacted quite differently. He remarked on how athletic Carlos looked. He was certain that his new son would become a football player and that he would probably be a punter because of his powerful kicks.

Why do parents react so differently to sons than to daughters? Are there actual differences between boys and girls besides anatomical? Or, are girls and boys treated differently because of the stereotyped ideas we have about what is proper "feminine" and "masculine" behavior? In this section, we will begin by looking at some differences that are commonly seen between boys and girls. We will then attempt to determine the basis for these differences. In particular, we will examine the biological origins of behavior and some theoretical explanations of social influences, such as culture, family, and television.

Explanation of Terms

Before we proceed further, we need to explain some gender terms that will be used repeatedly:

Gender: Refers to sexual identity or to the role attached to biological sex.

Gender is the perception of maleness or femaleness related to one's membership in a given society. *Gender* is often confused with sex, which typically refers to sexual anatomy and sexual behavior (e.g., masturbation and sexual intercourse). In short, gender is the environmental aspect of being male or female, sex is the biological dimension (Galambos, 2004; Hyde, 2004; Matlin, 2004).

Gender concept, or *constancy*, is the idea that one is a boy (or a man) or a girl (or a woman) (almost invariably) forever; the realization that gender is unchangeable.

Gender identity is the acceptance of one's basic biological nature as a male or a female; it is the ability to categorize oneself as a male or a female. Gender identity is independent of whether the person conforms to the cultural and social norms of his or her gender.

Gender typing, or gender-role development (formerly called sex typing or sex-role development), is the process by which a person learns a gender role that is considered appropriate by his or her culture. For example, a preschooler may say that boys should be praised for playing with trucks.

Gender-role stereotyping is an overextension of gender roles, the widely held beliefs about characteristics deemed appropriate for males and females (e.g., "All women are passive") or applying them too rigidly (e.g., "Men are unemotional").

Gender (Male - Female) Differences

In virtually every society studied, clear differences have been found between boys and girls. It should be noted that these differences are not steadfast and perfectly established. However, many consistent differences have been found between boys and girls. A consistent finding is that boys, on the average, are more aggressive both verbally and physically than girls. Boys engage in much more rough-and-tumble play than girls do. Also, boys react differently to their male peers than girls respond to their female peers. When boys try to get their way with male peers, they react by using commands, threats, and physical force. Girls rely on polite requests and persuasion. Boys play more boisterously and fight more often than girls and are more likely than girls to boss other children and to take risks. Boys typically approach potentially dangerous animals more closely than girls do, and climb in dangerous places like ledges.

Another well-established gender difference involves language where girls tend to excel in verbal ability. Mathematical differences are not consistent between boys and girls. For instance, boys do better than girls in algebra. But, girls do just as well in arithmetic and geometry. These cognitive differences show up at about age 10 or 11.

Empathy: The ability to understand how another person is feeling, and to act accordingly.

Many studies have found that girls tend to be more empathic than boys. *Empathy* is the ability to understand how another person is feeling, and to act accordingly. Gender differences in empathy generally appear at about age 4 or 5 years.

Many other gender differences have been noticed as well. Between the ages of 1 and 6 years, boys cry more often than girls, especially when frustrated. Girls comply with demands from adults better and report more fear and anxiety than boys. Also, girls have lower expectations for success, and boys appear to be more peer-oriented than girls at all ages.

Gender differences, such as boys being more aggressive than girls, do not include every individual. For example, there are girls who are more aggressive some boys. However, in any random group of boys and girls, a higher percentage of boys will be aggressive. In rough-and-tumble play, about 20 percent of the boys have higher scores on aggression than any of the girls, whereas the other 80 percent of boys are not very different from girls. It is important to remember that differences among the members of the same gender are usually greater than between the genders.

ORIGIN OF BIOLOGICAL GENDER DIFFERENCES

Those who espouse the biological origin of gender differences point out that males are different from females from the moment of conception. At conception, the one-celled baby receives one X chromosome from the mother and one Y chromosome from the father, if it is destined to be a male; and an XX chromosome pair, if it is destined to be a female. There are no further gender differences until about 5 or 6 weeks after conception, when those destined to be

Androgens: Male sex hormones secreted by the testes of the male and the adrenal glands of the female.

Testosterone: A male sex hormone produced by the testes that promotes the growth of male sexual characteristics.

Estrogen: A group of chemicals similar to hormones such as estradiol and estrone that increase female sexual development.

Androgenized human female: Females with masculinized external sex organs resembling those of a male.

Testicular feminization syndrome: Males with external genitalia resembling those of a female.

males show evidence of male sex hormones. The male sex hormone testosterone—produced mainly by the testes—initiates the formation of male body structures, including male genitalia. Female body structures do not begin to form until the embryo is 11 or 12 weeks old.

At birth, males have a significantly higher level of *androgens* (male sex hormones) including *testosterone,* whereas females have a higher level of *estrogen,* a hormone that increases female sex characteristics. Newborns also show gender differences in the internal reproductive system. Males have a prostate, seminal vesicles, and testes; females possess a vagina, a uterus, ovaries, and fallopian tubes. External genitalia for males include a penis and scrotum; for females, it is the labia and clitoris. There are also differences between the male and the female brains at birth.

Some investigators believe that biological differences between the genders, such as excess androgen and testosterone cause differences in the behavior between males and females. One source of possible clues to the biological origin of human behavior is the study of lower animals.

William Young, Robert Goy, and Charles Phoenix (1964), discovered that if female monkeys are given the male sex hormone testosterone before they are born, they engage in more aggressive play than untreated females. Young and his colleagues also discovered that if pregnant rhesus monkeys were injected with the male hormone testosterone, they had female offspring with malelike external genitalia and a pattern of social behavior that is typically male. The masculinized female offspring often threatened other monkeys, engaged in rough-and-tumble play, and would try to "mount" other monkeys, just as male monkeys do at the beginning of a sexual encounter. Researchers have also found that prolactin (a hormone capable of initiating and sustaining lactation) can cause maternal behavior in virgin female and male animals. But do animal studies tell us what we want to know about people? Here we need to be careful—animals are not people-- but such studies can provide us with clues.

The clearest evidence of the biological origin of gender differences in humans comes from *androgenized human females* who were born with ambiguous external sex organs. The external sex organs were apparently caused by ingestion of an androgen-like (masculinizing) hormone taken by the mothers during their pregnancies to prevent miscarriages (Berenbaum & Snyder, 1995).The hormone was taken at a critical time during the pregnancy when the genitals were developing in the female fetuses. The drug masculinized female fetuses, causing them to be born with a female internal reproductive system and external organs that resembled those of a male (e.g., a large clitoris that looked like a penis and fused labia folds that resembled a scrotum).

Limited evidence shows that a genetic anomaly can cause feminine characteristics in males. Males insensitive to the male hormone androgen may have a condition known as *testicular feminization syndrome*. The external genitalia resemble those of a female and the behavior is often more typical of a female than of a male (American Academy of Pediatrics, 2000). Males with this condition have small testes which usually do not descend and do not produce viable sperm, although victims of the disorder can engage in sexual activity and reach orgasm. There are also several feminine structures such as a normal clitoris and a short vagina, and occasionally a rudimentary uterus. Hence, biological factors, especially hormones, determine a child's gender development before birth (Reiner & Gearhart, 2004).

THEORIES OF THE ORIGIN OF ACQUIRED GENDER DIFFERENCES

Although some gender differences, such as genitalia, are biologically rooted, most behavioral, attitudinal, and cognitive differences appear to be acquired. We shall examine four views which attempt to explain these variations: *Psychoanalytic*, *cognitive-developmental*, and *gender-schema* theories.

Psychoanalytic Theory

As described earlier in this chapter, in psychoanalytic (Freudian) theory, gender roles are learned through identification, which is a strong desire to look, act, and feel like another person of the same gender (Freud, 1921). The process of identification is different for males than for females according to Freud and includes the Oedipus and Electra complexes.

A major problem with Freudian theory, which states that identification with the same-gender parent influences gender typing, is its difficulty of verification. The theory is based on a wide variety of assumptions and is highly biased toward a masculine perspective. Most researchers support the social cognitive theory or the cognitive-developmental theory of gender-role development.

Cognitive-Developmental Views of Gender-Role Acquisition

According to Lawrence Kohlberg (1966; 1969; 1985), the crucial factor in gender-role development is children's ability to categorize themselves as boys or girls. For Kohlberg, realization is a natural corollary of cognitive development. This realization of gender causes Sarah to match her behavior (and thinking) with what society deems important for her gender. For example, 5-year-old Sarah may cross her legs whenever she sits down because she has heard her mother tell her older sisters that is what girls are supposed to do. Thus, Sarah is actively socializing herself (David *et al.*, 2004).

According to Kohlberg, the discovery that the child is a boy or girl is not a simple one-step process. Rather, there are three steps in gender-role aquisition. **Step 1:** *Basic gender identity*. This stage begins at the age of 2 to 3 years when a child is acquiring a distinct sense of self. The child is able to label his or her gender correctly and to identify with other boys or girls, men or women. By their third birthdays, Carlos and Sarah can classify people as male or female and have considerable information about social expectations for the two genders. They may believe that girls are supposed to play with dolls and dress like their mothers, and that boys are supposed to be like their fathers and play with trucks.

Step 2: *Gender stability*. By age 4, children know many of the gender-role stereotypes for adult occupations. They expect women to be teachers and men to be firefighters and police officers. Children of 3 or 4 years of age also begin to develop stereotypes about gender characteristics: "(All) boys are loud, big, aggressive, independent, and competent;" and "Girls are quiet, nurturant, and emotional."

Step 3: *Gender constancy*. Gender constancy occurs at about 7 years when children move from Piaget's preoperational stage to the concrete-operational stage. The child now realizes that gender never changes despite alterations in clothing, activity, or appearance. Carlos knows that he does not become a girl if he plays with dolls. Children who understand gender constancy realize that they will never change: "Once a boy, always a boy (or a man)" and "Once a girl, always a girl (or a woman)."

Cognitive psychologists, like Kohlberg, believe that Carlos' grasp of gender constancy is related to his ability to conserve. Conservation is the ability to realize that quantities such as mass, weight, and volume (in this case genitals) remain unchanged despite changes in external appearance. Carlos realizes that he still has male genitalia even if he undergoes a change in appearance by putting on a dress (Ruble, 2000).

Another cognitive developmental view of gender role acquisition is socially directed cognitive theory based on the work of Albert Bandura and Walter Mischel (1965). According to Bandura and Mischel, gender roles are learned in two basic ways:
- *Direct reinforcement of gender-appropriate behavior*
- *Observational learning and imitation of gender-appropriate behavior*

Boys are reinforced for behaviors such as being tough, assertive, competitive, independent, and strong. They are also encouraged to play with action toys, such as trucks and guns. Girls are reinforced for being gentle, compliant, and staying close to their parents.

Observational learning of gender-appropriate behavior occurs by watching the behavior of same-gender models including parents, siblings, teachers, and peers (Fagot, Rodgers, & Leinbach, 2000). The roles played by different models vary from one culture to another. For instance, in African-American families, grandmothers play a more important role in childrearing than in many other cultures (Gibson, 2002; McAdoo, 2002).

Bem's Gender-Schema Theory

Gender-schema theory: A cognitive organizing structure for information relevant to gender typing.

Sandra Bem (1983; 1993; 1998) has proposed a stage theory of gender-role development which intertwines the cognitive-developmental views. According to Bem, the child's understanding of gender as well as attitudes and behavior which go with each gender can be thought of as a schema (Bauer, 1993). You will recall that schema is a Piagetian term meaning the organization of actions or thoughts into a unified whole or mental construct. An example of a gender schema is an organization of "appropriate" behavior for people on the basis of their gender such as saying that, "Trucks are for boys and dolls are for girls."

According to Bem, gender schemas are learned through observations and participation by the child in many events demonstrating gender-appropriate behavior. Furthermore, Bem purports that the child's gender schema consists of a network of associations embodying the culture's conception of gender roles which guide children in their behavior. The child learns through social experiences what kinds of things are directly associated with each gender, such as "girls play with dolls" and "boys play with trucks." For Bem, gender is a lens through which a person views the world and then decides how he or she should behave (Bem, 1993). To minimize gender-role stereotyping, Bem suggests that parents give boys dolls and give girls trucks to play with. Bem also suggests that children should be exposed to nontraditional occupations, such as a woman who installs cable lines and a man who works in a day-care center.

Bem also believes individuals have an easier time in life if they are more flexible in their views of femininity and masculinity. That is, they can adjust to more situations than the stereotypical male or female who is hindered by constraining images of masculine or feminine behavior. Bem has constructed a list of 60 personal traits including masculine, feminine, and neutral traits to rate one's degree of gender identity in which a person scores high on traits which have traditionally been considered to be masculine   or feminine.

PSYCHOLOGICAL ANDROGYNY: A NEW PERSPECTIVE ON GENDER TYPING

Society has always expected that boys and men should act and think one way, girls and women another. Failure to observe prescribed ways of thinking and behaving according to one's gender could lead to drastic consequences. Students have been expelled from school for not dressing "appropriately" for their gender, and homosexuals have been jailed for sexual acts that are considered to be "lascivious and unnatural." Many people also contend that failure to adhere to customary gender roles leads to psychological and social maladjustments.

Opponents of traditional gender roles claim adherence to a stereotyped way of thinking and behaving may be harmful. They point out that too much masculinity fosters excessive and inappropriate competitiveness, hostility, domination, and insensitivity. Critics argue that highly masculine boys often engage in problem behaviors such as delinquency, drug abuse, and sexual intercourse. Also, highly masculine teenage boys do poorly in school. Too many of them base their manhood on the caliber of gun they carry and on the number of children they have fathered (Sullivan, 1991).

Many psychologists suggest society would be better off if gender roles were more flexible. One suggestion is *psychological androgyny* (Greek *andro*, man; *gyne*, woman). This concept is derived from physical androgyny, in which the individual is a hermaphrodite, possessing physical and psychological characteristics of both the male and the female. Psychological androgyny should not be confused with the popular media concept of androgyny where physical appearance is ambiguous, neither distinctively male nor distinctively female.

Androgynous girls can make independent decisions, they can compete effectively if the need arises, and they can be caring, loving, nurturing, and sociable. Androgynous boys nurture, love, and express emotion. They are also strong, independent, and confident. For child developmentalists, psychological androgyny means a balance within a person of masculine and feminine traits.

Teaching Children to be Androgynous

Sandra Bem suggests that children should be taught early that gender is a biological fact defined by reproductive capacities and anatomy. She emphasizes that parents should stress that genitals, not clothes or behavior, define a person as a girl or a boy. Bem also states that parents need to do considerable interpreting and explaining of gender stereotypes. When reading a fairy tale, parents can point out that not all girls are weak, dependent, or need males to rescue them and that not all boys like to play basketball, nor do all girls like to cook.

Sandra Bem has gone a bit further to discuss gender role identity and has created four "gender role categories" based upon the separate dimensions of masculinity and femininity. According to Bem, a male or a female can be either high or low on the dimensions of masculinity and femininity which results in the four categorizations: *masculine gender role identity, feminine gender role identity, androgynous gender role identity, and undifferentiated gender role identity.*

Psychological androgyny: A balance within an individual of male and female gender characteristics, making it relatively easy for a person to break through the gender stereotypes.

Masculine gender role identity: One who perceives him or herself as possessing traditional masculine characteristics and few feminine characteristics.

Feminine gender role identity: One who perceives him or herself as possessing traditional feminine characteristics and few masculine characteristics.

Androgynous gender role identity: One who perceives him or herself as possessing both traditional masculine and feminine characteristics.

Undifferentiated gender role identity: One who perceives him or herself as lacking both traditional masculine and feminine characteristics.

An Evaluation of the Androgynous Lifestyle

Researchers have yet to determine the full impact of an androgynous gender role. It appears that women (and girls) would benefit more from such a change than men and boys would. Androgyny tends to make people more flexible and competent because they are not constrained to act in accordance with gender-typed expectations. They can be assertive and independent in one instance, and nurturant and passive in another (Davies & Banks, 1992).

THREE ENVIRONMENTAL FACTORS WHICH SHAPE GENDER-ROLE DEVELOPMENT: FAMILY, CULTURE, AND TELEVISION

Since children are not born with ideas about how to behave in relation to their gender, we need to look at environmental factors which are instrumental in shaping gender roles. Three important environmental factors are the family, culture, and television.

Influence of the Family on Gender Roles

The family influences a child's gender role (gender typing) by differences in treatment. Considerable evidence suggests differences in the treatment of boys and girls are particularly large in early childhood (Maccoby, 2003; McHale, Crouter, & Whiteman, 2003). One of the most basic ways in which parents encourage gender-role behavior is by selecting gender-consistent toys (Bowes & Goodnow, 1996). Parents encourage boys to play with masculine toys and to be more physically active. Boys are encouraged to engage in gross motor activity such as climbing, lifting, and running. Both the father and the mother talk differently to their sons than to their daughters (Leaper, Anderson, & Sanders, 1998). However, children might grow up in extremely gender-typed homes, yet as adults, they might work in occupations or be involved in a relationship they never imagined—the boy might work as a nurse's aid or a librarian, the girl might become a police officer (Maccoby, 1998; 2002).

Girls have more freedom in the clothes they wear, the kinds of games they play, and the people they play with (Maccoby & Jacklin, 1974). Parents encourage girls to engage in personal interaction, to be more nurturant, and to be involved in games of pretending and in plays that have domestic themes. Girls are also expected to be gentle, soft-spoken, reliable, and likable (Martin, 1995). Boys are expected to do better in math and sports than girls, while girls are expected to do better than boys in English.

The family constellation also appears to be a factor in gender-role development. Fathers who have two daughters tend to portray a more masculine image than fathers who have a son and a daughter. Exactly why this is so is not known. Nor do we know why adolescent girls who have a sister develop a less feminine pattern of interests than girls who only have brothers.

Gender typing in single-parent families. What happens to the development of a child's gender role when there is only one parent in the family? Albert Bandura's cognitive developmental theory, which emphasizes imitation, mutual parent-child interaction, and identification with the same-gender parent, predicts incomplete gender-role development in single-parent families. Kohlberg's cognitive-developmental theory, which emphasizes the role of intellectual processes and the influence of culture beyond the family, predicts little or no harm when the child is reared by one parent. The development of gender roles seems to depend on the timing of parental separation.

Boys whose fathers leave home when they are in preschool, are more adversely affected than those whose fathers leave after their sons are in regular school. Boys from divorced homes show less masculinity in toy preferences, they play more with females and younger children, and show less independence than male peers from father-present homes. After the first year of divorce, the boy's gender role seems to be affected more adversely than that of the girl's. Most of the studies on gender-role development in single-parent homes have focused on the impact of the father's absence. There is little information on what happens when the mother is absent although maternal employment provides some clues.

Gender-role development and maternal employment. The mother's employment also has an effect on her child's gender-role development. One reason is that the mother's work gives her less opportunity to provide a model of the traditional housewife and mother. When the mother works, the father tends to be more involved in traditional female household duties such as cleaning, child care, and preparing meals, thus presenting a more nontraditional view of gender role than when the mother is not employed.

Research indicates that the effect of the mother's employment is greater on the girl's gender-role development than on the boy's. Daughters of working mothers appear to have higher educational and career aspirations and higher self-esteem compared with their male counterparts (Hoffman, 2000). The girls have higher levels of achievement orientation and take more part in physical activities. Daughters of working mothers are less rigid concerning ideas about gender roles than daughters of nonworking mothers and are more likely to develop egalitarian ideas, believing that both men and women can work outside the home and make important decisions. Sons of working mothers develop traits such as independence and responsibility.

There also appears to be some adverse impact if the mother works. Children of working mothers often show greater dependency, greater attention-seeking, and greater anxiety.

The father's influence on gender-role development. According to the Oedipus complex, the young boy identifies with, or has a strong desire to look, act, and feel like, his father. The identification occurs as a defensive adaptation by the boy to avoid the father's anger for his son wanting his mother for sexual purposes. Other investigators have paid particular attention to the ways that fathers treat sons differently than daughters, for instance, putting more pressure on their sons to achieve than on their daughters (Lytton & Romney, 1991).

Upon first seeing their newborn daughters, fathers tend to emphasize the daughters' beauty and delicacy, whereas, they fuss over their sons' strength and coordination. Fathers are less accepting of their sons' playing with cross-gender toys than of their daughters doing so. The father is more likely to offer his young daughter a truck to play with than to offer his son a doll. Fathers also tend to reward their children for playing with same-gender items and to punish cross-gender play. Fathers are more physical and rougher with their sons compared with mothers. However, the parent's behavior is not always consistent. For example, the father may tell his son not to hit other people, yet hit his son (euphemistically called discipline) for hitting his sister (Holden & Miller, 1999).

The Role of Culture in Gender-Role Development

Every culture has rules and expectations about the activities, attitudes, and social positions that are considered appropriate for males and for females (Best, 2001. Many cultures, including our own, assign a more important status to males than to females. Moreover, in most societies (including our own) men are expected to be aggressive, powerful, and competitive. In male-dominated societies, girls who are "tomboys" are tolerated, whereas males who are "sissies" are rejected and ridiculed.

Margaret Mead's study. The effect of culture on children's gender-role development is illustrated in a classic study by anthropologist Margaret Mead (1963). While studying primitive people in New Guinea, (a South Pacific Island) in 1935, Mead discovered three tribes—the Arapesh, the Mundugumor, and the Tchambuli—with vastly different gender roles. Both men and women in the Arapesh tribe were nonaggressive and exhibited Western feminine temperament. Both men and women were nurturing, caring, and feeling. The men helped other members of the tribe and showed concern about others' needs and feelings.

The Mundugumor tribe were fierce head hunters and cannibals. The men and women were aggressive and dangerous. The women were often brutal and were every bit as violent as some men in our culture. Both men and women were totally uninhibited in their sexual behavior.

The third tribe, the Tchambuli, had reverse gender roles. The Tchambuli women were dominant leaders who fished and manufactured trade goods. The men were passive, emotional, and easily embarrassed. One of their goals was to please women by putting on theatricals.

Mead concluded that the reversals in traditional gender roles found in the New Guinea tribes could not be explained in biological terms. Clearly, the culture appeared to contribute heavily to the different forms of gender-role development.

The Role of Television in Gender-Role Development

Three-year-old Sarah spends about three hours a day watching television. Her favorite program is *Teletubbies* which originated in England and was introduced into the United States in 1998. The program has no plot and the four Teletubbies look like alien babies dressed in neon-colored pajamas who are waddling around looking at flowers, chatting softly to each other in baby talk. Sarah's mother sees no harm in letting her daughter watch the program. In fact, Sarah's mother has read that Teletubbies can help children learn a language easily because they identify with the alien babies (Mulrine, 1998). There has been some controversy surrounding this program and the potential negative influences it may have on gender role development in children.

Sarah's mother knows that television is an especially potent source of gender-role expectations. Unfortunately, about 70 percent of the major characters who initiate any kind of action on TV are men. The men are portrayed as aggressive, active, and competent, while women cook, clean house, care for the children, and try to look beautiful. Since children come to the TV set with preformed attitudes and select programs according to their gender, their stereotyped attitudes are reinforced (Plowman, Stephen & McPake, 2010; Browne, 1998). Consequently, children grow up with the idea that females are passive and their opportunities are limited. Males grow up with the idea that they should be dominant and play to win, be highly active, and display authority.

This direction has changed a bit in recent years to incorporate more gender inclusive roles and less biased depictions of male and female characters. For example, *Dora, the Explorer* is a popular cartoon story about Dora, a brave and adventurous little girl. *Sesame Street*, as described in an earlier chapter, has also incorporated less masculinated roles and information into its programming as well.

FEARS IN EARLY CHILDHOOD

Children develop many new fears between the ages of 2 and 6 years. They are usually most afraid of dogs or other large animals. Almost all preschoolers are afraid of animals, doctors, strange people, loud and strange noises, and falling. Other common forms of fear include public speaking or performance ("stage fright"), eating in front of someone, and using public rest rooms (Kleinknecht, 2000).

Fears of tangible stimuli decline in preschool, while those of intangible stimuli (darkness, monsters, abandonment, and getting lost in a crowd or in a strange place) increase during this period (Bouldin & Pratt, 1998). Girls tend to be more fearful than boys, and children from poorer homes are more fearful than those from middle-class homes.

Why are Children Afraid?

One reason for children's fears is a result of a frightening or a painful experience. The 3-year-old boy who has been confronted by a snarling, barking dog may shudder at the thought of the experience, even though he did not get bitten. Another reason for fears is the inability to distinguish appearance from reality. A father may scare his 3-year-old son when he puts a gorilla costume and mask on, even if the child sees his father dress. Similarly, Halloween can be a terrifying experience for children under 6 years of age. Hence, age is a factor in fear.

In one study (Cantor & Wilson, 1984) in which researchers attempted to determine what types of television stimuli would elicit fear in preschool and elementary school aged children, the younger children reacted with fear to transformations, whereas the older ones did not. Preschoolers were frightened by a physical transformation on television from a man to a green monster shown on "The Incredible Hulk." The older children did not react with fear; They knew that the transformation was superficial. Similarly, a 3-year-old may be petrified at the sight of a "moving" dinosaur on a visit to a museum; his 6-year-old brother may find the whole episode very interesting. Whereas the 3-year-old thinks the dinosaur's movements are genuine, the older boy knows that it's a motor that is moving the dinosaur's legs, and that the "animal" is not real.

Preschool children commonly fear abandonment, particularly when it is precipitated by threats such as the mother saying, "I'm going to leave you, if you don't come now," or by an actual experiences of being left. The fear may reach such abnormal proportions that the children may be afraid to go to bed for fear that they will wake up alone, or, they may crawl out of bed in the middle of the night to check if their parents are still in the house. They may also refuse to go to school.

Phobias

Phobia: An intense, irrational anxiety reaction to a specific situation.

Children 3 to 6 years old may develop an irrational, involuntary fear that is inappropriate to the situation and interferes with normal activities or with their state of well-being (American Psychiatric Association, 1994; Carey, 1990). This type of unrealistic fear is called a *phobia*. Phobias include fear of the dark, high places, mice, and snakes, and a general avoidance of the feared stimulus. Fortunately, many phobias are mild and allow children to function without difficulty.

Panic disorder: An intense fear or anxiety that usually occurs without warning.

In more severe (clinical) types of phobia, called *panic disorder,* the child may have episodes without warning in which there is an overwhelming fear of imminent death, of going insane, or of losing control over things. The child may suffer from heart palpitations, breathlessness, and dizziness or a choking sensation (Barlow, 2001).

Causes of phobias. There are many causes of phobias. Some phobias are closely connected to particular cultures or geographic areas. For instance, fear of ocean storms is more common among people of the Faroe Islands in the North Atlantic. Likewise, fear of hurricanes is more common among those who live in hurricane ravaged areas. For example, Hurricane Katrina ravaged Louisiana in 2005 and created devastating circumstances for thousands of families. It was considered one of the worst natural disasters in U.S. history.

For psychoanalysts, a phobia is the reemergence of a very threatening or anxiety-producing memory. The traumatic experience may appear in disguised form such as a girl who has been sexually molested being afraid of posts because she was tied to the bed post when she was raped. From a psychoanalytic point of view, the girl is not aware of the reason for her fear of posts because the cause of this fear exists in her unconscious.

There is also some evidence that phobias have a biological, possibly hereditary, origin. This is suggested by the fact that identical twins have a higher concordance rate (both twins have phobias more often) than fraternal twins (Lichtenstein & Annas, 2000).

Preventing and Treating Fears

Children's fears can be prevented by avoiding threats such as, "If you're not good, I'll put you in the basement so that the boogie man can get you." Nor should parents threaten to abandon a child if he or she misbehaves. The parents should also avoid ridicule such as, "You're afraid because you're a baby."

Systematic desensitization: A behavior modification model (therapy) where the subject is exposed gradually to a feared object for the purpose of overcoming the fear.

One method that therapists use with some success to treat children's fears is *systematic desensitization* (SDT), a behavior modification model based on the social cognitive theory (Bandura, Grusec, & Menlove, 1976). A key element of SDT is gradual (little by little) exposure to the feared object, while helping the patient remain calm and relaxed. The exposure to the feared object may be through imagery or through actual experience. The goal is to have the subject pair the newly learned relaxed response with the feared (phobic) stimulus. Systematic desensitization has been used successfully in the treatment of a number of anxiety disorders, ranging from fear of spiders and flying to posttraumatic stress disorder (Robbins, 2000). Let's look at an application of SDT.

Using SDT to help children overcome their unrealistic fear of dogs, Albert Bandura and his colleague (Bandura & Menlove, 1968) had children watch a fearless agemate play with a dog. At each stage of treatment, an unafraid child approached the dog closer than before. In the last stage of treatment, the fearless child played with the dog in a closed pen. Finally, after watching the fearless child (model), the phobic children could be coaxed bit by bit to approach the dog and to spend time with it, including feeding the dog and removing the leash.

Systematic desensitization works best if the children practice the approaching techniques over and over again. The principle at work is simple: Fear and relaxation are incompatible. The key is to recondition people so that the feared stimulus elicits relaxation.

One form of medical treatment for panic disorder is antidepressants such as Zoloft (sertraline) which has been approved by the FDA. The treatment period usually lasts from 6 to 9 months. A note of caution: We must always be aware of the side effects of medication given to children. Some adverse side effects of Zoloft include dry mouth, upset stomach, agitation, decreased appetite and suicidal tendencies.

BEHAVIORS IN EARLY CHILDHOOD

One day, while babysitting my 4-year-old grandson Kenny, I studied his activities for an hour. At the beginning of the hour, Kenny was attempting to soothe his sister who had just been frightened by the neighbor's dog. "It's OK, Sarah," Kenny said, as he patted his sister. A few minutes later, Kenny and Sarah got into a fight. After the scuffle, they both watched cartoons on television. At the end of the hour, both children were playing in the front yard. Such behaviors are typical of children in early childhood. Let's look at these behaviors a little closer.

Prosocial Behavior: Helping Others

Adults are sometimes amazed at how helpful and cooperative young children can be. Children as young as 2 ½ or 3 years may try to soothe another child and to offer sympathy and affection. Behavior that benefits other people such as helping, cooperating, sharing, and giving comfort is called *prosocial*.

Prosocial behavior:
Behavior that benefits other people, such as helping, cooperating, sharing, and giving comfort.

Prosocial behavior is often accompanied by empathy, the sharing of another person's emotions and feelings (Ladd, 2005). Empathy is the psychological state that corresponds to prosocial behavior in the same way that sympathy corresponds to helping a person in distress.

Prosocial behavior appears to be consistent in a number of ways. Preschool children who share, help, and cooperate in one situation are likely to do so in another. The consistency also lasts over a period of time. Preschoolers who are highly prosocial, exhibit the same positive traits 5 or 6 years later and tend to be consistently active and self-confident.

Influences on prosocial behavior. There are consistent gender differences in prosocial behavior, with girls being slightly more prosocial than boys. Some investigators suggest that girls are more prosocial because they are expected to be more helpful and sympathetic than males. Others believe that girls are more prosocial because they receive more affection and less punishment.

Age is a factor in the development of prosocial behavior (Ladd, 2005; Eisenberg & Morris, 2004). Whereas 3-year-old Carlos will usually try to help another child who is crying, he will normally not respond to more subtle clues of distress, such as a pained expression. The older child may respond to the slightest of clues. Children become more prosocial as they grow older because they can identify more subtle emotional clues and because they are more aware of adult expectations and approval.

How can parents promote prosocial behavior? Parents can influence prosocial behavior by loving and respecting their children so that they feel secure and confident (Eisenberg *et al.*, 1991). Parents also can set examples by cooperating with neighbors, offering to help others, and empathizing with those in distress. Seeing prosocial behavior modeled in real-life situations is usually more effective than seeing it depicted in films, books, or puppet plays.

Reinforcement of prosocial behavior is also influential. In a classic study, Nathan Azrin and Ogden Lindsley (1956) demonstrated that reinforcement can increase cooperation in young children. The reinforcement can be material (e.g., candy) or social ("You're a good boy for helping Sarah"). However, reinforcement has its drawbacks, particularly for later behavior.

The negative effect of reward on later behavior was demonstrated by Mark Lepper and David Greene (1978). These researchers first rewarded one group of 3- to 5-year-old children for drawing a picture, while children in another group were not rewarded for their drawing. During free play a week or two later, the rewarded children spent half as much time drawing as the unrewarded group. There may also be a decrease in prosocial behavior if the reward is excessive.

Many parents expect their children to behave in loving, cooperative ways automatically. However, parents should actively promote prosocial behavior. Parents who give clear cognitive messages ("You should help McKensie" and "Let Sariya share your candy; She would like to have some") have children who are more prosocial. Hence, parents should emphasize the good in their children's social relationships and provide guidance in, and support for, their children's cooperative and nonconfrontational behavior (Mize & Pettit, 1997).

Some forms of prosocial behavior, such as cooperation, can be increased by training children to adopt a "we," rather than an "I," attitude. Prosocial behavior can also be increased by appealing to the children's pride, to their desire to grow up, and to their concern for others (Eisenberg & Fabes, 1998). as well as seeing models of prosocial behavior on television (Fisch, 2004).

Aggression

Three-year-old Carlos' mother is worried about a recent change in her son's behavior: he has become quite aggressive. The other day he threw dirt in a girl's face, and just this morning, he pushed his brother while trying to retrieve a ball. She wonders if this is normal behavior.

Some aggression is normal in 3-year-olds because they do not have the skill, power, or language to get their way in a less aggressive manner. By age 5 or 6, when the child has gained greater dexterity, strength, and language ability, both *hostile* and *instrumental aggression* decrease. Hostile aggression is aimed at gaining social control over another person and may involve threats by gesture or word, or by actually striking a child to intimidate or persuade. Instrumental aggression usually occurs for the purpose of achieving some goal, such as pushing a child off the swing to use it.

Hostile aggression: Behavior aimed at gaining social control over another person.

Instrumental aggression: Behavior designed to achieve some goal.

Origin of aggression. There are many suspected causes of aggression. Biological factors undoubtedly play a role. The male hormone testosterone may help to explain why males have a tendency toward more aggression than females. Temperament may also have an impact on aggression since irritable and hard-to-soothe infants are more hostile and aggressive in preschool.

Most teachers know that the child who is disciplined the most harshly at home is often the bully in school. Physical punishment may result in high levels of aggression, especially if it is used inconsistently (Stormshak *et al.,* 2000). Destructive sibling rivalry also contributes to a high level of aggression by the early school years (Garcia *et al.,* 2000).

Children often imitate aggressive behavior, even if it is not reinforced. A classic study of unreinforced aggressive imitation by preschoolers was conducted by Albert Bandura and his colleagues (Bandura, Ross, & Ross, 1963). This classic study in the field of child development was coined the "bobo Doll Experiment." Three groups of 3- to 6-year-olds, consisting of 24 children in each group, saw an adult model display one of three different forms of behavior. One group was exposed to a model playing quietly in a corner with toys for 10 minutes. The second group saw the model assemble Tinker Toys for 1 minute, then push, throw, and kick a five-foot inflated doll (Bobo) for the rest of the 10 minutes. Children in the third group saw no model. After the sessions, children who had seen the aggressive model were much more aggressive when they were given a chance to play with toys than those in the other two groups.

Reducing aggression. A variety of techniques has been tried to reduce aggression. Aggression can be reduced by ignoring it. Punishment has also met with some success, but harsh punishment (*e.g.*, spanking, and isolating a child in her or his room for hours) usually causes more problems than it solves. Milder forms of punishment, such as having a child go to his room for a short period of time, can be effective. Situations can be structured in which behaviors, such as cooperation and sharing, are reinforced, causing a decrease in aggression.

Since aggression is frequently caused by frustration, one way to reduce it is to help a child when he or she is frustrated. Some evidence also suggests that children's TV programs should be monitored closely to reduce aggression. In the year 2000, an effort was made to reduce aggression on television by requiring all new televisions sold in the United States with a screen size of 13 inches or larger to include v-chips (a means of controlling violence) as standard equipment. Unfortunately, this requirement has had little publicity and has been minimally complied with (Cantor, 2000).

The key to controlling aggression is prevention. Parents play a most important role. First, parents should provide an appropriate model: Children usually act out what they see. Least aggressive children have parents who are *authoritative*. In this type of childrearing, misbehavior is dealt with by reasoning and by paying attention to the issues, rather than by fear and punishment or by loss of love. The parents are loving and consistent, yet demanding (Ballantine, 2001). They also recognize the child's interests and become directly involved in their child's school activities, such as sports and homework. This involvement helps the child to become more communicative and cooperative (Chen *et al.,* 2000).

Parents who become directly involved in their children's successes and failures are more aware of the kinds of help their child needs. Such parents are more likely to provide teaching and encouragement within what Vygotsky calls

Authoritative parenting style: A type of child rearing in which parents reason with their children and pay attention to the issues in a loving, yet demanding way.

the zone of proximal development, activities that a child is almost able to perform on his or her own or can perform with a little help.

Play

Much of 4-year-old Carlos' daily activity consists of play. Before breakfast, Carlos plays with the family dog, then spends some time in the bathroom making faces at himself in front of a mirror, and then jumps on the living room couch. Once seated for breakfast, Carlos may draw his mother's wrath by playing with his food, tossing it up in the air, and attempting to catch it with his mouth.

After breakfast, Carlos resumes his favorite pastime: playing. He may throw a ball and run after it, chase the birds in the front yard, and jump. All of these activities help Carlos expend his physical and mental energy, and learn about the world around him.

Although many people think of Carlos' play as an idle activity, nothing could be further from the truth. In fact, play is an educational process which helps children learn by means of discovery and exploration (Guldberg, 2009). The child, whose play consists of digging in the garden, may discover that plants have roots through which they receive food. Play also allows children to release aggressive impulses by kicking a ball and not be punished for their behavior. It provides Carlos an opportunity to reverse the role he usually plays in life a timid child, by pretending he is a powerful tiger. Group play gives the child an opportunity to be a leader as well as a follower, a situation that seldom occurs outside of play.

A strong advocate of the importance of children's play was the Russian psychologist Vygotsky (1962). Vygotsky was particularly interested in the symbolic and make-believe value of play such as when Carlos substitutes a stick for a horse and "rides" the stick as if it were a horse. According to Vygotsky, this type of imaginary play should be encouraged by parents because it advances the child's cognitive development, especially creative thought.

Mildred Parten's classic study of children's play. During the 1920s, Mildred Parten (1932) conducted one of the most exhaustive studies of the nature of preschool play. After observing children's play in a nursery, Parten distinguished six kinds of play, ranging from the most nonsocial to the most social, and catalogued the proportion of time the children spent at each type. Parten found that as children grow older, their play becomes more sociable and cooperative (see Table 9.1). At 5 or 6 years of age, the children begin to share things and to take turns ("I'll lend you my red crayons, if you give me your blue ones") and cooperate more by helping one another on projects such as building a house out of sand. Table 9.1 shows Parten's six types of play.

Although Parten's study provided us with broad insights into children's play, today's children are less sociable than those in Parten's study. One reason for this decreased sociability may be the increased sophistication of toys that encourage solitary play.

Culture may also be a factor in determining whether a child plays alone or with other children. In Korean-American preschools where teachers encourage individual academic achievement and task persistence rather than social interaction with other children, Korean-American preschoolers engage in much more solitary play than American preschoolers.

Today's children are different from those in Parten's time in part because they spend more time alone in front of a television or a computer (Guldberg, 2009). The playing habits of today's children have also changed dramatically because of the high divorce rate and the increase in mothers working outside the home.

Table 9.1
Parten's Study of Social Play in Early Childhood

Type and Age of Child	Description
Unoccupied behavior (First 2 years)	The child is apparently not playing but occupies himself with watching anything that happens to be of momentary interest. When there is nothing exciting taking place, the child plays with his own body, gets on and off chairs, stands around, follows the teacher, or sits in one spot, glancing around the room.
Onlooker behavior (First 2 years)	The child spends most of his time watching the other children play. He often talks to the children but does not enter into the play himself.
Solitary independent play (First 2 years)	The child plays alone and independently with toys different from those used by children within speaking distance. He pursues his own activity without reference to what others are doing.
Parallel activity (3 – 4 years)	The child plays independently with toys like those which the children around him are using, but he plays beside, rather than with other children.
Associative play (5 – 6 years)	The child plays with other children. The conversation concerns the common activity; there is a borrowing and loaning of play material; following one another with trains or wagons; mild attempts to control which children may or may not play in the group. All children engage in similar, if not identical, activity.
Cooperative or organized supplementary play (5 – 6 years)	The child plays in a group that is organized for the purpose of making some material product, striving to attain some competitive goal, dramatizing situations of adult and group life, or playing formal games. There is a marked sense of belonging or of not belonging to the group. The control of the group is in the hands of one or two of the members. The efforts of one child are supplemented by those of another.

Source: Adapted from M. Parten (1932).

One type of play that has not changed since Parten's time is gender-stereotypical behavior. Boys and girls spend about three times as much time playing with same-gender peers than with opposite-gender peers just as they did when Parten conducted her research some 80 years ago (Nepl & Murray, 1997). Today's preschool children also enact roles which are stereotypical for their gender in pretend play much as they did when Parten conducted her study. Girls portray the roles of the mother, daughter, wife, baby, and bride; boys tend to assume the roles of father, husband, and policeman. Preschool boys are more competitive than girls. For example, boys tend to play games that have clear winners and losers and then bluster about their skills. Girls tend to play more theatrical games and place very little emphasis on winning. Boys form large competitive groups, whereas girls gather in small groups just as they did during Parten's time.

Major theories explaining the nature and purpose of play are summarized in Box 9.1.

Recent research on play. While today's researchers continue to study children's social play that involves interactions with peers in much the same manner as in Parten's time, they also emphasize the *cognitive* aspect of play. For example, contemporary researchers spend considerable time studying sensorimotor play, such as a 1-year-old's reaction to a toy that makes a noise

Box 9.1: Theories of Play

Most psychologists believe that children's play serves a purpose. Some psychologists believe that a major function of play is its role in advancing the child's cognition. Other psychologists believe that play persists if it is rewarded.

Cognitive Theory of Play

Psychologist Jean Piaget, the main proponent of the cognitive theory of play, sees play as advancing children's cognitive development. During play, children learn about new and complex objects and agents, how to consolidate and enlarge concepts and skills, and how to integrate thinking with action in a relaxed, pleasurable way (Piaget, 1962). Since a child's level of cognition varies from one developmental stage to another, the quality of play varies accordingly. In the preoperational stage, the play is make-believe, involving symbolic representation. Because of the child's egocentricity in this stage, make-believe, or symbolic play, is not generally a social type of play. Also, because of the child's egocentricity, the make-believe is distorted such as thinking that a rock has feeling.

Piaget believed that play provides children with a means of resolving daily conflicts and realizing unsatisfied desires. This can be done symbolically: children who have been beaten, cursed, and shouted at continually relive their lives more satisfactorily through their toys. Freud, Erikson, and Piaget all view play as allowing children an opportunity to make responses they might otherwise be afraid to make for fear of failure or social ostracism. Through the process of assimilation, the child rearranges his or her unpleasant experiences to better suit his or her level of cognitive functioning. Piaget sees the child as repeating pleasant play experiences for the sheer joy the repetition generates.

Learning Theory of Play;

Learning theorists state that rewarded play will persist, though initially all children have similar play patterns. Play varies among cultures and subcultures because certain types of play are rewarded and others are discouraged. The particular types of play that are reinforced depend on the values and behavior that are treasured in that particular society as demonstrated by Roberts and Sutton-Smith.

Roberts and Sutton-Smith (1962) studied three separate societies. They found that (1) in cultures where responsibility and authority are emphasized, children tend to play games of chance in which they can respond to passive roles as players and provide themselves with some hope of escaping from their dull existence; (2) in those societies that value individual achievement or performance, such as American society, children like to play games of physical skill in which they can compete in a more relaxed manner; and (3) in cultures where children are raised to be obedient, they tend to play games of strategy in which they can control others in the game, providing themselves with an opportunity to displace their aggressive tendencies.

when squeezed. Today's researchers also study children's pretend/symbolic (sociodrama) play, such as a 3-year-old "fixing his car" as he strokes the leg of a chair, which he says is his "car."

Today's play therapists are also paying considerable attention to Vygotsky's theory of pretend play. Vygotsky, said pretend play is a cognitive process which creates a zone of proximal development and provides a window into areas of competence that the child is striving to master but which are still out of reach. Hence for Vygotsky, pretend play foreshadows the child's next higher level of mental functioning.

Today's therapists are also using play to determine its representative value such as when the child enacts an important life situation. For instance, in one study, an 8-year-old boy who enjoyed playing hide-and-go-seek with his therapist was "working through" his trauma of being abandoned by his biological mother when he was in preschool. The boy delighted in being found but was threatened when the therapist hid too well for the child to find her, reminding the boy of the time when his mother disappeared and never returned. Therapists have also noticed that depressed children play significantly less, particularly symbolic play, and shift from one type of play to another more often than nondepressed children. According to some investigators, play is always unconsciously purposeful (Landreth, 2000).

Play also provides children with an opportunity to express their feelings. This is often done with the use of inanimate objects such as dolls or trucks. If Marlene says that the doll is sad or that the truck is mad, she may be reflecting her own feelings. Therapists use play as a means of letting children work off frustrations while analyzing their conflicts and coping methods (Drewes, Carey, & Schaefer, 2003)

PEER RELATIONSHIPS

When Sarah and Carlos reach early childhood at about 3 years of age, their social behavior becomes much more reciprocal. They stand closer to their peers than they did before and make frequent eye contact with one another. There is also more attentive listening. Carlos and Sarah also use more attention-getting devices such as calling another child by name, or saying "Hey!" By about 5 or 6 years of age, children's social development becomes more discriminating so that some children are distinctly preferred by their *peers* over other children, a phenomenon called popularity. The term peers is derived from the Latin word "equals" and literally means individuals of approximately the same age and of equal or similar backgrounds.

Popularity with Peers

Peers: Individuals of approximately the same age and background.

Why are some children popular with their peers and others not? Numerous studies have revealed that popular children differ from their nonpopular peers in many ways. Popular children possess skills to make friends, they are not too aggressive, and do not to seek attention as often.

There is a distinct link between children's popularity and parental characteristics. Children who have a warm, positive relationship with their peers have parents with the same characteristics (Isley *et al.,* 1999). Children who are popular and concerned about other children's feelings tend to have mothers with the same traits.

Functions of Peer Relationships

Psychologists point out that peers serve many useful functions in both preschool and in later years (Ladd, 2005). During preschool, peer involvement exposes the child to new attitudes and competencies. Preschoolers begin to see the world differently through interaction with their peers. While dealing with their peers, children learn how to get along with others and how to master aggressive impulses. They also gain a gender-role identity and learn how to empathize with others (Hartup, 1978). If some of their peers have different racial characteristics or are disabled, children learn to make either positive or negative judgments about these differences (Johnson & Johnson, 1980), and they usually act accordingly for years to come.

SUMMARY

In early childhood, children are in Freud's phallic stage of psychosexual development. The Oedipus and Electra complexes are key concepts in Freud's theory. These complexes are conflicts which are resolved when the child identifies with a parent of the same gender. The superego, the child's conscience, develops between the ages of 3 and 6 years.

According to Erik Erikson, the chief developmental crisis in early childhood is initiative versus guilt. The child attempts to gain autonomy by changing his relationship with his parents.

Gender differences are found in every society. This is mostly due to the different roles that males and females are taught. A role incorporating elements of both the male and the female, known as psychological androgyny, is recommended.

The origin of acquired gender differences has been explained by psychoanalytic, cognitive-developmental, and gender-schema theories. Psychoanalytic theory focuses on the identity development of children related to their conflicts with the opposite sex parent. Cognitive-developmental theory purports that there is a link between gender identity and intellectual development and supports the importance of observation and imitation; gender-schema theory combines elements of the cognitive-developmental and the social cognitive theories. Three important factors which influence the development of gender roles are the family, culture, and television. The mother's employment is a factor in the development of gender roles, and the father's influence is also crucial.

Children have many fears in early childhood and they are unable to distinguish appearance from reality. they typically fear loud noises, animals, strange people, abandonment and sometimes develop phobias. Treatment procedures, such as systematic desensitization, have been successful in reducing fears.

Children show prosocial behavior by 3 years of age. The way parents treat their children plays an important role in the children's prosocial and aggressive behavior.

Children's play is an important aspect of their development. Much of a preschooler's play is spent in the company of peers who serve many useful functions.

IMPORTANT TERMS

Androgens
Androgynous gender role
    identity
Androgyny
Androgenized human female
Authoritative parenting
Castration anxiety
Conscience
Ego ideal
Electra complex
Empathy
Erikson's Initiative
Estrogen
Feminine gender role identity
Gender
Gender concept (constancy)
Gender-schema theory
Gender identity
Gender role

Gender-role stereotyping
Gender typing
Hostile aggression
Identification
Initiative
Instrumental aggression
Masculine gender role identity
Panic disorder
Peer
Phallocentric bias
Phobia
Pretend play
Prosocial behavior
Psychological androgyny
Superego
Systematic desensitization
Testosterone
Testicular feminization syndrome
Undifferentiated gender role identity

RELATED RESOURCES

Readings

Blaise, Mindy (2005). *Playing it Straight : Uncovering Gender Discourses in the Early Childhood Classroom,* New York: Routledge.

Evans, Richard I. (1981). *Dialogue with Erik Erikson.*New York: Praeger.

Kulish, Nancy (2008). *A story of Her oOwn : the Female Oedipus Complex Reexamined and Renamed.* Lanham, Md : Jason Aronson.

Marsh, Jackie editor (2005). *Popular Culture, New Media and Digital Literacy in Early Childhood.* London; New York: RoutledgeFalmer.

Parens, Henri (2008). *The Development of Aggression in Early Childhood.* Lanham, MD: Jason Aronson.

Riley, Dave (2007). *Social and Emotional Development : Connecting Science and Practice in Early Childhood Settings.* St. Paul, MN: Redleaf Press.

Saracho, Olivia N. and Spodek, Bernard editors. (2007). *Contemporary Perspectives on Social Learning in Early Childhood Education.* Charlotte, NC: Information Age Pub.

Websites

Institute for Psychoanalytic Training and Research
http://iptar.org/

Jean Piaget Society: Society for the Study of Knowledge and Development
http://www.piaget.org/index.html

Early Childhood News - Fostering Prosocial Behavior in Young Children
http://www.earlychildhoodnews.com/earlychildhood/
article_view.aspx?ArticleID=566

The Child Anxiety Network
http://www.childanxiety.net/Specific_Phobia.htm

Education.com - Television aggression
http://www.education.com/reference/article/television-aggression-creating-monsters/

PART FIVE

MIDDLE CHILDHOOD
(6 TO 12 YEARS)

Chapter 10

Physical Development in Middle Childhood (6 to 12 years)

Chapter Topics		Learning Objectives
What are some causes of variations in height and weight in middle childhood?		Know the factors related to height and weight variations in middle childhood: gender, ethnicity.
What are the causes and effects of childhood obesity?		Understand the genetic and environmental causes of obesity and the physical and psychological effects of childhood obesity.
What are the implications of malnutrition in middle childhood?		Understand the causes and consequences of malnutrition in middle childhood.
What are some of the health problems that exist in middle childhood.		Recognize the various health problems that exist in middle childhood: chronic conditions, vision and hearing problems, heart disease.
What are the gender differences in motor skills in middle childhood?		Understand the gender differences in motor skill development in middle childhood.
Chapter Summary		

Middle childhood: A period of development from about age 6 until 12.

A big event happened two days after Sara's sixth birthday - her first baby tooth fell out! Her lost tooth is one indication that Sara is entering a new phase of development known as *middle childhood*, commonly known as the school years. This period lasts from about age 6 until about age 12 years.

In addition to loss of baby teeth and replacement by permanent teeth, middle childhood is marked by increases in height, weight, and strength. The brain also undergoes change, resulting in more efficient thinking and better motor skills.

Physical development is most rapid in middle childhood in the lower parts of the body, especially in the legs. This accelerated leg growth causes changes in overall appearance.

Children can be quite different physically from one another in middle childhood. One reason for these variations may be heredity. Environmental factors such as illnesses, diet, and exercise also influence physical development, as does obesity.

We saw the importance of good nutrition in early childhood in chapter 7.Nutrition continues to play a major role in middle childhood as well. School-aged children need plenty of nutritious food. The importance of nutrition can be seen by studying malnutrition early in life. Children who are malnourished early in life show physical and psychological deficits in middle childhood as well as in later life.

There are many health and safety concerns in middle childhood. Chronic illness is on the rise in this country. Visual and hearing problems—often associated with psychological difficulties—are common. School-aged children need guidelines for good dental health as inadequate care of teeth is common.

Precursors to heart disease are often found in middle childhood. For example, one factor correlated with later heart disease is Type A behavior, marked by an extremely competitive and achievement-oriented lifestyle. Lastly, injury, most often as a result of car accidents, is the leading cause of death during middle childhood.

Motor development in middle childhood consists mostly of refining skills learned earlier. Handedness is usually overemphasized, often with negative consequences for those children who are left-handed. Left-handedness is misperceived as a negative occurrence.

PHYSICAL GROWTH IN MIDDLE CHILDHOOD (AGES 6 TO 12)

Increases in Height and Weight

The most obvious physical growth in middle childhood is an increase in height and weight (Nurse, 2009). Carlos, an average 6-year-old, is about 46 inches tall and weighs approximately 48 pounds. He is about one-fourth of an inch taller than Sara, and a couple of pounds heavier. By the end of middle childhood, Carlos will reach almost 5 feet and weigh slightly more than 90 pounds. Because of her earlier accelerated growth (pubescent growth spurt), by about age 12 years, Sara will be approximately an inch taller and about 4 pounds heavier than Carlos and will also have begun to mature sexually.

The growth rate slows down in middle childhood. At 6 years of age, children have reached about two-thirds of their adult height. By 12 years of age, boys have reached about 80 percent and girls 90 percent of their adult heights. These ratios are comparable for weight. At age 6 years, Carlos has attained about one-third of his adult weight; Sara about two-fifths. At age 12, Carlos' weight is almost two-thirds of his adult weight; Sara's about four-fifths.

A significant aspect of growth during middle childhood is an increase in strength. This is largely due to concentrated gain in muscle mass. Most boys double their muscular strength during middle childhood, and girls (who do not have as much muscle mass) do become significantly stronger as well (Maccoby, 1980).

Changes in Body Proportions

In accordance with the cephalocaudal principle of development we discussed in Chapter 4 (from head to foot), the head grows much more rapidly in early childhood than the lower parts of the body. In middle childhood, this process is reversed, giving the lower parts of the body—the trunk and the legs—a chance to catch up and grow to near-adult size (Wong *et al.*, 2001). This acceleration in growth makes the school-aged child look tall and thin.

The child's appearance also changes in middle childhood because of accelerated growth of the lower portion of the face, making it longer and thinner. The faster growth causes the eustachian tubes, connecting the middle ears to the throat, to assume a more vertical position, and to drain fluids out of the ear more easily. The result is fewer ear infections in those children who suffer from chronic infections.

Brain Development

If we watch a 6-year-old and a 12-year-old engage in activities such as riding a bike, climbing a ledge, or throwing a ball, the older child is much more skillful. The greater skill possessed by the older child is the result of a better working relationship between the two hemispheres of the brain, a process known as cerebral lateralization. In addition to controlling motor functions, cerebral lateralization also controls psychological functions. For instance, in most individuals, the left hemisphere is more involved in language processing and in the control of the right side of the body. The right side of the brain is involved in processing spatial information, such as drawing three-dimensional shapes. The increase in cerebral lateralization also results in more subtle, coordinated action, and more complex thought. There are other changes in the brain which affect the child's skills and behavior.

Between the ages of 5 and 7, there is a sharp rise in the surface area of the brain's frontal lobes, resulting in more complex thinking. There is also a growth spurt in head circumference, indicating a growth in brain size and in the number of neurons. By about age 9 or 10 years, the brain achieves its adult size in terms of total weight. Myelination (covering of neural fibers with an insulating sheath tissue) also expands in middle childhood, causing an increase in the speed of neural transmissions between different parts of the brain. Another change is the pattern of brain waves. This shift toward more alpha activity, which indicates engaged attention, results in brain function similar to adults.

However, there are significant differences between the brain of the child and the adult. These differences are particularly noticeable in the control of emotion and behavior. In childhood, emotion and behavior are controlled primarily by the amygdala, an almond-shaped collection of nuclei located beneath the temporal lobe. The amygdala controls emotions such as anxiety, anger, and depression. According to neuroscience, the multidisciplinary study of the nervous system and its function, the amygdala also controls behavior such as aggression, ability to get along with peers, and delinquency. When the child enters late adolescence, the control center for emotions and behavior shifts to the prefrontal cortex, located just behind the forehead.

Variations in Physical Growth

If you were to study a group of elementary schoolchildren of the same age, you would probably find considerable differences between the tallest and the shortest children. A child of average height on his seventh birthday would still be within the normal range of height if he did not grow at all for the next two years. This variability continues to widen with age.

One reason for this variation is ethnicity. Variations in normal heights among ethnic groups were vividly illustrated by Howard Meredith (1969) who studied several cultures around the world. Meredith found a range of about 9 inches between the mean heights of tallest and shortest of the same-aged children. The tallest children tended to come from northern and central Europe, eastern Australia, and the United States. The shortest children were mostly from Asia, Oceania (the 20,000 or so islands of the Pacific Ocean), and South America. Although genetics may account for some of these differences, environment also appears to play a crucial role.

Among the environmental factors influencing growth are medical care, nutrition, and sanitation. As living conditions improve, girls tend to start their prepubertal growth spurt (signaling impending sexual maturity) and menarche (first menstrual period) sooner. Finally, children with illnesses, such as recurring colds, ear infections, sore throats, and skin infections tend to be smaller. Chronically sick children also tend to come from economically depressed homes where nutrition and medical care are inadequate.

Due to the large variations in the physical growth of children, researchers are suggesting that separate growth standards be established for different populations. The use of different standards for growth appears to be particularly crucial due to the large influx of Asian families who tend to be smaller than their American counterparts.

ABNORMAL GROWTH

Although the physical development of most children is normal, some children are below their agemates in height and weight. In some instances, there appears to be no genetic, biological, or medical basis for the abnormality.

Deprivation Dwarfism

Deprivation dwarfism. A growth disorder in children between 2 and 15 years of age due to severe emotional deprivation and decreased growth hormone secretion.

Deprivation dwarfism is a failure of the body to grow normally due to a deficiency of the human growth hormone known as somatotropin. The disorder is caused by extreme deprivation of affection or stress, such as family conflict, which leads to disturbed sleeping (Gardner, 1979; Montgomery, Bartley, & Wilkinson, 1997). Since the growth hormone is released during sleep, the child's irregular sleeping patterns result in reduced secretion of the hormone. The disturbance can also be due to injury, disease, or radiation that is used to treat tumors of the middle ear or eye. In some instances, the disturbance can be *idiopathic*, that is, there is no recognizable cause, or the origin is spontaneous.

Idiopathic: A disease without a recognizable cause, or of spontaneous origin.

"Treating" short children. Over recent decades, doctors have attempted to treat growth hormone deficiency by injecting short patients with synthetic growth hormones. However, this practice carries many risks. One problem is a high likelihood of a negative reaction to the drugs. There is also the frightening possibility of someone being artificiallystretched10 or 12 inches beyond his or her genetically designed height (Hindmarsh *et al.,* 1990; Takano *et al.,* 1990). Such error might lead to failed joints and diseases such as cancer (Hintz, 2003). Nevertheless, in 2003, the Food and Drug Administration approved the use of a growth hormone (Humatrope) to treat healthy, short boys whose adult height is predicted to be less than 5 feet 3 inches and girls with a predicted adult height of less than 4 feet 11 inches. The hoped-for gain in height is 1 to 3 inches and the treatment is expected to take several years (Chemaitilly *et al.,* 2003).

Obesity

Obesity: A deviation of at least 20 percent over "ideal" body weight.

Obesity is defined as a deviation from normal weight. It is a medical term describing individuals who are at least 20 percent over their "ideal" weight for height, age, gender and body type (Crouse, 2010; Steinburg, 1996). More than one out of every four children between the ages of 6 and 11 is obese (Moran & Arizona, 1999). An alarming statistic is the recent increase in the rate of obesity in the American population, from 15 to 20 percent during the 20-year-period from 1980 to 2000 (U.S. Department of Health and Human Services 2000c)

Superobesity: A weight at the 95th percentile.

Another alarming statistic is the recent increase in *superobesity*, a weight at the 95th percentile (95 percent of children of the same age and gender weigh less). During the last three decades, superobesity has soared by 98 percent among school-aged children (Crouse, 2010; Gazzinga & Burns, 1993).

Effects of Obesity

Obesity has a range of physical and psychological consequences. This disorder is significant because of its long-term consequences, since obese children tend to become overweight adults and experience serious health conditions (Santrock, 2005; Whitaker *et al.,* 1997). Also, the obese child faces risks of serious medical complications such as elevated cholesterol levels, diabetes (the number one disease associated with obesity), high blood pressure, and heart, liver, and kidney disease. Fat found in the upper body brings greater risk than does fat carried in the lower part of the body. Obesity is more dangerous for the girl than for the boy. Being overweight as a girl can bring on early menstruation which is also a risk factor for breast cancer.

Adverse psychological effects of obesity include a negative self-image and difficulty making friends with agemates, who may ridicule the overweight child. Negative peer reaction can result in low self-esteem and depression (Lumeng *et al.*, 2003). Obese children frequently have difficulty in school. Overweight children of the most concern are the severely obese, or the superobese. Their quality of life, including psychological and social adjustment, perceived competency, self-respect, and school functioning, is similar to that of children diagnosed with cancer (Schwimmer, Burwinkle, & Varni, 2003).

What Causes Obesity?

If you were to ask your friends what causes obesity, many of them would likely answer, "eating too much." While there appears to be some truth to this simple answer (Cunningham, 1990), overweight children don't always eat more. Furthermore, children can become obese by eating as few as 50 extra calories each day. There appear to be three main contributors to obesity: genetics, environment, and a consequential combination of the two.

Genetic predisposition. There is substantial evidence that obesity has a genetic component (Stunkard *et al.*, 1990). In one study conducted over several decades (Chen *et al.*, 2004), the investigators linked specific genes and their chromosomal locations to body mass measurements (obesity). Children clearly seem to inherit a tendency toward fatness, so that every child is not equal risk. If both parents are obese, there is a 50 percent chance that their obese infants will become obese adults. Only 20 percent of obese infants with parents of normal weight become obese adults.

Environmental factors. Some researchers believe that the cause of obesity is lack of exercise. According to this theory, obesity is the result of not enough energy expended, rather than higher-than-average caloric intake.

A related environmental factor that appears to contribute to obesity is technology (e.g. television, computers, Ipods, and hand held video games) (Giammattei *et al.*, 2003). Children who watch television and play with computers consistently for long periods of time tend to exercise less and eat more (Robinson, 1998). Perhaps even more damaging is the fact that children who watch a lot of television tend to eat foods that are advertised on TV, mostly junk food. These foods are high in fats calories, salt, sugar, and cholesterol, all of which contribute significantly to obesity (McGuire & Beerman, 2010; Robinson & Killer, 1995; Sallis, 1993).

Combination of genetic and environmental factors. Since body weight is regulated by numerous mechanisms that maintain a balance between energy intake and energy expenditure, many researchers believe that obesity is the result of an interaction between genetic and environmental factors. Environmental circumstances, such as fast-foods and excessive TV viewing and computer interaction, allow the fullest impact of genetic traits on obesity. Caregivers should look beyond the weight itself and consider emotional factors. Is the child depressed? Does the child feel rejected?

Treating Childhood Obesity

The first thing to remember in treating obesity is the principle of modern medicine, "First, do no harm." But harm has been done in the treatment of obesity by exploiting well-intentioned health messages. For example, cigarette advertisers have exploited the belief that smoking is an effective slimming agent. Also, the dietary guidelines during the latter half of the 20th century have resulted in a rise in disordered eating such as anorexia nervosa (O'Dea, 2005). Society continually portrays exploitive and unrealistic images of thinness and health. In turn, these messages damage self-esteem and self-confidence of those who do not meet the unrealistic ideals.

Timing is important in the treatment of obese children. It is critical to address health and weight at the first sign there is a problem. The longer a child remains overweight, the greater the probability that he or she will be an obese adult. Once fat cells are deposited in the body, especially at a young age, it is difficult to eliminate them. Secondly, every obese child should be monitored closely, since he or she is at high risk for medical problems such as high blood pressure and diabetes. A third point to remember is that a single-pronged effort, such as just eating less, or just exercising more, is seldom effective (Ribeiro *et al.,* 2003); rather, it is the combination of the two that is most effective in weight management.

Behavior therapy: Therapy that involves learning principles in the elimination of unwanted behaviors.

One form of treatment which appears to offer some hope for combating obesity is *behavior therapy* (also called behavior modification) (Yanovski & Yanovski, 1999). Behavior therapists assume that maladaptive behaviors, such as eating too much and not exercising enough, are learned and conditioned (reinforced). Hence, the basic strategy in behavior therapy involves unlearning maladaptive behaviors and learning more adaptive behaviors in their place. Behavior therapists help children change their eating habits through reinforcement, modeling, and manipulation of situational cues. Usually the children are taught to monitor their own behavior and to record the results in a food diary (Wisotsky & Swencionis, 2003).

Many researchers claim that pediatric obesity can be successfully treated only if the family dynamics are considered. The family can play a role in the treatment of obesity because parents generally buy the food, prepare it, and determine how and when it is served (Rudloff & Feldmann, 1999). Some researchers (e.g., Flodmark *et al.,* 1993) believe that family based therapy can prevent the progression of obesity to superobesity.

These teachers are pleased with their students' enthusiastic participation in exercise which tends to combat obesity.

Preventing childhood obesity. Fewer than 5 percent of patients in weight-loss programs have had success for an extended period— one year or more. Since the treatment of childhood obesity has had relatively little success, prevention is extremely important. The prevention should begin at birth by breast-feeding babies which is thought to reduce the risk of the children becoming obese adults (Elliot, Kjolhede & Rasmussen, 1997). Children should be encouraged to stay active, and stay away from fast-food restaurants. The goals set for the child should be realistic — as opposed to a semistarvation diet. Children should be rewarded (with praise or a hug, for example) for complying with a nutrition program that emphasizes an increase in healthy foods like fruits and vegetables, and a reduction in unhealthy foods such as french fries, fast food, and sweets. (McGuire & Beerman, 2010; Sondike, Copperman, & Jacobson, 2000).

NUTRITION AND PHYSICAL GROWTH

School-aged children need plenty of healthy food (Goday & Sentongo, 2009). Since average body weight doubles during middle childhood and children's play requires great expenditures of energy, caloric requirements should be increased for both boys and girls. On the average, school-aged children need 2,200 calories each day, including about 35 grams of protein and a considerable amount of carbohydrates (the primary source of energy) which are found in potatoes and whole grains (McGuire & Beerman, 2010). Recently, the Food and Nutrition Board of the Institute of Medicine recommended higher levels of calcium for children 10 to 18 years of age than was previously recommended.

Not all children fit the norm for required food intake. A large, very active girl will need to eat more than a small, inactive boy. Furthermore, late-maturing girls need fewer calories than early-maturing girls of the same age. A girl's nutritional needs are greatest between 14 and 17 years of age; for boys, the greatest nutritional need is one to two years later.

No factor in development occurs in isolation from other factors. A single factor, such as food, can be considered by itself only for theoretical purposes. For example, whereas a good diet usually results in a girl having her first period at about age 12, there are exceptions. One of these is strenuous exercise. When girls use a large number of calories in an activity like dancing, gymnastics, or skating, they may not have their first periods when they are normally due, even though their diet is adequate. The strenuous exercise may prevent their bodies from reaching a specific level of body fat (15%) in proportion to muscle tissue necessary for menstruation to begin. Yet, exercise is important. Only about 17 percent of American middle-aged children have a daily physical education class and an average of only about 20 minutes of physical education a week (U.S. Department of Health and Human Services, 2000a).

Malnutrition

Although we normally think of America as being "the land of plenty," many families, including those living in poverty and the homeless, have difficulty providing enough food for their children. In the developing countries of Africa, Asia, and Latin America, more than four out of five children under the age of 5 are undernourished (Goday & Sentongo, 2009).

Marasmus: Extreme wasting of a young child as a result of insufficient protein and too few calories

Effects of malnutrition. The effects of food shortage are most evident if the deprivation is severe (Alaimo, Olson, & Frongillo, 2001). The dramatic effects of severe food deprivation is usually seen in young children (6 to 18 months of age) who suffer from a disease known as *marasmus* (first introduced in chapter 4). Marasmus affects babies who receive insufficient protein and too few calories. Victims of marasmus become very frail, wrinkled in appearance, growth stops, and body tissues begin to waste away. Children affected by the disorder remain small and usually suffer from social and intellectual impairment.

Kwashiorkor: A nutritional disorder due to little, if any, protein.

Another severe nutritional disorder, which is common in third-world countries, is *kwashiorkor*. Victims of kwashiorkor receive enough calories, but little, if any protein, usually caused by early weaning from the mother's breast which is the primary source of protein in underdeveloped countries. Children who suffer from kwashiorkor develop swollen faces, legs, and abdomens, and thinning hair (Liu *et al.,* 2003).

In western industrialized countries, a large number of children from all socioeconomic families suffer from iron and zinc deficiencies. One function of iron is the transportation of oxygen to the tissues. Zinc is involved in transporting carbon dioxide and in maintaining the acid-base balance of the body fluids. Iron and zinc shortages are most critical for young children because their rapid early growth requires more of these minerals than the children's diet normally provides. If the vitamin and mineral deficiencies are not corrected early, permanent physical and intellectual retardation are possible.

Nutritional Supplements for Undernourished Children

Fortunately, much of the damage caused by malnutrition can be reversed through a supplemental diet and improvement in social conditions, including intellectual stimulation. The sooner an enriched diet is provided to the children, the greater are the chances for catch-up growth (Grantham-McGregor, Walker, & Chang, 2000). The value of a supplemental diet was illustrated in a longitudinal study that was conducted over two decades in four rural Guatemalan villages by Ernesto Pollitt and his colleagues (1993). The children were provided with either protein and caloric supplements, or just caloric supplements in the form of a sweetened drink. Most of the children received the supplement prenatally and throughout the first 2 years of life or longer. The rest of the children received the supplement after age 2.

The results of the Guatemalan study revealed that the experimental children who received both the protein and the caloric supplement, made statistically significant improvements—although small—in cognitive development both during infancy and early childhood. Even more encouraging, is increased performance by the experimental children in number, vocabulary, knowledge, reading achievement, and information-processing tasks when compared with the control group who received the sweet drink alone.

In the Guatemalan study, Pollitt and his colleagues discovered that the benefits from food supplementation were moderated by several factors. For example, the positive consequences for long-term cognitive performance were greatest if the food supplementation was begun before the children reached 2 years of age. Also, children in the lowest socioeconomic groups benefited more than children in the higher socioeconomic groups. Food supplementation was most beneficial if it was combined with improvements in the children's social conditions.

The beneficial effects of combining food supplementation with improved social conditions was demonstrated in a Colombian study of malnourished children by Charles Super, Guillermo Herrera, and Jose Mora (1990). These investigators found that physical growth was enhanced when the food supplement program was combined with an early in-home education program. In another study (Grantham-McGregor *et al.,* 1994), Jamaican babies who had been hospitalized during infancy because of severe malnutrition, showed improvement on a variety of cognitive tasks after leaving the hospital as a result of participation in a 3-year supplemental food and education program.

HEALTH AND SAFETY CONCERNS

Illnesses in Middle Childhood

While many middle-childhood illnesses are similar to those of the preschool years, they differ in important ways. Although stomach pains continue to be common, the causes change somewhat. During the preschool years, stomach pains usually stem from a mild reaction to food or overexcitement. During middle childhood, the causes of stomach illness are often psychological, concerns such as anxiety over tests, feelings of inferiority, fear of punishment, or a strong desire for attention, approval, and acceptance. In addition, a school-aged child's stomach problems may be aggravated by medical conditions.

Ethnicity and gender also seem to be factors in illnesses in middle childhood. African-American families report fewer illnesses per child than do white families of similar income. And, both White and Black families report more illnesses for girls than for boys of the same age.

Although there is considerable decline in upper respiratory illnesses, sore throats, strep throats, and middle-ear infections in middle childhood (Marchant & Shurin, 1983), many children still have six or seven respiratory infections a year. Of particular concern is the increase in *chronic illnesses,* ailments which last for a long time and show little change (Crouse, 2010).

Chronic illness: An ailment which lasts for a long time and show little change.

Asthma. Asthma accounts for nearly one-third of chronic illness in childhood Asthma is a respiratory illness marked by wheezing, coughing, shortness of breath, and feelings of suffocation. To get an idea of how an asthmatic child feels, imagine that you just ran two blocks as fast as you could. This is the way many asthmatic children feel most of the time. The incidence of asthma has increased by about 100 percent during the last two decades and deaths from asthma have nearly doubled during this time. In fact, asthma is the most frequent cause of school absence and childhood hospitalization (Newacheck & Halton, 2000).

One cause of asthma is the children's smaller airways in the bronchial tubes (the passages that connect the throat and lungs) which are extremely sensitive to pollutants such as cigarette smoke, molds, and mildew (Cabana *et al.,* 2004). The bronchial tubes fill with mucus which leads to coughing, wheezing, and even cancer and death. One form of treatment for children with asthma is exercise, provided the asthma is under control and participation is evaluated on an individual basis. Medical treatment consists of anti-inflammatory drugs such as Flovent, an inhalant corticosteroid hormone produced by the adrenal glands.

The need for exercise.

An ever-increasing health problem is the result of too little exercise. In recent years, school-aged children have been exercising less despite evidence that regular exercise can help prevent heart problems and improve school performance. Children should be encouraged to be more active and competitive. They should be given opportunities to play tag, jump rope, play neighborhood games, and the like.

Exercise is beneficial in two ways: physiological and psychological. Physiologically, exercise stimulates the production of endorphins, morphine-like brain chemicals that can trigger feelings of euphoria and relaxation. Repetitive rhythmic exercise such as swimming or running can exert a tranquilizing effect on the brain and nervous system, similar to rocking a baby.

Among the psychological benefits of exercise are the mood-enhancing effects which boost self-esteem. Regular exercise increases self-confidence and self-efficacy, the belief that one can master a particular task. Also, when children exercise regularly, they develop a feeling of control and improve their school performance. Although exercise through sports can be beneficial, there are two groups of school-aged children who are particularly susceptible to injuries from sports. One group is those who have rarely seen the inside of a gym and suddenly make a team. The other group is those who are in shape and belong to a team but overtax their bodies severely.

Strenuous exercise appears to be particularly harmful to preteenage (10 to 12-year-old) girls. Girls of this age, who participate in highly competitive sports (e.g. swimming, cycling, and gymnastic tournaments), are highly susceptible to three co-occurring issues: amenorrhea (absence of regular menstrual cycle), osteoporosis (softness and brittleness of the bones), and anorexia nervosa and bulimia nervosa (eating disorders).

Visual Development and Problems

Vision is better in most school-aged children than in preschoolers. Until about 6 years of age, children are moderately farsighted,able to see things at a distance more clearly than objects that are near. In middle childhood, children's vision is keener and they can focus their eyes better. Box 10.1 presents a quiz that will allow you to test your knowledge of vision and eye care.

Visual impairment. Visual impairment is a significant loss of vision, ranging from partial to total blindness. Partial sight refers to a visual acuity of 20/70 to 20/200 with correction. This means that the child with partial visual impairment must be within 20 feet to see an object which a person with average sight can see from 70 to 200 feet away from him. Legal blindness denotes visual acuity (sharpness of vision) of 20/200 or worse in the better eye with correction. A person with 20/200 vision must be within 20 feet to see what a person with normal vision can see at 200 feet. Another definition of legal blindness is a field of vision of no more than 20 degrees when looking straight ahead (Corn & Koenig, 1996).

Box 10.1

Eye Quiz

There are many misconceptions about our eyes. Here is a chance for you to test your knowledge about children's vision (as well as that of adults). Which statements are true and which are false?

1. Reading in dim light will hurt children's eyes.
2. Not wearing proper glasses will hurt the eyes.
3. Using computers or video display terminals will not harm the eyes.
4. Children can sit closer to the television set than adults without hurting their eyes.
5. Only an ophthalmologist can provide total eye care.
6. Eating carrots will improve vision.
7. The need for glasses is a major cause of headaches.
8. Diabetes can cause eye damage.
9. A child must be legally blind to qualify for federal and/or state aid.
10. For children under 12, the most hazardous sport to the eyes is hockey.

Answers and Discussions:

*1. **False**. Using dim light does not damage the eyes. Not too long ago, all nighttime reading was done by candlelight or by gas or kerosene lamps. Good lighting makes reading easier and prevents fatigue.*

*2. **False**. Glasses are simply aids to improve vision. Improper glasses will not damage the eyes physically, except when the child has cross-eyes (strabismus), or "lazy eye" (amblyopia), one eye not being used as it loses its ability to see.*

*3. **True**. Although using computers or video display terminals will not harm the eyes, prolonged periods of close work may cause eye strain or fatigue. In such cases, the child should look up, or across the room frequently. If vision blurs, an ophthalmologist should be consulted.*

*4. **True**. Children can sit closer because they have greater ability than adults to focus up close without strain.*

*5. **True**. The ophthalmologist is a medical doctor (M.D. or osteopath) who is the only one educated, trained and licensed to provide total eye care, including medical eye examinations, diagnosing diseases and disorders of the eye, and using appropriate medical and surgical procedures for treatment.*

*6. **False**. Although carrots are rich in Vitamin A, which is essential for sight, many other foods also contain Vitamin A. A well-balanced diet, with or without carrots, provides all the nutrients necessary for good vision. Excessive doses of Vitamin A may be harmful.*

*7. **False**. Almost all headaches are caused by contraction of the muscles in the neck, or the base of the head, dilation of the blood vessels in the head (migraine headaches), or by diseases of the head, eyes, ears, or teeth.*

*8. **True**. Diabetes can cause glaucoma (build-up of fluid pressure in the eyeball) and cataracts (lenses which become nontransparent).*

*9. **False**. The eye damage need not be severe for the child to qualify for federal and/or state aid, for free books with large print, eyeglasses, and magnifying devices.*

*10. **False**. The greatest percentage of sports eye injuries by middle-aged children is baseball; for teenagers the most hazardous sport for the eyes is basketball.*

Source: American Academy of Ophthalmology

Refractive errors: The bending (deflection) of light rays from a straight path after they enter the eye.

Myopia: Defect in vision so that objects can only be seen distinctly when they are very close to the eyes. Distant objects appear blurred.

Types of eye problems. A common type of eye problem in childhood is *refractive errors*. In order to see, the light must bend before it reaches a light-sensitive area of the retina. Sometimes the bending, or refraction, is too great; in other cases, the refraction is too small. One refractive eye condition is *myopia*, or nearsightedness, which is the inability to see distant objects clearly. Light waves entering the eye are bent too much, and objects become focused in front of the retina. The result is that objects can be seen distinctly only when held close; distant objects appear blurred. Progressive forms of myopia usually begin just before puberty, but often as early as age 6.

Hyperopia: Ability to see distant objects, but difficulty seeing close ones.

Astigmatism: A visual defect marked by distorted vision due to unevenness of the cornea.

Retinopathy of prematurity: A visual defect where there is a leakage of fluids and blood into the retina.

Braille: A system of reading and writing that enables the blind to see by touching raised dots that represent numerals and letters of the alphabet.

Another refractive condition, *hyperopia*, or farsightedness, is caused by a flattened corneal surface, resulting in a shortened eyeball. Light waves entering the eye are not bent (refracted) enough, creating an image behind the retina. Farsighted people are able to see distant objects clearly, but have difficulty with close ones, which appear blurry.

A third optical defect is *astigmatism* (distorted vision), which is usually caused by unevenness in the surface of the cornea (the outer layer of the eye) or the lens. Rays of light are refracted differently and thus do not converge on a single point. The result is blurred or distorted vision at any distance of a viewing object. Individuals with astigmatism often have headaches, since the eye and brain must strain to compensate for the visual distortion.

Still, another type of visual defect is *retinopathy of prematurity* (formerly called retrolental fibroplasia), where there is a leakage of fluids and blood into the retina. Visual defects include decreased visual acuity, severe myopia, scarring and retinal detachment, and glaucoma. This condition is often associated with too much oxygen, low birth weight, and prematurity (Teplin, 1995).

Effects of visual impairment. Children with visual problems are at a great disadvantage in the classroom. They may give the impression of daydreaming or distracted behavior. Their academic performance is usually unsatisfactory. They may also have difficulty reading written material on the blackboard.

A child with impaired vision may confuse words and letters that look similar, such as *"dad"* and *"bad"* or *"m"* and *"n."* The visually impaired child may blink, frown, or make facial contortions while reading or while attending to the teacher. The child with visual impairment may fail to complete assignments involving considerable eye use, blink, or frown, while reading or while attending to the teacher. Outside the classroom, visual impairment can affect a child very early in life by interfering with his or her attachment to the caregiver because of difficulty in making eye contact (Troster & Bramberg, 1992).

Prevention of visual problems. During recent years, ophthalmologists have become convinced that much visual impairment can be prevented. Visual impairment from infection can be prevented by taking precautions against communicable diseases, such as rubella. Vaccination of all young children under 2 years of age is one such precaution.

Treatment of visual problems. Visually impaired children can be helped in a variety of ways. For children whose vision is impaired slightly, glasses or contact lenses are effective. Some children need other optical devices even while wearing glasses. A magnifying glass may be used by children who have difficulty with near-vision tasks such as reading. Distance vision may be enhanced by a small hand-held version of the telescope. Refractive errors, such as those which cause astigmatism, can usually be corrected with prescription glasses.

Most children who are blind use *Braille*, a system of reading and writing that uses combinations of raised dots based on a six-dot cell. The use of Braille has been greatly enhanced with the use of the personal computer. Specialized software and peripherals have made it possible to translate almost any material into Braille. Many blind children (and adults) are using computer-based reading systems that convert printed material into synthesized speech. These machines can scan books, magazines, and any kind of printed material and convert the words into a clear, accurate reading voice (Wehman, 1997).

Hearing Problems

Conductive hearing loss: Hearing impairment caused by damage to the outer or middle ear, usually by an excess of ear wax.

There are two major types of hearing impairment: *conductive* and *sensorineural.* Conductive hearing loss stems from damage to the outer or middle ear. The problem is associated with conducting or transporting sounds through the outer and middle ear. The most common cause of the damage is a simple blockage in the external canal by cerumen, or "ear wax." Sensorineural hearing loss is caused by damage to the cochlea (the primary organ of hearing located in the inner ear) which changes sound into neural impulses that are interpreted by the central nervous system, causing us to hear things. Sensorineural damage may also involve the cranial nerve that carries the neural information from the cochlea to the central nervous system. Common causes of sensorineural damage include viral and bacterial diseases, noise, and heredity.

Sensorineural hearing impairment: A hearing problem caused by damage to the cochlea, the primary organ of hearing, or by damage to the cranial nerve.

Symptoms of hearing impairment. Hearing loss should be suspected if a child was born prematurely and/or had low birth weight. A clue to possible hearing impairment occurs when the baby stops babbling. In school-aged children, hearing loss should be suspected if there is chronic inattention, frequent failure to respond when spoken to, and poor performance in school despite adequate intelligence. There may also be medical indications of hearing impairment: frequent ear aches, fluid running from the ears, and frequent colds or infections. Often the parents are the first to suspect hearing impairment in their child (Hall, Hill, & Elliman, 1990).

Recently, it has become easier to spot hearing loss in children. New advances in electrophysiology and applied computer technology have made it possible to identify hearing problems at any age — even while the child is still in the newborn nursery (Bowe, 1993). In 1993, the National Institutes of Health recommended that all infants receive hearing screening within the first three months of life. Table 10.1 shows the effects of various degrees of hearing loss.

Effect of hearing loss. Children with hearing impairment usually suffer in a variety of ways. They are ridiculed more often, have difficulty making friends, and suffer from loss of self-esteem. Hearing-impaired children may also suffer from intellectual impairment, motor deficiency, visual problems, seizure disorders, and psychiatric disorders such as depression (Koester & Meadow-Orleans, 1990; Sinkkonen, 1994). Usually, schoolwork also suffers. Deaf children tend to be delayed 3 to 5 years in their educational achievement; those whose hearing is less impaired are somewhat less delayed.

The average deaf student graduates from high school with language and academic achievement levels below that of the average fourth-grade hearing student. The average academic achievement for high school graduates who are hard of hearing is at the fifth-grade level (Holt, 1993). On a more positive note, many hard-of-hearing children appear to be quite normal. Abelfotouh and Telmesani (1993) found no significant difference between the prevalence of depression in deaf and hearing adolescents.

Decibel: The unit of intensity by which sound is measured.

Helping children with hearing problems. There are many ways of helping hearing-impaired children. Some children may benefit from a hearing aid, sometimes installed as early as 1 year of age. Normal hearing can sometimes be restored by having the cerumen (ear wax) removed from the external auditory canal. Antibiotics have been effective in controlling bacterial infections and in preventing subsequent damage to the ear. Sometimes surgical procedures are effective in restoring hearing. Unfortunately, sensorineural hearing loss (nerve deafness) is typically not treatable by surgical intervention. However, artificial cochlear implants, or "bionic ears," are being tested and may soon be on the market, enabling people who are profoundly deaf to hear, often for the first time in their lives.

Table 10.1

Measurement of Hearing Loss, in Decibels*

Severity of Hearing Loss	Decibels of Hearing Loss	Effects on Child
Slight	27-40	Has mild hearing loss; has difficulty with faint or distant sounds; will not usually have difficulty in school, although may need speech correction.
Mild	40-55	Can understand conversational speech three to five feet away (face-to-face); may need a hearing aid; may have vocabulary and speech problems; may not hear 50 percent of conversation if voices are quiet.
Marked	55-70	Has difficulty understanding loud conversations; speech is likely to be impaired.
Severe	70-90	Can hear loud sounds no more than 1 foot away; has poor speech and language development; may be able to discriminate vowels but not all consonants. If loss is present before one year of age, speech and language will not develop.
Extreme or Profound	over 90	May be able to hear some sounds, but unable to understand amplified speech; relies on vibrations rather than on tonal sounds to detect loud sounds.

*The threshold of hearing is 0 decibels, which is the softest sound that can be detected with some regularity by a person with normal hearing. A soft whisper is about 20 decibels; the roar from a large jet engine is about 150 decibels.

The cochlear implant sorts out sound and converts it into electrical impulses, bypassing the disabled hair cells in the cochlea and stimulating the auditory nerve directly, rather than amplifying the sound like the conventional hearing aid. A major weakness of the cochlear implant is that the sounds that are heard tend to be muffled.

Dental Development, Problems, and Care

Dental development is an important aspect of middle childhood. The first significant event is the loss of baby, or primary teeth, which begins at about age 6 years. The loss of the first baby tooth is often signaled as a rite of passage into middle childhood. But, it can also have psychological complications.

Some children become very self-conscious when they lose a tooth in the front of their mouth and realize that they look different. A child's speech may be affected if self-consciousness prevents him or her from opening the mouth for proper talking.

By age 11 or 12, all permanent teeth are in place except for two sets of molars. The first set erupts at about age 6; the second set of molars erupts at about age 13; the third set of molars, called wisdom teeth, erupt by the age 21. The child may have speech difficulties after the permanent teeth erupt, particularly in pronouncing "s," "z," and "th."

Problems in dental care. One problem in the proper development of permanent teeth in middle childhood is inadequate care of the primary or baby teeth. If decayed primary teeth are neglected, they may damage the permanent teeth that are forming within the jaw, requiring orthodontic work to straighten the teeth when the child is older.

Malocclusion: Improper alignment of opposing teeth in the upper and lower jaws.

Another problem that may cause *malocclusion*, or improper alignment of opposing teeth in the upper and lower jaws is thumb or finger sucking after the primary teeth erupt. Often, sucking is caused by insecurity, which may require counseling for both the parents and the child. Children who suck their fingers or thumbs may develop overbites requiring braces.

A major problem until recently was the high rate of dental cavities or caries. This situation has improved considerably within the last few decades. Whereas in the 1940s it was rare for a child not to have any dental cavieties, In 2000 it was found that one-half of American children aged 5 to 17 years have no cavities or other tooth decay (U.S. Department of Health and Human Services, 2000b). A major reason for this improvement is the use of fluoridation in the water, which reduces tooth decay by as much as 50 to 70 percent. Other reasons for improvement are a better diet, fluoridated vitamins, and fluoride in toothpaste and mouthwash.

Recent critical changes in pediatric dentistry.[1] Children's dentistry in the 21st century has come a long way from that of the 1950s and 1960s. For instance, 4 or 5 decades ago, infant dental checkups were virtually unheard of. Today, they are the norm. Early treatment enables the dentist to catch developing abnormalities. Equally important, visiting the dentist early (by age 1) helps to educate parents about proper care of their children's teeth.

A major advance in dental care is the use of sealants, a clear plastic similar to super-strength adhesive, which is painted on the teeth. The sealant fills in tiny indentations on the tooth's surface where food can be trapped easily. Sealants normally last 5 to 10 years.

There has also been a change in the thinking of what a child can eat. For instance, sugar is not the evil it was once thought to be. The sugar in apple juice, for instance, is easily dissolved by saliva. The sugar normally found in snacks is absorbed gradually by bacteria. The major cause of dental problems is sweet and starchy foods that are allowed to remain in the mouth for long periods of time. Another problem with sugar occurs when it is found in sticky foods or candy such as caramel.

Promoting good dental health. If social cognitive theorist Albert Bandura) is correct, one way to develop good dental habits in children is for parents to take proper care of their own teeth. The parents should set good examples, including going to the dentist regularly. Furthermore, they should try to hide whatever anxiety they have about going to the dentist if the children are to grow up feeling comfortable about their own dental visits (Winer, 1982). Here are some more pointers for promoting good dental health in children:

- Provide a well-balanced diet of fruits, vegetables, cereals, dairy products, meat, yogurt, and milk which are necessary for proper tooth development. Discourage starchy or sugary snacks because they assist in the production of acid that leads to tooth decay.

- Provide supplemental fluoride (one part per million), if local drinking water does not contain fluoride. If in doubt, contact local health department.

---

1. Dentistry of the near future is likely to take on a new "look": Synthetic bone material that will replace lost or diseased bone; a vaccine that will prevent oral herpes; and nearly invisible orthodontic appliances.

- Teach the child good brushing habits.

- Arrange for the child to see a dentist on a regular basis (every 6 months), beginning with the child's first birthday.

- Practice measures that will aid in avoiding cavities

  —Brush the teeth after every meal and at bedtime

  —Reduce sugar and sweets eaten by the child

  —Beware of foods that contain large amounts of sugar (bubble gum, sodas, and cookies).

- Teach children to floss. Children should floss by themselves at age 8, with occasional checks by an adult.

Coping with an evulsed (broken) tooth. A tooth that is broken as a result of an accident, can often be saved (as well as the smile) by following four steps:

- Find the tooth as soon as possible.

- Handle the tooth by the crown, not by the root; rinse it gently with water only (never use soap, chemicals, or a rubbing motion).

- Put the loose tooth back in its socket and hold it there securely (if the tooth cannot be put back in its socket, place it in a glass of milk, or place the broken tooth in a Save-A-Tooth kit, available from the local drug store).

- Call the dentist immediately to fix the problem of the evulsed tooth by using a splint much like an orthopedic surgeon would fix a broken leg.

Heart Disease

A pattern of behavior that might increase the risk of future heart disease can be recognized and addressed in childhood. Coronary heart disease (damage to the heart due to an insufficient supply of blood) has long been a leading cause of death and chronic illness in the United States. The problem occurs when the coronary blood vessels, which supply blood to the heart, are narrowed or closed by build-up of a substance called plaque. The result is blockage of the flow of oxygen and nutrients to the heart. Childhood heart disease a serious concern in today's medical world (Hugh, 2009).

Three factors commonly thought to cause heart disease are high blood pressure, smoking, and high levels of cholesterol—the "bad" type, low-density lipoprotein—in the blood. In the 1950s, a fourth suspected cause was added: A constellation of behaviors known as Type A. Still another form of behavior associated with heart disease is Type D.

Type A behavior: Behavior that is aggressive, impatient, hard-driving, and with a sense of urgency.

People who exhibit *Type A* behavior are extremely competitive and achievement-oriented, they are aggressive, impatient, hard-driving, have a sense of time urgency, speak quickly and emphatically, and find it difficult to relax. Type A people struggle to achieve more and more in less time.

As adults, certain Type A people appear to be at risk for heart problems. Those who are most at risk also have a high level of cynical hostility and proness to anger. The cynicism is marked by antagonistic and manipulative behavior, and by moodiness, suspicion, resentment, and distrust of others.

Since it is possible to identify some Type A characteristics in childhood, teachers and parents should help children channel their undesirable characteristics into more acceptable behavior. Children who find it irritating to stand in line (a symptom of the Type A disposition) can be trained to use the time to reflect on their homework or to study the behavior of their teachers or other students.

Some researchers (e.g., Ravaja *et al.,* 2000) believe that the most predictive factors for heart disease in Type A people is hostility plus a tendency to depression. Other researchers believe that proneness to anger, on its own, is a significant risk factor for coronary heart disease due to insufficient blood supply.

Type B behavior: A pattern of behavior characterized by a relaxed, unruffled life style.

Another form of behavior which has been identified is Type B. *Type B* people are the opposite of Type A. They seldom feel hurried, are not very competitive, and are slow to anger. Type B people are patient when they have to wait, they seldom feel guilty when they relax and do nothing, and they usually walk and eat slowly. People with Type B behavior do not develop heart problems as often and seldom as severe as those with Type A behavior.

Type D behavior: A personality type characterized by a general tendency to cope with stress by keeping negative emotions to oneself.

Recently, a new behavior pattern, called Type D, for distressed, has been associated with heart disease. People with *Type D* personality are likely to cope with stress by keeping their emotions to themselves, they tend to experience more negative emotions, and they are more likely to inhibit self-expression in their social interactions. Type D people are also more likely to experience a suppressed immune system, greater recurrence of cancer, and higher mortality rates.

ACCIDENTS AND SAFETY PRECAUTIONS

Statistics indicate that 1 in 4 children will have a serious accident before he or she grows up. What types of accidents do children have? What is the cause? How can they be prevented? And, what should a caregiver do if the child has an accident? Answers to these questions are discussed next.

Whereas a few years ago, the leading cause of accidents or death in children over 1 year of age was cancer, today it is unintentional injury. (National Safety Council, 2001). School-aged children are particularly vulnerable to injuries. If they run into something, they are likely to suffer a bone fracture because their bones are softer and are injured more easily than those of young adults. Children in middle childhood (particularly boys) are more likely to take risks by submitting to peer pressure, to do something dangerous, partly due to a feeling of invulnerability. Older children receive less supervision than younger children, yet they do not have mature judgment (U.S. Department of Health and Human Services, 2000d). The tragic result is often accidents—the leading cause of death in middle childhood.

A serious concern is gun accidents. American children are 12 times more likely to die from gunfire than their counterparts in the rest of the industrialized world.

Bicycle accidents are also very common in middle childhood. Most bicycle accidents (95 percent) involve a collision between a bicycle and a car. The highest rate of bicycle fatalities is sustained by children between 10 and 14 years of age, followed by children between the ages of 5 and 9 years. Since boys take more risks, three-and-a-half times as many boys as girls are involved in bicycle accidents. Today, the most common cause of injury and death in both middle and late childhood is motor vehicle accidents, either as a pedestrian or as a passenger.

Pedestrian accidents usually involve being hit by a car and are the second-leading cause of accidental death, after passenger-car fatalities. About 2,000 children are killed by cars each year, most of the victims are between 5 and 9 years of age. A major source of fatalities involving middle-aged children is school buses, which account for one-half of all school-injury deaths (Miller & Spicer, 1998).

Most eye injuries involve children between the ages of 6 and 14. The injuries are usually sustained while playing sports, particularly baseball (Rome, 1995). However, B.B. guns also cause many eye injuries.

Since many children have accidents with guns, their access should be carefully guarded (Schacter *et al.,* 2003). Better still, there should be no guns in a house if children are present.

Finally, we must remember that there is a psychological component to most accidents that occur in middle childhood. Most children this age have an inflated level of self-efficacy (the belief in one's ability to perform a particular task). Boys and girls in middle childhood often underestimate the danger in certain activities such as sliding head first in baseball. Their chances of getting hurt are compounded by their recent increase in strength and speed. (Kontos, 2004). Hence, children in elementary school need additional supervision and must be warned of the dangers of engaging in high-risk activities such as baseball and basketball.

MOTOR DEVELOPMENT

Although children learn relatively few motor skills during the school-age period, they continue to improve in activities such as running, jumping, and throwing. Boys and girls rapidly become faster, stronger, and better coordinated. Much of the improvement in motor skills is due to neurological maturation resulting in a more efficient connection between mind and body, or between neurons and actions (Kagan & Herschowitz, 2005; Pelligrino, 2009).

By the time children are in first grade, they are able to play many games involving gross muscle skills. The 6-year-old has some skill in playing soccer, football, tennis, hockey, swimming, jump rope, and in dancing. The greatest advance is in the use of small muscles to perform fine motor skills. Let's use the hand as an example of the child's progress in fine motor skills.

By age 6, Sara's greater hand proficiency, which relies mostly on the small muscles, enables her to assemble models, sew, weave, and paint. Sara can also copy complex figures such as a diamond and use scissors to cut out a paper doll. The 6-year-old can also print accurately and neatly, as well as write legibly (Van Galen, 1993). By age 8 or 9, Sara can use household tools such as screwdrivers, saws, pliers, and can openers—objects which require hand-eye coordination. A significant motor improvement in middle childhood is an increase in reaction time, the interval between stimulation and response. An 11-year-old reacts twice as quickly to a loud sound as a 5-year-old (Band *et al.,* 2000).

Progress in fine motor skills can be demonstrated in the use of a pencil. Preschool children often use a fist grip while keeping the hand and arm off the desk top, and the writing is quite large. In the first grade, children use wrist movements resulting in smaller marks. In the second or third grade, the child rests the side of his hand on the desktop and moves the pencil with his fingers, resulting in smaller marks.

Gender Differences in Motor Skills

Throughout middle childhood, boys have a slight edge over girls in motor skills (Pelligrino, 2009). Boys generally outperform girls in throwing, catching, hitting balls, running, climbing, and lifting. Around puberty, boys continue to make gains, but girls decline in motor performance. However, girls are better coordinated, more flexible, and superior in balance than boys (Lansdown & Walker, 1991). Girls are also superior to boys in gymnastics, ballet, and dancing.

Investigators suggest that males outperform girls after puberty because they have more muscle mass and greater strength. But why does female motor performance decline, particularly since girls continue to grow taller, heavier, and stronger? The answer may lie in the expectations of society. We expect females to be weaker, less aggressive, and less competitive than males, particularly as they get older.

Both boys and girls benefit from sports. Among the benefits are enhancement of children's social relationship and self-esteem, and mastery of certain skills.

HANDEDNESS

Although there are 23 million Americans like Tommy, he is criticized for being left-handed. His parents and relatives continually upbraid him for using the "improper" hand, and he has even been threatened with punishment if he doesn't start using the "right" hand. No one ever says anything to his friend, Jimmy, who is right-handed.

Self-fulfilling prophecy: The idea that a person's expectations produce the result that was expected.

These negative comments appear to have a profound effect on left-handers. Left-handed children have been judged to be more demanding, impatient, subjective, dependent, and hypochondriac, particularly in societies that frown on left-handers, such as Italy. Left-handers make up a relatively large percentage of delinquents, perhaps because of predictions made about them and the manner in which they are treated, a phenomenon known as *self-fulfilling prophecy* (Rosenthal & Jacobson, 1968). While the solution would seem to be to switch to right-handedness, the problem cannot be solved so simply (Basic *et al.*, 2004). It seems clear that any attempt to force children to change from their left hand to their right poses potential problems, nor do such attempts appear warranted.

Although children with genetically caused mental retardation are much more likely than usual to be left-handed, there appear to be several advantages to being left-handed. Left-handed people tend to do better at spatial tasks and to recover more quickly from brain damage than right-handers. Left-handedness also seems to favor athletes (Groulios *et al.*, 2000). Some of our most famous people were left-handers: Benjamin Franklin, Michelangelo, Pablo Picasso, and Leonardo da Vinci. Left-handers and mixed handers are more likely than their right-handed agemates to develop outstanding verbal and mathematical talents.Summary

Physical development in middle childhood is less rapid than in earlier years. Children undergo changes in body proportions and in brain sophistication. By middle childhood, there is considerable variation in physical development from one child to the next. Abnormal variations in growth are evident during this stage. Common disorders include deprivation dwarfism, a form of retarded physical growth, and obesity.

Proper nutrition is necessary for normal physical growth. Malnutrition affects physical, intellectual, and social development. While some health problems in middle childhood are similar to those in preschool, others, such as chronic illnesses, increase. One contributor to heart disease may be Type A behavior. Accidents are a major problem, particularly among boys. In general, the child's vision improves, although refractory problems, such as myopia and hyperopia, become quite common. Hearing problems are often associated with difficulty in school.

Both boys and girls improve their motor skills in middle childhood, with boys having a slight edge. Left-handedness is sometimes viewed as a problem by parents and/or society, although changing a child's handedness is ill-advised.

IMPORTANT TERMS

Asthma
Astigmatism
Behavior therapy (behavior
    modification)
Braille
Chronic illness
Conductive hearing impairment
Decibel
Deprivation dwarfism
Hyperopia
Idiopathic
Kwashiorkor
Marasmus

Malocclusion
Middle childhood
Myopia
Obesity
Refractive error
Retinopathy of prematurity
Self-fulfilling prophecy
Sensorineural hearing impairment
Superobesity
Type A behavior
Type B behavior
Type D behavior

RELATED RESOURCES

Readings

Drewett, Robert (2007). *The Nutritional Psychology of Childhood.* Cambridge; New York: Cambridge University Press.

Heinberg, Leslie J. and Thompson, J. Kevin editors (2009). *Obesity in Youth : Causes, Consequences, and Cures.* Washington, DC: American Psychological Association.

Jürimäe, T. (2000). *Growth, Physical Activity, and Motor Development in Prepubertal Children.* Boca Raton: CRC Press.

O'Donohue, William T.; Moore, Brie A. and. Scott, Barbara J. editors (2008). *Handbook of Pediatric and Adolescent Obesity Treatment.* New York: Routledge.

Pelligrino, Lucian T., editor (2009). *Handbook of Motor Skills: Development, Impairment and Therapy.* New York: Nova Science Publishers.

Shepphird, Sari Fine (2010). *100 Questions & Answers About Anorexia Nervosa.* Sudbury, Mass.: Jones and Bartlett Publishers.

Websites

American Academy of Opthalmology
http://www.aao.org/

United Stated Department of Agriculture
http://www.usda.gov/wps/portal/usda/usdahome

United States Department of Health and Human Services
http://www.dhhs.gov/

Centers for Disease Control and Prevention - 2009 Swine Flu
http://www.cdc.gov/h1n1flu/qa.htm

National Eating Disorders Association
http://www.nationaleatingdisorders.org/information-resources/resources-and-links.php

The Obesity Society
http://www.obesity.org/

National Hearing Conservation Association
http://www.hearingconservation.org/

National Institutes of Health
http://www.nih.gov/

National Safety Council
http://www.nsc.org/Pages/Home.aspx

Chapter 11

Cognitive Development in Middle Childhood (6 to 12 years)

Chapter Topics		Learning Objectives
What are the major characteristics of Piaget's concrete operations stage of cognitive development?		Recognize conservation, horizontal decalage, seriation, classification, and dealing with numbers.
What are the four major theories of moral development?		Understand Piaget's two stage theory of moral development, Kohlberg's moral dilemmas, Selman's role-taking dilemmas, and Bandura's social cognitive approach to moral development.
What is the Information Processing theory of memory?		Know the three kinds of memory systems: sensory, short term (working memory), and long term.
What are the major characteristics of conventional intelligence testing		Be familiar with the psychometric approach to intelligence testing and its strengths and weaknesses.
How does language improve in middle childhood?		Understand the advances made in language development during middle childhood.
What are some important factors in school that affect a child's development?		Understand the issues that emerge in school during middle childhood: teacher influence, disabilities, and, inclusion.
Chapter Summary		

Concrete operations: The third stage of Piaget's four stages of cognitive development during which a child becomes capable of logical thinking about concrete materials, but not about hypothetical or abstract events or experiences.

Sara and Carlos have reached a new threshold in life: middle childhood. During this period, which extends from about age 6 until 12, several important developments occur. They now enter a new stage of cognitive development known as *concrete operation*. This means that Carlos' and Sara's thinking has moved another notch closer to that of adults. According to some theorists, such as Jean Piaget, this is the first time a child is capable of moral and logical thinking about concrete materials, but not about hypothetical or abstract events or experiences.

In this chapter, we will look at other cognitive developments in middle childhood, including advances in memory and language. We will pay particular attention to the psychometric approach to measuring intelligence. In the final section of this chapter, we will discuss the role of the school in cognitive development, as well as education of the disabled child.

PIAGET'S STAGE OF CONCRETE (OBSERVABLE) OPERATIONS (FROM ABOUT 7 TO 11 YEARS)

"I can hardly believe how Sara's thinking has matured," comments Sara's grandmother at the girl's seventh birthday party. "She seems to be able to figure things out *logically,* and to recognize other people's points of view," said the grandmother.

Operation: Piaget's term for a logical internalized action which can be observable or abstract.

According to Piaget, an *operation* is an internalized (mental) action. In middle childhood, operations must be concrete, or *observable*, involving things that are familiar or experienced. Piaget claims that concrete things can be experienced through senses other than vision. For instance, 7-year-old Carlos, who is in the stage of concrete operations, knows that ice is cold by touching it.

Concrete operations is the third stage of Piaget's cognitive development, from ages 7 to 11, during which the child is capable of logical reasoning as long as it is applied to concrete or specific examples but not to abstract thinking. Abstract thinking involves ideas or situations that are not immediately apparent to the senses such as "trust" and "democracy."

Sara's logical thinking is evident in her ability to recognize another person's point of view, showing a decline in egocentrism. In addition to being more logical and less egocentric, 7-year-olds are capable of a variety of other "operations." Although they are capable of performing some operations during the preoperational period, children show dramatic improvements in middle childhood (the stage of concrete operations) by doing the following:

- *Conservation.* **The ability to realize that changes in spatial arrangements of objects or liquids, for example, do not change their number or amount.**

- *Seriation.* **Arranging items in order according to size, length, weight, etc.**

- *Classification.* **Grouping items according to some dimension, such as length, color, or shape.**

- *Dealing with numbers.* **The ability to count and to understand cardinal and ordinal numbers, and one-to-one correspondence.**

Let's look at each of these operations which are now within the capability of 6- to 12-year-olds in a little more detail.

Conservation

Conservation: Piaget's term for the knowledge that objects or substances remain quantitatively the same despite changes in appearance.

We learned earlier that when Sara and Carlos were in the preoperational stage they were not able to realize that the amount of liquid remained the same if it was poured from a glass of one shape into a glass of another shape. In other words, they had not learned to conserve matter. *Conservation* is Piaget's term for the knowledge that properties of an object or substance remain the same quantitatively in amount or number even if its appearance is changed in some superficial way.

Conservation can be tested by comparing two groups of children—one in the preoperational stage and the other in the concrete-operational stage. If two rows with six pennies each are shown to the children, and then rearranged, so that one row contains five pennies and the other seven, preoperational children will usually say that the total number of pennies changed with the rearrangement. These children are not yet able to conserve. Concrete-operational children—who are able to conserve—will say that the total number of pennies remains the same because the same number of pennies that were taken away from one row were added to the other row. To be able to conserve, children must possess an understanding of three basic principles: *Identity constancy*, *reversibility*, and *decentration*.

Identity constancy: The ability to realize that things stay the same despite changes in appearance, size, or form.

Reversibility: In Piaget's theory, the notion that something that has been changed can be returned to its original state by undoing the process that led to the change.

Sara has knowledge of identity constancy if she knows that she will always remain a girl even if she wears boys' clothes. Reversibility means that the transformation can be reversed if one penny is transferred from the row with seven pennies to the one with five, both rows will have six pennies again. Decentration involves focusing on more than one relevant dimension of a physical problem, so that flexible, reversible thought becomes possible. Although one of the rows has fewer pennies, the conserving child knows that this deficiency is compensated for by the additional penny in the other row.

Horizontal decalage: Unevenness in learning within a particular stage of development.

Horizontal decalage. Piaget discovered that some forms of conservation (for example, number) are understood much sooner than others (e.g., weight and volume). He called these developmental inconsistencies *horizontal decalage* meaning "gap" in French. Typically, children can solve tasks involving conservation of number (like the one with two rows of pennies just described) at age 6 or 7. Conservation of area (see Figure 11.1) does not occur until the age of 9 or 10 years. While horizontal decalage refers to unevenness in learning within a particular stage, vertical decalage refers to uneven development through the four Piagetian stages—sensorimotor, preoperational, concrete operational, and formal operational, which means that not all children of a particular age reach these stages at the same time.

Decentration: A child's ability to focus on more than one aspect of a problem.

Seriation and Transitivity

Children in the preoperational stage have limited ability in arranging items along some quantitative dimensions, such as length (ordering in sequence). Further, 4- and 5-year-olds can reproduce only one side of a staircase effect created by sticks of varying lengths. The ability to make inserts in a seriation problem does not occur until the age of 7 or 8 years when the child is in the stage of concrete operations and acquires an understanding of "bigger than...but smaller than".

Figure 11.1

Some Conservation Tasks and Ages at Which They are Typically Learned

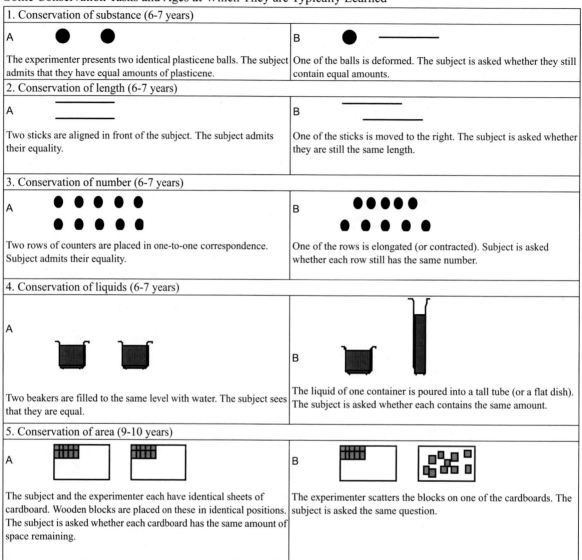

Source: Lefrancois, G.R. (1983) *Of Children,* 4th Ed.

Transitivity: Explains relations in a serial order, for example, "If Tom is taller than Mark, but shorter than John," then "Tom's height is between that of Mark's and John's."

The preoperational child also has difficulty with a seriation concept known as *transitivity*, which describes relations in a serial order or the ability to logically combine relations to understand certain conclusions. For example, the preoperational child does not realize that Brian is taller than Sara, if he is told that Brian is taller than Carlos, and Carlos is taller than Sara. Transitive ability is limited in middle childhood to actual (concrete) objects that are present physically. However, concrete operators cannot apply this type of relational logic to abstract symbols, such as "Xs," "Ys," and "Zs." This deficiency indicates that elementary schoolchildren are not ready for algebra.

Classification

You may recall that preoperational children's ability to "put together those [things] that are alike," or to classify objects on the basis of one or more dimensions, such as size, color, and shape, is inconsistent. When given a task of sorting red triangles, yellow squares, and so on, children of 4½ years sort out some materials by color (red triangles and red squares in one pile) and others by shape (red squares and blue squares in another pile). This limited ability to sort objects (classify) changes when the child enters the stage of concrete operations.

As a concrete-operational child, Sara is able to sort the objects in the example above into classes or piles with several dimensions. Sara can now sort objects into one pile of small red squares, another pile of large red squares, and a third pile of large red triangles, etc. This ability to classify is due to improvement in memory.

Dealing With Numbers: Understanding Numerical Concepts

It is a matter of common observation that preoperational children as young as 3 or 4 years of age can count "one, two, three;" that is, they understand the notion of *numerosity*—that number refers to specific amounts. However, even 5-year-olds have difficulty counting some items such as large groups of scattered objects. Five-year-olds also have more difficulty counting objects arranged in a circle, rather than in a straight line. In addition, movable items like toys and dishes are easier to count than immovable items like buttons on a dress.

Even older preoperational children have difficulty with numbers involving relationships. If shown eight yellow roses and three red ones and asked, "Are there more yellow roses, or more flowers?," preoperational children are likely to say that there are more yellow roses, even though they are capable of counting. Preoperational children are unable to segregate the concept of "flowers" from the subclassifications of "yellow roses" and "red roses." On the other hand, concrete-operational children understand these types of *hierarchical relationships* because they have learned that some sets of categories "fit into" others. For example, concrete operators know that "all roses" belong to the category of "flowers."

In middle childhood, children can understand that numbers have a rule-based flavor. That is, operations with number yield consistent results. For instance, 6 plus 3 is always 9. Furthermore, this operation can be reversed and still yield consistent results, so that 6 minus 3 is always 3. School-aged children (concrete operators) understand other aspects of numbers. When Carlos' mother angrily asks him to pick up his clothes, Carlos knows that this is the second time that he has been asked to perform this chore. He now knows that numbers have a particular order, which indicates that he is aware of the *ordinal* aspect or the property of numerical relations (e.g., first, second, and third). Carlos also knows that he has been to Disneyland a total of three times, which illustrates his knowledge of *cardinal numbers,* or absolute numerical size used in counting, for example, 1, 2, 3.

Seven-year-old Carlos also understands *one-to-one correspondence*. In choosing players for a game, Carlos and his friends can do so in several ways. They can count the number of children present and then arbitrarily divide the total number of individuals in half, randomly assigning one subgroup to one team, and the other subgroup to the opposing team. Or, Carlos can suggest that

Numerosity: The idea that number refers to specific amounts.

Hierarchical relationships: Sets of categories that "fit into" classes of a different order.

Ordinal numbers: Numbers that have a particular order such as first, second, and third.

Cardinal numbers: Numbers that are used in counting and denote numerical size, such as 1, 2, 3.

One-to-one correspondence: Matching each item in a group with single items from another group.

two captains be chosen, then each captain can take turns in choosing a member for his team, again illustrating one-to-one correspondence.

MORAL DEVELOPMENT: FOUR THEORIES

Morality: The standard one uses to judge the correctness of an action or behavior.

"Grow up," an angry father chided his son. "Stop hanging around the public square, wandering up and down the street. Go to school. Night and day you torture me. Night and day you waste your time having fun," the father ranted (Beatty, 1968, p. 10). Though this may sound like something modern parents say, it is taken from Sumerian clay tablets more than 4 thousand years old. These tablets reveal Sumerian parents' concern with their children's *morality*, a word derived from the Latin word *morali*, meaning "custom." Children's morality is as big a concern in today's society as it was thousands of years ago as indicated in statements made by our politicians. For example, character education became an integral part of our educational system in late 1990s.

Morality describes the standard one uses to judge the correctness of action or behavior. Abraham Lincoln set a standard for honesty when he walked three miles to return six cents. Joan of Arc, the young French heroine, set a standard for bravery. Standards of hard work and persistence were set by the Wright brothers when they tried to design an airplane that would fly. We will examine how four child development theorist explain the moral development of the child.

Jean Piaget's Two-Stage Theory of Moral Development

Jean Piaget, known for his work in cognitive development, also formulated a two-stage theory of moral development: *Heteronomous morality* (also called moral realism, absolutistic morality, and morality of constraint) and *autonomous morality* (also called morality of cooperation). These two stages coincide roughly with Piaget's preoperational and concrete-operational stages of cognitive development. The two stages are summarized in Table 11.1.

Heteronomous morality: Piaget's first stage of moral development in which children view moral rules as permanent features handed down by authorities and cannot be changed.

Heteronomous morality. In Piaget's heteronomous morality, which lasts until about 6 ½ years of age, children judge actions, rather than intentions. If 6-year-old Sara sees Carlos break one cup while trying to get some forbidden candy in a cupboard, and if she also sees McKensie break 10 cups while helping her mother, McKensie would be perceived as being naughtier than Carlos. A child in the heteronomous stage considers the *objective* damage, not the intentions of the individuals. According to Piaget, children in the heteronomous stage of morality subscribe to a *moral realism,* a confusion between moral and physical laws. Moral laws are viewed as predetermined and permanent aspects of the world just like physical laws. Since Sara is still egocentric, she cannot imagine more than one way of looking at a moral issue, and she evaluates responsibility for an act by its consequences.

Moral realism: Piaget's term for children's confusion between moral and physical laws.

Moral absolutism: Piaget's belief that young children assume that identical rules prevail universally and are unchangeable because they have been created by an authority.

In the heteronomous stage, children view acts as either totally right or totally wrong, depending on what powerful adults tell them, on the amount of damage done, and whether the act is punishable. Children in the heteronomous stage also assume that, at all times and in all places, identical rules prevail; rules are unchangeable since they have been created by an authority. Piaget called this type of thinking *moral absolutism.*

Table 11.1

Piaget's Two Stages of Moral Development

Dimension of Morality	Stage I: Morality of Constraint, or Heteronomous Morality (up to about 6½ years)	Stage II: Morality of Cooperation or Autonomous Morality (over 6½ years)
Moral concepts	Morality of constraint.	Morality of cooperation.
Point of view	Child views an act as either totally right or totally wrong, and thinks everyone sees it the same way. Child cannot put himself or herself in place of others.	Child can put himself or herself in the place of others. Not absolutistic in judgments; he or she sees possibility of more than one point of view.
Intentionality	Child tends to judge an act in terms of actual physical consequences, not the motivation behind it.	Child judges acts by their intentions and not by their consequences.
Rules	Child obeys rules because they are sacred, unalterable and reflect parental authority.	Child recognizes that rules were made by people and can be changed by people. The child considers himself or herself just as capable of changing rules as anyone else.
Respect for authority	Unilateral respect leads to feeling of obligation to conform to adult standards and to obey adult rules.	Mutual respect for authority and peers allows child to value own opinion and ability more highly and to judge other people more realistically.
Punishment	Child favors severe, expiatory ("eye-for-an-eye") punishment. Feels that punishment itself defines the wrongness of an act; an act is bad if it elicits punishment.	Child favors milder, reciprocal punishment that leads to restitution of the victim and helps the culprit recognize why his or her act was wrong, thus leading to her reform.
Immanent justice	Child confuses moral law with physical law and believes that any physical accident or misfortune that occurs after a misdeed is a punishment willed by God or by some other supernatural force.	Child does not confuse natural misfortune with punishment. Child realizes that punishment is not inevitable for a wrongdoing.

Source: Adapted partly from Kohlberg, 1964, and Hoffman, 1970.

Expiatory punishment: Punitive measures unrelated to the misbehavior.

Immanent justice: Piaget's view of young children's morality when they confuse moral law with physical law and believe that only deviation from the rules will inevitably result in punishment.

Autonomous morality: Piaget's second stage of moral development, in which individuals view rules as flexible, socially agreed upon principles that can be changed when it is deemed necessary to do so.

Six-year-old Sara, who is in Piaget's heteronomous morality stage, favors *expiatory punishment*, punitive measures that are unrelated to the misbehavior. Thus, she might favor not letting Carlos watch TV because he misbehaved at the dinner table. Children in the heteronomous stage also believe in *immanent justice*. They confuse moral law with physical law by believing that any accident or misfortune, such as a boy falling and hurting himself while running away after hitting his sister, is punishment for the misdeed. In other words, children in the heteronomous stage believe that wrongdoing inevitably leads to punishment.

Autonomous morality. Sara, aged 9, has undergone considerable change in her moral thinking since she was a preschooler. She is now less egocentric and her viewpoint has widened so that she adopts a more flexible attitude toward moral standards. She realizes that there can be more than one code of right and wrong. Sara is now in Piaget's stage of *autonomous morality*.

In determining the rightness or wrongness of an act, Sara takes intentions into account. Thus, McKensie would be considered as a moral, helpful person even though she broke 10 cups while helping her mother. Carlos would be considered a naughty person, even though he broke only one cup, because he was trying to get forbidden candy. These changes in Sara's thinking are possible since she has moved from the preoperational stage to the stage of concrete operations.

Kohlberg's Moral Dilemmas: The Child as a Moral Philosopher

Lawrence Kohlberg (1922–1987), a developmental psychologist, measures a child's moral development with the following story:

"A woman in Europe is near death from a special kind of cancer. There is one drug that doctors think might save her—a form of radium that a druggist in the patient's town recently discovered. The drug is expensive; about ten times what it would cost the druggist to make (the druggist paid $200 for the radium, but he wants $2,000 for the drug). The sick woman's husband, Heinz, cannot borrow the money, nor can he get the druggist to take less money. Realizing that the druggist simply wants to make money on the drug, the desperate Heinz breaks into the drugstore to steal it" (Kohlberg, 1964, p. 391).

Kohlberg then asks a child whether Heinz should have stolen the drug. Depending on the answer, the child is asked further specific questions. Kohlberg is not so much concerned with the childs answer as he is with the child's reasoning. Kohlberg believes that "decision-making capacities rather than fixed behavior traits" determine the level of an individual's moral judgment (Kohlberg, 1964, p. 391). Kohlberg also believes that many people are capable of working out moral judgments on their own, rather than merely "internalizing" the standards of parents, teachers, and peers.

Kohlberg's Levels and Stages of Moral Development

After studying children's and adults' responses to hypothetical moral dilemmas, Kohlberg concluded that there are six distinct stages of moral reasoning (See Figure 11.2). These stages unfold in an age-related fashion much like Piaget's stages of cognitive development. Kohlberg also grouped the stages of morality into levels: preconventional, conventional, and postconventional. Stages 1 and 2 are combined to form the preconventional level of morality. Stages 3 and 4 are combined to form the conventional level of morality, and Stages 5 and 6 combine to form the postconventional level of morality.

Figure 11.2
Critical Thinking in Kohlberg's Levels of Moral Development

Level I. Preconventional Level (Ages 4 to 10)
Stage 1: "I must do what I'm told so I won't be punished."
Stage 2: "You scratch my back and I'll scratch yours."
Level II. Conventional Level (Ages 10 to 18)
Stage 3: "I want to do what's nice and to please others."
Stage 4: "I will obey the law." (Concern for the larger community.)
Level III. Postconventional Level (Reached by only a few adults)
Stage 5: "Because society has agreed on these laws, I will follow them, but they can be changed."
Stage 6: "I will try to follow the law, but in some cases I may follow my own conscience if I think that the law is not right."

Preconventional morality: Kohlberg's first level of morality when children's behavior is subject to external controls.

At Level I, *preconventional morality*, children's behavior is subject to external controls. At Stage 1, Level 1, children gauge morality by whether an act elicits punishment or reward. Thus, they might say that Heinz should not steal the drug because he might be put in jail. At Stage 1, Level I, children believe that if punishment does not occur, the act must be good. At this stage, children are oriented toward punishment and obedience and toward the belief that,

Conventional morality:
Kohlberg's second level of morality when children conform to social expectations to gain the approval of others.

Postconventional morality:
In Kohlberg's theory, the third and final level of moral reasoning which conforms to personally accepted and internalized moral principles, rather than to the principles of others.

"Might is right." At the second stage of preconventional morality, Level I, Stage 2, children conform to social expectations to gain rewards. Justice is seen as an exchange system. Children might try to solve Heinz's dilemma by saying that he should steal the drug because he might need someone to steal it for him some day.

At Level II, *conventional morality*, children continue to conform to social expectations to gain others' approval, and to maintain good relations. The moral reasoning at Stage 3 is often associated with "The Golden Rule": "Treat others as if they were yourself." This reasoning is found in many religions and has also been heard as, "Do unto others as you would have them do unto you."

At Stage 3, Level II, there is also a desire to maintain rules and authority which support proper stereotypical behavior. At Stage 4, Level II, conventional morality, law and order become the watchwords. Laws are upheld, except in extreme cases. There is also a shift in focus from the child's family and close groups to larger social groups for moral norms. Kohlberg labeled this stage social system and conscience. Children focus on their duties, respect authorities, and follow rules and laws. There is less emphasis on pleasing others and more on adhering to a complex set of regulations to maintain order within society and to promote the good of all people.

Internalized principles guide individuals' thinking and behavior at Level III, *postconventional morality*. At Stage 5, Level III, individuals act to achieve the "greatest good for the greatest number of people." Individuals are aware that people may hold a variety of values and opinions, and that values are relative. These relative rules should be upheld to preserve social order, but they can be changed. There are some absolute values like life and liberty that must be upheld regardless of circumstances.

At Stage 6, Level III, achieved by less than 1 percent of adults, postconventional morality—as exemplified by Dr. Martin Luther King, the civil rights leader—self-chosen ethical principles are developed and followed. Although laws are not always believed to be valid, they should generally be upheld. When laws violate universal ethical principles, one's conscience should dominate. These universal principles include justice, equality of human rights, and respect for the dignity of others (Kohlberg, 1976). Hence, Kohlberg's highest stage of morality often presents a dilemma. For instance, until 2003, gay men were caught in moral conflict between their right to privacy in consensual sex and the law forbidding such behavior.

According to Kohlberg, the level of moral development reached by a child depends increasingly on logical reasoning and on sophisticated perspective-taking, the ability to consider a situation from another person's point of view. Thus, a person with low, logical development is not likely to move beyond Stage 3 or 4. The importance of perspective-taking in moral development is also emphasized by Robert Selman.

Selman's Role-Taking in Moral Dilemmas

Selman's role-taking in moral dilemmas: Studying a person's moral development by evaluating his or her perspective when presented with structured moral dilemmas.

Like Lawrence Kohlberg, Robert Selman believes that Sara's moral development can be understood by studying her perspectives when she is presented with dilemmas. Here is a classic study of a structured moral dilemma proposed by Selman.

"Holly is an 8-year-old girl who likes to climb trees. She is the best tree climber in the neighborhood. One day while climbing down from a tall tree, she falls, but does not hurt herself. Her father sees her fall. He is upset and asks her to promise not to climb trees anymore. Holly promises.

Later that day, Holly and her friends meet Shawn, whose kitten is caught in a tree and can't get down. Something has to be done right away or the kitten may fall. Holly is the only one who climbs trees well enough to reach the kitten and get it down, but she remembers her promise to her father" (Selman, 1976, p. 302).

Selman asks children several questions about the story, including:

* *Does Holly know how Shawn feels about kittens?*
* *What does Holly think will happen if her father finds out that she climbed the tree?*

Selman believes that children are most likely to understand how another person thinks or feels if he or she can take another person's perspective. Selman calls this perspective role-taking. Since preoperational children are highly egocentric, they cannot fully realize that each person has his or her own thoughts and feelings which serve as the basis for action (Flavell, 1985). Children are not able to see from another's perspective until they are between 6 and 8 years of age. According to Selman, once children acquire some role-taking ability, they move through a progression of stages which are closely related to Piaget's stages of cognitive development (Selman, 1980). Selman divided the development of moral role-taking into five stages, numbered 0 through 4, which overlap one another. As Carlos and Sara move through these stages, they learn to differentiate between their own perspectives and those of others and to understand others' views and the relations between these views and their own.

Stage 0: Egocentric role-taking (About ages 3 to 6): At this first stage, children make judgments based on their own egocentric viewpoints, which they think is the only one possible. When asked how Holly's father will react to her climbing the tree, children at this stage answer that he will be "happy because he likes kittens." These children assume that since they like kittens, everyone else does.

Stage 1: Social-informational role-taking (About ages 5 to 9): At Selman's Stage 1, children realize that people interpret situations differently. However, children at Stage 1 believe that these differences are due to having received different information from different sources. The children don't realize that people can have different views about the same information. Hence, they are still unable to reflect on the thinking of others and are unable to predict how others will react. Despite this limitation, children at this stage are beginning to realize the importance of intention. Thus, if asked whether Holly's father would be angry, they might say, "If he didn't know why she climbed the tree, he would be angry." Then, they say that if the father knew why Holly climbed the tree, he would realize that she had a good reason and he would not be angry.

Stage 2: Self-reflective role-taking (ages 7 to 12): Children now reflect on their own thinking as well as on that of others. At Selman's Stage 2, children know that they have a particular point of view and that others are aware of their perspective. Hence, they can anticipate other people's reactions to their own behavior or thinking. However, children at this stage are still not able to consider their own perspective *and* that of another person at the same time.

Stage 3: Mutual role-taking (ages 10 to 12): At Stage 3, children are able to consider their own viewpoints and that of another person simultaneously. Children can also see themselves from the point of view of another person or from the perspective of a disinterested third party. Children can now speculate about what people are thinking. They often use reciprocal relations between group members to regulate behavior, no longer relying upon a strong external source to define right and wrong. Thus, Holly might say to her friend, "I won't tell your mom what you did, if you don't tell my mother what I did."

Stage 4: Social and conventional system role-taking (about 14 years to adulthood): Holly realizes that there are integrated networks of perspectives and tries to understand another person's point of view by comparing it with that of the social system ("generalized other") in which others operate. Holly realizes that most people act in accordance with the expectations of their social group, and that some rival values cannot be reconciled.

Piaget's, Kohlberg's, and Selman's theories of moral development all emphasize the cognitive aspect. Furthermore, research confirms that children's moral role-taking skills emerge in an invariant sequence as the child develops as Selman claims. Research also confirms that children vary in the ages at which they acquire certain role-taking skills. Next, we will examine a theory which differs sharply: Bandura's social cognitive theory.

Bandura's Social Cognitive Theory of Moral Development

The social cognitive theory, espoused by Albert Bandura, holds that observation, reinforcement, punishment, and imitation explain children's moral behavior. When rewarded for behaving properly, the child is likely to repeat the behavior. The child also is likely to imitate the behavior of a model, such as a parent, who behaves morally and sets up a judicious system of punishments and rewards. To be influential, the model must have a warm relationship with the child and possess characteristics which appeal to the child. Children then identify with, or take on, the characteristics of models such as parents, teachers, and peers.

According to social cognitive theorists, when children fail to adhere to models, they feel guilty and anxious, even when the models are far away and have no way of knowing about the children's misdeeds. For social cognitive theorists, such children have internalized parental standards and achieved a certain level of morality. According to this view, a child who is moral in one situation will generalize the morality to all other situations. Hence, if morality generalizes from one situation to the next, then a child who always tells the truth to his mother would always tell the truth to anyone else. Such a view is debatable.

Critique of Theories of Morality

As with most theories, each view of moral development hasstrengths and weaknesses. Itis clear that children's understanding of morality increases with age as cognitive-developmentalists such as Jean Piaget claim (Browne-Miller, 2009; Boom & Molenar, 1989; Stewart & Pascual-Leone, 1992). In one study (Masters & McCoy, 1985) of 5-, 8-, and 12-year-old children who heard stories about other children who were upset, 8-year-olds were more likely to suggest verbal support (praising the other child or reassuring him that his sadness would pass) than 5-year-olds. The 12-year-olds provided more verbal support than the 8-year-olds. Cognitive-developmental theories have also stimulated our thinking about the association between cognitive maturity and moral development.

Most scientists agree with Kohlberg that the sequence of children's responses to moral dilemmas is invariant across cultures. For instance, young children give more preconventional (Level I) responses and older children give more conventional (Level II) responses. Hence, children's moral reasoning seems to progress generally from lower to higher stages. However, Kohlberg's model (Levels I, II, and III) may not apply equally to all cultures. Specific events in any given culture (war, famine, and prosperity) help shape the moral judgments of those people.

Studies have generally confirmed that moral role-taking skills emerge in an invariant fashion as Selman claims (Browne-Miller, 2009). Furthermore, laboratory studies of moral role-taking correlate with how often children engage in altruistic behavior such as helping another child or sharing food or candy.

Most researchers agree that the social cognitive theory expounded by Albert Bandura has both positive and negative aspects. On the positive side, children learn by observing and imitating a model such as a parent or a teacher. On the negative side, children may imitate negative behavior such as violence depicted on television. However, children do not imitate blindly or automatically—cognition plays a vital role according to Bandura. In attending to a model's behavior, children interpret behaviors they observe on the basis of their own personality, their past experiences, and their ability to remember the behavior that is portrayed by a model.

A persistent criticism of cognitive-developmental theories of morality such as Kohlberg's, is their failure to deal with the relationship between thinking and behavior (Lapsley, Narvaez & Nucci, 2004). Although cognitive-developmentalists claim that there is a link between moral judgment about a hypothetical dilemma and actual moral behavior, such a relationship has not been established. We are unable to predict how a person will behave by giving him or her a test about some theoretical moral situation that he or she might experience later.

A charge against Kohlberg's moral theory is that it has a masculine bias which devalues women's distinctive psychological perspectives. Carol Gilligan (1982; Gilligan & Attanucci, 1988) says that while morality for males is based on principles of rights and noninterference, for females it is based on *caring* or responsibility. Gilligan also says that whereas men and boys typically emphasize individuation and separateness, women and girls emphasize attachment and connectedness to others from infancy onward. Hence, Gilligan claims that the standards for morality should be different for men than for women. According to Gilligan, whereas men's views of morality should be judged on issues of justice and fairness, women's morals should be judged on the basis of care for individuals. and avoidance of harm

Although Gilligan says morality standards should be different for girls and women than for boys and men, he claims that the moral standards for girls and women can be just as valid as the standards for boys and men. Research studies have found no support for Gilligan's view that women predominantly use a "care" orientation and men a "justice" orientation.[1] Most theorists, including the Russian psychologist Vygotsky, agree that morals for both men and women are affected more by cultural and educational differences than by biological ones.

---

1.   Ironically, Gilligan's claim that women's morals should be based on different criteria than men's was used by Citadel College's attorneys when the college was sued because of its all-male admissions policy.

INFORMATION-PROCESSING AND MEMORY

During middle childhood (6 to 12 years), Sara's and Carlos' abilities to remember information increase considerably (Bauer, 2007). Furthermore, Sara and Carlos can "look in" on their own memory, a process called metamemory. But how does the child remember things? What neurological changes, if any, occur? One way to gain some insight into the memory process is to think of the mind as a computer. This approach, called information processing, views the human mind as a symbol-manipulating system through which information flows.

Both the human mind and the computer have hardware and software. The hardware in a computer consists of the random-access memory which integrates information we receive from the keyboard with what we retrieve from long-term storage on the hard drive. Mental hardware, according to cognitive psychologists, consists of three components: sensory memory, short-term (working) memory, and long-term memory.

The mental hardware of human thinking is generally believed to refer to mental and neural structures that are built-in and allow the mind to operate. Mental hardware allows us to "run" mental software to accomplish particular tasks such as reading, answering math questions, and finding our way home.

Information-processing scientists often use flow-charts to solve problems and to complete tasks, somewhat similar to the way in which programmers get computers to perform a series of mental operations. The information-processing approach is also being used to track the steps children use to solve problems such as how to get along with others. A key advantage of the information-processing approach is its emphasis on the way in which one's genetic heritage combines with diverse environmental circumstances to affect a child's development. Those who follow Piaget's thinkingsee children as taking an active part in their own development.

Stages in processing human memory. Like the computer, human memory processes information in three distinct stages: input or encoding, storage, and retrieval. In the encoding stage, sensory information is transformed into neural impulses that can be processed further and stored for later use. This is similar to the keyboard changing entries into electronic symbols that can be stored on a computer disk and used later.

In encoding, we usually identify the distinctive features of a stimulus, such as whether the event is a sound, a visual image, or a smell. Also, during encoding we often use labels. We may label an experience as unique, or scary. Personal computers typically store information on diskettes or hard drives.

The second stage of the memory process, *storage*, stores the information in the memory if we plan to retain it for any length of time or to use it more than once. Just as in a computer, bits of memory are stored briefly, then discarded; other items are stored on a permanent basis.

The third stage of memory, *retrieval*, calls up certain memories as stored information to be used again, in much the same way as we call up a computer program that has been named and stored by striking certain keys that provide the computer with cues to retrieve it. In short, retrieval is the process of recalling, or bringing a memory into consciousness.

Three Kinds of Memory Systems: The Three-Stores Model

We have discussed the three stages of memory process: encoding, storage, and retrieval. Now let's look at the hardware of the mental system that encodes, stores, and retrieves memory.

The most widely accepted information-processing model of memory is the one proposed by Richard Atkinson and Richard Shiffrin (1968). The Atkinson and Shiffrin model emphasizes three interacting *memory stores* that are common to all individuals. These stores process memory in three successive stages: sensory, short-term (or working memory,) and long-term. A memory store is a set of neurons that serves to retain information over time.

Memory store: A set of neurons that serves to retain information over time.

Sensory-memory store. The sensory-memory store receives information from the environment through the sense organs and retains it for a fraction of a second. Sensory memory lasts just long enough to give us a sense of continuity, but not long enough to interfere with new sensory input (Loftus, 1992). An example of sensory memory is a bright flash of lightning during a thunderstorm at night. There is also auditory sensory memory where information is held about the precise details of a sound for several seconds. Sensory memory can be retained for a period longer than a fraction of a second if it is transferred to the short-term memory store, also called the working-memory store (Baddeley, 2000).

Short-term, or working-memory, store. This compartment deals with the preservation of recent experiences and with the retrieval of information from the sensory-memory and the long-term memory stores. Short-term memory has a small capacity and is of short duration — about 30 seconds. However, the information can be retained longer through mental strategies such as rehearsal, the repetition of information that has entered short-term memory.

Recently, many scientists have broadened the term "short-term" memory and call it "working memory" (Baddeley, 2000). This expansion of the concept of short-term memory (which is viewed as a passive, temporary holding area) to working memory is based on the belief that working memory contains many subcompartments where information is actively processed by means such as reasoning and language comprehension (Shiffrin, 1993; Wickelgren, 1997).

Today, we think of short-term memory as a three-part or subcompartment in working memory. One subcompartment in working memory is the articulatory loop which holds visual and spatial information (Baddeley, 1992; Baddeley & Hitch, 1994; Baddeley, Gatherole, & Papagno, 1998). Another subcompartment in working memory is the phonological rehearsal loop which involves holding and manipulating verbal information. Finally, there is the central executive subcompartment which supervises and coordinates the other two subcompartments as well as material received from long-term memory.

Long-term memory store. Everything we "know" is stored in the long-term memory store which in theory has unlimited capacity. Information in long-term memory may last for a lifetime provided that drugs or disease do not damage the brain's memory circuits. Information can pass in either direction between short-term and long-term memory. Like the short-term memory store, the long-term memory store contains several subdivisions. One subdivision, called semantic memory, is much like a dictionary or encyclopedia. It is filled with general facts and information. Another system, called episodic memory, contains specific events that have personal meaning for us, something like a diary.

As information flows from one memory store to another (for example, from the sensory-memory store to the short-term memory store) we can operate on it and transform it by using mental strategies. A mental strategy is the software of the memory systems. It is a deliberate, controllable operation that is performed for the purpose of attaining a particular goal. Mental strategies include rehearsal, elaboration, categorization, and chunking. Metamemory, knowledge about one's own memory, also helps the memory process. Let's look at these strategies—the software of a computer model for retaining information in short-term memory, in more detail.

Mental Strategies for Improving Short-term (Working) Memory

Rehearsal: Simple repetition of material that is being learned.

Rehearsal. As soon as Carlos sat down in the school bus the other morning, he started talking to himself. When asked what he was saying, Carlos answered that he was repeating the chores he had to do after he got home: carry out the garbage, check the parrot's water, and feed the dog. Simple repetition of material that is being learned is called *rehearsal.*

The effectiveness of rehearsal depends on a variety of factors, including age. The older a child is, the more effective is his or her rehearsal strategy. In one experiment (Flavell, Miller, & Miller, 1993), only 10 percent of 5-year-olds repeated the names of objects they had been shown previously and asked to remember. The children's rehearsal was judged by their lip movements. On the other hand, 50 percent of 7-year-olds and 85 percent of 10-year-olds used a rehearsal strategy.

Elaboration: Remembering something by going beyond the information given.

Elaboration. Remembering something through *elaboration* involves going beyond the information given. Elaboration involves linking items to be remembered in some type of meaningful order. This technique is particularly helpful whenever the task is to associate two or more stimuli, such as a foreign word and its English equivalent. Thus, in trying to remember the French name for pen, *plume*, we might visualize someone writing with a feather. When asked to remember the words dog, fish, pipe, and swimming, a child might enhance his or her memory using elaboration by visualizing a scene involving a dog swimming behind a fish while smoking a pipe.

One type of elaboration common in school-aged children is visualizing objects in space. A child who is asked to do several chores may improve his memory of things to be done by visualizing himself walking to each place where a chore needs to be done. For example, the child might visualize himself walking to the garage while carrying out the trash, and, while he is there, going over to one corner of the garage to see if the rabbits have food, then walking to his bedroom to make up his bed (Terry, 2003). School-aged children use elaboration most effectively if they construct the elaboration themselves. Preschool children remember better when someone else makes up the elaboration for them.

Categorization: Grouping items into categories that represent shared abstract qualities, for example, "bread, milk, and sugar" are all "food."

Categorization and chunking. As children grow older, they become more adept at grouping items into categories that represent shared abstract qualities. We group carrots, bread, milk, and pickles in the category of food. The ability to *categorize* is common at age 10 or 11, although younger children can be taught to do so as well.

Chunking: The arrangements of material into meaningful units.

Chunking, the rearrangement of material into meaningful or familiar patterns, also improves short-term memory. For example, look at the following 15 letters:

YMO IOT FIS GNI HCT

You can see how easy it is to remember these letters if you use the chunking technique by rearranging the letters as:

MY FOOT IS ITCHING

Although the existence of separate memory stores has dominated thinking about memory for many decades, some theorists believe that there is one generic memory store. These theorists generally see short-term memory as a tiny portion of long-term memory in activation such as when one is reciting an unfamiliar phone number to have it available for a brief period. Despite the many disagreements about the structure of memory, one of the aspects on which theorists agree is metamemory.

Metamemory: Understanding of the processes of memory.

Metamemory. *Metamemory* is knowledge about memory. Carlos realizes that certain types of information are more difficult to remember than others. Sara knows that she can remember a poem by rehearsing it. The concept of metamemory is important because an individual's ability to use memory strategies depends on the understanding of how memory works and how it can be applied to a particular task. A student who wishes to commit a lecture to long-term memory must realize that notes are needed.

By the time children reach middle childhood, they know a great deal about memory. Even kindergartners and first graders know what it means to learn, to remember, and to forget. Children realize that past events are remembered with great difficulty, that studying something for a period of time will make it easier to remember, and that it is more difficult to remember many items than a few.

Metacognition: The ability to evaluate a cognitive task to determine how to accomplish it, and then to monitor and adjust one's performance of that task.

An ability that is related to metamemory is *metacognition*, a higher form of thinking. Metacognition, which is sometimes called "thinking about thinking," is the ability to evaluate a cognitive task and then determine the best way to accomplish the task. In other words, metacognition helps children monitor their understanding of what they read and enables them to develop strategies (e.g., reading slowly, rereading difficult passages, and trying to visualize information) to clear up any difficulties.

THE PSYCHOMETRIC APPROACH TO MEASURING INTELLIGENCE

When they were 7 years old, McKensie, Sara, and Carlos were given a test in which they were asked to define words such as "orange" and "envelope." They were also asked to complete partial statements, such as "An inch is short; a mile is ____." At age 11, the same three children were given a test again and asked to define the words "skill," "juggler," "constant," and "courage." They were also asked to find the errors in a picture and to complete the statement, "The streams are dry ____ there has been little rain." McKensie, Sara, and Carlos were taking the Stanford-Binet Intelligence Scale, a frequently used individual intelligence test, which is highly verbal.

The Wechsler Intelligence Scale for Children (Fourth Edition), or WISC-IV

Wechsler Intelligence Scale for Children-(Fourth Edition) or WISC-IV: An individually administered intelligence test that includes a measure of both general intelligence and a variety of mental and performance scores.

A widely used *individual* intelligence test—administered to one person at a time for children of school age—is the *Wechsler Intelligence Scale for Children (Fourth Edition)*, or *WISC-IV*. The WISC is the most commonly used individual intelligence test designed for children 6 through 16 years (Prifitera, Saklofske & Weiss, 2008; Eechsler, 2003). The test measures verbal and performance abilities and there is also a total score. The separate subtests, or subscales, measure many abilities, including vocabulary, general knowledge, memory, and visual awareness.

The WISC is given by a trained examiner who reads the questions to one child at a time. If the child scores much higher on the WISC than what is indicated by his or her chronological age, the child is usually placed in a "gifted and talented class." If the child does poorly on the WISC, special attention is given to his or her weakness. For example, a child who does poorly on the verbal subtest may have a language problem and will receive special attention in this area.

Group test: A test administered to a group of individuals simultaneously, as opposed to an individual test which is given to one person at a time.

While some intelligence tests, such as the WISC-IV, are administered to one child at a time, other intelligence tests are given to a group of children simultaneously. Such tests are called *group tests*. A popular group intelligence test is the *Otis-Lennon School Ability Test*, designed for children from kindergarten through the twelfth grade. This test requires an understanding of verbal and numerical concepts, and an ability to follow directions. Another group intelligence test is the *California Test of Mental Maturity (CTMM)*.

Validity of Intelligence Tests

Intelligence tests generally predict school success with a fairly high degree of certainty (Sattler, 2008). This is especially true for highly verbal children from middle-class families. In certain instances, intelligence tests are valid for clinical assessment of anxiety problems or neurological and perceptual deficiencies (Kaufman, 2009). Intelligence tests also help to identify children who are especially bright, assisting a teacher to decide whether a child can benefit from an enriched program. Despite the many uses of intelligence tests, there are many controversies surrounding their employment.

One argument against the usefulness of intelligence tests is scoring errors (e.g., not recording responses correctly and adding scores on individual subtests incorrectly) made by the people administering the tests (Sattler, 2008; Alfonso *et al.*, 1998). Another weakness of intelligence tests is their general unreliability in predicting success in a career, good health, and happiness. However, intelligence tests have been found to be good predictors of job success if the job requires the same kind of skill that is learned most often in school.

Many psychologists have expressed concern that intelligence is more than what intelligence tests measure. Since intelligence tests do not assess skills directly, we can only infer the child's ability based on how he or she scores. One result is an underestimation of minority groups whose skills are often different from those in the White middle-class culture.

Critics point out that the psychometric approach to measuring intelligence tells us nothing about how a person goes about answering questions and solving problems. Nor do traditional (standardized) tests tell us why people with low intelligence scores often behave intelligently in life by making good decisions, acting instantly and appropriately to save someone's life, or making wise personal choices. Consequently, some social scientists have rejected the psychometric approach to the study and measurement of intelligence in favor of other approaches such as Robert Sternberg's triarchic theory of intelligence (2000).

Sternberg's Triarchic (Three-Factor) Theory of Intelligence

Triarchic theory of intelligence: Sternberg's theory that there are three types of intelligence; analytical, creative, and practical.

Sternberg says that the limited scope of traditional intelligence tests makes it difficult to measure some aspects of intelligence such as street smarts (common sense and shrewdness in everyday life), social skills (getting along with people), and creativity (Sternberg, 2000; 2004). To meet these deficiencies, Sternberg has proposed a three-dimensional cognitive theory of intelligence[2] based on the principles of information processing. Sternberg's model includes a step-by-step analysis of cognitive processes which are applicable in any sociocultural context.

Componential (analytical) intelligence: One dimension of Sternberg's triarchic theory of intelligence typically included on conventional intelligence tests and measures analytical thinking.

The first dimension of Sternberg's triarchic theory of intelligence includes what we normally measure with conventional intelligence tests, which he calls *componential intelligence*, which forms the basis of information processing. It measures all of what we call analytical thinking; planning, organizing, remembering facts, and applying them to new situations.

Experiential (creative) intelligence: A second aspect of Sternberg's intelligence model which measures creativity.

Sternberg calls the second aspect of his intelligence model *experiential intelligence*. A person who possesses this type of intelligence is creative, can see new or unusual connections between things, and can relate to experiences in insightful ways. To do this, a person must be able to profit from his or her mistakes and capitalize on his or her experiences. Sternberg also proposes that the way a child deals with a novel situation is one of the best measures of reasoning ability. Yet, automatization of familiar skills such as driving a car is also a form of intelligence according to Sternberg because of the ease with which the task is performed, freeing cognitive resources for other tasks.

Contextual (practical) intelligence: A third dimension of Sternberg's triarchic theory of intelligence which assesses a person's ability to manipulate the environment for his or her needs. This dimension deals with the practical side of life such as the ability to stay out of trouble and having a knack for getting along with others.

Sternberg calls the third aspect of his triarchic theory *contextual intelligence*, the way an individual is able to manipulate his or her environment for his or her own needs. Thus, the girl who is afraid of being robbed by a gang on her way home from school may use contextual intelligence by persuading other children who live near her home to walk with her.

Although Sternberg has little quarrel with the types of intelligence tests that are normally used in school, he does not think they go far enough. He believes that there are times when experiential or contextual intelligence is more than the intelligence measured by traditional intelligence tests. For instance, Sternberg points out that traditional intelligence tests do not measure novelty and automatizations of information processing. According to Sternberg, these skills are necessary to measure creativity and practical knowledge as well as the ability to adapt to one's environment.

Differences Among Intelligence Test Scores

Only a few years after Alfred Binet introduced the first intelligence test in 1905, mental testers noticed discrepancies among individual scores. These differences

---

2. Recently, Sternberg changed the names of his three types of intelligence. The terms componential intelligence, experiential intelligence, and contextual intelligence have been replaced by the terms analytical intelligence, creative intelligence, and practical intelligence, respectively.

have shown up consistently until the present. Those who have the lowest scores are often members of ethnic minority groups and the poor, who are often also members of minority groups). For example, *taken as a whole*, scores of White children are approximately 15 points higher than those of Blacks (African-Americans) (Brody, 1992; Loehlin, 2000), with other ethnic groups, such as Native Americans and Hispanics, scoring at some intermediate level.

Usually, three explanations are given for discrepancies among intelligence test scores: Heredity, an impoverished environment, and cultural bias. Let's look at each argument.

The argument for heredity. Many pioneer mental testers interpreted differences among intelligence test scores as the result of innate differences in intelligence. A person was believed to be born with a certain mental capacity, which was genetically determined and therefore would remain relatively stable over time. According to this theory, some people are born smarter than others—a difference known as heritability—and no amount of training or variation in the environment will change the level of intelligence.

One of the most heated controversies regarding the innateness and stability of intelligence erupted when Arthur Jensen, a UC Berkeley professor, published an article in 1969 with the title, *How Much Can We Boost IQ And Scholastic Achievement?* Jensen argued that hereditary factors have a major influence on racial differences in intelligence. According to Jensen, 80 percent of the differences are due to heredity. Jensen argued that Blacks do as well as Whites on a lower level of intelligence which he calls *associative learning ability*. This includes mastering tasks through repetition and rote learning. According to Jensen, Blacks do not do as well on another level of intelligence, which he calls *cognitive learning ability* which is of a higher order and involves problem solving and abstract reasoning. In cognitive learning, we manipulate, elaborate, and transform incoming information mentally.

Critics charge that Jensen used biased tests, misused statistical techniques, and misrepresented data. Whereas Jensen claims that the heritability of intelligence (percentage of differences in a trait believed to be due to inherited factors) is about 80 percent, many investigators disagree. Recent estimates place the heritability of intelligence in the range of 50 to 60 percent (Plomin, Fulker, & DeFries, 1997).

Another person who differentiated between higher and lower mental functions was the Russian psychologist Vygotsky. Although Vygotsky did not become embroiled in alleged racial differences in intelligence as Jensen did, Vygotsky claimed that humans inherit the lower or elementary mental functions.

Vygotsky believed that our higher mental functions develop as a result of social interactions and through the use of signs and symbols that allow us to think in more complex ways. Language is another important tool which helps us to move to higher forms of intelligence, according to Vygotsky.

The debate about racial differences in intelligence scores was renewed in the 1990s in a highly controversial book, T*he Bell Curve* by Richard Herrnstein and Charles Murray. Herrnstein and Murray (1994) point out that Asian and Asian-American students typically test 3 to 5 points higher on intelligence tests than Caucasian students and that African-American children score about 12 points lower than Euro-American children.

The evidence for environment. A classic study of the effect of environment on children's IQs was conducted by Sandra Scarr and Richard Weinberg (1976; 1983). These two investigators evaluated the impact of

Associative learning ability: Arthur Jensen's view of one type of intelligence which measures the ability to learn through lower-form methods such as repetition and rote learning.

Cognitive learning ability: According to Arthur Jensen, a component of intelligence that involves manipulation, elaboration, and transformation of information mentally.

environment on African-American children who were adopted into Caucasian middle-class homes from African-American working-class families. The children's expected IQ, had they remained at home, was an average of 85. Their actual score was 97, just about the national average, even though the children had been adopted more than a year after birth. Those adopted closer to birth had even higher IQs.

This type of evidence strongly suggests that environment is a major factor in promoting the types of abilities which are measured by standardized intelligence tests. These are the same abilities that are important for success in school. But suppose that children who succeed in school are then transferred to a new culture. Will they perform equally well on an intelligence test in the new culture? Or, do intelligence tests have a *cultural bias*? Apparently they do.

Cultural bias: The perception that scores on intelligence tests draw on the background of the culture in which they are administered, and do not reflect the test taker's true intelligence.

The cultural-bias argument. One of the persistent criticisms of intelligence tests is that they draw on a background that is culture-specific (Lynn, 1996). Since different cultures do not emphasize the same skills or knowledge, children from diverse cultures are likely to answer the same question differently. For example, if an American child who was raised in Puerto Rico is asked to name the color of a lemon, he or she will usually answer "green," because lemons in Puerto Rico are often green.

Attempts to Construct a Culture-Fair Intelligence Test

Since every intelligence test reflects the values, interests, and experiences of one culture more than that of another, it is impossible to construct an intelligence test that gives all children—regardless of culture—an equal chance. This was a goal of mental testers in the past.

Culture-fair intelligence test: An intelligence test on which language differences and other cultural effects are negligible.

Today, the aim is to construct an intelligence test that is *culture-fair*, that is, the test is constructed so that language differences and other cultural effects are negligible. To date, no such test has been constructed. However, we can say that some tests are *more culture-fair* than others. One such test is the *Raven Progressive Matrices Test*, shown in Figure 11.3 which basis its scores on the test taker's ability to detect, evaluate, and match graphic patterns. However, even this simple test poses a problem for some children from cultures in which fill-ins or matching exercises are uncommon. Also, people with more education score higher than those with less education (Greenfield, 2003).

Raven Progressive Matrices Test: A test designed to be culture-fair by requiring people to identify, distinguish, and match patterns of varying complexity.

Another line of endeavor in the effort to construct a culture-fair test is performance tests which require few, if any, instructions. Here again we run into difficulty. For children from some cultures, even the notion of sitting down and taking a test is a completely foreign experience.

Hence, the issue of cultural relevance looms more important than ever. Since cultural diversity in the United States is increasing, devising a culture-fair test is becoming more difficult. As a result, many states, including California, have sharply curtailed the use of intelligence tests.

Figure 11.3
Sample item from Raven Progressive Matrices Test

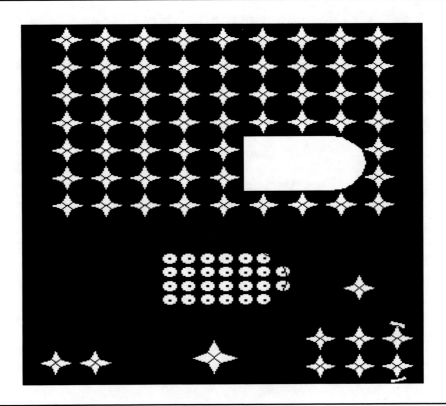

Note: As simple as this test appears—the answer is "6"—some children have difficulty with it due to cultural factors or lack of acquaintance with tests of any kind. In some cultures, the children are not even familiar with two-dimensional representations of figures.

LANGUAGE REFINEMENT IN MIDDLE CHILDHOOD

Metalinguistic awareness: The ability to understand hidden meanings in a language, and to achieve comprehension when information is fuzzy or incomplete.

"My, you're a good boy today," Carlos' mother says to him. "Yes, I am," Carlos answers somewhat sheepishly. In this brief exchange, Carlos detects a hidden meaning that is not obvious immediately from the content of the utterance. Carlos knows that when his mother remarks about his good behavior she is also referring to the many times when he hasn't been so good, without saying so directly. This ability to achieve comprehension when the information is unclear or incomplete, or to detect hidden meanings, known as *metalinguistic awareness,* develops throughout middle childhood and forms the basis of humor.

A little later that day, Carlos asks his mother whether they are still going to Disneyland. "We're going, aren't we?" he asked. "Remember," the mother replies, "I said we *might* go, I *didn't promise*." "I know," Mark said. In this exchange, we see another development in Carlos' language—the use of *tag questions.* Carlos' use of, "aren't we?" in a question. "We're going, *aren't we?"* is an example of a tag question. A tag question is a declarative statement with a question added to indicate uncertainty or to request confirmation. Tag questions are much more complex grammatically than *"yes/no," "who," "what,"* and

Tag question: A declarative (explanatory) statement with a question added to indicate uncertainty or to request confirmation.

"where," questions. Complete mastery of tag questions is not attained until the end of middle childhood or in early adolescence.

Finally, we should note that Carlos realizes that his mother did not promise him that they would go to Disneyland for sure. This illustrates that as a concrete-operational child, Carlos is learning more precise word meanings (Shulman & Capone, 2010).

Acquisition of More Precise Word Meanings

In a 1973 study, David Palermo demonstrated how children learn to apply words in increasingly precise ways. Three- to seven-year-olds were shown two cardboard apple trees and asked whether one tree had more or less apples on it than the other. While most of the 3-year-olds used the words "more" and "less" interchangeably, most of the 7-year-olds understood the distinction. Younger children vaguely equated both words with quantity, whereas older ones focused on the words' properties of contrast. Although 7- and 8-year-olds do not confuse words with one another as much as preschoolers, they still have difficulty. For example, they often confuse the words "ask" and "tell." Or, they may interpret the word "tell" correctly but interpret "ask" the same way.

Children's Humor

Anyone who has spent time with elementary schoolchildren knows that they never seem to run out of jokes and riddles. Telling jokes or riddles is a form of language play. This is why children who are most advanced in language usually have the best sense of humor. The ability to use humor and what one finds funny is linked to cognitive development (Chapman & McGheen, cited in Masten, 1986).

Because of the link between cognitive development and humor, the jokes and riddles of school-aged children are more sophisticated than those of preschoolers. A typical form of preschool humor is similar to this: "You know what?" the child asks. "What?" asks an adult. "That's what," answers the child. A youngster in middle childhood would find such a joke dumb or silly. He is more likely to use a joke involving concrete-operational thinking, such as the following:

"Mr. Jones went into a restaurant and ordered a whole pizza for dinner. When the waiter asked if he wanted it cut into six or eight pieces, Mr. Jones said: "Oh, you'd better make it six! I could never eat eight!" (McGhee, 1976, p. 422).

On the other hand, 7- and 8-year-olds are not likely to understand jokes based on ambiguities in grammatical structure or on different semantic interpretations which require formal operations such as:

"I saw a man-eating shark in the aquarium," states one teenager.

"That's nothing, I saw a man eating herring in a restaurant," jokes another.

Helping Children to Communicate

Numerous studies indicate that children can be taught to communicate more effectively. Here are a few pointers:

• **Teach children to focus on the differences among the stimuli that they are talking about (Pratt, McLaren, & Wickens, 1984).**

- **Encourage children to monitor what they hear carefully and to ask questions if they do not understand something (Patterson & Kister, 1981).**

- **Give children a written message before presenting it aurally so that they can read the message while they are listening to it (Olson & Hildyard, 1983).**

THE MIDDLE CHILDHOOD STUDENT IN SCHOOL

For Sara and Carlos, starting school is an important watershed. They must now leave the security of their home and family, perhaps for the first time, and become new social creatures, learning to get along with all kinds of new people. At the same time, the children's cognitive development makes them more curious than ever about the world around them.

The types of experiences Carlos has in school, particularly in elementary school, can enhance his potential or doom him to failure or mediocrity. Hence, school is a place where children develop—or fail to develop—many competencies that help them to define their self-concepts, abilities, and how they get along with their peers.

The way in which Carlos and Sara are regarded by their teachers can have a pronounced effect on their future prospects. Children tend to perform at the level expected of them.

A Teacher's Influence and the Self-fulfilling Prophecy

The effect that a teacher's expectations can have on a student's performance was demonstrated by Robert Rosenthal and Lenore Jacobson (1968). Their central theme was that "one person's expectations for another person's behavior can quite unwittingly become a more accurate prediction for its having been made." Rosenthal and Jacobson called this phenomenon *self-fulfilling prophecy*.

Self-fulfilling prophecy: The idea that a person's expectations of another person produce the result that was expected.

Rosenthal and Jacobson obtained their data from an experiment conducted by several elementary school teachers. First, an intelligence test was administered to all students from the first grade through the sixth grade before the beginning of the school year. Each teacher was given the names of five students identified as potential "academic spurters" or "intellectual bloomers" who would show a spurt in intellectual development during the school year. In fact, the names of the academic spurters or intellectual bloomers were chosen at random without the teachers' knowledge, so the superior potential of the bloomers existed only in the teachers' imaginations.

At the end of the school year, all children were tested again. The intellectual bloomers showed considerable improvement in IQ: 30 percent of the academic spurters gained an average of 22 IQ points; all pupils in Grades 1 and 2 gained at least 10 IQ points. Moreover, the teachers rated the intellectual bloomers as more curious, more interesting, happier, and more likely to succeed than those in the control groups. Although no concerted effort was made by the teachers to treat the experimental students differently, such as by spending more time with them, subtler influences may have been at work. Teachers' reactions may have varied between the two groups of students in tone of voice, facial expressions, touch, and posture. In short, there appears to be a clear link between teacher characteristics and expectations and student achievement.

Textbooks in the Educational Process

Textbooks have historically reflected the practices and values of society. For instance, three or four generations ago when men were considered to be the dominant force in our society, most textbooks depicted pictures of men rather than of women. This was particularly true of people in important positions. Doctors were typically depicted as being men and maids as women. However, during the last couple of decades women have been portrayed more often in important roles. Even the language in textbooks has been changed: *mankind* has been replaced by *humanity*, *cameraman* by *camera operator*, and *fireman* by *firefighter*.

Another recent change in textbooks is the inclusion of new (often controversial) themes. In the 1970s, children's textbooks broke new ground by discussing divorce, sex, nuclear fears, sibling rivalry, interracial adoption, and stepfamilies. Two themes that were added to the textbooks published in the 1980s were AIDS and drugs. The 1990s added other themes such as helping the homeless, avoiding war, preserving the environment, and teaching children how to get along with others who differ in color or ethnicity. Due to the increase in teenage (and pre-teenage) pregnancy, current textbooks are placing increased emphasis on sex education that goes beyond male and female reproductive systems and puberty. These new topics include proper use of condoms, sex refusal skills, and how to cope with sexual harassment.

Two new areas which are now being included in textbooks are *multiculturism* and *political correctness*. In the multicultural approach, the emphasis shifts from the traditional "Anglocentric" approach which centered on the White European male to one that validates all cultures and ethnic groups. The politically correct point of view represents a profeminist, progay rights, prominority studies perspective, and one that is mistrustful of tradition. Disabled Children in School

Although most children are able to perform reasonably well in school, some (about 5 percent) have limitations which prevent them from performing normally. Let's look at a few of these handicaps, or *disabilities*: Mental retardation, learning disability, and attention-deficit hyperactivity disorder (ADHD).

Mental retardation. Prior to the establishment of guidelines by the American Association on Mental Retardation (1994), mental retardation was defined almost exclusively in terms of a score on an intelligence test such as the Stanford-Binet or the Wechsler Intelligence Scale for Children.

Furthermore, in addition to using a cut-off score of 85 IQ, working practitioners also categorized mental retardation according to severity. The least severe type of mental retardation was called "borderline" with an IQ of 71 to 85. These individuals were rarely identified before they began school. The next category of mental retardation was called "mild" (IQ of 55 to 70), constituting some 90 percent of all people with mental retardation. The next category was called "moderate" (IQ of 40-54) followed by "severe" (IQ of 25 to 39), and "profound" mental retardation (IQ below 25.)

The current definition of mental retardation refers to *substantially below-average intelligence and problems adapting to an environment that emerge before the age of 18.* The cut-off score for mental retardation is from 70 to 75, reinforcing the notion that scores on intelligence tests (IQs) are not precise measurements. Consequently, the current view of mental retardation de-emphasizes IQ and places more reliance on adaptive skills which are often

Multiculturism: An emphasis that validates all cultures, rather than just one.

Political correctness: A view that represents all groups in a culture and is mistrustful of tradition.

Disability: A handicap such as mental retardation, dyslexia, and attention-deficit hyperactivity disorder.

Mental retardation: A disorder which occurs before age 18, characterized by an IQ below 70 to 75difficulty in adapting to one's environment.

measured by assessment tools such as the *Vineland Test of Adaptive Intelligence* (Venn, 2004).

Adaptive skills refer to a person's ability to perform in two or more tasks that are needed to function in one's environment or to get along in the world. One of the best-known instruments available for the assessment of adaptive behavior is the *AAMR Adaptive Behavior Scale*. This scale categorizes adaptive behavior functioning into five major categories, including personal self-sufficiency (e.g., how well a child can handle basic needs such as eating and toileting), community self-sufficiency (e.g., how well a child can function appropriately in common, everyday situations such as traveling about the neighborhood), personal-social responsibility (e.g., getting to school on time), social adjustment (e.g., individual acting inappropriately with other individuals) and inappropriate personal adjustment (e.g., excessive hugging or kissing).

Learning disability:
Difficulty processing basic information resulting in interference with the understanding of language and difficulty in communicating with others.

Learning disability. About 5 percent of children in middle childhood have difficulty processing basic information that interferes with their understanding of language, either written or spoken (Lerner, 1993). These types of obstacles to learning are called *learning disabilities*. Learning disabilities have no obvious physical cause such as blindness or hearing impairment, and are not the result of slowness of thinking as in the case of mental retardation. The most common form of learning disability is difficulty learning to read, particularly unfamiliar words, called *dyslexia*, also referred to as a developmental reading disorder. Let's look at a dyslexic child named Louella, a 10-year-old.

Dyslexia: An impairment in the ability to read.

One of Louella's problems is difficulty communicating to others what she has seen or heard. Louella also has difficulty processing certain information. She is often unsure in which direction to write, and confuses *"b's"* with *"d's,"* and *"p's"* with *"q's."* She often sees words in reverse order, such as seeing "saw" as "was." Louella has difficulty calling objects by their correct names; a "cup" may become a "drinking thing." Although Louella does poorly in school, her IQ is slightly above average, as is her family background, as well as her physical and emotional condition.

The most common explanation of the cause of learning disability, including dyslexia, is minimal brain damage causing a disruption in phonological processing--difficulty in breaking words into their component sounds. New imaging techniques indicate that dyslexic children have faulty wiring in the brain so that they cannot make the connection between the symbols(e.g., "kuh," "aah," and "tuh") and the word the symbols represent "cat." Children with dyslexia only hear the sound of the entire word "cat," hence they are unable to sound out words. They cannot pull the words apart into their constituent sounds, what scientists call phonemes — the smallest discernible segments of speech. A learning disability such has dyslexia might be inherited to some degree (Pennington, 1990) if it emerges before the age of 7 (American Psychiatric Association, 1994).

Attention-deficit hyperactivity disorder: A syndrome characterized by inattention, pervasive impulsivity, distractibility, and great activity at inopportune times.

Attention-deficit hyperactivity disorder (ADHD). About 3 percent of schoolchildren (about six times more common in boys than in girls) have *attention-deficit hyperactivity disorder* (ADHD), the technical term for what is usually called hyperactivity. ADHD is one of the most commonly diagnosed mental health disorders of childhood. The hallmark symptom of ADHD is distractibility. The mind wanders while the child is reading a book, having a conversation, or doing schoolwork. Also, ADHD victims do not pay attention; they are excessively active and impulsive, often being very disruptive. The

ADHD child fails to finish what he or she starts and doesn't seem to listen, focusing only on what he or she is interested in. The child has difficulty concentrating on school work. An ADHD child can't sit still for more than 10 or 15 minutes and is always getting into trouble (Brown, 1982; Weiss, 1990). Finally, recent evidence indicates that a higher proportion of children with ADHD grow into adulthood with the disorder than formerly believed, resulting in problems such as poor social competence and drug abuse.

There are many theories about the causes of ADHD, America's No. 1 childhood psychiatric disorder. Some investigators believe that ADHD is largely genetic, that is, inherited (Elia *et al.*, 1999) but familial and school environments have also been implicated (Woodward, Taylor, & Dowdey, 1998).

Treatment for ADHD has often involved drugs such as the stimulant Ritalin (methylphenidate) (Searight, Nahlik, & Campbell, 1995). Another drug is Norpramine (desipramine), however, it is seldom used due to fear of heart damage (Rappley, 2005). Each year, more than 1 million schoolchildren receive some form of medication for attention-deficit hyperactive disorder (Reilly, 1998). Although some drugs appear to be effective, there is no way to predict which children will show improvements and which ones will have adverse effects, including nausea and vomiting (Hartlage & Telzrow, 1982; Pelham & Hinshaw, 1992). Despite the lack of knowledge about the effects of drugs to treat ADHD children, the use of stimulants, antidepressants, and other psychiatric drugs increased significantly during the 1990s (Goode, 2000). In some classrooms, up to 20 percent of the students are taking Ritalin. Psychotherapy, combined with medication, has shown promise in the treatment of ADHD, particularly if it involves both the child and the parents to develop techniques for management of the child's behavior (Hechtman, 2005; Medd, 2003).

Educating Disabled Children

Mainstreaming: The integration of handicapped and nonhandicapped children, as much as possible.

Many suggestions have been made and tried in attempts to educate children with disabilities (Grigorenko, 2008). One common denominator that seems to run through all of these suggestions is *mainstreaming*, which is the integration of handicapped with nonhandicapped children, *as much as possible*. This means that some disabled children need to have a combination of segregated and mainstreamed classes, being separated from nondisabled classmates as little as possible, with specialized services provided within the regular classroom.

Public Law 94-142: The Education of All Handicapped Children Act of 1975, which requires all children with disabilities be given free, appropriate public education.

A major purpose of mainstreaming is to avoid stigmatizing disabled children as being different from nonhandicapped children and to offer them the same educational and social opportunities. To meet this end, the US Congress passed the *Education of All Handicapped Children Act of 1975* (Public Law 94-142) guaranteeing every child across the nation, between the ages of 3 and 21, the right to a free, appropriate public education (Grigorenko, 2008).

Individuals with Disabilities Education Act (IDEA):
Spells out broad mandates for services to all children with disabilities and includes evaluation and eligibility determination, appropriate education and the individualized education plan, and the least restrictive environment.

Inclusion: Placing disabled students in need of special services in regular classrooms rather than segregating them.

In 1986, Public Law 99-457, Education of the Handicapped Act Amendments mandated preschool services to all handicapped 3- to 5-year-olds and encouraged states to provide early intervention services to handicapped children from birth through their second years. In 1990, PL 94-142 was amended further and the title changed to *"Individuals with Disabilities Education Act,"* now called *IDEA*. Autism and traumatic brain injury were added as two separate categories of disability. In 1997, IDEA was amended tocall for (1) nondiscriminatory and multidisciplinary assessment of educational needs; (2) parental involvement in developing each child's educational needs, (3) education in the least restrictive environment, and (4) an individualized plan for each child. This legislation, updated in 2004, makes it clear that not all children learn in the same manner and ensures a free, appropriate public education for all children with disabilities.

There are many ways that teachers can help children with disabilities besides mainstreaming. One alternative is *inclusion*, the practice of placing disabled students in need of special services in the regular classroom rather than segregating them (Smith, 2004). Often, regular classroom teachers need specialized training to help some children with a disability and state educational agencies are required to provide such training (Wardle, 2003). Another technique is to take advantage of the child's strengths. If a child finds it hard to process visual information, the work can be modified to an auditory format if the child has good hearing. Persistent training can often result in a dyslexic child minimizing his or her reversal problems (*e.g.,* mistaking *"b's"* for *"d's"*; *"p's"* for *"q's"*). In some instances, children's school performance has improved when they receive additional attention from their parents, better medical care, and improved nutrition.

Often a child with a learning disability can be helped by pinpointing specific deficits that hamper his or her performance in school (Grigorenko, 2008). For instance, the teacher needs to spend considerable time with a student on the connections between letters and sounds if *boy* sounds like *toy* which sounds like *soy*. The child who cannot read and is worried about what his or her classmates and teachers think, can be helped by being told to relax and that he or she can learn to read with a little assistance from the teacher.

Attention-deficit hyperactivity disorder can be controlled by removing distracting stimuli, such as pictures on the walls, and by creating a comfortable, serene atmosphere. Many ADHD children can learn to read manually by using the American Sign Language (ASL). ASL relies on a set of hand movements for each meaningful word part, or morpheme. Reading Machines help the blind to "read" by converting print into electronic (synthesized) speech. Devices such as closed-circuit television can enlarge print size for a student who has a limited visual capacity. Specially designed computer games and CD-ROM books have helped dyslexic children recognize hard-to-hear sounds.

Electronic mail (e-mail) allows children who are deaf to communicate with one another as well as with hearing individuals. Deaf children may also subscribe to online news groups devoted to deafness and other disabilities. Disabled children can also be helped if schools have on-site clinics which integrate treatment of physical and mental problems (Bussing *et al.,* 1998). If disabled children are not given additional help to cope with their problems, they usually become anxious and concerned that they are different from other children, and their prospects for future success may diminish. School experience is particularly important for children with disabilities because it is an important setting for social, emotional, and cognitive development.

SUMMARY

Children are in the Piagetian stage of concrete operations from about age 7 to 11 years. Their egocentricism has declined, and they become more proficient at tasks such as conservation, seriation, classification, and dealing with numbers.

Moral development is influenced by a variety of factors, including the child's cognitive development, role-taking, and imitation. According to cognitive-developmentalists Piaget, Kohlberg, Gilligan, and Selman, moral development coincides with cognitive development.

Piaget divides moral development into two stages: Morality of constraint and morality of cooperation. Kohlberg's theory of morality extends Piaget's model to include six stages of moral reasoning which are organized on three levels: Preconventional, conventional, and postconventional. Selman has five stages of morality, with an emphasis on the importance of role-taking. Bandura emphasizes the importance of modeling and observation in moral development.

Children's memory improves considerably in middle childhood. They are able to rely more on short-term memory and metamemory, the understanding of how memory works. Middle-childhood youngsters also become quite proficient at using a variety of strategies for remembering.

The intelligence of children in middle childhood is assessed by individual tests such as the *Stanford-Binet* and the *Wechsler Intelligence Scale for Children (Fourth Edition)*, and by group tests such as the *Otis-Lennon School Ability Test*. Although intelligence tests are good predictors of school success and success in occupations that emphasize school-type abilities, they have many shortcomings.

Sternberg claims that conventional tests do not evaluate every aspect of intelligence. Others fault current intelligence tests for not being culturally fair. Hence, attempts have been made to construct new culture-fair tests. To date, no culture-fair test has been devised, and differences among performances in intelligence tests continue.

Children develop a greater understanding of language in middle childhood. Much of the development is the refinement of language skills. When Carlos and Sara are in middle childhood, they develop a more precise understanding of vocabulary, and their humor reflects their growth in language.

School sets the stage for the child's performance and image, which last beyond middle childhood. Teachers play a crucial role in self-fulfilling prophecies, which often limit student performance, particularly that of minorities. New textbooks address social issues and present an inclusive view of society.

School presents specific issues for disabled children. As much as possible, they should be mainstreamed; that is, placed in regular classes. Among atypical, or disabled children, are the mentally retarded, the learning disabled, and those with attention-deficit hyperactivity disorders.

IMPORTANT TERMS

Adaptive skills
Associative learning ability
Attention-deficit hyperactivity
   disorder (ADHD)
Autonomous morality
Cardinal number
Categorization
Chunking
Cognitive learning ability
Componential intelligence
Conservation
Concrete operations
Contextual intelligence, Sternberg's
Conventional morality, Sternberg's
Cultural bias
Culture-fair intelligence test
Decentration
Disability
Dyslexia
Elaboration
Experiential intelligence, Sternberg's
Expiatory punishment
Formal operations
Group test
Heteronomous morality
Hierarchical relationships
Horizontal decalage
IDEA
Identity constancy
Immanent justice
Inclusion
Information processing
Intelligence
Individuals with Disabilities
   Education Act (IDEA)
Learning disability
Long-term memory

Mainstreaming
Memory store
Mental retardation
Metacognition
Metalinguistic awareness
Metamemory
Moral absolutism
Moral realism
Moral role-taking, Selman's
Morality
Multiculturism
Numerosity
One-to-one correspondence
Operation
Ordinal number
Political correctness
Postconventional morality
Preconventional morality
Public Law 94-142
Raven Progressive Matrices Test
Rehearsal
Reversibility
Self-fulfilling prophecy
Selman's role-taking dilemma
Sensory memory
Short-term memory
Sternberg's Triarchic Theory of
   Intelligence
Tag question
Transitivity
Wechsler Intelligence Scale for
   Children—(Fourth Edition)
   (WISC-IV)
Wechsler Preschool and Primary
   Scale of Intelligence
Working memory

RELATED RESOURCES

Readings

Fraser, Steven editor (1995). *The Bell Curve Wars: Race, Intelligence, and the Future of America.* New York: BasicBooks.

Lipina, Sebastián J. (2009). *Poverty and Brain Development during Childhood: An Approach from Cognitive Psychology and Neuroscience* (Washington, DC: American Psychological Association).

Lockwood, Alan L. (2009). *The Case for Character Education: a Developmental Approach.* New York: Teachers College Press.

Nisbett, Richard E. (2009). *Intelligence and How to Get It: Why Schools and Cultures Count.* New York: W.W. Norton & Co..

Proulx-Schirduan, Victoria (2009). *Mindful Education for ADHD Students: Differentiating Curriculum and Instruction Using Multiple Intelligences.* New York: Teachers College Press; London: Continuum.

Rief, Sandra F. (2010). *The Dyslexia Checklist: a Practical Reference for Parents and Teachers.* San Francisco, Calif.: Jossey-Bass.

Smith, J. David (2009). *Ignored, Shunned, and Invisible: How the Label "Retarded" has Denied Freedom and Dignity to Millions* (Westport, Conn: Praeger).

Websites
American Association on Intellectual and Developmental Disabilities
http://www.aamr.org/

Council for Exceptional Children.
http://www.cec.sped.org

Learning Disability Association of America.
http://www.ldanatl.org

National Center for Learning Disabilities.
http://www.ncld.org

Chapter 12

Social Emotional Development in Middle Childhood (6 to 12 years)

Chapter Topics		Learning Objectives
How does self-concept development during middle childhood?		Recognize the theoretical perspectives on development of a self-concept: Freud, Erikson, Piaget, and Bandura.
What peer-related factors effect social emotional development in middle childhood?		Understand the peer group, peer pressure, interracial peer groups, and popularity in relation to social emotional development in middle childhood.
What family-related factors effect social emotional development in middle childhood?		Understand discipline, parenting styles, maternal employment, divorce, and family constitution in relation to social emotional development in middle childhood.
What types of psychological and emotional disturbances exist in middle childhood?		Explain the characteristics, causes, and potential treatments for several types of psychological and emotional disturbances in middle childhood: childhood depression, separation anxiety disorder, and obsessive compulsive disorder.
Chapter Summary		

Middle childhood: The elementary school period, from the age of about 6 to 12 years.

One way to describe *middle childhood* (ages 6 to 12), is *change*. During this period, children's self-concept and self-esteem become much more prominent. According to Freud, this development is due largely to a dominant superego; according to Erikson, this change is the result of the child's desire to produce.

Middle childhood also brings a change in discipline. The child now shares the responsibility for his or her discipline with his or her parents. Peers and school also help to control behavior. Sometimes the child is faced with a contradiction between what he or she is taught at home and what he or she learns in school.

Children in middle childhood may face challenges such as divorce, being raised by a single parent, or remarriage by divorced parents which affect their social emotional development adversely. The child may develop severe psychological and emotional disturbances, including

THE DEVELOPMENT OF A SELF-CONCEPT

Human beings have a desire to answer questions like "Who am I?" or, "How do I fit into this society?" Possibly, you have asked yourself questions like this not only lately but many times in the past. The answers to such questions provide a person with his or her *self-concept*, a sense of oneself as a separate individual who possesses a unique set of characteristics.

Self-concept: A sense of oneself as a separate individual who possesses a unique set of characteristics.

Self-concept begins in infancy at about 18 months of age when Sara realizes that she is separate from other people and things and begins to develop a sense of uniqueness and an image of herself which includes the global self (or self-esteem), the physical self (or body esteem), the athletic self, and the academic self. The struggle to come to grips with a sense of self is a lifelong process. Let's look at the progression of Sara's self-concept from infancy through middle childhood.

At 1½ years, Sara discovered many things that began to form her self-concept. Sara learned that she could control the movement of her hands and feet, that the wall did not move when she did, and that her hands and feet were always nearby. On the other hand, her mother and father would come and go. Young Sara discovered that if she bit a teething ring, it felt different than if she bit her hand. Sara also discovered that the person she saw in the mirror was herself. By about 2 years of age, Sara was able to recognize a distinction between herself and others. These experiences helped Sara to develop an understanding of the permanence of self. She had also started developing a distinct personality with an individual style of coping with the world.

The next major step toward developing a self-concept occurred during the preschool period (ages 3 to 6). At age 3, Sara was able to think of herself mostly in terms of visible characteristics or "externals." She would describe herself in concrete terms such as eye color, pony-tailed hair, and family residence ("I live in that big house over there"). A year or two later, Sara was likely to describe herself not only in obvious physical terms but also in terms of activities ("I like to play ball"). Toward the end of the preschool period, we see the beginning of *social comparison* when children evaluate themselves by comparing their characteristics, abilities, values, and other qualities with those of other individuals, particularly their peers. Social comparison serves as an important means by which children evaluate themselves and develop their self-image and self-esteem (Ladd, 2005).

Social comparison: The desire to evaluate one's behavior, abilities, and expertise to perform effectively in social situations.

Researchers have noticed that there is a marked increase in the use and complexity of social comparison in the early elementary school years. Eight-year-old Carlos knows that he is stronger than his friend Wayne, but not as strong as his father. Carlos also knows that he is not as good at baseball as his friend Jimmy.

The shift in judgment of abilities, behavior, appearance, and other characteristics from the self to others, or social comparison, is due to a variety of factors (Ladd, 2005). When children begin elementary school, their behavior is being continually evaluated by their peers, teachers, and parents. Changes in physical size, strength, and skill necessitate constant reevaluation. What children could not do only a few months previously, may be well within their capability today. Schoolchildren's developing cognitive abilities enable them to make more critical evaluations of people's reactions to them. By the time children reach 7 or 8 years of age, their social comparisons become quite prominent.

A highlight in middle childhood is children's description of self-concept in abstract terms such as "smart," "dumb," and "nice." The use of abstractions means that elementary schoolchildren begin to build an integrated personality theory to describe their motives, feelings, and thoughts. Toward the end of middle childhood, children also begin to be concerned with self-control.

Development of the Private Self

In the chapter on social emotional development in preschoolers, it was mentioned that preschool children tend to describe themselves in concrete terms ("I have blue eyes" and "I play baseball"). At around 8 years of age, there is a developmental shift toward emphasis on internal, or psychological, self-descriptions. Carlos now realizes that he has a public self (or selves) that others see and a private self (or selves) that is not available for public scrutiny. The course of this development was vividly illustrated by Robert Selman, first discussed in chapter 11. Selman posed story dilemmas such as the following:

"Eight-year-old Tom is trying to decide what to buy his friend Curry for a birthday present. By chance, he meets Curry on the street and learns that Curry is extremely upset because his dog, Reno, has been lost for two weeks. In fact, Curry is so upset that he tells Tom, "I miss Reno so much that I never want to look at another dog...". Tom goes off only to pass a store with a sale on puppies. Only two are left and these will be gone soon" (Selman, 1980).

After hearing the story, children were first asked whether Tom should buy Curry one of the puppies. To probe the children's understanding of the distinction between the private self and one's public image, they were asked follow-up questions. Sample questions included, "Can you ever fool yourself into thinking that you feel one way when you really feel another?" and, "Is there an inside and an outside to a person?"

Selman found that prior to middle childhood, children did not distinguish between private feelings and public behavior. They took Curry's statement that he never wanted to look at another dog again at face value. According to Selman, children at this stage are at the physicalistic level because the self is equated with specific body parts. A child at this stage might say that her mouth tells her hand what to do or that her ideas come from her tongue (Selman, 1980).

At about 8 years of age, most children say that Curry would be quite happy to have another puppy. They realize that there can be a difference between inner states (psychological experience) and outward appearances. Children now understand that each person has a private, subjective (inner) self and a public self. Eight-year-olds also understand the possibility of self-deception. By 8 years of age, children also understand that it is possible to tell oneself that one should do one thing, while in reality he or she is doing something quite different (Selman, 1980). For example, a child might tell herself or himself that she or he should not ride a bike on a certain street, yet be persuaded to do so.

As a result of understanding the private self and the ability to make social comparisons, the child's self-concept takes on new dimensions in middle childhood. Eight-year-old Carlos not only sees himself as the physical self, an image based on his movement skills, strength and appearance, but also as the active self, and image that includes skills that influence other people. He also sees the social self, which reflects his activities based on approval or disapproval of others, and the psychological self, with an awareness of his knowledge, motivation, and learned skills. This increased awareness of the self provides Carlos with motivation toward further development of the self-concept.

Self-Esteem: An Evaluation of One's Own Worth

So far, we have discussed self-concept in a descriptive and nonjudgmental manner, but usually when we describe ourselves (or others), we do so with either a *positive* or a *negative* connotation. When we evaluate our own (or others') qualities along a positive/negative dimension (*e.g.,* "good" or "bad"), we are referring to *self-esteem*. Self-esteem generally rises during the late elementary school years and then declines with the advent of puberty. This decline is particularly marked for girls (Wigfield & Eccles, 1994).

Self-esteem: An individual's overall and specific positive and negative self-evaluation.

The importance of self-esteem for proper development has been noted by a number of investigators. Erik Erikson views self-esteem as a critical index of mental health. In fact, high self-esteem is a necessary first step toward successful adjustment (Klein, 2000). Children with high self-esteem are more satisfied with themselves and are more likely to achieve identity status, which formulates a mature conception of an integrated set of goals, values, and beliefs. Children with high self-esteem are less likely to be depressed or anxious, and are more likely to do well in school and to be adjusted socially (Baumeister *et al.,* 2003).

Measuring self-esteem. Susan Harter (1998), a researcher, has devised a questionnaire for children aged 8 and older which assesses their self-esteem—or self-worth—in five domains. The questionnaire, known as the *Self-Perception Profile for Children (SPPC)*, evaluates children's scholastic competence, athletic competence, social acceptance, behavioral conduct, and physical appearance. Figure 12.1 shows a sample question from Hater's questionnaire. Harter discovered that young children (aged 4 to 7) do not have a general sense of self-esteem. However, children's self-esteem is well established by age 8 or 9 because their concept of the self has extended beyond self-appraisal.

Figure 12.1

A Sample Item from Harter's Self-Perception Profile for Children;

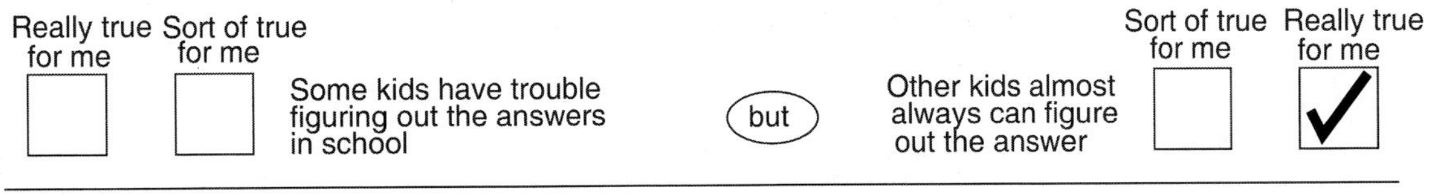

Choices to the left of center indicate degrees of poor self-esteem or self-worth; those to the right indicate degrees of positive self-esteem.

Source: Harter, 1985.

Prior to about age 7, children adopt an all-or-nothing view of being "loved" or "not loved." As the children mature, their perception of themselves broadens and becomes multidimensional (Klein, 2000). For example, 8-year-old Carlos may see himself as competent academically, but awkward on the basketball court. Sara, also 8 years of age, may see herself as being loved and admired, but somewhat of a loner. Children's perception of themselves (positive or negative) forms the basis for their self-esteem, which can be global as well as multidimensional and both positive and negative.

According to Harter, self-esteem depends on two factors. First, the smaller the discrepancy between a child's achievement in something that he or she values (*e.g.*, being good in a sport) and the goal he or she sets, the greater the child's self-esteem. Second, the more support a child receives (particularly from parents and peers) in areas that matter to him or her, the greater his or her self-esteem.

Parenting styles and children's self-esteem. Research has linked parenting styles to self-esteem. In an extensive study of 10- to 12-year-old boys, Stanley Coopersmith (1967) found that parents of children with high self-esteem showed their children love and respect and accepted them while making greater demands for academic performance and good behavior. The parents structured their children's world in ways that they believed were proper and appropriate, then allowed the children considerable freedom within these limits.

Coopersmith found that clear, consistent rules let children know what is expected of them and provide them with guidelines for gaining internal control. According to Coopersmith, children's self-esteem is most evident when the parents have firm but reasoned control, when they use positive encouragement of independence, and when they foster a warm, loving atmosphere. Coopersmith also discovered that the parents of children with high self-esteem have high self-esteem themselves. The parents lead active, rewarding lives, while permitting their children to dissent openly. Coopersmith found that the amount of time spent with children does not affect children's self-esteem as much as the *quality* of parenting.

Coopersmith also studied parenting styles of children with low self-esteem. The parents had fewer rules; the limits were few and poorly defined, and when broken, harsh control techniques were used. Although the limits were often vague, absolute compliance was demanded. The effect on the children was one of confusion and a feeling of powerlessness. The parents were usually withdrawn, resulting in the children not having meaningful contacts with adults.

The parenting style which fits best with Coopersmith's findings on self-esteem is Diana Baumrind's model of authoritative parents (1971; 1978;

1982; 1989; 1991). The parents direct children's activities in a rational, issue-oriented manner. The parents do not flaunt their authority, taking it for granted that they have more physical power than their children. Verbal give-and-take between parents and their children is welcomed, and the parents encourage their children to discuss the reasoning behind their own (parents') actions (Branden, 1994). If the child disagrees, he or she is allowed to explain the reasoning behind the objections. Yet, the adult perspective prevails, high standards are set for the children, and they are encouraged to be individualistic and independent. Baumrind's authoritative style of parenting should not be confused with *authoritarian parenting* where parents emphasize and often demand, obedience and make most of the decisions for their children. The result is that the children feel subdued, they have low self-esteem, are highly aggressive, and out of control.

Authoritative parenting: Diana Baumrind's term for a parenting style in which parents emphasize (often demand) unquestioning obedience.

Bidirectionality of self-esteem: An interactive process in which adults affect a child's behavior and self-evaluation, but the child's characteristics (e.g., personality and behavior) also influence the thinking and behavior of adults.

Bidirectionality of self-esteem. Although it seems obvious that the way Sara turns out, including the amount of self-esteem she possesses, is a one-way street from parents to children, this is not always the case (Jenkins *et al.,* 2005). First, there is little doubt that parents shape the child, but the kind of parenting style chosen may unwittingly be based on the child's temperament. Hence, children play an important role in shaping the child-rearing practices used by their parents, a phenomenon known as reciprocal influence. In other words, parents influence and direct their children but their children also influence the parents, and in reality play an active role in their own socialization (Bronfenbrenner & Morris; 1998; Kuczynski, 2002).

The way a child affects the behavior of adults is illustrated by Kathleen Anderson and her associates (Anderson, Lytton, & Romney, 1986) who worked with mothers of 6- to 11-year-old boys. Some of the boys were judged to be normal while others were diagnosed as "conduct-disordered"—they were defiant, aggressive, destructive, or had other serious problems. When the mothers were paired with conduct-disordered boys, they (the mothers) were more coercive and demanding than when paired with more normal boys. This held true for mothers of normal boys as well as for mothers of conduct-disordered boys. We can see that children *do* have an influence on how they are treated (Miller-Loncar *et al.,* 1997).

FOUR THEORETICAL PERSPECTIVES ON THE DEVELOPMENT OF SELF-CONCEPT

Self-concept is defined as a person's perception of him or herself as an individual with specific characteristics and behaviors. Several theories of personality offer a perspective on the development of Sara's and Carlos' self-concept: Freud's Psychosexual Theory, Erikson's Psychosocial Theory, Piaget's Cognitive Development Theory, and Bandura's Social Cognitive Theory.

Freud's Psychosexual Theory - Latency Stage (Ages 6 to 11)
According to the Freudian model, Sara and Carlos, now 9 years old, are nearing the end of the latency stage. They have functioning superegos (consciences) that keep the id (the home of powerful instincts, such as hunger and the sexual urge) in check, they have resolved their Oedipal or Electra conflicts, and they have assumed an appropriate gender role. Carlos' and Sara's sexual energies have

become oriented toward adapting to their culture, including school. Freud would say that the sexual energies have been repressed and channeled into school activities. Sara and Carlos can now work on acquiring the facts, skills, and attitudes that will help them to assume an effective adult role.

Freud's ideas that school-aged children repress their sexuality, or lack interest in sex and channel their energies into schoolwork and other non-neurotic social activities, have been largely discredited. Many contemporary researchers believe that school-aged children engage in a variety of sexual behaviors including masturbation and cross-gender exploits such as asking "sexual" questions (Calderone & Johnson, 1981). Much of this sexual behavior is hidden because of society's disapproval.

Erikson's Psychosocial Theory - Stage IV: Industry Versus Inferiority (Ages 6 to Puberty)

According to Erik Erikson, school-aged children continue in their attempts to resolve past crises. For instance, the 9-year-old child continues to try to resolve the initiative crisis (most prominent from age 3 to 6) by trying to do things on his or her own. Sometimes children feel overly guilty, such as when they hit someone. However, school-aged children spend most of their time resolving the crisis of *industry versus inferiority*. A successful resolution of this crisis means that children will want to produce and will no longer be satisfied with play. In our culture, school-aged children strive to learn the "three R's"—l reading, writing, and arithmetic. They also learn skills such as how to use tools and ride a bicycle. Mastering new skills allows children a degree of independence, heightens their sense of worth, and provides a feeling of self-control that is a crucial defense against emotional problems (Bradley & Corwyn, 2005).

According to Erikson, if the school-aged child fails at certain tasks and feels worthless and inadequate, the result is inferiority. In the more extreme cases, he or she may withdraw with the feeling, "I can't do anything right."

> **Industry versus inferiority:** In Erikson's theory, the fourth stage of psychosocial development occurs in middle childhood, when a successful resolution of conflicts results in the child becoming a competent and productive member of society.

Piaget's Cognitive-Developmental Theory

A major change in the elementary schoolchild's thinking is a shift toward the cognitive-developmental theory proposed by Jean Piaget. Remember, Piaget viewed the child as being able to actively build psychological structures and cognitive development that takes place in stages. The cognitive-developmental theory seems to be more applicable to self-concept in middle childhood than in early childhood because the thinking processes are much more advanced than they were in preschool. Rather than thinking solely from his own point of view as he did in preschool, Carlos is able to decenter and to think from another's point of view. Carlos' increasing flexibility makes his thinking less rigid. No longer does 8-year-old Carlos think of himself as a "good" or a "bad" boy. He now knows that most of the time he is good, once in a while, he misbehaves.

One branch of cognitive-developmental theory is the information-processing approach. According to this view, Carlos processes information about himself according to the type of cognitive structure, called the *self-schema* (plural, self-schemata), he possesses.

Self-schema is an internal cognitive portrait of the self that is used to organize information about the self. Since self-schemas depend on the way that Carlos and Sara filter, interpret, and organize their information, they have different views of the world and of themselves. Their particular views also

> **Self-schema:** An internal cognitive portrait of the self that is used to organize information about the self.

influence how they react to the world around them. For example, if Sara has a positive self-schema--that is, she has high self-esteem--, she is likely to notice compliments which further enhance her self-image. In contrast, if Carlos has a negative self-schema, or low self-esteem, he is likely to be more aware of comments which confirm his negative feelings and lower his self-esteem still further.

Bandura's Social Cognitive Theory

According to social cognitive theorists such as Albert Bandura, the school-aged child's self-concept is particularly affected by his or her observation and imitation of models. This is due to the child's keener sense of self-awareness and observation than when he or she was in preschool. The school-aged child is most sensitive to being influenced by individuals (models) he or she perceives as powerful or rewarding. Models can be parents, teachers, or other children. In fact, by the time a child is 8 or 9 years old, other children may be copied more than parents or teachers. A child who has an older brother is likely to be more physically active and daring than one without an older brother.

Many investigators have questioned the use of reinforcement of behavior through reward or punishment—sometimes advocated by social cognitive theorists—in shaping behavior. One problem is that the opposite of the desired behavior may be reinforced unintentionally. In one study (Snyder, 1977) of families with problem children, the families unconsciously reinforced their children's displeasing behavior (with smiles or favorable comments and the like). In this study, families with well-behaved children punished their children more than families with problem children.

SOCIAL EMOTIONAL DEVELOPMENT

"Goodbye, Mom," says 8-year-old Carlos as he scurries out the front door. "I hardly ever see that boy any more," the mother says to a friend. "I guess he doesn't need me anymore," the mother adds dejectedly. Carlos' behavior is typical of boys his age. There is a major shift in children's relationships with their parents in middle childhood—away from parents *towards* peers. A word of encouragement to the mothers before we go on: "Mom, your children still love you and need you—but in a different way!"

School-aged children need their parents (and grandparents) for guidance, for lasting, dependable bonds, and for affirmation of competence or value as a person. Parents (and teachers) are also looked upon as providers of new skills. Peers fulfill other needs.

The Peer Group

Peer group: Individuals of equal or similar backgrounds and approximately the same age.

Peer groups usually form naturally among children of approximately the same age who live in the same neighborhood and go to school together. They often have similar ethnic or racial backgrounds and interests (baseball, hockey, and "hanging around") (Pellegrini *et al.*, 2002). Of particular interest, is the way peer groups influence other children—both positively and negatively, although researchers do not dismiss the influence of parenting skills (Ladd, 2005; Collins *et al.,* 2000). Often peer groups can become cliques intent on excluding their peers ("Stay away from us, we don't like you") or including their peers ("Come with us, we want to be your friends").

Positive influence of peer groups. Peer groups provide children with a realistic appraisal of their abilities, a feat next to impossible in the home because of the power parents exercise over their children. Furthermore, parental prejudices and biases hinder children from making objective appraisals of themselves. It is more helpful for children to make their own appraisals by comparing themselves with their peers. Peer groups also help children establish a new form of control. If Carlos hogs the ice cream, leaving very little for his peers, he soon learns that authority is established by the children themselves. Rather than ruling by decree, peer group authority occurs through negotiation, compromise, discussion, and sanctions, which are often more effective than those imposed by parents, where control comes from the top.

Toward the end of middle childhood, (from about 8 to 12 years) children begin to form small groups called cliques. Cliques range from 2 to 12 individuals and are usually of the same gender. Cliques usually share ideas, hang out together, and often develop an in-group identity in which they believe that their clique is better than other cliques.

Peer groups in middle childhood appear to have considerable influence on a child's achievement in school (Ryan, 2001). For instance, the level of a student's achievement is influenced more by his or her peer group if the members are high achievers than if they are low achievers. A student's achievement in school is also influenced more if the child's peer group dislikes school than if it enjoys school. However, a peer group is not equally influential on all academic characteristics. Parents play a bigger role in their children's perceptions on the usefulness of school than peers do.

An important function of the peer group in middle childhood is companionship and intimacy (Ladd, 2005). Individual friendships in middle childhood are highly segregated. Whereas 35 percent of friendships in preschool are cross-gendered companionships, by age 7 or 8, cross-gender friendships are almost nonexistent. Girls rely more on their female friends than on boys, since their friendships with other girls are more intimate, affectionate, and worth-enhancing.

Acceptance by one's peers has a positive effect on self-image and a feeling of belongingness. Rejection by one's peers in middle childhood consistently predicts behavioral and emotional disturbance later on, such as aggression, hostility, delinquency, depression, and withdrawal.

Adverse peer group pressure. Several investigators have addressed the issue of children's extreme susceptibility to engage in delinquent behavior as a result of peer pressure. Not all children seem to be equally influenced by their peers. The susceptibility is related to child-rearing practices. In a study of children in the fifth through ninth grades, Lawrence Steinberg (1986) found that children who were raised by authoritative parents (who reason with children, listen and compromise, and set firm limits) were less susceptible to adverse peer pressure. These children were also less likely to get into trouble when they were on their own after school. Children who came from either dictatorial (authoritarian style) or lax (permissive) homes were most likely to succumb to negative peer pressure, as were children who were loners and who did not get along with their peers (Patterson, Reid, & Dishion, 1992).

Age is also a factor in yielding to peer pressure. Children of 10 or 11 years of age are much more likely to succumb to peer pressure than younger children. This tendency increases to the age of about 15 and then decreases. Some scientists view the age-related increase in conformity to negative peer pressure as an attempt to model accepted adult behavior, rather than as social deviance (Jessor, 1998).

Prejudice and Discrimination

Prejudice: An unjustified negative, stereotyped attitude toward an individual — who often belongs to a minority group — based solely on the individual's membership in a particular group

A major task in children's social development is learning to work and play in harmony with other children (and adults) of various ethnic and cultural backgrounds. Unfortunately, this is not an easy task in America where racism is rampant. In middle childhood, children usually begin to develop negative stereotyped attitudes toward minorities, a phenomenon known as *prejudice* (Ruble *et al.,* 2004). ("My mommy told me not to play with black children" or "You're white, we don't want to play with you.") In some instances, children do not show prejudice until the end of middle childhood. The display of prejudice is heavily dependent on family, community, and historical pressures (Ruble, *et al.,* 2004). With considerable reduction in racial prejudice in the United States, many children who learn to be prejudiced, actually develop more positive feelings toward other groups as they age (Barrett, Lyons, & Valle, 2004). A counterpart of prejudice is *discrimination*, behaving unfairly toward a particular group of people. A task for our society is to find ways to deal with the problems of prejudice and discrimination so that everyone is treated equally and justly.

Discrimination: Behaving unfairly toward a particular group of people.

Brown vs. Board of Education of Topeka, Kansas: Court-ordered desegregation of "separate but equal" segregated schools.

One method that is used to minimize prejudice and discrimination is school integration. However, a wide body of evidence shows that court-ordered desegregation, such as that first handed down in 1954 (*Brown vs. Board of Education of Topeka, Kansas*), is not enough to promote total integration. Although the court struck down the so-called "separate-but-equal" segregated schools as unconstitutional and directed school systems to act with "all deliberate speed" in implementing change, two-thirds of African-American students still attend schools that have a majority of Black or Latino students. One method which seems effective in promoting greater interracial acceptance in elementary school is assigning students from different ethnic backgrounds to the same ability groups for instruction (Ramsey, 1995)[1]. Finally, cooperative effort by children should not only involve close physical contact, but also the contact should be frequent and last for an extended period of time.

Popularity

By age 6 or 7, Sara and Carlos begin to make distinctions among people and to seek the company of certain children with some consistency. Children who are preferred by others with some regularity are *popular*; those who are ignored or rejected are *unpopular*. The topic of popularity has received considerable attention lately since there appears to be a clear link between lack of popularity in early childhood and poor school adjustment, school dropout, delinquency, and psychopathology in adolescence and adulthood (Kupersmidt, Coie, & Dodge, 1990).

Who is the popular child? Popular children tend to share a number of characteristics. Despite the maxim that "beauty is only skin deep," popular children tend to be physically attractive. Even 6-month-old infants can easily discriminate between attractive and unattractive faces (Langlois *et al.,* 1991). Popular children tend to be healthy, vigorous, and well-poised. Popular boys tend to mature early, although early maturing girls are seldom popular. Girls who mature "on time" tend to be the most popular.

Popular children have a number of behavioral characteristics in common. They are likely to have a good sense of humor, they are not too aggressive, they do not seek attention often, and they feel good about themselves. Perhaps most importantly, popular children know how to get along with other children, that is, they possess social skills. Popular children tend to share things more than unpopular children, they cooperate more, and they help others more. Popular children also possess superior cognitive skills. They tend to do well in school and to score higher on intelligence tests than unpopular or rejected children (Butkowski *et al.,* 1993; Franco & Levitt, 1997).

Although we normally think of popular children as being prosocial, that is, their actions benefit other persons without any expected reward for themselves, a few children are popular even though they are antisocial. This small subtype consists of aggressive children who are often getting into fights, defy adult authority, and usually do poorly in their schoolwork. These children are popular because they are often good athletes, and sometimes even because they exploit others (Rodkin *et al.,* 2000).

Who is the unpopular child? Certain characteristics exist in unpopular children. The most outstanding trait is aggression. By aggression is meant all acts in which harm is intended to another person. In a longitudinal study of popularity, Frank Vitaro, Richard Tremblay, & Claude Gagnon (1992) found that children who were unpopular were more likely to be rated as "fights most" than popular children. Other forms of negative behavior by unpopular children include social withdrawal, annoying behavior, and bossiness (Coie, 1990). Unpopular children tend to be mistreated at home (Pollak *et al.,* 2000).

Unpopular children are often not aware that they are disliked. Nor are they usually aware of the reasons for their unpopularity. Often they have a positive view of themselves and deny their role in peer difficulties (Sandstrom & Coie, 1999).

Helping the unpopular child. The traditional adult response to helping an unpopular child is to pressure him or her to socialize (interact) more with

---

1. A precedent to the Brown vs. Board of Education of Topeka, Kansas, was the US Supreme Court ruling in 1948 in the Mendez vs. Westminster School District of Orange County (California) case which struck down the practice of segregating American schoolchildren of Mexican descent.

other people. The solution is not that simple. The solution seems to be to provide social skills that will change the *quality* of the unpopular child's interactions. One such attempt was undertaken by Sherri Oden and Steven Asher (1977) with third- and fourth-graders.

In this study, unpopular children participated in six sessions over the course of a month. Each unpopular child was paired with a moderately popular child and both were taken to a separate room where they played games together. Prior to each session, except the first, a "coach" instructed the unpopular child for 5 to 7 minutes in several different social skills: Getting involved and paying attention, cooperating—taking turns and sharing, communicating—talking, listening, and validating, looking at the other person, giving support, and the like.

After each pair of children played together, the coach again discussed social skills with the unpopular child. A few days later, all the children in the classroom rated their classmates on work and play. Each rating showed a higher acceptance of the unpopular children. This evaluation held true a year later even though many of the classmates were new and had not participated in the study the year before. According to some authorities (*e.g.*, Mize & Ladd, 1990), children as young as 3 or 4 years of age can be taught proper social skills.

Another technique for helping unpopular children is modeling. In one type of modeling program, unpopular children are shown films of popular children in complex social behaviors. According to Albert Bandura's social cognitive theory, children can learn new forms of behavior by merely observing the behavior of a model, making mental notes, and then using these representations to copy the model's behavior at some future date. Hence, rejected or unpopular children can learn skills that lead to peer acceptance (LaGreca, 1993).

FAMILY INFLUENCE IN MIDDLE CHILDHOOD

When Sara was 3 years old, her parents were concerned about their daughter establishing daily routines such as washing her hands before mealtime, going to the bathroom on time, and controlling her temper tantrums. When Sara reached middle childhood, new issues arose; one of these was discipline. Although the parents' philosophy on discipline remained basically the same, the parents realized that they should not use the same techniques as before.Sara's parents were also concerned about how involved they should become in her school, especially in their daughter's homework.

Other family factors which affect children are the mother's employment outside the home, divorce, and single-parent families (including one-third of the mothers who have never been married.)

Discipline

Discipline: Techniques of socialization intended to teach children how to regulate their own behavior.

All parents exercise some form of control over their children's behavior. While some use heavy-handed tactics such as spanking, others adhere to the Latin definition for *discipline*, meaning "knowledge" or "instruction." An important aspect of control or discipline of children is the amount of supervision parents should use as the children get older. Research indicates that middle childhood should serve as a transitional period when parents switch to a different form of supervision. In this new form of supervision, parents exercise general oversight, while permitting their children to be in charge of moment-by-moment decision-making. This type of supervision is called *coregulation*.

Coregulation: A transitional form of parental supervision in which the children receive general oversight but are permitted to be in charge of their moment-by-moment decision-making.

In coregulation, children are given greater independence than when they were younger, yet they are given considerable support since children are seldom capable of making most adult-type decisions in middle childhood. Coregulation means the parents and children share the disciplinary powers. To accomplish this task, children and parents need to communicate clearly; moreover, the parents must take time to get to know their children well so that they can make informed decisions about when to step in. Proper coregulation enables children to monitor their own behavior such as adopting acceptable standards, avoiding undue risks, and recognizing when they need help from adults.

Coregulation is consistent with Freud's belief that middle childhood youngsters are preoccupied with mastering adult standards because of the emerging prominence of the superego. The superego acts like a parent, giving the ego orders and threatening it with punishment if it "misbehaves" (Freud, 1940/1964). Of course, children are often willing to share control of their own behavior because their developing cognitive abilities enable them to see the necessity for some form of discipline or control.

Parenting Styles

A considerable body of research shows that not all parents treat their children the same way. Some parents make greater demands for chores, some allow more deviant behavior (e.g., fighting and disruption in school), some try harder to motivate their children.

So, which style of parenting is the right one? If you visit the Internet and click through the thousands of Web sites offering information on how to rear children properly, you may be more confused than ever. However, developmental psychologists have been able to group the various parenting styles into a handful of categories. For example, Diana Baumrind (1971) has identified three major parenting practices based on the particular type of parental authority: *Authoritarian, authoritative,* and *permissive*.

Authoritarian parents: Diana Baumrind's term for a parenting style that emphasizes strict enforcement of rules. Obedience is viewed as a virtue and the children are expected to mind without argument.

Authoritarian parents are highly demanding and unresponsive to their children. The parents have a high set of standards for their children's behavior and emphasize obedience, respect for authority, and order. Authoritarian parents have rigid expectations about their children's behavior and are emotionally distant and unresponsive. Whereas we normally think of the father in the family as being the authoritarian figure, the mother can also be highly authoritarian. Furthermore, maternal authoritarianism independently predicts children's conduct problems 5 to 10 years after birth.

Authoritative parents:
Diana Baumrind's term for a parenting style that uses firm enforcement of rules, but allows give-and-take between parents and child.

Permissive parents: In Baumrind's terminology, parents who make few demands on their children and allow them to determine their own schedules and activities.

Authoritative parents maintain a balance between being demanding and responsive. The rules are firmly enforced, and the children's conduct is monitored consistently. Authoritative parents are warm and supportive of their children's behavior and encourage them to express their ideas and opinions (Kuczynski & Lollis, 2002). Despite allowing the children considerable freedom, authoritative parents set high standards for their offspring (Fletcher, Steinberg, & Sellers, 1999).

Permissive (neglectful or indulgent) parents use a nonpunitive method of discipline and expect socially responsible and mature behavior from their children. Permissive parents are nurturant, communicative, and accepting of their children, but are very tolerant of their children, and there is very little parental control.

Effect of Baumrind's parenting styles. Each parenting style has a different effect on children's behavior. Children with authoritarian parents tend to be unfriendly, relatively withdrawn, apprehensive, and lacking in curiosity. They are usually obedient and self-controlled.

Children raised by authoritative parents tend to be competent, self-controlled, independent, assertive, and inquiring. The children tend to do well in school and to be responsible, self-reliant, and friendly.

Children raised by permissive parents tend to be dependent, immature, and to misbehave frequently. The children also tend to be impulsive, aimless, and lacking in self-control. Often, children raised by permissive parents experiment with drugs, sex, and alcohol.

Baumrind discovered that there are gender differences in the way boys and girls respond to parenting styles. Sons of authoritarian parents have more difficulties with social relations than daughters and are more defiant toward people in authority. The daughters are more independent than their brothers, while the sons tend to be more socially responsible than their sisters.

Since most parenting styles emphasize control, a key question is how much control is best. Most studies (e.g., Kurdeck, Fine, & Sinclair, 1995) have concluded that a moderate level of control — including a limited amount of supervision and monitoring — produces the best results. Lawrence Kurdek and Mark Fine (1994) found that high levels of parental monitoring had no greater impact on drug use by children than moderate levels. Moderate levels of supervision seem to result in higher student grades.

Maternal Employment

When one of the authors of this text began the study of psychology in 1946, the word "mother" conjured up an image of a housewife who stayed home and took care of the house and children while her husband went to work. Today, only about 10 percent of American households are made up of a breadwinner-husband, homemaker-wife, and children. A major reason for this change is maternal employment outside the home. Whereas in 1947 the proportion of employed married mothers was 20 percent, by 2000, the figure had reached nearly 71 percent (U.S. Census Bureau, 2002). While some mothers work for economic reasons (to supplement the husband's income or because they are the sole family supporter), others work to further their careers, and to have a more fulfilling life (Duncan & Chase-Lansdale, 2001). What effect does maternal employment have on the children? Are there any harmful effects? Any benefits?

Effects of maternal employment on school-aged children. A vast body of research has enabled investigators to make some generalizations about the effects of maternal employment on children. Generally, the findings are positive, especially for older girls. Daughters of working mothers have higher educational plans and express plans to work in adulthood more often than daughters of nonworking mothers. They are also more independent, outgoing, are high achievers, and show better social and personal adjustment. Daughters of employed mothers also have higher career aspirations, regardless of the family's socioeconomic status (Hoffman, 2000). Daughters of working mothers appear to have higher self-esteem compared with sons of working mothers. This may be due to working mothers paying somewhat less attention to their sons.

If a mother works, social class is a factor, particularly for boys. Sons of middle-class unemployed mothers are more dependent, conforming, and inhibited than those of working mothers. Traditional stereotypes, which dictate specific gender behaviors, are more pronounced (rigid) for boys of working mothers from low-income families than from middle-class families. Also, boys from lower-class families whose mothers work experience more strain in the father-son relationship, they admire their fathers less, and are less well-adjusted than sons of mothers who do not work outside the home.

Bruce Baldwin (1985) states that working parents do not spend enough time with their children. Instead, they shower their children with gifts, trying to buy the children's affection. Working parents seldom spend time teaching their children how to do tasks such as mowing the lawn, but instead hire lawn service. According to Baldwin, these children do not learn to perform well, they do not learn responsibility, and have no self-discipline, resulting in children who want to have everything *now* without working for it. Yet, many mothers who work teach their children responsibility, self-discipline, and other necessary skills. A critical factor appears to be the mother's attitude toward employment. Since many women feel better about themselves if they are employed, they are able to assume their mothering duties with a more positive attitude. We must also remember that some benefits go beyond the children. One side benefit is the breakdown of the stereotype that the "woman's place" is in the home.

The effect of a mother's employment on her child's development is unclear and often contradictory as illustrated in a series of studies (seven in all) by the National Longitudinal Survey of Youth (NLSY) (Olsen, 2003). The NLSY is a survey of women who have been interviewed annually since 1979 when they were 14 to 22 years old. Beginning in 1986, the children (approximately 5,000) of these women have also been assessed several times.

One of the most striking contradictions among the findings of the NLSY series is the effect of the mother's employment when her child is under 3 years of age. Using the data from the NLSY series, Nazli Bayder and Jean Brooks-Gunn (1991) and Jay Belsky and David Eggebeen (1991) found adverse effects on the children if the mother went to work when the children were very young. However, in studying many of the same children, Elizabeth Harvey (1999) concluded that early maternal employment does *no* significant harm to the children.

Nuclear family: A family structure consisting of a mother, a father, and their biological child or children.

Blended (reconstituted) family: A family created from a combination of stepchildren, stepparents, and stepsiblings.

Children of divorce suffer in many ways.

Children of Divorce

Prior to about 1960, most children (about 90 percent) grew up in a home with both their biological mother and father, in what is called a *nuclear family.* The nuclear family has been viewed historically as the institution that had the responsibility for providing the child with a happy, stable home with devoted parents. Today, slightly more than half (56 percent) of children live with their biological mother and father and no one else (Fields, 2001). Even this low figure is a 5-percent decrease over the number of nuclear families in the late 1980s (Popenoe, 1993).

One reason for the low number of nuclear families, is an increase in the number of unmarried—often divorced—mothers; another reason is the high rate of divorce. Nearly 60 percent of contemporary American marriages will end in divorce, affecting a million children every year (Levine, 1990; National Center for Health Statistics, 1997). What is the impact of divorce and how can children be helped to cope? We will look at these issues, including what happens if the custodial parent decides to remarry and form a *blended* or a *reconstituted family.*

The impact of parental divorce. The most comprehensive study of the effects of divorce on children is the *Children of Divorce Project,* begun in 1971 and directed by Judith Wallerstein. (Wallerstein, 1984a, 1985; Wallerstein & Blakeslee, 1989; Wallerstein, Lewis, & Blakeslee, 2000). The study involved 60 divorced families with 131 children, ranging in age from 2 to 18 years, including families from a variety of backgrounds. The children were interviewed at various periods immediately following divorce and periodically for the next 30 years.

Wallerstein's overall conclusion was that the effects of divorce are not uniform and are much less optimistic than is generally believed—families do not recover spontaneously after a few years. According to Wallerstein, the negative effects of divorce are cumulative; the impact increases over time. Wallerstein found that 5 years after the marital breakup, about one-quarter of the children seemed to be resilient; they showed relatively few ill effects and seemed to be able to cope with their changed lives. Yet, children this group felt lonely, unhappy or sorrowful about the divorce and harbored vivid, detailed memories of the breakup after 10 years. About one-half of the children "muddled through life coping as best they could." About one-quarter were so bruised by the divorce that they were unable to recover even after 10 years. After 20 years, many of the children were struggling to create strong love relationships of their own. They had little tolerance for conflict in their personal lives, believing that every argument represented the permanent slamming of a door. One-third of them said that they did not want to have children and that they would never want a child to go through what they endured when they were young. Six years after divorce, when the children were entering adolescence, family life continued to improve for mothers with daughters but there was considerable conflict between mothers and sons.

Wallerstein and her colleagues also found that over 70 percent of divorced women with children dropped their standard of living in the first year after their marital breakup. Furthermore, few of the children were helped financially with their college education, despite the fact that many of the fathers could have afforded to do so. Other studies have found that two out of three teenage suicides occur among children of divorced parents. Children of divorced parents have a shorter life expectancy, higher mortality rates, more illnesses, and

Sleeper effect: Judith Wallerstein's term for the negative effects of divorce on the children which occur some time after the family breakup.

tend to receive less cognitive and social stimulation, with divorced parents generally providing "minimal parenting."

Wallerstein found that some girls from divorced families suffer from the *Sleeper Effect*. They function reasonably well (their grades are good; they have friends, and they are not depressed) until they become old enough to have a serious relationship. Girls from divorced families become afraid to get involved, fearing that they may repeat their parents' marital failure. Adolescent girls from divorced families also worry about being betrayed, they have difficulty establishing a realistic view of men, and have difficulty exercising good judgment in their choice of partners.

Wallerstein's study is criticized because it failed to track a control group. Critics argue that the absence of a control group makes it difficult to judge whether the problems experienced by children of divorced parents are the result of the divorce or are due to other factors such as poverty or family discord. The critics also say that other factors such as the age of the child at the time of divorce and gender should also be taken into account.

Several studies (*e.g.*, Hines, 1997) indicate that the effect of divorce on children varies with the age of those involved. Preoperational children are confused by divorce because they do not have enough concrete experience to assimilate the idea of permanent separation. However, preschoolers seem to fare better than children of other ages. In follow-up studies conducted by Wallerstein 20 years after the parents' divorce, many children who were preschoolers at the time of the family breakup said that they had no memory of their family before the divorce (Wallerstein, 1984, 1987; Wallerstein, Lewis, & Blakeslee 2000).

The children's gender is a factor in the effect of divorce. Boys are usually affected more deeply than girls and feel the impact longer. Moreover, boys are more likely to be angry with their mothers whom they blame for the loss of their fathers (Hetherington, Cox, & Cox, 1982; Hetherington & Stanley-Hagan, 2002). The gender of the departed parent is also important, particularly for adolescents. Teenagers seem to suffer most if they lose a parent of the same gender.

To hold or to fold a bad marriage? Since the effects of divorce can be so devastating, some people have wondered if children would be better off if the parents stayed together even though they do not get along. The Virginia Study of Divorce and Remarriage by Mavis Hetherington, Martha Cox, and Roger Cox (1982) provides some insight. These researchers followed two groups of preschool children. One group resided in divorced families while the other lived in intact households. Both groups had some families with high and low levels of conflict. In the first year following divorce, children from divorced families had more problems adjusting. By two years following divorce, children from intact, conflict-ridden homes were more poorly adjusted.

These findings suggest that, in the long run, it is probably better for families to break up if they cannot get along (Cherlin *et al.*, 1991). Caution is warranted, however. We are just beginning to understand that children from divorced families suffer in many ways. Furthermore, the effects vary according to factors such as the child's understanding, age, and relationship with the parents. Until we know the full impact of divorce, we must resist stating firm conclusions.[2] We do know, however, that children from families with low levels of marital conflict are almost never better off if their parents divorce. Oddly enough, children from highly conflicted families are seldom better off following a divorce (Braver *et al.*, 2004).

Effects of divorce on grandchildren. Studies indicate that the same problems (lower education, marital discord, and parental tension) which are associated with divorce are "handed down" not only to their children but to their grandchildren as well. Furthermore, the grandchildren are affected adversely by their grandparents' divorce even if they had not yet been born at the time of their grandparents' marital breakup (Amato & Cheadle, 2005).

Helping children of divorce. There are many guidelines parents can use to ease the adverse effects of divorce on their children. Children need advance warning about the intended marital breakup so that they can adjust. Children should be told the truth about the reason for the divorce, and they should also be told that they are not the cause of the family dissolution. Also, the children should be reassured that they are loved and that they will not be abandoned.

Both parents should maintain frequent contact with their children throughout a divorce proceeding and after the legal breakup of the marriage. There should also be a sharing of parental decisions until the child grows up. Reliable, frequent contact with the noncustodial parent is particularly beneficial for the boy (Kelly, 1987). While visits by the absent parent may help, a more active relationship is desirable. The child should have many opportunities to participate in the daily activities of the noncustodial parent. Such activities help to reduce the child's dependence on one parent, and make the likelihood of maladjustment more remote.

Joint physical custody: A shared parenting arrangement in which both the father and the mother take equal responsibility for the care and upbringing of their child.

To allow for more contact between the child and the divorced parents, some courts grant *joint physical custody*—a shared parenting arrangement in which both the biological father and the mother take equal responsibility for the care and upbringing of their child. This practice is a controversial one, and not all psychologists and legal professionals advocate it. Some researchers (e.g., Maccoby & Mnookin, 1992) say that joint physical custody does not improve a child's lot in life, even if the divorce is amicable, and may worsen it in a bitter divorce. Others report better cooperation with former spouses and greater financial resources than in sole custody, with no association between the child's adjustment and the form of child custody (Pearson & Thoennes, 1990). A key factor is frequency of child-father contacts (Arditti & Keith, 1993).

Judith Wallerstein and Sandra Blakeslee (1989) suggest four major ways to help children whose parents are divorced:

- **The children should be aware of what they're going through. Many children are not aware that how they feel at 19 years of age is connected to their parents' divorce 10 or 15 years earlier. These children need to separate the past from the present.**

- **The parents should seek support for their child from sympathetic adults: grandparents, aunts, and teachers. An older confidant often provides more needed attention, stability, and validation for the child than the divorced parents.**

---

2. We must also remember that long-term behavioral and psychological problems seen in many children of divorced parents are usually due to factors in addition to the divorce itself and the resulting absence of a parent. Children of divorced parents are also damaged by parental discord and arguments that preceded the family breakup.

- **The children should draw a line between their needs and those of their divorced parents. Children can be compassionate toward their divorced parents, but they also need to take care of themselves.**

- **Parents should pay attention to how their children's lives are affected by custody arrangements, and consider modifying them if necessary.**

Helping divorced parents. There are many organizations and programs that are designed to help divorced parents and those in the process of getting divorced. The largest of these organizations is Parents Without Partners, with a national membership of about 180,000. It has numerous local chapters with programs designed to alleviate the problems of divorced parents (Koek & Martin, 1988). *Divorce mediation,* consists of a series of meetings between divorcing parents and a trained professional, often court-appointed, who helps with issues such as child custody and property settlement. Divorce mediation has resulted in more out-of-court settlements and has reduced conflict between parents and their children.

Divorce mediation: A series of meetings between divorcing parents and a trained professional with the idea of reducing family conflict and legal battles.

Increasingly, children of divorcing parents are included in the mediation process (Gentry, 1997). Advantages include a focus on the needs of the children and giving them some sense of control at a time when they feel helpless. Disadvantages of involving children in mediation include imposing undue pressure or burden on the children to make decisions for which they may not be ready and placing them in a situation where they are faced with a conflict in loyalty to one or both parents.

The One-Parent Family

Whereas we normally think of a family as consisting of a mother, a father, and their biological children, such is not always the case. Historically, one-quarter to one-third of American children have lived at some time before the age of 18 years in a single-parent household. Up until about 1900, the biggest reason for one-parent families was death. One in five children could expect to see a parent die before the age of 30 at the turn of the twentieth century; today, the figure is one in fifteen.

Since 1970, the number of one-parent families has more than doubled in the United States due mostly to the rising rates of divorce and parenthood outside of marriage. Single-parent families are more common among African-Americans and Latinos than among White Americans. Although single parents usually have extremely limited resources of time, money, and energy, in some cases they raise competent, successful, and well-adjusted children.

A major reason for one-parent households currently is children born to unmarried mothers. About 1 in 3 of all births are to unmarried parents. Divorce is still the single largest cause of one-parent families. Following divorce, most children (84 percent) reside with their mother in a single-parent home (Cherlin & Furstenberg, 1994).

Is it possible to raise a child properly in a one-parent family? Apparently so (Bornstein, 1995). Children grow up better adjusted when they have a good relationship with one parent than when they grow up in a two-parent home where there is discord and discontent. Many studies (*e.g.*, Amato & Keith, 1991) have failed to find significant differences between children of divorce and children in families with two biological parents. However, a substantial body of research has shown that, on average, children who are raised from birth in two-parent families have better outcomes (e.g., cognitively and behaviorally) compared with children who were raised by a single mother. The research also points to the many problems that are common in one-parent families.

Over half of one-parent households headed by women live on a family income below the poverty level (Miller & Davis, 1997; National Center for Children in Poverty, 2000). The mother in a single-parent household is often isolated, which may cause her to devote less attention to her children. Also, she has no one to act as a buffer between her and her children when she is not functioning well as a parent. Several studies have found that 3 out of 4 of all juveniles in state reform institutions come from father-absent homes, and that children from single-parent homes achieve poorly in school more often. (Menaghen, Kowaleski-Jones, & Mott, 1997; Miller & Davis, 1997). Also, many studies have found a link between the absence of the biological father and the daughter's early sexual activity and pregnancy. If the single mother is divorced, there is a 75 percent chance that she gets less than the full amount of child support from the absent father or none at all (Children's Defense Fund. 2000).

The Blended Family

For most parents, divorce is a temporary situation. About 65 percent of women and over 75 percent of men remarry within 3 years of divorce to form a new group of persons called the *blended family* (Bumpass & Raley, 1995). This new unit usually consists of a biological mother, her children, and a stepfather. In 2007, about one child under the age of 18 in every 5 families was living in a reconstituted family.

Blended (reconstituted) family: A family consisting of a biological parent, a stepparent, and one or more children.

Effect on children. The transition to a blended household is fraught with difficulties (Biller, 1993; Fischman & Hamel, 1981; Hagan, *et al.,* 1992; Kurdek, 1991). Children often feel resentment because they believe that the stepparent is intruding into their lives or has caused the parental breakup. The children may direct their anger at the absent parent or toward the stepparent. The children's loyalties often lie with the absent parent, which interferes with forming ties with the stepparent. Stepchildrens' hostility might intensify if they wish to live with the absent biological parent or if they are jealous of the attention the stepparent receives from the custodial biological parent, and express these feelings by misbehaving (Kutner, 1990). A major problem is the lack of emotional bonding between stepparent and stepchildren. One authority, Mavis Hetherington, has labeled stepfathers as "polite strangers" who often demonstrate a "disengaged parenting style" (Hetherington *et al.,* 1992). Usually, girls suffer more from parental remarriage than boys.

Stepparents often experience rejection when they try to assume the parental role. In many instances, stepparents—particularly the stepfather—remain detached deliberately (Gibbons, 1993). However, boys will occasionally accept their stepparents with open arms, while stepdaughters seldom do so (Aquilino, 1991).

Easing the problem of blended families. Stepfamilies need guidelines for forming new intimate relationships (Kurdek, 1991). Courses in remarriage preparation, counseling, and honest discussions of feelings among stepfamily members can ease many problems (Jacobson, 1980; Kheshgi-Genovese & Genovese, 1997). Since stepchildren generally feel more rejected than children in nuclear homes, they need to be constantly reassured that they are *welcome* in the new home. Older children need to have considerable space, such as a room of their own and less supervision by stepparents. Stepparents should take an active role in the supervision and discipline of their stepchildren only gradually. They should *first* build a friendly relationship with their stepchildren.

PSYCHOLOGICAL AND EMOTIONAL DISTURBANCES IN MIDDLE CHILDHOOD

Robert, 8 years old, receives the highest grades in his second-grade class. He is also quiet and cooperative. Whenever Robert's mother talks to his teachers, they praise him. Yet, there are many times when Robert seems bored, has no initiative, feels worthless, hopeless, and is unable to sleep at night. He also has headaches and other pains.

Lately, Nadia seems petrified at the thought of going to school. When her parents tried to force her on the school bus the other day, she broke out in a sweat, complained of chest pains and dizziness, and became short of breath. Nadia has no interest in friends and is obsessed with suicide and death. Sariya experiences a repetitive need to wash her hands after touching anything. She is often upset because she feels like she has germs on her hands and washing them does not help.

All three of these children have a psychological or emotional disturbance. Robert suffers from *childhood depression*; Nadia has a type of separation anxiety disorder known as *school phobia.*; and, Sariya is plagued by *obsessive compulsive disorder.*[3]

Childhood Depression

Childhood depression: A feeling of boredom, no initiative, worthlessness, hopelessness, and inability to sleep at night.

About once a month, Mark feels "blue" or "down in the dumps" for three or four days. Is Mark's depression normal or is it a cause for concern? Since Mark's depression is not too severe and lasts for only a few days, there is little need to worry. Almost everyone suffers from mild periods of sadness, unfortunately, some children suffer from major depression.

---

3. For more information on children's mental and emotional disturbances, write to: Meridell Achievement Center, P.O. Box 203638, Austin, TX. Or call 1-800-366-8656.

Contrary to conventional thinking, major depression can afflict prepubertal children — those under about age 12 (Gotlib & Hammen, 2009; Rey & Burmaher, 2009; Wolk & Weissman, 1996). The peak age for major depression is 16 years (Connelly *et al.*, 1993). Physicians view depression as a lifetime illness (Hirschfeld, 1996).

Symptoms. Although some characteristics of childhood depression are age-specific (American Psychiatric Association, 1994), the basic symptoms are similar in childhood and in adulthood. In the more extreme cases, a major symptom of depression is attempted suicide. Another symptom is a child's extreme sadness and the admission of that sadness.

Several investigators have indicated that depressed individuals tend to be less effective in interpersonal functioning (Kovacs, 1997). Other symptoms include a feeling of worthlessness, helplessness, withdrawal, continual crying, and lowered initiative. Still other symptoms of childhood depression include boredom, irritability, inability to concentrate or sleep at night, but napping during the day, extreme feelings of guilt, giving up activities or hobbies, loss of appetite and weight, and extreme fatigue (Gotlib & Hammen, 2009; Rey & Burmaher, 2009). Children who report high levels of depression also tend to have high levels of anxiety and fear (Ollendick & Yule, 1990; Thapar, 1997). About 1 in 10 children between the ages of 6 and 12 experience these symptoms.

We must remember that the symptoms for a disorder normally found in American textbooks such as depression, apply mostly to Caucasian American, mainstream children and adults and may manifest itself differently in different cultures. For example, depression among the Chinese manifests itself through bodily symptoms such as constipation, loss of appetite, and fatigue, with little emotion displayed which is common among White individuals born in America. Disorders such as depression may also appear predominantly in one culture and not in another (American Psychiatric Association, 2000).

Causes. The roots of childhood depression are largely unknown, although there are a number of suspected causes (Gotlib & Hammen, 2009; Ray & Burmaher, 2009). One suspected cause is biological, including an abnormal supply of hormones and abnormal electroencephalograms (records of electrical discharges from the brain). Some scientists suggest that depression is inherited, since parents of depressed children tend to be depressed. Children also tend to be depressed if they do not receive enough support and approval from their families.

Helping mildly depressed children. Although children with severe depressive disorders (often called major or clinical depression) need professional help, milder forms—a basic case of the doldrums—may be alleviated by people with little or no professional training. The first step in informal "treatment" is to recognize when depression is most likely to occur. Children often feel depressed after a summer vacation when it's time to go back to school. They may become depressed on the first rainy or cloudy day in the fall, signaling the end of a laid-back summer. During these times, the parents should encourage the child to talk.

The depressed child should be urged to get plenty of rest and to maintain good eating habits. The child should not skip breakfast and he or she should eat five or six small meals or snacks throughout the day. The food should be nutritional, since depression can be caused by a lowered state of energy. The child should remain active—but not to the point of overtaxation. Instead of ignoring unpleasant feelings, the child should acknowledge them. The depressed child should make a list of everything he or she likes and dislikes in school, and also be aware of any recent changes in his or her personal life.

Children who are depressed are often isolated.

Sometimes, developing a new routine during depressed periods helps, as does listening to music. Whenever possible, the family should try to do fun things. Parents should also refrain from criticizing the child when he or she is depressed, since criticism increases the child's guilt and feeling of worthlessness. If possible, parents should postpone major changes, such as moving to another town, until their children finish school.[4]

Treatment of severely depressed children. We have to be mindful of the cultural variations in the treatment of childhood depression. Some cultures emphasize seeking assistance from family members. Other cultures view any sign of mental illness as a disgrace to the family that must be hidden from everyone (Suzuki, Meller, & Ponterotto, 2000).

Little is known about the treatment of severely depressed children. There has been some success using a behavior-modification approach, where attempts are made to increase desirable behaviors and decrease unwanted responses. Behavior-modification emphasizes socially appropriate interactions with others, altering maladaptive thinking, and self-evaluation.

Drug therapy has also been used to treat depression. The most widely used antidepressant is Tofranil (imipramine). Like other drugs, Tofranil has met with little success in the treatment of children's depression. As a result, the Food and Drug Administration approved Prozac (fluoxetine), the most widely used antidepressant in the world, for children's depression. Prozac does not produce the unwanted side effects that are induced by other antidepressants such as anxiety, insomnia, and nausea.

However, in an apparent contradiction, in 2004, the Food and Drug Administration ordered a black box warning on all antidepressant drugs, issuing its strongest warning. The FDA warning linked antidepressant drugs to increased suicidal thoughts and behavior among children and adolescents taking them. Yet, no antidepressant drugs for children are banned since scientists claim

---

4. For more information on depression, write to: the National Institute of Mental Health, Room 15C-05, Dept. P, 5600 Fisher's Lane, Rockville, MD, 20857.

that the drugs can be of significant benefit for children when they are used appropriately[5].

Most therapists believe that drugs are most effective in the treatment of depression when they are combined with counseling such as talk therapy (Mayer, 2009). If a severely depressed child is not given any form of therapy, there is a one in six chance of suicide some time during his or her lifetime.

Separation Anxiety Disorder

Separation anxiety disorder: A violent, lengthy reaction to being separated from a customary caregiver.

Ever since Sara was 9 months old, she would express rage and despair when her parents were leaving without her. If the protest is not too severe and lasts for a short time, the child is experiencing *separation anxiety*. If the child reacts violently for a considerable length of time to the separation (e.g., cries for several hours without stopping), we have a classic case of *separation anxiety disorder* (Silverman & Dick-Niederhauser, 2004).

Symptoms. A key symptom of separation anxiety disorder is extreme fear of separation from the parents or caregiver. Often, there are physical symptoms such as nausea, stomachaches, and dizziness. The symptoms may last for several weeks. In some instances, the disorder may appear even if the separation does not involve any unpleasantness. Consider 11-year-old Nadia who refused to spend the night at her best friend's home next door because her parents were going out of town for a week. When Nadia was told that her grandmother would come to stay with her, her physical symptoms and fear seemed to disappear instantly.

Cause. The cause of separation anxiety disorder is unknown, although there are some common elements. The parents tend to be professionals and they often suffer from separation anxiety disorder themselves. However, the family is usually caring and closely-knit. Children with separation anxiety disorder are usually average or above-average students. In many instances, the child had some trauma, such as death of a significant figure, preceding the disorder.

School phobia: An overwhelming fear of going to school and active resistance to attending school.

School phobia.[6] One type of separation anxiety disorder which has received considerable attention is *school phobia*, an unrealistic dread of school, so extreme that the child refuses to go to school. About 16 out of every 1,000 children develop this disorder.

The most obvious symptom of school phobia is an overwhelming fear of going to school and active resistance to attending school. The fear of school can be so intense that the child cannot be coaxed into the school bus or into the school building. If the school-phobic child manages to get to school, he or she may cry, complain of aches and pains, and cannot be calmed down. A child with school phobia may constantly talk about his or her fear of school, complain about stomachaches or headaches, or become unusually clingy. Often the school phobic child will ask for repeated reassurance from the parent such as, "Can you stay at school with me?" or "Do I have to go?"

Cause. There are many theories about the cause of separation anxiety disorder, including school phobia. From a psychoanalytic perspective, school phobia is related to fear of separation from parents—particularly from the mother. The child may be afraid that the mother is in danger of serious illness or

---

5. For more information on antidepressant drugs, visit the Food and Drug Administration on the web at: www.fda.gov/cder/drug/antidepressants/default.htm
6. To learn more about phobias, write to: National Alliance for the Mentally Ill, Colonial Place Three, 2107 Wilson Blvd. Suite 300, Arlington, VA 22201. Phone: 703-524-7600.

death. To protect his or her mother from harm, the child feels that he or she has to stay home to avert this threat. All of the child's thinking and feeling—except his or her dread of going to school—are unconscious according to psychoanalytic thinking.

There is some evidence that the parents of school-phobic children are also phobic. Many of the parents show significant signs of depression and anxiety. There is also evidence of panic disorder among parents of school-phobic children (Martin *et al.,* 1999). Hence, school phobia may be inherited.

Treatment. A variety of ways have been suggested for dealing with separation anxiety disorder including school phobia (Stallard, 2009). One way is to have familiar people and objects with the child at the time of separation. Another way is to suggest that the stranger, such as a new babysitter, be sensitive and unobtrusive (Shaffer, 2000). Many therapists believe that the first element in treatment of school phobia should be an early return to school to break the phobic cycle.

A technique for treating phobias through gradual introduction to the feared stimulus is Joseph Wolpe's *systematic desensitization therapy (SDT),* a form of behavior modification (Wolpe, 1958). The basic idea in SDT is that people are not able to experience two contradictory emotions, such as pain and pleasure, simultaneously. Thus, a child who has a dread of school (pain) might be told beforehand that after school he or she will see a movie featuring his or her favorite actor (pleasure). Wolpe believes that pleasure and relaxation (which is taught by the therapist) can inhibit a pain response, if the pain is not excessive.

A favorite technique in SDT is to rank the individual's feared stimuli from the least feared to the most feared. Next, the patient relaxes to offset the pain resulting from the feared stimulus. The patient is then asked to think about the least-threatening stimulus. The stimuli that are next most feared are presented in sequence to the subject verbally until the patient feels comfortable with every stimulus.

The final phase of SDT could include gradual exposure to the feared stimulus itself. For example, a person who has an intense fear (phobia) of blood, might first be shown a scalpel, then a vial of blood, then taken on a tour of a hospital, including the surgery room, then watch an operation in which there is considerable blood. When there are no more rungs to climb, the subject is considered to have been treated successfully.

Some therapists recommend a combination of psychotherapy and drugs such as Tofranil (imipramine) or Xanax (alprazolam) to treat phobias. While pharmacological (drug) treatment often works, drugs have many undesirable side effects, and a second opinion is usually advisable. Although drugs may provide immediate relief for anxiety disorders such as phobia, their long-term effect on developing children is largely unknown. Since school phobia often represents other problems in the child's family, such as alcoholism or marital conflict, treatment should include the parents.

Obsessive-Compulsive Disorders (OCD)

Children may have two sets of chronic-related behavioral patterns, *obsessions* and *compulsions,* which often occur in combinations. Unwanted recurring thoughts and impulses experienced as senseless or repugnant, such as thinking that one's hands are dirty after washing them dozens of times, are called obsessions. One of the most common themes in obsessional thoughts is fear of

Systemic desensitization therapy (SDT): A form of behavior modification therapy in which the subject is exposed gradually to a feared object for the purpose of overcoming the fear.

Obsession: Unwanted recurring thoughts and impulses.

Compulsion: A repetitive, stereotyped act performed to relieve fear.

germs and contamination, which is what we see in Sariya's case (Riskind *et al.*, 1997). Impulses to perform certain acts repeatedly, such as washing one's hands in a particular way 150 times a day, are called compulsions. Compulsive acts range from mild kinds of superstitious behavior (such as one will get hurt if he or she steps on the cracks in sidewalks) to a rigid, senseless routine, such as opening and closing a door 50 times before entering a building to make sure that the door is unlocked (American Psychiatric Association, 2000). Obsessive-compulsive disorders[7] affect 1 to 2 percent of children and are typically chronic, yet fluctuating (vary in degree of severity) (Piacentini *et al.*, 2003).

A key feature of obsessive-compulsive behavior is perfectionism (*e.g.,* excessive concern over the smallest mistakes) and excessive doubts about one's actions (Frost & Stekette, 1997). Another characteristic is the feeling of being responsible for almost everything that happens, especially unfavorable outcomes (Ladoucer, Rheaume, & Auble, 1997). Obsessive-compulsive victims know that their behavior is irrational, yet, they believe that harm will come to them if they do not perform the rituals. Often, the victims will minimize or deny the disorder (King, Leonard, & Marsh, 1998).

Cause. According to Freud, the nagging thoughts and repetitive actions hold anxiety back by suppressing it from conscious awareness. The obsessive-compulsive child who opens and closes the door several dozen times before he enters a house may be repressing his fear of being locked in a closet for punishment.

Most current theories explain the origin of obsessive-compulsive behavior as biological in nature, involving increased sensitivity to the neurotransmitter serotonin. The hereditary basis of obsessive-compulsive disorder is based in part on research findings that the disorder is more common in twin pairs than in other pairs of relatives.

Cognitive-behavioral therapy: A form of psychotherapy with a cognitive emphasis on attitudes and a behavioral emphasis on changing maladaptive responses by reinforcing more acceptable behavior.

Treatment. Over the last couple of decades, *cognitive-behavioral therapy* has emerged as the treatment of choice for obsessive-compulsive disorders (Stallard, 2009; March *et al.*, 1997). This form of behavior therapy consists of a two-pronged thrust—a cognitive emphasis on thoughts and attitudes and a behavioral emphasis on changing maladaptive responses by reinforcing more acceptable ones.

The first step in the treatment consists of changing the individual's negative self-statements (*e.g.,* "I am not going to go to the party because no one will speak to me") to more rational, constructive coping responses. For example, John may be urged to initiate conversations. When other people begin responding to him, John is likely to develop a sense of mastery and self-efficacy, a belief in his ability to perform competently in whatever he attempts. Thus, anxiety-provoking stimuli are replaced by more realistic and less frightening thoughts and behavior.

Another method of treating obsessive-compulsive disorders is drugs. The pharmacological (drug) approach has met with some success, indicating that this disorder may have a biological basis (Baxter, 2000). The first-line pharmacological agents that are used in treating obsessive-compulsive disorders are the selective serotonin reuptake inhibitors (SSRIs), such as Prozac, that sometimes lift people from a state of depression by blocking the reabsorption and removal of serotonin from synapses. However, drugs such as Prozac can

---

7. For further information on Obsessive-Compulsive Disorders, write to: Obsessive-Compulsive Foundation, P.O. Box 9573, New Haven, CT, 06535.

produce sleep disturbances and behavioral changes and their long-term effects are unknown. An improved version of Prozac is being developed (Appleton, 2000). Although drug treatment for children with obsessive-compulsive disorders has met with some success, its use must be scrutinized carefully. For instance, although Anafranil (clomipramine), an antidepressant, is quite effective in reducing the severity of OCD, its adverse side effects, including seizures and anorexia nervosa, may outweigh the benefits (Grados & Riddle, 2001).

Warning: Although drugs are prescribed routinely for adults with mental illnesses and there is some evidence of their effectiveness, extra precautions need to be taken when medication is prescribed for childhood mental illnesses. Many of the drugs that are prescribed for mental disorders in children are "Off Label," which means that they are dispensed without formal study or approval of their use. Another problem with drugs prescribed for children with mental disorders such as obsessive-compulsive disorders is the short period of time—usually only a few weeks—to determine the effectiveness of the drugs and their adverse side effects. Most experts agree that drugs should be used to treat children's psychological problems only when they are combined with psychotherapy or talk therapy.

SUMMARY

Self-concept is a sense of oneself and develops considerably in middle childhood through social comparison, and also by children realizing that they have an inner self and a public self. Self-esteem, which consists of an evaluation along a positive/negative dimension, has many facets. It is linked to patterns of childrearing, although children also influence the type of parenting they receive.

According to Freud, middle childhood is a period when sexual strivings are relatively dormant. A major reason is the dominance of the superego, which keeps the id under control. According to Erikson's fourth crisis, industry versus inferiority, the child strives to produce in middle childhood. Piaget's cognitive-developmental theory states that self-concept develops as a result of the advanced thinking capability of the school-aged child. The information-processing approach states that self-concept is developed through self-schemata based on prior experience. Bandura's social cognitive theory claims that self-concept develops when models are copied. Social cognitive theorists question whether reinforcement is effective.

The peer group plays an important role in a child's psychosocial development. Some children are more susceptible than others to peer pressure. The type of discipline, age, and personality appear to be crucial variables in yielding to peer pressure. Some children are more popular than others. Those who are liked more often possess certain characteristics, such as social skills and confidence.

Several family factors influence children's development. One of these is discipline, with the authoritative type being the best. Divorce, maternal employment, single parenthood, and stepfamilies also influence children's social emotional development.

Psychological and emotional problems can occur in middle childhood. These include childhood depression, separation anxiety disorder, and, obsessive compulsive disorder.

IMPORTANT TERMS

Authoritative parents
Authoritarian parents
Bidirectionality of self-esteem
Blended family
Brown vs. Board of Education of
    Topeka, Kansas
Childhood depression
Coregulation
Discipline
Discrimination
Divorce mediation
Erikson's stages
Industry versus inferiority, Erikson's
Joint physical custody
Middle childhood

Nuclear family
Obsessive compulsive disorder
Peer
Permissive parents
Phobia
Prejudice
School phobia
Self-concept
Self-schema
Self-esteem
Separation anxiety disorder
Sleeper effect
Social comparison
Stepfamily
Systematic desensitization therapy

Related Resources

Readings

Gullotta, Thomas P. and Blau, Gary M. editors (2008). *Family Influences on Childhood Behavior and Development: Evidence-Based Prevention and Treatment Approaches.* New York: Routledge.

Mayer, Matthew J. editor (2009). *Cognitive-behavioral Interventions for Emotional and Behavioral Disorders: School-based Practice.* New York: Guilford Press.

Rey, Joseph M. and Birmaher, Boris (2009). T*reating Child and Adolescent Depression* (Philadelphia: Wolters Kluwer Health/Lippincott Williams & Wilkins).

Riddick, Barbara (2010). *Living with Dyslexia : the Social and Emotional Consequences of Specific Learning Difficulties/Disabilities.* London; New York: Routledge.

Stallard, Paul (2009). A*nxiety: Cognitive Behavior Therapy with Children and Young people.* London; New York: Routledge.

Wallerstein, Judith S. (2003). *What about the Kids?: Raising Your Children Before, During, and After Divorce.* New York: Hyperion.

Wallerstein, Judith S. (2000). *The Unexpected Legacy of Divorce: a 25 year Landmark Study.* New York: Hyperion.

Websites

American Academy of Child and Adolescent Psychiatry
http://www.aacap.org

International Obsessive Compulsive Disorder Foundation
http://www.ocfoundation.org

The Child Anxiety Network
http://www.childanxiety.net/Specific_Phobia.htm

PART SIX

ADOLESCENCE
(12 TO 18 YEARS)

Chapter 13

Physical Development in Adolescence (12 to 18 years)

Chapter Topics		Learning Objectives
What are some physical changes during puberty?		Know the characteristics that define puberty.
What gender differences exist during puberty?		Understand the differences between males and females during puberty.
How do eating disorders play a role in adolescent lives?		Recognize eating disorders, their characteristics, gender differences, and consequences.
What are the issues surrounding the prevalence of obesity?		Understand obesity and its consequences.
What major drugs are used by adolescents?		Know the major drugs used by adolescents: depressants, stimulants, and psychedelics.
What are the major sexually transmitted diseases that afflict adolescents?		Be familiar with the major symptoms of AIDS, chlamydia, and genital herpes.
What kinds of illness and death effect the lives of adolescents?		Understand acne and suicide as examples of issues that adolescents face.
Chapter Summary		

Sara, aged 12½ years, is on the threshold of a major physical development. She is about to have her first menstrual period, or menarche. This single event, called puberty, which generally signals sexual maturity for the first time in females. Carlos, who is also 12½, is a couple of years behind Sara in reaching sexual maturity. The ability to reproduce is the culmination of rapid growth during a two- to three-year period, known as pubescence. Hence, pubescence is the changes leading to sexual maturity and puberty is sexual maturity following pubescence.

Pubescence is characterized by a variety of physical changes. In addition to rapid gain in height and weight, pubescence involves changes in primary and secondary sex characteristics. Primary sex characteristics include the organs directly involved in sexual reproduction; secondary sex characteristics help differentiate mature males from females but are not necessary for reproduction. Secondary sex characteristics include growth of facial hair in the boy and breast development in the girl.

The attainment of sexual maturity or the ability to reproduce (puberty) is the beginning of a transitional period known as adolescence. The end of adolescence varies considerably from culture to culture, and from one domain (legal, sociological, and cognitive) to another.

Many factors affect development during adolescence including nutrition, eating disorders, drug abuse and sexually transmitted diseases c. We will examine each of these, as well as illness and death, although the teenage years are generally healthy.

ADOLESCENCE: THE "IN-BETWEEN" STAGE

Adolescent: A person approximately between the ages of 12 and 18 years and has reached sexual maturity but not many of the benchmarks of adulthood such as being self-supporting or having discovered an identity.

Adolescence: Stage of development between childhood and adulthood.

One of the terms we hear most often in discussions about young people is "adolescents." By *adolescents* we mean children who are approximately between the ages of 12 and 18. A related term, *adolescence*, is the stage of development between childhood and adulthood. Adolescence begins with the physical changes that precede a child's ability to reproduce, a phenomenon known as puberty.

It is difficult to imagine a time when the concept of adolescence did not exist. Yet, historically, a person was considered either a child or an adult, the dividing line being puberty or the ability to reproduce for the first time. Two hundred years ago, children 11 or 12 years old would have been considered an adult, earning a living and taking on many of the responsibilities now reserved for adults. Today, the onset of puberty is generally considered the beginning of adolescence — a transitional period between childhood and adulthood. The end of adolescence, or the beginning of adulthood isn't so readily identifiable, although many criteria are used to identify this important benchmark.

Legal adulthood (the end of adolescence) is usually recognized when the individual reaches the age of 18 years. However, an individual is not responsible for legal contracts in some states until the age of 21. Young people can marry and enlist in the armed forces at age 18 without parental consent but can't go into bars.

Age of Majority: A legal term to describe when an individual reaches adulthood.

Emancipation: For children, the legal equivalent of divorcing their parents.

One term used by lawyers to describe the attainment of adulthood is the *Age of Majority* when an individual acquires both the rights and responsibilities of adulthood. Another legal term is *emancipation:* For children, emancipation is the legal equivalent to divorcing their parents. Stated another way, emancipation is legal statement (often before the child reaches 18 years of age) which declares parents are no longer responsible for their child and the child no longer answerable to his or her parents.

Although most scientists agree on the criteria marking the beginning of adolescence, there is considerable confusion about the age when adolescence ends and adulthood begins. Even the beginning of physical adulthood is difficult to determine. Is it at age 18 when the person has reached adult height? Is it at age 20 when the brain reaches its maximum weight of about 3 pounds? In short, there is no definite upper limit which signifies the end of adolescence and the beginning of adulthood. The transition from adolescence to adulthood occurs later in youth with disabilities than in those without disabilities (Sawin, Cox, & Metzger, 2000).

PUBESCENCE: THE PHYSICAL TRANSITIONS LEADING TO SEXUAL MATURITY

Twelve-year-old Sara has been undergoing drastic physical changes during the last 2 or 3 years. She now has pubic hair, her hips have broadened, and her breasts are approaching adult size. In another 6 months, she will have her first period, or menarche, signifying that she has reached sexual maturity and will be able to reproduce for the first time. This period of progress toward sexual maturity is known as *pubescence.* Carlos will undergo similar changes about 2 years later. Let's define a few relevant terms.

Pubescence: A 2- or 3-year-period of rapid growth beginning at about age 10 for girls and age 12 for boys that lead to sexual maturity or puberty.

Puberty: Sexual maturity for the first time following pubescence. The end point of sexual maturation preceded by the process known as pubescence. (Many psychologists think of puberty as a combination of pubescence *and* the first time a person is capable of sexual reproduction.

- **The pubescent growth spurt—an early sign of impending sexual maturity (puberty) when height, weight, and bodily proportions change dramatically.**

- *Puberty*—**the attainment of sexual maturation for the first time.**

- **Menarche—the beginning of menstruation in girls.**

- **Primary sex characteristics—physical features (ovaries, uterus, labia, clitoris, and vagina in females; penis, scrotum, and testes in males) that involve the reproductive organs directly.**

- **Secondary sex characteristics—anatomical and physiological signs of sexual maturity that distinguish males from females outwardly, such as facial hair in boys and rounded hips in girls, but are not necessary for reproduction.**

The Pubescent Growth Spurt

The pubescent growth spurt is one of the first signs of approaching sexual maturity, or puberty (Lawton, 2009). There is a sharp increase in height and weight in both boys and girls, although not at the same age. Sara will experience this increase between the ages of approximately 10 and 12; Carlos between about ages 12 and 14 (Bogin, 1990).

Human growth hormone:
A biochemical substance secreted by the pituitary gland.

During the pubescent growth spurt—which lasts 2 to 3 years—boys increase in height by as much as 9 inches and gain as much as 50 pounds. Girls increase their height by about 4 inches and gain up to 30 pounds. By the end of the growth spurt, adolescents reach about 98 percent of their ultimate height. Shortly after the growth spurt ends, a child reaches sexual maturity, or puberty, for the first time. The key instigator of the growth spurt is a biochemical substance, the *human growth hormone,* secreted by the pituitary gland. Adolescents continue to grow more slowly after the growth spurt ends until about age 18 for girls and 20 for boys.

A key initial indication of the pubescent growth spurt in girls is a deepening and widening of the hips; in boys, it is a broadening of the shoulders. The changes in the girls' hips are due to the fat settling around the pelvic area. The result is the rounded appearance typical of mature women.

Male-female differences. Besides the widening and deepening of the hips in girls and a broadening of shoulders in boys, there are other gender differences during the pubescent growth spurt (Lawton, 2009). Boys accumulate more muscle than girls, and the heart and lungs develop at a faster rate, thereby allowing more oxygen-bearing red blood cells to be carried throughout the male body. This results in the boys' higher blood pressure when the muscles contract. Boys reach their adult heights later than girls (at about 17 or 18 years of age versus at about 15 or 16 years of age for girls). Also, boys begin to neutralize chemical wastes such as lactic acid more efficiently than girls. This results in greater physical strength for boys. Following puberty, boys can exercise for longer periods and exert more force per ounce of muscle than girls. Another difference between boys and girls is in the accumulation of fat. Around age 8, girls gain more fat than boys on their legs, arms, and trunk. This gain in fat accelerates between the ages of 11 and 16. On the other hand, the arm and leg fat of adolescent boys decreases (Siervogel *et al.*, 2000).

The role of hormones in sexual maturity. The journey toward sexual maturity starts in the brain with a small organ called the pituitary gland which produces the growth hormones that are responsible for the growth spurt. At about the same time as the growth spurt begins (at age 10, 11, or 12), the pituitary gland stimulates the gonads (ovaries in the female; testes in the male). The messages sent to the gonads by the pituitary gland are the gonadotropic hormones. Another set of hormones, called the adrenocorticotrophic hormones, are sent to the adrenal glands, small organs located atop the kidneys. However, neither the gonadotropic hormones nor the adrenocorticotrophic hormones play a direct role in a person's sexual maturity. This task is left up to the male and female sex hormones, produced by the testes in the male and ovaries in the female, respectively.

Androgens: Male sex hormones that are produced by the testes. The most prominent androgen is testosterone.

Estrogens: Female sex hormones that are responsible for sexual maturation.

Testosterone: A hormone that is responsible in males for the development of primary and secondary sex characteristics and the production of sperm.

Progesterone: A hormone, that in females, regulates the menstrual cycle and prepares the uterus for pregnancy.

The testes produce the male sex hormones, referred to collectively as *androgens*, the most important of which is *testosterone* which plays a key role in the development of primary and secondary male sex characteristics. A group of chemically similar hormones that cause female sexual development are *estrogens*, such as estradiol, which are produced mainly by the ovaries, but also by the adrenal glands. The ovaries also produce *progesterone* which is of primary importance in preparing the uterus for pregnancy and in maintaining the pregnancy. Both males and females possess the *same* sex hormones, but in different amounts. For example, the testes produce small amounts of the "female" hormone estrogen.

Primary Sex Characteristics

Primary sex characteristics: Anatomical and physiological organs that are directly involved in reproduction.

Primary sex characteristics include anatomical and physiological organs that are directly involved in reproduction, and are usually present at birth. In the male, these organs include the penis, the testes which produce sperm cells, and the prostate which produces semen (Lawton, 2009). The primary male sex characteristics also include the ejaculatory tract, which brings sperm through the prostate gland; and seminal vesicles, small glands that lie behind the bladder and open into the ejaculatory ducts where the fluids they secrete combine with the sperm. During the pubescent growth spurt, these organs enlarge dramatically and become functionally mature. Boys first ejaculate between the ages of 13 and 14.

Menarche: A girl's first menstruation.

Primary sex characteristics in the female include the vagina, uterus, ovaries, labia, and clitoris. The most identifiable primary sex characteristic in females is the first period, known as the *menarche*. The first menstrual period usually occurs when the girl is about $12\frac{1}{2}$ years old, although the timing can vary considerably due to factors such as stress (girls under undue stress begin to menstruate earlier) and the level of physical exercise (the more strenuous the physical exercise, the later the first period). Ovulation—the release of an egg (ovum) from an ovary—follows the onset of menarche by several months.

Secondary Sex Characteristics

Secondary sex characteristics: Anatomical and physiological signs of sexual maturity that outwardly distinguish males from females (e.g., breast development in females; and the appearance of underarm and pubic hair in both genders).

Secondary sex characteristics are the anatomical and physiological signs of sexual maturity that outwardly distinguish males from females (Lawton, 2009). They are not directly involved in reproduction. Secondary sex characteristics in both males and females include pubic hair, a lowering of the voice (more in males than in females), and axillary (armpit) hair. Other secondary sex characteristics include rounding of the body, broadening of the hips, and breast development in girls. Secondary sex characteristics in boys include growth of facial hair, development of musculature, a broadening of the shoulders, and an increase in the density of the bones.

PUBERTY: THE ATTAINMENT OF SEXUAL MATURITY

Puberty is the point at which a child is able to reproduce sexually for the first time (Murray, 2009). The timing of puberty or sexual maturation depends, as in all forms of development, on a complex interaction between genetic and environmental factors. The importance of genetic factors in sexual reproduction can be seen by comparing the differences in menarche (the first menstrual period, from the Greek word *arche*, meaning "beginning") of identical and fraternal twin girls. For identical twin girls, the average difference in menarche is about 2 months, whereas the average difference between fraternal twin sisters is about 8 months. Nontwin sisters, who are less alike than fraternal twin sisters, begin their first periods about 12-18 months apart. Unrelated women have their first periods about $18\frac{1}{2}$ months apart[1].

Although genetic factors appear to have considerable influence on the timing of puberty, environmental factors such as stress and health also play an

---

1. The timing of the menarche (a girl's first period) does not necessarily mean that the girl is able to get pregnant the first time she has sexual intercourse. Initial periods may not be accompanied by ovulation, the release of a mature ovum (reproductive cell) from the ovary.

important role. Malnutrition can slow puberty markedly (Susman, Dorn, & Schiefelbeih, 2003).

In one study (Tanner, 1981), girls from affluent homes (environment) reached menarche several months sooner than girls from economically poorer families. Negative environmental factors can also speed up puberty. Some research (e.g.,Wierson *et al.*, 1993) suggests that stress, such as the parents' divorce, is related to an earlier onset of menarche. Smoking, drinking alcohol, and obesity are also associated with early menarche (Danielle *et al.*, 2000; Kaplowitz *et al.*, 2001).

The Secular Growth Trend: Declining Age of Maturity

Secular growth trend: Changes in physical or behavioral development from one generation to the next.

McKensie's and Curry's mother is a pediatrician who has been monitoring her children's physical development from the day they were born. The mother-doctor has discovered that her daughter is maturing and growing taller at a younger age then she did. Curry follows a similar pattern of earlier development when compared with his father, a tendency which has occurred during the last 100 years, known as the *secular growth trend* which refers to patterns over time, especially across generations. About 15 percent of Caucasian girls are showing outward signs of secondary sex characteristics such as the budding of breasts and growth of pubic hair by age 8. The comparable figure for African-American girls is earlier (Herman-Giddens *et al.*, 1997). This trend has been most noticeable in technologically advanced societies where the average age of menarche (a girl's first menstruation) has been declining three to four months per decade for the last century (Schickedanz *et al.*, 2000). Girls in Great Britain, the United States, and Europe begin menstruating $2^{1}/_{2}$ to $3^{1}/_{4}$ years earlier than their agemates a century ago, with the onset of menarche decreasing during this period from slightly more than 14 years to about $12^{1}/_{2}$ years (Tanner, 1990).[2] Boys also appear to be maturing earlier. In addition, there is some evidence that children have been growing taller at a more rapid rate with an average height gain of nearly $^{1}/_{3}$ inch per decade (Freedman *et al.*, 2000).

While environmental factors such as diet may speed up the process of sexual maturity, there may be other reasons (Lawton, 2009). One of these is obesity. Very overweight girls tend to mature earlier. The link may be a protein called leptin which is produced by fat cells and is necessary for the progression of pubescence. Overweight girls also have more insulin circulating in their blood which appears to stimulate the production of sex hormones by the ovaries and adrenal glands. Obesity is also linked to culture. For instance, in African-American and Latino families which value the larger body size, the girls tend to mature earlier than girls in Anglo cultures. Figure 13.1 graphs the sequence of events in sexual maturation for males and females, and the range of ages at which they typically occur.

---

2. Earlier menarche is characteristic of girls who live in urban, higher socioeconomic status households, the housing is of better quality, and there are assets in the home such as a TV, computer, and a refrigerator.

Figure 13.1
Sequence of Events in the Sexual Maturation of Males and Females

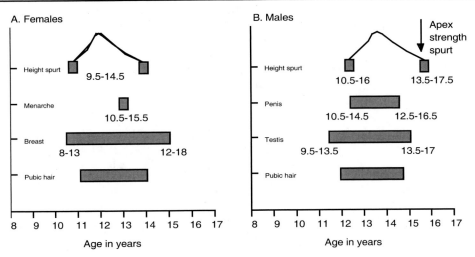

The numbers represent the variation among individuals in the ages at which each aspect of sexual maturation occurs. For example, menarche can occur any time between the ages of 10$^{1/2}$ and 15$^{1/2}$.

Source: Marshall and Tanner, 1970.

Psychological Impact of Puberty

The influence of puberty goes beyond being sexually mature, stronger, and taller. There are many psychological consequences (Murray, 2009). The 11-year-old sexually mature girl has a different attitude toward boys, as well as a different outlook on life, than one who has not begun the growth spurt. At puberty, the rate of clinical depression more than doubles to about 15 percent, affecting about 1 in 5 teenage girls and about 1 in 10 teenage boys (Graber, 2004), a point parents and teachers should remember when their charges become despondent and difficult to manage. The timing of puberty also has a different effect on boys than on girls.

Early versus late sexual maturity (puberty) in males. Brian reached sexual maturity at age 12, while Howard did not achieve this benchmark until age 16. Compared with Howard, early-maturing Brian has many advantages, one of which is physical superiority that enables him to excel in competitive sports. Socially, Brian is more popular, often being chosen as a leader, partly because of his larger physique and his superior physical abilities. Brian also gets along better with his agemates and parents. He has learned to play an adult role in interpersonal relationships and is considered more mature than the average adolescent his age. Compared with Howard, Brian has little need to strive for status. Intellectually, Brian is above-average; emotionally, he is relaxed, confident, and independent. As an adult, Brian will probably be placed in a supervisory or managerial position and will be successful.

The advantages that early male bloomers enjoy carry over into adulthood. Mary Cover Jones (1957) studied twenty33-year-old men and found that although some of the early adolescent differences had disappeared, boys who had matured early continued to enjoy many advantages. They achieved success sooner in their chosen careers and seemed to sustain a good image of themselves.

Early versus late sexual maturity (puberty) in females. Studies of early- and late-maturing females are scant and often contradictory. In general, the studies favor late maturity for girls. These girls tend to be more popular, have a more positive self-concept, are more socially poised, more at ease, and more socially perceptive.

Early-maturing girls have been portrayed as being uncomfortable in their adult bodies, more aloof, withdrawn, and somewhat rebellious and unconventional (Dick *et al.*, 2000). There also appears to be an association between age at puberty (menarche) in females and onset of schizophrenia (Cohen *et al.*, 1999). In males, the opposite appears to be true. It is not known what variables account for this gender difference. Some investigators believe that hormones are involved.

Body image and puberty. The adolescent is influenced by others' reactions to his or her body, as well as by his or her interpretations of these reactions—a phenomenon called *body image.* Moreover, through exposure to television, movies, and magazines, Sara may think that an early maturing girl possesses the mythical body ideal.

Body image: A child's interpretation of the reactions of others to his or her body.

Puberty can also result in a negative body image. The teenager may be troubled by the acne on his face and feel that he is not attractive because of his facial appearance. Or, the 14-year-old boy with large feet and long legs may be conscious of his disproportionate body.

NUTRITION

Of all the environmental influences on physical development, none is more potent than nutrition. We can see its effect in the timing of sexual maturation: The better the nutrition, the earlier the sexual maturation. Proper nutrition results in greater height throughout childhood. In one study in Stuttgart, Germany, adolescents were about 2 inches taller between World War I and II when food was more plentiful (Tanner, 1963) than during the wars.

Several key nutrients have been identified for proper development (McGuire & Beerman, 2010). One of these is protein, which sustains growth, although protein is not as critical in adolescence as in early childhood. Protein is believed to be primarily responsible for the age of menarche in girls and muscle development in boys.

American adolescents often have iron-deficiency anemia because they do not eat enough iron-fortified bread and iron-rich red meat, dried fruits, and leafy green vegetables. Iron is needed for muscle development and is thus particularly important for physically active adolescent boys (Blum & Nelson-Mmari, 2004). All too often, teenagers consume processed and fast foods. These foods are high in fats, calories, salt, sugar, and cholesterol, a waxy fat-like substance. The cholesterol can build up on artery walls and block the flow of blood to organs such as the heart, causing heart attacks and strokes.

Since girls mature earlier than boys, their nutritional needs reach a peak earlier than boys. The girls' greatest nutritional need is from about age 11 to 14, then there is a gradual decline until physical maturity is reached. This means that the adolescent girl must receive all the nutrients she needs from a fewer number of calories than the boy (about 2,300 calories per day for the girl; 3,000 for the boy). The nutritional needs of the boy continue to rise from about age 11 to 18.

It is particularly important for adolescents to have extra calcium for healthy bones and teeth (Balint, 1998). That's because almost half of an adult's bone mass is formed during the adolescent years, and calcium is a major component of bones. Final adult height may be limited by lack of calcium during adolescence. The calcium need can be met by choosing milk (4 to 5 glasses daily) and other dairy products like yogurt, ice cream, and cheeses. Leafy dark green vegetables are also a source of calcium (Epstein, 1991).

Osteoporosis: A disease caused by a deficiency of calcium that thins and weakens bones.

Calcium deficiency in childhood may lead to loss of bone mass, a condition common in postmenopausal women, called *osteoporosis* (literally "porous bones"), a disease that thins and weakens bones to the point where they break easily. This is because 90 percent of adult bone mass is formed by the end of the teenage years. Hence, osteoporosis is a pediatric disease with geriatric consequences. About 85 percent of American teenage girls (about 65 percent of American teenage boys) are calcium deficient. An average teenager requires about 1,300 milligrams of calcium daily.

Unfortunately, today's teenagers are drinking more carbonated beverages and less milk, which has calcium they need for strong bones. In addition to the daily need of about 1,300 milligrams of calcium, bones also need magnesium, present in leafy, green vegetables, nuts, and whole grains. Hence, teenagers should limit sodas and drink about 3 cups of skim or fat-free milk each day. The body will not absorb calcium without vitamin D which is found in liver oils, fortified milk, eggs, tuna, salmon, and sunlight. However, excessive calcium intake should be avoided because it can lead to heart problems.

Another important ingredient for proper bone development is phosphorus which affects oxygen delivery and is a major structural component of bone. Phosphorous is found in a variety of foods such as dairy products, meat, fish, and beans. In addition to a proper diet, adolescents can strengthen their bones by taking part in weight-bearing exercises at least 5 days a week.

Eating Disorders

Even though nutrition is the most influential environmental factor in physical development, many children and adolescents do not eat enough nutrients because they deny themselves food. This condition, known as *anorexia nervosa*, is particularly common among adolescent girls and is becoming increasingly more prevalent in boys as well (Smolak & Thompson, 2009). Other adolescents take in large quantities of food and then purge themselves, or rid their bodies of the food, a condition known as bulimia nervosa. Still, other adolescents have difficulty with *obesity*, even though they may not eat excessive amounts of food.[3]

Anorexia nervosa: A severe, progressive eating disorder in which individuals refuse to eat normally and may become skeleton-like, while denying their behavior and appearance.

Anorexia nervosa. Anorexia nervosa is an alarmingly common preoccupation with thinness and with a self-imposed weight loss of at least 15 percent of minimal normal weight. The disease is a progressive disorder, meaning that the longer a person has the illness, the worse it gets. More than 90 percent of its victims are Caucasian adolescent females and about 10 percent are males, an increase from 0.3 percent in 1994 (American Psychiatric Association, 2000; Smolak & Thomspon, 2009). The disorder is ten times more common in females than in males (Herzog *et al.,* 1995). By the end of high school, more

---

3. For more information about eating disorders, write to: National Association of Anorexia Nervosa and Associated Disorders, P.O. Box 7, Highland Park, IL, 60035, or call (847) 831-3438.

than half of the students have dieted seriously and some die from too much dieting (Brown, Childers, & Waszak, 1988). Mortality rates from anorexia nervosa are estimated to be between 4 and 30 percent of its victims, despite treatment (Herzog *et al.*, 2000; Wicks-Nelson & Israel, 1991).

The most obvious physical symptom of anorexia nervosa is a dangerous level of weight loss. Many victims lose more than 50 percent of their normal weight. Other symptoms of anorexia nervosa include constipation, skin deterioration, loss of hair, brittle nails, hollow cheeks, delayed puberty, damaged reproductive organs, hypothermia (below normal body temperature because of the body's inability to maintain heat), and depression. There may be loss of blood pressure, and persistent vomiting to correct perceived "loss of control." Female anorexics may also have a cessation of menstruation (amenorrhea) due to a low body mass index. Females suffering from anorexia who fall below 15% body fat due to their extreme starvation, will cease to menstruate. (The causal link between a low percentage of body fat and amenorrhea is illustrated by the fact that high level elite, female athletes who have 13 percent body fat because of their high level of muscle mass.) Other possible symptoms of anorexia include: Heart murmur, bradycardia (slow heart rate), and reduced bone density. A major psychological symptom is an intense fear of becoming obese, which does not diminish with weight loss (American Psychiatric Association, 2000).

Possible Causes of Anorexia Nervosa. Since there is no known physical cause of anorexia, such as malignant tumors, support for a biological explanation is at best incomplete. However, since anorexia nervosa tends to run in families, there may be a genetic influence (Smolak & Thompson, 2009; Strober *et al.*, 2000). The prevailing view is that anorexia nervosa is a psychological disorder. Some investigators believe that the disorder is an obsession with the victim's fears of growing up. Other experts see the disease as an effort to cope with the frightening demands of approaching maturity by attempting to forestall the event. Still other theories root the cause of anorexia in childhood sexual abuse. Another cause of anorexia nervosa may be the extraordinary premium placed by society on models and celebrities who are unrealistically thin. In fact, in our culture, the thin, prepubertal body is idealized in television, movies, music videos, and magazine images, to the shape of dolls given to young girls.

Some investigators see anorexia nervosa as an extreme symptom of family malfunctioning. They theorize that the disorder may a way for a girl to assert autonomy as a reaction to overprotective parents. Some researchers believe that anorexia nervosa may be due to excessive exercise (Eisler & le Grange, 1990). Finally, some investigators view the disorder as resulting from a distorted perception of one's body. According to this view, the victim regards herself as fat even when she is grossly emaciated (Cash & Hicks, 1990). Still other investigators associate the cause of anorexia nervosa with a drive for perfectionism (Ghizzani & Montomoli, 2000).

Treatment. Anorexia nervosa is very difficult to treat. Overall, results of all types of treatment for anorexia nervosa are very disappointing (Gowers and Green, 2009; Kreipe & Uphoff, 1992). In many respects, the treatment of anorexia nervosa is as challenging today as it was over 100 years ago when it was first formally recognized as a disorder. A major problem is the patient's denial that a problem exists. The anorexic patient needs constant assurance that the point of treatment is normalization of weight, not to produce obesity (Harris, 1991).

Before treatment can begin, the anorexic patient must have a complete physical and neurological examination to determine the extent of damage. If the victim is below about 80 pounds or is vomiting, hospitalization is necessary. During hospitalization, the anorexic patient is maintained on a nutritional, high-caloric diet to promote weight gain and to restore physiological homeostasis (Gowers and Green, 2009; Moukaddem *et al*, 1997).

Another form of treatment for anorexia nervosa involves confronting the patient repeatedly with his or her image in mirrors, photographs, and on videotape to induce a more realistic self-appraisal. Regardless of which method is used, anorexic victims usually need long-term treatment and support.

Bulimia nervosa. While some teenagers attempt to lose weight through extreme dieting, others engage in eating binges—usually in secret—and then purge themselves by induced vomiting as many as 40 times a day, by taking large doses of laxatives, or by compulsive exercising (Smolak & Thompson, 2009). Victims of this disorder, known as *bulimia nervosa*, may consume up to 50 candy bars, a dozen donuts, and a whole pizza at one sitting. Or, they may consume thousands of calories within a few minutes. The result of these binging episodes is the act of purging.

Bulimia nervosa: An eating disorder that primarily affects adolescent girls and young women and is characterized by eating binges followed by purges through vomiting, laxatives, and compulsory exercise.

Available evidence for bulimia indicates that, like anorexia nervosa, bulimia afflicts mostly teenage girls. As many as 3 percent of girls between 13 and 20 are bulimic (McGilley & Pryor, 1998).

The major cause of bulimia nervosa seems to be the cultural emphasis on thinness (the "boyish" look) and a poor body image (Gowers and Green, 2009). The disorder is more common among females in middle and upper classes where thinness is highly emphasized and idealized as representing power and success. The girl who is most at risk reaches puberty early and believes that beauty is essential for her happiness. For some unknown reason, early maturing girls typically acquire and retain higher fat levels than late-maturing girls. Because of this higher level of fat, the early maturing girl is a likely candidate for bulimia. Psychoanalytic theory states that bulimia is an attempt to use food to satisfy love and attention that is not received from parents. There is also some evidence that bulimia nervosa may be the result of a genetic predisposition.

The effects of bulimia nervosa can be devastating. Laxatives and diuretics used as purging agents can deplete the body of critical electrolytes, calcium and potassium, bringing on cardiac arrhythmia and heart attacks. The self-induced vomiting can cause hernias, chronic sore throat, and rotten teeth due to being continually coated with vomited stomach acid. Bulimics can even drown in their own vomit from accidental aspiration of food (food entering the lungs).

Cognitive-behavioral therapy: A form of psychotherapy that combines cognitive therapy with behavioral therapy.

Treatment for bulimia nervosa includes psychotherapy to help the patient understand the causes of the disorder and how it can be controlled. The most effective form of psychotherapy for bulimia nervosa is *cognitive-behavioral therapy*, which addresses both the cognitive aspects of the disorder as well as the behavioral components (Gowers, 2009). In addressing the cognitive aspect, the patient is confronted with her body weight, food, and low self-esteem. Behavioral intervention addresses the patient's eating habits, binge eating, purging, and ritualistic exercise (McGilley & Pryor, 1998).

Antidepressant medicine is often used for depressed victims of bulimia nervosa, especially for those who are at high risk of suicide. The most effective medication for bulimia nervosa reported to date is the antidepressant Prozac (fluoxetine hydrochloride) (Goldstein *et al*, 1995). Prozac tends to reduce the frequencies of binge-eating, and improves the bulimic's mood. The antidepressant Norpramin (desipramine) is also used, although its effectiveness is highly questionable due to the severe toxicity of the drug. Regardless of which form of treatment is used, bulimia nervosa continues to be a major problem because of its relapses and chronicity (the disorder lasts for a long time).

Obesity. Obesity is one of the three most striking types of eating disorders mentioned in medical literature (Smolak & Thompson, 2009. Obesity is a deviation of at least 20 percent over "ideal" weight and is of particular concern because obese teenagers tend to become obese adults (Power, Lake, & Cole, 1997) who are subject to many health risks, including cardiovascular difficulties. There is also concern that obesity has increased significantly among adolescents within the last three decades. Another concern about obesity is the presence of weight-related type II diabetes—also known as adult-onset diabetes— which is being diagnosed more frequently in adolescents.

Although various diet programs exist to combat obesity, they have had limited success. Perhaps one reason for this inability to treat obesity more successfully is the narrow approach of most weight-control programs which are interested mainly in the number of pounds lost, often through dieting. However, chronic dieting may be ineffective because it may train the body to store fat in anticipation of famine, since it can't tell the difference between starvation and dieting.[4]

The most successful programs to treat obesity take a multifaceted approach (O'Donohue, Moore, & Scott, 2008). They involve not only dieting, but exercise, psychotherapy and a change in eating habits (Bray & Tartaglia, 2000). In many successful weight-loss programs for teens, the parents are also involved. Moreover, the adolescent has to be given responsibility and independence to control his or her own weight.

A major reason why treatment for eating disorders has been relatively unsuccessful is comorbidity, the presence of other disorders. For example, many individuals with an eating disorder also have psychiatric problems. Hence, to treat a person with an eating disorder effectively, we must also address other abnormal conditions such as a low level of self-esteem.

PSYCHOACTIVE SUBSTANCE ABUSE

Psychoactive substance abuse: A pattern of misuse of drugs that have negative effects on a person.

Historically, the main concern about children's health was illness and death from organic diseases such as cancer and infections from communicable diseases. While the incidence of morbidity and mortality from traditional sources has declined, today's risks are largely psychological or behavioral. A major health problem faced by young people today is *psychoactive substance abuse* which means a pattern of the use of illegal or illicit drugs that have a detrimental effect on a person's health, consciousness, mood, and social and occupational roles (Jung, 2010). The psychoactive substances that are most abused currently by adolescents are alcohol, tobacco, and marijuana.

---

4. In 1994, more than a dozen diet programs were being investigated by the Federal Trade Commission regarding their claims in advertising and promotional literature about weight loss.

Psychoactive substances or drugs are generally classified into three categories (Inaba & Cohen, 2007):

Depressants, or "downers" such as alcohol, barbiturates and opiates. Depressants calm neural activity and slow down bodily functions.

Stimulants, or "uppers" which increase bodily functions such as heart rate and breathing. Examples of stimulant drugs include caffeine, nicotine, and more powerful amphetamines and cocaine.

Hallucinogens, or psychedelic ("mind-manifesting") drugs such as LSD that distort perceptions and evoke sensory images in the absence of sensory input.

Following a drop-off in popularity during the 1960s, alcohol once again became the dominant drug in high schools and on college campuses. In the early 1990s, approximately 90 percent of all high school seniors had tried alcohol at least once and about two-thirds of 8th graders had already tried alcohol. Fortunately, there has been a decline in the prevalence of alcohol use by teenagers in the last decade. The high prevalence of alcohol use by seniors during the 1990s declined to 47 percent in 2003 (Johnston, O'Malley, & Bachman, 2003).

Alcohol

Alcoholism: A physiological, and perhaps psychological, dependence on alcohol.

Joan is a 16-year-old high school junior who likes to go to movies and parties. She also likes to drink alcohol and often drinks alone. She has no control over how much she drinks. She now has a disease called *alcoholism*[5]—a physiological, and perhaps psychological, dependence on alcohol. Physiological dependence, or addiction, means that the body has built up a chemical dependence on alcohol so that withdrawal—resulting from lack of alcohol—causes unpleasant physical symptoms. Psychological dependence means a powerful compulsion to drink.

Joan's drinking problem began early. At age 12, she would occasionally sneak into the kitchen and drink a can of beer. Within 6 months, she was having two cans of beer three or four times each week. Within the year, she was also drinking wine. By age 14, Joan was drinking one six-pack of beer or one quart of wine three or four times a week. Occasionally, she would also drink whiskey. Drinking made her feel "grown-up."

Joan had trouble getting liquor. To avoid suspicion, she would steal alcohol from her parents' supply once or twice a week. At other times, she would get her older friends to buy liquor for her, sometimes she would use her older sister's identification card and purchase liquor herself; occasionally she would stand in front of a liquor store and ask strangers to buy liquor for her. She was now an alcoholic. No one seemed to suspect the problem although there were many signs.

In school, Joan's grades slipped from A's and B's to D's and F's. She was increasingly absent from school, often without adequate explanation. Her social relationships began to deteriorate, and she would ignore or abuse family

---

5. In 1956, the American Medical Association concurred in the disease concept of alcoholism due to a character weakness rather than a behavioral disorder (Many authorities consider alcoholism our nation's No. 1 health problem and the most untreated treatable disease in the United States).

members. She also became secretive; for example, she would refuse to reveal her plans for the day.

Joan's parents noticed unusual behavioral signs such as extreme drowsiness and blackouts. Often Joan's speech would become garbled and incoherent. Joan became listless, moody, and less talkative. Shortly after she received her driver's license, Joan had two accidents within a month. In both cases, Joan said that she had blacked out and didn't know what happened. A visit to the doctor revealed other symptoms such as increased pulse rate, decreased blood pressure, irregular heart beat, flushed areas on the nose and cheeks, and malnutrition. The doctor's diagnosis: Joan was an alcoholic.

Effects of alcohol. For hundreds of years, it has been evident that individuals behave more aggressively while under the influence of alcohol (Bushman & Cooper, 1990; Jung, 2010). Alcohol intoxication has been linked to violent crimes such as assault, spousal abuse, and rape (Dawkins, 1997). Alcohol does its damage to the body in three ways: *(1)* Substitution of alcohol for food, leading to malnutrition, *(2)* Destruction of cells, tissues, and even entire organs, such as the liver, and *(3)* Hyperlipidemia, or higher-than-normal levels of fat deposited on hips, thighs, and stomach (Suter, Schutz, & Jequier, 1992).

Alcohol use is especially devastating to adolescents. One reason is that alcohol often serves as a "stepping stone" to more dangerous behavior. For instance, the teenager who begins his or her errant ways by drinking a glass or two of alcohol each week may soon be using other drugs such as marijuana as well. A combination of alcohol and other drugs leads to more risky behavior such as careless driving and motor vehicle accidents. Adolescent alcohol and drug use has also been linked to suicide, dropping out of school, delinquency, and aggression (Kushner *et al.*, 2000).

Causes of excessive drinking. A common explanation for the cause of excessive drinking is the *self-handicapping strategy*, which says that individuals who are unsure of their ability to perform successfully may rely on excessive alcohol consumption to provide themselves with a plausible justification for failure. Presumably, individuals who are unsure of their performance can say that the reason they performed poorly was their intoxication, rather than their limited abilities. In this way, they maintain their self-esteem. Students who use self-handicapping strategies such as drinking alcohol tend to do poorly in school and to drop out of school early (Martin, Marsh, & Debus, 2001).

Many studies have attempted to link the cause of drinking, particularly alcoholism, to heredity (NIAAA, 2000). Most studies suggest that the risk for developing alcoholism is attributable to genetic factors in the 25- to 40-percent range. This conclusion is supported in a number of ways. For example, prealcoholics (individuals without current drinking problems who later become alcoholics) tend to have alcoholic relatives (Peterson *et al.*, 1994). There is also evidence that genetic factors make it more difficult to metabolize the ethanol (a product obtained from grain by fermentation and distillation). Heredity might also create greater physiological dependence on alcohol (or on some other drug).

Self-handicapping strategy: A tendency to rely on a crutch such as alcohol due to fear of failure.

Detoxification: The removal of toxic substances such as alcohol from the body.

Withdrawal: The physical reaction that accompanies the cessation or interruption of drug use by an addicted person.

Treatment for problem drinking. Most treatment programs for alcohol problems have been designed for the most extreme form—alcoholism. The most popular medical model is *detoxification*, or rapid removal of the alcohol (10 to 20 percent each day) from the patient's bloodstream. Some doctors also prescribe a colon cleanser such as a mild laxative. As detoxification is occurring, the patient may need to be administered drugs such as Valium or Librium. Drugs help to prevent complications of *withdrawal* such as seizures, deliriums (extreme mental excitement, marked by confused speech and hallucinations), and cardiac arrhythmia (irregular heart action).

Some therapists believe that a more effective treatment for alcoholism attempts to alleviate the cause of the drinking, including depression, low-self-esteem, and self-handicapping strategy (Jung, 2010). These are the goals of Alcoholics Anonymous, an organization of alcoholics whose purpose is to stay sober and help other recover by offering a non judgmental atmosphere in which alcoholics discuss issues affecting their lives and their recovery from alcohol addiction. The first step is for the patient to admit that he or she has a drinking problem (McCarthy, 1991).

The American Medical Association states that alcoholism should be viewed as a treatable psychiatric and medical disease, and that therapeutic rather than punitive strategies should be employed to combat alcohol use (Gans & Shook, 1994). These treatments include a comprehensive evaluation of the patient, a program with an abstinence philosophy (*i.e.,* any alcohol use is abuse), the belief that drug use is a chronic disease, and the use of support groups, including the child's family. The American Medical Association further asserts that in some instances it may be necessary to remove the alcoholic child from the family—at least for a while.

Among the items discussed in treatment are how to restructure the child's life so that he or she will stop drinking alcohol. One way is to restructure the child's relationship with his or her family and peers. There also needs to be discussions of risk-taking behaviors—a common trait of alcoholics. Finally, most clinicians believe that medication should never be forced on an adolescent because a teenager may perceive the medicine as a form of control by an adult just when he or she is striving for independence.

Many researchers have endorsed the individualized approach to the treatment of alcohol abuse which has been approved by the American Medical Association. First, researchers have identified various adolescent types of alcohol abuse. Each type needs a different form of treatment. For instance, since heavy drinkers often resort to drinking alcohol when they are faced with daily hassles, helping them cope with their families, peers, and love relationships has been shown to lessen their drinking problems. Similarly, helping another type of drinker, known as a problem drinker, has been helped by assisting the abuser with his aggressive and delinquent behavior.

Smoking: A Major Cause of Death

In 1964, the U.S. Surgeon General issued a report explicitly showing the relationship between smoking and diseases such as lung cancer, heart disease, and emphysema (a pulmonary disease of breathlessness and coughing, with production of sputum). Since that time, numerous authorities have indicated the heavy toll from smoking in health and lives (Council on Scientific Affairs, 1990). Each year, more than 400,000 Americans die from tobacco use (more than from all other drugs combined). Smoking is harder on women than on men. Women who smoke are twice as likely as male smokers to develop lung cancer. There are eleven known human carcinogens (cancer-causing substances) in cigarette smoke. One of these is arsenic, a very poisonous metallic element, which if used habitually as in the case of everyday smokers, can cause convulsions, paralysis and death. Illness and death are not the only effects of tobacco use. There is a heavy financial toll over a period of years once a person gets addicted--about $50 billion a year for all smokers in the U.S. (USDHHS, 2000).

Fortunately, cigarette smoking is decreasing among adolescents. For example, in one study of eighth-, tenth-, and twelfth-graders who said they had ever smoked cigarettes, the percentage of smokers dropped by 8 to 10 percentage points from 1998 to 2003 (Johnston, O'Malley, & Bachman, 2005).

Why do children begin to smoke? Initial use of tobacco can be explained by the *social cognitive theory* which states that children are more likely to begin smoking if others around them condone its use or smoke themselves. If a child's best friend smokes, the chances are 9 out of 10 that he or she will also begin to smoke. Moreover, the older a child is, the more likely the child is to imitate his or her peers. Smoking in the family is also a persuasive factor. If one parent smokes, a child is twice as likely to smoke than when neither parent smokes. If both parents smoke, the chances of the child smoking increase significantly by about four to one. The literature also states that children are more likely to begin to smoke if they are depressed. In some instances, children begin smoking as a form of rebellion against authority.

Social cognitive theory: The view that behavior, environment, and person/cognition are the key factors in development.

Piagetian theory suggests that children begin to smoke because they imagine themselves in a "personal fable," in which they believe that they are somehow immune to natural disasters, such as accident or death (Feroli & Burstein, 2003). Piagetian theory further suggests that many young adolescents' thinking is concrete, egocentric, and not particularly future-oriented. This type of thinking results in an inability to understand the long-term consequences of destructive behavior such as smoking.

It is not difficult to determine why young people continue to smoke once they start—smoking is physiologically (and perhaps psychologically) addictive (Koch, 2000).

A note to students who smoke: If you wish to quit this destructive habit, now is the time to do it. Attempts to quit later will be *more difficult* and *more painful* (O'Dell *et al.*, 2004).

Prevention of tobacco use. We need to take steps to curtail some of the policies of our government, such as providing subsidies to tobacco farmers and pressuring other nations to buy American tobacco products. Furthermore, we need to target tobacco companies who have now admitted that they attempt to get children to smoke. Of course, young people need to be kept adequately informed of the dangers of smoking. We need to prohibit all media advertising (newspapers, magazines, and bulletin boards) of tobacco products, since young people are highly sensitive to any form of advertising. Easy access to tobacco products, such as vending machines, should be outlawed.

One way to curtail smoking is to combat the problem globally. Such a step has already been taken by the World Health Organization (WHO). In 2002, WHO joined forces with the international governing bodies of motor racing, football, and the Olympic Games, as well as with well-known athletes in a drive to sweep Big Tobacco out of sporting arenas worldwide.

Marijuana

Although marijuana use declined during the late 1970s and early 1980s, its consumption increased in the 1990s and 2000s (Jung, 2010). Marijuana is the most widely used illicit drug in the United States (Johnston *et al.*, 2004). About 5 percent of teenagers use it on a daily basis.

Effects of marijuana use. The use of marijuana has particular relevance for students. Users have impaired short-term memory and comprehension. They have difficulty concentrating, have more problems than nonusers in acquiring new information, and tend to have lower motivation to do well in school. Because marijuana users often inhale the unfiltered smoke deeply and hold it as long as they can, the lungs and pulmonary system are often damaged. The marijuana user may also develop respiratory infections. Another possible effect is paranoia and psychosis. Prolonged marijuana use can create psychological dependence, which raises the tolerance level, thus necessitating a greater amount of marijuana than formerly to obtain the previous high. Marijuana can contribute to poor grades because it impedes memory and learning.It can also cause car accidents because it reduces perception, alertness, attention span, judgment, and motor skills needed to drive a vehicle (Solowij *et al.*, 2002).

Causes of marijuana use. The reasons for using marijuana, or any other drug, are numerous and complex. Among the strongest predictors of drug abuse during adolescence are peer influences. Of course, peer pressure is minimized if the child's home life is stable and there is a good parent-child relationship (Farrell & White, 1998). Another major factor in the use of drugs is family structure. For instance, children are more likely to use drugs if their parents are divorced (Runeson, 1990). Also, children in stepfamilies are more likely to use drugs than children living in nuclear families (Ganong & Coleman, 1993).

Social-control theory: A belief that an unfavorable family environment causes children to become involved in deviant behavior such as delinquency and drug abuse.

The belief that there is a relationship between family structure involving problems such as divorce and drug use, is called *social-control theory.* This theory proposes that family problems create an environment that is one of rebellion against conventional institutions and practices, often leading to deviant behavior such as delinquency and drug abuse (Bailey & Hubbard, 1990).

Treatment and prevention of drug abuse. If children increasingly look to their peers for support and approval as they mature, controlling the behavior of the peer group might result in modifying drug behavior (Barnea, Teichman, & Rahav, 1992). One way to do this is to provide peer groups with adequate supervision and proper modeling. At the same time, it is important to deal with the teen's difficulties such as depression and inability to get along with others, since children with psychological problems are more likely to abuse drugs, including marijuana.

"Gateway" drugs: Drugs such as marijuana and alcohol which are believed to be forerunners of the use of "harder" drugs.

The ideal goal is to prevent children from using drugs in the first place. Some suggest that this should be attempted early in junior high or even in elementary school by targeting *gateway drugs* (marijuana, alcohol, and cigarettes which are believed to be a forerunner of the use of "harder" drugs such as cocaine and heroin.) However, these programs have met with limited success, particularly in trying to stop the use of alcohol. Nor does teaching children to "Say no to drugs" appear to be helpful. The relapse rate after treatment (falling or slipping back to drug abuse) is about 85 percent (Gilvarry, 2000). A better technique is to teach children that not everyone is taking drugs (Donaldson, Graham, & Hansen, 1994).

Table 13.1
Comparative Substance Abuse by Adolescents and Effects

Type	Ever Used in Lifetime (percent)	Effects
Alcohol	80.	Can lead to alcoholism; physiological and perhaps psychological addiction and aggression. Causes Fetal Alcohol Syndrome in babies born to alcoholic mothers. Linked to more traffic accidents than any other single factor.
Tobacco	72.0	Causes lung and throat cancer, heart attack, high blood pressure and low birth weight in babies born to mothers who smoke. No known minimal safe amount. Physiological, and possibly psychological, addiction. Long-term effects include emphysema; lung, mouth, and throat cancer; and cardiovascular damage. A recent concern is passive smoking, damage to non-smokers by breathing someone else's cigarette smoke. Tobacco is the most commonly abused drug during pregnancy.
Marijuana and hashish	51.5	In low doses, creates a feeling of relaxation and euphoria; higher doses cause an increase in heart rate, lung problems, bloodshot eyes, dry mouth, and increased appetite; contributes to traffic accidents and impedes schoolwork.
Inhalants (solvents, aerosol sprays)	15.	Nausea, sneezing, coughing, nosebleeds, and fatigue are common. Inhaling vapors deeply may cause unconsciousness or death.
Hallucinogens (LSD, PCP)	10.3	Slowing down of body movements and time; delusions and hallucinations. Large doses can cause convulsions and coma, heart and lung failure, depression, anxiety, and violent behavior.
Cocaine; crack	7.8	Effects include dilated pupils and elevated blood pressure; psychological and physiological dependence; ulceration of mucous membranes. Preparation of freebase can result in death or injury from fire or explosion of volatile solvents.
Heroin	1.2	Initial feeling is one of euphoria followed by drowsiness, nausea and vomiting. Overdose may produce shallow breathing, convulsions, coma, and possibly death. Danger of contracting AIDS from contaminated syringes and needles. Addicted pregnant women may give birth to addicted babies.
Stimulants (amphetamines, methamphetamines)	10.5	Increased heart and respiratory rate, blurred vision, and tremors usually result. Amphetamine injection can result in stroke, high fever, or heart failure. Prolonged use can result in amphetamine psychosis.
Sedatives (barbiturates, methaqualone)	15.0	Small amounts produce calmness and relaxed muscles; large doses cause depression, coma, and death. Can lead to physical and psychological dependence.
Tranquilizers (Valium, Librium, Equanil, Miltown)	11.9	Can cause dependence similar to that of barbiturates or alcohol use. Drowsiness, confusion, skin eruptions, and edema are common. Paradoxical reactions such as anxiety and rage can occur.

Ecstacy (MDMA): A drug which affects the body like a stimulant and a psychedelic.

Update on drug abuse. Several studies (*e.g.*, Gfroerer, 1996) indicate that illicit drug use by teenagers is on the increase. One survey (Johnston, 1993) of 50,000 junior and high school students revealed that marijuana was the drug of choice for students in the 1990's; at the turn of the 21st century, it was *ecstacy*, a powerful stimulant. Ecstacy, (MDMA-3-4 methylenedioxymethamphetamine), causes increased heart rate, high blood pressure, high body temperature, dilation of the pupils, appetite loss, dry mouth and nausea (Inaba & Cohen, 2007). Its most popular effects are those evident in the feeling of happiness and pleasure, making it widely popular in college students and young adults. Cocaine use has held steady at low levels; alcohol use has risen slightly. A relatively recent development in substance abuse is the use of injected steroids (Ballard & Wood, 2005).

Within the past three years, the abuse of methamphetamine has reached epidemic proportions. Methamphetamine (or meth as it is popularly known) has been tried illegally by more than 12 million Americans, and 1.5 million are regular users. Meth is also legally available in low doses for the treatment of attention-deficit disorder and narcolepsy, a chronic ailment consisting of recurrent attacks of drowsiness and sleep.The immediate effect of meth is a feeling of euphoria (king of the hill), fearlessness, confidence, hyperalertness, and sexiness that lasts for hours on end. Meth then starts destroying lives. As the immediate effect of meth wears off, the person feels drained, helpless, and deeply depressed. Long-term effects include destruction of both the mind and the body.

Table 13.1 compares the rates of use of various substances by adolescents and explains their effects.

SEXUALLY TRANSMITTED DISEASES (STDS)

Sexually transmitted diseases (STDs), also referred to as venereal diseases, are spread mostly through sexual contact. The incidence of STDs has reached epidemic proportions, particularly among the young (Lawton, 2009). Most cases of gonorrhea and syphilis occur within the 15- to 29-year-old age group. Approximately 25 percent of sexually active adolescents are infected with some form of STD each year. Adolescent females are at higher risk than males for all sexually transmitted diseases because of their lower genital tract and vaginal mucus.

Acquired Immune Deficiency Syndrome (AIDS)

Acquired Immune Deficiencies Syndrome (AIDS), is a fatal sexually transmitted disease. Death, however, is not a direct result of the disease, but instead from pneumonia, infections, or cancers that wreak havoc on the individual's compromised immune system.[6] AIDS stands for *Acquired Immune Deficiency Syndrome*. It causes by a crippling of the entire immunological system. The result is susceptibility to a variety of fatal diseases. The virus that causes AIDS is transmitted through bodily fluids, usually blood or semen.

The initial stage of AIDS causes a weakening of the immune system which renders the individual vulnerable to a wide range of opportunistic infections and tumors such as fevers, night sweats, weight loss, chronic fatigue, and swollen lymps. Although relatively few cases of AIDS have been found among adolescents because of the long incubation period between infection with the HIV virus and AIDS diagnosis, the number is increasing (Centers for Disease Control and Prevention, 2002; Conway *et al.*, 1993; Lawton, 2009).[7] There may also be more AIDS among adolescents than is generally believed since the incubation period—when the disease is difficult to identify—is so long. On average, it takes about 11 years from the time an individual is infected with HIV until he or she has AIDS. ***The rapid increase in the occurrence of AIDS.*** An alarming fact about AIDS is the rate with which it has spread. Although the first case of AIDS was identified in 1981 (O'Donnell & Bernier, 1990), by 1987, about 1 million were infected; more than 20 million were infected worldwide by 1992 (Greene, 1993). In 1999, 33 million people were infected with the AIDS virus, 2.6 million of whom died from the disease worldwide. By 2005, an estimated 58 million people had been infected with AIDS worldwide; the disease has now reached epidemic proportions among children (CDC, 2003). In fact, of the approximately 5 million new infections each year worldwide, almost 60 percent involve children younger than 15 (Summers, Kates, & Murphy, 2002). Drug abusers and people who receive blood transfusions are also likely candidates for AIDS, as are babies born to infected mothers.

Ignorance about AIDS among children. The lack of proper knowledge about AIDS among children and adolescents is disturbing. Many believe that AIDS can be spread by mosquito bites, by touching a person with AIDS, or by toilets. Moreover, many of the terms used to explain AIDS are not accurately understood by children. Most children and adolescents do not know that it is at least twice as easy for a male to infect a female with any sexually transmitted disease, including AIDS, than it is for a female to infect a male (U.S. Centers for Disease Control, 2000).

Limiting the damage from AIDS. AIDS is an incurable disease. However, there are some precautions that can be taken. Blood screening can reduce the risk of contraction by transfusion. Teenagers who are sexually active should limit the number of sexual partners. Preventive measures should be taken. Sexual partners should be aware of any cuts or breaks in the skin and avoid exposing them to anyone else's bodily fluids or secretions. Also, there are many over-the-counter spermicides, such as nonoxynol-9, which have been shown to kill the AIDS virus (HIV) and many other organisms.[8] These should be used in combination with a condom as a preventive measure. Of course, the best preventive measure is to avoid having sex with a person that you suspect of having AIDS.

Testing for AIDS. Anyone who could possibly be at risk should be tested for AIDS. This includes the following: Anyone who has shared needles or

---

6.   The initial stage of AIDS involves being infected with the Human Immunodeficiency Virus (HIV). However, not all HIV-infected people develop AIDS. Many remain in good health and show no symptoms but are capable of spreading the virus to others through unprotected sexual contact; sharing of intravenous needles; and, less often, through blood transfusions. People who carry the AIDS virus should inform health officials immediately. Furthermore, they should not share razors, toothbrushes, or other personal articles since these items may be contaminated with the blood, semen, or saliva of an AIDS victim.

7.   The AIDS virus has been known to remain dormant for more than 10 years before the immune system begins to wear away and symptoms begin to appear.

8.   Women need to be careful about relying too much on over-the-counter remedies for problems such as vaginal yeast infection, one of the most common symptoms of AIDS and HIV-infection in women. Please see a doctor!

received blood products from surgery, anyone who has ever had unprotected sex (whether heterosexual, homosexual, or bisexual), and pregnant women. Other individuals who should be tested for AIDS include individuals living in low-income circumstances, Latinos, and African Americans (Centers for Disease Control and Prevention 2002). (The test for AIDS is relatively simple: A small amount of blood is drawn from the arm for laboratory analysis.) There is an oral test, where a sample of fluid is taken from people who are afraid of needles.

There is some hope in the case of infection through new treatments which slow the progression from HIV to AIDS.

Chlamydia: The Silent STD

Chlamydia: The most common sexually transmitted disease caused by a parasite.

Chlamydia is the most prevalent sexually transmitted disease in the United States, involving approximately 4½ million new cases each year. Most women and many men with chlamydia have no symptoms of the disease. In females, the disease causes infection of the urinary tract and can lead to pelvic inflammatory disease (PID), a serious abdominal infection. Teenage girls who are at greatest risk of becoming infected with chlamydia are unmarried, of low socioeconomic status, and have multiple sex partners. If the adolescent female with chlamydia becomes pregnant, the baby is likely to have complications such as low birth weight and even death.

In men, untreated chlamydia can spread to the testicles, causing painful swelling and possibly sterility. Chlamydia can also cause inflammation of the urethra, the structure serving as a channel for the semen. Chlamydia is usually treated with oral doses of tetracycline, such as doxycycline. Pregnant women with chlamydia should be treated with erythromycin. Chlamydia and gonorrhea are the most common *curable* STDs.

Herpes Simplex, Type 2 (Genital Herpes)

Genital herpes: An incurable, highly contagious lifelong sexually transmitted disease.

Genital herpes (herpes, from Greek "to creep") is an incurable, highly contagious, lifelong infection. The disease is characterized by a pattern of infection, latency (present but invisible and inactive), and reactivation. A telltale sign of herpes is genital blisters, although some women with sores on the cervix may be unaware of a problem. About 45 million Americans have herpes, an increase of about 30 percent since the late 1970s (Bren, 2002).The disease affects an estimated 16,000 American women in its more serious form and contributes to over 7,000 deaths a year; more than 20 million suffer reactivations. Certain forms of the disease are nearly always contracted from infected sexual partners. The disease can be transmitted to the fetus, causing severe damage to its central nervous system.

There is no cure for herpes, although antiviral medications can reduce the duration of blisters and fever. One medication is the drug Zovirax (acyclovir) which appears to be successful in reducing subsequent outbreaks of genital herpes in late pregnancy (Braig *et al.*, 2001). One difficulty in treating genital herpes is identification of the infection. Often, it mimics (looks like) common skin conditions and goes untreated.

Other common sexually transmitted diseases include syphilis, gonorrhea, and genital warts (see Table 13.2).[9]

---

9. Anyone with STD should see a private physician or call the Hot line for AIDS U.S. Public Health Service: 1-800-342-AIDS.

Table 13.2
Some Common Sexually Transmitted Diseases Annually in America

Disease	Approx. Number of New Cases Each Year in the U.S.	Description, Effects, and Treatment
Chlamydia	4-10 million	The most common sexually transmitted disease. Girls 15 to 19 years of age have the highest infection rates of any age group. In the male, the most obvious symptom is pain during urination and discharge from the penis; in the female, vaginal discharge and abdominal pain. Often (80-90 percent) the disease has no symptoms, and can go undetected for years. Chlamydia can cause pelvic inflammatory disease (PID), ectopic pregnancy, and sterility in women; men can also become sterile. Tetracycline is the usual treatment.
Gonorrhea	650,000	In both men and women, there is a yellow discharge that is most noticeable in men during urination. Causes abnormal menses in women. Eighty percent of women who contract the disease are asymptomatic in early stages. Major hazard to both men and women is sterility, arthritis, meningitis, and kidney damage. PID often occurs in women; in men, infection throughout genital and urinary system is often a cause of gonorrhea. The total number of gonorrhea cases has declined in the past 15 years but has increased among young African Americans. The condition is easily treated with antibiotics such as penicillin.
Genital Warts	1 million (greatest increase recently among Caucasian males)	Painless growth caused by viral infection that appears on the genitals or anus; in females may occur inside the vagina without external symptoms. As many as one-third of all sexually active teenagers have genital warts. (Genital warts are similar to plantar warts and are usually painless, but may itch.) Certain strains may show up in the throat. In a more serious form, the warts may obstruct the birth canal in the female, and have been linked to cervical cancer. The warts can be removed by cryosurgery (freezing) or alcohol-based podophyllin solution but the infections remain for the life of the patient.
Herpes Simplex, Type 2	1 million (about 25% of American women and 10% of men have herpes simplex)	Causes painful bumps and sores in the genital region. Progressive headaches, stiff neck, and fever are other symptoms. In women, symptoms are more painful and prolonged than in gonorrhea. Women may be unaware of sores on the cervix. No reliable cure, but can be controlled by antiviral drug Acyclovir; ointment 2-deoxy-D-glucose which had looked promising, now seems ineffective. Undiagnosed herpes during pregnancy is a serious threat, which can cause miscarriage, stillbirth. Presence of herpes may require a Cesarean section.
Syphilis	100,000	Marked by four stages: Primary, secondary, latent, and tertiary. In the primary stage, there is a reddish-brown sore on mouth, or genitalia, or both. In the secondary stage, there is a skin rash which may cover entire body. In the latent stage, symptoms may disappear for 1 to 40 years, but damage is being done. In the tertiary stage, ulcers may form on organs such as lungs or liver. Effects include brain damage, paralysis, and sometimes death. Treatment of choice is penicillin. Complete cure is possible in early stages. Syphilis infection rates are highest among 15- to 19-year-old African American girls.
Acquired Immune Deficiency Syndrome (AIDS)	20,000 (Quite likely, the figure is much higher) (30 million to 100 million are infected with the AIDS virus worldwide)	AIDS was first described as a separate disease entity in 1981. A virus, the human immune deficiency virus (HIV), attacks key immune defense cells, crippling the entire immune system. There is loss of appetite and weight, tiredness, "flu" that does not go away, night sweat, swollen lymph nodes, diarrhea, and susceptibility to other diseases. Risk of contracting AIDS may be increased by open syphilis sores, making teenage sex a medical minefield. Death is usually due to cancer. There is no known cure, but the drug AZT, still in the experimental stage, offers promise. The latest treatment for AIDS is the "cocktail approach," which means using several drugs in combination, including protease inhibitors which appear to extend life by slowing the progression from HIV to AIDS.

Herpes, chlamydia, and some other STD diseases, such as gonorrhea, may be asymptomatic for years and therefore go untreated.

ILLNESS AND DEATH IN ADOLESCENCE

There are no medical conditions unique to adolescence. The majority of deaths are due to accidents (especially motor vehicle accidents), homicide, and suicide. Each year, about one-third of the adolescents involved in sports experience an injury that is severe enough to require medical treatment. The injuries are sustained most often from contact and collision while playing basketball, football, and soccer. Occasionally, the cause of injury is physical fights between players (Cheng *et al.*, 2000). Acute chronic diseases are responsible for about 20 percent of deaths during adolescence. Communicable diseases and respiratory problems so prevalent at one time, have decreased considerably. The leading cause of death from disease among teenagers is cancer which is now considered to be a chronic, life-threatening illness rather than an inevitably fatal disease (Ritchie, 2001).

In this section, we will look at one form of illness, which although ordinarily not serious, is quite troublesome to teenagers: Acne. Then we will look at a common cause of death among adolescents: Suicide.

Acne (Vulgaris)

A common illness in adolescence, *acne*, is an inflammatory skin condition characterized by pimples and blackheads. The cause of acne is bacterial buildup inside oil-clogged pores. *Acne vulgaris*, as this condition is known technically, is often found on the face, upper chest, back, and shoulders. Most acne is worse in the winter and improves in the summer. About 80 to 90 percent of teenagers suffer from this disorder, with boys being more susceptible to acne than girls.

Acne (Vulgaris): An inflammatory skin condition which is common in adolescence.

Acne tends to be more common among girls with highly irregular menstrual cycles and to flare up a few days prior to each period. Acne can be aggravated by habitual rubbing, squeezing, picking of the skin, and by heavy application of cosmetics. Acne can have negative psychosocial consequences for the affected individual, including diminished self-esteem and social withdrawal due to embarrassment, and depression. Hence, treatment is important, especially since satisfactory results can usually be achieved (Brown & Shalita, 1998).

Treatment. An effective treatment for mild acne consists of dietary restrictions (cutting back on foods with a high fat content, such as pork, potato chips, and milk) and frequent washing with antibacterial detergent soaps or skin cleansers. Antibiotics, particularly tetracycline, are also an effective form of treatment. A recent development, a variation of vitamin A, called Accutane, appears promising in the treatment of severe acne (Webster & Freeman, 2003). In girls, when acne appears to come and go with the menstrual cycle, a birth control pill containing synthetic female hormones can sometimes cure acne. However, pregnant women should not take the drug since it is known to cause miscarriages and severe birth defects. In the more serious cases of acne, surgical treatment can be used in conjunction with medical treatment. Another recent treatment is laser therapy where a doctor passes a light over the affected areas to kill the bacteria and shrink the oil glands.

Cerebral Palsy: A Nerve and Muscle Disorder

Cerebral palsy: A nerve and muscle disorder that is caused by damage to the brain's motor centers.

Cerebral palsy, or perinatal encephalopathy, is a catch-all term that describes any dysfunction of the motor centers and pathways of the brain acquired before, during, or in the first few months after birth (Roijen *et al.*, 2001). "Cerebral" refers to the brain and "palsy" refers to weakness, lack of control, or paralysis of any voluntary muscle owing to a disorder of the nervous system. One result of this disorder is difficulty or inability to walk. Since the throat and diaphragm muscles are usually affected, labored or distorted speech occurs in about 70 percent of affected children. There are often sensory and perceptual deficits, learning difficulties, severe emotional and personality problems, and intellectual retardation. The degree of impairment varies from very mild to severe, but the malady is not fatal (Liptak *et al.*, 2001).

Cerebral palsy is not a disease; rather, it is a group of symptoms involving motor and sensory systems (Steiner, Morton, & Walsh, 1991). It is not contagious, nor is it progressive (gets worse with time). Best estimates indicate that cerebral palsy affects approximately 1 to 3 children per every 1,000 (Nelson & Ellenberg, 1978; Hay *et al.*, 1997). Early warning signs include inability to lift the head or push up on arms by 3 months of age, floppy or limp body posture, and use of only one side of the body to crawl. Another early warning sign of cerebral palsy is low Apgar scores. Also, the disorder may affect the child's ability to maintain posture and balance. It is estimated that 50 to 75% of persons with cerebral palsy have some type of speech impairment, which is a major concern in the classroom (Watson, 1995). Since cerebral palsy is a permanent non-progressive brain disorder, there is no cure. Treatment includes physiotherapy, speech therapy, and medications.

Types

There are several types of cerebral palsy based on the type of tonal dysfunction (abnormal resistance of muscles to passive elongation or stretch) and extremities affected. The most common type (50 to 65 percent of all cases) is called spastic.

Spastic palsy is characterized by a loss of voluntary muscle control, causing a lack of balance between the antagonistic muscles and suppressor areas of the brain. The result is simultaneous contraction of the extensor muscles, such as those used in extending the arm, and the flexor muscles, such as those used in pulling the arm toward the body (Liptak *et al.*, 2001; Stevenson, 2001). Movement is attained through a series of spasms, making movement jerky, exaggerated, and poorly coordinated. When the spastic person walks, knees are bent and pointed inward and the person stands on the toes. Urinary incontinence is common (Roijen *et al.*, 2001).

Athetosis is more disabling than spasticity and affects about 15 to 20 percent of the cerebral palsied. The condition is marked by purposeless, involuntary twisting and writhing movements, especially in the wrists, fingers, and face. The person walks with serpentine movements, the arms waving wildly, the head drawn back, the mouth open, and the neck extended. Usually the tongue protrudes and the mouth drools. Gross motor tasks such as walking require considerable effort; fine motor skills such as picking up a pencil are usually very difficult. Often, speech is labored, hoarse, and unintelligible owing to involvement of the muscles of the tongue, lips, throat, and diaphragm. Intellectual functioning is often normal.

Ataxia is a third type of cerebral palsy. It is caused by damage to the cerebellum, which controls balance and coordination such as that required for walking. Consequently, a key symptom of ataxia is poor balance and lack of motor coordination. While walking, the person may sway and stagger, appearing intoxicated; speech is often slurred.

Treatment: Treatment for cerebral palsy involving a team approach (doctor, language specialist, etc.) can result in improved speech and more coordinated movement. Realistically, the goal in the treatment of cerebral palsy is to help the child achieve maximum potential, rather than normality. If children with cerebral palsy have sufficient coordination to use a keyboard, they can do their written work on a computer. Children with unclear speech can use speech and voice synthesizers, communication boards, talking notes, and page turners.

Suicide

Everyone was shocked to learn that 15-year-old Jimmy had committed suicide. Yet, there were signs that he was not adjusting to his mother's death. His grades in school were falling, he was droopy, listless, and appeared to have given up hope. Rather than being concerned with Jimmy's emotional well-being, his teachers and father were more concerned about his declining grades. The teachers thought that Jimmy had a learning disability, but Jimmy's father thought that his son was not trying hard enough. In conferences with the teachers and the school psychologist, the father said he was certain that Jimmy would improve within a week or two. When the school psychologist pointed out that Jimmy missed his mother and was listless because of the fantasies about her, the father rejected this theory. "After all," the father said, "My wife is dead. I know she is dead... and I am sure that Jimmy doesn't even think about it." When told that the boy had been contemplating suicide, the father dismissed this as a trick. Yet, two weeks later, using his father's gun, Jimmy took his own life.

In the United States, over 5,000 people under the age of 25 commit suicide each year and another 1 million contemplate suicide. This phenomenon has increased by 300 percent since the mid-1950s in both male and female adolescents (Rotherman-Boris, Walker, & Ferns, 1996). About 12 percent of all teenage deaths are caused by suicide. In 2000, suicide was the fifth leading cause of death among children aged 5 to 14 years and the third leading cause of death among adolescents 13 through 18 years in the United States (National Center for Health Statistics, 2000). Just four years later (in 2004), suicide was the second leading cause of death among teenagers.

So serious is the problem of suicide among teenagers, that several high schools have instituted suicide prevention programs. These programs usually have several elements in common: They last the entire year and parents, teachers, counselors, and psychologists are involved. All programs are presented positively. The programs usually provide training in recognizing potential suicide and methods of helping the suicidal person.

Those who have studied suicide, find that there are certain patterns. Female adolescents attempt suicide about three times more often than males, but males "succeed" more often. This is because men use more drastic means to end their lives, such as guns. Boys who feel that they are unable to cope with their situation are about four times more likely to commit suicide than girls. There are also racial and gender differences: Caucasian males have the highest suicide rate, followed by African American males, Caucasian females, and African American females. Also, teenage suicide often occurs in clusters. Depressed people are more likely to commit suicide if they knew a person who took his or her own life or if the initial suicide was advertised in the media (Grossman & Kruesi 2000).

Symptoms of possible suicide. The most important predictor of possible adolescent suicide is a previous attempt. Common symptoms of suicidal tendencies are depression (twice as common in adolescent females than in males), feeling lonely, and feeling like a failure. The suicide rate for people with severe depression is 22 to 36 times greater than for the general population. Sudden changes in behavior—particularly if the changes are drastic—such as a good student unexpectedly becoming truant or a person who normally loves to eat suddenly losing his appetite, are strong indicators of potential suicide. The suicidal adolescent may suddenly turn to drugs (Crumley, 1990), delinquency, or promiscuity, or might run away. Often, the suicidal person is unable to sleep, and shows signs of pathological bereavement, such as being unable to function normally after the death of a parent (Bowlby, 1980; Wagner, 1997). Eighty percent of people who plan suicide give some detectable hint such as "I'm going to end it all," or "There's no point in carrying on."

Overall, suicide appears in two types of young people. One group is very intelligent but solitary and withdrawn, with unrealistically high standards. The second type, a larger group, is antisocial and express their anger, disappointment, and depression toward others and themselves by bullying or destructiveness (American Academy of Pediatrics 2000; Fergusson, Woodward, & Horwood, 2000).

According to many investigators, hopelessness (the belief that suicide is the only way out of an unsolvable problem) appears to be a sensitive indicator of potential suicide (Beck *et al.*, 1990). Symptoms of potential suicide can often be detected in preschool or in the primary grades. Dysfunctional coping behaviors such as substance abuse, setting fires, talking back to teachers, fighting with peers, skipping classes, and truancy are often symptomatic of extreme turmoil within the mind of the child and may be indicators of intended suicide. Usually these problems have persisted for some time (Haliburn, 2000).

Researchers have noticed that the cause of children's suicide is often familial (Brent *et al.*, 2002). For instance, there is a higher risk of suicide in children if their parents had attempted suicide, whether the attempt was successful" or incomplete. The risk of suicide is increased still more if the children had been sexually abused or if there is a climate of parental hostility toward the children.

Helping suicidal persons. Before discussing ways to help suicidal persons, there are some things *not* to do:

- Never ignore a suicidal threat or attempt.

- Don't abandon the potential victim until you've obtained outside help.

- Don't assume that the situation will take care of itself.

- Don't argue or debate moral issues.

- Don't dare the person to take his or her life.

- Don't make a "no-suicide" contract with the suicidal person. Such a "no-harm" agreement is often a false reassurance that the risk of suicide has disappeared, when in fact it seldom has.

- Do not agree with the person that he or she has nothing to live for.

- Don't trivialize the person's plight (Do not say, "Oh, you'll get over it").

- Don't ignore warnings ("I won't be around after tomorrow"), even if they are subtle ones.

- Don't promise to keep the intended suicide secret.

- Avoid saying, "Don't say that!" if a child threatens suicide. Such a comment sounds negative and judgmental—as well as unhelpful.

- Avoid ignoring a suicide attempt as a way of escaping a problem a suicidal person is unable to solve (Brown *et al.*, 2000). Often, just a little help from another person can prevent suicide.

Here are some ways in which a suicidal person can be helped:

- Call 1-800-SUICIDE to be connected with a crisis center in your area.

- Be aware of the person who suddenly becomes drawn to music, movies, books, or Internet sites that focus on death.

- Be sensitive to signs of potential suicide: depression, inability to cope with everyday tasks, feeling of loneliness, difficulties in social relationships, substance abuse, eating disorder, family conflict, failure in school, and a family history of suicide.

- Show composure to communicate a sense of control of the situation.

- Be a sympathetic listener. What may seem trivial to you, such as getting a "C" on a test, may have enormous emotional significance for the potential suicide victim.

- Answer the child's questions honestly, even if the answer is, "I don't know."

- Be frank and ask the person if she or he has thoughts of suicide (the person often feels relieved after admitting to such ideas).

- Find out the person's frustration and try to remove the problem.

- Show the person other options ("Why don't you go back home until you can find another job?," and "Talk to your mother about this").

- Tell the person you care about what happens to him or her.

- Remove potential means of suicide (guns, drugs, and toxic substances) as soon as possible.

- Arrange for the person to meet with a mental-health professional schooled in suicide prevention. If this is not possible, call a suicide hotline. (Local listings can be found in the phone book under "Suicide").

- Suicide attempts can usually be prevented if the parents spend more time with their children and give them the attention and love that they need desperately.

- Suicide attempts can also be prevented if we address the psychodynamics of the suicidal person. Psychodynamics deals with the quality of the suicidal person's relationships with others, the nature of his or her conflicts, the role of anxiety in the intended suicide, the hopelessness, and the rage.

Caution. Since experts frequently disagree about the accuracy of predictions of suicide potential—even with the best of help—following the guidelines above does not guarantee that the suicidal person will not attempt to take his or her life. Many investigators believe that today's adolescents face more stresses and have fewer supports than they did in the past (McIntosh, 2000).

SUMMARY

Adolescence is a transitional period between childhood and adulthood. It begins with the onset of puberty, which is the attainment of sexual maturity when a person is able to reproduce. There is a tendency toward earlier sexual maturation in teenagers today. This is known as the secular growth trend.

The end of adolescence is difficult to determine and there are no valid criteria to determine this benchmark. In some societies, adolescence ends at puberty. In our society, there are many criteria: Legal, sociological, psychological, and cognitive.

Both genders undergo considerable change during puberty. These changes include sharp growth in height and weight. There are also changes in primary sex characteristics, which involve organs directly related to reproduction, and secondary sex characteristics, which include breast development in females and growth of facial hair in males.

The timing of puberty varies. Typically, the girl has her first period, or menarche, at about age 12½; the boy's sperm becomes mature (capable of reproduction) at about age 14. Genetic factors and environment appear to play a role in puberty.

Good nutrition is important for proper physical development during adolescence. Protein, calcium, and iron are essential nutrients.

Among the eating disorders are anorexia nervosa, marked by self-starvation; and bulimia nervosa, characterized by excessive eating and purging. Both disorders are more common among female adolescents but do not spare males. Obesity is also a societal problem.

Drug abuse among adolescents continues to be a significant concern. A new epidemic is the increase in tobacco smoking by teenage girls, who now outnumber boys who smoke.

Sexually transmitted diseases are a major problem among adolescents. The most common is chlamydia. Other sexually transmitted diseases include AIDS, genital warts, gonorrhea, and syphilis.

A common illness in adolescence is acne.

A much more serious problem is suicide.

IMPORTANT TERMS

Acne (vulgaris)

Acquired Immune Deficiency Syndrome (AIDS)

Adolescence

Adolescent

Age of majority

Alcoholism

Androgens

Anorexia nervosa

Body image

Bulimia nervosa

Ceberal palsy

Chlamydia

Cognitive-behavioral therapy

Conduct disorder

Detoxification

Ecstacy (MDMA)

Emancipation

Estrogens

"Gateway" drugs

Genital herpes

Human growth hormone

Industry versus inferiority

Menarche

Osteoporosis

Primary sex characteristics

Progesterone

Psychoactive substance abuse

Puberty

Pubescence

Pubescent growth spurt

Secondary sex characteristics

Secular growth trend

Seizure disorder (Epilepsy)

Self-handicapping strategy

Sexually transmitted disease

Social cognitive theory

Social-control theory

Somatotropin

Spasticity

Testosterone

Tonic-clonic seizure

RELATED READINGS

Gutierrez, Peter M. (2009). *HIV Prevention: a Comprehensive Approach.* London; Boston, MA.: Elsevier/Academic Press.

Gutierrez, Peter M. and Osman, Augustine (2008). *Adolescent Suicide: an Integrated Approach to the Assessment of Risk and Protective Factors.* DeKalb, IL: Northern Illinois University Press.

Jamieson, Daniel Romer (2008). *The Changing Portrayal of Adolescents in the Bedia since 1950.* New York: Oxford University Press.

Lawton, Sandra A. editor (2009). *Sexual Health Information for Teens: Health Tips about Sexual Development, Reproduction, Contraception, and Sexually Transmitted Infections Including Facts about Puberty, Sexuality,Birth control, Chlamydia, Gonorrhea, Herpes, Human Papillomavirus,Syphilis, and More.* Detroit, MI: Omnigraphics.

Thomas, R. Murray (2009). *Sex and the American Teenager: Seeing Through the Myths and Confronting the Issues.* Lanham, Md.: Rowman & Littlefield Education.

Pipher, M. (2000). *Reviving Ophelia: Saving the Selves of Adolescent Girls.* Westminster, MD: Ballantine.

Websites
Centers for Disease Control and Prevention
http://www.cdc.gov/

National Eating Disorders Association
http://www.nationaleatingdisorders.org/information-resources/resources-and-links.php

The Obesity Society
http://www.obesity.org/

Drug Information Online
http://www.drugs.com/

National Institutes of Health
http://www.nih.gov/

Chapter 14

Cognitive Development in Adolescence (12 to 18 years)

Chapter Topics		Learning Objectives
How does formal-operational thinking differ from other types of thinking?		Understand Piaget's formal operational thinking in adolescence.
How does egocentrism influence an adolescent's thoughts?		Understand adolescent idealism and egocentrism factors in adolescent thinking.
What is the relationship between cognitive development and moral reasoning?		Understand Kohlberg's theory of moral development in adolescence.
What are some influential factors in achievement in high school?		Be familiar with the characteristics of American Education.
What factors play a role in the choice of a vocation for adolescents?		Recognize parental influences, gender, and vocational assessments as factors in vocational choice for adolescents.
Chapter summary		

Seventeen-year-old Sara thinks that she is "grown-up." She is a senior in high school, has a boyfriend, and drives a car. At times, she is able to think logically (Piaget's stage of formal operations), to consider hypothetical objects and events, and to understand abstract principles. At other times, she's concerned about the world around her and often reflects on a better one, different from the one in which she is living. She is also beginning to develop her own sense of right and wrong, indicating that she is at Kohlberg's postconventional moral stage. Sara is also grappling with a vocation.

Even though Sara usually exhibits mature behavior, she can be quite childish. At times, she is overly self-conscious, believing that everyone is thinking about her. These signs of immaturity indicate that Sara is not quite grown up; she is still an adolescent. In this chapter, we will look at cognitive development during this important period.

PIAGET'S FORMAL OPERATIONS (AGES 11 TO 14 OR 15)

Twelve-year-old McKensie, excited and nervous, is about to go on her first date. What should she wear? She looks in her wardrobe—as well as in her mother's—and finds four dresses, three skirts, three blouses, and two sweaters that might be suitable. By considering all possible combinations after trying each one on, McKensie finally settles on an outfit acceptable not only to herself, but also to her girlfriend and to her mother.

The manner in which McKensie solved her problem illustrates the thinking typical of Piaget's stage of formal operations, the highest level of cognitive development (Inhelder & Piaget, 1958). McKensie took a generalized approach to solving her problem by systematically isolating each outfit until she had explored all possible solutions. She was aware of the tentativeness of each hypothesis, testing each one mentally, then proceeding to the next one.

In contrast to the stage of concrete operations, the child in the stage of formal operations like McKensie is able to manipulate abstract ideas and symbols. McKensie can now consider general laws and think about what is hypothetically possible, as well as what is real. She is also able to speculate, and to use logical operations in an adult manner to solve problems. This type of thinking is typical in scientific endeavors and is usually reached when the child is somewhere between 12 and 15 years of age. Cognitively, according to Piaget, such a child is now an adult because he or she has reached the stage of formal operations.

Piaget's Pendulum Problem

Jean Piaget illustrated formal-operational thinking with his classic pendulum problem. A child is first shown the pendulum, an object hanging from a string. The child is then provided with objects of different weights, strings of different lengths to attach to the objects, and a bar from which to hang the strings. The objective is to determine the period of the pendulum, the time it takes to complete a swing from one side to the other side and back. Is the critical factor (or variable) the length of the string, the weight of the pendulum, the height from which the weight is released, or the degree of force with which the pendulum is propelled?

Preoperational thinking. When given the pendulum problem at age 6, Carlos approaches the task haphazardly. He might put a heavy weight on a short string, push it, then try swinging a long pendulum with a light weight and a long string. Following this random approach, Carlos is at a loss to know what to do next, or to report what actually happened. Many preoperational children conclude erroneously that the force of the push makes the pendulum go faster.

Concrete-operational thinking. Concrete-operational children approach the pendulum problem using a partially systematic approach. For example, they might test for the effect of string length, but without systematically holding the weight constant. Concrete-operational children fail to realize that height and force with which the pendulum is released are also influential factors. Since more than one critical factor is varied, concrete operational children are unable to solve the problem. They may occasionally hit on a partially correct answer, but since they are tied to the here and now, they are incapable of thinking of all possibilities, and hence, are unable to solve the pendulum problem.

Solving the pendulum problem through hypothetico-deductive reasoning. Using *hypothetico-deductive reasoning* and working systematically, the formal-operational child will first come up with a general theory that includes all possible factors that may influence the swing of the pendulum. Drawing from these various possibilities, the child deduces a number of specific hypotheses that may help to solve the problem. Usually, formal-operational children come up with four possible hypotheses: length of string, the weight of the object hung on the string, the height from which the weight is released, and the force behind the push.

The formal-operational child will systematically vary one factor at a time, while holding the other critical elements constant. In one condition, Carlos might use the same length string, push the weight with the same force, release the pendulum from the same height each time, but use different weights. Carlos will then observe the results as carefully as he can, keep track of the results, and draw the appropriate conclusions (Miller, 2002). In another condition, he might push the same weight with varying force while holding the length of string and height constant. Carlos continues in this way, varying one factor at a time, until he has identified the critical variable, the length of the string.

When a child is capable of hypothetical-deductive reasoning, he can develop a specific prediction, or hypothesis, about how one variable is related to another and can design an experiment to test it. He considers as many relationships among variables as he can imagine and examines them systematically, one by one, to eliminate the false and arrive at the true. When the child is capable of hypothetical reasoning, he has a tool to solve problems such as fixing the family car as well as tackling more difficult tasks such as constructing a political theory which might eliminate some of society's major problems.

Flexibility is one reason why formal-operational Carlos can solve the pendulum problem. If a particular hypothesis does not work, the formal child discards it immediately and goes on to another possibility. For example, if Carlos discovers that the strength of his release is not the critical factor, he will search for another variable such as the height from which the pendulum is released. Carlos' flexibility enables him to come up with an infinite number of possible solutions because he is able to go beyond reality, or what he has

Hypothetico-deductive reasoning: The ability to consider all possible solutions to a problem, then systematically evaluate each possible solution one by one to arrive at the correct solution.

actually experienced. This includes both the real (experienced, concrete) world and the much wider view of possibility.

A broader view of the world by formal-operational children was demonstrated by John Flavell (1985). When formal-operational adolescents were asked to describe what would happen if the earth stopped revolving around the sun, they proposed such hypotheses as millions of people would have to move to warmer climates, farming outdoors would be impossible in many places, and there would not be any seasons. Concrete-operational children responded to the query by first referring to reality, and to things which they could sense immediately or experience. For example, they would answer that it would "always be cold" or "always be warm." Concrete operators, whose thinking is tied to objective reality, might even answer that it is impossible to think about objects and events that don't exist or could never happen.

Abstractions: Ideas or situations not immediately apparent to the senses.

The formal-operational child is at an advantage because of his or her ability to grasp *abstractions*—ideas or situations that are not immediately apparent to the senses. Sara can now think about what might be, rather than what is. Formal-operational Sara can also think about infinity, whereas only a few years ago she had difficulty figuring out how far it was to her school. Sara's ability to think abstractly enables her to plan for the future. She is also able to think about the consequences of her actions (e.g., "If I have unprotected sex, then...").

Since Sara can think about abstract situations, she often develops new goals that are contrary to what is generally accepted. Using political and philosophical doctrines, formal-operational Sara may mentally design an ideal society or reflect on such weighty abstractions as morality and justice. Formal-operational children can also reflect on the way things "ought to be" as well as on "the way they are." For concrete operational children the possibilities equal reality; for formal-operational adolescents, there are infinite possibilities. Thus, for the concrete child, religion may mean attending church and nothing more. The formal-operational child might reflect on a religious society with or without churches.At this age, the child cannot only further the development of thinking about what was learned earlier, but to add a new, qualitative dimension to his or her thinking (Andrich & Styles. 1994). Table 14.1 compares the scope of thinking in childhood to that in adolescence.

The Poker-Chips Problem and Propositional Thinking

Proposition: A statement that does not always refer to real objects or events.

A significant feature of formal-operational thinking is the ability to use *propositions*: statements that do not always refer to real objects or events. We can see propositional thinking in a study by Daniel Osherson & Ellen Markman (1975). A pile of poker chips is placed on a table. The experimenter tells Cindy that some statements will be made about the chips, and she is to respond to each statement as "True," "False," or "Uncertain."

In one condition, the examiner conceals a chip in his hand and says, "Either the chip in my hand is green or it is not green," or he says, "The chip in my hand is green and it is not green." In another condition, the examiner holds up either a red or green chip and makes the same statements. Sara, now 12, can evaluate the logic of the statements as propositions. She understands that "either/or" statements are always true, and that the "and" statements are always false. She realizes that propositional statements do not always refer to real objects or events.

Since much of the thinking in formal operations is no longer restricted to reality or is factually incorrect, language plays a far more critical role at this stage than earlier. The use of language helps the formal-operational thinker to deal with abstract terms by using representations that are entirely separate from concrete reality. This enables the child to solve complicated mathematical problems, and to deal with abstract concepts such as, "What is truth?" and "What is justice?" Formal-operational Carlos can apply these abstract concepts to a variety of situations including his home, the school, and the government (King & Kitchener, 1994).

Table 14.1
A Comparison of Childhood and Adolescent Thought

Childhood	Adolescence
Thought is limited to here and now	Thought is extended to possibilities
Problem solving is dictated by details of the issue	Problem solving is governed by planned hypotheses testing
Thought is limited to concrete objects and situations	Thought is expanded to ideas as well as to concrete reality
Thought is focused on one's own perspective	Thought is enlarged to perspective of others

Source: Sprinthall and Collins, 1984, p. 93.

A New Outlook on Life

Piaget believes that formal-operational thinking affects every aspect of an adolescent's life. Piaget says that formal thinking causes Sara to alter her feelings about herself, to develop new goals, to adopt new values and beliefs, and to develop a new relationship with her parents. As a result, formal-operational Sara will view the world differently than before. She is now a bit of a philosopher, preoccupied with the idealistic world of the possible as well as with real world.

What Brings About Formal Operations?

Psychologists are particularly interested in the role environment plays in advancing Sara to the stage of formal operations, but neurological factors also play a role in reaching the highest stage of thinking. Sara

Formal operations are likely to be developed in technologically advanced Western societies in major cities and in academic settings. Exposure to schooling that stresses logic, preliterate mathematics, science, and English appears to enhance formal operations. In preliterate societies, where formal schooling is rare or nonexistent, no one can solve Piaget's formal-operational problems, but there may be a different way of looking at this issue.

Of course, schooling itself does not guarantee advancement to the stage of formal operations. Adolescents and adults who score slightly below average on intelligence tests rarely reason at the formal-operational level. About one-third to one-half of late adolescents seem to be incapable of abstract thought (ideas or situations not immediately apparent to the senses), a highlight of formal operations as Piaget defined it (Gardiner & Kosmitzki, 2005).

Are There Gender Differences in Formal-Operational Thinking?

There has been a significant amount of research to determine whether there are male-female differences in formal-operational thinking involving social and scientific reasoning. Popular belief suggests that men have greater talent in areas such as mathematics, science, and engineering. Women are generally believed to be superior in language ability. Studies (e.g., Voyer, Voyer, & Bryden, 1995) have shown that, on average, males outperform females in tasks in which spatial abilities (the skill to visualize the relationships of objects in space) play a significant role.

A classic study which highlighted gender differences during the formal-operational period was conducted by Eleanor Maccoby and Carol Jacklin (1974). Maccoby and Jacklin found four fairly well-established gender differences between boys and girls:

- Beginning at around age 11 years, girls exhibit greater verbal ability than boys.

- Boys are superior to girls in visual-spatial tasks in adolescence, but not in early childhood.

- At about age 12 or 13 year, boys move ahead of girls in mathematics.

- Males are more aggressive than females. Gender differences in aggression are greatest among preschoolers and decrease through the college years.

More recent studies have tended to confirm the gender differences found by Maccoby and Jacklin. However, the differences are not as great as Maccoby and Jacklin claim. Moreover, girls have reduced their historical weakness in mathematics more than boys have closed the gap in language skills.

Evaluation of Piaget's Formal Operations

Piaget's theory has enabled us to develop a better understanding of cognitive development. However, there is constant criticism of his theory because of its lack of specificity about the prerequisites necessary for advancing from one stage to the next (Morra, 2008). Although Piaget does say that the transition from concrete-operational to formal-operational reasoning occurs gradually over a period of several years, he is vague in his explanation of this transition. Piaget says that maturational changes are necessary for such cognitive advancement.

One line of investigation seeks to determine if children can learn formal operations sooner than Piaget claimed. A number of studies (Ennis, 1971; Paris, 1973) have demonstrated that elementary schoolchildren are capable of some forms of propositional logic, a cornerstone of formal thinking. For example, 8-year-olds can draw a correct conclusion when given the following problem:

Premise 1: If Jack washes the dishes, then his father will be very pleased.
Premise 2: If Jack's father is very pleased, then Jack gets 50¢.
Premise 3: Jack washes the dishes.
Conclusion: Jack gets 50¢.

On the other hand, when premises are stated in the negative, elementary schoolchildren have considerable difficulty. Here is an example of a negative premise:

> Premise 1: If there is a knife, then there is a fork.
> Premise 2: There is not a knife.
> Erroneous Conclusion: There is not a fork. (Kodroff and Roberge, 1975).

It is not surprising that elementary schoolchildren have difficulty with negative premises because adolescents and adults often experience difficulty as well. This finding may suggest that there is not as much difference between formal-operational and concrete-operational thinking as Piaget suggested (Morra, 2008).

ADOLESCENT IDEALISM AND EGOCENTRISM

Adolescent idealism: An adolescent's thinking about the way things should be instead of confining his or her thinking to the way things are.

"When I get to be President of the United States, there will be no more wars, no more homeless people, and no more poverty," 16-year-old Carlos says to his parents. Although his mother responds in a half-hearted agreement, Carlos' father calls his son a daydreamer who is living in a fantasy world. Carlos' desire for a better society is typical of teenage thinking and forms the basis for *adolescent idealism*, which is reasoning about the way things should be instead of the way things are. While adolescent idealism often irks adults, it fulfills several important functions.

One function of adolescent idealism is to provide an opportunity and experience to plan for the future. In this way, Carlos is able to develop goals and organize his current activities in a meaningful way. He is also able to tie the present to the future. Moreover, idealistic thinking is an attempt to change *what is* to *what should be*. Unfortunately, this attempt at change is often the basis of a conflict between parents and their teenager. The teenager is merely attempting to try out his ideas in the home where he feels safe. When Carlos receives feedback on his idealism, he may next try it out on the larger audience, such as his teachers. If Carlos' ideas are rebuffed, he may withdraw and resort to daydreams, have temporary stupors, or become moody. Parents need to listen to their teenagers' ideas, even when they seem unrealistic. It is also important for parents to avoid public criticism and ridicule of their teenagers.

Adolescent egocentrism: An adolescent's focus on his or her ideas as being the only possible solutions to problems.

Egocentrism in adolescent thought. One constant criticism adults have of teenagers is that they think they have all the answers. This is because adolescents tend to focus on their own ideas as the only possible solution to problems. Adolescents believe that they have the answers, if only others would listen. They also feel that others are focused on them as much as they are on themselves. Carlos and Sara also think that they are special and unique (Rycek *et al.*, 1998). These types of self-preoccupation are forms of egocentrism, which Piaget believed accompanies the emergence of all stages of intellectual development. Let's consider *adolescent egocentrism* in a little more detail, including imaginary audience, the personal fable, and test anxiety.

Imaginary audience: A kind of egocentrism common in adolescence, including a suspicion that others are "always looking at me, and they are making fun of me."

Imaginary audience. Sara, age 14 years, spends much of her time thinking that she is like an actress who is constantly on stage, and that others are preoccupied with her appearance and behavior. She also complains that other girls are whispering about her, that boys are making fun of her, and that people look at her strangely. While some of Sara's complaints may be based on fact, she probably exaggerates the extent to which others are preoccupied with her. Sara's extreme suspicion of others and her excessive sensitivity to them is due to a type of egocentrism called *imaginary audience.* The cause of Sara's problem is her inability to differentiate adequately between her own thoughts and those of others, which she assumes are constantly focused on her. Sara's preoccupation with herself is characteristic of Piaget's early formal operations. Sara assumes that since she spends considerable time thinking about herself, others must be thinking about her also. Although both male and female adolescents' thinking is centered on themselves, females possess a higher level of egocentrism, including emphasis on an imaginary audience.

Personal fable: The familiar belief of adolescents that bad things happen to other people, but not to them.

Personal fable. A counterpart to the imaginary audience is the *personal fable* discussed in an earlier chapter, the familiar belief of adolescents that bad things happen to other people, not to them. Adolescents see themselves as omnipotent, invincible, and even immortal, and are not subject to the same law as everyone else. Thus, the adolescent boy may see himself as unique and somehow immune from harm, an attitude that is characteristic of the young reckless driver, the bungee jumper, the drug abuser, the gang member, and some armed services recruits who think that only the "enemy" will be shot in a war.

Personal fables may be behind some of the promiscuous sexual activity. Although teenage girls know that sexual intercourse produces babies, many think that only other girls will become pregnant, and that nothing will ruin their lives. Adolescents' personal fable is also evident in their belief that they have avoided the effects of AIDS even though they engaged in unprotected sex. The personal fable lets the teenage girl deny responsibility for the pregnancy or the STD. A teenager may blame her partner, her hormones, or even the devil for her sexual misfortune (Schifter & Madrigal, 2000).In fact, in many instances, adolescents contract the disease but are not aware of it because the HIV infection may be present for several years before the symptoms are or evident.

Test anxiety: Stress that causes difficulty in preparing for a test and in taking it.

Test anxiety. An adolescent's egocentrism is often evident in Sara's self-consciousness and anxiety when taking a test. *Test anxiety* can cause Sara to become so distracted by negative thoughts that she may fail to follow instructions and neglect or misinterpret obvious informational clues provided by the questions. As anxiety mounts, Sara may say things to herself such as, "My stomach hurts," and "What will I tell my parents if I fail?" Sara can become so preoccupied with self-deprecatory thoughts that she devotes only a limited amount of attention and concentration to the test (Wine, 1971). The result can be difficulty in retrieving facts that Sara has learned well.

MORAL DEVELOPMENT

Eighteen-year-old Carlos is fuming because a high school senior he knows received a 6-month jail sentence for stealing food. "Although, from a legal point of view, it is wrong to steal," says Carlos, "What was Timothy supposed to do? He had no job and had been kicked out of his home." Those who have studied models of moral development will recognize that Carlos' thinking is typical of Kohlberg's postconventional moral thought, Level III. When Carlos was at Level I (ages 4 to 10), the preconventional level, he was concerned with obeying those in authority to avoid punishment. At Level II (from 10 to 18 years), Carlos had internalized the standards of others and was interested in maintaining the status quo, doing what was considered right, and obeying the law. Now that Carlos is at the postconventional level, his individual principles of conscience are beginning to emerge (Browne-Miller, 2009).

Kohlberg's Level III: Postconventional Moral Thought (Young Adulthood or Never)

Individuals at Kohlberg's third level of morality rely on an internal control of conduct, both in observing standards of behavior and in reasoning about right and wrong. Individuals at Level III acknowledge the possibility of conflict between two socially accepted standards such as obeying the law versus doing what they believe is right, which might mean breaking the law. This means that postconventional reasoners occasionally feel compelled to act illegally if the laws are at variance with their moral principles. For example, acts of civil disobedience were committed by idealists Henry David Thoreau, the American naturalist, and by Martin Luther King, Jr., the American civil rights leader. According to Kohlberg, these men were justified in breaking the law in view of their postconventional moral stance (Kohlberg, 1971).

The attainment of postconventional moral thought appears to be a function of formal thinking. According to Kohlberg, formal thinking is necessary, but not sufficient, for advancement to Level III (Carpendale, 2000). About 60 percent of individuals above the age of 16 advance to the level of formal thought (Stage 5), but only about 10 percent of them show a principled level of moral reasoning (Stage 6). Table 14.2 summarizes Kohlberg's levels of moral development.

An Application of Kohlberg's View of Moral Development

Having discussed Kohlberg's moral reasoning, let's review how a child would respond at each of Kohlberg's three levels. Kohlberg was not so much concerned with whether the child thinks a particular form of behavior is moral or immoral, as he is with the reasoning behind the decision (Browne-Miller, 2009). Hence, children can come up with two opposite conclusions about a particular act and still be at the same moral level.

You might remember Heinz's dilemma mentioned in Chapter 11, and that Heinz stole the drug in an attempt to save his wife's life. Here are typical pro and con responses to Heinz's dilemma using Kohlberg's moral stages.

Level I: Preconventional Morality (Ages 4 to 10 years)

Pro-stealing: "If you let your wife die, you will get in trouble. You'll be blamed for not spending the money to save her and there will be an investigation of you and the druggist for your wife's death."

Anti-stealing: "You shouldn't steal the drug because you'll be caught and sent to jail if you do. If you do get away, your conscience would bother you, thinking how the police would catch up with you at any minute."

Note that at Level I, Sara makes moral decisions on the basis of self-interest, either to avoid punishment or to gain reward. The reasoning is hedonistic, self-centered, and lacking in empathy. Level I can often be seen in adults. Here is an example: "I was merely a little cog in the machinery that carried out the directives of the German Reich"— this statement was made by Adolph Eichmann, accused of assisting in the death of millions of Jews during World War II.

Level II: Conventional Morality (Ages 10 to 18 years)

Pro-stealing: "No one will think you're bad if you steal the drug, but your family will think you're an inhuman husband if you don't. If you let your wife die, you'll never be able to look anyone in the face again."

Anti-stealing: "It isn't just the druggist who will think you're a criminal, everyone else will too. After you steal it, you'll feel bad thinking how you've brought dishonor on your family and yourself; you won't be able to face anyone again."

At this level, Carlos continues to regard conformity as the basis for morality, and he strongly believes in supporting and preserving the laws and rules of the current social system. Whereas at the preconventional level Sara conforms to social norms and laws to avoid undesirable consequences of "improper" actions, at the conventional level she believes that active maintenance of the social order is important in its own right.

Level III: Postconventional Morality (Reached by about 60 percent of adults)

Pro-stealing: "If Heinz does not do everything to save his wife, then he is putting some value higher than the value of life. It doesn't make sense to put respect for property above respect for life itself. Men could live together without private property at all. Respect for human life and personality is absolute, and accordingly men have a mutual duty to save one another from dying" (Rest, 1979, p. 37).

Anti-stealing: "If you stole the drug, you wouldn't be blamed by other people, but you'd condemn yourself because you haven't lived up to your own conscience and standards of honesty."

At Kohlberg's Level III, people define their values in terms of principles, whether philosophical, religious, or personal. A postconventional adolescent is no longer tied to the rules of authority or to society but responds to a particular situation by concerns which transcend the maintenance of social order. When faced with a conflict between the law and the right thing to do, the postconventional individual follows his conscience, often at great personal risk. Mahatma Ghandi, the Indian leader who protested British rule, exemplified Level III, Stage 6, postconventional morality, when he addressed the court before being sentenced: "I… submit to the highest penalty… for what in law is a deliberate crime… appears to me to be the highest duty of a citizen." Kohlberg also says that his levels and stages are hierarchical, so that a person moves through them one by one and that no level or stage can be skipped, although the majority of research has been inconclusive on this point (Rest, 1983).

Table 14.2

Kohlberg's Stages of Moral Development

Level and Stage	Content of Stage		
	What is Right	Reasons for Doing Right	Social Perspective of Stage
LEVEL I—PRECONVENTIONAL. Stage 1—Heteronomous Morality	To avoid breaking rules backed by punishment, obedience for its own sake, and avoiding physical damage to persons and property.	Avoidance of punishment, and the superior power of authorities.	*Egocentric point of view.* Doesn't consider the interests of others or recognize that they differ from the actor's; doesn't relate two points of view. Actions are considered physical rather than in terms of psychological interests of others. Confusion of authority's perspective with one's own.
Stage 2—Individualism, Instrumental Purpose, and Exchange	Following rules only when it is in someone's immediate interest; acting to meet one's own interests and needs and letting others do the same. Right is also what's fair, what's an equal exchange, a deal, an agreement.	To serve one's own needs or interests in a world where you have to recognize that other people have their interests too.	*Concrete individualistic perspective.* Aware that everybody has his own interest to pursue and these conflict so that right is relative in the concrete individualistic sense.
LEVEL II—CONVENTIONAL. Stage 3—Mutual Interpersonal Expectations, Relationships, and Interpersonal Conformity	Living up to what is expected by people close to you or what people generally expect of people in your role as son, brother, friend, etc. "Being good" is important and means having good motives, showing concern about others. It also means keeping mutual relationships, such as trust, loyalty, respect, and gratitude.	The need to be a good person in your own eyes and those of others. Belief in the Golden Rule. Desire to maintain rules and authority which support stereotypical good behavior.	*Perspective of the individual in relationships with other individuals.* Aware of shared feelings, agreements, and expectations which take primacy over individual interests. Relates points of view through the concrete Golden Rule, putting yourself in the other guy's shoes. Does not yet consider generalized system perspective.
Stage 4—Social System and Conscience	Fulfilling the actual duties to which you have agreed. Laws are to be upheld except in extreme cases where they conflict with other fixed social duties. Right is also contributing to society, the group, or institution.	To keep the institution going as a whole, to avoid the breakdown in the system "if everyone did it," or the imperative of conscience to meet one's defined obligations (easily confused with Stage 3 belief in rules and authority).	*Differentiates societal point of view from interpersonal agreement or motives.* Takes the point of view of the system that defines roles and rules. Considers individual relations in terms of place in the system.
LEVEL III—POSTCONVENTIONAL or PRINCIPLED. Stage 5—Social Contract or Utility and Individual Rights	Being aware that people hold a variety of values and opinions, that most values and rules are relative to your group. These relative rules should usually be upheld, however, in the interest of impartiality and because they are the social contract. Some nonrelative values and rights like *life* and *liberty*, however, must be upheld in any society and regardless of majority opinion.	A sense of obligation to law because of one's social contract to make and abide by laws for the welfare of all and for the protection of all people's rights. A feeling of contractual commitment, freely entered upon, to family, friendship, trust, and work obligations. Concern that laws and duties be based on rational calculation of overall utility, "the greatest good for the greatest number."	*Prior-to-society perspective.* Perspective of a rational individual aware of values and rights prior to social attachments and contracts. Integrates perspectives by formal mechanisms of agreement, contract, objective impartiality, and due process. Considers moral and legal points of view; recognizes that they sometimes conflict and finds it difficult to integrate them.
Stage 6—Universal Ethical Principles	Following self-chosen ethical principles. Particular laws or social agreements are usually valid because they rest on such principles. When laws violate these principles, one acts in accordance with the principle. Principles are universal principles of justice: the equality of human rights and respect for the dignity of human beings as individuals.	The belief as a rational person in the validity of universal moral principles and a sense of personal commitment to them.	*Perspective of a moral point of view from which social arrangements derive.* Perspective is that of any rational individual recognizing the nature of morality or the fact that persons are ends in themselves and must be treated as such.

Source: Kohlberg, 1976, pp. 34 and 35.

What Causes Adolescents to be Moral?

As children get older, they spend an increasing amount of time away from home, and they have more opportunities to break rules. Many children, however, voluntarily follow their parents' teachings and obey the laws even when the parents are not present. Why do they? Martin Hoffman, (1979) provides us with some insights.

Hoffman says that effective types of parental socialization are those associated with children who voluntarily follow rules even when no one is watching. Among the desirable parental behaviors that promote moral behavior in children are:

• **The parents reason with their children, pointing out the consequences of misbehavior on others, particularly on other children.**

• **The parents appeal to a child's pride and desire to be thought of as "grown up."**

• **The parents' reasoning with their child is accompanied by affection. This enables the child to free himself or herself from fear of being punished and to concentrate on the needs and feelings of others.**

Cultural Differences in Moral Development

Numerous studies indicate that moral development varies from one society to the next. Studies also indicate that individuals in technologically advanced societies move through Kohlberg's moral stages more rapidly and to higher levels than individuals from more primitive societies. Individuals from primitive cultures usually do not reach Stage 4, a level attained by most high school adolescents in Western cultures (Edwards, 1981). Why do these differences exist?

One possibility is that Kohlberg's dilemmas of moral reasoning are more applicable to some cultures than to others. Another related argument is that moral development is related to the complexity of society (the simpler the governmental, educational, and legal institutions, the lower the morality of its members). There is yet another, perhaps more plausible explanation. That is, that moral development depends on the types of values and skills emphasized in a particular society. In traditional peasant and tribal communities, where the primary emphasis is on cooperation with one another, individuals usually do not progress beyond Kohlberg's Stage 3. In societies such as the Israeli *kibbutzim* where children are raised communally from an early age, a greater proportion of them reach Stage 5 than American children (Kohlberg, 1985).

Kibbutzim: Collective farms in Israel where children are raised communally.

It seems that the higher levels of Kohlberg's moral stages cannot be reached unless certain moral environmental antecedents are present. These include the family, peers, schools, and institutions which reflect the type of culture found in Western industrialized nations. If such is the case, then there is doubt about one of Kohlberg's major claims; that his model of moral development applies equally to all children everywhere.

Evaluation of Kohlberg's Postconventional Level of Morality

There is wide support for Lawrence Kohlberg's general sequence of moral development. In over 1,000 studies around the world (Taiwan, Turkey, Mexico, Kenya, India, the Bahamas, Israel, and the United States), older children have consistently shown higher levels of moral judgment than younger ones (Rest, 1983). One confusing aspect continues to be different end points for children from various cultures. Studies suggest that no adults reach Stage 6 in more primitive societies. Kohlberg's model of morality is also at variance with feminist thinkers who believe that morals are different for men than for women.

Feminist thinkers such as Carol Gilligan argue that Kohlberg ignores the social context of moral behavior. According to Gilligan, women typically approach moral conflict differently than men. She says that women tend not to base decisions on personal, self-chosen principles as men do, but to consider the consequences of their moral decisions for others (Gilligan, 1977; 1982). According to Gilligan, women's primary ethic is *care* and *responsibility*, for men it is *individual rights* and *justice*.

According to Gilligan, women tend to define themselves through their *relationships with others*, thus intimacy is a primary issue. Males tend to define themselves according to their *occupations*. This difference is due to men's and women's early experiences. Gilligan makes her point by comparing the answers by 11-year-old Jake and his agemate Amy to Heinz's dilemma: What should Heinz do about getting a drug for his ailing wife? Using a mathematical approach, which shows that life has greater value than property, Jake believes that Heinz is obligated to steal the drug. Amy is a little more uncertain. She knows that stealing the drug or letting Heinz's wife die would both be wrong. She searches for alternatives, such as getting a loan, stating that it would profit Heinz little if he stole the drug and was sent to jail, leaving his wife by herself.

Although Amy would likely be judged lower on Kohlberg's scale than Jake, her reaction is one that has traditionally defined the "goodness" of women. Hence, the very traits that have marked women as moral (caring, the avoidance of pain, and empathic) are classified as deficient on Kohlberg's scale. Consequently, women typically score lower than men, who are usually found at Kohlberg's Stage 4, women at Stage 3.

A major criticism of Kohlberg's theory of moral development is the overwhelming emphasis on moral thought and not enough emphasis on moral behavior. Moral reasons have sometimes been used to justify immoral or criminal behavior. Robin Hood, the legendary English outlaw of the 12th century, justified robbing the rich because the money was given to the poor.

Kohlberg also argued that parents play a relatively minor role in their child's moral development because parent-child relationships are usually power-oriented which provide children with little opportunity for mutual give and take or moral development are more likely to be provided by children's peer relations (Brabec, 2000). Ample studies indicate that parents do influence children's developing moral thought (Gibbs, 2003).

AMERICAN EDUCATION

Although America has an education system that is maintained by the community and is available to all children at virtually no cost, public education in this country is a relatively new phenomenon. For instance, it was not until 1875 that the State Supreme Court of Michigan set a national precedent when it ordered the city of Kalamazoo to collect funds for a village high school so that every child could attend free of charge.

A major reason for the Kalamazoo ruling was the realization that every child must have access to an education regardless of the family's financial condition. Another reason was the realization that children get smarter when they attend school. Since, the Kalamazoo case, scientific studies have indicated that the longer a person goes to school, the more intelligent he or she becomes as measured by IQ tests., This shows the importance of access to high schools and colleges in addition to elementary schools.

High school is a three- or four-year institution. It has its origins in both the Latin grammar school and in the Academy, which fostered the learning of useful knowledge, rather than subjects that were simply ornamental. In 2005, approximately 14 million students attended public and private high schools in the United States. This number represents approximately 96 percent of teenagers 14 to 17 years old, compared with 11 percent in 1900. In 1995 over 80 percent of Americans, 25 years old and older had earned their high school diplomas (U.S. Bureau of the Census, 1997); in 1900, the figure was about 2 percent.

Traditionally, high schools have fostered two types of development: academic and nonacademic. The cognitive or academic skills emphasize mathematics, writing, biology, and chemistry, which have been the traditional responsibility of the school. The nonacademic skills have been primarily designed to prepare children with the types of abilities they will need in adulthood such as driving a car, getting along with others, and being an effective homemaker. Since the late 1960s, serious questions have been raised about the effectiveness of American public education, including the high school.

Dissatisfaction with American Education

There is widespread agreement that America's children are not receiving an adequate education (Milner, 2010; Eccles, 2004; Hemmings, 2004). Those concerned about American public education have indicated that it has been losing credibility, prestige, and public confidence. The weakness of American public education was highlighted in the 1980s following the publication of *A Nation At Risk: The Imperative for Educational Reform* (National Commission on Excellence in Education, 1983). This publication warned that "the educational foundations of our society are presently being eroded by a rising tide of mediocrity that threatens our very future as a nation and a people."

One study (Applebee *et al.*, 1994) of 30,000 fourth, eighth, and twelfth graders across the country found that their writing skills were "mediocre" and that quality was the "exception."[1] The raw data most damaging to American public education are scores on the SAT which have declined nearly every year since 1963 in both the verbal and in the mathematics portions of the test. The mean mathematics score declined from 502 in 1963 to 466 in 1981; the verbal scores showed a greater decline (Oldenquist, 1983). One ray of hope is that the combined verbal and math score on the SAT increased slightly (17 points) from 1982 to 1995 (Tirozzi & Uro, 1997).

The low academic performance of American students was highlighted in an international comparison involving eighth graders in 45 countries. The study found that America's best math students were in the middle of the pack

---

1. This decline is not peculiar to the United States. In a recent study of British 17-year-olds, fewer than half knew when World War II ended, more than 1 in 4 could not divide 65 by 5. However, almost all knew that 18 was the minimum age when people could buy alcohol legally.

compared with students in Singapore, and not even in the top quarter of Japanese students. In a recent study of general knowledge of science and mathematics by U.S. 12th graders, they were among the lowest scoring students from 41 nations participating in the study (Schmidt, McKnight, & Raizen, 1997). There are also indications that the decline in vocabulary and reading by American students is as dramatic as that in science and mathematics. This decline is reflected in SAT scores.

Causes of Dissatisfaction with American Education

One explanation for the decline in American education is a decreased academic emphasis. Only one-third of the high schools in the nation offer more than one year of mathematics and science instruction. In 1990, slightly more than one-half of the high school graduates in the United States had taken more than two science courses and only one year of algebra. Recent studies also indicate that 20 percent of those who graduate from high school are illiterate and are unable to function effectively in society.

Nelson's work (2000), which addresses the weaknesses of American education, levels its harshest criticism at textbooks. In particular, the study gave an unsatisfactory rating to science, mathematics, and technology textbooks. The study found that the books do not flesh out the four basic ideas driving today's research in the science, mathematics, and technology research: how cells work, how matter and energy flow from one source to another, how plants and animals evolve, and the molecular basis of heredity. The researchers state that much of the typical curriculum today is obsolete, that there is no coherence across grade levels or subject matter, and that too many topics are covered to be taught effectively during an average school year.

Mass education: Universal schooling of all children with public support.

Another reason that is often advanced for the academic decline in American public schools is the broader base of students. For example, the nation's student population is much more diverse than it was 30 years ago (Milner, 2010). This trend toward *mass education*, universal schooling of all children with public support, began over 200 years ago. Mass education was pioneered by Andrew Jackson (1767-1845) who was elected president of the United States in 1828. Jackson and others, such as Horace Mann, chief administrative officer of the Massachusetts public schools, could see the need for education that combined practical needs with utopian goals for all children.

How Can American Education be Saved?

To be competent adults in today's society, adolescents must have the ability to read at relatively high levels, use personal computers for tasks such as word processing, communicate effectively both orally and in writing, and work effectively in groups with persons of various backgrounds (Milner, 2010; Hemmings, 2004). A variety of suggestions have been made to enhance the image and effectiveness of schools in America. One of these is greater emphasis on academic subjects. Others feel that the problem of poor quality American education lies with incompetent teachers (Dilworth, 1992). These critics suggest raising the level of professionalism in teaching by adding certification of special teaching ability. This would be equivalent to what doctors go through when they become specialists. Some critics, such as James D. Koerner (1963), advocate luring talented people into the teaching profession who lack only the teaching credential that is obtained by completing specialized education courses and doing practice teaching. Another suggestion is instituting competency tests for all students and teachers.

According to Jean Piaget, education should have two major goals: (1) Produce individuals who are capable of doing new things by being creative and inventive, and (2) Provide opportunities for students to observe, analyze possibilities, and draw inferences about perceived relationships. Using these parameters, students can develop formal and abstract thinking through discussion groups, debates, and problem-solving sessions.

Many studies have found that the most needed change in high school is in the atmosphere of the learning environment. Many schools are filled with tension and anger. Students express their unhappiness through defiance of authority, vandalism, absence, and school shootings. Teachers get back by using repressive disciplinary measures and expelling students for minor violations, while school administrators blame both the teachers and the students for the problems. Little is being done to alleviate the problems aside from putting more police on campus. Rather than relying on disciplinary measures, the teachers should encourage the students to develop a favorable self-image (Carlson, Uppal, & Prosser, 2000).

One way to create a more positive atmosphere might be to give students more autonomy rather than relying on authority. The road to adulthood is a gradual one, beginning with the child's total dependence on his or her caregivers, to finally being governed by oneself, a concept known as autonomy (Rodgers, 1998). In an autonomy-supported classroom, children govern themselves, their actions are freely chosen, and they take full responsibility for their behavior. Rather than being taught facts and skills as in the traditional classroom, in the autonomy-supported classroom, there is a cooperative exchange of viewpoints between peers and a search for answers that make sense. Instead of deferring to an authority figure, the students become active researchers who collect evidence and analyze each other's reasoning critically in search of the truth. In an autonomy-supported classroom, the children become well-adjusted adults who function effectively in society.

Participatory education: A program in which students participate in the real world in activities such as career education, arts and crafts, and government.

GOALS 2000: An act designed to set voluntary standards for core subjects such as history and mathematics.

Some say that there should be a division between cognitive and *participatory education*. According to this view, cognitive or intellectual goals should be the primary function of high schools and programs outside the school could concentrate on participatory education. Participatory education includes experience in the real world in activities such as arts and crafts and government. Toward this end, *GOALS 2000: Educate America Act* was passed in 1994 (Short & Talley, 1997). This act was designed to set voluntary national standards so that everyone is aware of what a child should know in core subjects such as history and mathematics. Another objective of GOALS 2000 is that "... every school in the United States will be free of drugs, violence, the unauthorized presence of firearms, and alcohol." The act created a hands-on role for the federal government in schools across the country to achieve goals such as teacher training and parental participation in the education program. A major objective is to have all children in America be ready to learn when they start school.

Many critics believe that schools should teach children to be creative, the ability to think in novel and unusual ways, and to come up with unique solutions to problems (Kaufman & Baer, 2004). One way is to provide children with opportunities to brainstorm in which they play off each others' ideas and say whatever comes to mind. Another way to teach creativity in the classroom is to invite speakers who are creative such as writers, poets, and scientists.

Harold Stevenson and Shin-ying Lee (1990), who have compared U.S. students with their peers in other countries, make the following suggestions for improving American education:

1. Give teachers more time to prepare lessons and to correct students' work.

2. Improve teacher training by having prospective teachers work with, more experienced, capable teachers.

3. Set higher standards for students.

Many theorists have suggested that one way to improve American education is to create new teaching-learning models. Vygotsky has proposed a number of designs including the reciprocal teaching model where a teacher and two to four pupils form a collaborative learning group. Group members take turns leading dialogues on the content of a text passage and flexibly apply four cognitive strategies. These strategies include: (1) questions about the content of a passage and rereading the original text if there is disagreement, (2) summarizing the passage, (3) clarifying ideas, and (4) predicting upcoming content based on the passage.

Studies show that elementary and junior high school students have made impressive gains in reading comprehension when exposed to reciprocal teaching. Equally impressive, reciprocal teaching has enabled children to learn practical skills that they would not have been able to perform on their own by being provided with a more skilled partner, a concept Vygotsky calls the zone of proximal development.

The debate between the traditionalists and the reformers is central to the question of how best to improve public education. *Traditionalists* claim that schools should return to the "basics," in which a key feature is rote memory, that is, learning something in a mechanical way without thought of the meaning. For instance, traditionalists insist that every child needs to learn the multiplication table. Traditionalists also insist that every child needs to learn certain mathematical concepts such as "pi," which is the key to calculating the circumference of a circle.

Reformers argue that math can be learned in ways other than rote memory. For instance, 12 plus 12 can be learned by the child visualizing two rows of 12 crates each. Reformers claim that insisting that the child learn the basics of math by rote memory may prevent the child from acquiring more sophisticated concepts of geometry. Then, there is the calculator that the child can use.

The most heated debate between the traditionalists and the reformers centers around the best way to teach reading and spelling. Traditionalists advocate the *code-based approach to reading* which emphasizes the components of reading such as the sounds of letters and their combinations. This view states that the individual components of words should be processed first, then combined into words, and then the words should be used to derive the meaning of written sentences and passages (Treiman *et al.*, 1998). This method of teaching reading where the child must first master the phonetic code that matches the printed alphabet to spoken sounds is probably the way your

Traditionalists: Individuals who espouse the belief that schools should return to the "basics," such as rote memory.

Reformers: Individuals who believe that schools should change to become more effective, such as de-emphasizing rote memory and other forms of traditional basic learning and concentrate on more imaginative forms of learning such as teaching spelling through creative writing.

Code-based approach to reading: Teaching reading by presenting the basic skills that underlie reading such as the sounds of the letters and how the letters and sounds are combined to make words.

grandmother learned to read. Now there is a new method called the whole-language approach to reading.

Whole-language approach to reading: Teaching reading by exposing children to complete writing of sentences, stories, poems, charts, and lists. Instead of being taught how to sound words out, the children learn whole words and phrases at a time, gradually becoming proficient readers.

In the *whole-language approach to reading* that is advocated by reformers, the children are exposed to complete writing of sentences, stories, poems, charts, and lists. Instead of being taught how to sound out words, children are encouraged to make guesses about the meaning of words based on the context in which they appear. Through such a trial-and-error approach, children learn whole words at a time, gradually becoming proficient readers according to its proponents (Graham & Harris, 1997).

Reformers claim that spelling programs should consist of frequent writing, with the children correcting any misspelled words in their final drafts. Reformers insist that there is no need to practice lists of spelling words since spelling is learned naturally, just like a language, while the children write for real purpose (Graham, 2000). This method is called the *whole-language approach to reading*, which appears to benefit kindergartners who are just starting to read, with gradual introduction of phonics as their reading skills improve.

Another controversy over ways to improve education is the extent to which education should be "techno-sized," particularly the extent to which children should be computer-dependent and be "on-line." Almost all American public schools have computers as part of their instructional programs, and 95 percent can access the Internet (U.S. Bureau of the Census 2000). Computer-assisted instruction has proved useful in teaching academic skills as early as preschool (Hitchcock & Noonan, 2000). Many educators and developmental psychologists agree that classroom computerization can benefit students and provide a superior educational environment. However, they see many drawbacks.

Critics claim that chat rooms, games, and Internet advertisements which dominate the ways in which children are interacting with computers today do not teach children how to think logically or rationally. Nor does the structure of the web teach children moral and ethical thought, which is grounded in logic (Nelson, 2000a). The web may hinder the development of moral thinking. For example, the structure of a chat room, which makes it possible to talk (type) "over" anyone at any time, is antithetical to polite conversation or to proper morals. Computers seem to be designed more for entertainment and information-gathering, not to promote thinking.

Influences on Achievement in School

Why do some students do better in school than others? Is it the size of the school? The quality of the teachers? Availability of teaching aids? Undoubtedly, these factors contribute toward higher student achievement, but they are not key factors. A study from the 1960s suggests that student characteristics are more significant than school factors in predicting academic success. *Equality of Educational Opportunity* (better known as "*The Coleman Report*") by a leading sociologist, James Coleman and his colleagues (1966) looked at third-, sixth-, ninth-, and twelfth-grade students in 4,000 schools throughout the country. Using some 45 measures, these investigators found very little difference between schools in the amount of student achievement. There was much more difference within the best and worst schools than between schools. In any given school, we usually find a few students with a 4.00 grade-point average, and a few students who fail almost every class they take.

One critical factor in school achievement is student characteristics such as intelligence and gender. Other factors are socioeconomic status, family structure, and influence of parents.

Student characteristics. Investigators have noted that children's cognitive development is a major determinant of their success in school. Researchers, such as Arthur Jensen (1980), believe that intelligence accounts for about one-third of the total variance in academic achievement. Intelligent students (those who score high on intelligence tests) have a greater understanding of abstract concepts and, accordingly, need less time to learn material. Intelligent students are able to retain the material they learn; they also possess a larger vocabulary, and read with more comprehension.

The child's personal adjustment also affects his or her performance in school. Children who have good images of themselves tend to do better than those who think of themselves as dumb. When children's self-concepts are high, they have confidence in their own ability and try harder. Children with negative self-concepts often shun tasks or goals that are well within their capabilities. One way of helping these children is to retrain them so that they attribute their failures to a lack of effort rather than to a lack of ability (Dweck, 1999). Children may also minimize academic performance because they want to use their ethnicity as a basis for friendship. This appears to be particularly true of many African-American adolescents (Hamm, 2000).

Much research indicates that children's affective (mood) states, particularly depression, are related to academic achievement. Depression may affect academic performance because of the distractibility that accompanies it. The depressed person is not able to persist at a learning task, he or she has a lower expectation of success, and has a poor memory.

Gender. A clear gender difference has been noted in student performance in mathematics and science. Girls outperform boys in every type of math ability until about the sixth grade when boys begin to outperform girls. The gender difference favoring adolescent boys is particularly pronounced among superior students. For example, boys outnumber girls 2 to 1 among students who score over 500 on the new SAT and 5 to 1 among those who score over 600. One interesting finding is that the gender difference in math, which has traditionally favored adolescent boys, is decreasing, particularly where formal-operational thinking is involved.

Gender differences in science follow a similar path to that of math. Girls outperform boys in science until about age 9, but boys outperform girls through adolescence.

A number of researchers have noted that beginning in middle childhood, females appear to have difficulties with competitive achievement, particularly when they are in rivalry with males. For instance, Matina Horner states:

"When success is likely or possible, threatened by the negative consequences they expect to follow success, young women become anxious and their positive achievement strivings become thwarted."

(Horner, 1972, p. 171)

Fear of success: Matina Horner's term for the concern of some young women that academic, business, or professional success, might lead to undesirable consequences such as rejection.

Horner says that this fear exists because, for many women, the anticipation in a competitive situation produces conflicts, threats of social rejection, and loss of femininity. In other words, there is a belief that the girl who gets a better grade in math than her boyfriend may be thought of as too aggressive, and be rejected by the boyfriend. Note that *fear of success* is not the same as fear of failure. Persons fearing failure do not try because of anticipated loss of face; when success is feared, little effort is put forth because achievement may result in adverse consequences.

Socioeconomic status. Most people believe that socioeconomic status (income, education, and occupation of parents) is among the most important factors in a student's achievement in school. The Coleman report concluded that socioeconomic status is a significant variable associated with student achievement. However, many other studies show that socioeconomic status is only weakly correlated with school performance.

Family structure. Conventional wisdom suggests that in addition to the family's socioeconomic status, family structure (one-parent, two-parents, or stepparent) also affects the child's school performance. Studies generally do not support such a belief. In a study of a large national representative sample of high school students, Herbert Marsh (1990) concluded that family configuration has remarkably little effect on student performance during the last two years of high school. A similar conclusion was reached by Lansford *et al.* (2001) in their study of children's family structure, including adoptive, two-parent biological, single-mother, stepfather, and stepmother households. The investigators concluded that a child's performance in school depends largely on family processes such as the amount of time the parents spend with the children, whether the family has fun together, and whether family members show concern for one another.

Influence of parents. The major influence on school achievement is the atmosphere in the home, which is usually set by the parents. In one study (Simpson, 1962) of 743 high school boys, working-class boys with ambitious educational aspirations were most likely to have parents with high career standards who encouraged their sons to enter a profession. Other studies show that the mother's educational aspirations for her teenager are more influential than a peer's, even when the peer is a best friend.

Self-efficacy: The belief that the student can succeed because of his or her ability.

Self-efficacy. Children who do well in school, usually have a high degree of *self-efficacy*, the belief that they can *succeed* because of *their own ability*. Students who are high in self-efficacy, have a high degree of self-understanding, self-confidence, and social reflection. They set challenging goals and use appropriate strategies to achieve these goals. These students persist despite difficulties, and when their goal seems unattainable, they seek help from others. The parents of successful students are also high in self-efficacy, that is, they are high in their belief that they have the ability to motivate their children to succeed in school. Finally, we should not forget the importance of efficacious schools where teachers regard their students as capable of high academic achievement and set challenging academic standards for them.

Many educators and psychologists believe that students show more interest in their schoolwork and learn best if they are given individual attention by their teachers.

Influence of parenting style. Many studies indicate that parenting methods play an important role in the child's achievement in school. The model which appears to be most productive is Diana Baumrind's *a*uthoritative style. One study (Dornbusch *et al.*, 1985) of more than 8,000 high school students in the San Francisco Bay area found that authoritative parenting helps children in a variety of ways:

- **The parents respect knowledge, and they encourage their children's intellectual curiosity.**

- **Children are taught to look at both sides of an issue.**

- **Parents admit that sometimes their children know more than they do.**

- **Children are made to feel free to participate in family discussions, including politics.**

- **Parents praise children for getting good grades, and encourage them to try harder and offer help when needed.**

School disconnectedness. During the past couple of decades there has been a growing realization that one reason why many children, particularly those from urban minority backgrounds, do not do well in school is due to their feeling of alienation. As a result of this absence of school connectedness, the children become more involved in risk-taking behavior, they perform poorly in their school work, and their health declines. Children are likely to feel more connected (attached) to their school by meeting many of their social, emotional, and health needs through the school (Mansour *et al.*, 2003). Also, school connectedness is enhanced if school personnel display more interest in the children, a technique which is particularly effective with children from low socioeconomic backgrounds.

School Dropouts

Although there has been a reduction in dropout rates in the nation's schools, high school dropout remains an immense problem. Overall, in 2005, approximately 11 percent of people 16 to 24 years old dropped out of high school. The figure is quite distorted when we consider the dropout rate of minorities separately (NCES, 2003). Whereas 7.3 percent of Caucasians dropped out of high school in the United States in the 1990s, the figure was 13 percent for African Americans, and almost 30 percent for Latinos (U.S. Bureau of the Census, 1997).

Why Do Students Drop Out of School?

Although we normally think that students drop out of school for obvious reasons such as illness, failing in school, death in the family, or fear of violence at school, often, the reason is the culmination of a long-term process. Many children at risk of dropping out of school were identified in the first grade. For example, a child is more likely to drop out of school if he or she is placed in a lower academic track when he or she is in elementary school. A child is also more likely to drop out of school if his or her parents have shown no interest in the child's performance in school. Furthermore, if the parents get divorced when the child is young, he or she is more likely to drop out of school (Alexander, Entwisle, & Horsey, 1997). Students also drop out of school if the teachers focus more on discipline than on learning and if there is little opportunity for student participation (Rumberger & Thomas, 2000). Many of the risk factors for dropping out of school are also risk factors for violence (Hunt *et al.*, 2002).

Title IX: A federal law which prohibits public schools from forcing pregnant and parenting female students to drop out of public school.

Prior to the 1970s, the pregnant student was less likely to complete high school than her nonpregnant colleague. About the only option pregnant girls had to complete their education was to study at home since they were barred from attending public school. With the passage of the 1972 *Title IX* of the Education Amendments Act (Section 106.40), pregnant and parenting girls are no longer prohibited from attending public school. The law also requires public schools to treat childbirth in the same way that they treat absences due to other temporary disabilities[2]. As a result of this legislation, many pregnant girls are just as likely to graduate from high school as their nonpregnant peers (Leadbeater, & Way, 2001).

Later Careers of School Dropouts

What happens to children after they drop out of school? Longitudinal studies indicate that the effect is not the same for boys as it is for girls. Boys who drop out of school are likely to move "downward"—that is, they usually end up in occupations that are lower paying and lower in status than their fathers' occupational positions. For example, those from white-collar backgrounds (their fathers hold professional or skilled jobs) are likely to be employed in blue-collar (semi-skilled) positions (factory work, waiting on tables, or clerking in a store). They also have more difficulty finding a job. In 2005, 1 in 4 high school male dropouts was looking for work, compared with 1 in 20 who graduated from high

---

2. This landmark gender equity legislation bars gender bias in athletics and other educational programs and states: "No person in the United States shall, on the basis of sex, be excluded from participation in, be denied the benefits of, or be subjected to discrimination under any educational program or activity receiving Federal financial assistance."

school. More than one-fifth of recent male high school graduates who did not continue their education are unemployed (U.S. Department of Education, 2000).

This young couple is enjoying their graduation ceremony. They also have many pleasant memories of the friends they made in high school. At the same time, they are, no doubt, thinking about their futures: Should they continue with their education in college,? Should they skip college and go into the work force immediately,? and What about marriage?

Girls who drop out of school tend to marry at a younger age than those who graduate. They also tend to have a higher divorce rate. Oddly enough, the girl's dropout is not an important factor in social mobility. Girls from white-collar backgrounds who drop out of school are just as likely to marry someone from the same family background as their peers' who completed high school.

THE PURSUIT OF A VOCATION

Most parents encourage their children to decide on a vocation while they are still in high school. Usually, teenagers have thought about a vocation by the time they are in grade nine or ten, but they are often uncertain about their career choice. Often, they make a choice only to change their minds shortly after. This vacillation indicates that choosing a vocation is not simple. Many factors are involved. In this section we will discuss two of these: Parental influence and gender. We will also look at a few "tests" that are used to help children make the right vocational choice.

Parental Influences

Historically, it has been thought that the school and individual factors such as vocational attendance, IQ, self-esteem, and motivation, play a major role in a child's occupational choice. Recent research indicates that the major role may be played by the family (Glasgow et al., 1997).

A significant family factor in the girl's choice of vocation is the mother's employment outside the home. Daughters of mothers who work outside the home are less likely to see certain occupations as exclusively masculine or feminine than daughters of nonemployed mothers. Moreover, if a mother provides a dual-role (housewife and employed), the daughter is more likely to aspire to a definite career, regardless of her plans to marry and to have a family.

Parental encouragement appears to have a major influence on children's aspirations and achievements. Parental encouragement plays a larger role in their sons' choice of a vocation than socioeconomic status. Parental confidence-building messages and career guidance can also help girls to set career goals that match their abilities. So can models of accomplished women. Although many fathers of teenagers support their children, the effect of father involvement is still unclear.

Gender Differences in Choice of a Vocation

Gender differences are consistently found in the vocational plans of male and female adolescents. Vocational plans of adolescent boys are considerably more realistic, more ambitious, more achievement-oriented, and better differentiated than those of females. Furthermore, adolescent females tend to choose vocations which are predominantly nurturing such as teaching, nursing, social work, library work. Males tend to choose more high-status professions—business, law practice, and medicine. Also, although females use computers for surfing the Internet and e-mail, they are far less likely to enter careers in technology and science than males.

As we have already noted, one reason for gender differences in the choice of a vocation is fear of success among women. Matina Horner (1972) suggests that women do not aspire to high status careers because of the negative image and consequences that might result. Perhaps an equally important reason for gender differences in occupational choice is society's expectations; boys are expected to follow one line of endeavor and girls another. Much of this thinking is changing. The occupational choices are becoming less linked to traditional gender-role stereotypes (Wulf & Steitz, 1997). For example, whereas three decades ago about 1 out of every 7 medical doctors was a woman, at the turn of the 21st century the figure had almost doubled to 1 female doctor for every 4 male doctors (U.S. Bureau of the Census, 2002).

Although women have more flexibility in their vocational choices, there are still many obstacles (Eccles, Wingfield, & Byrnes, 2003). Schools often shortchange girls by steering them away from science and math into female gender-typed pursuits such as nursing and library science. Some young women do not enter male stereotyped vocations such as engineering and medicine because they lack confidence in these areas.

Interest and Aptitude Tests

At one time, it was felt that a person could enter any vocation and be successful as long as he or she was smart enough and worked hard. We now realize that this is not necessarily the case. An individual who is not interested in a particular line of endeavor is seldom successful. Also, children may not be successful even if they are interested in a particular vocation because they do not have the aptitude. Aptitude means an individual's *potential* for acquiring certain skills.

Interest tests. One of the better-known tests to measure one's interest in a given area is the *Kuder General Interest Survey, Form E* (Kuder, 1975). The Kuder measures interest in 10 areas; outdoor, mechanical, computational, scientific, persuasive, artistic, literary, musical, social service, and clerical.

Another well-known interest test is the *Strong-Campbell Inventory.* This test asks subjects questions such as: How they would feel about participating in various occupations, how well they like certain subjects in school, and what they like to do for recreation.

There are no right or wrong answers on interest tests. Hence, they are not tests in the true sense.

Aptitude test: A "test" of a person's ability to learn a new skill.

Aptitude tests. *Aptitude tests* are a relatively recent phenomenon in American education. Aptitude measures ability or tries to estimate future performance in various types of behavior such as the child's potential for success in school. The most common use of aptitude tests is admission to a college or university. Also, college graduates are sometimes chosen for well-paying jobs based upon their scores on aptitude tests. Until 1994, one of the more widely used aptitude tests was the *Scholastic Aptitude Test* (SAT), which made its debut in 1926. Each year, about 2 million candidates took the SAT.

Scholastic Aptitude Test: An aptitude test often used, prior to 1994, to determine one's acceptability to college.

New SAT: A revision of the SAT with greater emphasis on writing and math.

In 2005, there was an exhaustive revision of the SAT. A major purpose of this new version of the SAT, called the *New SAT,* requires an essay in the hope of producing better writers. Grammar is emphasized so that students are asked to fix poorly used gerunds (e.g., nouns such as the verb "write" changed to the noun "writing") and the like. The New SAT goes beyond basic algebra and geometry for the first time to include Algebra II content. There are also some deletions from previous SAT tests such as analogies "somnolent is to wakeful" as "graceful is to _____.[3]" The New SAT could favor girls over boys, affect how English is taught in high school, make the SAT more subjective, and create an uproar among teachers and parents.

ACT Assessment Program: A college admissions test that includes a Student Profile Section, the ACT Interest Inventory, and high school grades.

The second most widely used college admissions test is the *ACT Assessment Program.* The *ACT* Assessment Program consists of a registration form that includes (1) the Student Profile Section consisting of a demographics inventory, high school activities and accomplishments, and academic and extracurricular plans for college, (2) the ACT Interest Inventory which is a survey of the student's vocational preference, and (3) the high school course grades in history, Math, English, Reading, and Science Reasoning. Both the SAT and the ACT are sometimes called "achievement" tests because they call for specific information that the student learned in school. Students' scores on both the SAT and the ACT are fairly reliable predictors of the grades high school students are likely to achieve in college.

Dynamic testing for aptitude. Traditionally, a child's potential for future learning (aptitude) has been measured by what a child has learned in the past. The assumption is that children who have learned more in the past will likely learn more in the future. Critics argue that a child's learning potential can be measured more accurately-- be more valid-- if the test assessed a child's potential for future learning directly. One suggestion is dynamic testing.

Dynamic testing: Intelligence testing in which a subject learns something in the presence of an examiner.

Dynamic testing is based on Vygotsky's zone of proximal development and scaffolding. The zone of proximal development is a "zone" that surrounds a learner that includes all the skills, knowledge, and concepts that the person is close to acquiring but cannot yet master without help. Scaffolding is the

---

3. clumsy."

temporary support that is provided to help a learner master the next task in a given learning process. In dynamic testing, learning potential can be estimated by the amount of material a child learns during interaction with an examiner and/or from the amount of help the child needs to learn new material (Grigorenko & Sternberg, 1998). To obtain a more comprehensive view of a child's potential, dynamic testing could be combined with a traditional intelligence test such as the WISC-IV which measures a child's knowledge and skills up to the time of testing.

SUMMARY

Only about two in five high school graduates reach Piaget's stage of formal operations. Key characteristics of this stage are the ability to think abstractly, to engage in hypothetico-deductive reasoning such as that used in solving the pendulum task, and thinking in terms of possibilities.

Adolescents in the stage of formal operations are egocentric. They are highly idealistic and self-conscious, being oversensitive and suspicious of others without legitimate cause.

Most adolescents are at Kohlberg's conventional level of morality. Some reach the postconventional stage, where morality relies on an internal control of conduct. Some adolescents are still at the preconventional level.

Cultural factors play a role in the development of morality, and moral judgment varies from culture to culture. There is some question as to whether Kohlberg's model of morality can be applied universally. More than one model of morality may be needed for measuring proper standards of moral thinking and moral actions.

High school plays an important role in the lives of most adolescents, and more than 80 percent of adults have graduated from high school. A major concern is the quality of education provided by our schools. Many suggestions have been made for improvement.

Among the factors that play a role in a child's achievement in school are student characteristics and socioeconomic status of the family. However, no single factor is as important as parental encouragement, especially from the mother.

A major concern in our schools is the high rate of dropouts. In some instances, this rate is two-thirds. Students drop out for a number of reasons, including poor academic performance and personal problems.

Many factors are involved in the choice of a vocation. Parental influence and gender play vital roles in the choice. Tests are often used to help the adolescent make the right vocational choice.

RELATED RESOURCES

Readings
Gilligan, C. (1982). *In a Different Voice: Psychological Theory and Women's Development.* Cambridge, Mass.: Harvard University Press.

IMPORTANT TERMS

Abstraction	Mass education
ACT Assessment Program	New SAT
Adolescent egocentrism	Participatory education
Adolescent idealism	Personal fable
Aptitude test	Preconventional morality
Authoritative parenting	Propositional thinking
Code-based approach to reading	Reformer
Dynamic testing	Scholastic Aptitude Test (SAT)
Fear of success	Scholastic Assessment Test (SAT)
Formal operation	Systematic reasoning
GOALS 2000: Educate America Act	Test anxiety
Hypothetico-deductive reasoning	Title IX
Imaginary audience	Traditionalist
Kibbutzim (Plural of kibbutz)	Whole-language approach to reading

Gilligan stresses that there are gender differences in psychological development. Women have a different orientation to the social world as well as toward themselves than men. This difference, according to Gilligan, leads to a different basis for the development of moral reasoning in women than in men.

Senge, P. *et al.*, (2000). *Schools that Learn.* Westminster, MD: Doubleday.
Written by bestselling author Professor Peter Senge, this book offers practical advice for educators, administrators, and parents on how to apply learning organization principles to help strengthen and rebuild our schools. The book brings together practices that are being tried across the country in both affluent and depressed areas and offers a wealth of practical tools, anecdotes, and advice that educators and teachers can use.

Chapter 15

Social Emotional Development in Adolescence (12 to 18 years)

Chapter Topics		Learning Objectives
What theoretical perspectives exist on the topic of adolescent personality?		Understand theoretical perspectives of adolescent personality: G. Stanley Hall, Margaret Mead, Sigmund Freud, Anna Freud, Erik Erikson, and James Marcia.
What are the differences between peer and parent relationships in adolescence?		Recognize Sara the differences in personal relationships with peer and with parents during adolescence.
What are the issues related to adolescent sexuality?		Understand the variety of issues related to adolescent sexuality: sexual behaviors, trends in sexual behaviors, teenage pregnancy, and parental dialogue with adolescents about sexuality.
What is juvenile delinquency?		Know the causes and treatments for juvenile delinquency.
Chapter summary		

Sara will soon celebrate two very important events: Her eighteenth birthday and graduation from high school. She is now physically capable of reproducing sexually and is almost completely grown. Sara has broken away considerably from her parents and now relies more on her peers, although she still maintains contact with her parents on important issues. Occasionally, Sara is caught between the wishes and ideology of her peers and her parents. She is also troubled by pressure to make good grades, to get into college, and by the responsibility of taking care of the house while her mother works.

Sara is also troubled by being treated more like a child rather than like an adult. She must endure a prolonged childhood that is likely to be stretched out even more by her need to attend college. At times, Sara is impetuous and at other times she is very hesitant. Sometimes she has confident self-assurance ("I can do it myself, I don't need anybody to help me"), while at other times she is petrified at the thought of failing. Such unpredictability, turmoil, and conflict are trademarks of most American teenagers. Some teenagers react to their stresses by gaining weight; others cannot sleep. Still others are continually fatigued or listless. Many react by drinking or by drug abuse.

Sara has read that things weren't always like this. Up until the mid-19th century, children labored in the fields alongside their parents. By the time a girl was Sara's age, she would probably have been married and had two or three children. However, this knowledge doesn't help Sara. She feels irrelevant, yet she wants to feel needed by her family and peers. She doesn't know who she is and where she fits in. Nor does she feel very connected to her peers. The idealism which bonded teenagers in the 1960s and 1970s is gone. Much of Sara's time is spent on the Internet. She shops, talks to her friends, and even looks on the Internet for a job after graduation. Sometimes Sara feels that the only things that bind her to other teenage girls are her computer, IPod, cell phone, and birth control pills.

From her reading and discussions with her parents, Sara has learned that her generation is much more at risk than earlier ones. With the divorce rate hovering near 60 percent, about one-half of all teenagers are living in single-parent families and have only limited access to their custodial parent, who is usually working. Alcohol and drugs appear to be the norm.

The search for various types of identity (sexual, vocational, etc.) is paramount in the minds of adolescents. A serious problem is teenage pregnancy. The high rate of juvenile delinquency and the rash of school shootings recently are also troubling. Also, because she is conscious of world conditions, Sara knows that sexually transmitted infections such as AIDS, teen births, and sexual abuse remain common health hazards for adolescents, particularly in impoverished nations (WHO 2005).

THEORETICAL PERSPECTIVES ON ADOLESCENT PERSONALITY

Among those who can provide us with some answers to Sara's and Carlos' problems of development are G. Stanley Hall, Margaret Mead, Sigmund Freud, Anna Freud, and Erik Erikson.

G. Stanley Hall: "Storm and Stress" of Adolescence

The first psychologist to formulate a theory of adolescence was G. Stanley Hall, the first president of the American Psychological Association, and a major figure in developmental psychology (Cairns, 1983). Hall proposed two controversial ideas about individual development based on Darwin's theory of evolution (Buss, 2004).

Ontogeny recapitulates phylogeny: G. Stanley Hall's belief that an individual's development recapitulates the entire history of the species.

Ontogeny recapitulates phylogeny. Hall believed that the development of an individual organism recapitulates the entire evolutionary history of the species. The infant's and toddler's developing skill in using tools "recapitulates" the tool-using discoveries of the cave people. The 6-year-old who plays "cops and robbers" might be reliving the lives of early hunters and fishermen who lived in caves. Middle childhood corresponds to an ancient period of historical development when human reason, morality, feelings of love, and religion did not reach today's standards. According to Hall, more mature benchmarks of development are reflected in adolescence that provide the child with the first opportunity to develop individual talents and abilities (Hall, 1904). Hall states that adolescence is a time of "storm and stress," which reflects the turbulent state of a bygone Western civilization.

Figure 15.1
G. Stanley Hall; (1846-1924)

Hall was the "father" of adolescent psychology who believed that the "storm and stress" of adolescence is inevitable. Hall was strongly influenced by Charles Darwin, the famous evolutionary theorist, and applied the scientific and biological dimensions of Darwin's view to the study of adolescent development. Hall believed that environment played a minimal role in child development, particularly during the early years.

Storm and stress of adolescence: G. Stanley Hall's view that the emotional turmoil, conflict, and defiance typically experienced by adolescents is inevitable.

The storm and stress of adolescence is inevitable. Hall's view that the *storm and stress* (heightened emotionality, conflict, and defiance of adults) usually seen in adolescents is inevitable, is more controversial than his theory of recapitulation (Collins & Laursen, 2004). Many theorists, including Margaret Mead, claim that Hall's theory is overstated, if not totally false (Arnett, 1999). The dominant opinion today is that the storm and stress which most American adolescents experience is not inevitable, but the result of environmental pressure, such as parental criticism and high expectations which push the child to achieve beyond his or her capabilities.

Although Hall's theory of adolescence is not nearly as prominent today as it once was, its importance cannot be overlooked. His thinking forms the basis for the views of Sigmund Freud, Jean Piaget, and Erik Erikson. Furthermore, Hall identified the major dimensions of adolescent development—intellectual, emotional, moral, sexual, and social. However, Hall's emphasis on recapitulation, with its biological emphasis as a basis for child development, has waned in favor of a more environmental view, such as that proposed by anthropologist Margaret Mead.

Margaret Mead: Cultural Influence on Personality Development

Margaret Mead (1901–1978), a noted authority on personality and culture, studied adolescence in the Pacific Islands of Samoa and New Guinea. Mead argued that the "storm and stress" typical of American adolescents is not innate or inevitable. In her books, *Coming of Age in Samoa* (1928), *Male and Female* (1949), and *Growing Up in New Guinea* (1953), Mead claimed that local customs greatly affect adolescents' feelings and behavior. In *Culture and Commitment* (1970), Mead suggested that the training adolescents receive depends on the nature and needs of their society.

Although Mead conceded that biological and psychological factors affect adolescence, she placed greater emphasis on cultural determinants. She pointed out that in underdeveloped cultures such as Samoa, there was general casualness, particularly toward sexual relations among adolescents. Mead also pointed out that in Samoa young children were permitted to see expressions of sexuality, watch babies being born, witness death, do important work, and engage in sex play, resulting in adolescence that was relatively free of stress.

Mead claims that in the United States, where children are protected from adult responsibilities, the shift from childhood to adulthood is more discontinuous and therefore more stressful. Mead also claims that even semi-restrictive societies introduce unnecessary conflicts, making the transition to adulthood much more difficult. Often, myths are perpetuated about normal sexual activities, such as saying that masturbation causes warts and blindness.

Figure 15.2
Margaret Mead; (1901-1978)

Noted anthropologist who claimed that adolescents need not necessarily go through a period of turmoil, which G. Stanley Hall called "storm and stress."

Evaluation of Mead's theory. Margaret Mead's claim that storm and stress, so common among Western teenagers and practically nonexistent among Samoan adolescents, is the result of culture, has been disputed by a number of investigators. Derek Freeman (1983) claims that there was more conflict and stress among Samoan girls than Mead recognized. Freeman also claims that delinquency was more prevalent among Samoan adolescents than in any other age group in that culture. Still, there are many scientists who defend Mead's work. Her findings stand as a beacon for cultural factors in the storm and stress of adolescence. Mead's work has caused investigators to re-examine biologically oriented theories by psychologists such as G. Stanley Hall, Arnold Gesell, and Sigmund Freud, who believe that "biology is destiny."

If Mead's theory that adolescent turbulence is linked to cultural factors is correct, then there should be a relationship between the amount of stress today's teenagers are subjected to and their emotions and behavior, a point verified by many investigators. Most investigators agree that today's adolescent is under greater stress than his or her counterpart of 50 or 100 years ago. Among these greater stresses are a more dangerous world, easy sex, ominously higher rates of drinking and smoking, gang violence, AIDS, school shootings, and drug abuse.

With divorce rates hovering around 60 percent, today's teenagers are more on their own than ever before. Moreover, the single parent usually has to contend with poverty, since about 55 percent of single-parent families are living at poverty levels.

With these additional strains, we would expect more problems of distress among today's teenagers than four or five decades ago. One index is the suicide rate, about 18 per 100,000 teenagers, double that of the 1970s. If we look at the inner cities where most indicators of economic and social conditions point toward the negative, we see dramatic evidence of the teenagers' turbulence. Among African American teenagers, where the unemployment rate is 40 to 70 percent, 90 percent of African American teenage mothers are unmarried, the school dropout rate reaches as high as 60 percent, and "crack" has become a medium of commerce and violence. This supports the view of Margaret Mead that there is a relationship between the high turmoil among today's teenagers and the many stresses with which they are confronted.

Sigmund Freud: Genital Stage (About Ages 11 to 14)

According to Sigmund Freud, personality development culminates during the *genital stage* and is accompanied by considerable turmoil and emotionality. However, this turmoil is of short duration, and Freud sees it as necessary in developing a mature, well-integrated personality, particularly if the adolescent is to cope successfully with crises. One of these crises is dealing with the physiological changes involving puberty.

The sexual urges which were repressed in latency reappear in the genital stage in full force. These physical urges are no longer directed toward the parents, but toward peers of the opposite gender, which eventually results in sexual reproduction. The teenager is able to resolve his or her sexual feelings toward the parent of the opposite gender because of incest taboo. This is done through a defense mechanism known as *reaction formation* (replacing an anxiety-producing feeling with the expression of its opposite, or a more acceptable form of behavior).

According to Freud, when adolescents are trying to free themselves from sexual dependency on the opposite-gender parent, they usually go through a homosexual stage seen in hero worship of the same-gender adult. If the teenager overcomes this stage, he or she moves on to a mature (genital) stage of sexuality. If the adolescent does not make the switch from same-gender worship

Genital stage: In Freudian theory, the final stage of psychosexual development in which the focus returns to the sex organs and there is attraction to the opposite gender.

Reaction formation: Replacing an anxiety-producing feeling with the expression of its opposite or a more acceptable form of behavior.

to the opposite gender, the result might be homosexuality[1]—a very controversial aspect of Freudian theory.

Figure 15.3
Sigmund Freud (1856-1939)

Sigmund Freud developed the theory of psychoanalysis. He believed that the only mature form of sexual behavior is coitus with a member of the opposite gender.

Evaluation of Freud's genital stage. The Freudian genital stage has received mixed reviews from investigators. Freud's theory of dual orgasm, clitoral and vaginal, has been confirmed by laboratory evidence provided by William Masters and Virginia Johnson (1966). Nevertheless, many of his other claims are in doubt.

Freud's contention that the only mature form of orgasm for the girl is vaginal, is disputed. Clitoral orgasm, for instance, is apparently characteristic of many normal, well-adjusted adult women (Masters & Johnson, 1966). Moreover, Freud's belief that masturbation, petting to orgasm, and homosexuality are aberrant forms of sexual behavior appears to have been stimulated by his ignorance and prejudice. Freud's contention that masturbation declines with age is also in dispute. Older adolescents and nonvirgins (from about 16 to 19) are more likely to masturbate than younger ones (13- to 15-year-olds).

Scientists generally agree that Freud's explanation of sexual (and moral) development "flies in the face of sociological and historical evidence" (David *et al.,* 2004). Freud's ideas reflect the beliefs and practices of middle-class Victorian society at the end of the nineteenth society. However, recently there has been a trend toward greater acceptance of Freud's ideas.

Anna Freud: Ego Defenses

Anna Freud (1895–1982), Sigmund Freud's daughter and a psychoanalyst in her own right, was particularly interested in adolescence. She saw this period as a time of considerable stress, since teenagers are attempting to reintegrate their personalities after physical changes have occurred. Anna Freud saw stress as a symptom that the adolescent is probably dealing successfully with new feelings and changes. According to Anna Freud, adolescents in stress (those who argue with their parents a lot, for instance) are attempting to emancipate themselves from their parents and are trying to come to terms with their own needs, wants,

---

1. A "homosexual" is now commonly referred to as "gay"; a gay female is called a "lesbian."

and desires (Edgcumbe, 2000). She sees the conflict between teenagers and their parents as a normal part of children's development toward increased independence and autonomy as they strive to attain adulthood. The absence of a conflict during adolescence, or the presence of behaviors such as considerateness, submissiveness, and goodness, while convenient for the parents, may be an indication of the adolescent's reluctance to grow up (Freud, A., 1972). Research indicates that many teenagers who are disobedient often settle down once they have jobs and families of their own, verifying Anna Freud's contention that aberrant behavior in adolescence can be a normal forerunner of acceptable behavior in adulthood (Vaillant, 2002).

According to Anna Freud, there is a precarious balance between the id, representing raw impulses like the sexual drive and anger, and the weak ego, which represents the reality of the environment (Edgcumbe, 2000). To regain psychological balance, the ego must avoid overassociation with the superego (conscience that controls the moral scruples) and the id (the reservoir of all instinctual, unconscious drives that pursue pleasure). If the raw impulses of the id are repressed too much by the superego, the result is inflexibility in personal relations or slavishness to social rules. If the ego is dominated by the id, the result is total loss of control over one's desire for gratification (Freud, A.,1946).

Figure 15.4
Anna Freud (1895-1982)

Anna Freud, Sigmund Freud's daughter, was a psychoanalyst in her own right. For many years, she was a director of the Hampstead Child-Therapy Clinic in London, England. Anna extended her father's psychosexual theory, clarifying the mechanisms of defense and applying the theory to the practice of child psychiatry. Like her father, Anna Freud focused on the conflicts and tensions inherent in various stages of life. However, Anna placed less emphasis on the unconscious than her father.

One reason for increased conflict during adolescence is the resurgence of Oedipal feelings. The teenage boy, whose sexual feelings were relatively dormant during the latency stage, often idolizes his mother again, and a girl may have similar feelings of closeness to her father, vying with her mother for the father's attention. The father may exacerbate his daughter's emerging sexuality to which he feels attracted by unconsciously drawing *away* from her. The father may also idolize his daughter to the point that he strongly disapproves of any young man that his daughter is attracted to by setting impossibly high standards for his daughter or her boyfriend. The mother may add to the problem by openly flirting with her daughter's boyfriend. The effect on the girl is usually one of confusion, guilt, and anxiety. To restore equilibrium, defense mechanisms (mental devices for coping with anxiety-arousing situations and for resolving conflicts) are often produced. Two of the more important defense mechanisms during adolescence, according to Anna Freud, are *intellectualization* and *ascetism*

Intellectualization: A defense mechanism marked by detachment from a stressful situation by dealing with it in abstract, intellectual terms.

Intellectualization. Intellectualization is an attempt to gain detachment from a stressful situation, such as conflict over one's sexuality by dealing with it in abstract, intellectual terms. Intellectualization may entail behavior such as holding an all-night abstract discussion on religion, politics, or philosophy. Intellectualization displaces an anxiety-provoking problem onto a small detail, thus helping the troubled person escape from the world of emotions into a world of intellectual concepts. We see this in the medical doctor who is continually confronted with human suffering, but who avoids involvement with his patients by becoming immersed in solving problems such as the Mideast crisis. Intellectualization is a problem only when it becomes so pervasive that the individual is unable to experience any kind of feeling.

Ascetism. Ascetic individuals often become religious zealots and lead overcontrolled lives that require renunciation of "worldly" behaviors and possessions. An example is the person who devotes his life to combating some particular evil (abuse of drugs, sexual promiscuity, etc.), which represents his own unconscious instincts. Anna Freud says that ascetism is a phase of puberty which indicates a simultaneous fear of, and defense against, sexuality. Others have argued that *ascetism* is the result of the teenager's increased ability in abstract thought, or an attempt to find an identity.

Ascetism: An overcontrolled life that requires renunciation of "worldly" behavior and possessions.

Erik Erikson's Crisis V: Identity Achievement Versus Identity Diffusion (About Ages 12 to 18)

Although McKensie is 16 years old she is still unclear about who she is, where she fits in, and what she wants out of life. At times, she feels helpless and alone. For Erikson, these feelings of anxiety, confusion, disorientation, and deep isolation are symptoms of an *identity crisis* (Erikson, 1968). Erikson says that when a person experiences an identity crisis there is a sudden disintegration of the framework of values and goals that the person relies on to give meaning and purpose to daily life.

Identity crisis: Feelings of anxiety, confusion, disorientation, and deep isolation that are common in adolescence.

Erikson pays special attention to a type of identity crisis which he calls diffusion. *Identity diffusion* means that the person lacks a commitment to any goals or values and significantly does not meet any of the usual demands of adolescence such as completing school assignments, looking for a job, or thinking about the future. Marlene seems not to care about anything because "nothing matters."

Identity diffusion: An adolescent's lack of values, traits or commitments; the opposite of identity achievement.

According to Erikson, if children are to negotiate their development successfully they must resolve their identity crisis and achieve a "sense of personal sameness and historical continuity" (Erikson, 1968, p. 17). If Sara is not able to resolve her identity, she will not be able to form intimate relationships and may remain isolated for the rest of her life.

Virtue of fidelity: A sense of belonging to someone.

An important identity crisis involves the *virtue of fidelity*, a sense of belonging to a loved one, or to friends and companions. When Sara is in a loving relationship, she can share her thoughts and feelings, receive feedback, and feel free to change. Despite this intimacy, which often accompanies love, Erikson does not view adolescent love as being identical with that of mature, adult love. He says that males cannot reach both adult intimacy and adult love until they have achieved a stable identity.

For Erikson, there are several other identity crises that an adolescent must resolve for proper development. One of these is the sexual crisis ("What pattern of sexual behavior is acceptable?"). Another crisis is ideological ("What should I believe in?"). There is also an occupational crisis in adolescence. Having resolved the various identity crises, the teenager acquires a more mature conception of the self: An *ego identity*.

***Ego identity:** A mature sense of oneself.*

Achievement of an ego identity. *The achievement of an* ego identity involves a pattern of beliefs about the self which tells Sara how she is like other people and how she differs from them. Among the components of ego identity are sexual, social, physical, and moral characteristics which make up the self. All of the ego must be sorted into a unified whole so that the teenager has mature direction and meaning to his or her life (Erikson, 1959; Marcia, 1980; 1996).

The adolescent who has achieved an ego identity also has a much more developed sense of trust. However, contrary to infancy when it was important for the child to trust others, the teenager who has achieved an ego identity has more trust in himself. Moreover, the trust that Carlos had in his parents is transferred to other people, who become his mentors and often loved ones. Adolescents who have achieved an ego identity have a stable self-concept and a sense of well-being. They are at home in their bodies, they know where they are going, and they feel assured of recognition from significant people (Erikson, 1968).

Early teenagers such as these 13-year-olds love to be the center of attention. Erickson and Marcia would say that the girls are trying to establish an identity.

James Marcia's Identity Statuses: Crisis and Commitment

Identity statuses: James Marcia's four levels of identity formation that depend on the presence of crisis and commitment.

Crisis: A period of decision-making when previous choices, beliefs, and identifications are questioned by the child.

Commitment: A relatively stable set of roles and ideals.

Identity foreclosure: Marcia's term for an individual identity status in which a commitment to family, work, political, and religious values is established prematurely, without a crisis.

Identity diffusion: Marcia's term for an adolescent's identity status when he has made no specific commitment and there is no active search for an identity.

Erikson's theories of identity formation have been tested and elaborated by James Marcia, a professor at Simon Fraser University in Canada. Marcia defines four levels of identity formation which he calls *identity statuses* which are determined on the basis of whether the adolescent has gone through crises and whether he has made a regular commitment (Marcia, 1980; 1994). *Crisis*[2] refers to a period of decision-making when previous choices, beliefs, and identifications are questioned by the child. *Commitment* refers to the choices of a relatively stable set of roles and ideals involving areas such as occupational choice, religion, and political ideology. According to Marcia, the search for identity involves four categories: Identity achievement, identity foreclosure, identity diffusion, and identity moratorium.

1) *Identity foreclosure (commitments are made, but they come from authority figures; there is no self-search).* Jason is in this category because he has made plans (commitment) to enter law school. He has a definite ideological position—one which represents ultraconservatives. But Jason's commitment is not self-chosen, it reflects his father's wishes. Being a wealthy conservative lawyer, Jason's dad wants his son to follow in his footsteps. Instead of thinking things through on his own (going through a period of exploration), Jason has reached a premature commitment to a ready-made identity formulated by his father.

For the time being, Jason appears to be happy with his decision to enter law school. He talks about his vocational plans with considerable self-assurance, and sometimes is even smug about plans for his life. He feels a closeness to his family, and becomes dogmatic when his allegiance to his family is questioned. Nevertheless, Jason has not experienced the "crisis" of deciding what suits *him* best.

2) I*dentity diffusion (no specific commitment is made and there is no active search due to an unresolved identity crisis or to an absence of a crisis).* Tommy is unclear about who he is and where he is headed. In fact, he has no goal. When asked what he wants to do with his life, he replies nonchalantly, "Nothing, man." Actually, Tommy has considered several options but has not made a firm occupational or ideological commitment, nor is he actively trying to reach any specific goal.

Tommy has mentioned a few times that it would be "nice" to be a doctor or a teacher. He takes a smorgasbord approach to religion, in which one faith is as good as another. Both political and social interests are low. "Politics just don't interest me," he says casually. While some see Tommy as a carefree playboy, others see him as bordering on psychotic.

Tommy is unable to get some direction to his life because he has never experienced an identity crisis. Of course, there is also the possibility that if Tommy had experienced a crisis he would not have been able to solve it. People like Tommy are just drifting along. Some drop out from active participation in the mainstream of society. Many turn to drugs or to mystical experiences, seldom resolving the task of growing up. According to Marcia, identity diffusion is the least developmentally advanced of the statuses and most characteristic of young adolescents who feel lost.

---

2.   Most researchers now use the term *exploration* rather than crisis.

Identity moratorium:
Marcia's term for an identity crisis which is in progress, and the search for commitments continues.

3) *Identity moratorium (identity crisis is in progress and the search for commitment continues).* Priscilla is trying to "find herself." She has thought about entering a variety of professions, but cannot make her mind up. She has also tried numerous political and ideological stances without being certain which ones she favors. She also finds it troublesome to go from one relationship to another, not being quite certain about what she wants in a man. Nor is she certain about her position on sexual intercourse. The idea of contracting AIDS scares her, yet she knows that many of her single friends are having sex.

Despite these crises, in all likelihood Priscilla will be able to achieve an ego identity. She is already on a psychological route to a mature self-definition. This is apparent because of the many positive signs while she is still in the identity moratorium. For example, although Priscilla has strong feelings and is very self-conscious, she is open to new experiences and is comfortable dealing with other people. She is also attempting to make decisions about her future and is examining different options. Finally, Priscilla is engaged in self-directed, conscious, and positive behavior to learn about and define her sense of self. When will she achieve an ego identity? Quite likely within a year or two after graduation from high school, maybe sooner.

Identity achievement:
Marcia's term for individuals who have been through an identity crisis and have made some important decisions regarding their goals in life and what they believe in.

4) *Identity achievement (identity crisis is past and commitments have been made deliberately).* Sara has defined her goal in life (teaching) after much thought about what to do (the crisis period) with her life. She has already been accepted at a local state college and is now committed to becoming a teacher. Sara realizes that she may have to alter her goal from time to time (if she becomes ill, she may have to graduate a year later; she may not always be able to get the professors she wants). If necessary, she is willing to make adjustments.

Having achieved an ego identity, Sara is likely to get along with her new classmates since she is sociable and seldom feels threatened by people. She is also cooperative and at ease in discussions of controversial issues. Moreover, Sara is not afraid to express an opinion contrary to those of her parents and peers, and she holds to her position firmly without hostility.

Sara also has a sense of humor which makes it easier for her to perform under stress. Young people like Sara who have achieved an identity, are much less likely to become depressed and commit suicide. Rather, they look to the future with confidence.

According to Marcia, decisions about a person's identity are developed in bits and pieces. Synthesizing the various components of identity is a long drawn out process (Marcia & Carpendale, 2004).

Achievement of identity for minority teens. With the high influx of minorities into the United States recently, a major problem has been the achievement of an identity ego for minority teenagers. The following quotations are an adaptation of stages of Jean Phinney's (2003) identity development for minority adolescents:

- **Diffusion. "I'm not interested in learning about the contributions of African American people." (African American adolescent)**

- **Foreclosure. "If it were possible, I would be Caucasian because they have more job opportunities and are more accepted." (Mexican-American male)**

- **Moratorium. "To understand the present status of my people, we need to know what they have gone through in the past. One way to obtain**

this understanding is to study African American art." (African American female)

- **Achievement. "Being light-skinned, in the past I always tried to "pass" as White. Now I actually enjoy telling people I am a mixture of African American, Caucasian, and Mexican." (African American female)**

PERSONAL RELATIONSHIPS IN ADOLESCENCE: PEERS VERSUS PARENTS

Sara and Carlos, both 13 years of age, have close relationships with two sets of individuals: their parents and their peers. In many instances, Sara and Carlos feel that they are in a tug of war. The parents would like to hold onto their children, yet Sara and Carlos feel increasingly attracted to their peer group. The parents feel that they are losing their grip on their children, often wondering whether their children love them or need them.

Relationships With Parents

Sara's and Carlos' parents are troubled because their values are often rejected although they may be embraced in later years. Contrary to what parents might think, adolescents do not want to sever their relationships with them entirely. What teenagers want is more room to grow. In one word, they need more *independence*. This struggle is nothing new, it began a long time ago.

Carlos' struggle for independence began as early as 1½ or 2 years of age when he had temper tantrums and tried to express himself verbally. Throughout his life, Carlos has increased his knowledge of himself and the world around him. He has learned many skills that promote autonomy. His increased intelligence causes him to be more curious and independent. These various developments enable Carlos to construct his own ideas of what to do, what is right, and what is wrong.

What Carlos needs from his parents is acceptance of his experiments and mistakes (Gullotta & Blau, 2008). Although he often disagrees, Carlos uses his parents as a sounding board. Seeing that their children are often afraid and uncertain, parents frequently give their children mixed messages. For instance, parents may encourage their daughter to go to college and live in the dorm. When they see that she has some reservations, they may say, "You can always live *at home* while going to college," causing her to vacillate still more.

Parents worry about their children's "rebelliousness." The problem is seldom serious. In a 34-year longitudinal study of sixty-seven 14-year-old suburban boys, the majority adapted to their life experiences (Offer, Offer, & Ostrov, 2004). The relatively few adolescents who are like ticking time bombs set to explode in later life tended to come from broken homes and as adults continued to reject cultural norms and remained maladjusted.

Parents need to know that their teenagers respect them and attempt to resolve their differences with dialogue rather than through conflict or rejection (Gullotta & Blau, 2008). Almost two-thirds of adolescents are "extremely" close or "quite close" to their parents and only about 1 in 10 is "not close." Moreover, adolescents and their parents tend to agree about a variety of major issues, such as religion, marriage, and morality. Carlos and Sara tend to disagree with their parents about drugs, sex, dress styles, hair length, and hours of sleep.

Several studies show that children's interactions with fathers are different from those with their mothers. Adolescents talk to their mothers about personal, more intimate topics, such as dating, financial independence, sex, and popularity. Fathers are usually consulted about long-range plans, such as which job to take, and how to resolve a moral conflict.

What should parents do? Perhaps the most important single bit of advice for parents of adolescents is to let go of their children. Allowing children greater independence gives them practice in becoming more competent. Fortunately, many parents realize that their teenagers need more independence since they will soon leave home and establish their own lives. Some parents continue to exercise maximum control over their teenagers in such matters as clothing, school courses, and going out with friends (Collins *et al.*, 1997). Usually, immigrant parents are more controlling with their teenagers than nonimmigrant parents (Phinney & Ong, 2001).

Often, the cause of the excessive control of teenagers is the parents' realization that their growing adolescent will soon leave home and establish his or her own life. Consequently, as the adolescent presses for greater autonomy, the parents press for more togetherness. This imbalance, which Urie Bronfenbrenner, the ecologist, calls the *chronosystem*, promotes friction between the parent and teenager. The friction can be imposed externally, such as a father restricting his teenage daughter from talking to boys, or internally, such as the girl wanting more freedom. To reduce conflict, parents need to keep changing. For instance, what worked with a ten-year-old girl, such as forbidding her to talk to boys, will cause problems if the same restrictions are imposed when the girl is a teenager.

The best way to raise independent and competent children is to use Diana Baumrind's authoritative method. The parent-child relationship is warm but demanding and fosters high self-esteem and social and moral maturity. Authoritative parents value and listen to their children's opinions and explain the rules. The parent's listening should be *active*, sending back and affirming the child's message. For instance, if a teenager is upset about failing her exam, the parent should say something like, "You are angry about flunking your exam, aren't you?" rather than, "Well, try harder next time and you'll do better" (Gordon, 1975).

Chronosystem: In ecological systems theory, temporal changes in children's environments, which produce new conditions that affect development. The changes can be imposed externally or from within the organism.

Peer Groups in Adolescence

In this section, we will first look at the structure of adolescent peer groups. Then we will examine the functions performed by peer groups. Finally, we will look at peer pressure, particularly when it is negative, and the reasons why some children are more susceptible to peer pressure than others.

Structure of adolescent peer groups. If we compare peer groups in middle childhood with those in adolescence, we find many differences. Peer groups in middle childhood tend to be homogeneous, consisting of boys or girls of about the same age, from approximately the same backgrounds, and with similar disdain for members of the opposite gender. Beginning at about age 12, peer groups begin to fragment, forming new groups with new common denominators (Larson & Wilson, 2004).

A highlight of teenagers is their desire for attention. Which teenager do you think is trying the hardest to be the center of attention?

Clique: A small, exclusive group of people who interact frequently.

Crowd: The joining of several cliques into a larger group of peers.

One change in adolescence is the development of two basic subgroups: *Cliques* and *crowds* (Brown, 2004). Cliques are composed of four to six young people—usually female—with strong emotional ties to one another. There is considerable intimate sharing and much negative gossip about nonmembers (e.g., "Did you see the weird boyfriend she had?"). A major concern among female adolescent cliques is body image. There is considerable discussion about body weight and a preoccupation with thinness. There is also considerable body comparison: "How does my body compare with hers?"

The crowd consists of a large group of male and female adolescents who are loosely bound by similar characteristics (age, common interests, and background). In high school, there may be a crowd of athletes, students with high academic aspirations, car buffs, and cheerleaders. A crowd is often composed of several cliques. As members of a crowd become older, they begin to mix more frequently with members of the opposite gender. At about age 16 or 17, heterosexual relationships become more stable and the appeal of the crowd lessens.

Investigators have found that there are qualitative differences in the way boys and girls structure their closest relationships. Girls of 11 or 12 years of age focus primarily on doing things together in their close friendships. Around the age of 14 years, girls are more interested in emotional support and now need someone who can be loyal and trustworthy. One reason for this shift is the girl's greater interest in the opposite gender and her growing erotic interests. During the late teen years, there is a decline in peer friendship among girls. Having worked out many earlier fears, older female teenagers have less anxiety about being "abandoned or betrayed." Older teenage girls are also more tolerant of differences in peers and have a larger pool of potential friends to draw from. Robert Selman (1981) mentions this shift by girls to a larger world when the adolescent progresses in moral development from Stage 3 (mutual role-taking—ages 10 to 12) to Stage 4 (social and conventional role-taking—ages 12 to 15).

Boys seldom form friendships as intimate as those of girls. One reason may be the greater competition among boys. Another reason may be the boys' greater reliance on authority. Moreover, boys are usually less articulate. Both boys and girls are attracted to athletics. One reason sports are so popular–particularly in early adolescence—is that young people seem to be attracted to the aggression involved (Bukowski, Sippola, & Newcomb, 2000).

Box 15.1
Tween Peer Groups

One type of peer group that has received considerable attention lately from psychologists and the media is the "tweens." Tweens are children from about 8 to 12 years of age who disown adults whom they consider to be "dumb-witted" and "boring." Tweens do not consider themselves children and are in a hurry to grow up.

Instead of playing with Barbies and Legos, tweens assume adult roles in a variety of ways. Tween boys try to look grown up by acting "cool and tough." Girls try to act grown up by wearing low-rise jeans, tight tops, and body lotions with names like "Heat" and "Lollipop Bling."

This rush to adulthood is the result of several factors. One reason is parental absence, forcing children to assume an adult role by cooking for themselves and taking care of younger siblings and the house. The media, the clothing industry, and cosmetic companies have seized upon the void created by parental absence by treating the children as if they are adults. The television, videos, and the Internet expose the children to adult materials at ever-younger ages. Clothing and cosmetic companies have also seized on the opportunity to make the children feel grown up by using adult-type products.

The pressures that are placed on tweens to grow up quickly take their toll in a variety of ways. The toll includes physical problems such as stomach pains that are caused by ulcers or asthma. There are also emotional problems such as persistent fears and high anxiety as well as behavioral problems such as truancy and defiance. Children need time to grow up with as little external pressure as possible. Over 100 years ago, Friedrich Froebel (1782-1852), the German education reformer who founded the kindergarten system, stated that children need to be nurtured and not hurried in their development.

Functions of adolescent peer groups. Child developmental theorists (e.g., Freud, Erikson, and Piaget) are generally agreed that adolescent development is strongly shaped by peers (Brown, 2004). Like girls, boys want friends who are amiable and cooperative. Boys expect their male friends to help them in times of trouble with authority. Both boys and girls expect friends to help each other confront and make sense out of ambiguous and anxiety-provoking situations. The first time a boy tries to kiss a girl, his best friend may be only a few feet away nodding his approval. Like the female counterpart, by age 17 or 18, the boy seldom needs the assurance and support of his best friend.

The major function served by a peer group is to help teenagers break away from their parents and to provide emotional support. The teenager who wants to break away from his parents is often confused by a mass of possible life-styles, values, and ideologies. Peer-group norms provide tentative guidelines until the adolescent feels confident enough to develop his own set of norms, and eventually, his own identity (Erikson, 1950). In other words, peer groups may help young people fill the void which was created when they began to separate from their parents.

One way that peers can help one another is to share confidential information about intimate fears and plans. Teenage girls can relate their feelings about a transition to active sexuality by providing each other with an open atmosphere in which they can share their erotic fantasies and behaviors. By checking with others, girls can rest assured that their feelings are normal and that they don't have to feel embarrassed or guilty. Implicit in this sharing of intimate information, is the need for trustworthiness—the ability to keep whatever one knows or hears about another person private. Girls want to be able to tell their friends "everything," without worrying that their friends will spread stories.

The peer group also serves as a testing ground. The teenager can adopt a variety of roles or life-styles, and then determine which one is right for him or her according to the reaction by peers. Peer influence is particularly strong between the ages of 12 and 14. Boys this age talk alike, go everywhere together, and do the same things. Cohesiveness is also seen in girls. For example, every member of a clique may "dislike" a particular nonpeer-group member.

Peer pressure. Peer groups help to shape the attitudes of their members toward two central issues: school and teenage culture. A peer group may reinforce its members for disliking school or for "getting by with doing as little work as possible in school." Or, peer groups can reinforce parents' admonitions to "stay out of trouble." Peer pressure is greatest when the standards for appropriate behavior are unclear.

> **Peer pressure:** Influence in either a positive or a negative direction by individuals of one's own age group and of equal or similar backgrounds.

Teenagers who live with only one parent run a greater risk of succumbing to peer pressure toward delinquency. This is the finding of a nationwide study of 6,710 twelve to seventeen-year-olds living with only their mothers (Dornbusch *et al.*, 1985). In this study, teenagers were more likely to exhibit antisocial behavior such as truancy, running away from home, smoking, having discipline problems in school, and getting into trouble with the law, if they lived with one parent.

A major reason why some teenagers are more susceptible to negative peer pressure than others appears to be their philosophical outlook. The home lives of most delinquent youths are stressful, disorganized, and poverty stricken, leaving them poorly equipped to succeed. The result is low self-esteem and despair. Juvenile delinquents often realize that their goals can be attained by a more direct, aggressive form of behavior such as stealing and selling drugs. Moreover, the further children are from their parents emotionally, the more susceptible they are to adverse peer pressure. If the parents support their children and use an authoritative style of discipline (the children's misbehavior is dealt with by reasoning, the parents pay attention to the issues, they are loving, consistent, yet demanding), the children hold their parents in high regard, an attitude which serves as a buffer against antisocial peer pressure (Sim, 2000).

A note of optimism. Parental wishes often prevail over those of peers. Parents are more likely to be influential when the issue involves scholastic goals or future-oriented decisions and aspirations ("Who am I to be?"). Adolescents who experience greater warmth and control from their parents and whose parents have greater knowledge of their activities, are more likely to reflect the values of their parents.

ADOLESCENT SEXUALITY

Sexual behavior usually begins in early adolescence and progresses from petting above the waist, to petting below the waist, to sexual intercourse. By the end of adolescence, the majority of teenagers have engaged in sexual intercourse. According to the Centers for Disease Control data from 2002, the average American girl has had her first sexual intercourse at age 17, one year later than the average American boy. However, there are many American teenagers who have had their first sexual intercourse long before the age of 17 or 18. Boys are more likely than girls to have their first sexual intercourse before age 13 (CDC,

2002). There are also ethnic differences in the timing of the first incident of sexual intimacy. African Americans and Latinos are more likely to have sexual intercourse earlier than Caucasian teenagers (Kaiser Family Foundation *et al.*, 2003).

National surveys of sexual practices, beginning with the studies conducted by Alfred Kinsey and his associates (1948, 1953), indicated that sexual activity among boys was a constant 50 to 70 percent rate from the 1940s until the 1980s. However, during this period the number of sexually active girls climbed from a low of 10 percent in the 1940s to a high of over 50 percent in the 1980s. Since the 1980s, sex rates have declined to 48 percent among teenage boys and to 43 percent among teenage girls (Brener *et al*, 2002). The decline in sex rates among teenage girls has been accompanied by a 30 percent drop in pregnancy rates (Manlove, Ryan & Franzetta, 2003).

Pregnancy rates vary considerably among ethnic groups. Latina adolescents continue to have the highest of adolescent pregnancy and birth rates (*Child Trends*, 2001). The rates have fallen most sharply among African American teenagers. However, despite the dramatic drop in pregnancy and birth rates among U.S. teenagers, they are still more likely to become pregnant and give birth than teenagers in any other western country (Alan Guttmacher Institute, 2002).

Influences on children's sexual behavior. One of the clearest influences on adolescent sexual behavior is the parents' attitude toward sex. In one significant study of high school students (Treboux & Busch-Rossnagel, 1990), if the parents had a positive attitude toward sex, their children were more likely to have sexual intercourse. Peers also play a role. In one study (DiBlasio & Benda, 1990), sexually active teenagers believed that their friends were also sexually active. Religious participation may also influence sexual behavior. Teenagers who attend church regularly and who value religion have less permissive attitudes toward sex. More recently, we have found a significant influence on adolescent sexuality to be the media and its covert and overt messages about sex and sexual behavior (Jordan, 2009). One way that investigators obtain information about adolescents' sexuality is through sex surveys.

Sex Surveys

"Mom, there's a man at the door," says 17-year-old Sara. "Ask him what he wants," the mother yells back. "He wants to talk to you," Sara replies. The mother discovers that the stranger is conducting a survey of teenage attitudes toward sex and their sexual practices and would like the parents' permission to question Sara. This scenario is repeated over 2,000 times in households selected randomly from a nationwide sample of 20 city and suburban neighborhoods and rural locations in more than 100 areas of the continental United States. The study just described resembles the one conducted by Robert Sorenson (1973). Sorenson's study is typical of every sex research project from Alfred Kinsey's original surveys undertaken in the 1940s to the present day.

Respondent: An individual who answers questions.

Among the questions asked is whether the *respondents* (the individuals answering the questions) have ever necked, done French kissing, fondled breasts, masturbated, or had sexual intercourse. Other questions are designed to elicit information about the age of the respondent at the time of the first sexual encounter and whether the subject had ever experienced an orgasm.

Social scientists have been particularly interested in adolescents' early sexual activity. A number of causal factors have been implicated. These factors include early entrance into puberty, a history of sexual abuse or parental neglect, and absence of a father (Ellis *et al.*, 2003). Self-esteem plays a different role for boys than for girls. Boys with high self-esteem engage in sex early, whereas girls with high self-esteem engage in their first sexual activity much later than the average girl (Spencer *et al.*, 2002).

There appears to be a special risk for girls who engage in sexual activity very early. Often they are victims of sexual violence or abuse. Young girls often report that their first sexual experience was unwanted or not voluntary.

Limitations of sex surveys. An important limitation of sex surveys is *sample bias* since the responses are not representative of all teenagers. In any survey of sex attitudes and behavior, there are always some subjects who do not consent to take part in the study. In Sorenson's study, the parents of 331 teenagers refused to give permission for their children to be interviewed (115 students refused to take part in the study even though their parents gave them permission).

Many surveys on sex also suffer from a *demographic bias* (incorrect representation of larger populations of vital and social statistics such as births, deaths, and marriages). Typically, the sample used in sex surveys contains a larger proportion of Caucasian, middle class, and college or high-school-educated people who are not representative of the general population.

Sample bias: A distortion of the results of a study because the sample is not representative of the larger population.

Demographic bias: An incorrect representation of vital and social statistics such as births, deaths, and marriages because it is not representative of the larger population.

Petting

Some researchers believe that *petting* (erotic caressing below the waist which does not include sexual intercourse) represents the greatest change in premarital sexual experience for American teenagers in the twentieth century. As with other forms of sexual behavior, petting has increased most dramatically among girls. A positive feature of petting is that it offers a shared sexual activity without the risk of pregnancy (Crooks & Baur, 1990).

Petting is usually part of a larger sequence of actions that make up sexual behavior. The sequence of petting usually goes from lip kissing, to tongue kissing, to touching the breasts through clothing, to touching the breasts under clothing, to touching the genitals through clothing, to genital contact (sexual intercourse).

Petting: Erotic caressing, usually below the waist, which does not include sexual intercourse.

Masturbation

One of the most widespread, but least talked-about, sexual behaviors is *masturbation*, or sexual self-stimulation. This is in contrast to many cultures that accept masturbation as a normal part of human sexuality. Scholars generally agree that masturbation is harmless and should be treated as a normal part of sexuality. Kinsey found that about 82 percent of men and 20 percent of women had masturbated by age 15. About 90 percent of the men had masturbated by age 20; about 42 percent of girls by age 19 (Kinsey, Pomeroy & Martin, 1948).

Masturbation: Sexual self-stimulation.

Gender differences in masturbation. There are differences between boys' and girls' masturbatory experiences. In our society males generally have more liberal attitudes toward masturbation than females (Elkind, 1998). For the adolescent boy, masturbation reinforces his commitment to sexual behavior in early adolescence. Moreover, masturbation tends to focus the male's feelings of sexual desire on his penis. Males report having masturbatory fantasies that involve sexual aggression, dominance, and unattainable sexual "luxury," such as a harem at one's command.

For most males, masturbation provides the first orgasm within a few years of the onset of puberty. Many women begin to masturbate only after they have begun to have sexual intercourse. Women also masturbate less frequently than men do.

Premarital Sexual Intercourse

Are teenagers having sex earlier and more frequently than ever before? Are there fewer adolescent virgins than in the past? One answer to these questions is provided by the Kinsey studies (Kinsey, Pomeroy & Martin, 1948), which despite their drawbacks (too few people from rural areas and too little data on African Americans), are still considered reliable.

The Kinsey studies of the late 1940s found that 3 percent of girls and 39 percent of boys had sexual intercourse by the age of 16. Currently, by the end of adolescence, most American boys and girls have had sexual intercourse at least once.

In addition to more of today's teenage girls having sexual intercourse, they also have their first sexual experience earlier (Jordan, 2009). This earlier sexual experience means that today's girls have more sexual partners during their teenage years than their parents did. Another concern is that the younger teenage girls are when they begin having sexual intercourse, the less likely they are to use contraception, and the more likely they are to get pregnant (Miller & Heaton, 1991).

Gender differences. Since girls differ from boys in their sexual attitudes (e.g., masturbatory fantasies are different), we can expect gender differences toward sexual intercourse. Girls are more likely to choose someone they know well and like as a first partner for sexual intercourse. A boy's first sexual partner is more likely to be someone he knows casually (he may not even know the girl's last name). Girls are also more likely to continue having intercourse with their first partner, whereas boys are more likely to keep changing sex partners.   As is typical of earlier studies, the rate of sexual intercourse is higher among boys than among girls.

Causes of Increase in Premarital Sexual Intercourse

Investigators have been trying to determine the causes for the high rate of sexual intercourse among young people.

The "New Sexual Morality": A sexual revolution in the 1960s and 1970s which viewed sex as acceptable between consenting, if not committed adults, and argued for abolishment of the "double standard" for sexual behavior.

The "New Sexual Morality." Many blame the increase in premarital sex and pregnancy on the attitudes and behavior promoted by the sexual revolution of the 1960s and 1970s. This revolution was called the "new sexual morality," when sex was looked upon by many people as fun and games. Three benchmarks of this new sexual ethic include:

1. Anything consenting people want to do sexually is considered moral, as long as it does not hurt anyone. Theoretically, all sexual behavior is viewed as a private matter between consenting adults and adolescents, married or unmarried. Adherents of this idea believe that there should be no universal moral sexual code, and regardless of marital status or age, people should decide for themselves whether their sexual behavior is moral. A majority of adolescents have consistently agreed with this view during the last four decades.

Double standard: An unwritten code of sexual behavior permitting men more freedom than women.

2. There should be a decline in the *double standard*, the idea that sexual activity outside marriage is less objectionable for males than for females. Therefore, females can be just as permissive sexually as males.

3. Sex is acceptable only within a loving and affectionate, if not committed, relationship; promiscuity, exploitation, and unprotected sexual intercourse are unacceptable.

Although the "New Sexual Morality" of the 1960s and 1970s played a major role in the increase in premarital sex and pregnancy, many investigators believe that the surge toward more freedom in premarital sex started much earlier. Investigators believe that the sexual revolution started immediately after World War I with the return of the doughboys (infantrymen), since the percentage of U.S. women engaging in premarital sexual intercourse more than doubled between 1920 and 1950.

Influence of the media. Although few teenagers will admit that their sexual behavior is influenced by media such as television and videos (only about 3 percent say that they are), psychologists believe that the media plays a large role in the dramatic increase in premarital sex (Jordan, 2009). One reason is the amount of exposure (Roberts, Henriksen & Foehr, 2004). Teenagers watch about 24 hours of TV per week and about 2 hours of music videos a day. The content of 75 percent of the videos is based on a sexual theme. Moreover, the sexual content is often distorted, such as sexual intercourse lasting for hours, whereas the average duration is 7$\frac{1}{2}$ minutes.

Often the media—particularly television—awaken and exploit teenagers' sexual urges. One of the messages that television gives is, "Everybody is doing it." Television offers very little information on the hazards of premarital sex or how to cope with problems such as contracting a sexual transmitted infection (STI) or pregnancy. Usually, there is very little accurate information about sex in the media. Further, there is far more sexual violence on the screen than in real life. On the other hand, there is little information in the media on unwanted births, the exploitation of sexual urges, and induced abortions (Roberts, Henriksen & Foehr, 2004).

One of the concerns about television is the negative influence of relatively new television-related technology such as the Internet (or World Wide Web). The Internet has the potential of exposing children to levels of sexual violence that would be unimaginable on commercial TV. Also, it is relatively easy for a child to "meet a nice person" on the Internet who happens to be a violent pedophile.

Ignorance about sexuality. A major point of concern is the adolescent's ignorance about physiology and reproduction. Only about half of Caucasian and a fifth of African American teenagers can describe the time of greatest fertility in the menstrual cycle[3]. There is also considerable ignorance about sexually transmitted diseases. Few teenagers know how AIDS is transmitted (most often through exchange of semen or blood). Hence, many teenagers submit to their urges without realizing the potential harm.

---

3. The woman is most likely to become pregnant, assuming that she menstruates regularly, every 28 days (and many do not), if sperm are deposited in the vagina between days 9 and 18 of her menstrual cycle, counting from day one of her menstrual period.

Influence of peers. One of the undeniable influences on premarital sex is peers. In some instances, teenagers become sexually active if they think their peers will respect them. In other instances, teenage girls may believe that their boyfriends will be more committed to them if they become sexually active and become a mother. Many teenage boys also report that they experienced pressure to engage in sexual activities they did not feel ready for. Most of the pressure came from their peers.

The personal fable: The "it-can't-happen-to-me" ("no-harm-can-come-to-me") attitude among some adolescents.

The personal fable. Some teenagers engage in sex because of the "it-can't-happen-to-me" attitude. The girl may rationalize that she is not the type of girl who will get pregnant. She may think that she can get pregnant only if she does drugs as well as having sex. Many girls are convinced that they can get pregnant only if they want to, and some believe that pregnancy cannot occur if they are young. Other girls think that they can prevent pregnancy by having intercourse in a certain position.

As a result of the personal fable and ignorance about the physiology of the body, only 14 percent of teenage girls use contraceptives the first time they have sexual intercourse. Moreover, there is usually a delay of about one year between initial sexual intercourse and the first use of prescription methods of birth control. There is also a tendency for teenagers to choose the least reliable ways of preventing pregnancy and to use contraceptives inconsistently and less effectively (Cooley & Chase-Lansdale, 1998). Some researchers (e.g., Cole & Slocumb, 1995) have discovered that even if adolescents are quite knowledgeable about human sexuality, there is no relationship between their understanding of sex and condom use while having sex.

Teenage Pregnancy: Children Having Children

There is an increasing number of teenage pregnancies worldwide, although the rate has fallen to a record low (Centers for Disease Control and Prevention, 2001).[4] Although teenage pregnancy in the United States has been reduced by a third in the last decade, this country still has the highest rate of teenage pregnancy in the industrialized world, double that of its nearest rival—England (Alan Guttmacher Institute, 2002).

Of particular concern is the trend toward an increasing number of pregnancies at a younger age (Alan Guttmacher Institute, 1994). Since 1942, the birth rate has doubled for girls 10 to 14 years of age (Center for Health Statistics, 1995). Currently, approximately 10 percent of girls in the United States between the ages of 15 and 19 years become pregnant each year, with around half of these pregnancies culminating in a live birth. This trend toward pregnancy and childbearing at a younger age is occurring throughout the world.

Consequences of teenage pregnancy. Teenage pregnancies represent the highest medical risk category for both the baby and its mother (Stevens-Simon & White, 1991; Ventura, 1994). Preterm (formerly called premature) birth, and its consequent low birth weight, are twice as likely to occur if the mother is a teenager than if she is in her mid-20s. Other possible complications for babies include disorders such as hyaline membrane disease (a respiratory distress disorder common in preterm infants) and brain damage from oxygen deprivation due to the mother's underdeveloped pelvic area and a slow and difficult passage through the birth canal (Phipps, 2002). The younger the

---

4. For more information on teenage pregnancy, write to: National Organization of
    Adolescent Pregnancy and Parenting (NOAPP), P.O. Box 2365, Reston, VA, 22090.

teenager is when she gets pregnant, the more likely she is to have an untreated sexually transmitted infection such as gonorrhea, genital herpes, syphilis and chlamydia, the most common STIs among adolescents (WHO, 2005). Also, once the baby arrives, it is more likely to die during the first year than a baby born to a mother in her 20s (Children's Defense Fund, 2000).

Babies born to teenage mothers have a greater risk of poor perceptual abilities, motor incoordination, and neurological impairments such as blindness, deafness, and mental retardation. The children are more likely to have low IQs and to do worse in school. Often, the children have emotional problems, cause havoc in school, and become high risks for juvenile delinquency and drug abuse. The children are more likely to have accidents, injuries, poisonings, to be hospitalized, and are also at risk of being abused or ending up in foster care. Moreover, children of adolescent mothers are at a higher risk of repeating their parents' pattern of early parenthood (Dash, 1990). Finally, children of teenage mothers may never see their fathers.

In addition to the children of teenage mothers being at risk for a variety of problems, the young mothers are also subject to many hazards. For instance, birth complications such as preeclampsia (a condition unique to pregnancy due to vascular and kidney disease), prolonged labor, and iron-deficiency anemia are common among teenage mothers. The teenage mother can also have difficulty delivering her baby as a result of cephalopelvic disproportions caused by a pelvis that is too small to allow normal delivery (Dash, 1990). Teenage mothers are more likely to die during delivery than those in their 20s. Many of these problems are related to preexisting conditions in the teenage mother, such as poor nutrition, drug abuse, low parental warmth and involvement, poor school performance, and adult models of unmarried parenthood. Many adolescent mothers seem to turn to parenthood as a means to move into adulthood when educational avenues and careers are not available to them (Luker, 1996).

There are many psychological hazards of teenage pregnancy in addition to medical risks for the mother and her baby. One is the disruption of the pregnant teenager's growing-up process. Only one out of five pregnant girls, aged 17 and under ever finishes high school. Consequently, she is seldom able to develop vocational skills which would make her self-sufficient (Walters, Roberts, & Morgen, 1997). Also, having a baby before age 20 cuts a woman's chances of getting married in half, whether to the baby's father or to someone else (Graefe & Lichter, 2002). Usually she becomes disenchanted with life, goes on welfare, and then projects this negative attitude on her children.

The teenage father's life is also affected. He may have guilt feelings about getting the girl pregnant and may resent being forced into an unwanted ("shotgun") wedding.   The teenage father is also not likely to reach his educational goal (Thornberry, Smith & Howard, 1997).

Parental Influences on Healthy Sexual Attitudes

There are many things that parents can do to influence a normal and healthy development of sexual attitudes and behavior while raising their children.

- **Encourage free communication. Teenagers who feel that they can approach their parents without fear of criticism or blame are more likely to have a healthier attitude toward sex and to postpone sexual intercourse as well as to use safety precautions when they decide to have sex. Almost one-third of American teenagers have never talked to** their parents about sex and close to one-half are nervous or afraid to bring it up. Almost two-thirds have never discussed birth control with their parents. Parents need to communicate all aspects about sex (birth control, how to say "No," and male versus female attitudes toward sex), not just abstinence.

- Encourage children to learn about sex. Many parents believe that if their children are exposed to sexual information, such as that provided by school sex education programs, the children are more likely to engage in sex. Ample evidence shows that the opposite is true (Jemmott, Jemmott & Fong, 1998).

- Acknowledge children's sexuality. All too often, parents want to gloss over their children's strong sexual drives by admonishing the child to simply "Say no!" It would be better if the parents acknowledged the child's sexual drive and point out the consequences of irresponsible sex.

If a child is sexually active, parents need to acknowledge such behavior. If a 15-year-old girl comes home at five o'clock in the morning with her skirt on backward and wearing some man's sweater, parents should not look the other way and say, "Did you have a nice time at the movies?" (Sorenson, 1973, p. 61). Rather, they should say something like, "I hope you used birth control. If not, I would be glad to talk to you about it." In such instances, reference to a birth control clinic—especially in poor, urban areas where teenagers' access to health care is limited—appears to be especially effective.[5] Research indicates that the most effective way to prevent adolescent pregnancy is knowledge and distribution of contraceptives (Franklin & Corcoran, 2000). Issues of responsibility also need to be raised ("What do you plan to do if you get pregnant?"). Children who are sexually active should be asked if they feel manipulated or pressured, and given support in making good choices.

Use of Piaget's Formal-Operational Reasoning to Deal with Children's Sexuality

Since the teenager's reasoning about sexuality is often immature, some authorities suggest encouraging teens to use Piaget's formal operations. Formal operations enable the adolescent to *envision alternatives* (using birth control, refusing, or delaying sexual intercourse), to *evaluate alternatives* ("If I have my baby adopted, then I may feel guilty; if I keep the baby, then I'll have to support it"), and to engage in *perspective-taking* which is the need to understand the partner's viewpoint (males need to know why birth control is important for the female partner, girls need to know that the male's request for intercourse without protection is not an affirmation of love). Piaget also suggests that formal operators are better able to estimate the odds of an event occurring. Those who are not able to do so, often confuse chance with probability[6] and are usually surprised when a pregnancy occurs because they had sex "only a few times" (Gordon, 1990).

---

5. Some states have proposed a birth control implant to prevent pregnancy.
6. Chance is something that happens without apparent cause and is unpredictable. Probability is the proportion of times that the outcome would occur if an experiment (such as flipping a coin to determine how many times a head comes up) were repeated indefinitely.

Helping the Teenage Mother

The teenage mother needs help. This assistance should begin before the baby is born. The pregnant teenager needs proper nutrition and good prenatal (and postnatal) care since girls with inadequate prenatal care are more likely to have problems with pregnancy or delivery (Robertson, 1981). One of the urgent needs in this country is comprehensive maternity care services for all pregnant women, regardless of their age, marital status (single, married, separated, or divorced), or ability to pay.

The teenage mother needs counseling to persuade her to stay in school (Solomon & Liefeld, 1998). If she drops out of school, she should enroll in a remedial education program as soon as possible. Teenage mothers who manage to complete their education are more able to control future pregnancies and to find work. They have a better chance of reaching the same income level as their nonpregnant classmates and entering into a stable marriage. In addition, schools often teach parenting skills.

The teenage mother needs psychological counseling to deal with her emotions. Young mothers are often confused, anxious, and afraid. The teenage mother needs to learn how to cope with the emotional responsibility of raising a child and what to expect from a newborn. Often, the teenage mother has unrealistic expectations of her baby. At the same time she needs counseling to complete her own cognitive, social, and emotional development which were interrupted by the pregnancy (Lowenthal & Lowenthal, 1997). Whenever possible, teenage mothers should continue to reside in their parents' homes. The parents can provide emotional support (assuring their daughter that she is still attractive, that she is able to take care of a child, and that she can still realize her dreams) and help the daughter with child care responsibilities, particularly if the baby is at risk due to complications such as low birth weight (Pope, 1993).

Finally, the teenage mother needs to take sex education classes. Such classes are likely to teach her how to avoid future unwanted pregnancies, since she is not likely to change her sexual behavior (Corcoran, Miller, & Bultman, 1997).

JUVENILE DELINQUENCY

Although adult crime has decreased considerably in the United States during the last decade, the statistics are much more pessimistic for juveniles. For instance, in 2007, violent juvenile crime arrests were about 50 percent above the crime level arrests for juveniles of a decade earlier. About one-half of all major crimes—murder, rape, armed robbery—in the United States are committed by children under 18 years of age (Langman, 2009; Kauffman, 1997). Arrests for *juvenile delinquency*—illegal acts committed by children under 18 years of age—are highest among adolescents between 15 and 16 years of age. Legal infractions which constitute juvenile delinquency range from littering to murder (Farrington, 2004).

Juvenile delinquency: Illegal acts committed by children under 18 years of age.

The ratio of boys to girls appearing in juvenile court is four to one. Boys are usually arrested for stealing and mischief, girls for running away from home and for sex offenses. Increasingly, girls are involved in more serious crimes. Furthermore, 16 out of every 100 juveniles that are arrested for a crime, commit a total of four or more crimes—ranging from theft to murder—before the age of 18. More than a half million youths are members of gangs (Howell, 1998).

A problem of increasing concern in American high schools is violence and fear of violence. Fear of violence is three times as common among African-Americans and Hispanic youth as among European-American youth (MMWR, July 30, 2004). A major cause of the fear is children bringing weapons to school. In every high school in America, two or three students bring a weapon (gun, knife or club) to school (Eccles, 2004). One California study has found that seven times as many 12- to 17-year-old boys as girls had their own guns (Sorenson & Vittes, 2004).

Causes of Juvenile Delinquency

Ever since 1946, when television broadcasting began in the United States, there has been a fear of a link between watching violence on TV and crime. This link has been confirmed by a variety of studies (Anderson & Dill, 2000). Concern over the influence of violence on television has resulted in the development of a "V-Chip" for new television sets in the United States which can block the depiction of violence.

Research has consistently linked physical punishment (spanking) to juvenile delinquency. One study (Pettit, 2004) has found that the use of patient parenting at age 5 and the use of conversation rather than physical punishment decreases the likelihood of delinquency 10 years later.

Many other factors have been attributed as causes of juvenile delinquency in addition to depiction of violence on TV. There is a correlation between low IQ and delinquency. There is an eight-point difference in IQ between juvenile delinquents and nondelinquents. Proponents of this view believe that the lower IQ makes it difficult for children to distinguish between right and wrong. However, it is unlikely that this difference in IQs is a significant factor.

There are personality differences between juvenile delinquents and children who do not get into trouble with the law. Some children with poor social skills become aggressive because it is the only way that they know how to communicate with others. These children are rejected by their peers which leads them to be more frustrated and more antisocial. Many juvenile delinquents come from single-parent families with little or no parental involvement (Sampson, 2000). Those who become delinquents are more likely to be impulsive, destructive, suspicious, hostile, and defiant. Some of them may have an inherited predisposition to commit crime. There is also a link between the parents' knowledge of the whereabouts and activities of their adolescents and the children's delinquent behavior. The greater the parental knowledge, the less likelihood there is of delinquent behavior.

Progression toward delinquency. Often there is a predictive progression toward juvenile delinquency (Walker *et al.*, 1998). The first stage in a child turning to crime is usually an unsatisfactory home life. The homes of delinquent children often lack warmth and the discipline might consist of harsh punishment such as spanking with a belt or stick. There is very little control over the children, and the parents often have difficulty keeping track of their children's whereabouts and activities. Often the discipline is highly inconsistent, there is little positive parental involvement with the children, and the children feel alienated and powerless. The second stage in a child turning to crime is failure in school. The third stage is associating with delinquent peers or older law-breaking teenagers rather than other youths their own age. The fourth stage is joining a gang. Often, juvenile delinquency follows shortly after. Hence, early identification of potential delinquency is very important (Greenwood, 1995).

Potential delinquency can often be identified early by looking for subtle forms of behavior. The future delinquent may bite his or her lips or nails continually. He or she may lower his or her voice, tense his or her muscles, make facial grimaces, or complain of not feeling well.

Advanced signs of potential delinquency are more obvious. The child may lash out verbally at others at the slightest provocation. He or she may threaten teachers or withdraw from others. Another important sign is destruction of property. If a child with this profile joins a gang whose members have committed several crimes, he or she is almost certainly headed for more trouble.

During recent years there has been an increasing urgency to create a criminal imprint or profile of children involved in school shootings. Many symptoms have been identified. Often, children involved in school shootings are loners. They are often bullied physically or psychologically (teased, ridiculed, or rejected). Often, children involved in school shootings have talked about harming others and have developed a plan to harm others. Usually, they have access to firearms and a prior history of violence (Yablonsky, 2000).

Treating the Juvenile Delinquent

One of the tasks in dealing with juvenile delinquents is to identify those children who are likely to become career criminals. This identification can sometimes be done as early as preschool.

Children who become career criminals are often antisocial in preschool and elementary school. They often start fights with their peers and are disrespectful to their teachers. They may challenge authority figures such as the school principal and call their teachers derogatory names. Often they are the class bully. At home, they are either punished severely or neglected completely. They are usually the first in their class to use drugs and to have sex. Often, they are less involved in school activities and are more involved with older, law-breaking youths (Farrington, 2004).

Most people would say that these deviant youth or "criminals" should be placed in a penal institution such as a juvenile hall or reform school. Placing children in penal institutions with the idea of punishing them makes the children more bitter and more likely to continue a life of crime. Numerous studies show that placing a juvenile delinquent in a residential penal institution usually aggravates the delinquency problem. Residential incarceration in a penal institution may backfire for several reasons. First, placing an adolescent in an atmosphere of toughness and defiance often results in increased antisocial behavior which may become habitual. Second, an adolescent may turn to more serious crime as a result of being placed in a juvenile detention facility if he makes friends with other (particularly older) deviant youth (Dishion *et al.*, 2002).

Most children in trouble with the law needprompt psychotherapy, the sooner, the better (Compas, 2004). The psychotherapeutic approach to solving juvenile delinquency was pioneered by psychoanalyst August Aichhorn (1878-1949) of Austria in the early part of the 20th century. In his book, *Wayward Youth*, Aichhorn subscribed to the philosophy that happy, well-adjusted children seldom, if ever, knowingly commit illegal acts. According to this view, certain identifiable factors cause children to commit crimes. Many youth feel disconnected from the mainstream of society. Psychologically, they do not have the ego strength to cope with adjustments necessary to deal with rejection, a broken family, feelings of insecurity, and worthlessness. When these factors are removed, the children's behavior usually changes. Let's look at the Lyman-Wiltwyck Schools study as an example of this remedial approach.

In this study (McCord & Sanchez, 1982), the records of juvenile inmates who spent time in one of two different institutions (Lyman and Wiltwyck) were compared over a 25-year period following initial release. One of the schools was the Lyman School in Massachusetts, a prison for teenagers. No effort was made to offer psychological treatment. Punitive discipline was employed, including a disciplinary cottage where inmates were required to be absolutely silent. There was some vocational training.

The Wiltwyck School in New York, a reform school, used a different approach. The facility was unwalled and the staff conducted individual and group therapy sessions. The inmates had considerable autonomy, including self-government.

Both institutions had inmates with similar demographic backgrounds. Both had inmates who were severely disturbed and had committed violent crimes. The Lyman School had mostly Caucasian boys, the inmates of the Wiltwyck School were predominantly from minority groups.

Recidivism: Repeat of criminal offenses.

A 25-year follow-up study of both schools showed some striking differences. While there was a 9 percent *recidivism* rate (repeat of criminal offenses) among inmates from the Wiltwyck School five years after initial release, there was a 67 percent recidivism rate among those released from the Lyman School.

Justice officials are now paying particular attention to the state of Massachusetts, which has been using a social-problems approach rather than the law-enforcement model involving punitive measures. The state of Massachusetts deals with juvenile delinquents on the premise that they require less incarceration, not more, and that they should be in smaller facilities (15 beds per facility). Only 55 of every 100,000 children in Massachusetts is in custody (compared with 450 per 100,000 in California). Also, only 15 percent of delinquents are held in secure, locked facilities in Massachusetts (compared with almost 100 percent in California).

In the Massachusetts model, education, skills, and behavioral development are emphasized, with a teacher-student (inmate) ratio of one to four in juvenile facilities. Those children who have committed a crime, but have not been placed in a juvenile facility, are given intensive supervision at home or placed in a variety of small, community-based programs.

The result of these rehabilitative programs for juvenile delinquents in Massachusetts has been very encouraging. Only 23 percent of those committed to the state's youth services in Massachusetts are incarcerated as repeat offenders, contrasted with over 60 percent in California. On the monetary side, the cost of the Massachusetts program is only about one-half the national average.

Another form of treatment which has met with some success with serious young offenders is Bronfenbrenner's ecological model of development (Bronfenbrenner & Morris, 1998). This treatment model attempts to change systems and processes such as parental discipline, familial emotional reactions, and peer associations. This ecological model is sensitive to individual and sociocultural differences among juvenile offenders. The treatment model uses principles of family therapy (a form of psychotherapy in which all family members participate) and behavior therapy (a form of treatment that is based on direct observation of actual behavior).

SUMMARY

G. Stanley Hall viewed the storm and stress of adolescence as inevitable. Margaret Mead disagreed with Hall, claiming that much of the turbulence is the result of cultural pressures.

According to Sigmund Freud, the genital stage signifies mature adult sexuality. During this stage, teenagers must resolve their renewed sexual striving toward a parent of the opposite gender.

Anna Freud saw adolescence as a period of considerable conflict; an adolescence devoid of turmoil might indicate a resistance to growing up. To cope with conflicts, a teenager engages in intellectualization and ascetism.

Erik Erikson sees adolescence as a period when there is a striving to attain an ego identity. A mature ego identity involves a knowledge of how one is similar to and different from other people.

James Marcia purports that an identity cannot be formed unless there is a crisis and a commitment. He identified four identity statuses: Identity achievement, foreclosure, diffusion, and moratorium.

Adolescents are often caught in a tug of war between their parents and their peers. Contrary to popular belief, most children like and need their parents, but they also need their peers and have a strong desire to be more independent.

Peer relationships change when children enter adolescence. Usually, girls are more intimate with their peers than boys.

Adolescent sexuality is often studied through surveys which are usually biased. They are useful, however, in indicating that sexual attitudes and behaviors are more liberal than they were in the past. There is also a decline in the double standard of sexual behavior for males and females. A majority of teenagers have had sex before they reach the age of 18.

The rate of teenage pregnancy in the United States is among the highest in the world. These early pregnancies have negative consequences for the girl, her baby, the father, and the young mother's family. It is important that the teenage mother stay in school and receive counseling.

A persistent problem is juvenile delinquency. One way to combat juvenile crime is to give teenagers help, rather than punishment.

IMPORTANT TERMS

Ascetism

Bias

Chronosystem, Bronfenbrenner's

Clique

Commitment

Crowd

Demographic bias

Double standard

Ego identity

Exploration

Genital stage

Identity achievement

Identity crisis

Identity diffusion

Identity foreclosure

Identity moratorium

Identity status, Marcia's

Intellectualization

Juvenile delinquency

Masturbation

Moratorium

"New sexual morality," The

Ontogeny recapitulates phylogeny, G. Stanley Hall's

Peer pressure

Personal fable

Petting

Reaction formation

Recidivism

Respondents

Role confusion

Sample bias

Storm and stress, G. Stanley Hall's

Virtue of fidelity

GLOSSARY OF CHILD DEVELOPMENT TERMS

A

Abstraction. Ideas or situations not immediately apparent to the senses.

Accommodation. In Piagetian theory, adjustment of a schema (model) to make it fit better with the world of reality. A process that restructures the child's existing schemes so that new information is understood better.

Acne (vulgaris). An inflammatory skin condition common in adolescence.

Acquired Immune Deficiency Syndrome (AIDS). A serious disease, believed to be always fatal, usually transmitted either through sexual contact or through exposure to infected blood (often by sharing needles with a narcotics addict); a disease that gradually weakens the immune system and disables the victim.

ACT Assessment Program. A college admissions test that includes a Student Profile Section, the ACT Interest Inventory, and high school grades.

Acuity. That aspect of visual perception having to do with the sharpness of images; the ability to distinguish details.

Adaptation. Piaget's idea of a child adjusting to its environment through the processes of assimilation and accommodation.

Adaptive skills. Abilities such as social skills typically required to function in the everyday world.

Adolescence. A developmental transition period between late childhood and adulthood, around ages 12 to 18. Adolescence begins with the physical changes of puberty.

Adolescent. Young man or woman, not fully grown, between the ages of about 12 and 18.

Adolescent egocentrism. A common feeling among adolescents that they have all the answers and that they are special and unique.

Adolescent growth spurt. A period of time, that precedes sexual maturity, when there is a sharp increase in height and weight. This increase starts roughly two years earlier for girls than for boys and lasts two to three years.

Adolescent idealism. A young person's thinking about the way things should be instead of confining his or her thinking to the way things are.

Adoption. A legal term for the act of creating a lawful relationship between an adult and a child that did not exist naturally.

Age of majority. A legal term to describe when an individual reaches adulthood (usually age 18), and acquires both the rights and responsibilities of adulthood.

Age-stages. Unique periods that occur during particular times in a child's life.

Agemates. Children of approximately the same age.

Aggression. Any response made with the intention of harming another person. Aggression also includes all acts in which harm was intended but not done, for example, a boy throwing something at another child but missing him.

AIDS. (See Acquired Immune Deficiency Syndrome).

Ainsworth's Strange Situation. A study of a baby's reaction to a series of eight episodes to determine the quality of a child's attachment to its caregiver.

Alcoholism. A psychological and physiological dependence on alcohol in which the person has no control over the drinking or behavior when drinking; a chronic, progressive, and potentially fatal disease.

Allele. A member of an alternate form of a gene pair that is located at a specific point on a homologous (partner) chromosome. It controls one of two or more alternative inherited traits.

Alpha Fetoprotein Test. A blood test to detect the possibility of a defective formation of the spinal cord or brain of a fetus due to secretion of the chemical alpha fetoprotein by the liver into the amniotic fluid.

Altruism. A type of prosocial behavior in which a person voluntarily aids or benefits another without expecting any type of external reward.

Ambivalent attachment. An insecure form of behavior in which the baby shows both approach and avoidant behaviors.

Amniocentesis. A medical procedure performed during pregnancy, consisting of the withdrawal of amniotic fluid through a needle inserted in the mother's abdomen to determine the presence of chromosomal abnormality in the fetus.

Amphetamines. A class of drugs acting as central nervous system stimulants.

Anaclitic depression. Rene Spitz's term for a syndrome developed by most children reared in an orphanage due to lack of social stimulation.

Anal-explosive personality. According to Freud, difficulty controlling one's anger and aggressive feelings.

Anal-retentive personality versus anal-explosive. According to Freud, a person who is obsessively precise and compulsive versus one who is anger-prone and aggressive.

Anal stage. In Freudian theory, the second psychosexual stage of infancy (at the age of 1 to 3 years), during which children receive pleasure through anal stimulation. Toilet training is critical during this period.

Androgynous gender role identity. One who perceives him or herself as possessing both traditional masculine and feminine characteristics.

Androgens. Male sex hormones produced by the testes present in each gender, but in different amounts.

Androgenized human females. Females with masculinized external sex organs resembling those of a male.

Androgynous. Having some characteristics typical of males and other characteristics typical of females.

Animism. The belief, held by preoperational children, that inanimate objects are alive, and therefore have emotions or intentions.

Anorexia nervosa. A serious eating disorder, seen most commonly in young women, marked by self-starvation.

Anoxia. A medical term for the physical effects on a baby who is completely deprived of oxygen in the brain; reduced oxygen content.

Antisocial behavior. Bullying or being cruel to others, being disobedient at school or at home, having trouble getting along with others, not feeling sorry after misbehaving, lying, and cheating.

Apgar scale. A standard medical assessment of a newborn that uses such criteria as appearance, pulse, and grimace; evaluation of a newborn's physical condition.

Apnea. To be without breath; an interruption in breathing.

Aptitude test. A test that rates a person's potential for learning skills required by various occupations.

Artificial insemination by a doner (AID). The introduction of sperm nonsexually into a woman's body for the purpose of causing pregnancy.

Artificialism. The belief that environmental events like snow and rain are human inventions.

Ascetism. In Anna Freud's terminology, a defense mechanism commonly used by adolescents in which there is self-denial to avoid the possible loss of control over one's impulses.

Assimilation. In Jean Piaget's terminology, the process of taking in new information and interpreting it in such a manner that it conforms to a currently held schema (model) of the world.

Associative learning ability. Arthur Jensen's view of one type of intelligence which measures the ability to learn through lower-form tasks such as repetition and rote memory.

Asthma. A lung disease that periodically inflames and narrows air passages, making it difficult to breathe.

Astigmatism. A visual defect marked by distorted vision due to unevenness of the cornea.

Attachment. The establishment in later infancy of a tie between a baby and another person (usually the mother) that binds them together and lasts for a considerable period of time.

Attention-deficit hyperactivity disorder (ADHD). A syndrome characterized by inattention, pervasive impulsivity, distractibility, and great activity at inopportune times and places. ADHD emerges before the child is 7 years of age.

Atypical child. A child below or above the average in traits such as intelligence, health, motivation, and depression.

Auscultation. The process of listening for sounds in some of the body cavities, especially the chest and abdomen, to detect or judge some abnormal condition.

Authoritarian parents. Diana Baumrind's term for a parenting style that emphasizes strict enforcement of rules. Parents view obedience as a virtue; children are expected to mind without argument. Parents feel it is necessary to control their children.

Authoritative parents. Diana Baumrind's term for a parenting style that uses firm enforcement of rules, but allows verbal give-and-take between parents and child. There is respect for the child's individuality with a desire to instill social values; the child is encouraged to be independent. Parents are nurturing and loving and consider children's needs.

Autism. A severe disorder of childhood involving mutism, sensory blocking, and unawareness of others.

Autonomous morality. Piaget's second stage of moral development in which individuals view rules as flexible, socially agreed upon principles that can be changed when it is deemed necessary to do so.

Autonomy. Independence; the ability of the child to self-regulate or determine his or her own behavior. According to Erik Erikson, autonomy is fostered from birth to 3 years as the child is offered guided opportunities for free choice.

Autonomy versus shame and doubt. In Erik Erikson's theory, the second critical period for the formation of traits such as independence and self-assertion; it takes place when the child is a toddler. Failure to resolve this crisis satisfactorily leads to self-doubt and shame (rage turned against the self).

Autosomal inheritance. An inherited trait that is determined by genes on any chromosome other than the sex (X or Y) chromosomes.

Autosome. Any chromosome that is not a sex (X or Y) chromosome.

Average child. A composite of all children within the typical range for their gender, at whatever age of development is being discussed.

Aversive conditioning. Pairing punishment with an undesirable response such as bedwetting with the hope that the pain associated with punishment will prevent recurrence of the undesirable response.

Avoidant attachment. A type of insecure relationship between a baby and its primary caregiver in which the child does not cry when left alone and is just as likely to be comforted by a stranger as by its primary caregiver and it avoids contact upon the caregiver's return.

B

Babbling. Speech-like sounds made by an infant which consist of vowel-consonant combinations such as "mama" and "dada."

Barbiturates. Addictive drugs that depress activity of the central nervous system, resulting in a lessening of brain activity, making the patient dull and less active.

Basic trust versus mistrust. In Erikson's theory, the critical alternative of psychosocial development, in which infants develop a sense of how reliable people are. Basic trust is developed if babies feel that their parents can be relied upon.

Bayley Scales of Infant Development (Second Edition) (BSID-II). A test that is frequently used to measure infants' intelligence, but designed to evaluate the developmental abilities of children from 1 month to $3\frac{1}{2}$ years of age. The current version has three components: a mental scale, a motor scale, and an infant behavior profile.

Behavior modification. (See behavior therapy).

Behavior therapy. Practical procedures for changing behavior by combining reinforcement, modeling, and manipulation of situational cues.

Behavioral genetics. A quantitative study of how genetic and environmental factors combine (interact) to produce individual differences in human behavior and psychological traits.

Behavioral state. A periodic variation in an infant's cycle of wakefulness, activity, and sleep.

Behaviorism. A learning theory school of psychology that concerns itself with observable behavior, rather than thoughts and feelings. Hence, observable behaviors and events (environment) are studied (rather than hereditary factors) to determine their effect on behavior.

Bidirectionality of self-esteem. An interactive process in which adults affect a child's behavior and self-evaluation, but the child's characteristics influence the behavior and thinking of adults.

Biographical method. A systematic and lengthy study about a subject's behavior.

Biological systems (bioecological) theory. Bronfenbrenner's view of the child as developing within a complex system of relationships that are affected by multiple levels of the surrounding environment.

Biological theory. A model of development that views all organisms as having a basic set of material characteristics such as survival, metabolism, and regulation.

Birthing room in a hospital. A combination of labor, delivery, and recovery room.

Blastocyst. The zygote a few days after fertilization, when the tiny inner mass of cells forms a hollow, fluid ball and implants itself into the wall of the uterus approximately two weeks after conception.

Blended (reconstituted) family. A family created from a combination of stepchildren, stepparents, and stepsiblings.

Body image. A child's interpretation of the reactions of others to his or her body.

Bonding. The process by which a mother becomes attached to her baby during the period immediately following birth, which some believe is a physical bond that affects the strength of the child's later relationships.

Braille. A system of reading and writing that enables the blind to see by touching raised dots that represent numerals and letters of the alphabet.

Brazelton Neonatal Behavioral Assessment Scale. A measure of a newborn's neurological condition. The Brazelton Scale includes tests of the newborn's reflexes, motor capacities, muscle tone, and capacity for responding to objects and people.

Breech position. The delivery of a baby feet or buttocks first due to misalignment of the fetus in the uterus.

Brown versus Board of Education of Topeka, Kansas. A 1954 U.S. Supreme Court decision that ruled that segregated schools are inherently unequal.

Bulimia nervosa. An eating disorder in which a person typically eats huge quantities of food then purges him- or herself with induced vomiting, large doses of laxatives, fasting, or excessive exercise.

C

Caffeine. A natural drug with stimulant properties found in coffee and tea.

Calcification. Deposit of lime salts in the tissues and bones.

Calorie. The energy-producing value in food when oxidized (combined with oxygen) by the body.

Carcinogen. Any cancer-producing substance, for instance, tobacco.

Cardinal numbers. Numbers used in counting and denote numerical size such as 1, 2, 3.

Carolina Abecedarian Project, The. An intensive, highly qualified program designed to test whether quality intervention can prevent mental retardation and improve academic performance for children from impoverished families.

Case study. An intensive investigation of the behavior of a single person, family, or group over a period of time.

Castration anxiety. In Freudian theory, part of the Oedipus complex, in which the boy fears castration by the father, leading to repression of sexual feelings for the mother and identification with the father.

Categorization. Grouping items into categories that represent shared abstract qualities, for example, "bread, milk, and sugar" are all "food".

Catharsis. The psychoanalytic belief that aggressive impulses can be discharged by engaging in actual or symbolic acts of aggression that do not affect another person.

Causality. An awareness that one's actions can be the cause of an effect.

Centration. Piaget's term for the child's ability to consider only a limited aspect of a situation when making conclusions; it is characteristic of the preoperational stage.

Cephalocaudal principle. Literally, "head-to-tail". Refers to the principle that growth begins at the top and works its way down; the upper parts of the body develop before the lower parts.

Cerebral cortex. The covering layer of the cerebrum, the two connected hemispheres of the brain.

Cerebral lateralization (dominance). The process by which one side of the brain takes control of certain mental functions, such as speech and emotions.

Cerebral palsy. A nerve and muscle disorder that involves a lack of muscular coordination, shaking, and unclear speech.

Certified nurse-midwife. A person who is a nurse and has special training in childbirth management.

Cesarean delivery. The removal of the fetus through a surgical incision of the abdominal and uterine walls.

Child abuse. Physical or sexual assault, neglect, or psychological maltreatment of a child by a parent or another caregiver.

Child-centered kindergarten. Education that involves all of a student's needs and considers the child's physical, cognitive, and social development as well as the individual's interests and learning styles.

Child clinical nutrition. The recovery of children from illness through proper diet.

Child development. The scientific study devoted to understanding the physical, cognitive, and psychosocial aspects of human growth and change from conception through adolescence.

Child dietetics. The practical application of nutritional science to children.

Child life specialist. A person who addresses the psychosocial needs of a child.

Child public health nutrition. Nutritional care of children, especially high-risk children.

Childhood depression. A mood disorder characterized by such symptoms as a prolonged feeling of boredom, no initiative, worthlessness, hopelessness, and inability to sleep at night or to have fun, weight change, and thoughts of death or suicide.

Chlamydia. The most common sexually transmitted disease; caused by a parasite.

Chorionic Villus Sampling (CVS). A new method for testing a fetus for birth defects. This procedure can be performed earlier in pregnancy than amniocentesis and provides quicker results.

Chromosome. A rod-shaped particle found in every living cell; it carries genes. Every normal human being has 46 chromosomes in the body cells; 23 in human germ cells (ova and sperm).

Chronic illness. An ailment which shows little change and lasts for a long time and require special healthcare.

Chronological age. The number of years that a person has lived.

Chronosystem. In ecological systems theory, proposed by Urie Bronfenbrenner, temporal changes in children's environments, which produce new conditions that affect development. The changes can be imposed externally or from within the organism. Children can make the changes as they get older.

Chunking. The grouping of information into meaningful units for easier handling by short-term memory.

Classical conditioning. A reflexive procedure in which an organism is exposed to a neutral stimulus (for example, a bell) that is repeatedly paired with a natural stimulus (for example, food); eventually the organism responds to the neutral stimulus, such as a bell, as it would to the natural stimulus.

Classification. Jean Piaget's term for the tendency to group objects into categories or classes on the basis of particular sets of characteristics.

Clinical method. A technique popularized by Jean Piaget in which observations are combined with questions tailored to the individual (and hence differ from child to child).

Clique. A small exclusive group of people.

Cloning. The reproduction of a genetic copy of an individual.

Cocaine. A crystalline drug used as a central nervous system stimulant and local anesthetic.

Code-based approach to reading. Teaching reading by presenting the basic skills that underlie reading such as the sounds of the letters and how the letters and sounds combine to form words.

Codominance. The inheritance of a trait by heterozygous genes that are equally strong and expressive.

Cognition. Knowing. The use of language, thought, reason, problem solving, imagination, and mental activity through which human beings acquire and process knowledge.

Cognitive-behavioral therapy. A newer form of psychotherapy that combines the techniques of cognitive therapy with those of behavior therapy.

Cognitive development. Changes in the individual's mental powers and qualities that permit understanding.

Cognitive-developmental theory. Piaget's theory of cognitive development which stresses the underlying processes of human thought and states that children actively construct their understanding of the world. Piaget claims that children go through four stages of development.

Cognitive learning ability. According to Arthur Jensen, a higher form of learning involving abstract reasoning and problem solving.

Cognitive-sociocultural theory. Vygotsky's approach that emphasizes how cognitive development proceeds as a result of social interactions between members of a culture. Vygotsky believed that children actively construct their knowledge.

Cohort. A group of persons of approximately the same age who have had similar major life experiences, such as cultural training, economic conditions, and education.

Cohort effect. Factors unique to individuals of approximately the same age that sometimes present a problem in cross-sectional research.

Colic. A sudden abdominal discomfort and distended stomach.

Color blindness. An inherited defect of vision resulting in the inability to distinguish between certain colors, most often between red and green.

Commitment. According to Marcia, the extent of personal investment in an occupation, a set of religious values, or a political position.

Compensatory preschool education program. A program that attempts to make up for early disadvantages of some children. An example of such a program is Project Head Start.

Communal custody. A model for separating child sex offenders by placing them in special communities where they can lead near-normal lives.

Componential intelligence. One dimension of Sternberg's triarchic theory of intelligence, typically included in conventional intelligence tests. Sternberg's term for the analytic aspect of intelligence.

Compulsion. Repetitive, stereotyped act not normally indulged in that is performed to relieve fear.

Conception. The penetration of the egg cell from the female by one sperm cell from the male, resulting in a zygote (baby); also called fertilization.

Conceptual learning ability. According to Arthur Jensen, a component of intelligence that involves manipulation, elaboration, and transformation of intelligence mentally.

Concordance rate. The percentage of cases in which a particular attribute is present in both members of a pair if it is present in one member.

Concrete-operational stage. The third of Piaget's four stages of cognitive development; it begins at about age 7 and ends at about age 11. A key characteristic is the development of logical thinking about concrete materials, but *not* about hypothetical or abstract events or experiences.

Conditioned fear. Fear that can be evoked by a previously neutral stimulus as a result of that stimulus having been paired with a stimulus that produces fear naturally.

Conductive hearing problem. Hearing impairment caused by damage to the middle ear, usually by an excess of ear wax.

Conscience. In Freudian theory, the superego, or internalized sense of right and wrong that usually controls one's conduct and produces emotional discomfort when violated.

Conscious. Awareness of our thoughts, feelings, and beliefs that reside in the mind.

Conservation. Piaget's term for the child's ability to realize that some aspects of an object or a substance remain unchanged no matter how its form may be altered; amount remains the same if nothing is added or taken away.

Contact comfort. Harry Harlow's term for a pleasant and reassuring feeling infants derive from touching or clinging to something soft and warm, usually the mother.

Contextual intelligence. A third dimension of Sternberg's triarchic theory of intelligence that assesses a person's ability to manipulate the environment for his or her needs. Sternberg's term for the practical aspect of intelligence.

Contextual theory of child development. A view of the child as developing within a complex system of relationships, some near and others more distant.

Control group. In an experiment contrasting two groups, the group that is *not* given treatment.

Conventional morality. In Lawrence Kohlberg's theory of moral development, the second level, in which a child's morality is rule-based because of his or her desire to please other people and to conform to social rules. The standards of authority figures are internalized.

Cooing. Prelinguistic speech without meaning, consisting mostly of repeated vowel sounds.

Coregulation. A transitional period during middle childhood in the control of behavior when the parents and children share disciplinary powers; parents exercise general supervisory control but the children regulate themselves from one moment to the next.

Correlational study. A study that determines the direction and extent of a relationship between certain events or variables, but *not the cause*.

Counterconditioning. A set of classical conditioning techniques for substituting new and opposite responses for either an unwanted response such as fear of spiders or for forbidden behavior such as child abuse.

Crisis. According to Erikson, a turning point in an individual's development that is resolved in either a positive or a negative direction. Normal personality development is the result of a resolution of crises in a positive direction. Marcia's term for a period of identity development during which the adolescent is choosing from among meaningful alternatives.

Critical period. A specific span of time when a psychological or physical event will have its greatest impact. This impact is sometimes irreversible.

Crossing over. An exchange of genetic material between a pair of chromosomes during the first phase of meiosis.

Cross-sectional design. A method of study in which groups of subjects of different ages are observed and tested once on a particular variable.

Cross-sequential (mixed) design. A method of study combining the cross-sectional and longitudinal patterns in which individuals are tested more than once and the results are analyzed.

Crowd. The joining of several cliques into a larger group of peers.

Cultural bias. The perception that scores on intelligence tests draw on the background of the culture in which they are administered, and do not reflect the test taker's true intelligence.

Culture. The traditions, activities, beliefs, behaviors, values, and language shared by members of a society.

Culture-fair intelligence test. An intelligence test on which language differences and other cultural effects are negligible.

Cytomegalovirus (CMG). A viral parasitic infection that is contracted from raw or undercooked meat or by physical contact with the feces of cats who have the disease. A form of herpes that is a major cause of birth defects in the unborn baby. In newborns, CMV may take the form of jaundice and low birth weight.

D

Day care. A program designed to provide part-time care for children (generally those of preschool age) outside the home, usually because the mother works.

Decentration. Piaget's term for the child's ability to focus on more than one aspect of an object or situation. Piaget demonstrated this concept through his conservation experiments.

Decibel. The unit of intensity by which sound is measured.

Deductive reasoning. A form of reasoning that proceeds from the general (premise) to the particular (conclusion). Drawing an appropriate logical inference from two or more pieces of information.

Defense mechanism. An unconscious mental device for coping with anxiety-arousing situations and for resolving conflicts that protect the individual from psychic pain and allows him or her to control primitive impulses.

Deferred imitation. In Piagetian theory, the child's ability to imitate an action that the child observed earlier.

Delinquency. Illegal acts committed by juveniles (individuals under 16 or 18 years of age, according to the definition of adulthood in a particular state and the nature of the act).

Demographic bias. An incorrect representation of vital and social statistics such as births, deaths, and marriages of larger populations.

Denver II Test (formerly called the Denver Developmental Screening Test). A test designed to measure young children's development in four areas from birth to 6 years of age, and includes separate assessments of gross and fine motor skills, language, and personal-social ability.

Deoxyribonucleic acid. (See DNA).

Dependent variable. In an experiment, a phenomenon whose measured changes are attributed to, or correspond to, concomitant changes in the independent variable. The response that is measured.

Deprivation dwarfism. A growth disorder after 2 years of age in which the child receives adequate nutrition, but fails to grow normally because of emotional abuse and neglect. A similar condition in babies under 2 years of age is called failure-to-thrive syndrome.

Depth perception. The ability to see three-dimensional space and to estimate distances.

Detoxification. Removal of toxic properties of a poisonous substance such as alcohol.

Development. The overall process that results in babies becoming children, children into adolescents, and adolescents into adults. This process includes physical, cognitive, and psychosocial changes.

Developmental norms. Standards developed by Arnold Gesell to identify the stages at which different forms of behavior emerge.

Developmental psychology. A multidisciplinary science of human development concerned with identifying and explaining the changes that individuals undergo across the life span; the scientific study of the course of human development from conception until death.

Developmental quotient. A comparison of a person's developmental age (score on motor, language, adaptive behavior) with the person's chronological age.

Diabetes mellitus. A disorder in which the body cannot make use of sugars and starches in a normal way either due to lack of insulin or the inability of the body to use insulin properly.

Diabetic retinopathy. Visual impairment caused by diabetes.

Diagnosis. Identifying a disease from its symptoms.

Diagnostic and Statistical Manual of Mental Disorders-Fourth Edition (DSM-IV). A manual for classifying psychological disorders, containing descriptions of the major categories of disorders, as well as a description of specific criteria that must be met before a diagnosis can be assigned.

Dialectic reasoning. An ability beyond Piaget's formal reasoning where the individual deals with problems that have not yet been delineated.

Diethylstilbestrol (DES). A synthetic female hormone, used in the past to prevent miscarriage, now known to produce abnormalities of the reproductive system in young women whose mothers received the drug during their pregnancies.

Difficult baby. Chess's and Smart's term for a child who has an irritable temperament, irregular biological rhythms, resists changes, and is slow to adapt.

Diffusion status. Marcia's term for the identity status of people who have not made any commitments to goals or beliefs. Often they "drop out," thus avoiding the responsibility of growing up.

Dilation. The first stage of labor accompanied by uterine contractions.

Disability. A handicap such as mental retardation, dyslexia, and attention-deficit hyperactivity disorder.

Discipline. Techniques of socialization intended to teach children how to regulate their behavior.

Discrimination. Behaving unfairly toward a particular group of people.

Dishabituation. Renewed interest in a stimulus that has changed in some way since the last time it was seen or experienced.

Disorganized/disoriented attachment. A form of attachment in which a child is confused and exhibits contradictory behavior.

Divorce mediation. A series of meetings between divorcing adults and a trained professional to reduce family conflict during the period surrounding divorce proceedings.

Dizygotic (fraternal) twins. Offspring that result from 2 ova fertilized by two different sperm at approximately the same time. Such twins share about half their genes, like any other siblings.

DNA (Deoxyribonucleic Acid). The chemical of which genes are made; it is formed in the nuclei of the cells and structured to provide genetic information.

Dominant inheritance. Gregor Mendel's law that states that when an offspring receives genes for contradictory traits (e.g., for blue eyes and for brown eyes), only the dominant trait (in this case brown eyes) will be expressed.

Double standard. A more flexible sexual standard for males than females.

Doula. A caregiver who provides emotional and physical support during childbirth and often helps with the care of the baby after it is born.

Down syndrome (Trisomy 21). A disorder usually caused by an extra 21st chromosome; major features include mental retardation and heart defect. Other characteristics include unusual physical features and a shortened life expectancy.

DSM-IV. (See Diagnostic and Statistical Manual of Mental Disorders (DSM-IV).

Dynamic testing. Intelligence testing in which a subject learns something in the presence of an examiner.

Dyslexia. A category of learning disabilities involving sever impairment in the ability to read unfamiliar words and to spell correctly often caused by brain damage; a person with this difficulty may have normal intelligence and normal physical and emotional health.

E

Early childhood. The preschool years from age 3 to 6.

Easy baby. Chess's and Smart's term for a child who has a generally happy temperament, has regular biological rhythms, is flexible, and accepts new experiences willingly.

Ecology of child development. The environmental effects on a child's development within a larger family context than normally studied. The ecology includes brothers and sisters, grandparents, babysitters, pets, school teachers, the parents' jobs, and the safety of the neighborhood.

Ecstasy (MDMA). A drug affecting the body like a stimulant.

Education for All Handicapped Children Act of 1975. (Public Law 94-142). This act requires that all children with disabilities be given a free appropriate public education. It has been renamed Individuals with Disabilities Act (IDEA) with some additional provisions for children with disabilities.

Ego. In Freud's tripartite division of personality, that part, corresponding to the perceived self, whose function it is to establish realistic interactions between the raw impulses of the id and the reality of the child's environment. Language and thought are both ego functions.

Egocentrism. Piaget's term for a child's ability to see things only from his or her point of view; a cognitive state that is characteristic of Piaget's preoperational period.

Ego ideal. The superego's idealized sense of how a person should behave.

Ego identity. According to Erik Erikson, a mature conception of oneself.

Elaboration. Going beyond the information given to remember something better.

Electra complex. In Freudian theory, a universal conflict in females during the phallic stage of psychosexual development, at about age 4 or 5, when the girl becomes attracted to her father and is hostile toward the mother. The conflict is resolved when the girl represses her sexual feelings for the father and identifies with her mother. The male counterpart is the Oedipus complex.

Electronic fetal monitoring. Mechanical devices (machines) for monitoring oxygenation and fetal heartbeat during labor and delivery; often used in high-risk deliveries.

Emancipation. For children, the legal equivalent of divorcing their parents.

Embryonic disc. A period in pregnancy from 2 to 8 weeks when the unborn baby's structures develop rapidly; mass of cells projecting into the cavity of the blastocyst and eventually becoming a baby.

Embryonic stage. The second stage of pregnancy (2 to 8 weeks) marked by differentiation of body parts and systems and ending with the appearance of bones.

Embryonic stem cells. Cells formed during the first few days of pregnancy and may hold the key to the treatment of diseases and injuries such as Alzheimer's, Parkinson's, diabetes, and spinal cord injuries.

Empathy. The ability to participate in the feelings of another person and to respond accordingly; appreciation of another's feelings.

Encoding. The conversion of information into a form that can be stored in memory.

Engrossment. The parent-child bond; the parent's strong attraction to his or her son or daughter at birth, as well as enormous pride and elation over the new offspring.

Enuresis. Bed-wetting; inability to control urination after about age 5 years.

Environment. All the factors surrounding and influencing an organism that are not inherited. The prenatal environment includes amniotic fluid, the uterus, the food and drugs that the mother ingests, and the mother's emotional condition.

Epigenetic principle. Erikson's term for the idea that each part of personality has a particular time in the life span in which to develop, if it is going to develop at all.

Equilibration. In Piagetian theory, a form of mental self-regulation that the child uses to bring coherence and stability to his or her view of the world when confronted by inconsistencies in experience. An aspect of adaptation designed to make sense out of the world. A reorganization of schemes from a state of disequilibrium to one of equilibrium involving a periodic restructuring of schemes into new structures.

Equilibrium. Adapting successfully to one's environment.

Estrogens. Major female sex hormones that stimulate the development of secondary sex characteristics and maintain the primary reproductive function of the female body. Also present in males but in smaller amounts than in females.

Ethology. The branch of biology that studies the behavior of animals in their natural habitats; the findings are sometimes applied to the study of children.

Experiential intelligence. A second aspect of Sternberg's intelligence model that measures creativity, ability to make unusual connections between things, and to relate to experience in insightful ways.

Experimental group. Subjects that undergo some change in their environment and are then measured to determine the effect of the change.

Experimental method. A procedure of collecting and treating data on a specific subject. A key feature is manipulation of the independent variable to determine its effect on the dependent variable.

Expiatory punishment. Punitive measures unrelated to the misbehavior.

Exploration. According to James Marcia, the choices of a relatively stable set of roles and ideals that an adolescent must go through to form an identity.

Expulsion. The birth of a baby.

Extrinsic reinforcement. External rewards such as praise, grades, or money.

F

Fagan Test of Infant Intelligence. A nonverbal, individual intelligence test used with infants, that is useful for screening infants at risk for mental retardation.

Failure-to-thrive syndrome Failure of infants to develop normally despite adequate diet and absence of medical problems; usually the cause is parental emotional abuse and neglect. In children beyond 2 years of age, a similar condition is called deprivation dwarfism.

Fallopian tubes. Tube-like organs about 4 inches (10 cm.) long in the female reproductive system that extend from the uterus to the ovaries; conception normally takes place in one of the fallopian tubes.

Fear of success. Matina Horner's term for the concern of some young women that academic, business, or professional success might lead to undesirable consequences, such as rejection and identification as being nonfeminine.

Feminine gender role identity. One who perceives him or herself as possessing traditional feminine characteristics and few masculine characteristics.

Fertilization. See Conception.

Fetal alcohol syndrome (FAS). A constellation of about 20 known birth defects in children born to mothers who consume alcohol during pregnancy. Symptoms include physical abnormalities such as growth retardation or facial malformation and/or mental disabilities such as hyperactivity.

Fetal anoxia. A condition resulting from an insufficient amount of oxygen in the body tissues.

Fetal stage. The third and final period of prenatal development (8 weeks to birth). There is an increase in detail of body parts and considerable body growth.

Fetoscopy. A medical procedure permitting direct viewing of the fetus in the uterus.

Fixation. Visual direction and focus on a particular stimulus for a period of time. In psychoanalytic theory, the likelihood that experiences during an earlier psychosexual stage affect behavior later in life; a preoccupation with the issues and tasks of an earlier stage of psychosexual development; failure to move from one psychosexual stage to another as expected.

Fontanels. Small openings in the infant's skull bones that are covered with a soft tissue. At birth, there are six fontanels in a baby's skull.

Formal operations. In Piaget's theory, the fourth and final stage of cognitive development, ages 11 and beyond, in which the child achieves the ability to use abstract, symbolic and flexible thinking, to think logically about hypothetical statements and ideas, and to solve problems systematically.

Foundling home. An institution for abandoned children.

Fragile X syndrome. A chromosomal sex-linked disorder that is the most common cause of inherited mental retardation and also causes anomalies such as protruding ears and a prominent jaw.

Fraternal twins. (See Dizygotic twins).

Free-standing birth center. A facility for delivering babies that is a compromise between home birth and hospital birth.

G

Gamete. A mature sex cell; the female ovum and the male sperm cell involved in reproduction. Contains only half the genetic material present in other body cells.

"Gateway" drugs. "Softer" drugs such as marijuana that some people claim are forerunners of "harder" drugs like cocaine.

Gender. The perception of maleness or femaleness related to one's membership in a given society. Gender is often confused with sex, which typically refers to sexual anatomy and sexual behavior.

Gender constancy. An awareness of the stability of one's maleness or femaleness—"Once a boy (or girl), always a boy (or girl)."

Gender difference. A significant difference between girl's and boy's scores on one or many studies on some measurement.

Gender identity. An awareness of one's maleness or femaleness and that of others.

Gender role. "Appropriate" behavior for one's gender; these behaviors and attitudes are usually set by culture.

Gender-role stereotype. Too rigid application of gender roles. For example, in our society which has clear gender-role stereotypes, *all* men are thought of as being competent, skillful, assertive, aggressive, and able to get things done. *All* women are thought of as being warm, thoughtful, tactful, gentle, quiet, and lacking in logic.

Gender typing. The process by which children acquire the values, motives, and behaviors considered appropriate for their gender in their particular culture.

Gender-schema theory. A theory proposed by Sandra Bem that children socialize themselves to their gender roles by developing the concept of what it means to be male or female.

Gene therapy. A procedure involving replacing a defective gene with a normal one.

Genes. Areas on chromosomes that carry hereditary instructions for various traits. The biological units of heredity that are composed of DNA (deoxyribonucleic acid).

Genetic. Traits determined by genes as opposed to environment.

Genetic code. The biochemical messages created by genetic factors that guide the emergence of individual characteristics and tempo of growth and apparently the many predispositions for behavior.

Genetic counseling. The determination and provision of information to prospective parents about their genetic makeup, particularly with regard to the possibility of genetic defects in their children.

Genetics. A branch of biology that deals with heredity and variations in plants and animals, and the process by which hereditary characteristics are transmitted from parents to offspring.

Genital herpes. An incurable, highly contagious lifelong sexually transmitted disease.

Genital stage. In Freudian theory, the fifth and final stage of psychosexual development (ages 11 to about 14), in which the focus returns to the sex organs and to the opposite gender as a source of sexual satisfaction, and usually leads to normal adult sexual development.

Genome. The full set of genes in each cell of an organism, with the exception of the sperm and egg cells.

Genotype. In genetics, the hereditary constitution or genetic makeup of an individual that is inherited from his or her parents, which may differ from physical appearance (phenotype).

Gentle birth. A technique, also known as the Leboyer method, designed to make the first moments of a baby's life as tranquil and pleasant as possible; delivery rooms are dimly lit and quiet.

Germinal stage. First two weeks of prenatal development; principle features include rapid cell division, increasing complexity, and attachment of conceptus to the wall of the uterus at the end of this stage.

Gestalt. The tendency to integrate pieces of information into meaningful wholes.

Gestational diabetes mellitus. A form of diabetes that is diagnosed for the first time during pregnancy.

Glia. Cells that surround neurons and hold them in place. One of two major types of cells that make up the nervous system.

Goals 2000: Educate America Act. Voluntary national standards of achievement in core subjects.

Gonorrhea. A bacterial disease, usually obtained through sexual intercourse with an infected person, that can damage the baby before birth.

Goodness-of-fit model. Thomas' and Chess' model that states that an effective match between child-rearing practices and the child's temperament leads to favorable development and psychological adjustment.

Grammar. The structure of language made up of morphology and syntax.

Group test. A test administered to a group of individuals simultaneously.

Growth hormone. A biochemical substance secreted by the pituitary gland that controls growth.

H

Habituation. A process by which an organism gets used to and ceases to respond to a particular stimulus through repeated exposures to a form of learning.

Handedness. An individual's hand preference.

Head Start. (See Project Head Start)

Hemophilia. A recessive genetic blood disorder in which the blood fails to clot normally. Because the gene is sex-linked, hemophilia occurs only in men; women carry the abnormal gene without developing the disease.

Heredity. The transmission of mental and physical qualities from parents to their children through information carried in the chromosomes, resulting in resemblances and differences among organisms. The basic unit of heredity is a gene, which occupies a specific location on chromosomes in the nucleus of every cell in the body.

Heritability. A trait that stems entirely from genes, such as eye color; a mathematical index of the extent to which *differences* in a population—known as variance—such as height are the result of genetic factors.

Herpes Simplex, Type 2 (Genital herpes). A disease with two stages (active and latent) that causes damage to the baby if it is delivered during the active phase of the illness. The latent stage can last forever or for as short a span as 2 weeks.

Heteronomous morality. Piaget's first stage of moral development in which children view normal rules as permanent features that are handed down by authorities and cannot be changed.

Heterosexual. An attraction to, and sexual interest in, members of the opposite gender.

Heterozygous. Pertaining to a gene pair in which each allele contains different chemical instructions for the composition of a particular trait; having two different alleles at a corresponding site on a pair of chromosomes.

Hierarchical relationships. Sets of categories that fit into categories of a different order.

Holophrase. A one-word sentence; babies become capable of uttering it at about 1 year of age.

Homosexuality. A sexual attraction between persons of the same gender. Gay is the accepted term for homosexual; a gay female is called a lesbian.

Homozygous. Pertaining to a gene pair in which the alleles are identical and contain the same chemical instructions for the composition of a particular trait.

Horizontal decalage. Piaget's term for a child's uneven performance at any given stage of development when the same logical problem is presented in different forms (e.g., the child does not learn all forms of conservation at the same time).

Hormones. Biochemical substances found in the blood in very small amounts, and that influence the functioning of various body systems.

Hostile aggression. Behavior aimed at gaining social control over another person.

Human Genome Project. An international research project to find the precise location of genes for specific traits by mapping human chromosomes. This effort was virtually completed in 2001, although analysis continues.

Human genome. The complete set of 25,000 or so genetic instructions found in most human cells that make people the individuals they are. The entire inventory of nucleotide base pairs that comprise the genes and chromosomes of humans.

Human growth hormone. A biochemical substance secreted by the pituitary gland.

Hydrocephalus. A condition involving increased accumulation of cerebrospinal fluid in the brain.

Hyperopia. A visual defect causing farsightedness.

Hypothetico-deductive reasoning. The ability to consider all possible solutions to a problem that might exist, then systematically evaluate them one by one, to eliminate the false and arrive at the true.

I

Id. In Freud's tripartite division of personality, the reservoir of all instinctual, unconscious drives. If unchecked, the id seeks immediate gratification of primitive needs such as being held, fed, or changed.

IDEA. (See Individuals with Disabilities Education Act).

Identical twins. Twins who develop from the same egg, which splits in half, and have identical genetic makeups. It is not always apparent at birth if twins are identical or fraternal, although tests can be conducted to be certain.

Identification. The Freudian notion of the process by which an individual acquires the characteristics of a model, such as a parent or teacher; an important personality development of early childhood. In psychoanalytic theory, the child incorporates traits of the same-gender parent.

Identity. An individual's sense of uniqueness and belonging.

Identity achievement. Marcia's term for the identity status of individuals who have been through the identity crisis and have made some important decisions regarding their goals in life and what they believe in.

Identity constancy. The ability to realize that things stay the same despite changes in appearance, size or form; the ability to realize who a person is, who he should be, and what he is likely to become.

Identity crisis. Erik Erikson's term for a sudden disintegration of the framework of values and goals that a person relies on to give meaning and purpose to daily life.

Identity diffusion. James Marcia's term for the identity status of individuals who do not have a firm commitment to values and goals and are not trying to reach them.

Identity foreclosure. In Marcia's theory, the attempt to resolve an identity crisis prematurely, such as by marrying early.

Identity moratorium. Marcia's term for an identity crisis which is in progress and the search for commitments continues.

Identity status. Marcia's term for the level of identity formation an adolescent has attained.

Identity versus identity diffusion (formerly called role confusion). In Erikson's theory, the fifth crisis of psychosocial development, when adolescents must discover who they are, where they are going, and where they belong. Failure to resolve this crisis results in an underdeveloped ego and role confusion.

Idiopathic. A disease without a recognizable cause, or of spontaneous origin.

Imagery. The ability to associate words with the objects or ideas to which they refer.

Imaginary audience. A kind of egocentrism common in adolescence; the suspicion that "others are always looking at me, they are making fun of me."

Immanent justice. Piaget's stage of moral development, up to about 6½ years, that involves the child's notion that you *always* get punished for behaving inappropriately. Conversely, the child believes that if he or she got punished, he or she must have done something bad.

Imprinting. A learning mechanism specific to some social species that occurs early in the life of the individual within a limited critical period that results in the formation of attachment or bond to a kindred member of the species.

Incest. Any sexual interaction between individuals who are so closely related that marriage between them would be illegal.

Inclusion. Educating a child with special education needs full time in the general school program.

Incomplete dominance. A condition in which a stronger (dominant) allele fails to mask all the effects of a weaker (recessive) allele.

Independent variable. A characteristic that is manipulated by researchers in an experiment by randomly assigning subjects to treatment conditions.

Independent variable. In an experiment, the variable under the experimenter's control that is correlated with changes observed in the dependent variable.

Individual ability test. A test that is administered to one individual at a time.

Individual differences. The principle that each child is unique.

Individuals with Disabilities Education Act (IDEA). IDEA is the new name for P.L. 94-142. It spells out broad mandates for services to all children with disabilities and includes appropriate education and the least restrictive environment possible.

Induction. A form of reasoning by which we conclude that what is true of certain individuals is true of a class; what is true at certain times will be true in similar circumstances at all times.

Inductive reasoning. A form of logical reasoning that proceeds from the particular to the general.

Industry versus inferiority. In Erikson's theory, the fourth stage of psychosocial development, occurring in middle childhood, in which a successful resolution of conflicts results in the child becoming a competent and productive member of society. Failure to learn the skills of one's culture results in feelings of inferiority.

Infancy. The period from birth until about 18 months to 2 years of age.

Infant-directed speech (Motherese). The type of speech adults generally use with young children.

Infantile autism. A rare, severe disorder of childhood involving mutism and unawareness of others. Autistic children do not cuddle and do not like to be picked up.

Infertility. Inability to conceive after trying to have a baby for 1 year.

Informal family day care. An arrangement in which a group children is cared for in the home of a nonrelative.

Information-processing approach. Study of intellectual development based on the belief that human cognitive activities are similar in many ways to the workings of a computer; mental capacities and processes that support thought. A strategy for explaining cognitive development based on an analogy with the workings of a digital computer.

Informed consent. An important consideration in studying subjects that requires the subject or his or her guardian or parent to understand the nature of the study and that the study is undertaken voluntarily.

In loco parentis. A legal term empowering school administrators and teachers to act as substitute parents.

In vitro fertilization. Conception in a glass dish. An egg is removed surgically from a woman's body and combined in a dish with a man's sperm. The fertilized egg (embryo) is then injected into the uterus of the woman from whom the egg was removed, or into a different woman.

Initiative versus guilt. In Erikson's theory, the third stage of psychosocial development, occurring early in childhood, in which children try out new things and begin to evaluate the consequences of their behavior. Failure to develop initiative results in excessive guilt.

Insecure attachment. A description of the quality of a toddler's relationship with another person, usually a parent. The insecurely attached child will be distant to the mother after being separated in the *Strange Situation* according to Mary Ainsworth.

Instinct. An inborn pattern of behavior that is consistent throughout a species.

Instrumental aggression. Aggressive behavior designed to achieve some goal.

Intellectual development. Changes in one's mental abilities, activities, or organization over a period of time (see *cognitive development*).

Intellectualization. In Anna Freud's terminology, a psychological defense mechanism marked by participation in abstract intellectual discussions to avoid unpleasant, anxiety-producing feelings.

Intellectual power. A type of thinking measured by traditional intelligence tests.

Intelligence. A broad term that refers to an individual's abilities in diverse cognitive areas such as language, mathematics, and problem solving. The ability to score well on standardized intelligence tests.

Intelligence quotient (IQ). A score on a test of intelligence originally calculated by dividing a person's mental age by his or her chronological age and multiplying by 100, (IQ = MA/CA x 100); now an index of a person's intelligence, relative to the statistical average for his or her age group.

Intelligence test. An evaluation instrument that measures an individual's abilities in diverse areas such as language, mathematics, and problem solving.

Interview method. A procedure in which people are asked to state their attitudes, opinions, or histories.

Intimacy. Erikson's term to mean commitment to a particular person; the development of a close, trusting and enduring relationship with another person.

Intrinsic reinforcement. Behavior that is internally interesting and challenging for its own sake, rather than for some external consequence, such as a reward.

IQ. See Intelligence quotient.

Irreversibility. Piaget's term for the inability to think about how you arrived at the state in which you find yourself. The inability to "go backward" or reverse a particular sequence of events or thoughts.

Isolette. A completely enclosed Plexiglas crib, used for low-birth-weight babies, that permits full temperature regulation; formerly called an incubator.

J

Joint physical custody. Shared parenting arrangement in which both the father and the mother take equal responsibility for the care and upbringing of their child.

Juvenile delinquency. Illegal acts committed by children.

K

Karotype. A chart containing pictures of an individual's chromosomes.

Kaufman Assessment Battery for Children (K-ABC-II) Test. An intelligence test designed to be nondiscriminatory toward minority and learning-disabled children.

Kibbutzim. Collective farms in Israel, where children are raised communally from an early age.

Kindergarten. A school or class that serves as a transition between nursery school and the first grade.

Klinefelter syndrome. A disorder resulting in genetically male individuals who have an extra X chromosome. It is not usually diagnosed until after puberty.

Kwashiorkor. A nutritional disorder due to little, if any, protein.

L

Labor. The process of uterine muscular contractions during childbirth that literally push the baby out of the uterus.

LAD. See Language Acquisition Device.

Lamaze method of childbirth. A method of "natural childbirth" developed by Lamaze. The pregnant woman and her husband are trained in breathing and relaxation techniques that are used during labor and delivery.

Language Acquisition Device (LAD). According to Noam Chomsky, an inborn mental mechanism containing universal linguistic information that enables the child to build a system of language rules; a subcategory of nativism.

Lanugo. Fine, soft prenatal hair that sometimes is present on the newborn baby; it disappears shortly after birth.

Latency stage. In Freudian theory, the fourth stage of psychosexual development (ages 6 to 11) when there is relative sexual quiescence. During this period, libidinal energies are quiet.

Learning. Relatively permanent changes in behavior that occur as a result of experience or practice.

Learning disability. A disorder that a child is presumed to have if his or her school performance is considerably below expected performance according to his or her IQ. It is assumed that the poor performance is not due to emotional or motivational difficulties or to serious motor or sensory disabilities.

Learning theory. A theory that most behavior is the result of experience.

Libido. The driving force or sexual energy in Freud's psychoanalytic theory of personality development that provides the motivation for human thought and behavior.

Locomotion. The ability to move from one place to another.

Logical reasoning. The thinking that consists of two types: deductive and inductive.

Linguistic speech. The ability to communicate through meaningful utterances; besides words and grammar, it includes pronunciation, intonation, and rhythm to convey meaning.

Long-term memory. "Permanent" memory from past experience. Information that is stored must first have been in short-term memory, but not all information in short-term memory enters long-term memory (compare with *Short-term memory*).

Longitudinal design. A method of study involving prolonged, repeated observations of the same group of subjects at different times. The subjects may be studied for a decade or even for an entire lifetime.

Low-birth-weight baby. A baby whose weight is less than 2,500 grams (5½ pounds).

Lymphatic system. A group of tissues through which an alkaline fluid, called lymph, passes and provides immunity against infections.

M

Mainstreaming. The practice of placing handicapped and nonhandicapped children in the same classroom as much as possible.

Malocclusion. Improper alignment of the teeth with the jaws closed.

Marasmus. Extreme wasting of a young child as a result of insufficient protein and too few calories.

Masculine gender role identity. One who perceives him or herself as possessing traditional masculine characteristics and few feminine characteristics.

Mass education. Universal schooling of all children with public support.

Masturbation. Sexual self-stimulation; erotic stimulation of the genitals other than by sexual intercourse, usually resulting in orgasm.

Maturation. In developmental psychology, the physical, neural, physiological, biochemical, and behavioral changes that take place in an organism over time as a result of the organism's genetic timetable.

McCarthy Scales for Children's Abilities. An intelligence test designed for minority, preschool, and kindergarten children.

Mechanistic (learning) theory. An explanation of development that uses concepts and theoretical models derived from physics and chemistry. The individual is viewed as a machine; children's development is assumed to be a variation of material processes.

Meconium. Fetal waste matter. Feces that an infant passes in the first few days following birth, consisting mainly of bile, cell debris, and white cells ingested in the uterus.

Meiosis. A type of cell division in which the gametes receive one of each pair of chromosomes; a cell-reduction process by which sex cells are produced.

Memory store. A set of neurons that serves to retain information over time.

Menarche. A girl's first menstruation at puberty.

Metacognition. An awareness of one's thinking process. For example, you know you think differently in math than in English.

Mental age (MA). Assessment of a child's intellectual abilities and knowledge by administering an intelligence test and then matching the child's score with the average age of children who have scored similarly. For instance, an intellectually average 5-year-old would have a mental age of 5; a very bright boy of 5 might have a mental age of 7 or 8 years.

Mental representation. The ability to use symbols—images, words, numbers, pictures, or other configurations -- to represent real objects; the ability to conceive of objects mentally, rather than by physical manipulation. An ability that allows one to represent aspects of the world inside one's head.

Mental retardation. Mental subnormality generally defined as an IQ below approximately 70 to 75 and impairment in adaptive ability that originated before age 18.

Mental strategy. A deliberate, controllable cognitive operation that is performed for the purpose of attaining a particular goal.

Metabolism. The complex chemical reactions that provide and use energy in an organism.

Metacognition. An awareness of one's thinking process (i.e., "thinking about thinking"). You know that you think differently in math than in English.

Metalinguistic awareness. The ability to understand hidden meanings in one's own language, and to achieve comprehension when information is fuzzy or incomplete.

Metamemory. An individual's knowledge about his or her own memory processes. For example, the child's realization that a list of digits is more difficult to retain than a meaningful passage, is a form of metamemory.

Method of approximations. A variation of operant conditioning in which the researcher encourages the subject to produce the desired responses by reinforcing those behaviors that approximate the correct performance.

Micropreemie. A very premature baby weighing less than 2 pounds and is about 12 inches long.

Microsystem. In Bronfenbrenner's sociological systems theory, the activities and interaction patterns in the child's immediate surroundings.

Middle childhood. The elementary school period from the age of about 6 to 12 years.

Midwife. A person specially trained to help women in childbirth.

Minamata disease. A severe form of mercury poisoning, named after Minamita Bay, Japan, where fish containing mercury caused the disease.

Mitosis. The process by which the nucleus duplicates itself during cell division, leading to multiplication of somatic (nonreproductive) cells. The duplication results in identical cells.

Modeling. Albert Bandura's term for what a model (parent, teacher, or sibling) does. According to Bandura, such behavior is often copied by a child.

Monozygotic (identical) twins. Two individuals with identical genes who began life as a single zygote that divided.

Montessori School. A type of preschool with a child-centered curriculum that focuses on motor, sensory, and language education.

Montessori's sensitive period. Montessori's term for a period in early childhood when children are able to acquire a great deal of knowledge and skill with very little effort.

Mood disorder. Psychological dysfunction involving depression and/or mania (abnormal elation).

Moral absolutism. Piaget's belief that young children assume that identical rules prevail universally and are unchangeable because they have been created by an authority.

Morality. The standard that one uses to judge the correctness of an action or behavior.

Moral realism. Piaget's term for children's confusion between moral and physical laws.

Moratorium. Marcia's term for the status of people who are currently involved in an identity crisis about their goals and beliefs, but alternatives are being explored in an effort to find values and goals to guide the individuals' lives. During the moratorium, no action is taken on making personal commitments.

Morpheme. The smallest unit with meaning in a language.

Morphology. A word that has the smallest unit of sound with meaning.

Morula. A cluster of cells that develop from a single-cell zygote.

Motherese. (Now called **Infant-directed speech**.) A description of the language mothers—and often other adults and older children—tend to use when speaking with an infant or toddler; the sentences are short, simple, slow, high-pitched, and repetitive.

Multiculturalism. An emphasis that validates all cultures, rather than just one.

Mutation. A sudden permanent change in a gene, in the arrangement of a gene, or in the amount of chromosomal material that may then be transmitted to future generations.

Myelin. A fatty substance that coats the neurons in the nervous system and helps speed up the transmission of neural signals. Myelin also plays an important part in the maturation of the brain.

Myelination.The coating of neural fibers with myelin (a white fatty substance) that results in an increase in the speed of neural impulses.

Myopia. A visual defect (nearsightedness) making it difficult to focus distant objects. Myopia occurs when light entering the eye is focused in front of the retina instead of on it because the lens of the eye is too curved or the eyeball is too long.

N

Nativism. The theory that human development, such as speech, arises from an inborn capacity. The belief that innate features of the brain guide the process of language acquisition, as well as other perceptual skills in a predictable manner.

Natural childbirth. See Prepared (natural) childbirth. A relatively painless way of delivering a baby with minimal use of drugs.

Naturalistic study. A study of subjects in their natural surroundings, such as children playing uninterruptedly on the school grounds.

Nature-versus-nurture controversy. A debate over the relative importance of heredity and environment in influencing human development.

Nature. The processes that guide an organism to unfold structures and traits according to its genetic code; biological and genetic factors that influence development.

Negative reinforcement. A process that increases the probability of a response if it is followed by the removal, delay, or decrease in intensity of an unpleasant or aversive stimulus.

Neglected attachment. A lack of an emotional bond between a confused baby and its depressed mother.

Neoanalyst. A new category of psychoanalysts who focus less on the unconscious and more on conscious choice and self-direction.

Neonatal intensive care unit (NICU). A special room in a hospital for preterm and low-birth-weight babies.

Neonate. The technical term for a newborn infant up to about 4 weeks of age.

Neonatal period. The first four weeks after a baby is born.

Neurons. Specialized cells that receive and transmit information to other cells in the body.

Neuroscience. A multidisciplinary study of the nervous system and its function.

New SAT. A revision of the Scholastic Assessment Test, with increased emphasis on reading, writing, and mathematics.

"New sexual morality, The". A sexual revolution in the 1960s and 1970s that viewed sex as acceptable between consenting, if not committed, adults, and advocated abolishment of the "double standard" for sexual behavior.

New York Longitudinal Study. A study identifying three different types of temperament in newborn children: easy, difficult, and slow-to warm-up.

Niche-picking. The process of deliberately seeking environments compatible with one's genetic makeup.

Night terror. A sleep disorder in which a child suddenly wakes up from his or her sleep in a state of panic. The child may cry out, run, perspire heavily, and become totally disoriented. Usually there is amnesia for the episode.

Nondisjunction. Failure of a pair of chromosomes to separate at meiosis.

Norm. A statistical standard involving averages derived from the results of research of a large, representative sample of a given population. The norm is usually determined through systematic and controlled observation.

Normative information. The average age or grade that different forms of behavior can be expected to emerge in normal children.

Nuclear family. A family structure consisting of a mother, a father, and their biological child or children.

Numerosity. The idea that number refers to specific amounts.

Nurture. A term used to refer to the way a child is reared, including qualities of warmth, loving, caring, and attention to physical needs; a reference to environment in general.

O

Obesity. A condition characterized by an abnormal amount of fat on the body. A deviation of at least 20 percent over "ideal" body weight considering the child's age, build, gender, and height.

Object permanence. In Piaget's theory, a child's understanding that an object continues to exist even when it is not being looked at, touched, or heard. This ability is fully attained by about 2 years of age.

Objectivity. A judgment that is not biased by the investigator's preconceptions.

Observational learning. A process in which an individual learns new responses by observing the behavior of another (a model) rather than through direct experience.

Obsession. Unwanted recurring thoughts, impulses, and images that cause an individual significant anxiety.

Obsessive-compulsive disorder. An anxiety disorder in which there is extreme preoccupation with certain thoughts and repetitive performance of certain behaviors, both of which occur in a ritualistic manner.

Obstetric medication. The use of drugs in childbirth.

Oedipal complex. (See Oedipus complex)

Oedipus (Oedipal) complex: In Freudian theory, a girl's or boy's sexual attraction to a parent of the opposite gender.

One-to-one correspondence. Matching each item in a group with single items from another group.

Ontogenetic theory. A theory proposed by Arnold Gesell that states that the development of a child is genetically prescribed and unfolds according to a blueprint known as maturation.

Ontogeny recapitulates phylogeny. A belief that an individual's development repeats its ancestral evolutionary stages.

Operant conditioning. The modification of behavior as a consequence of rewards or punishments that the behavior produces; a form of learning in which voluntary responses are controlled by their consequences.

Operation. A Piagetian term for logical internalized actions. According to Piaget, operations are not present during the sensorimotor or preoperational stages of development. An operation allows the child to combine, separate, order, reorder, and transform information and objects in his or her mind, an ability that appears at about age 7.

Optimal (sensitive) period. The best time for learning a particular task; the task may be learned later, but with greater difficulty.

Opiates. A class of highly addictive drugs (opium, codeine, morphine, and heroin) that often result in the birth of premature babies who are vulnerable to respiratory infection.

Oral stage. In Freudian theory, the first psychosexual stage of infancy, occurring in the first year of life, during which the child's attention is focused on the mouth.

Ordinal numbers. Numbers that have a particular order such as *first, second, third.*

Organismic theory. Jean Piaget's view of development that holds that organisms control their environment by their thoughts and actions, rather than being passive machines.

Organization. Piaget's term for children constantly rearranging their existing knowledge to produce new and more complex mental structures.

Ossification. The process of mineralization of the bones. The process of replacing cartilage in the bone by mineral deposits, particularly calcium.

Osteoporosis. Loss of bone mass due to calcium deficiency, a condition common in postmenopausal women causing bones to become more fragile and fracture more easily.

Otitis media. A middle ear infection.

Overregularization. An inappropriate extension of the general rules of language to irregular instances, for example, saying "camed" instead of "came."

Ovulation. A process by which the ovum separates from the ovarian wall and is released from the ovary.

Ovum. The unfertilized egg of the female, when fertilized, it develops into a child; the female gamete.

Oxytocin. A pituary hormone that stimulates the uterus to contract, thus inducing childbirth, and stimulates the breasts to produce milk (lactation).

P

Palmar grasp. A common spontaneous reflexive movement in newborns.

Panic disorder. An episode of intense fear or anxiety that occurs suddenly, usually without warning.

Participatory education. A program in which students participate in the real world in activities such as career education, arts and crafts, and government.

Paternal engrossment. A father's attraction to his newborn child, including enormous pride and elation.

Peer group. A group of individuals of one's own age and of equal or similar backgrounds.

Peer pressure. Influence in either a positive or a negative direction by individuals of one's own age group and of equal or similar backgrounds.

Peers. Individuals of approximately the same age and of equal or similar backgrounds who possess unique values and standards of behavior and a social structure of leaders and followers.

Penis envy. In Freudian theory, the unconscious desire in little girls to have a penis.

Permissive parents. In Diana Baumrind's terminology, parents who allow their children to determine their own schedules and activities; few demands are made on the children.

Personal fable. The feeling of a typical adolescent that no one understands his or her unique feelings or problems; a counterpart to the idea of the *imaginary audience*., a sense of uniqueness and indestructibility.

Personality. An individual's unique way of behaving and feeling.

Petting. Erotic caressing, usually below the waist, that does not include sexual intercourse.

Phallic stage. In Freudian theory of personality, the period from about 3 to 6 years of age in which the child receives gratification in the genital area; the period of the Oedipus complex.

Phallocentric bias. A belief that men are superior to women.

Phenotype. Observable characteristics of an individual due to inheritance (compare with *Genotype)*.

Phenylketonuria. An inherited disorder in which babies are born lacking a liver enzyme (phenylalanine hydroxylase) resulting in severe mental retardation, seizures, and psychotic episodes.

Phobia. An irrational, intense anxiety reaction to a specific situation; the reaction is inappropriate to the situation and interferes with normal activities.

Phoneme. Any of the basic sounds in a language.

Physical development. Changes in body, sensory capacity, and motor skills that occur over a period of time.

Physiologic jaundice. A yellowish tinge to a newborn's skin and eyes due to a rise in the pigment bilirubin.

Pincer grasp. The use of the opposing thumb to grasp objects between the thumb and the fingers

Pivot word. A word that can be combined with a variety of other words to produce simple two-word phrases, for example "*My* doggie," and "*My* mommy."

P. L. 94-142 (IDEA). A federal law guaranteeing every disabled child between 3 and 21 years of age a free, appropriate education in the least restrictive environment possible.

Placenta. The disc-shaped organ, also known as the afterbirth, by which the embryo is attached to the wall of the uterus. Nutrients and oxygen pass from the mother to the unborn baby through the placenta. Waste products pass from the fetus to her mother.

Placenta previa. A placenta that is implanted in the lower uterine segment in front of the fetus so that the exit from the womb is partly or completely blocked.

Plasticity. The degree to which a developing structure such as the brain is capable of being molded and modified by experience, regardless of genetic codes at work.

Political correctness. A view that represents all groups in a culture and is mistrustful of tradition.

Polygenic inheritance. An interaction of a number of different genes to produce certain traits. Environment also affects the traits.

Postconventional morality. In Kohlberg's theory of moral development, the third and final level, in which individuals conform to personally accepted and internalized moral principles rather than to the principles of others. Also called *principled moral thought*.

Postmaturity. Delivery of a baby after 42 weeks from the first day of the mother's last menstrual cycle.

Postpartum depression. An emotional disturbance of varying degrees in which the mother feels hopeless, despondent, and has difficulty relating to her newborn baby.

Posttraumatic stress disorder: A disorder in which a very stressful event such as a car accident results in later emotional symptoms such as nightmares.

Poverty. An annual income of $18,850 or less for a family of four according to Federal guidelines for 2004.

Preconscious (foreconscious). According to Freudian (psychoanalytic) theory, part of the mind just beneath the surface of awareness, that can be easily brought to consciousness.

Preconventional morality. In Kohlberg's theory of moral development, the first level of moral reasoning in which children conform to external standards and decisions to avoid punishment and to gain rewards.

Preeclampsia. A maternal infection during pregnancy that affects both the mother and her unborn baby. The mother is advised not to lie on her back because this causes the uterus to press on the blood vessels that supply it.

Prejudice. An unjustified negative, stereotyped attitude toward an individual that is based solely on the individual's membership in a particular group.

Prelinguistic vocalization. A child's attempt at communication by using sounds without words or grammar.

Premature baby. A baby born before the due date and is always of low birth weight. (A premature baby is now called preterm.)

Prenatal. Before birth; the period from the time of conception until the start of labor.

Preoperational stage. In Piaget's theory, the second period of cognitive development, between the ages of 2 and 7, during which children acquire the capacity for representational thought, but *not* for operations or reversal of actions.

Prepared (natural) childbirth. A procedure, used by Fernand Lamaze, in which the mother prepares for childbirth by learning about the physiological processes involved and by learning a series of exercises—as well as surgery and the use of medication, if necessary—that make labor and delivery easier. The father is usually involved.

Presbyopia. Farsightedness; the blurring of near objects.

Preschool. A program designed to provide children with educational experiences before they start formal school.

Preterm (premature) baby. A child born before 37 weeks of gestation, dated from the mother's first day of the last normal menstrual period.

Primary sex characteristics. Characteristics directly related to reproduction, specifically, the male and female sex organs.

Private speech. A form of language common at age 5 when the child talks out loud with no intent of communicating with others.

Problem-finding stage. An ability beyond Piaget's formal thinking that enables an individual to discover problems that have not yet been delineated, to describe these problems, and to raise questions about ill-defined questions.

Progesterone. A hormone that, in females, regulates the menstrual cycle and prepares the uterus for pregnancy and the maintenance of pregnancy.

Prognosis. The likely course of a disease.

Project Head Start. A compensatory preschool education program for children from low-income families begun in 1965.

Propositional thinking. A form of reasoning, characteristic of Piaget's formal operational stage that evaluates the logic of verbal assertions without making reference to concrete, real-world circumstances.

Prosocial behavior. A type of behavior intended to aid or benefit another person, including sharing, helping, and cooperating.

Proteomics. The science of cataloguing and analyzing every protein in the human body.

Proximodistal principle. Literally, near-to-far; the parts of the body near its center, such as spinal cord, develop before its extremities.

Psychoactive substance abuse. A pattern of use of illegal or illicit drugs that have a detrimental effect on a person's health, consciousness, and mood and on social and occupational roles.

Psychoanalytic theory. A view of humanity that focuses on emotional factors and personality development as the central forces in development; Freud's approach to therapy emphasizing free association, dream interpretation, and transference.

Psychodynamic approach. Freud's view that various processes are generally beyond people's awareness (unconscious) and control our thoughts, feelings, and behavior.

Psychosexual development. In Freud's theory, the idea that development takes place in stages (oral, anal, phallic, latency, and genital), each stage being characterized by a zone of pleasurable stimulation and appropriate objects of sexual attachment.

Psychosocial theory. Erikson's theory of development that stresses the strong role that social and environmental forces play in the resolution of each crisis of development.

Puberty. Physical transition from childhood to adulthood, including the ability to reproduce for the first time.

Pubescence. The period of physical changes that leads to reproductive maturity, or puberty.

Public Law 94-142. The Education for all Handicapped Children Act of 1975 that requires that all children with disabilities be given free, appropriate public education. With some changes, this law is now called IDEA, *Individuals with Disabilities Education Act*.

Pupillary reflex. A reaction to the amount of light entering the eye by constricting or expanding the pupil.

Q

Qualitative change. A process of change that is generally gradual and continuous, but sometimes involves "leaps" or stages.

Quantitative change. A fairly straightforward alteration in development that can be measured and reported such as height, weight, or vocabulary.

Quickening. Fetal movements that can be felt by the mother. It usually occurs between the 18th and 20th weeks of pregnancy.

R

Radiation. High-energy particles such as heat, light, sound, and diagnostic X rays that can damage an unborn baby.

Radical behaviorism. A view that behavior can be explained almost exclusively as the result of learning and experience. B. F. Skinner's method of studying acts and events by observing and measuring them directly.

Radical behaviorist. One who takes an extreme position on the importance of environment in shaping the development of a child.

Random sampling. A number of items of any sort drawn from a larger group in such a manner that every individual item has the *same* chance to be chosen as any other.

Rationalization. In Freudian theory, a defense mechanism in which a person may give a "good" reason for unacceptable behavior.

Raven Progressive Matrices Test. A presumably culture-free test of intelligence that relies on the scores of the test-taking ability of the test takers and on their ability to detect, evaluate, and match graphic patterns.

Reaction formation. Replacing an anxiety-producing feeling with the expression of its opposite or a more acceptable form of behavior.

Reaction range. In genetics, a concept that sets the limits on the range of possible outcomes in response to different environments.

Recall. The ability to reproduce something from memory with a minimum of cues; requires both storage and retrieval (compare with *Recognition*).

Recessive trait. A characteristic or trait that is expressed only if an organism is homozygous for the trait (has two alleles carrying it).

Recidivism. Repeat of criminal offenses.

Recognition. A type of memory involving an ability to realize that one has seen or experienced something before (compare with *Recall*).

Reconstituted (blended) family; stepfamily. A family consisting of a biological parent, a stepparent, and one or more children.

Reflex. A primitive, unlearned, and involuntary action that can be elicited by specific forms of stimulation.

Refractive error. The bending of light rays from a straight path after they enter the eye.

Reformers. Individuals who believe that schools should change to become more effective, such as deemphasizing rote memory and other forms of traditional basic learning.

Regression. In Freudian Theory, a defense mechanism in which a person returns to an earlier form of behavior, such as wetting one's underwear instead of using the toilet.

Rehearsal. A strategy for remembering that involves extended repetition of material after it has been presented.

Reinforcement. In operant conditioning, the consequences of a behavior that makes the response either more or less likely to be repeated.

Reliability. The degree of consistency between repeated measurements of individuals with the same measurement device.

Remineralization. A process designed to reduce tooth decay by delivering calcium and phosphate to replace lost minerals.

Replicability. The use of the same procedures in a study as other researchers have used and obtained the same results.

Representation. See mental representation.

Representational thought. The capacity to think about the properties of things while not in direct contact with them. This ability begins to appear at about 1½ years of age.

Repression. In Freudian theory, a defense mechanism of forgetting painful or threatening material by blocking it off in the unconscious and preventing it from reaching consciousness.

Respondents. Individuals answering questions.

Retention. The process of retaining information in memory so that it can be used at a later date.

Retinopathy of prematurity. A disorder of the eye such as leakage of blood into the retina that is often associated with too much oxygen, low birth weight, and preterm birth.

Retrieval. The process of recovering information that is stored so that we can be consciously aware of it.

Reversibility. In Piaget's theory, the notion that something that has been changed can be returned to its original state by undoing (reversing) the process that led to the change.

Rh factor. An inherited protein substance found in the blood of most people; individuals who have this substance are said to be Rh-positive. Rh factor is a system of blood groups that is independent of the ABO system.

Rh factor incompatibility. A problem in newborns, such as anemia and jaundice, caused by interference of a pregnant woman's Rh-negative blood with her baby's Rh-positive blood.

Role. A pattern of behavior that one is expected to exhibit when occupying a particular position within a group.

Role confusion. Erikson's outdated term for the lack of a strong sense of identity, often seen in adolescence, resulting in an inability to answer questions such as: "Who am I?, Where am I going?, and Where do I fit in?"

Rubella (German measles). A usually benign disease that can cause severe birth defects in an unborn baby. A rubella vaccine is given to children aged 12 to 15 months and a booster is given at 5 years of age or older.

S

Sample bias. A distortion of the results of a study because the sample that is studied is not representative of the larger population.

SAT, New. A revision of the Scholastic Assessment Test with more emphasis on writing and math.

Scaffolding. Vygotsky's term for an instructional process in which the teacher continually adjusts the amount and type of support he or she offers as the child continues to develop more sophisticated skills.

Scheme (pl. schemes) or Schema (pl. schemata). In Piagetian theory, an organized pattern of behavior or thought that a child develops in relation to a particular activity, such as that involved in catching or throwing a ball. A generalized idea that captures the important components of a situation or a concept, but not every detail.

Scholastic Assessment Test (SAT). An achievement test designed to determine a person's level of knowledge in a given subject area. A test designed to measure a high school student's ability to do college work. A revised version is the New SAT.

School phobia. An unrealistic fear of school that may be caused by separation anxiety.

Scientific method. A rule for procedure that yields factual data and knowledge about the functional relations of the data; this means of inquiry depends on observations to establish findings, uses further observations to test alternative explanations for the findings, then uses new observers to test the validity of the observations.

Secondary sex characteristics. Anatomical and physiological signs of sexual maturity (such as breast development and growth of pubic hair) that do not involve the sex organs.

Secular growth trend. The tendency over several generations for the rate of some changes in development to occur at a more rapid rate and at an earlier time.

Secure attachment. Mary Ainsworth's term for a relationship in which an infant has come to trust and depend on its caregiver as a base from which to explore.

Self-concept. The sense of self as a separate individual who possesses a unique set of characteristics.

Self-efficacy. The extent to which a person believes he or she can perform behaviors necessary to bring about a desired outcome.

Self-esteem. An evaluation of oneself along a positive or negative dimension; includes feelings of worthlessness, pride, and discouragement.

Self-fulfilling prophecy. The idea that a person's expectations of another person produce the result that was expected. For example, children will do well in school if they are told that they are intelligent.

Self-handicapping strategy. A tendency to protect one's self-esteem due to fear of failure by relying on a crutch such as alcohol.

Self-schema. According to the information-processing approach, a set of "knowledge structures" or cognitive generalizations about the self, derived from past experience, that organize and guide the processing of self-related information and help children decide how to act.

Selman's role-taking in moral dilemmas. Taking another person's perspective in moral conflicts to understand how that person thinks or feels.

Sensitive period. Montessori's term for a period in early childhood when children are able to acquire a great deal of knowledge and skill with very little effort.

Sensorimotor stage. In Piaget's theory, the first of four stages of cognitive development that the child goes through; it takes place during approximately the first 2 years of life. Schemata during this period are developed primarily through the senses and motor activities because the infant is incapable of mental representation.

Sensorineural hearing impairment. A hearing problem caused by damage to the cochlea, the primary organ of hearing.

Sensory memory. The retention, for a brief instant, of information received through the sense organs; there is usually awareness of images and sensations that disappear quickly.

Separation anxiety. Distress, unhappiness and fear experienced and expressed by a child when a person to whom that child is attached goes away; it usually begins in the second half of the first year of life. A term used by John Bowlby for the reaction of young children when they are placed in an institution.

Separation anxiety disorder. A condition involving *excessive* anxiety that lasts for at least 2 weeks when the child is separated from a caregiver to whom he or she is attached. The degree of anxiety is far greater than in separation anxiety.

Seriation. The hierarchy of levels within a classification.

Sex chromosomes. The pair of chromosomes that determine a person's gender. They are of two types: Females have XX chromosomes; males XY.

Sex-linked inheritance. A hereditary process by which certain genes located on sex chromosomes (X and Y) determine gender and are transmitted differently to males than to females. Color blindness is an example.

Sexually transmitted disease. Any of several diseases (syphilis, gonorrhea, and herpes) spread by sexual contact. Also called *venereal disease*.

Shape constancy. The realization that an object's shape remains the same despite changes in the shape of its retinal image.

Shaping. Skinner's term for controlling and gradually changing a response by reinforcing successive approximations to a goal.

Short-term memory. Now generally called working memory, short-term memory retains new information for a period of up to about 30 seconds. The content fades rapidly unless it is stored in long-term memory or is actively preserved through rehearsal (compare with *Long-term memory*).

Sickle-cell trait. A mild form of sickle-cell anemia in which individuals have one dominant allele for normal blood cells and one recessive sickle-cell allele and who show signs of anemia only when they are seriously deprived of oxygen such as when they exercise strenuously or are at extreme altitudes. This disorder is most common among African-Americans.

Sidestream tobacco smoke. Smoke from another person's burning cigarette.

Significate. A term used by Piaget for the actual object or event represented by a signifier.

Signifier. A term used by Piaget for symbols and signs.

Size constancy. The realization that an object's actual size remains the same despite changes in its distance from the viewer and in the size of the object's retinal image.

Sleep apnea. Abnormal breathing and heart rate while asleep.

Sleeper effect. Judith Wallerstein's term for the negative effects of divorce on daughters that occur some time after the family breakup.

Sleepwalking. Walking in one's sleep or moving about aimlessly and not remembering the incident after waking up.

Slow-to-warm-up baby. Thomas's and Chess's term for a child who is withdrawn, makes mild responses, and is hesitant about accepting new experiences.

Small-for-date baby. An infant who weighs less than $5\frac{1}{2}$ pounds or less than 90 percent of all babies of its gestational age; may or may not be preterm (premature).

Small-for-gestational age. A baby who weighs less than 90 percent of babies of the same gestational age.

Social behavior. The ways in which people interact with one another, including negative attitudes such as prejudice, the way they attempt to influence one another, and why they like or dislike one another.

Social cognitive theory. A behavioristic theory of child development that stresses observation, imitation, and modeling; a major proponent is Albert Bandura. The theory holds that gender roles are learned through socialization. This theory is Bandura's expansion of social learning theory.

Social comparison. Judgments of abilities, behavior, appearance, and other characteristics in relation to those of others.

Social-control theory. A belief that an unfavorable family environment causes children to become involved in deviant behavior such as delinquency and drug abuse.

Social referencing. A type of communication in which babies keep a watchful eye on the caregiver to monitor the acceptability of their behavior.

Social speech. A form of speech intended to be understood by someone else (listener).

Socioeconomic status. The grouping of people within a society on the basis of income, occupation, and education.

Sorting out cells. The classification of cells by function.

Sperm. The male reproductive cell that can fertilize an ovum; the male germ cell.

Spontaneous abortion (miscarriage). The natural expulsion of the embryo from the uterus before it can survive outside the womb; death of a fetus before 20 weeks of gestation.

Stage theory. A period of development that is assumed to be qualitatively different from previous or subsequent periods. Stages are assumed to occur in a particular sequence, though their timing can vary.

Standardization. The process of testing a large, representative group of people to determine the standard or average for a specific behavior or trait such as intelligence.

Stanford-Binet Intelligence Scale. A frequently used individual intelligence test that can be given to children age two or over; test assesses verbal, nonverbal, quantitative, and memory items.

Stem cells. A group of cells, some of which are inside the blastocyst, called embryonic stem cells, that can cause the formation of any tissue or organ such as the heart and lungs.

Stepfamily. (See Reconstituted family).

Stephanie's Law. A Kansas law that allows sex offenders to spend an indefinite period of time in prison and in mental institutions.

Stillborn.The delivery of a dead infant after 20 weeks of gestation.

Storage. The retention of information in memory.

Storm and stress. G. Stanley Hall's view that adolescence is normally a time of strong and variable emotions.

Strange Situation. An experimental procedure developed by Mary Ainsworth to determine the attachment between a caregiver and a baby.

Stranger anxiety. A child's wariness of strange people and places; this characteristic occurs when the baby is between 6 and 12 months of age.

Substance abuse. A pattern of pathological use of drugs such as alcohol or cocaine resulting in a disturbance in social relationships or deterioration of occupational functioning. Substance abuse often leads to a dependence commonly known as addiction.

Sudden Infant Death Syndrome (SIDS). An unexplained death of an apparently healthy infant; typically strikes children between 1 month and 1 year of age; also known as *crib death*.

Superego. In Freud's tripartite division of personality, that part, corresponding most nearly to the conscience that controls moral scruples.

Superobesity. A weight at the 95th percentile or above.

Surfactant. A substance that coats the lungs and is necessary for normal breathing. A chemical that enables the lungs to transmit oxygen from the air to the fetal bloodstream and exists in insufficient quantities in preterm babies, resulting in difficulties in breathing.

Surrogate mother. A woman who bears a child conceived by artificial insemination for an infertile couple.

Swaddling. Wrapping a child snugly in a blanket or clothes to prevent free movement.

Symbolic representation (thought). The use of symbols (numbers, pictures and words) to represent real objects.

Symptom. A sign that something may be wrong.

Synaptic pruning. The process of weeding out unnecessary cells.

Syndrome A medical term that refers to a group of symptoms that characterize a physiological or a psychological disorder.

Syntax. Form or structure of a language or the way that language arranges words into meaningful phrases, clauses, and sentences.

Synthetic drugs. Drugs that can be manufactured.

Syphilis. A sexually transmitted infection that is a serious threat to an unborn baby, often resulting in a miscarriage or in a stillbirth.

Systematic desensitization. A form of behavior modification (therapy) where the subject is exposed gradually to a feared object for the purpose of overcoming the fear. The patient is also taught to relax, which is incompatible with the fear response.

T

Tabula rasa. John Locke's description of a child's mind as a blank slate at birth with no preformed dispositions. The blank slate is "filled in" by experience.

Tag question. A declarative (explanatory) statement with a question added to indicate uncertainty or to request confirmation.

Tay-Sachs disease. A disorder for which there is no treatment. Symptoms of the disease include blindness and muscle degeneration. Death occurs by age 5.

Telegraphic speech. A form of verbal communication, first used at about 18 months, that contains only words carrying meaning, omitting many parts of speech.

Temperament. An individual's innately determined style of approaching other people and situations; the physical foundation of personality, including mood and sensitivity, which can be observed during the first months of life.

Teratogen. Any outside agent, such as a disease or a chemical, that is capable of causing a birth defect.

Teratology. The science that deals with hazards from the environment (drugs, alcohol, and radiation) that interfere with normal prenatal development, possibly producing birth defects.

Testicular feminization. Males with external genitalia resembling those of a female.

Test anxiety. Stress that causes difficulty in preparing for an exam, as well as in actually taking the exam.

Testes. The male sex organs, located in the scrotum; the source of sperm and male sex hormones.

Testosterone. A male sex hormone produced by the testes that promotes the growth of male sexual characteristics. Also present in the female, but in a lesser amount.

Theory. A system of concepts that provides a framework for organizing and interpreting observations; the underlying principles of a given phenomenon.

Theory of mind. An individual's thoughts about how mental processes work.

Time sampling. The observation of behavior for a given period of time. There is no manipulation of variables; used to predict future observations.

Title IX. A federal law that prohibits public schools from forcing pregnant or parenting female students to drop out of school.

Toddlerhood. The period of psychosocial development that starts when the child first begins to walk and ends at around 2½ or 3 years.

Toxoplasmosis. A viral parasitic infection that is contracted from raw or undercooked meat or by physical contact with the feces of cats who have the disease.

Tracking (pursuit) ability. Following a moving object visually.

Traditionalists. Individuals who espouse the belief that schools should return to the "basics," such as rote memory.

Trait. A specific characteristic of a person, animal, or plant, that is at least partly genetic, for example, a child's brown eyes.

Transductive reasoning. A form of reasoning from the particular to the particular, without concern for logic or generalizations. For example, "Mother bought an umbrella, so it must be raining." The two events are believed to be connected because they have been experienced together in the past.

Transitional object. A toy or some other object—usually one that is soft and cuddly—that a child uses as a bedtime companion.

Transitivity. A Piagetian logical operation involving a mental arrangement of a set of objects according to some quantitative characteristic such as relations in a serial order.

Triarchic Theory of Intelligence. Robert Sternberg's view that there are three types of intelligence: componential, contextual and experiential or, analytical, creative, and practical, respectively.

Trisomy 21. An extra chromosome in a pair of number 21 chromosomes resulting in Down syndrome.

Turner syndrome. A disorder resulting in a genetically female individual with 45 (only one X) chromosomes.

Type A behavior. A type of personality, which includes traits such as competitiveness, achievement orientation, aggression, impatience, and hostility. In adults, Type A personality is correlated with coronary disease.

Type B behavior. A personality type that is easygoing, relaxed, and not easily aroused to anger.

Type D behavior. A personality type characterized by a general tendency to cope with stress by keeping negative emotions to oneself.

U

Ulnar grasp. The awkward ability for an infant to hold an object between their fingers and their palms

Ultrasound. A medical procedure using high-frequency sound waves to detect the outlines of a fetus and to discover if the baby is progressing normally.

Umbilical cord. A rope-like structure that connects the fetus to the placenta. The cord allows the blood of the fetus to receive oxygen and nutrients.

Unconscious. In psychoanalytic theory, that part of a person's mind that contains impulses and desires not directly known to the person.

Undifferentiated gender role identity. One who perceives him or herself as lacking both traditional masculine and feminine characteristics.

V

Validity. The degree to which a test measures what it is supposed to measure. For example, a valid psychology test measures the student's knowledge of psychology, not of art or music.

Variable. A specific factor or characteristics that can take on a particular value in research. Quality or characteristic that scientists measure or manipulate in an experiment.

Vernix caseosa. A cheesy varnish on a newborn that serves as a protection for the neonate against infection, and drops off shortly after birth.

Viability. The ability of the fetus to survive extrauterinely, reached at about the sixth month of pregnancy.

Vicarious reinforcement. Learning (second-hand) by watching the consequences to others of their behaviors.

Virtue of fidelity. According to Erikson, a sense of belonging to a loved one or to friends and companions.

Visual acuity. The sharpness of the visual image at the retina.

Visual cliff. A device for testing depth perception in human or animal babies by watching their reaction to a simulated drop-off.

W

Wechsler Intelligence Scale for Children (Revised) (WISC-IV). A standard individual intelligence test for school-aged children that includes verbal and nonverbal performance subtests, yields an overall score, and is designed to be administered individually.

Wechsler Preschool and Primary Scale of Intelligence—Revised (WPPSI-R). An intelligence test for children between 3 and 8 years, that is designed to be administered individually, and includes separate verbal and performance subtests.

Whole-language approach to reading. Teaching reading by exposing the readers to complete writing of sentences, stories, poems, and the like instead of concentrating on individual words and sounds.

WISC-IV. See Wechsler Intelligence Scale for Children-Revised.

Working (short-term) memory. An inclusive term for short-term memory systems designed to maintain recently acquired information and information retrieved from long-term memory for about 30 seconds to 4 minutes.

Z

Zone of Proximal Development, Vygotsky's. The area between what a child can do by himself or herself and what the child can achieve with the help of a competent adult or peer.

Zygote. The fertilized egg formed by the union of a sperm cell and an egg cell at the moment of conception.

BIBLIOGRAPHY

AAP (American Academy of Pediatrics). (February, 2005). Breastfeeding and the use of human milk. *Pediatrics*, Vol. 115(2), 496-506.

Abelfotouh, M. A., & Telmesani, A. (1993). A study of some psychosocial characteristics of blind and deaf male students in Abb City, Asir Region, Saudi Arabia. *Public Health,* 107, 261-269.

Abramson, L. (1991). Facial expessivity in failure to thrive and normal infants: Implications for their capacity to engage in the world. *Merrill-Palmer Quarterly,* 37, 159-182.

Addis, A., Moretti, M. E., Ahmed Syed, F., Einarson, T. R., & Koren, G. (2001). Fetal effects of cocaine: An updated meta-analysis. *Reproductive Toxicology*, 15. 341-369.

Adler, S. A., Gerhardstein, P., & Rovee-Collier, C. (April, 1998). Levels-of-Processing Effects in Infant Memory? *Child Development*, 69(2), 280-294.

Agin, D. P. (2010). More than genes: what science can tell us about toxic chemicals, Development, and the risk to our children (Oxford; New York: Oxford University Press).Ainsworth, M. D. S. (1979). Attachment as related to mother-infant interaction. In J. S. Rosenblatt *et al.* (Eds.), *Advances in the Study of Behavior*, Vol. 9. New York: Academic Press.

_____ (1993). Attachment as related to mother-infant interaction. *Advances in Infancy Research,* 8, 1-50.

Ainsworth, M. D. S., Bell, S. M., & Stayton, D. J. (1972). Individual differences in the development of some attachment behaviors. *Merrill-Palmer Quarterly*, 18, 123-143.

Ainsworth, M. D. S., Blehar, M. C., Waters, E., & Wall, S. (1978). Patterns of attachment: A psychological study of the strange situation. *Child Development*, 48, 1208-1216.

Alaimo, K., Olson, C. M., & Frongillo, E. A. (July, 2001). Food insufficiency and American school-aged children's cognitive, academic, and psychosocial development. *Pediatrics*, 108(1), 44-51.

Alan Guttmacher Institute (1981). *Teenage Pregnancy: The Problem that Hasn't Gone Away.* New York: Author.

_____ (1994). *Sex and America's Teenagers.* New York: Author.

_____ (2002). Teen pregnancy: Trends and lessons learned. In *Policy Analysis: Issues in Brief.* New York: Author.

Alexander, K. L., Entwisle, Dr. R., & Horsey, C. S. (April, 1997). First grade forward: Early foundations of high school dropout. *Sociology of Education,* 70, 87-107

Alfonso, V. C., Johnson, A., Patinella, L; & Rader, D. E. (1998). Common WISC-III examiner errors evidence from graduate students in training. *Psychology in the Schools*, 15(2), 119-125.

Allen, Hugh D. editor (2008). *Moss and Adams' heart disease in infants, children, and adolescents: including the fetus and young adult.* (Philadelphia: Wolters Kluwer Health/Lippincott Williams & Wilkins).

Allen, J. E. (May 8, 2000). How do you know its attention deficit hyperactivity disorder? *Los Angeles Times*, S3.

Allen, M. C., & Capute, A. J. (1986). Assessment of early auditory and visual abilities in extremely premature infants. *Developmental Medicine and Child Neurology*, 28, 458-466.

Aloise-Young, P.A., Graham, J.W., & Hansen, W.B. (1994). Peer influence on smoking initiation during adolescence: A comparison of group members and group outsiders. *Journal of Applied Psychology, 79,* 281-287.

Altman, L. K. (May 9, 1975). Evacuation: Youngsters and pregnant go first. *The New York Times*, 15.

Altrocchi, J. (1990). *Abnormal Behavior.* New York: Harcourt, Brace, Jovanovich.

Alvidrez, J., & Weinstein, R. S. (1999). Early teacher perceptions and later student academic achievement, 91(4), 731-746. *Journal of Educational Psychology,* 91(4), 731-746.

Agin, Dan (2010) More than genes: what science can tell us about toxic chemicals, development, and the risk to our children (New York: Oxford University Press).

Amato, P. R., & Cheadle, J. (2005). The long reach of divorce: Divorce and child well-being across three generations. *Journal of Marriage the Family*, 67, 191-206.

Amato, P. R., & Keith, B. (1991). Parental divorce and the well-being of children: A meta-analysis. *Psychological Bulletin,* 110, 26-46.

American Academy of Pediatrics, (2000). Suicide and suicide attempts in adolescents. *Pediatrics,* 105. 871-874

_____ (February 1, 2005). Breastfeeding and the use of human milk. *Pediatrics,* 115(2), 496-506.

American Association on Mental Retardation (1994). *Mental Retardation: Definition, Classification and System of Supports.* Washington, DC: Author.

American Psychiatric Association (1994). *Diagnostic and Statistical Manual of Mental Disorders.* (4th ed.) Washington, DC: Author.

American Psychiatric Association. (2000). *Diagnostic and Statistical Manual of Mental Disorders* (4th ed. text revision). Washington, DC: Author.

Amunts, K., Schlaug, Janice L., Steinmetz, H., Schleicher, H., Darbring haus, A., & Ziles, K. (1997). Motor cortex and hand motor skills: Structural copliance in the human brain. *Human Brain Mapping,* 5, 206-225.

Anderson, C. A., & Dill, K.E. (2000). Video games and aggressive thoughts, feelings, and behavior in the lab and in life. *Journal of Personality and Social Psychology,* 78, 772-790.

Anderson, D. R., Huston, D. C., Schmitt, K. L., Linebarger, D. L., & Wright, J. C. (2001). Early childhood television viewing and adolescent behavior. *Monographs of the Society for Research in Child Development,* 66(Serial No. 264).

Anderson, K. E., Lytton, H., & Romney, D. M. (1986). Mothers' interactions with normal and conduct-disordered boys: Who affects whom? *Developmental Psychology,* 22, 604-609.

Anderson, R. N. (2002). *Deaths: Leading Causes for 2000.* National Vital Statistics Reports, 50(16). Hyatsville, MD: National Center for Health Statistics.

Andolsek, K. M. (January, 1997). Advice from family physicians on infant sleeping patterns. *American Family Physician,* 55, 295-299.

Andrich, D., & Styles, I. (1994). Psychometric evidence of intellectual growth spurts in early adolescence. *Journal of Early Adolescence.* 328-344.

Anglin. (1993). Vocabulary development: A morphological analysis. *Monographs of the Society for Research in Child Development,* 58 (10, Serial No. 238).

Apgar, V. (1953). A proposal for a new method of evaluation of the newborn infant. *Current Researches in Anesthesia and Analgesia,* 32, 260-267.

Appl, D. J. (Fall, 1998). Children with down syndrome: Implications for adult-child interactions in inclusive settings. *Childhood Education,* 39-43.

Appelbaum, M. (September/October, 2001). Child care and children's peer interaction at 24 and 36 months. The NICD study of early child care. *Child Development,* 72(5), 1478-1500.

Applebee, A. N., *et al.* (1994). *NAEP 1992: Writing Report Card.* Washington, DC: U.S. Department of Education.

Appleton, W. S. (2000). *Prozac and the New Antidepressants: What You Need to Know about Prozac, Zoloft, Luvox, Wellbutrin, Effexor, Serzone, Vestra, Celexa, St. John's Wart, and Others* (rev. ed.). New York: Plume Books.

Aquilino, W. S. (1991). Family structure and home leaving: A further specification of the relationship. *Journal of Marriage and the Family,* 53, 999-1010.

Arias, E., MacDorman, M. F., Tro Strobino, D. M., & Guyer, B. (2002). Annual summary of vital statistics: 2002. *Pediatrics,* 112, 1215-1230.

Arditti, J. A., & Keith, T. Z. (1993). Visitation frequency, child support payment, and the father-child relationship postdivorce. *Journal of Marriage and the Family,* 55, 699-712.

Aristotle, De Anima (1952). On the soul. Book 3, Chapter 4, Section 430. J. A. Smith (Trans). Chicago: Encyclopedia Britannica.

Arnett, J. J. (May, 1999). Adolescent storm and stress, reconsidered. *American Psychologist,* 317-326.

Arvin, A. M., & Prober, C. G. (October, 1997). Herpes Simplex Virus Type 2—A persistent problem. *The New England Journal of Medicine*, 1158-1159.

Ashmead, D. H., *et al.* (1993) Visual guidance in infants' reaching toward suddenly displaced targets, *Child Development*, 64, 1111-1127.

Atkinson, L., & Goldberg, S. (Eds.) (2004). *Attachment Issues in Psychopathology and Intervention*. Mahwah, NJ: Erlbaum.

Atkinson, R. C., & Shiffrin, R. M. (1968). Human memory: A proposal system and its control processes. In K. W. Spence & J. T. Spence (Eds.), *Advances in the Psychology of Learning and Motivation Research and Theory*. Vol. 2. New York: Academic Press.

Autti-Raemoe, I. (2000). Twelve-year follow up of children exposed to alcohol in utero. *Developmental Medicine and Child Neurology*, 42.

Ayers, L. (1909). *Laggards in Our Schools*. New York: Russell Sage Foundation.

Azrin, N. H., & Lindsley, O. R. (1956). The reinforcement of cooperation between children. *Journal of Abnormal and Social Psychology*, 52, 100-102.

Baddeley, A. (2000). Short-term and working memory. In E. Tulving & F. M. Craik (Eds.), *The Oxford Handbook of Memory*. New York: Oxford University Press.

Baddeley, A. D. (1992). Working memory. *Science*, 255, 556-559.

Baddeley, A., Gatherole, S., & Papagno, C. (1998). The phonological loop as a learning device. *Psychological Review*, 105(1), 158-173.

Baddeley, A. D., & Hitch, G. J. (1994). Developments in the Concept of Working Memory. *Neuropsychology*, 8, 485-493.

Bahado-Singh, R. O., Choic, S. J., Oz, U., Mendilciolglu, I., Routher, M., & Persutte, W. (2003). Early second-semester individualized estimation of trisomy 18 risk by ultrasound. *Obstetrics and Gynecology*, 101, 463-468.

Bailey, D. B., Skinner, D., & Sparkman, K. L. (February, 2003). Discovering fragile X syndrome: Family experiences and perceptions. *Pediatrics*, 111(2), 407-415.

Bailey, S. L., & Hubbard, R. L. (1991). Developmental changes in peer factors and the influence on marijuana initiation among secondary school students. *Journal of Youth and Adolescence*, 20, 339-360.

Baillargeon, R. (1992). The object concept revisited: New directions in the investigation of infants' physical knowledge. In C. E. Granrud (Ed.), *Carnegie -Mellon Symposia on Cognition:* Vol. 23. *Visual Perception and Cognition In Infancy*. Hillsdale: NJ: Erlbaum.

Baldwin, R. (1985). *Cornucopia Kids Life-Style Management for Busy People*. Wilmington, NC: Direction Dynamics.

Bale, J. E., Jr., Zimmerman, B., Dawson, J. D., Souza, I. E., Petheram, S. J., & Nurph, J. R. (1999). Cytomegalovirus transmission in child care homes. *Archives of Pediatrics and Adolescent Medicine*, 153, 75-79.

Ballantine, J. (Fall, 2001). Raising competent kids: The authoritative parenting style. *Childhood Education*, 46-47.

Ballard, C. L., & Wood, R. I. (2005). Intracerebroventricular self-administration of commonly abused anabolic androgenic steroids in male hamsters (*mesocricetus auratus*): Nandrolone, drostalolone, oxymetholone, and stanozolol. *Behavioral Neuroscience*, 119, 752-758.

Band, G. P., Van der Molen, M. W., Overtoom, C. C. E., & Verbaten, M. N. (2000). The ability to activate and inhibit speeded responses: Separate developmental trends. *Journal of Experimental Child Psychology*, 75, 2630290.

Bandura, A. (1999). Social cognitive theory of personality. In L. A. Pervin & O. P. John (Eds.), *Handbook of Personality and Research*, (2nd ed.). New York: Guilford.

_____ (1977). *Social Learning Theory*. Englewood Cliffs, NJ: Prentice-Hall.

_____ (1982). The self and mechanisms of agency. In J. Suls (Ed.), *Psychological Perspectives on the Self*. Vol. 1. Hillsdale, NJ: Erlbaum.

_____ (1986). *Social Foundation of Thought and Action: A Social Cognitive Theory*. Englewood Cliffs, NJ: Prentice-Hall.

_____ (1989). Social cognition theory. In R. Vasta (Ed.), *Annals of Child Development*. Vol. 6. Greenwich, CT: JAI Press.

_____ (1997). *Self-Efficacy: The Exercise of Control*. New York: Freeman.

_____ (2000). Social cognitive theory. *Annual Review of Psychology*. Vol. 52. Palo Alto, CA: Annual Reviews.

Bandura, A., Barbaranelli, C., Vittorio Caprara, G., & Pastorelli, C. (2001). Self-efficacy beliefs as shapers of children's aspirations and career trajectories. *Child Development, 72,* 187-206.

Bandura, A., Grusec, J. E., & Menlove, F. L. (1976). Vicarious extinction of avoidance behavior. *Journal of Personality and Social Psychology*, 5, 16, 23.

Bandura, A., & Menlove, F. L. (1968). Factors determining vicarious extinction of avoidance behavior through symbolic modeling. *Journal of Personality and Social Psychology,* 8, 99-108.

Bandura, A., & Mischel, W. (1965). Modification of self-imposed delay of reward through exposure to live and symbolic models. *Journal of Personality and Social Psychology*, 2, 698-705.

Bandura, A., Ross, D., & Ross, S. A. (1961). Transmission of aggression through imitation of aggressive models. *Journal of Abnormal and Social Psychology*, 63, 575-582.

_____(1963). Vicarious reinforcement and imitative learning. *Journal of Abnormal and Social Psychology*, 67, 601-607.

Bang, K. M., Lockey, J. M., & Keye, W. (May, 1983). Reproductive hazards in the workplace. *Family Community Health*, 6, 44.

Baraket, L. P., Kunin-Batson, A., & Kazak, A. E. (2003). Child health psychology. In I. B. Weiner (Ed.), *Handbook of Psychology*. Vol. 9. New York: McGraw-Hill.

Barker, D. J. P. (1995). The Wellcome Foundation Lecture, 1994. The fetal origins of adult disease. *Proceedings of the Royal Society of London. Series B: Biological Sciences*, 262, 37-43.

Barlow, D. H. (2001). *Anxiety and its Disorders*. New York: Guildford Press.

Barnea, Z., Teichman, M., & Rahav, G. (1992). Personality, cognitive, and interpersonal factors in adolescent substance use: A longitudinal test of an interacting model, *Child Development, 2,* 187–201.

Barr, Ronald G.; Hopkins, Brian and Green, James A. editors (2000). *Crying as a sign, a symptom, & a signal: clinical, emotional and developmental aspects of infant and toddler crying* (Cambridge: Mac Keith Press).

Barnett, S. B., & Maulik, D. (2000). Guidelines and recommendations for ultrasound in perinatal applications. *Journal of Maternal and Fetal Medicine*, 10, 75-84.

Barrett, M., Lyons, E., & Valle, A. D. (2004). The development of national identity and social identity processes: Do social identity theory and self-categorization theory provide useful heuristic frameworks for developmental research? In M. Bennett & F. Sani (Eds.), *The Development of the Social Self*. Hove, England: Psychology Press.

Basic, S., Hajnsek, S., Poljakovic, A., Basic, M., Culic, V., & Zadro, I. (2004). Determination of cortical language dominance using functional transcranial Doppler sonography on left-handers. *Clinical Neurophysiology*, 115, 154-160.

Bauer, Patricia J. (2007). *Remembering the times of our lives: memory in infancy and beyond* (Mahwah: Lawrence Erlbaum Associates).

Bauer, P. J. (1993). Memory for gender-consistent and gender-inconsistent event sequences by **twenty-five-month-old mothers.** *Child Development, 64,* 285-297.

Baumeister, R. F., Campbell, J. D., Krueger, J. I., & Vohs, K. D. (2003). Does high self-esteem cause better performance, interpersonal success, happiness, or healthier lifestyles? *Psychological Science in the Public Interest*, 44((1), 1-44.

Baumrind, D. (1971). Current patterns of parental authority. *Developmental Psychology Monographs*, 4(1), 1-103.

_____ (1978). Parental disciplinary patterns and social competence in children. *Youth and Society*, 9, 239-276.

_____ (1982). Are androgynous individuals most effective persons and parents? *Child Development*, 43, 44-75.

_____ (1989). Rearing Competent Children. In W. Damon (Ed.) *Child Development: Today and Tomorrow*, 349-370. San Francisco: Jossey-Bass.

_____ (1991). Parenting styles and adolescent development. In R. M. Lerner, A. C. Petersen, & J. Brooks-Gunn (Eds.), *Encyclopedia of Adolescence*. New York: Garland.

Baxter, L. R. (March 21, 2000). Cited in A. Fuentes, Finding hope and despair in treating compulsive disorders. *New York Times*, D7.

Bayder, N., & Brooks-Gunn, J. (1991). Effects of maternal employment and child-care arrangements on preschoolers' cognitive and behavioral outcomes: Evidence from the children of the National Longitudinal Survey of Youth. *Developmental Psychology, 27*, 932-945.

Bayley, N. (1965). Research in child development: A longitudinal perspective. *Merrill-Palmer Quarterly of Behavior and Development*, 1, 184-190.

_____ (1993). *Bayley Scales of Infant Development* (Second Edition) (BSID-II). San Antonio, TX: The Psychological Corporation.

Beatty, J. (March 16, 1968). Trade winds. *Saturday Review*, 10.

Beck, A. T., Brown, G., Berchick, R. J., Stewart, B. L., & Steer, R. A. (1990). Relationship between hopelessness and ultimate suicide: A replication with psychiatric outpatients. *American Journal of Psychiatry*, 147, 190-195.

Bellamy, C. (2000). *The State of the World's Children 2000.* New York: Oxford University Press (in cooperation with UNICEF).

Bellinger, D., Stiles, K. M., & Needleman, H. L. (1992). Low-level lead exposure, intelligence and academic achievement: A long-term follow-up study. *Pediatrics*, 90, 855-861.

Belsky, J. (2001). Emmanuel Miller Lecture: Developmental risks (still) associated with early child care. *Journal of Child Psychology and Psychiatry and Allied Disciplines*, 42, 845-859.

Belsky, J., & Eggebeen, D. (1991). Early and extensive maternal employment and young children's socioemotional development: Children of the National Longitudinal Survey of Youth. *Journal of Marriage and the Family, 53*, 1083-1110.

Bem, S. L. (1974). The measurement of psychological androgyny. *Journal of Consulting and Clinical Psychology*, 42, 155-162.

_____ (1983). Gender schema theory and its implications for raising aschematic children in a gender-schematic society. *Signs*, 8, 598-616.

_____ (1993). *The Lens of Gender: Transforming the Debate on Sexual Inequality.* New Haven, CT: Yale University Press.

_____ (1998). *An Unconventional Family.* New Haven, CT: Yale University Press.

Benbow, C. P., Lubinski, D., Shea, D. L., & Eftekkara-Sanjani, H. (2000). Sex differences in mathematical reasoning ability at age 13: Their status 20 years later. *Psychological Science*, 11, 474-480.

Bendelius, J. (2003). The nutritional challenge of genetic enzyme-deficiency syndromes. *School Nurse News, 20*, 16-17.

Berenbaum, S. A., & Snyder, E. (1995) Early hormonal influences on childhood sex-typed activities and playmate preferences: Implications for the development of sexual orientation. *Developmental Psychology, 31*, 31-42.

Berk, L. E. (1994). Vygotsky's theory: The importance of make believe play. *Young Children*, 50, 30-38.

Best, D. (2001). Cross-cultural gender roles. In J. Worrell (Ed.), *Encyclopedia of Women and Gender.* San Diego: Academic Press.

Bethia, L. (March 15, 1999). Primary prevention of child abuse. *American Family Physician, 59*(6), 1577-1585.

Bettleheim, B. (1983). *Freud and Man's Soul.* New York: Knopf.

Biller, H. B. (1993). *Fathers and Families: Paternal Factors in Child Development.* Westport, CT: Auburn House.

Bingol, N., Fuchs, M., Diaz, V., Stone, R. K., & Gromisch, D. S. (1987). Teratogenicity of cocaine in humans. *Journal of Pediatrics*, 10, 93-96.

Bisnaire, L. M. C., Firestone, P., & Rynard, D. (January, 1990). Factors associated with academic achievement in children following parental separation. *American Journal of Orthopsychiatry*, 60(1), 67-75.

Blanco, J., Gabau, E., Gomez, D., Baena, N., Guitart, M., Egozcue, J., & Vidal, F. (October, 1998). Chromosome 21 disomy in the spermatozoa of the fathers of children with trisomy 21 in a population with a high prevalence of down syndrome: Increased incidence in cases of paternal origin. *American Journal of Human Genetics*, 63, 1067-1072.

Blehar, M. C. (1974). Anxious attachment and defensive reactions associated with day care. *Child Development*, 45, 683-692.

Blum, R. W., & Nelson-Mmari, K. (2004). Adolescent health from an international perspective. In R. M. Lerner & L. D. Sternberg (Eds.), *Handbook of Adolescent Psychology* (2nd ed.). Hoboken, NJ: Wiley.

Bobak, I. M., Jensen, M. D., & Zalar, M. K. (1989). *Maternity and Gynecologic Care* (4th ed.), St. Louis: Mosby.

Bogin, B. (1990). The evolution of human childhood. *BioScience*, 40(1), 16-24.

Bonser, S., Hewson, D., & Jupp, J. (February, 1990). Retention control training for nocturnal enuresis: A case study. *School Psychology: International*, 11(1), 55-62.

Boom, J., & Molenaar, P. C. (June, 1989). A developmental model of hierarchical stage structure in objective moral judgements. *Developmental Review*, 9, 133-145.

Bornstein, M. E. (Ed.), (1995). *Handbook of Parenting, Vol. 3. Status and Social Conditions and Parenting.* Hillsdale, NJ: Lawrence Erlbaum.

Bouchard, Jr., T. J., (June 17, 1994). Genes, environment, and personality. *Science,* 264, 1700-1701.

Bouchard, Jr., T. J., & McGue, M. (2003). Genetic and environmental influences on human psychological differences. *Journal of Neurobiology,* 54, 4-45.

Boukydis, C. F. Z., & Lester, B. M. (1998). Infant crying, risk status and social support in families of preterm and term infants. *Early Development and Parenting*, 7, 31-39.

Bouldin, P., & Pratt, C. (1998). Utilizing parent report to investigate young children's fears: A modification of the fear survey schedule for children—II: A research note. *Journal of Child Psychology and Psychiatry*, 39(2), 271-277.

Bowe, F. (1993). Statistics, politics, and employment of people with disabilities: Commentary. *Journal of Disability Policy Studies,* 4(2), 83-89.

Bower, T. G. R. (1982). *Development in Infancy.* New York: Freeman.

_____(2002). Space and objects. In A. Slater M. Lewis (Eds,). *Introduction to Infant Development.* New York: Oxford University Press.

Bowes, J. M., & Goodnow, J. J. (1996). Work for home, school, or labor force. *Psychological Bulletin*, 119, 300-321.

Bowlby, J. (1951). Maternal care and health. *World Health Organization Monographs* (No. 2).

_____ (1958). The nature of the child's tie to his mother. *International Journal of Psychoanalysis*, 39, 350-373.

_____ (1969). *Attachment and Loss*. Vol. 1. *Attachment*. New York: Basic Books.

_____ (1973). *Attachment and Loss*. Vol. 2. *Separation, Anxiety, and Anger*. London: Hogarth Press.

_____ (1980). *Attachment and Loss*. Vol. 3. *Loss: Sadness and Depression*. New York: Basic Books.

_____ (1988). Contexts of child rearing: Problems and prospects. *American Psychologist*, 34, 844-850.

_____ (1988). *A Secure Base*. New York: Basic.

Brabeck, M. M. (2000). Kohlberg, Lawrence. In A. Kazdin (Ed.), *Encyclopedia of Psychology.* Washington, DC & New York: American Psychological Association and Oxford University Press.

Brachlow, A., Jordan, A. E., & Tervo, R. (2001). Developmental screenings in rural settings: A comparison of the child developmental review and the Denver II Developmental Screening Test. *Journal of Rural Health*, 17, 156-159.

Bradford, Helen (2009). *Communication, language and literacy in the early years foundation stage* (London: Routledge).

Bradley, R. H., & Corwyn, R. F. (2005). Productive ability and the prevention of behavior problems. *Developmental Psychology,* 41, 89-98.

Braig, S., Luton, D., Eibony, O., Edlinger, C., Boissinot, C., Blot, P., & Oury, E. G. (2001). Acyclovir prophylaxix in late pregnancy prevents recurrent genital herpes and viral shedding. *European Journal of Obstetrics, Gynecology, and Reproductive Biology*, 96, 55-58.

Branden, N. (1994). *Six Pillars of Self-Esteem*. New York: Bantam Books.

Braver, S. L., Hipke, K. N., Ellman, I. M., & Sandler, I. N. (2004). Strengths-building public policy for children of divorce. In K. I. Maton, C. J. Schellenbach, B. J. Leadbeater, & A. L. Solarz (Eds.), *Investing in Children, Youth, Families, and Communities. Strengths-Based Research and Policy.* Washington, DC: American Psychological Association.

Bray, G. A., & Tartaglia, L. A. (2000). Medicinal strategies in the treatment of obesity. *Nature*, 404, 672-677.

Brazelton, T., & Cramer, B. (1990). *The Earliest Relationships*. New York: Addison-Wesley Publishers.

Breastfeeding and HIV International Transmission Study Group, The. Late postnatal transmission of HIV-1 in breastfed children. An individual patient data meta-analysis. *HS 2004*, 189, 2154-66.

Bremmer, J. G. (1982). Object localization in infancy. In M. Poetgal (Ed.), *The Normal Developmental Basis of Spatial Orientation*. New York: Academic Press.

Brems, C. (2000). *Dealing with Challenges in Psychotherapy and Counseling*. Pacific Grove, CA: Brooks/Cole.

Bren, L. (March/April, 2002). Genital herpes: A hidden epidemic. *FDA Consumer*, 10-14.

Brener, N., Lowry, R., Kann, L., Kolbe, L., Lehnherr, L., Janssen, R., & Jaffe, H. (2002). Trends in sexual risk behaviors among high school students— United States 1991-2001. *Morbidity and Mortality Weekly Reports,* 856-859.

Brent, D. A., *et al.* (September, 2002). Familial pathways to early onset suicide attempt. *Archives of General Psychiatry*, 59, 801-806.

Bretherton, L., & Main, M. (2000). Mary Dinsmore Salthworthy Ainsworth (1913-1999): Obituary. *American Psychologist*. 55, 1148-1149.

Briere, J. N., & Elliott, D. M. (1994). Immediate and long-term impacts of child sexual abuse. *The Future of Children*, 4, 54-69.

Bridges, K. M. B. (1932). Emotional development in early infancy. *Child Development*, 3, 324-341.

Brock, E. T., & Shucard, D. W. (1994). Sleep apnea. *American Family Physician*, 49, 385-394.

Brody, J. E. (March 5, 1994). Folic acid emerges as a nutritional star. *New York Times,* B7, B9

Brody, N. (1992). *Intelligence* (2nd ed.). San Diego, CA: Academic Press.

Brodzinsky, D. M., & Pinderhughes, E. (2002). Parenting and child development in adoptive families. In M. H. Bornstein (Ed.), *Handbook of Parenting* Vol. 1. (2nd ed.). Mahwah, NJ: Erlbaum.

Bronfenbrenner, U., & Cecil, S. (1994). Nature-nurture reconceptualized in developmental perspective: A bioecological model. *Psychology Review,* 101, 568-589.

Bronfenbrenner, U. (1979a). *The Ecology of Human Development*. Cambridge, MA: Harvard University Press.

_____ (1979b). Contexts of child rearing: Problems and prospects. *American Psychologist,* 34, 844-850.

_____ (1986). Ecology of the family as a context for human development: Research perspectives. *Developmental Psychology,* 22, 723-742.

_____ (April, 1989). The developing ecology of human development. Paper presented at the biennial meeting of the Society for Research in Child Development, Kansas City.

_____ (March, 1995). Role research has played in Head Start. Paper presented at the meeting of the Society for Research in Child Development, Indianapolis, IN.

_____ (2000). Ecological theory. In A. Kazdin (Ed.), *Encyclopedia of Psychology*. Washington, DC & New York: American Psychological Association and Oxford University Press.

_____(2002). Ecological theory. In A. Kazdin (Ed.), *Encyclopedia of Psychology*. Washington, DC & New York: American Psychological Association and Oxford University Press.

_____(2004). *Making human beings human*. Thousand Oaks, CA.

Bronfenbrenner, U., McClelland, P., Wethington, E., Moen, P., & Ceci, S. J. (1996). *The state of Americans: This Generation and the Next*. New York: Free Press.

Bronfenbrenner, U., & Morris, P. A. (1998), The ecology of developmental processes. In R. M. Lerner (Ed.), *Handbook of Child Psychology: Theoretical Models of Human Development*. (5th ed. Vol. 1). New York: Wiley.

Bronstein, A., & Petrova, E. (1952). An investigation of the auditory analyzer in neonates and young infants. *Zhurnal Vysshei Nervnoi Deyatelnosti, Immemi, I. P. Pavalova*, 2, 333-343.

Brown, B. B. (2004). Adolescents' relationships with peers, In R. Lerner & L. Steinberg (Eds.), *Handbook of Adolescent Psychology*. New York: Wiley.

Brown, G. K., Beck, A. T., Steer, R. A., & Grisham, J. R. (2000). Risk factors for suicide in psychiatric outpatients: A 20-year prospective study. *Journal of Clinical and Consulting Psychology*, 68, 371-377.

Brown, J. D., Childers, R. W., & Waszak, C. S. (June, 1988). Television and adolescent sexuality. Paper presented at the conference on television and teens: Health implications. Manhattan Beach, CA.

Brown, J. E. (1983). *Nutrition for Your Pregnancy*. Minneapolis, MN: University of Minnesota Press.

Brown, R. T. (1982). A developmental analysis of visual and auditory sustained attention and reflection-impulsivity in hyperactive children. *Journal of Learning Disabilities*, 15, 614-618.

Brown, S. K., & Shalita, A. R. (June 20, 1998), Acne Vulgaris, *The Lancet*, 351, 1871-1976.

Browne, B. (1998). Gender stereotypes in advertising on children's television in the 1990s. A cross-national analysis. *Journal of Advertising*, 27(1), 83-97.

Browne-Miller, Angela (2009). *Raising thinking children and teens: guiding mental and moral development* (Santa Barbara: Praeger/ABC-CLIO).

Bruner, J. S. (1968). *Process of Cognitive Growth: Infancy*. Worcester, MA: Clark University Press.

Bukowski, R., Burgett, A. D., Gei, A., Saade, G. R., & Hankins, G. D. (2003). Impairment of fetal growth potential and neonatal encephalopathy. *American Journal of Obstetrics and Gynecology*, 188, 1011-1015.

Bukowski, W. M., Sippola, L. K., & Newcomb, A. F. (2000). Variations in patterns of attraction of same and other sex peers during early adolescence. *Developmental Psychology*, 36, 147-154.

Bumpass, L. L., & Raley, R. K. (1995). Redefining single-parent families: Cohabitation and changing family reality. *Demography, 32,* 97-109.

Burns, C. E. (2000). *Pediatric Primary Care: A Handbook for Nurse Practitioners*. Philadelphia: Saunder.

Burns, G. W. (1976). *The Science of Genetics*. New York: Macmillan.

Bushman, B. J., & Cooper, H. M. (1990). Effects of alcohol on human aggression: An integrative research review. *Psychological Bulletin*, 107(3), 341-354.

Bushnell, E. W., & Boudreau, S. P. (1993). Motor development and the mind: The potential role of motor abilities as a determinant of aspects of perceptual development, *Child Development*, 64, 1005-1021.

Buss, A. A., & Plomin, R. (1984). *Temperament: Early Developing Personality Traits*. Hillsdale, NJ: Erlbaum.

_____ (1986). The EAS approach to temperament. In R. Plomin & J. Dunn (Eds.), *The Study of Temperament: Changes, Continuities, and Challenges*. Hillsdale, NJ: Erlbaum.

Buss, D. M. (2004). *Evolutionary Psychology* (2nd ed.). Boston: Allyn & Bacon.

Bussee, W. W., & Lemanske, R. F. (Eds.) (2005). *Lung Biology in Health and Disease*. Vol. 195. *Asthma Prevention*. Boca Raton, FL: Taylor & Francis.

Bussing, R., Zima, B. T., Perwien, A. R., Belin, T. R., & Widawski, M. (June, 1998). Children in special education programs: Attention deficit hyperactivity disorder, uses of services, and unmet needs. *American Journal of Public Health,* 88(6), 880-886.

Butkowski, W. M., Gauze, C., Hoza, B., & Newcombe, A. F. (1993). Difference and consistency between same-sex and other-sex relationships during early adolescence. *Developmental Psychology,* 29, 255-263.

Butler, R. J., Redfern, E. J., & Forsythe, W. I. (1990). The child's construing of nocturnal enuresis: A method of inquiry and prediction of outcome. *Journal of Child Psychology and Psychiatry*, 31(3), 447-454.

Byard, R. W. (2004). *Sudden Death in Infancy, Childhood, and Adolescence* (2nd ed.). Cambridge, England: Cambridge University Press.

Cabana, M. D., Rand, C., Slish, K., Nan, B., Davis, M. M., & Clark, N. (2004). Pediatrician self-efficiency for counseling parents of asthmatic children to quit smoking. *Pediatrics*, 113, 78-81.

Cabrera, N. J., Tamis-LeMonda, T, Bradley, R.H., Hofferth, S., & Lamb, M.E. (January/February, 2000). Fatherhood in the twenty-first century. *Child Development,* 71(1), 127-136.

Cadwell, Karin (2009). *Continuity of care in breastfeeding: best practices in the maternity setting*(Sudbury: Jones and Bartlett Publishers).

Cairns, R. B. (1983). The emergence of developmental psychology. In P. H. Mussen (Ed.), *Handbook of Child Psychology*: Vol. 1. *History, Theory and Methods*. New York: Wiley.

_____ (1998). The making of developmental psychology. In: R. M. Lerner (Ed.), *Handbook of Child Psychology*: Vol. 1. *Theoretical Models of Human Development* (5th ed.). New York: Wiley.

Calderone, M. S., & Johnson, E. W. (1981). *The Family Book about Sexuality.* New York: Harper & Row.

Campbell, F. A., Pungello, E. P., Miller-Johnson, S., Burchinal, M., & Ramey, C. T. (2001). The development of cognitive and academic abilities: Growth curves from an early childhood educational experiment. *Developmental Psychology*, 37, 231-242.

Campbell, F. A., & Ramey, C. T. (1994). Effects of early intervention on intellectual and academic achievement: A follow-up study of children from low income families. *Child Development*, 65, 684-698.

Campbell, J. R., Hombo, C. M., & Mazzeo, J. *NAEP 1999: Trends in Academic Progress*. Washington, DC: U.S. Department of Education.

Campos, J. J., Anderson, D. I., Barbu-Roth, M. A., Hubbard, E. M., Hertenstein, E. M., & Witherington, D. (2000). Travel broadens the mind. *Infancy*, 1, 149-219.

Cantor, J. (August, 2000). Media violence. *Journal of Adolescent Health*, 275(2), 30-34.

Cantor, J., & Wilson, B. J. (1984). Children's fear responses to mass media: Testing some Piagetian predictions. *Journal of Communication*, 34, 90-103.

Capone, G. T. (2001). Down syndrome: Advances in molecular biology and the neurosciences. *Journal of Developmental and Behavioral Pediatrics*, 22, 40-59.

Carey, G. (July/August, 1990). Genes, fears, phobias, and phobic disorders. *Journal of Counseling and Development*, 68, 628-632.

Carley, A. (2003). Anemia. When is it iron deficiency? *Pediatric Nursing,* 29, 133.

Carlson, C., Uppal, S., & Prosser, E. (2000). Ethnic differences in processing contributing to the self-esteem of early adolescent girls. *Journal of Early Adolescence*, 20, 44-67.

Carlson, M., & Earls, F. (January, 1997). Psychological and neuroendocrinological sequelae of early social deprivation in institutionalized children in Romania. *Annals of the New York Academy of Sciences*, 419-428.

Carpendale, J. I. M., (2000). Kohlberg and Piaget on stages and moral reasoning. *Developmental Review*, 20, 181-205.

Carr, J. (1994). Long-term outcome for people with down syndrome. *Journal of Child Psychology and Psychiatry and Allied Disciplines,* 35, 425-439.

Cash, F., & Hicks, K. L. (June, 1990). Being fat versus thinking fat: Relationships with body image, eating behaviors, and well-being. *Cognitive Therapy and Research*, 14(3), 327-341.

Casper, R. (1993). Old and new facts about perinatal brain development. *Journal of Child Psychology and Psychiatry*, 34, 101-109.

Castoldi, A. F., Coccini, T., & Manzo, L. (2003). Neurotoxic and molecular effects of methylmercury in humans, *Review of Environmental Health*, 18, 19-31

Cavazzana-Calvo, M. (April 28, 2000). Gene therapy of human severe combined immunodeficiency (SCID-X1) disease. *Science,* 288, 669-672.

Center for Health Statistics (1995). *Vital Statistics of the United States, Volume I—Natality: 1992*. National Center for Health Statistics, Hyattsville, MO.

Centers for Disease Control and Prevention (April 25, 1997). Alcohol consumption among pregnant and childbearing-aged women — United States, 1991-1995. *Morbidity and Mortality Weekly Report,* 46, 346-350.

_____ (2000). Trends in the attendant, place and timing of births and in the use of obstetric interventions in the United States, 1989-1997. *Mortality and Morbidity Weekly Report,* 49.

_____ (2001). *Data and Statistics: Adolescent Pregnancy.* Atlanta: Author

_____ (2002). *Sexually Transmitted Diseases*. Atlanta: Author.

_____ (2002). Youth risk behavior surveillance—United States 2001. *Morbidity and Mortality Weekly Report,* 51(4). Atlanta: Author.

_____ (2003). *The Tobacco Atlas: Deaths*. http://www.5.who.int/tobacco/repository/stp84/36%209%20deaths.pdf.

_____ (September 17, 2004). Use of vitamins containing folic acid among women of childbearing age—United States, 2004. *Morbidity and Mortality Weekly Report,* 53, 847-850.

Chabon, J (1966). *Awake and Aware: Participating in Childbirth through Prophylaxis*. New York: Delacorte Press.

Chartrand, S. A., & Pong, A. (1998). Acute otitis media in the 1990s: The antibiotic resistance. *Pediatric Annals,* 27(2), 85-95.

Chaudron, L. H. (2003). Postpartum depression. What physicians need to know. *Pediatric Review,* 24, 154-161.

Chemaitilly, W., Trivin, C., Suberbielle, J. C., & Brauner, R. (2003). Assessing short-statured children for growth deficiency. *Hormone Research,* 60, 34-42.

Chen, S., Leu, M., Le, B., Cen, G., Chen, H., & Wang, L. (2000). Maternal authoritative and authoritarian attitudes and mother-child interactions and relationships in urban China. *International Journal of Behavioral Development,* 24, 119-126.

Chen, W., Li, S., Cook, N. R., Rosner, B. A., Srinivasan, S. R., Boerwinkle, E., & Berenson, G. S. (2004). An autosomal genome scan for loci influencing longitudinal burden of body mass index from childhood to young adulthood in white sibships. The Bogalusa Heart Study. *International Journal of Obesity,* 28, 462-469.

Cheng, T. L., Fields, C. B., Brenner, R. A., Wright, J. L., Lomax, T., Scheidt, P. C., & the District of Columbia Child/Adolescent Injury Research Network. (2000). Sports injuries: An important cause of morbidity in urban youth. *Pediatrics,* 105, 32.

Cherlin, A. J. *et al.* (1991). Longitudinal Studies of effects of divorce in Great Britain and the United States, *Science,* 25, 1386-1388.

_____ (1983). Mothers are always the problem—Or are they? Old wine in new bottles. *Pediatrics,* 71(6), 974-976.

Cherlin, A. J., & Furstenberg, F. F. (1994). Stepfamilies in the United States: A reconsideration. In J. Blake & J. Hagen (Eds.), *Annual Review of Sociology.* Palo Alto, CA: Annual Reviews.

Chess, S., & Thomas, A. C. (1982). Infant bonding! Mystique and reality. *American Journal of Orthopsychiatry,* 52(2), 213-222.

Child Trends. (2001). *Trends among Hispanic Children, Youth, and Families.* Washington, DC: Author.

Children's Defense Fund. (2000). *The State of America's Children: (Yearbook 2000).* Washington, DC: Author.

_____ (1996). *The State of America's Children.* Washington, DC: Author.

Chomsky, N. (1968). *Language and Mind.* New York: Harcourt, Brace, World.

_____ (1972). *Language and Mind.* (2nd ed.).New York: Harcourt, Brace, World.

_____ (1986). *Knowledge of Language: Its Nature, Origins and Use.* New York: Praeger.

Christensen, D. (2000). Sobering work: Unraveling alcohol's effects on the developing brain. *Science News,* 138, 28-29.

Ciaccio, N. V. (1971). A test of Erikson's theory of ego epigenesis. *Developmental Psychology,* 4, 306-311.

Cibelli, J. B., Kiessling, A. A., Cunniff, K., Richards, C., Lanza, R. P., & West, M. D. (November 26, 2001). Somatic cell nuclear transfer in humans: Pronuclear and early embryonic development. *The Journal of Regenerative Medicine, 2001,* 25-31.

Clarke-Stewart, K. A., & Hevey, C. M. (1981). Longitudinal relations in repeated observations of mother-child interaction from one to two-and-a-half years. *Developmental Psychology,* 17, 127-145.

Claverie, J. M. (February 16, 2001). What if there are only 30,000 human genes? *Science,* 291(5507), 1255-1257.

Cnattingius, S., Brondes, H., & Forman, M. (1993). Do delayed childbearers face increased risk of adverse pregnancy outcomes after the first birth? *Obstetrics and Gynecology,* 81, 512-516.

Cohen, R. Z., Seeman, M. V., Gotowiec, A., & Kopala, L. (July 6, 1999). Earlier puberty as a predictor of later onset of schizophrenia in women. *American Journal of Psychiatry,* 156(7), 1059-1064.

Coie, J. D. (1990). Toward a theory of peer rejection. In S. R. Asher & J. D. Coie (Eds.), *Peer Rejection in Childhood.* Cambridge, England: Cambridge University Press.

Cole, F., & Slocumb, E. (1995). Factors influencing sex: Sexual behaviors in heterosexual late adolescent and young adult collegiate males. *Image: Journal of Nursing Scholarship,* 27, 217-223.

Cole, M., & Cole, S. R. (1993). *The Development of Children* (2nd ed.). New York: Freeman.

Coleman, J. S., Campbell, E. Q., Hobson, C. J., McFarland, J., Mood, A. W., Weinfeld, F. D., & York, R. L. (1966). *Equality of Educational Opportunity.* Washington, DC: U.S. Government Printing Office.

Colin, V. L. (1996). *Human Attachment.* New York: McGraw-Hill.

Coll, C. G., Bearer, E. L., & Lerner, R. M. (Eds.). (2004). *Nature and Nurture.* Mahwah, NJ: Erlbaum.

Collins, E. S., & McKusick, V. A. (2001). Implications of the Human Genome Project for Medical Science, *Journal of the American Medical Association*, 295, 540-544.

Collins, R. C., & Deloria, D. (July/August, 1983). Head Start research: A new chapter. *Children Today*, 15-19.

Collins, W. A., & Laursen, B. (2004). Parent-adolescent relationships and influences. In R, Lerner & L. Steinberg (Eds.), *Handbook of Adolescent Psychology.* New York: Wiley.

Collins, W. A., Laursen, B., Mortensen, N., Luebker, & Ferreira, M. (1997). Conflict processes and transitions in parent and peer relationships: Implications for autonomy and regulation. *Journal of Adolescent Research*, 12, 178-198.

Collins, W. A., Maccoby, E. E., Steinberg, L., Hetherington, E. M., & Bornstein, M. H. (2000). Contemporary research on parenting: The case for nature and nurture. *American Psychologist*, 52, 218-232.

Colton, T. *et al.* (April 28, 1993). Breast cancer in mothers prescribed diethylstilbestrol in pregnancy. *The Journal of the American Medical Association,*" 269, 2096-2100.

Connelly, B. *et al.* (Spring, 1993). The prevalence of depression in a high school population. *Adolescence*, 28, 150-158.

Conway, T. *et al.* (June 9, 1993) Trends in HIV Prevalence Among Disadvantaged Youth. *Journal of the American Medical Association,* 269, 2887-2889.

Cook, B. G., & Semmel, M. I. (1999). Peer acceptance of included students with disabilities as a function of severity of disability and classroom composition. *The Journal of Special Education,* 33(1), 50-61.

Cooley, R. L., & Chase-Lansdale, P. L. (1998). Adolescent pregnancy and parenthood: Recent evidence and future directions. *American Psychologist,* 53, 152-166.

Coontz, S. (1997). *The Way We Really Are: Coming to Terms with America's Changing Families.* New York: Basic Books.

Cooper, R. T. (April 4, 1999). Head Start's fresh start, *Los Angeles Times*, B2.

Coopersmith, S. (1967). *The Antecedents of Self-esteem.* San Francisco: Freeman.

Cooter, R. B. (Ed.), (2004). *Perspectives on Rescuing Urban Literacy Education.* Mahwah, NJ: Erlbaum.

Corbett, M., & Meyer, J. H. (1987). *The Adolescent and Pregnancy.* Boston: Blackwell Scientific Publications, Inc.

Compas, B. (2004). Processes of risk and resilience during adolescence: Linking contexts and individuals. In R. Lerner & L. Steinberg (Eds.), *Handbook of Adolescent Psychology.* New York: Wiley.

Corcoran, J., Miller, P. O., & Bultman, L. (1997). Effectiveness of prevention programs for adolescent pregnancy. *Journal of Marriage and the Family*, 59, 551-567.

Corn, A. L., & Koenig, A. J. (1996). *Foundations of Low Vision: Clinical Functional Perspectives.* New York: AFB Press.

Corrigan, R. (1982). Methodological issues in language acquisition research with very young children. *Developmental Review*, 2, 163.

Council on Scientific Affairs. (June 27, 1990). The worldwide smoking epidemic. *Journal of the American Medical Association*, 263.

Cowan, C. P., & Cowan, P. A. (2000). *When Partners Become Parents: The big life change for couples.* Mahwah, NJ: Erlbaum.

Cramer, D. W., Schiff, I., Schenbaum, S. C., Gibson, M., Belislie, S., Albrecht, B., Stillman, R. J., Berger, M. M., Wilson, E., Stadel, B. V., & Seibel, H. (1985). Tubal infertility and the intrauterine device. *The New England Journal of Medicine*, 313, 941-947.

Crandell, L. E., & Hobson, R. P. (1999). Individual differences in young children's IQ: A social-developmental perspective. *Journal of Child Psychology and Psychiatry,* (40) (1), 455-464.

Crockenberg, S. C. (2003). Rescuing the baby from the bathwater. How gender and temperament influence how child care affects child development. *Child Development,* 74, 1034-1038.

Crooks, R., & Baur, K. (1990). *Our Sexuality* (4th ed.). Redwood City, CA: Benjamin Cummings.

Crouse, Janice Shaw (2010). *Children at risk: the precarious state of children's well-being in America* (New Brunswick: Transaction Publishers).

Crumley, F. E. (1990). Substance abuse and adolescent suicidal behavior. *Journal of the American Medical Association*, 263(22), 3051-3056.

Cunningham, F. G., Gant, N. F., Leveno, K. J., Clark, S. L., Hauth, J. C., & Wenstrom, K. D. (2001). *Williams Obstetrics* (21st ed.). New York: McGraw-Hill.

Cunningham, J. D. (1993). Experiences of Australian mothers who gave birth at home, at a birth centre, or in a hospital labour wards. *Social Science and Medicine*, 36, 475-483.

Cunningham, N. (1990). *Complete Guide to Early Child Care*. New York: Crown.

D'Antonio, M. (August, 1997). The dance of nature and nurture. *Child*, 20, 22, 24.

Dabelea, D., Knowler, W. C., & Pettit, D. J. (2000). Effect of diabetes in pregnancy on offspring: Follow-up research in the Pima Indians. *Journal of Maternal and Fetal Medicine*, 9, 83-88.

Dale, P., & Goodman, J. (2004). Commonality and differences in vocabulary growth. In M. Tomasello & D. I. Slobin (Eds.), *Beyond Nature-Nurture*. Mahwah, NJ: Erlbaum.

Danielle, D. M., Rose, R. J., Viken, R. J., & Caprio, J. (2000). Pubertal timing and substance use: Association between and with families across late adolescence. *Developmental Adolescence*, 36, 180-189.

Dash, L. (July/August, 1990). When children want children. *Society*, 27(5), 17-20.

David, B., Grace, D., & Ryan, M. K. (2004). The gender wars: A self categorization perspective on the development of gender identity. In M. Bennett & F. Sani (Eds.), *The Development of the Social Self.* East Sussex, England: Psychology Press.

David, H. P. (1981). Unwantedness: Longitudinal studies of Prague children born to women twice denied abortions for the same pregnancy and matched controls. In P. A. Ahmed (Ed.), *Pregnancy, Childbirth, and Parenthood*. New York: Elsevier.

Davies, B., & Banks, C. (1992). The gender trap: A feminist prostructuralist analysis of primary school talk about gender. *Journal of Curriculum Studies*, 24, 1-25.

Davis, B. G., Trimble, C. S., & Vincent, D. R. (January, 1980). Does age entrance affect school achievement? *The Elementary School Journal*, 80, 133-143.

Dawkins, M. P. (1997). Drug use and violent crimes among adolescents. *Adolescence,* 32, 395-405.

Dean, R. S., & Anderson, J. L. (1997). Lateralization of cerebral function. In A. M. Horton, Jr., D. Wedding, & J. Webster (Eds.), *The Neuropsychology Handbook: Vol. 1. Foundations and Assessment* (2nd ed.). New York: Springer.

Decasper, A. J., & Spence, M. J. (1986). Prenatal maternal speech influences perception of speech sounds. *Infant Behavior and Development*, 9, 133-150.

Decker, M. D., Dewey, M. J., Hutcheson, R. H., & Schaffner, W. (1984). The use and efficacy of child restraint devices. *Journal of the American Medical Association*, 252(18), 2571-2575.

Dejong, A. R., Emmett, G. A., & Hervada, A. (1982). Sexual abuse of children. *American Journal of Diseases of Children*, 136, 129-134.

Delgado, J., Ramirex-Cardich, M.E., Gilman, R. H., Laverello, H., Dahodwala, N., Bazan, A., Rodriguez, V., Cama, R. I., Tovar, M., & Lescano, A. (2002). Risk factors for burns in children: Crowding, poverty, and poor maternal education. *Injury Prevention*, 8, 38-41.

DeLaney, S. E. (1995). Divorce mediation and children's adjustment to parental divorce. *Pediatric Nursing*, 21, 434-437.

DeLoache, J. S. (1986). Memory in very young children. Exploitation of cues to the location of a hidden object. *Cognitive Development*, 1, 123-138.

Dennis, C. L. (2004). Can we identify mothers at risk for postpartum depression in the immediate postpartum period using the Edinburgh Postnatal Depression Scale? *Journal of Affective Disorders*, 28, 163-169.

Dennis, W. (1960). Causes of retardation among institutionalized children: Iran. *Journal of Genetic Psychology*, 96, 45-599.

Dezoate, J. A., MacArthur, AB. A., Tuck, B. (April 7, 2003). Prediction of Bayley and Stanford-Binet scores with a group of very low birthweight children. *Child: Care, Health & Development*, 28, 5, 3679372.

DeRegt, R. H., Minkoff, H., Feldman, J., & Schwartz, R. H. (1986). Relation of private or clinic care to the cesarean birth rate. *The New England Journal of Medicine*, 315, 619-624.

DeVries, R. (1969). Constancy of gender identity in the years three to six. *Monographs of the Society for Research in Child Development,* 34(3), Serial No. 127.

DiBlasio, F. A., & Benda, B. B. (1990). Adolescent sexual behavior: Multivariate analysis of a social learning model. *Journal of Adolescent Research*, 5, 449-466.

Dick, D. M., Rose, R. J., Viken, R. J., & Kaprio, J. (2000). Pubertal timing and substance use: Associations between and within families across late adolescence. *Developmental Psychology*, 36, 180-189.

Dick-Read, G. (1944). *Childbirth Without Fear: The Principles and Practices of Natural Childbirth*. New York: Harper & Row.

DiFranza, J. R., & Lew, R. A. (April, 1995). Effect of maternal cigarette smoking on pregnancy complications and sudden infant death syndrome. *The Journal of Family Planning*, 40, 385-394.

Dilworth, M. (1992). (Ed.) *Diversity in Teacher Education: New Expectations*. San Francisco: Jossey-Bass.

Dishion, T. J., Bullock, B. M., & Granic, I. (2002). Pragmatism in modeling peer influence: Dynamics, outcomes, and change processes. *Development and Psycholopathology*. 14, 969-981.

Dodge, K. A. (1983). Behavioral antecedents of peer social status. *Child Development*, 54, 1386-1399.

Doherty, Martin J. (2009). *Theory of mind: how children understand others' thoughts and feelings* (Hove: Psychology Press).

Doherty, W. J. (1997). The best of times and the worst of times: Fathering as a contested area of academic discourse. In A. J. Hawkins, & D. C. Dollahite (Eds.), *Generative Fathering: Beyond Deficit Perspectives*. Newbury Park, CA: Sage.

Donaldson, S. I., Graham, J. W., & Hansen, W. B. (1994). Testing the generalizability of intervening mechanism theories: Understanding the effects of adolescent drug use prevention interventions. *Journal of Behavioral Medicine*, 17, (2), 195-216.

Dooley, D. (2001). *Social Research Methods* (4th ed.). Upper Saddle River, NJ: Prentice-Hall.

Dornbusch, S. M., Carlsmith, J. M., Bushwall, S. J., Ritter, P. L., Leiderman, H., Hastorf, A. H., & Gross, R. T. (1985). Single parents, extended households, and the control of adolescents. *Child Development*, 56, 326-341.

Dowell. S. F., Kupronis, B. A., Zell, E. R., Stat. M., & Shay, D. K. (2000). Mortality from pneumonia in children in the United States, 1939 through 1996. *New England Journal of Medicine,* 342(19), 1399-1407.

Down, J. L. (1866). Observation on an ethnic classification of idiots. *Clinical Lectures and Reports*, 3, London Hospital.

Drake, A. J., & Walker, B. R. (2004). The intergenerational effects of fetal programming: Non-genomic mechanisms for the inheritance of low birth weight and cardiovascular risk. *Journal of Endocrinology*, 180, 1-16.

Drewes, A. A., Carey, L. J., & Schaefer, C. E. (Eds.), (2003). *School-based Play Therapy*. New York: Wiley.

Dreyer, P. H. (1982). Sexuality during adolescence. In B. Wolman (Ed.), *Handbook of Developmental Psychology*. Englewood Cliffs, NJ: Prentice-Hall.

Driscoll, C. D., Streissguth, A. P., & Riley, E. P. (1990). Prenatal alcohol exposure: Compatibility of effects in humans and animal models. *Neurotoxical Teratology*, 12, 231-237.

DSM IV (See American Psychiatric Association). 1994. *Diagnostic and Statistical Manual of Mental Disorders* (4th ed.). Washington, DC: Author.

Duncan, Greg J. and Chase-Lansdale, P. Lindsay editors (2001). *For better and for worse: welfare reform and the well-being of children and families* (New York: Russell Sage Foundation).

Dutton, G., N. (2003). Cognitive vision, its disorders and differential diagnosis in adults and children: Knowing where and what things are. *Eye*, 17, 289-304.

Dweck, C. S. (1999). *Self-theories: Their Role in Motivation, Personality, and Development.* Philadelphia: Psychology Press, Taylor & Francis.

Dykman, R., Casey, P.H., Ackerman, P.T., & McPherson, W.B. (February, 2001). Behavioral and cognitive status in school-aged children with a history of failure to thrive during early childhood. *Clinical Pediatrics*, 63-70.

Eagle, M. (2000). Psychoanalytic theory: History of the field. In A. Kazdin (Ed.), *Encyclopedia of Psychology.* Washington, DC & New York: American Psychological Association and Oxford University Press.

Eaves, L. J., & Stilberg, J. L. (2003). Modulation of gene expression by genetic and environmental heterogeneity in timing of developmental milestones. *Behavior Genetics*, 33, 1-6.

Eccles, J. S. (2004). Schools, academic motivation, and stage environment fit. In R. Lerner & L. Steinberg (Eds.), *Handbook of Adolescent Psychology.* New York: Wiley.

Eccles, J. S., Wigfield, a., & Byrnes, J. (2003). Cognitive development in adolescence. In I. B. Weiner (Ed.), R. M. Lerner, M. A. Easterbrooks, & J. Mistry (Vol. Eds.), *Handbook of Psychology.* Vol. 6, *Developmental Psychology.* New York: John Wiley and Sons.

Eckstein, E. (1980). *Food, People, and Nutrition.* Westport, CT: AV Publishing.

Edgcumbe, Rose (2000). *Anna Freud: a view of development, disturbance and therapeutic techniques* (London: Routledge).

Edelman, M. (1982). Human behavior and sociobiological models of natural selection. *The Philosophical Forum*, 13, 1-42.

Eden, A., & Mohammad, A. (1997). Iron deficiency in 1-3-year-old children. *Archives of Pediatric and Adolescent Medicine*, 151, 986-988.

Edwards, C. P. (1981). The comparative study of the development of moral judgment and reasoning. In A. L. Monroe, R. Monroe, & B. B. Whiting (Eds.), *Handbook of Cross-cultural Human Development.* New York: Garland.

Ehrlich, V. (1982). *Gifted Children: A Guide for Parents and Teachers.* Englewood Cliffs, NJ: Prentice-Hall.

Eisenberg, N., & Fabes, R. A. (1998). Prosocial development. In W. Damon (Series Ed.) & N. Eisenberg (Vol. Ed.), *Handbook of Child Psychology.* Vol. 3, *Social, Emotional and Personality Development.* (5th ed.). New York: Wiley.

Eisenberg, N., Fabes, R. A., Schaller, M., Carlo, G., & Miller, P. A. (1991). The reactions of parental characteristics and practices to children's vicarious emotional responding. *Child Development*, 62, 1393-1408.

Eisenberg, N., & Morris, A. S. (2004). Moral cognitions and prosocial responding in adolescence. In R. Lerner & L. Steinberg (Eds.), *Handbook of Adolescent Psychology.* New York: Wiley.

Eisler, I., & leGrange, D. (1990). Excessive exercise and anorexia nervosa. *International Journal of Eating Disorders*, 9(4), 377-386.

Ekman, P. (1997). Expression or communication about emotion. In N. L. Segal & G. E. Weisfeld (Eds.), *Uniting Psychology and Biology: Integrative Perspectives on Human Development.* Washington, DC: American Psychological Association.

Eley, T. C., Lichtenstein, P., & Stevenson, J. (1999). Sex differences in the etiology of aggressive and nonaggressive antisocial behavior: Results from two twin studies. *Child Development,* 70(1), 155-168

Elia, J., *et al.* (March 1, 1999). Treatment of attention deficit hyperactivity disorder. *New England Journal of Medicine,* 340, 780-788.

Elicker, J., Englund, M., and Sroufe, L. A. (1992). Predicting peer competence and peer relationships in childhood from early parent-child relationships. In R. D. Parke & G. W. Ladd (Eds.), *Family-Peer Relationships: Modes of Linkage.* Hillsdale, NJ: Erlbaum.

Elkind, D. (1998). *Grown Up and No Place to Go: Teenagers in Crisis* (rev. ed.) Reading, MA: Addison-Wesley.

Elliot, K.G., Kjohede, C.L; & Rasmussen, K.M. (1997). *Obesity Research,* 5, 538.

Ellis, B. J., *et al.* (2003). Does father-absence place daughters at special risk for early sexual activity and teenage pregnancy? *Child Development,* 74, 801-821.

Emde, R. N. (1992). Individual meaning and increasing complexity: Contributions of Sigmund Freud & Rene Spitz to developmental psychology, *Developmental Psychology,* 28, 347-359.

Engelhard, Jr., G. (1990). Gender differences in performance on mathematics items: Evidence from the United States and Thailand. *Contemporary Educational Psychology,* 15, 13-26.

Ennis, R. H. (1971). Conditional logic and primary children. *Interchange,* 2, 127-132.

Epstein, L. H., Valoski, A., Wing, R. R., & McCurley, J. (1990). Ten-year follow-up of behavioral family-based treatment for obese children. *Journal of the American Medical Association,* 264, 2519-2523.

Epstein, R. H. (April, 1991). Dem Bones, Dem Bones. *Inc,* 55-58.

Erikson, E. H. (1950). *Childhood and Society.* New York: W. W. Norton.

_____ (1968). *Identity, Youth and Crisis.* New York: W. W. Norton.

Eriksson, P. S., Pertilieva, E., Björk-Eriksson, T., Alborn, A., Nordborg, C., Peterson, D. A., & Gage, F. A. (1998). Neurogenesis in the adult hippocampus. *Nature Medicine,* 4, 1313-1317.

Eskenazi, B. (1993). Caffeine during pregnancy: Grounds for concern? *Journal of the American Medical Association,* 270, 2973-2974.

Eskenazi, B., Fenster, D., & Sidney, S. (July 10, 1991). A multivariate analysis of risk factors for preeclamsia. *Journal of the American Medical Association,* 266(2), 237-241.

Estes, L. S. (2004). *Essentials of Child Care and Early Education.* Boston: Allyn & Bacon.

Evans, Gary W. and Wachs, Theodore D. editors (2010). *Chaos and its influence on children's development: an ecological perspective* (Washington: American Psychological Association).

Fagan, J. F. (April, 1985). Early novelty preferences and later intelligence. Paper presented at the meeting of the Society for Research in Child Development, Toronto.

Fagot, B. I., Rodgers, C. S., & Leinbach, M. D. (2000). Theories of gender socialization. In T. Eckes, & H. M. Trautner (Eds.), *The developmental Social Psychology of Gender.* Mahwah, NJ: Erlbaum.

Fantz, R. (1961). The origin of form perception. *Scientific American,* 204, 71-72.

_____ (1965). Visual perception from birth as shown by pattern selectivity. *Annals of the New York Academy of Sciences,* 118, 793-814.

_____ (1967). Visual perception and experience in early infancy. In H. Stevenson, E. Hess, & H. Rheingold (Eds.), *Early Behavior Comparative and Developmental Approaches.* New York: Wiley.

Fantz, R., & Miranda, S. (1975). Newborn infant attention to forms of contour. *Child Development,* 46, 224-228.

Farrell, A. D., & White, K. S. (1998). Peer influences and drug use among urban adolescents: Family structure and parent-adolescent relationship as protective factors. *Journal of Consulting and Clinical Psychology,* 66(2), 248-258.

Farrington, D. (2004a). Conduct disorder, aggression and delinquency. In R. Lerner & L. Steinberg (Eds.), *Handbook of Adolescent Psychology.* New York: Wiley.

_____ (2004b). Conduct disorder, aggression and delinquency. In R. Lerner & L. Steinberg (Eds.), *Handbook of Adolescent Psychology* (2nd ed.). Hoboken, NJ: Wiley.

Fauci, A. (Ed.), (1998). *Harrison's Principles of Internal Medicine.* New York: McGraw-Hill.

Feldman, R., & Eidelman, A. I. (2003). Skin-to-skin kangaroo care accelerates autonomic and neurobehavioral maturation in preterm infants. *Developmental Medicine and Child Neurology,* 45, 274-281.

_____ (2003). Direct and indirect effects of breast milk on the development of premature infants. *Developmental Psychology, 43, 109-119.*

Fenson, L., Dale, P.S., Reznick, J.S., Bates, E., Thai, D.J., & Pethick, S.J. (1994). Variability in early communication development. *Monographs of the Society for Research in Child Development* Vol. 59, (Serial number 242).

Fentress, J. C., & McLeod, P. J. (1986). Motor patterns in development. In E. M. Blass (Ed.), *Handbook of Behavioral Neurobiology.* Vol. 8. *Developmental Psychobiology and Developmental Neurobiology.* New York: Plenum.

Fergusson, E. M., Woodward, L. J., & Horwood, L. J. (2000). Risk factors and life processes associated with the onset of suicidal behavior during adolescence and early adulthood. *Psychological Medicine,* 30, 23-39.

Feroli, K. L., & Burnstein, G. R., (March/April, 2003). Adolescent sexually transmitted diseases. *MCN,* 28(2), 113-118.

Field, D. (1981). Can preschool children really learn to conserve? *Child Development,* 52, 326-334.

Field, T. M. (2001). *Touch.* Cambridge, MA: MIT Press.

Fields, J. (2001). Living arrangements of children: Fall 1996. *Current Population Reports,* 70-74, US Census Bureau, Washington, DC

Firthel, Richard A. editor (2007). Focus on medical genetics and Down's syndrome research (New York: Nova Biomedical Books).

Fisch, S. M. (2004). *Children's Learning from Educational Television.* Mahwah, NJ: Erlbaum.

Fischman, B., & Hamel, B. (1981). From nuclear to stepfamily ideology. A stressful change. *Alternative Lifestyles,* 42(2), 181-204.

Flavell, J. (1963). *The Developmental Psychology of Jean Piaget.* New York: Van Nostrand.

_____ (1977). *Cognitive Development.* Englewood Cliffs, NJ: Prentice-Hall.

_____ (1985). *Cognitive Development.* (2nd ed.) Englewood Cliffs, NJ: Prentice Hall.

Flavell, J. H., Miller, P. H., & Miller, S. A. (1993). *Cognitive Development* (3rd ed.). Upper Saddle River, NJ: Prentice Hall.

_____ (2002). *Cognitive Development* (4th ed.). Upper Saddle River, NJ: Prentice Hall.

Fletcher, A. C., Steinberg, L., & Sellers, E. B. (August, 1999). Adolescents' well-being as a function of perceived interparental consistency. *Journal of Marriage and the Family,* 61, 599-610.

Flodmark, C., Ohisson, J., Ryden, O., & Sweger, T. (1993). Prevention of progression to severe obesity in a group of obese schoolchildren treated with family therapy. *Pediatrics,* 91, 880-884.

Flynn, J. R. (1999). Searching for justice: The discovery of IQ gains over time. *American Psychologist,* 54(1), 5-20.

Follari, Lissanna M. (2007). *Foundations and best practices in early childhood education: history, theories and approaches to learning*(Upper Saddle River: Pearson/Merrill Prentice Hall).

Fox, M. K., Pac, S., Devaney, B., & Jankowski, L. (2004). Feeding infants and toddlers study: What foods are infants and toddlers eating? *Journal of the American Diet Association,* 104, 22-30.

Franco, N., & Levitt, M. I. (April, 1997). Friendship, friendship quality, and the friendship networks in middle childhood: The role of peer acceptance in a multicultural sample. Paper presented at the Biennial Meetings of the Society for Research in Child Development, Washington, DC

Francouer, R. T. (1985). Reproductive technologies: New alternatives and new ethics. *SIECUS Report,* 14, 1-5.

Frank, D.A., Augustyn, M., Knight, W.G., Pell, T., & Zuckerman, B. (March 28, 2001). Growth, development, and behavior in early childhood following prenatal cocaine exposure. *Journal of the American Medical Association,* 285(12), 1613-1625.

Franklin, C., & Corcoran, J. (2000). Preventing adolescent pregnancy: A review of programs and practices. *Social Work,* 45, 40-52.

Free, T., Russell, F., Mills, B., & Hathaway, D. (July/August, 1990). A descriptive study of infants and toddlers exposed prenatally to substance abuse. *MCN,* 15, 253.

Freedman, D. S., Khan, L. K., Serfula, M. K., Sprinivasan, S. R., & Berenson, G. S. (2000). Secular trends in height among children during two decades: The Bogalusa Heart Study. *Archives of Pediatric and Adolescent Medicine*, 154, 155-161.

Freeman, D. (1983). *Margaret Mead and Samoa*. Cambridge, MA: Harvard University Press.

Freeman, S. B., Taft, L. F., Dooley, K. J., Allran, K., Sherman, S. L., Hassold, T. J., Khoury, M. J., & Saker, D. M. (1998). Population-based study of congenital heart defects in down syndrome. *American Journal of Medical Genetic*, 80, 213-217.

Freud, A. (1946). *The Ego and the Mechanisms of Defense*. New York: International Universities Press.

_____ (1972). Adolescence. In J. F. Rosenblith, W. Allinsmith, & J. P. William (Eds.), *The Causes of Behavior* (3rd ed.). Boston: Allyn & Bacon.

Freud, S. (1921). Group psychology—The analysis of the ego. In J. Strachey (Ed., & Trans.), *The Standard Edition of the Complete Works of Sigmund Freud*. Vol. 18. London: Hogarth Press.

_____ (1940/1964). An outline of psychoanalysis. In J. Strachey (Ed. and Trans.), *The Standard Edition of the complete Psychological Works of Sigmund Freud*. Vol. 23. London: Hogarth Press.

Frias, J. L., & Davenport, M. L. (2003). Health supervision for children with Turner syndrome. *Pediatrics,* 111, 692-702.

Fried, P. A. (1982). Marijuana use by pregnant women and effects on offspring: An update. *Neurobehavioral Toxicology and Teratology*, 4, 451-454.

Friedman, R. C., & Downey, J. I. (December, 2000). Psychoanalysis and Sexual Fantasies. *Archives of Sexual Behavior*, 29(6), 567-585.

Friend, M., & Davis, T. I. (1993). Appearance/reality distinction: Children's understanding of physical and affective domains. *Developmental Psychology*, 29, 907-914.

Frost, R. O., & Steketee, G. (1997). Perfectionism in obsessive-compulsive disorder patients. *Behavior Research and Therapy*, 15(4), 291-296.

Galambos, N. L. (2004). Gender and gender role development in adolescence. In R. Lerner & L. Steinberg (Eds.), *Handbook of Adolescence*. New York: Wiley.

Galambos, S. J., & Goldin-Meadow, S. (January, 1990). The effects of learning two languages on levels of metalinguistic awareness. *Cognition*, 34, 1-56.

Gale, C. R., & Martin, C. N. (2004). Birth weight and later risk of depression in a national birth cohort. *British Journal of Psychiatry*, 184, 28-33.

Galinsky, E., Howes, C., Kontos, S., & Shinn, M. B, *The Study of Children in Family Child Care and Relative Child Care: Highlights of Findings*. New York: Families & Work Institute, 1994.

Galluhue, D. L., & Ozmun, J. C. (2002). *Understanding Motor Development: Health and Human Performance*, (5th ed.). New York: McGraw-Hill.

Ganong, L. H., & Coleman, M. (1993). A meta-analytic comparison of the self-esteem and behavior problems of stepchildren to children in other family structures. *Journal of Divorce and Remarriage,* 19(3-4) 143-163.

Gans, J. E., & Shook, K. L. (1994). *Alcohol and Other Harmful Substances*. Chicago: American Medical Association.

Garbarino, J., Kostelny, K., & Dubrow, N. (1991). *No place to be a child. Growing up in a War Zone*. Lexington, MA: Lexington Books.

Garcia, M. M., Shaw, D. S., Winslow, E. B., & Yaggi, K. E. (2000). Destructive sibling conflict and the development of conduct problems in young boys. *Developmental Psychology*, 36, 44-53.

Gard, J. W., Alexander, J. M., Bawddon, R. E., & Albrecht, J. T. (2002). Oxytocin preparation stability in several common intravenous solutions. *American Journal of Obstetrics and Gynecology,* 186, 496-498.

Gardiner, H. W., & Komitzki, C. (2005). *Lives across Cultures, Cross-Cultural Human Development*. Boston: Allyn & Bacon.

Gardner, H. (March 29, 1979). Exploring the mystery of creativity. *The New York Times*, C1, C17.

_____ (Winter, 1998). A multiplicity of intelligences. *Scientific American,* 9(4), 19-23.

Garrison, J. (April 19, 2001). Toddler's time in child care linked to behavior problems. *Los Angeles Times,* 1, 24.

Gathercole, V. C. (1985). More and more about more. *Journal of Experimental Child Psychology*, 40, 73-104.

Gathercole, S. E., Pickering, S. J., Ambridge, B., & Wearing, H. (2004). The structure of working memory from 4 to 15 years of age. *Developmental Psychology,* 40, 177-190.

Gauthier, S. M., Bauer, C. R., Messinger, D. S., & Closius, J. M. (April, 1999). The Bayley Scales of Infant Development II: Where to start? *Developmental and Behavioral Pediatrics,* 20(2), 75-156.

Gazzaniga, J., & Burns, T. (1993). Relationship between diet and body fatness, physical activity in pre-adolescent children. *American Journal of Clinical Nutrition,* 58, 21-28.

Gentry, D. B. (1997). Including children in divorce mediation and education: Potential benefits and cautions. *Families in Society: The Journal of Contemporary Human Services*, 307-315.

George, L., Milas, J.L., Johansson, A.L.V., Nordmark, A., Olander, B., Granath, F., & Cnattingius, S. (October 16, 2002). Plasma folate levels and risk of spontaneous abortion. *Journal of the American Medical Association,* 288(15), 1867-1873.

Gerrard, J. A., & Chudasama, G. (2003). Screening to reduce HIV transmission from mother to baby. *Nursing Times,* 99, 44-45.

Gesell, A., & Ilg, F. L. (1943-1946). *Child Development: An Introduction to the Study of Human Growth* (Parts 1 & 2). New York: Harper.

Gesell, A., & Thompson, H. (1938). *The Psychology of Early Growth.* New York: Macmillan.

_____ (1929). Learning and growth in identical infant twins: An experimental study by the method of co-twin control. *Genetic Psychological Monographs*, 6, 1-24.

Gfroerer, J. (1996). *Preliminary Estimates From the 1995 National Household Survey on Drug Abuse.* U.S. Dept. of Health and Human Services. Public Health Services: Washington, DC

Ghizzani, A., & Montomoli, M. (2000). Anorexia nervosa and sexuality in women: A review. *Journal of Sex Education and Therapy*, 25, 80-88.

Giammattei, J., Blix, G., Marshak, H. H., Wollitzer, A. O., & Pettitt, D. J. (2003). Television watching and soft drink consumption: Associations with obesity in 11 - 13 year-old schoolchildren. *Archives of Pediatric and Adolescent Medicine*, 157, 882-886.

Gibbons, A (1993). Evolutionists take the long view on sex and violence, *Science*, 26, 987-988.

Gibbs, J. C. (2003). *Moral Development and Reality.* Thousand Oaks, CA: Sage.

Gibson, E., & Walk, R.D. (April, 1960). The visual cliff. *Scientific American,* 202(1), 64-71.

Gibson, P. A. (2002). African-American grandmothers as caregivers: Answering the call to help their grandchildren. *Families in Society*, 83, 35-43.

Gilbert, W. M., Nesbitt, T. S., & Danielson, B. (January, 1999). Child bearing beyond age 40: Pregnancy outcome. *Obstetrics & Gynecology*, 93(1), 9-14.

Gilligan, C. (1977). In a different voice: Women's conception of self and of morality. *Harvard Educational Review*, 47, 481-517.

_____ (1982). *In a Different Voice. Psychological Theory and Women's Development.* Cambridge, MA: Harvard University Press.

Gilligan, C., & Attanucci, J. (1988). Two moral orientations: Gender differences and similarities. *Merrill-Palmer Quarterly*, 34, 223-237.

Gilvarry, E. (2000). Substance in young people. *Journal of Child Psychology and Psychiatry*, 41, 55-80.

Gitlin-Weiner, K., Sandgrund, A., & Schaefer, C. (2000). *Play Diagnosis and Assessment,* (2nd ed.). New York: Wiley.

Glasgow, K. L., Dornbusch, S. M., Steinberg, L., & Ritter, P. L. (June, 1997). Parenting styles, adolescents' attributions, and educational outcomes in nine heterogeneous high schools. *Child Development*, 68(3), 507-529.

Goday, Praveen S. and Sentongo, Timothy S. editors (2009). *Nutritional deficiencies*, guest editors. (Philadelphia: W. B. Saunders).

Godfrey, K. M. (1998). Maternal regulation of fetal development and health in adult life. *European Journal of Obstetrics & Gynecology and Reproductive Biology*, 78, 141-150.

Goldin-Meadow, S. (1997). The resilience of language in humans. In C. T. Snowdon & M. Hausberger (Eds.), *Social Influences on Vocal Development*. Cambridge, England: Cambridge University Press.

Goldin-Meadow, S., & Mylander, C. (1998). Spontaneous sign systems created by deaf children in two cultures. *Nature*, 391, 279-281.

Goldschmidt, L., Day, N. L., & Richardson, G. AA. (2000). Effects of prenatal marijuana exposure on child behavior problems at age 10. *Neurotoxicology and Teratology*. 22, 325-336.

Goldstein, D. J., Wilson, M. G., Thompson, V. L., Potvin, J. H., & Rampey, Jr., A. A. (1995). Long-term fluoxetine treatment of bulimia nervosa. *British Journal of Psychiatry*, 166, 660-666.

Golinkoff, R., & Hirsh-Pasek, K. (July/August, 1999). Small talk. *Working Mother*, 46-50.

Golombok, S., Cook, R., Bish, R., & Murray, C. (1995). Families created by new reproductive techniques: Quality of parenting and social and emotional development of the children. *Child Development*, 66, 285-298.

Goode, E. (February 23, 2000). Sharp rise found in psychiatric drugs with the very young. *The New York Times*, A-1.

Goodman, J. H. (2004). Paternal postpartum depression: Its relationship to maternal postpartum depression and implications for family health. *Journal of Advanced Nursing*, 45, 26-35.

Gordon, D. E. (July, 1990). Formal operational thinking: The role of cognitive-developmental processes in adolescent decision-making about pregnancy and contraception. *American Journal of Orthopsychiatry*, 60(3), 346-354.

Gordon, J. (1975). *Parent Effectiveness Training*. New York: New American Library.

Gorey, K. M., & Leslie, D. R. (1997). The prevalence of child sexual abuse: Integrative review adjustment for potential response and measurement biases. *Child Abuse and Neglect*, 21(4), 391-398.

Gosden, R., Frasier, J., Lucifero, D., & Faddy, M. (1975-1977). Rare congenital disorders, imprinted genes, and assisted reproductive technology. *The Lancet*, 361.

Gottesman, I. I. (1993). Origins of schizophrenia: Past as prologue. In R. Plomin & G. E. McClearn (Eds.), *Nature, Nurture, and Psychology*. Washington, DC: American Psychological Association.

Gottfredson, L. (Winter, 1998). The general intelligence factor. *Scientific American*, 9(4), 24-29.

Gottlieb, G. (2004). Normally occurring environmental and behavioral influences on gene activity. In C. G. Coll, E. L. Bearer, & R. M. Lerner (Eds.) *Nature and Nurture*, Mahwah, NJ: Erlbaum.

Gotlib, Ian H. and. Hammen, Constance L. (2009). *Handbook of depression* (New York: Guilford Press).

Gowers, Simon G. and Green, Lynne (2009). *Eating disorders: cognitive behavior therapy with children and young people* (London: Routledge).

Graber, J. A. (2004). Internalizing problems during adolescence. In R. M. Lerner, & L. D. Steinberg (Eds.), *Handbook of Adolescent Psychology* (2nd ed.). Hoboken, NJ: Wiley.

Grados, M. A., & Riddle, M. A. (2001). Pharmacological treatment of childhood obsessive-compulsive disorders: From theory to practice. *Journal of Clinical Child Psychology*, 30(1). 67-79.

Graefe, D. R., & Lichter, D. T. (2002). Marriage among unwed mothers: Whites, blacks and Hispanics compared. *Perspective on Sexual and Reproductive Health*, 34, 286-293.

Graham, S. (2000). Should the natural learning approach replace spelling instructions? *Journal of Educational Psychology*, 92(2), 235-247.

Graham, S., & Harris, K.R. (1997). Whole language and process writing: Does one approach fit all? In J.W. Lloyd, E.J. Kameenui, & D. Chard (Eds.), *Issues in Educating Students with Disabilities*. Mahwah, NJ: Lawrence Erlbaum.

Grantham-McGregor, S., Powell, C., Walker, S., Chang, S., & Fletcher, P. (1994). The long-term follow-up of severely malnourished children who participated in an intervention program. *Child Development*, 65, 428-439.

Grantham-McGregor, S. M., Walker, S. P., & Chang, S. (2000). Nutritional deficiencies and later behavioral development. *Proceedings of the Nutritional Society*, 59, 47-54

Graue, M. E., & DiPerna, J. (2000). Redshirting and early retention: Who gets the "gift of time" and what are its outcomes? *American Educational Research Journal,* 37, 509-534.

Grazinano, A. M. (2001). *Developmental Disabilities*. Boston: Allyn and Bacon.

Green, N. S. (2002). Folic acid supplementation and prevention of birth defects. *The Journal of Nutrition*, 132 (8, Suppl., 2356S-2360S.

Greene, W. C. (September, 1993). AIDS and the immune system. *Scientific American*, 67-73.

Greenfeld, M. (1990). Disclosing incest: The relationships that make it possible. *Journal of Psychosocial Nursing*, 28(7), 120-123.

Greenfield, P. M. (February, 2003). Commentary. *Monitor on Psychology*, 34(2), 58.

Greenman, G.W. (1963). Visual behavior in newborn infants. In A. J. Solnit & S. A. Provence (Eds.), *Modern Perspectives in Child Development*. Kansas City, MO: Hallmark.

Greenough, W. T., & Black, J. E. (1992). Induction of brain structure by experience: Substrates for cognitive development. In M. R. Gunnar & C. A. Nelson (Eds.), *Symposia on Child Psychology*. Hillsdale, NJ: Erlbaum.

Greensher, J., & Mofenson, H. C. (1985). Injuries at play. *Pediatric Clinics of North America*, 32(1), 127-139.

Greenwood, P. W. (1995). The cost-effectiveness of early intervention as a strategy for reducing violent crime. Paper prepared for the University of California Policy Seminar Crime Project, Santa Monica, CA: RAND.

Grigorenko, E. L., & Sternberg, R. J. (1998). Dynamic testing. *Psychological Bulletin*, 124, 759.

Grigorenko, Elena L. editor (2008). *Educating individuals with disabilities: IDEIA 2004 and beyond* (New York: Springer Pub.).

Grimshaw, G. M., Adelstein, A., Bryden, M. P., & MacKinnon, G. E. (1998). First-language acquisition in adolescence: Evidence for a critical period for verbal language development. *Brain and Language*, 63, 237-255.

Grossman, J. A., & Kruesi, M. J. P. (2000). Innovative approaches to youth suicide prevention: An update of issues and research findings. In R. W. Marias, S. S. Canetto, J. L. McIntosh, & M. M. Ailcweman (Eds.), *Review of Suicidology*, 2000. New York: Guilford.

Groulios, G., Tsorbatzoudis, H., Alexandris, K., & Darkoukis, V. (2000). Do Left-handed competitors have an innate superiority in sports? *Perceptual and Motor Skills*, 90, 1273-1282.

Grufferman, S. Schwartz, A. G., Ruymann, F. B., & Mauer, H. M. (1993). Parents' use of cocaine and marijuana and increased risk of rhabdomyosarcoma in their children. *Cancer, Causes & Control,* 4, 217-224.

Grych, J. H., & Clark, R. (1999). Maternal employment and development of the father-infant relationship in the first year. *Developmental Psychology*, 35, 893-903.

Guldberg, Helene (2009). *Reclaiming childhood: freedom and play in an age of fear* (Milton Park: Routledge).

Gullotta, Thomas P. and Blau, Gary M.; research assistant, Ramos, Jessica M. editors (2008). *Family influences on childhood behavior and development: evidence-based prevention and treatment approaches* (New York: Routledge).

Gunnoe, M. L., & Mariner, C. L. (August, 1997). Toward a developmental-contextual model of the effects of parental spanking on children's aggression. *Archives of Pediatrics and Adolescent Medicine*, 768-775.

Gurbutt, Dawne J. (2007). *Sudden infant death syndrome: learning from stories about SIDS, motherhood and loss* (Seattle: Radcliffe Pub.).

Gurwitch, R. H., Silovsky, J. F., Schultz, S., Kees, M., & Burlingame, S. (2001). *Reactions and Guidelines for Children Following Trauma/Disaster.* Norman, OK: Department of Pediatrics University of Oklahoma Health Sciences Center.

Hagan, M. S., Hollier, E. A., O'Connor, T. G., & F Eisenberg, M. (1992). Parent-child relationships in nondivorced, divorced, single-mother, and remarried families. In E. M. Hetherington & W. G. Clingemped (Eds.), Coping with marital transitions. *Monographs of the Society for Research in Child Development*, 57(2-3, Serial No. 227).

Hagenas, L, & Arver, S. (1998). Klinefelter syndrome affects mostly boys: An undiagnosed chromosome abnormality. *Lakartidningen, 95.* 2686-2690.

Hagerman, R. J. (2000). Fragile-X syndrome. In P. L. Jackson and J. A. Vessey (Eds.), *Primary Care of the Child with a Chronic Condition,* (3rd ed.). St. Louis, MO: Mosby.

Haliburn, J. (2000). Reasons for adolescent suicide attempts. *Journal of the American Academy of Child Adolescent Psychiatry,* 13, 29.

Hall, D.M.B., Hill, P., & Elliman, D. (1990). *The Child Survey Handbook.* Oxford: Radcliffe Medical Press.

Hall, G. S. (1904). *Adolescence: Its Psychology and Its Relation to Physiology, Anthropology, Sociology, Sex, Crime, Religion, and Education (*2 vols.) New York: Appleton.

Hamilton, B. E., Martin, J. A., & Sutton, P. P. (November 23, 2004). Birth: Preliminary data for 2003. *National Vital Statistics Reports,* 53(9), 1-17.

Hamm, J. W. (2000). Do birds of a feather flock together? The various bases for African-American, Asian-American, and European-American adolescents' selection of similar friends. *Developmental Psychology,* 36, 209-219.

Hansen, D. *et al.* (August 28, 1999). Severe periconceptional life events and the sex ratio in offspring: Follow up study based on five national registers. *British Medical Journal,* 319, 548-549.

Harari, M. D., & Moulden, A. (2000). Nocturnal enuresis: What is happening? *Journal of Pediatrics and Child Health,* 36, 78-81.

Hard, M., Raha, S., Spino, M., Robinson, B. H., Koren, G., & Koren, G. (2001). Improvement in pyruvate dehydrogenase activity by acetaldehyde. *Alcohol,* 23, 1-8.

Harlap, S., & Shiono, P. (1980). Alcohol, smoking, and the incidence of spontaneous abortions in the first and second trimester. *The Lancet,* 2, 173-176.

Harlow, H. (1958). The nature of love. *American Psychologist,* 13, 673-685.

_____ (April, 1973). Harry are you going to go down in history as the father of the cloth mother? A conversation with Carol Tavris. *Psychology Today,* 65-77.

Harlow, H., & Harlow, M. K. (1962). The effect of rearing conditions on behavior. *Bulletin of the Menninger Clinic,* 26, 213-224.

Harris, P. L., & Kavanaugh, R. D. (1993). Young children's understanding of pretense. *Monographs of the Society for Research in Child Development,* 58 (1, Serial No. 231).

Harris, R. T. (April, 1991). Anorexia nervosa and bulimia nervosa in female adolescents. *Nutrition Today,* 30-34.

Hartlage, L. C., & Telzrow, C. F. (1982). Neuropsychological disorders in children: Effect of medication in learning behavior in hyperactivity. *Journal of Research and Development in Education,* 5(3), 55-75.

Harter, S. (1998). The development of self-representations. In W. Damon (Series Ed.) & N. Eisenberg (Vol. Ed.), *Handbook of Child Psychology*: Vol. 3. *Social, Emotional, and Personality Development* (5th ed.). New York: Wiley.

Hartup. W. W. (1978). Children and their friends. In H. M. Gurk (Ed.), *Issues in Childhood Social Development.* London: Methuen.

Harvey, E. (1999). Short-term and long-term effects of early parental employment on children of the National Longitudinal Survey of Youth, *Developmental Psychology,* 35(2), 445-459.

Hassold, T. J., & Patterson, D. (1998). (Eds.), *Down Syndrome: A Promising Future Together.* New York: Wiley-Liss, Inc.

Haupt, D. (February, 1998). Safety Alert. *Parenting.*

Haverkamp, B., & Daniluk, J. (1993). Child sexual abuse: Ethical issues for the family therapist, *Family Relations,* 42, 134-139.

Hay, D. R., Pedersen, J., & Nash, H. (1982). Dyadic interaction in the first year of life. In K. H. Rubin & H. S. Ross (Eds.), *Peer Relationships and Social Skills in Children.* New York: Springer.

Hay, W. W., Groothuis, J. R., Hayward, A. R., & Levin, M. J. (1997). *Current Pediatric Diagnosis and Treatment* (13th ed.). San Mateo, CA: Appleton-Lange.

Head Start Bureau. (2000). 2000 Head Start Fact Sheet. (On-line) Available: www.acf.dhhs.gov/programs/hsh/research/.

Heath, T. D. (1994). The impact of delayed fatherhood on the father-child relationship. *Journal of Genetic Psychology*, 155, 511-530.

Healy, J.M. (1994). *Your Child's Growing Mind*. New York: Doubleday.

Hembree, D. (March, 1986). High-tech hazards. *Ms*, 79.

Hemmings, A. (2004). *Coming of Age in U.S. High Schools*. Mahwah, NJ: Erlbaum.

Henshaw, S. K. (1993). Teenage abortion, birth, and pregnancy statistics by state, 1988. *Family Planning Perspectives*, 25, 122-126.

Herman-Giddens, M.E., Slora, E.J., Wasserman, R.C., Bourdony, C.J., Bhapkar, M.V., Koch, G.G., & Hasemeier, C.M. (April, 1997). Secondary sexual characteristics and menses in young girls seen in office practice: A study from the pediatric research in office settings network. *Pediatrics,* 88(4), 505-513.

Herrnstein, R. J., & Murray, C. (1994). *The Bell Curve: Intelligence and Class Structure in Modern Life*. New York: Free Press.

Herzog, D., Agras, W. S., Marcus, M. D., Mitchel, J., & Walsh, B. T. (May 20, 1995). Recent advances in eating disorders: Symposium of the American Psychiatric Association.

Herzog, D. B., Greenwood, D. N., Dorer, D. J., Flores, A. T., Ekeblad, E. R., Richards, A., Blais, M. A., & Keller, M. B. (2000). Mortality in Eating Disorders: A Descriptive Study. *International Journal of Eating Disorders*, 28, 20-26.

Hetherington, E. M., Clingempeel, W. G., Anderson, E. R., Deal, J. E., Hagan, S. M., Hollier, E. A., & Linder, M. S. (1992). Coping with marital transitions: A family systems perspective. *Monographs of the Society for Research in Child Development,* 57(2-3, Serial No. 227).

Hetherington, E. M., Cox, M., & Cox, R. (1978). The aftermath of divorce. In J. Stevens, & R. M. Matthews (Eds.), *Mother-Child, Father-Child Relationships*. Washington, DC: National Association for Education of Young Children.

_____ (1982). Effects of divorce on parents and children. In M. E. Lamb (Ed.), *Nontraditional Families: Parenting and Child Development*. Hillsdale, NJ: Erlbaum.

Hetherington, E. M., & Stanley-Hagan, M. (2002). Parenting in divorced and remarried families. In M. H. Bornstein (Ed.), *Handbook of Parenting*. Vol. 3. (2nd ed.). Mahwah, NJ: Erlbaum.

Hey, E. N. (1972). Thermal regulation in the newborn. *British Journal of Hospital Medicine*, 51-64.

High, P. C., LaGasse, L., Becker, S., Ahlgren, I., & Gardner, A. (2000). Literacy promotion in primary care pediatrics: Can we make a difference? *Pediatrics*, 105, 927-934.

Hindmarsh, P. C., Pringle, P. J., Disilvio, L., & Brook, G. G. D. (1990). Effects of 3 years of growth hormone therapy in short normal children. *Acta Paediatrica,* 366, 6-12.

Hinds, D. A., Stuve, L. L., Nilsen, G. B., Halperin, E. E., Eskin, E., Ballinger, D. G., *et al.* (2005). Whole genome patterns of common DNA variation in three human populations. *Science,* 307, 1072-1079.

Hines, A. M. (May, 1997). Divorce-related transitions, adolescent development, and the role of the parent-child relationship: A review of the literature. *Journal of Marriage and the Family*, 59: 375-388.

Hingson, R., Alpert, J. J., Day, N., Dooling, E., Kayne, H., Morelock, S., Oppenheimer, E., & Zuckerman, B. (1982). Effects of maternal drinking and marijuana use on fetal growth and development. *Pediatrics*, 70(4), 537-546.

Hintz, R. I. (2003). Confirming the diagnosis of growth hormone deficiency (GHD) and transitioning the care of patients with childhood-onset GHD. *Pediatric Endrocrinology and Metabolism*, 16 (Suppl. 3), 637-643.

Hirschfeld, R. M. A. (June 1, 1996). The long-term nature of depression. *Psychiatric Annals,* 26(6), 313-314.

Hitchcock, C. H., & Noonan, M. J. (2000). Computer-assisted instruction of early academic skills. *Topics in Early Childhood Special Education*, 20, 145-158.

Hofer, M. A. (1981). *The Roots of Human Behavior: An Introduction to the Psychology of Early Development*. New York: Freeman.

Hoff-Ginsberg, E. (1997). *Language Development*. Pacific Grove, CA: Brooks/Cole.

Hoffman, L. W. (2000). Maternal employment: Effects of social context. In R. D. Taylor & M. C. Wang (Eds.), *Resilience Across Contexts: Family, Work, Culture, and Community.* Mahwah, NJ: Erlbaum.

Hoffman, M. L. (1982). Development of prosocial motivation: Empathy and guilt. In N. Eisenberg (Ed.), *The Development of Prosocial Behavior.* New York: Academic Press.

_____ (1979). Development of moral thought, feeling, and behavior. *American Psychologist, 34,* 958-966.

_____ (2002). *Empathy and Moral Development,* New York: Cambridge University Press.

Holden, G. W., & Miller, P. C. (1999). Enduring and different: A meta-analysis of the similarity in parents' child rearing. *Psychological Bulletin, 125,* 223-254.

Holt, J.A. (1993). Stanford Achievement Test—8th edition: Reading comprehension subgroup results. *American Annals of the Deaf, 138, 172-175.*

Holt, L. H., Sears, M., & Sears, W. (1997). *The Pregnancy Book: A Month-by-Month Guide.* New York: Little, Brown, & Company.

Hopkins, B. (2000). Development of crying in normal infants: Method, theory and some speculations. In R. G. Barr, B. Hopkins. and J. A. Green (Eds.), *Crying as a Sign, a Symptom, and a Signal.* London: McKeith Press.

Horne, R. S., Parslow, P. M., Ferens, D., Watts, A. M., & Adamson, T. M. (2004). Comparison of evoked aroustability in breast and formula fed infants. *Archives of Diseases in Childhood, 89,* 22-25.

Horner, M. S. (1970). Femininity and successful achievement: A basic inconsistency. In J. M. Bardwick, E. Douvan, M. S. Horner, & D. Gutman (Eds.), *Feminine Personality and Conflict.* Belmont, CA: Brooks/Cole.

Houts, A. C., Berman, J. S., & Abramson, H. (1994). Effectiveness of psychological and pharmacological treatments for nocturnal enuresis. *Journal of Consulting and Clinical Psychology, 62,* 737-745.

Howell, C. J., Dean, T., Lucking, L., Dziedzic, K., Jones, P. W., & Johnson, R. B. (2002). Randomized study of long-term outcome after epidural versus non-epidural analgesia during labor. *British Medical Journal, 352,* 357.

Howell, J. C. (1998). *Youth Gangs in the United States: An Overview.* Washington, DC: Office of Juvenile Justice and Delinquency Prevention.

Howes, C., Phillips, D. A., & Whitebook, M. (1992). Thresholds of quality: Implications for the social development of children in center-based child care. *Child Development, 63,* 449-460

Hughes, Daniel A. (2009). *Attachment-focused parenting: effective strategies to care for children* (New York: W.W. Norton & Co.).

Hull, H. (1993). Polio eradication in sight, *World Health* (March/April 1993), 17-19.

Humphryes, J. (July, 1998). The developmental appropriateness of high-quality montessori programs. *Young Children, 4-12.*

Hunt, E. (1985). Verbal ability. In R. J. Sternberg (Ed.), *Human Abilities: An Information-Processing Approach.* New York: Freeman.

Hunt, M. H., Meyers, J., Davies, G., Meyers, B., Grogg, K. R., & Neel, J. (2002). A comprehensive needs assessment to facilitate prevention of school drop out and violence. *Psychology in Schools, 39(4),* 399-416.

Huston, A. C. (1992). *Big World, Small Screen: The Role of Television in American Society.* Lincoln: University of Nebraska Press.

Huston, A. C., & Aronson, S. R. (2005). Mothers' time with infants and time in employment as predictors of mother-child relationships and children's early development. *Child Development, 76,* 467-482.

Hutchison, M. K., & Sandall, M. (1995). Congenital TORCH infections in infants and young children: Neurodevelopmental sequelae and implications for intervention. *Topics in Early Childhood and Social Education, 15(1),* 65-82.

Hutt, S. J., Lenard, H. G., & Prechtl, H. E. R. (1969). Psychophysiology of the newborn. In L. P. Lipsitt & H. W. Reese (Eds.), *Advances in Child Development and Behavior.* Vol. 4. New York: Academic Press.

Huttenlocher, P. R. (2002). *Neural Plasticity: The Effects of Environment on the Development of the Cerebral Cortex.* Cambridge, MA: Harvard University Press.

Hyde, J. S. (2004). *Half the Human Experience* (5th ed.). Boston: Houghton Mifflin.

Inaba, D. S., & Cohen, W. E. (2007). *Uppers, downers, all arounders: Physical and mental effects of psychoactive drugs* (Medford: CNS Publications Inc.).

Inhelder, B., & Piaget, J. (1958). *The Growth of Logical Thinking.* London: Routledge.

Insel, P. M., & Roth, W. F. (1977). *Concepts: Health in a Changing Society.* Palo Alto, CA: Mayfield.

Irons, T. C. (1995). *Health and Illness.* Westerville: Hans & Cassady.

Isabella, R. A. (1993). Origins of attachment: Maternal interactive behavior across the first year. *Child Development,* 64, 605-621.

Isley, S. L., O'Neal, R. O., Clatfelter, D., & Parke, R. D. (1999). Parent and child expressed affect and children's social competence: Modeling direct and indirect pathways. *Developmental Psychology,* 35(2), 547-560.

Ismail, A. I. (1998). The role of early dietary habits in dental caries development. *Special Care Dentist,* 18, 40-45.

Jaccard, J., Blanton, H., & Dodge, T. (2005). Peer influence on risk behavior: An analysis on the effects of a close friend. *Developmental Psychology,* 41(1), 135-147.

Jackson, D. J., Lang, J. M., Swartz, W. H., Ganiats, T. G., Fullerton, J., Ecker, J., *et al.* (2003). Outcomes, safety, and resources utilization in a collaborative care birth center program compared with traditional physician-based perinatal care. *American Journal of Public Health*, 93, 999-1006.

Jackson, P. L. (2000). The primary care provider and children with chronic conditions. In P. L. Jackson & J. A. Vessey (Eds.), *Primary Care of the Child with a Chronic Condition.* St. Louis: Mosby.

Jacobson, D. S. (1980). Stepfamilies. *Children Today,* 9, 2-6.

Jacobson, J. L., & Willie, D. E. (1984). Influence of attachment and separation experience on separation distress at 18 months. *Developmental Psychology,* 20(3), 477-484.

Jemmott, J. B., Jemmott, L. S., & Fong, G. T. (1998). Abstinence and safer sex: A randomized trial of HIV risk-reductions interventions for young African-American adolescents. *Journal of the American Medical Association,* 279(19), 1529-1536.

Jenkins, J., Simpson, A., Dunn, J., Rashbash, J., & O'Connor, T. G. (January, 2005). Mutual influence of marital conflict and children's behavior problems shared and nonshared family risks. *Child Development*, 76(1), 24-39.

Jensen, A. R. (1969). How much can we boost IQ and scholastic achievement? *Harvard Education Review*, 39, 1-123.

_____ (1980). *Bias in Mental Testing.* New York: Free Press.

Jessor, K. (1998). *New Perspectives on Adolescent Risk Behavior.* New York: Cambridge University Press.

Jeynes, W. H., & Littell, S. W. (2000). A meta-analysis of studies examining the effect of whole language instruction on the literacy of low-SES students. *Elementary School Journal*, 101, 21-33.

Jin, S. H., Kim, T. I., Han, D. S., Shin, S. K., & Kim, W. H. (2002). Thalidomide suppresses the interleukin 1 (beta)-induced NF (kappa) B signaling pathway in colon cancer cells. *Annals of the New York Academy of Science,* 973, 414-418.

Johnson, D., Magee, J. C., Colbert, C. M., Christie, B. (March, 1996). Active properties of neuronal dendrites. *Annual Review Neuroscience,* 19, 165-186.

Johnson, D. E. (2002). Adoption and the effect on children's development. *Early Human Development*, 68, 39-54.

Johnson, D. W., & Johnson, R. T. (1980). Integrating handicapped students into the mainstream. *Exceptional Children*, 46, 89-98.

Johnson, J. (June, 2001). Children and funerals. *Mothering*, 106, 38-44.

Johnson, S., & Marano, R. E. (March/April, 1994). Love: The immutable longing for contact. *Psychology Today*, 27, 32-37, 64-66.

Johnston, L. (1993). *Monitoring the Future Study Questionnaires From the Nation's High School Seniors.* Ann Arbor: University of Michigan.

Johnston, L. D., O'Malley, P. M., Bachman, J. G. (2003). *Monitoring the Future: National Results on Adolescent Drug Use. Overview of Key Findings, 2002.* Bethesda, MD: National Institute on Drug Abuse.

Johnston, L. D., O'Malley, P. M., Bachman, J. G., & Schulenberg, J. E. (2004). *Monitoring the Future: National Results on Adolescent Drug Use. Overview of Key Findings.* NIH Publication No. 04-5506. Bethesda, MD: National Institute on Drug Abuse.

Johnson, M., & Robin, N.H. (May, 2000). Pediatrics and the human genome project. *Contemporary Pediatrics,* 100-112.

Johnston, C. A., Steel, R. G., Herrera, E. A., & Phills, S. (2003). Parent and child reporting of negative life events: Discrepancy and agreement across pediatric samples. *Journal of Pediatric Psychology,* 28(8), 579-588.

Jones, M. C. (1957). The later career of boys who were early—or late—maturing. *Child Development,* 36, 899-911.

Jones, R. E. (1997) *Human Reproductive Biology.* San Diego: Academic Press.

Jordan, Amy B. editor (2009). *Media messages and public health: a decisions approach to content analysis /* (New York: Routledge).

Jung, J. (2010). *Alcohol, Other Drugs, and Behavior* (California: Sage Publications).

Jusczyk, P. W. (1995). Language acquisition: Speech sounds and phonological development. In J. L. Miller & E. D. Eimas (Eds.), *Handbook of Speech, Language, and Communication.* Orlando, FL: Academic Press.

_____ (2002). Language development: From speech perception to words. In A. Slater & M. Lewis (Eds.), *Introduction to Infant Development.* New York: Oxford University Press.

_____ (2003). Language development: From speech perception to words. In A. Slater & M. Lewis (Eds.), *Introduction to Infant Development.* New York: Oxford University Press.

Kagan, J. (1979). Structure and process in the human infant: The ontogeny of mental representation. In M. H. Bornstein and W. Reese (Eds.), *Psychological Development from Infancy: Image to Retention.* Hillsdale, NJ: Erlbaum.

_____ (1984). *The Nature of the Child.* New York: Basic Books.

Kagan, J., & Herschkowitz, E. (2005). *Young Mind in a Growing Brain.* Mahwah, NJ: Erlbaum.

Kagan, J., & Snidman, N. (2004). *The Long Shadow of Temperament.* Cambridge, MA: Belknap Press.

Kahn, D. (Ed.) (1995). *What is Montessori Preschool?* Mountain View, CA: Educational Publications.

Kail, R., & Hall, L. K. (1994). Processing speed, naming speed, and reading. *Developmental Psychology,* 30, 949-854.

Kaiser Family Foundation, Hoff, T., Greene, L., & Davis, J. (2003). *National Survey of Adolescents and Young Adults: Sexual Health Knowledge, Attitudes and Experiences.* Menlo Park, CA: Henry J. Kaiser Foundation.

Kalichman, S. C. (1991). Psychopathalogy and personality of criminal sex offenders as a function of age. *Archives of Sexual Behavior,* 20(2), 187-197.

Kallman, F. J. (1946). The genetic theory of personality. *American Journal of Psychiatry,* 103-309-322.

Kaplan, E., & Kaplan, G. (1971). The prelinguistic child. In J. Elliott (Ed.), *Human Development and Cognitive Processes.* New York: Holt, Rinehart, Winston.

Kaplowitz, P. B., Slora, E. J., Wasserman, R. C., Pedlow, S. E., & Herman-Giddens, P. A. (August, 2001). Earlier onset of puberty in girls: Relation to increased body mass index and race. *Pediatrics,* 108(2), 347-353.

Karlsrud, K., & Schultz, D. (1993). Can You Spoil a Baby? *Parents,* 36.

Kauffman, J. M. (1997). *Characteristic of Emotional and Behavioral Disorders of Children and Youth* (6th ed.). Upper Saddle River, NJ: Merrill.

Kaufman, A. S. (1982). An integrated review of almost a decade of research on the McCarthy Scales. In T. R. Kratochwill (Ed.), *Advances in School Psychology.* Vol. 3. Hillsdale, NJ: Erlbaum.

Kaufman, A. S., & Kaufman, N. L. (1983; 2003). *Kaufman Assessment Battery for Children (K-ABC).* Circle Pines, MI: American Guidance Services.

Kaufman, James C. editor (2009). *Intelligent testing: integrating psychological theory and clinical practice* (Cambridge: Cambridge University Press).

Kaufman, J. C., & Baer, J. (Eds.), (2004). *Creativity Across Domains.* Mahwah, NJ: Erlbaum.

Kazdin, A. E. (2000). *Behavior Modification Applied Settings* (6th ed.). Pacific Grove, CA: Brooks/Cole.

Kelly, J. B. (August, 1987). Long-term adjustment in children of divorce. Converging findings and implications for practice. Paper presented at the Annual Meeting of the American Psychological Association, New York.

Kelly, S. J., Day, N., & Streissguth, A. P. (2000). Effects of prenatal alcohol exposure on social behavior in humans and other species. *Neurotoxicology and Teratology*, 22, 143-149.

Kempe, R. S., & Kempe, C. H. (1978). *Child Abuse*. Cambridge, MA: Harvard University Press.

Kempermann, G., & Gage, F. H. (May, 1999). New nerve cells for the adult brain. *Scientific American,* 280, 48-53.

Kessler, Daniel B. and Dawson, Peter editors (1999). *Failure to thrive and pediatric undernutrition: a transdiciplinary approach* (Baltimore: Brookes).

Keuhne, E. A., & Reilly, M. W. (2000). Prenatal cocaine exposure. In P. L. Jackson & J. A. Vessey (Eds.), *Primary Care of the Child with a Chronic Condition*. St. Louis, MO: Mosby.

Kheshgi-Genovese, Z., & Genovese, T. A. (1997). Developing the spousal relationship within stepfamilies. *Families in Society: The Journal of Contemporary Human Services*, 255-264.

Kimble, G. A. (1993). Evolution of the nature-nurture issue in the history of psychology. In R. Plomin & G. E. McClearn (Eds.), *Nature, Nurture, and Psychology*. Washington, DC: American Psychological Association.

King, P. M., & Kitchener, K. S. (1994). *Developing Reflective Judgment: Understanding and Promoting Intellectual Growth and Critical Thinking in Adolescents and Adults*. San Francisco: Jossey-Bass.

Kinney, H. C., Filiano, J. J., Sleeper, L. A., Mandell, F., Valdes-Dapena, & White, W. F. (1995). Decreased muscarinic receptor binding in the arcuate nucleus in sudden infant death syndrome. *Science,* 269, 1446-1450.

Kinsey, A. C., Pomeroy, W. B., & Martin, C. E. (1948). *Sexual Behavior in the Human Male*. Philadelphia: Saunders.

Kinsey, A. C., Pomeroy, W. B., Martin, C. E., & Gebhard, P. H. (1953). *Sexual Behavior in the Human Female*. Philadelphia: W. B. Saunders.

Klahr, D., & MacWhinney, B. (1998). Information processing. In D. Kuhn & R. S. Siegler (Eds.), *Information Processing*. New York: Wiley.

Klahr, D., & Wallace, J. C. (1976). *Cognitive Development: An Information-Processing View*. Hillsdale, NJ: Erlbaum.

Klaus, M. H., & Kennell, J. H. (1976). *Maternal Infant Bonding*. St. Louis: Mosby.

_____(1982). *Parent-Infant Bonding* (1st ed.). St. Louis, MO: Mosby.

Klaus, M. H., Kennell, J. H., & Klaus, P. H. (1995). *Bonding: Building the Foundations of Secure Attachment and Independence*. Reading, Mass.: Addison-Wesley.

Klee, L. (1986). Home away from home: The alternative birth center. *Social Science and Medicine*, 23, 9-16.

Klein, H. A. (Summer, 2000). Self-esteem and beyond. *Childhood Education,* 240-241.

Kleinknecht, R. A. (2000). Social phobia. In M. Hersen & M. K. Biaggio (Eds.), *Effective Brief Therapies: A Clinical Guide*. New York: Academic Press.

Knobloch, H., & Pasaminick, B. (1963). Predicting intellectual potential in infancy. *American Journal of Diseases of Children*, 107(1, 43-51).

Koch, W. (June 16, 2000). Big tobacco tells Florida it has reformed. *USA Today*, 13A.

Kodroff, J. F., & Roberge, J. J. (1975). Developmental analysis of the conditional reasoning abilities of primary grade children. *Developmental Psychology*, 11, 21-28.

Koek, K. E., & Martin, S. B. (Eds.) (1988). *Encyclopedia of Associations* (2nd ed.). Detroit: Gale Research Company.

Koerner, J. D. (1963). *The Miseducation of American Teachers*. Boston: Houghton-Mifflin.

Koester, L., & Meadow-Orlans, K. (1990). Parenting a deaf child; Stress, strength and support. In D. F. Moores & K. P. Measow-Orlans (Eds.), *Educational and Developmental Aspects of Deafness*. Washington, DC: Gallaudet University Press.

Kohlberg, L. (1964). Development of moral character and moral ideology. In M. L., & S. L. W. Hoffman (Eds.), *Review of Child Development Research*. Vol. 1. New York: Russell Sage Foundation.

_____ (1966). *Parent-Infant Bonding* (2nd ed.). St. Louis, MO: Mosby.

_____ (1966). A cognitive-developmental analysis of children's sex-role concepts and attitudes. In E. E. Maccoby (Ed.), *The Development of Sex Differences*. Stanford, CA: Stanford University Press.

_____ (1969). Stage and sequence. The cognitive-developmental approach to socialization. In D. A. Goslin (Ed.), *Handbook of Socialization Theory and Research*. Chicago: Rand McNally.

_____ (1971). From is to ought: How to commit the naturalistic fallacy and get away with it in the study of moral development. In T. Mischel (Ed.), *Cognitive Development and Epistemology*. New York: Academic Press.

_____ (1976). Moral stages and moralization: The cognitive developmental approach. In T. Lickona (Ed.), *Moral Development and Behavior: Theory, Research and Social Issues*. New York: Holt, Rinehart, & Winston.

_____ (1985). *The Psychology of Moral Development*. San Francisco: Harper & Row.

Kolb, B., & Whishaw, I. Q. (2003). *Fundamentals of Human Neuropsychology* (5th ed.). New York: Worth.

Konkol, R. J., & Olsen, G. D. (1996). *Prenatal Cocaine Exposure*. Baton Rouge, FL: CRC Press.

Kontos, A. P. (September, 2004). Perceived risk, risk taking, estimation of ability and injury among adolescent sport participants. *Journal of Pediatric Psychology*, 20(6), 448-455.

Kosterman, K., Haggerty, K. P., Spoth, R., & Redmond, C. (August, 2004). Unique influence of mothers and fathers in children's antisocial behavior. *Journal of Marriage and the Family*, 66, 762.

Kotch, J. B. *et al.* (1997). Stress, social support, and substantiated maltreatment in the second and third years of life. *Child Abuse and Neglect*, 21(11), 1025-1037.

Kovacs, M. (1997). Depressive disorder in childhood: An impressionistic landscape. *Journal of Child Psychology and Psychiatry*, 38(3), 287-298.

Krauss, R. M., & Glucksberg, S. (1969). The development of communication as a function of age. *Child Development*, 40, 255-266.

Kreipe, R. E., & Uphoff, M. (1992). Treatment and outcome of adolescents with anorexia nervosa. *Adolescent Medicine*, 3, 519-540.

Kuczynski, L. (2002). *Handbook of Dynamics in Parent-Child Relations*. Thousand Oaks, CA: Sage.

Kuczynski, L., & Lollis, S. (2002). Four foundations for a dynamic model of parenting. In J. R. M. Gerris (Ed.) *Dynamics of Parenting*. Hillsdale, NJ: Erlbaum.

Kuder, G. E. (1975). *General Interest Survey (Form E.) Manual*. Chicago: Science Research Associates.

Kuhn, D. (2004). What is scientific thinking, and how does it develop? In P. Smith & C. Hart (Eds.), *Blackwell Handbook of Cognitive Development*. Malden, MA: Blackwell.

Kupersmidt, J. B., Coie, J. D., & Dodge, K. A. (1990). The role of poor peer relations in the development of disorder. In S. R. Asher & J. D. Coie (Eds.), *Peer Rejection in Childhood*. Cambridge, England: Cambridge University Press.

Kurdek, L. A. (1991). Marital stability and changes in marital quality in newlywed couples: A test of the contextual models. *Journal of Social and Personal Relationships*, 8, 27-48.

Kurdek, L. A., & Fine, M. A. (1994). Family acceptance and family control as predictors of adjustment in young adolescents: Linear, curvilinear, or interactive effects? *Child Development,* 65, 1137-1146.

Kurdek, L. A., Fine, M. A., & Sinclair, R. J. (1995). School adjustment in sixth graders: Parenting transitions, family climate, and peer norm effects. *Child Development,* 66, 430-445.

Kushner, M. G., Neumeyer, I., Anderson, N., Neumeyer, B., & Mackenzie, T. (2000). Expectancies for alcohol to affect tension and anxiety as a function of time. *Addictive Behaviors,* 25, 93-98.

Kutner, L. (November, 1990). Agreeing to disagree. *Child*, 36-38.

Lancashare, J. (1995). National Center for Health Statistics data line. *Public Health Reports,* 110, 105-106.

Ladd, Gary W. (2005). *Children's peer relations and social competence: a century of progress* (New Haven: Yale University Press).

Ladd, G. W., & LeSieur, K. D. (1995). Parents' and children's peer relationships. In M. H. Barnstein (Ed.), *Handbook of Parenting*. Vol. 4, *Applied and Practical Parenting*. Mahwah, NJ: Erlbaum.

Ladoucer, R., Rheume, J., & Auble, T. F. (1997). Excessive responsibility in obsessional concerns: A fine-grained experimental analysis. *Behavior Research and Therapy*, 35(5) 423-427.

LaGreca, A. M. (1993). Social skills training with children: Where do we go from here? *Journal of Clinical Child Psychology*, 22, 288-298.

Lamb, Michael E. editor (2010). *The role of the father in child development* (Hoboken: Wiley).

Lamb, M. (1998) Nonparental child care: Context, quality, correlates, and consequences. In I. E. Sigel & K. A. Renninger (Eds.), *Handbook of child psychology* (5th ed.). Vol 4, *Child Psychology in Practice*. New York: Wiley.

Landine, J., & Stewart, J. (1998). Relationships between metacognition, motivations, locus of control, self-efficacy, and academic achievement. *Canadian Journal of Counseling*, 32, 200-212.

Landreth, G. L. (2000). *Innovations in Play Therapy: Issues, Process, and Special Populations.* Philadelphia: Taylor & Francis.

Landry, S.H., Smith, K.E., Swank, P.R., & Miller-Loncar, C.L. (March/April, 2000). Early maternal and child influences on children's later independent cognitive and social functioning. *Child Development,* 71(2), 358-375.

Langlois, J. H., Ritter, J. M., Foggman, L. A., & Vaughn, L. S. (1991). Facial diversity and infant preferences for attractive faces. *Developmental Psychology,* 27, 79-84.

Langman, Peter (2009). *Why kids kill: inside the minds of school shooters* (New York: Palgrave Macmillan).

Lansdown, R., & Walker, M. (1991). *Your Child's Development From Birth to Adolescence.* New York: Knopf.

Lansford, J. E., Ceballo, R., Abbey, A., & Stewart, A. J. (August, 2001). Does family structure matter? A comparison of adoptive, two-parent biological, single-mother, stepfather, and stepmother households. *Journal of Marriage and the Family*, 63, 840-851.

Lapsley, D. K., & Narvaez, D. (Eds.), (2004). *Moral Development, Self, and Identity.* Mahwah, NJ: Erlbaum.

Larson, J. E., Morrow, S. L., & Cohen, J. (January/February, 1997). Gene Therapy. *Science and Medicine*, 4-5.

Larson, R. W., & Wilson, S. (2004). Adolescence across place and time: Globalization and the changing pathways to adulthood. In R. Lerner & L. L. Steinberg (Eds.), *Handbook of Adolescent Psychology.* New York: Wiley.

Lawton, Sandra A. editor (2009). *Sexual health information for teens: health tips about sexual development, reproduction, contraception, and sexually transmitted infections including facts about puberty, sexuality, birth control, chlamydia, gonorrhea, herpes, human papillomavirus, syphilis, and more* (Detroit: Omnigraphics).

Lazar, M. H. (2005). How obesity causes diabetes. Not a tall tale. *Science*, 307, 373-375.

Leadbeater, B. J. R., & Way, N. (2001). *Growing up Fast.* Mahwah, NJ: Erlbaum.

Leaper, C., Anderson, K. J., & Sanders, P. (1998). Moderators of gender effects on parents' talk to their children: A meta-analysis. *Developmental Psychology,* 34(1), 3-27.

Leary, M. R. (2004). *Introduction to Behavioral Research Methods* (4th ed.). Boston: Allyn & Bacon.

Leboyer, F. (1975). *Birth Without Violence.* New York: Random House.

Lee, V. E., Brooks-Gum, J., Schnur, E., & Liaw, F. (1990). Are Head Start effects Sustained? A longitudinal follow-up comparison of disadvantaged children attending Head Start, no preschool and other preschool programs. *Child Development* 61, 495-507.

Legerstee, D. A., & Schaffer, A. (1998). Five- and eight-month-old infants recognize their faces and voices as familiar and social stimuli. *Child Development*, 69(1), 37-50.

Lepper, M. R., & Greene, D. (Eds.) (1978). *The Hidden Costs of Reward.* Hillsdale, NJ: Erlbaum.

Lerner, J. (1993). *Learning Disabilities* (6th ed.). Boston: Houghton Mifflin.

Lesser, J. B., & Salmon, D. K. (1997-1998). Anesthesia used during labor and delivery. *Parents*, 22-23.

Lester, T., & Small, S. A. (February, 1997). Sexual abuse history and problems in adolescence: Exploring the effects of moderating variables. *Journal of Marriage and the Family*, 131-142.

Levine, B. (January, 1990). Children of divorce. *Seventeen*, 95, 110-111.

Levy, H. L., & Ghavami, M. (1996). Maternal phenylketonuria: A metabolic teratogen. *Teratology,* 53, 176-184.

Lewis, R., Gaffin, D., Hoefnagels, M., & Parker, B. (2004). *Life* (5th ed.). New York: McGraw-Hill.

Li, C. Q. *et al.* (March 24-31, 1993). The Impact of infant birth weight and gestational age of cotinine-validated smoking reduction during pregnancy. *The Journal of the American Medical Association*, 1519-1524.

Lichtenstein, P., & Annas, P. (2000). Heritability and prevalence of specific fears and phobias in childhood. *Journal of Child Psychology and Psychiatry and Allied Disciplines*, 41, 927-937.

Ligezinska, M. *et al.* (1996). Children's emotional and behavioral reactions following the disclosure of extrafamilial sexual abuse: Initial effects. *Child Abuse and Neglect*, 20(2), 111-125.

Lillard, A. S. (1993). Pretend play skills and the child's theory of mind, *Child Development*, 64, 348-371.

_____ (2005). *Montessori: The Science Behind the Genius.* New York: Oxford University Press.

Linn, Susan (2008). *The case for make believe: saving play in a commercialized world* (New York: New Press).

Liptak, G.S., O'Donnell, M., Conaway, M., Chumlea, W. C., Wolrey, G., Henderson, R.C., Fung, E., Stallings, V. A., Samson-Fang, L., Cavert, R., Rosenbaum, P., & Stevenson, R. D. (2001). Health status of children with moderate to severe cerebral palsy. *Developmental Medicine and Child Neurology*, 43, 364-370.

Liu, J., *et al.* (June, 2003). Malnutrition at age 3 years and lower cognitive ability at age 11 years. *Archives of Pediatric and Adolescent Medicine,* 157, 393-600.

Loehlin, J. C. (2000). Group differences in intelligence. In R. J. Sternberg (Ed.), *Handbook of Intelligence.* New York: Cambridge University Press.

Loehlin, J. C., Willerman, L., & Horn, J. M. (1988). Human behavior genetics. *Annual Review of Psychology*, 39, 101-133.

Loftus, E. F. (1992). When a lie becomes memory's truth: Memory distortion after exposure to misinformation. *Current Directions in Psychological Science,* 1, 121-123.

Lopez-Jaramillo, P., Delgado, F., Jacome, P., Teran, E., Ruano, C., & Rivers, J. (1997). Calcium supplementation and the risk of preeclampsia in Ecvadorian pregnant teenagers. *Obstetrics and Gynecology,* 90, 162-167.

Lowenthal, B., & Lowenthal, R. (Fall, 1997). Teenage parenting: Challenges, interventions and programs. *Childhood Education: Infancy Through Early Adolescence*, 29-32.

Lu Rang, M. (October, 1981). Understanding your baby's sleep patterns. *American Baby*, 181.

Luker, K. (1996). *Dubious Conceptions: The Politics of Teenage Pregnancy.* Cambridge, MA: Harvard University Press.

Lumeng, J. C., Gannon, K., Cabra, H. J., Frank, D. A., & Zuckerman, B. (2003). Association between clinically meaningful behavior problems and overweight in children. *Pediatrics,* 112, 1138-1145.

Luthar, S. S. (1999). *Poverty & Children's Adjustment,* Thousand Oaks, CA: Sage Publications, Inc.

Luthar, S. S., Zigler, E., & Goldstein, D. (1992). Psychosocial adjustment among intellectually gifted adolescents: The role of cognitive developmental and experiential factors. *Journal of Child Psychology and Psychiatry and Allied Disciplines*, 33, 361-373.

Lykken, D. T. (1982). Research with twins: The concept of emergenesis. *Psychophysiology*, 19, 361-373.

Maccoby, E. E. (1998). *The Two Sexes: Growing Up Apart, Coming Together.* Cambridge, MA: Belknap Press/Harvard University Press.

Lytton, H., & Rommey, D. M. (1991). Parents' sex-related differential socialization of boys and girls: A meta-analysis. *Psychological Bulletin*, 109, 267-296.

Maccoby, E. E. (1980). *Social Development: Psychological Growth and the Parent-Child Relationship.* New York: Harcourt, Brace, Jovanovich.

_____ (2002). Parenting effects: Issues and controversies. In J. G. Borkowski, S. L. Ramey, & M. Bristol-Power (Eds.), *Parenting and the Child's Work.* Mahwah, NJ: Erlbaum.

_____ (2003). The gender of child and parent as factors in family dynamics. In A. C. Crouter & A. Booth (Eds.), *Children's influence on family dynamics.* Mahwah, NJ: Erlbaum.

Maccoby, E. E., & Jacklin, C. N. (1974). *The Psychology of Sex Differences.* Stanford, CA: Stanford University Press.

Maccoby, E.E., & Mnookin, R.H. (1992). *Dividing the Child: Social and Legal Dilemas of Custody.* Cambridge, MA: Harvard University Press.

Mackey, M. C. (1995). Women's evaluation of their childbirth performance. *Maternal-Child Nursing Journal*, 23, 57-72.

Mader, S. (1993). *Biology* (4th ed.) Dubuque, Iowa: W. C. Brown.

Main, M., & Solomon, J. (1990). Procedures for identifying infants as disorganized/disoriented during the Ainsworth Strange Situation. In M. T. Greenberg, D. Diechetti, & E. M. Cummings (Eds.), *Attachment in the Preschool Years. Theory, Research, and Intervention.* Chicago: University of Chicago Press.

Manlove, J., Ryan, S., & Franzetta, K. (2003). Patterns of condom use with teenagers' first sexual relationships. *Perspectives on Sexual and Reproductive Health,* 35, 246-255.

Mandler, J. M. (2004). *The Foundations of Mind: Origins of Conceptual Thought.* Oxford, England: Oxford University Press.

Mannessier, L., Alie-Daram, S., Roubinet, A., & Broussard, R. (2000). Prevention of Fetal Hemolytic disease. It is time to take action. *Transfusions in Clinical Biology*, 7, 527-532.

Mansour, M. E., *et al.* (June, 2003). Health-related quality of life in urban elementary schoolchildren. *Pediatrics,* 111(6), 1372-1381.

Maratsos, M. (2000). More overregularizations after all: New data and discussion on Marcus, Pinker, Ullman, Rosen and Xu. *Journal of Child Language,* 27, 183-212.

March, J. S., Frances, A., Kahn, D., & Carpenter, D. (1997). Expert consensus guidelines: Threat of obsessive-compulsive disorder. *Journal of Clinical Psychiatry,* 58(Suppl. 4), 1-72.

Marchant, C. D., & Shurin, P. A. (1983). Therapy of otitis media. In W. T. Speck & J. L. Blumer (Eds.), *The Pediatric Clinics of North America.* Philadelphia: Saunders.

Marcia, J. E. (1980). Identity in adolescence. In J. Adelson (Ed.), *Handbook of Adolescent Psychology.* New York: Wiley.

_____ (1994). The empirical study of ego identity. In H. A. Bosna, *et al.* (Eds.), *Identity and Development.* Newbury Park, CA: Sage.

_____ (1996). *Unpublished Review of John Santrock's Adolescence* (7th ed.). Dubuque, IA: Brown & Benchmark.

Marcia, J. E., & Carpendale, J. (2004). Identity: Does thinking make it so? In C. Lightfoot, C. Lalonde, & M. Chandler (Eds.), *Changing Conceptions of Psychological life.* Mahwah, NJ: Erlbaum.

Marcus, Carole L. editor (2008). *Sleep and breathing in children: developmental changes in breathing during sleep* (New York: Informa Healthcare).

Marcus, G., Vijayan, B., Bandi, R., & Vishton, P. M. (January, 1999). Rule learning by seven-month-old infants. *Science*, 283, 77-80.

Marcus, M. B. (October 2, 2000). Don't let the false alarms scare you off prenatal tests, but do get the facts first. *U.S. News & World Report*, 69-70.

Margolin, G., & Gordis, E. B. (2000). The effects of family and community violence on children. *Annual Review of Psychology*, 51, 445-479.

Marlow, N., Wolke, D., Bracewell, M. A., & Samara, M. (2005). Neurologic and developmental disability at six years of age after extremely preterm birth. *New England Journal of Medicine,* 352, 9-19.

Marquis, D. P. (1931). Can conditioned reflexes be established in the newborn? *Journal of Genetic Psychology*, 39, 479-492.

Marsh, H. W. (1990). Two-parent, stepparent, and single-parent families: Changes in achievement, attitudes, and behavior during the last two years of high school. *Journal of Educational Psychology*, 82(2), 327-340.

Marshall, W. A. and Tanner, J. M. (1989). Identity and intervention, *Journal of Adolescence* 12, 401-410.

Martin, A. J., Marsh, H. W., & Debus, R. L. (2001). Self-handicapping and defensive pessimism: Exploring a model of predictors and outcomes from a self-protection perspective. *Journal of Educational Psychology*, 93(1), 87-102.

Martin, C., Cabrol, S., Bouvard, M. P., Lepine, J. P., & Mouren-Simeoni, M. C. (July, 1999). Anxiety and depressive disorders in fathers and mothers of anxious school-refusing children. *Journal of the Academy of Child and Adolescent Psychiatry,* 38(7), 916-922.

Martin, C. L. (1995). Stereotypes about children with traditional and nontraditional gender roles. *Sex Roles,* 33, 727-751.

Martin, I. A., *et al.* (2003). Births: First data for 2002. *National Vital Statistics Reports,* 52(10). Hyattsville, MD: National Center for Health Statistics.

Martin, J. A., Park, M. M., & Sutton, P. D. (2002). Births: Preliminary data for 2001. *National Vital Statistics Reports,* 50(10). Hyattsville, MD: National Center for Health Statistics.

Masten, A. S. (1986). Humor and competence in school-aged children. *Child Development,* 57, 461-473.

Masters, W. H., & Johnson, V. E. (1966). *Human Sexual Response.* Boston: Little, Brown.

Mather, E. (2004). Health-related quality of life of severely obese children and adolescents. *Child Care and Health Development,* 30, 94-95.

Matlin, M.W. (2004). *The Psychology of Women* (5th ed.). Belmont, CA: Wadsworth.

Maurer, D., & Lewis, T. L. (2001). Visual activity and spatial contrast sensitivity: Normal development and underlying mechanisms. In C. A. Nelson and M. Luciana (Eds.), *Handbook of Developmental Cognitive Neuroscience.* Cambridge, MA: MIT Press.

Maxson, S. (2003). Behavioral genetics. In L. B. Weiner (Ed.), *Encyclopedia of Psychology.* Vol. 3. New York: Wiley.

Mayer, Matthew J. editor (2009). *Cognitive-behavioral interventions for emotional and behavioral disorders: school-based practice* (New York: Guilford Press).

McAdoo, H. P. (2002). African-American parenting. In M. H. Bornstein (Ed.), *Handbook of parenting.* Vol. 4, *Social conditions and applied parenting* (2nd ed.). Mahwah, NJ: Erlbaum.

McCall, R. B. (1983). A conceptual approach to early mental development. In M. Lewis (Ed.), *Origins of Intelligence: Infancy and Early Childhood* (2nd. ed.). New York: Plenum.

McCall, R. S., & Carriger, M. S. (1993). A meta-analysis of infant habituation and recognition memory performance as predictors of later IQ, *Child Development,* 64, 57-79.

McCance, K. L., & Huether, S. E. (1998). *Pathophysiology: The Biologic Basis for Disease in Adults and Children* (3rd ed.). New York: Mosby.

McCarthy, L. (July/August, 1991). Beyond AA. *Health,* 40-44.

McCarthy, L. F. (June/July, 1998). Pregnancy at 20, 30, 40. *Parenting,* 101-107.

McCarton, C. M. (, January, 1997). Results at age 8 years of early intervention for premature low-birth-weight infants. *Journal of the American Medical Association,* 277, 126-132.

McCord, W., & Sanchez, J. (April 1, 1982). Curing criminal negligence. *Psychology Today,* 79-82.

McDonald, S. D., Ferguson, S., Tam, L., Lougheed, J., & Walker, M. C. (2003). The prevention of congenital anomalies with periconcentional folic acid supplementation. *Journal of Obstetrics and Gynecology Canada,* 25, 115-121.

McDonough, L. C. (November, 1990). 10 medical myths even smart parents believe. *Child,* 32, 35, 121.

McGee, L. M., & Richgels, D. J. (2000). *Literacy's Beginnings* (3rd ed.). Boston: Allyn and Bacon.

McGhee, P. E. (1976). Children's appreciation of humor. A test of the cognitive congruency principle. *Child Development,* 47, 420-426.

McGilley, B. M., & Pryor, T. L. (June, 1998). Assessment and treatment of bulimia nervosa. *American Family Physician,* 57(11), 2743-2750.

McGuire, M. & Beerman, K.A. (2010). *Nutritional sciences: From Fundamentals to Food.* (California: Wadsworth Cengage Learning).

McHale, S. M., Crouter, A. C., & Whiteman, S. D. (2003). The family contexts of gender development in childhood and adolescence. *Social Development,* 12, 125-152.

McIntosh, J. L. (2000). Epidemiology of adolescent suicide in the United States. In R. W. Maris, S. S. Canetto, J. L. McIntosh, & M. M. Silverman (Eds.), *Review of Suicidology,* (2000). New York: Guilford.

McKusick, V. (1995). *Mendelian Inheritance in Man: Catalogues of Autosomal Dominant, Autosomal Recessive, and X-Linked Phenotypes* (10th ed.). Baltimore: Johns Hopkins University Press.

_____ (1998). *Mendelian Inheritance in Man A Catalogue of Human Genes and Genetic Disorders.* Vols. 1, 2, 3. (12th ed.). Baltimore: Johns Hopkins University Press.

McNeil, Jr., D. G. (February 10, 1979). 100 Love Canal families are urged to leave area. *The New York Times*, L21, 24.

McWhirter, J.J., McWhirter, B.T., McWhirter, A., & McWhirter, E.H. (1998). *At-Risk Youth: A Comprehensive Response* (2nd ed.). Belmont, CA: Brooks/Cole.

Mead, M. (1928). *Coming of Age in Samoa.* New York: Morrow.

_____ (1949). *Male and Female.* New York: Morrow.

_____ (1953). *Growing up in New Guinea.* New York: Mentor.

_____ (1963). *Sex and Temperament in Three Primitive Societies.* New York: Morrow.

_____ (1970). *Culture and Commitment: A Study of the Generation Gap.* New York: Doubleday.

Medd, S. E. (2003). Children with ADHD need our advocacy. *Journal of Pediatric Health Care,* 17, 102-104).

Meis, P. J. (February 6, 2003). Effects of progesterone on preterm births. Paper presented at the meeting of the Society for Maternal-Fetal Medicine, San Francisco.

Mellon, M. W., & McGrath, M. L. (2000). Empirically supported treatments in pediatric psychology: Nocturnal enuresis. *Journal of Pediatric Psychology, 25, 193-214.*

Meltzoff, A. N. (1985). Immediate and deferred imitation in fourteen- and twenty-four month old infants. *Child Development*, 56, 62-72.

_____ (1988). Infant imitation and memory: Nine-month-olds in immediate and deferred tests. *Child Development*, 56, 62-72.

_____ (2002). Elements of a developmental theory of imitation. In A. N., & W. Prinz (Eds.), *The Imitative Mind: Development, Evolution, and Brain Bases.* Cambridge, England: Cambridge University Press.

Meltzoff, A. N., & Moore, K. M. (1998). Object representation, identity and the paradox of early permanence: Steps towards a new framework. *Infant Behavior and Development*, 21, 201-235.

Menaghan, E. G., Kowaleski-Jones, L; & Mott, F. L. (March, 1997). The intergeneralization costs of parental social stressors: Academic and social difficulties in early adolescence for children of young mothers. *Journal of Health and Social Behavior*, 72-86.

Mendelowitz, D. (1998). Nicotine excites cardiac vagal neurons via three sites of action. *Clinical and Experimental Pharmacology & Physiology,* 24, 453-456.

Meredith, H. V. (1969). Body size of contemporary groups of eight-year-old children studied in different parts of the world. *Monographs of the Society for Research in Child Development*, 34(1).

Miller, A. G., Gordon, A. K., & Buddie, D. M. (1999). Accounting for evil cruelty; Is to explain to condone? Personality and Social Psychology Review, 3, 254-268.

Miller, B. C., Fan, X., Christensen, M., Grotevat, H. D., & Van Dulmen, M. (2002). Comparison of adopted and nonadopted adolescents in a large, nationally representative sample. *Child Development*, 71, 1458-1473.

Miller, B. C., & Heaton, T. B. (August, 1991). Age at first intercourse and the timing of marriage and childbirth, *Journal of Marriage and the Family,* 719-732.

Miller, J. E., & Davis, D. (November, 1997). Poverty history, marital history, and quality of children's home environments. *Journal of Marriage and the Family*, 59, 996-1007.

Miller, P. H. (2002). *Theories of Developmental Psychology* (4th ed.). New York: Worth.

Miller, T. R., & Spicer, R. S. (March, 1998). How safe are our schools? *American Journal of Public Health,* 88(3), 413-418.

Miller-Loncar, C., Landry, S. A., Smith, K. E., & Swank, P. R. (1997). *The Role of Child-Centered Perspectives in a Model of Parenting.* Orlando, FL: Academic Press.

Milner, H. Richard IV editor (2010). *Culture, curriculum, and identity in education* (New York: Palgrave Macmillan).

Minde, K. (2000) Prematurity and serious medical conditions in infancy: Implications for development, behavior, and intervention. In C. H. Zeanah, Jr., (Ed.), *Handbook of Infant Mental Health.* New York: Guilford.

Miringoff, M., & Mirringoff, M.I. (1999). *The Social Health of the Nation: How America is Really Doing.* New York: Oxford University Press.

Nippold, Marilyn A and Scott, Cheryl M editors. (2010). Expository discourse in children, adolescents, and adults: development and disorders (New York: Psychology Press).Mischel, W. (2004). Toward an integrative science of the person. *Annual Review of Psychology,* Vol. 55. Palo Alto, CA: Annual Reviews.

Mishra, S. P. (1981). Factor analysis of the McCarthy Scales for groups of white and Mexican-American children. *Journal of School Psychology,* 19, 178-182.

Mittendorf, R., Williams, M.A., Berkeley, C.S., & Cotton, P.E. (1990). The length of uncomplicated human gestation. *Obstetrics and Gynecology,* 75, 929-932.

Mize, J., & Ladd, G. W. (1990). A cognitive-social learning approach to social skill learning with low status preschool children. *Developmental Psychology,* 26(3), 388-397.

Mize, J., & Pettit, G. S. (April, 1997). Mothers' social coaching, mother-child relationship style, and children's peer competence: Is the medium the message? *Child Development,* 68(2), 312-332.

MMWR. (July 30, 2004). Violence-related behaviors among high school students—United States 1991-2003. *Morbidity and Mortality Weekly Report,* 53, 651-655.

Montagu, M. F. A. (June/July, 1950). Constitutional and prenatal factors in infant and child health. In J. L. Senn (Ed.), *Symposium on the Healthy Personality.* Transactions of Special Meetings of Conference on Infancy and Childhood, New York.

Montgomery, S. M., Bartley, M. J., & Wilkinson, R. G. (1997). Family conflict and slow growth. *Archives of Disease in Childhood,* 77, 326-330.

Moore, K. L., & Persaud, T. V. N. (2003). *The Developing Human: Clinically Oriented Embryology* (7th ed.). Philadelphia: Saunders.

Moran, R., & Arizona, G. (February 15, 1999). Evaluation and treatment of childhood obesity. *American Family Physician, 59*(4), 861-868.

Morra, Sergio (2008) *Cognitive development: neo-Piagetian perspectives* (New York: Lawrence Erlbaum Associates).

Morris, K. (1998). Short course of AZT halves HIV-1 perinatal transmission. *The Lancet,* 351(9103), 651.

Moscucci, O. (2003). Holistics obstetrics: The origins of natural childbirth in Britain. *Postgraduate Medicine Journal,* 79, 168-173.

Moss, N. E., & Carver, K. (1998). The effect of WIC and Medicaid on infant mortality—the United States. *American Journal of Public Health,* 88, 1354-1361.

Moukaddem, M., Boulier, A., Apfelbaum, M., & Rigaud, D., (1997). Increase in diet-induced thermogenesis at the start of refeeding in severely malnourished anorexia nervosa. *American Journal of Clinical Nutrition,* 66, 123-140.

Mullen, P. R., Martin, J. L., Anderson, J. C., Romans, S. E., & Herbesin, G. P. (1995). The long-term impact of the physical, emotional, and sexual abuse of children. A community study. *Child Abuse and Neglect,* 20(1), 7-21.

Murline, A. (April 6, 1998). TV for crib potatoes: A new PBS show from Britain targets 12-month-old viewers. *U.S. News and World Report,* 70.

Myers, N., & Perlmutter, N. (1978). Memory in the years from two to five. In P. Orstein (Ed.), *Memory Development in Children.* Hillsdale, NJ: Erlbaum.

Nair, *et al.* (May 2, 1997). Risk Factors for disruption in primary caregiving among infants of substance abusing women. *Child Abuse and Neglect,* 21(11), 1039-1051.

Navaez, D., Mitchell, C., Bock, T., Endicott, L., & Gardner, J. (2001). Guidelines for developing curricula for middle students that meet graduation standards while teaching character. *In Press.*

National Center for Children in Poverty, (2000). *Child Poverty in the United States.* New York: Author.

National Center for Education Statistics (NCES). (2003). *The Condition of Education, 2003.* (Publication No. 2003-067). Washington, DC: Author.

National Center for Health Statistics, U.S. Department of Health and Human Services (2000). *Vital Statistics of the United States, 1996.* Washington, DC: U.S. Government Printing Office.

National Center for Health Statistics. (1997). Births, Marriages, and Deaths for 1996. *Monthly Vital Statistic Report, 45(12).* Hyattsville, MD: Author.

_____(2000). *Health United States, 2000, with Adolescent Health Chartbook.* Bethesda, MD: U.S. Department of Health and Human Services.

National Commission on Excellence in Education (1983). *A Nation at Risk: The imperative for Educational Reform.* Washington, DC: U.S. Department of Education.

National Institute on Alcohol Abuse and Alcoholism. (1987). Seventh special report to the U.S. Congress on alcohol and health: DHHS Publication ADM 90-1656. National Research Council (U.S.). Panel on Adolescent Pregnancy and Childbearing. In C. Hayes (Ed.), *Risking the Future: Adolescent Sexuality, Pregnancy, and Childbearing.* Washington, DC: National Academy Press.

_____(2000). *Tenth Special Report to the U.S. Congress on Alcohol and Health.* Washington, DC: National Institute of Health (Publication No. 00-1583).

National Institutes of Health (1999). *HIV and Adolescents.* Bethesda, MD: Author.

Nazzi, T., Jusczyk, P. W., & Johnson, E. K. (2000). Language discrimination by English-learning 5-month-olds: Effects of rhythm and familiarity. *Journal of Memory and Language*, 43, 1-19.

Needham, A. (1998). Infants use of featural information in the segregation of stationary objects. *Infant Behavior and Development*, 21, 1-24.

Nelson, C. A., & Bosquet, M. (2000). Neurobiology of fetal and infant development: Implications for infant mental health. In C. H. Zeanah, Jr. (Ed.), *Handbook of Infant Mental Health* (2nd ed.). New York: Guilford.

Nelson, D, W. (Exec. Ed.). (1996). *Kids Count Data Book: State Profiles of Child Well-Being.* Baltimore, MD: Annie E. Casey Foundation.

Nelson, G. (Spring/Summer, 2000). *Designs for Science Literacy: Guiding k-12 Curriculum Reform,* 1-8.

Nelson, K. B., & Ellenberg, J. H. (1978). Epidemiology of cerebral palsy. *Advances in Neurology*, 19, 421-435.

Nelson, S.A. (May 2000a). Technology in schools: Whose best interest? *The Education Digest,* 45-47.

Neppl, T. K., & Murray, A. D. (1997). Social dominance and play patterns among preschoolers: Gender comparisons. *Sex Roles*, 36(5/6), 381-393.

Ness, R. B. *et al.* (February 4, 1999). Cocaine and tobacco use and the risk of spontaneous abortion. *The New England Journal of Medicine,* 140(3).

Nester, E. W., Anderson, D. G., Roberts, C. E., Pearsall, N. N., & Nester, M. T. (2004). *Microbiology* (4th ed.). New York: McGraw-Hill.

Newacheck, P. W., & Halfon, N. (2000). Prevalence, impact and trends in childhood disability due to asthma. *Archives of Pediatric and Adolescent Medicine,* 154, 287-293.

NICHD Early Child Care Research Network. (2005). *Child Care and Child Development: Results from the NICHD Study of Early Child Care and Youth Development.* New York: Guilford Press.

Niebyl, J. R. (1991). Drugs in pregnancy and lactation. In S. G. Gabbe, J. R. Niebyl, & J. L. Simpson (Eds.), *Obstetrics: Normal and Problem Pregnancies* (2nd ed.). New York: Churchill Livingstone.

Notzon, F. D. (June 27, 1990). International differences in the use of obstetric interventions. *Journal of the American Medical Association*, 263(24), 3286-3291.

Nucci, L. P. (2004). The development of moral reasoning. In P. Smith & C. Hart (Eds.), *Blackwell Handbook of Cognitive Development*, Malden, MA: Blackwell.

Nugent, J. Kevin; Petrauskas, Bonnie J. and Brazelton, T. Berry Editors (2009). *The newborn as a person: enabling healthy infant development worldwide* (HobokenS: Wiley).

Nurse, Angela D. (2009). *Physical development in the early years foundation stage* (London: Routledge).

O'Donnell, T. G., & Bernier, S. L. (1990). Parents as caregivers. *Journal of Psychosocial Nursing*, 28(6), 14-17.

O'Dea, J. (August 24, 2005). Prevention of child obesity: 'First., do no harm.' *Health Education Research*, 20(2), 259-265.

Oden, S., & Asher, S. R. (1977). Coaching children in social skills for friendship making. *Child Development*, 48, 495-506.

Offer, D., & Offer, J. D. (1974). Normal adolescent males: The high school and college years. *Journal of the American College Health Association*, 22, 209-215.

Offer, D., Offer, M. K., & Ostrov, E. (2004). *Regular Guys: 34 Years beyond Adolescence.* Dordrecht, Netherlands: Kluwer Academic.

Oldenquist, A. (1983). The decline of American education in the 60s and 70s. *American Education*, 19(4), 13.

Ollendick, T. H., & Yule, B. (1990). Depression in British and American children and its relation to anxiety and fear. *Journal of Consulting and Clinical Psychology*, 58(1), 126-129.

Oller, D. K. (2000). *The Emergence of the Speech Capacity.* Mahwah, NJ: Erlbaum

Olsen, R., Director. (2003). *National Longitudinal Surveys.* Bureau of Labor Statistics. www.BLS.Gov/NLS.

Olson, O. (1997). Meta-analysis of the safety of home birth. *Birth Issues in Perinatal Care,* 24, 4-13.``

Olson, D. R., & Hildyard, A. (1983). Writing and literal meaning. In M. Martlew (Ed.), The psychology of written language: A developmental approach. *Child Development*, 51, 97-106.

Ono, T., Squire, L. R., & Marcus, E. (May, 1993). *Brain Mechanisms of Perception and Memory.* New York: Oxford.

Ornoy, A., Segal, J., Bar-Hamburger, R., & Greenbaum, C. (2001). Development of school-age children to mothers with heroin dependency: Importance of environmental factors. *Developmental Medicine and Child Neurology*, 43. 668-675.

Osherson, D. N., & Markman, F. M. (1975). Language and the ability to evaluate contradictions and tautologies. *Cognition*, 2, 213-226.

Ostrer, H. (1998). *Non-Mendelian Genetics in Humans.* New York: Oxford University Press.

Oviatt, S. L. (1982). Inferring what words mean: Early development in infants' comprehension of common object names. *Child Development*, 53, 274-276.

Palermo, D. (1973). More about less: A study of language comprehension. *Journal of Verbal and Learning Behavior*, 13, 211-221.

Papalia, D. E., & Olds, S. W. (1990). *A Child's World: Infancy through Adolescence* (5th ed.). New York: McGraw-Hill.

Paris, S. G. (1973). Comprehension of language connectives and propositional logical relationships. *Journal of Experimental Child Psychology*, 16, 278-291.

Parke, R. D. (1977). Some effects of punishment on children's behavior—Revisited. In R. D. Parke & E. M. Hetherington (Eds.), *Contemporary Readings in Child Psychology.* New York: McGraw-Hill.

_____ (2004a). Development in the family. *Annual Review of Psychology*, 55, Palo Alto, CA: Annual Reviews.

_____ (2004b). The society for research in child development at 70: Progress and promise. *Child Development,* 72, 1-24.

Parten, M. (1932). Social play among preschool children. *Journal of Abnormal and Social Psychology*, 27, 243-269.

Patterson, C. J., & Kister, M. C. (1981). The development of listener skills for referential communication. In D. P. Dickson (Ed.), *Children's Oral Communication Skills.* Orlando, FL: Academic Press.

Patterson, G. R., Reid, J. B., & Dishion, T. J. (1992). *Antisocial Boys.* Eugene, OR: Castalia Press.

Paul, A. M. (January/February, 1998). Do parents really matter? *Psychology Today,* 46-78.

Pavlov, I. P. (1927). *Conditioned Reflexes.* New York: Liveright.

Pearson, J., & Thoennes, N. (April, 1990). Custody after divorce: Demographic and attitudinal patterns. *American Journal of Orthopsychiatry* 60(2), 233-247.

Pelligrini, A. D. (1993). Boys' rough and tumble play, social competence, and group composition. *British Journal of Developmental Psychology,* 11, 237-248.

Pellegrini, A. D., Kato, K., Blatchford, P., & Baines, E. (2002). A short-term longitudinal study of children's playground games across the first year of school: Implications for social competence and adjustment to school. *American Educational Research Journal,* 39, 991-1015.

Pelligrino, Lucian T. editor (2009). *Handbook of motor skills: development, impairment and* (New York: Nova Science Publishers).

Pelham, W. E., & Hinshaw, S. P. (1992). Behavioral intervention for attention deficit-hyperactivity disorder. In S. M. Turner, K. S. Calhoun, & H. E. Adams (Eds.), *Handbook of Clinical Therapy* (2nd ed.). New York: Wiley.

Pennington, B. F. (1990). Annotation: The genetics of dyslexia. *Journal of Child Psychology and Psychiatry*, 31(2), 193-201.

Pereira, L.A.A., Loomis, D., Conceicao, G.M.S., *et al.* (June, 1998). Association between air pollution and intrauterine mortality in Sao Paulo, Brazil. *Environmental Health Perspective*, 106(6), 325-329.

Perry-Jenkins, M., Repetti, R., & Crouter, A. C. (2000). Work and family in the 1990s. *Journal of Marriage and the Family,* 62, 081-998.

Peters, K. F., Menaker, T. J., Wilson, P. L., Hadley, D. W. (August, 2001). The human genome project: An update. *Cancer Nursing: An International Journal for Cancer Care*, 24(4) 287-299.

Peterson, P. L., Hawkins, J. D., Abbott, R. D., & Catalano, R. F. (1994). Disentangling the effects of parental drinking, family management, and parental alcohol norms on current by black and white adolescents. *Journal of Research on Adolescence,* 4, 203-227.

Pettit, G. S. (2004). Violent children in developmental perspective: Risk and protective factors and the mechanisms through which they may operate. *Current Directions in Psychological Science,* 13, 194-197.

Petrill, S. A., Saudino, K., Cherney, S. S., Emde, R. N., Fulker, D. W., Hewitt, J. K., & Plomin, R. (1998). Exploring the genetic and environmental etiology of high general cognitive ability in fourteen- to thirty-six-month-old twins. *Child Development,* 69, 68-74.

Phinney, J., & Ong, A. (2001). *Family Obligations and Life Satisfaction among Adolescents from Immigrant and Non-Immigrant Families: Direct and Moderated Effects.* Unpublished manuscript. Los Angeles: California State University.

Phinney, J. S., Feshbach, N. D., & Farver, J. (1986). Preschool children's response to peer crying. *Early Childhood Research Quarterly*, 1(3), 189-206.

_____(2003). Ethnic identity and acculturation. In K. M. Chun, P. B. Organista, & G. Martin (Eds.), *Acculturation*. Washington, DC: American Psychological Association.

Phipps, M. G., & Sowers, M. (2002). Declining early adolescent childbearing. *American Journal of Public Health,* 92, 125-128.

Piacentini, J., Bergman, R.L., Keller, M., & McCracken, J. (2003). Functional impairment in children and adolescents with obsessive-compulsive disorder. *Journal of Child and Adolescent Psychopharmacology*, 13, Supplement 1, S61-S69.

Piaget, J. (1926). *The language and thought of the child.* New York: Harcourt, Brace & World.

_____ (1929). *The child's conception of the world.* London: Routledge & Kegan

_____ (1952). *The Origins of Intelligence in Children.* New York: International Universities Press.

_____ (1955). *The Language and Thought of the Child.* New York: Meridian Books.

_____ (1962a). *Play, Dreams, and Imitation.* New York: Norton.

_____ (1962b). Comments on Vygotsky's critical remarks concerning *The Language and Thought of the Child*, and *Judgment and Reasoning in the Child.* In L. S. Vygotsky, *Thought and Language.* Cambridge, MA: MIT Press.

_____ (1963). *The Origins of Intelligence.* New York: Norton.

_____ (1972). *Psychology of Intelligence.* Totowa, NJ: Littlefield, Adams.

Piaget, J., & Inhelder, B. (1959). *La Genese des Structures Elementaire: Classifications et Sériations.* [The Use of Elementary Structures: Classifications and Seriations.] Neuchatel: Delachaux et Niestle.

_____ (1967). *The Children's Concept of Space.* New York: Norton.

_____ (May, 1998). The genetics of cognitive abilities and disabilities. *Scientific American*, 62-69.

Piatelli-Palmerini, M. (1980). *Language and Learning*. Cambridge, MA: Harvard University Press.

Pierce, B. A. (1990). *Family Genetics Sourcebook*. New York: Wiley.

Pinett, M.G., Wax, J., Blackstone, J., Curtin, A., & McCrann, D. (2004). Timing of early amniocentesis as a function of membrane fusion. *Journal of Clinical Ultrasound*, 32, 8-11.

Pinker, S. (1994). *The Language Instinct*. New York: Harper Collins.

Plomin, R. (1986). *Development, Genetics, and Psychology*. Hillsdale, NJ: Erlbaum.

_____ (1997). Identifying genes for cognitive abilities and disabilities. In R. J. Sternberg & E. L. Grigorenko (Eds.), *Intelligence, Heredity, and Environment*. New York: Cambridge University Press.

_____ (2002). Behavioural genetics in the 21st century. In Willard W. Hartup & Rainer K. Silberesen (Eds.), *Growing Points in Developmental Science: An Introduction*. Philadelphia: Psychology Press.

Plomin, R., & DeFries, J. G. (1985). *Origins of Individual Differences in Infancy: The Colorado Adoption Project*. Orlando, FL: Academic Press.

_____ (May, 1998). The genetics of cognitive abilities and disabilities. *Scientific American*, 62-69.

Plomin, R., DeFries, J. C., McClearn, G. E., & Rutter, M. (1997). *Behavioral Genetics* (3rd ed.). New York: Freeman.

Plomin, R., Fulker, D. W., & DeFries, J. C. (November, 1997). Nature, nurture, and cognitive development from 1 to 16 years: A parent-offspring adoption study. *Psychological Science*, 8(6), 442-447.

Plomin, R., Owen, M. J., & McGuffin, P. (1994). The genetic basis of complex human behaviors. *Science*, 264, 1733-12739.

Plomin, R., & Rutter, M. (1998). Child development, molecular genetics, and what to do with genes once they are found. *Child Development*, 69, 1223-1242.

Plowman, Lydia & McPake, Joanna (2010). *Growing up with technology: young children learning in a digital world* (London: Routledge).

Pollak, S. D., Cicchetti, D., Hornung, K., & Reed, A. (2000). Recognizing emotion in faces: Developmental effects of child abuse and neglect. *Developmental Psychology*, 36, 679-688.

Pollitt, E. P., Gorman, K. S., Engle, P. L., Martorell, R., & Rivera, J. (1993). Early supplementary feeding and cognition. *Monographs of the Society for Research in Child Development*, 58(7), Serial No. 235.

Poma, P. A. (1999). Effects of obstetrician characteristics on cesarean delivery rates: A community hospital experience. *American Journal of Obstetrics and Gynecology*, 180, 1364-1372.

Pope, S. (1993). Low-birth-weight infants born to adolescent mothers. *Journal of the American Medical Association*, 269, 1396-1400.

Popenoe, D. (1993). American family in decline 1960–1990: A review and appraisal. *Journal of Marriage and the Family*, 55, 527-555.

Porter, R. H., Makin, J. W., Davis, L. B., & Christensen, K. M. (1992). An assessment of the salient olfactory environment of formula-fed infants. *Physiology and Behavior*, 50, 907-911.

Porter, R. H., & Winberg, J. (1999). Unique salience of maternal breast odors for newborn infants. *Neuroscience and Biobehavioral Reviews*, 23, 439-449.

Power, C., Lake, J. K., & Cole, T. J. (1997). Measurement and long-term risks of child and adolescent fatness. *International Journal of Obesity and Related Metabolic Disorders*, 21, 507-526.

Pratt, M. W., McLaren, J., & Wickens, G. (1984). Rules as tools: Effective generalization of verbal self-regulative communication training by first-grade speakers. *Developmental Psychology*, 20, 893-902.

Prifitera, Aurelio; Saklofske, Donald H. and Weiss, Lawrence G. editors (2008). *WISC-IV clinical assessment and intervention* (Amsterdam: Academic).

Puckett, Margaret B. (2007). *Understanding infant development* (St. Paul: Redleaf Press).

Rae, C., Joy, P., Harasty, J., Kemp, A., Kuan, S., Christodoulou, J., Cowell, C. T., & Coltheart, M. (2004). Enlarged temporal lobes in Turner syndrome: An X-chromosome effect? *Cerebral Cortex*, 14, 156-164.

Rakic, P. (1995). Corticogenesis in human and nonhuman primates. In M. S. Gazzinga (Ed.), *The Cognitive Neurosciences.* Cambridge, MA: MIT Press.

Ramakrishna, U. (2004). Maternal circulating nutrient concentrations in pregnancy. *American Journal of Clinical Nutrition,* 79, 17-21.

Ramey, C. T., & Ramey, S. L. (1992). Effective early intervention. *Mental Retardation,* 30, 337-345.

_____ (1998). Early intervention and early experience. *American Psychologist,* 53, 109-120.

Ramirez, J. M. (2003). Hormones and aggression in childhood and adolescence. *Aggressive and Violent Behavior,* 8, 621-644.

Rampage, C., Eovaldi, M., Ma., C., & Weigel-Foy, C. (2002). Adoptive families. In F. Walsh (Ed.), *Normal Family Processes: Growing Diversity and Complexity* (3rd ed.). New York: Guildford Press.

Ramsey, P. G. (1995). Growing up in the contradictions of race and class. *Young Children.* 50, 18-22.

Rappley, M. D. (January 13, 2005). Attention deficit-hyperactivity disorder. *The New England Journal of Medicine,* 352, 165-173.

Rathus, S. A., Navid, J. S., & Fichner-Rathus, N. (2000). *Human Sexuality in a World of Diversity* (4th ed.) Boston: Allyn & Bacon.

Ratner, N. B. (2001). Atypical language development. In J. B. Gleason (Ed.), *The Development of Language* (4th ed.). Boston: Allyn and Bacon.

Ravaja, N., Kauppinen, T., & Keltikangas-Jarvinen, L. (2000). Relationship between hostility and physiological coronary disease risk factors in young adults: The moderating tendencies of depressive tendencies. *Psychological Medicine,* 30, 381-393.

Raver, C. C., & Zigler, E. F. (January, 2004). Another step back? Assessing readiness in Head Start. *Young Children,* 58-63.

Reason, J. (2000) The Freudian slip revisited. *Psychologist,* 23, 610-611.

Reese, H. (1982). Behavior analysis of life-span developmental psychology. *Developmental Review,* 2, 150.

Reifsnider, E., & Gill, S. L. (2000). Nutrition for the childbearing years. *Journal of Obstetrics, Gynecology, and Neonatal Nursing,* 29, 43-55.

Reilly, K.M. (1998). Pharmacotherapy for ADHD. *Consensus in Child Neurology,* 16-20.

Reiner, W. G., & Gearheart, J. P. (2004). Discordant sexual identity in some genetic males with cloacal exstrophy assigned to female sex at birth. *New England Journal of Medicine,* 350, 333-341.

Reinking, D., & Wu, J. H. (Winter, 1990). Reexamining the research on television and reading. *Reading Research and Instruction,* 29(2), 30-43.

Reissland, N., Shepherd, J., & Herrera, E. (2003). The pitch of maternal voice: A comparison of mothers suffering from depressed mood and non-depressed mothers reading books to their infants. *Journal of Child Psychology and Psychiatry,* 44(2), 255-261.

Relier, J.B. (2001). Influence of maternal stress on fetal behavior and brain development. *Biology of the Neonate,* 79, 168-171.

Remez, L. (1997). Planned home birth can be as safe as hospital delivery for women with low-risk pregnancies. *Family Planning Perspectives,* 29, 141-143.

Renzulli, J. S., & Reis, S. M. (1991). The schoolwide enrichment model: A comprehensive plan for the development of creative productivity. In N. Colangolo & G. A. David (Eds.), *Handbook of Gifted Education.* Needham Heights, MA: Allyn & Bacon.

Rest, J. R. (1979). *Development in Judging Moral Issues.* Minneapolis: University of Minnesota Press.

_____ (1983). Morality. In P. H. Mussen (Ed.), *Manual of Child Psychology.* Vol. 3, *Cognitive Development.* New York: Wiley.

Revkin, A. C. (July 11, 2000). Milestone report on mercury emissions. *The New York Times,* A12.

Rey, Joseph M. and Birmaher, Boris editors (2009). *Treating child and adolescent depression* / editors(Philadelphia: Wolters Kluwer Health/Lippincott Williams & Wilkins).

Reynolds, A. (February, 2001). Breastfeeding and brain development. *The Pediatric Clinics of North America,* 48(1), 159-171.

Reynolds, A. J., Temple, J. A., Robertson, D. L., & Mann, E. A. (May 9, 2001). Long-term effects of an early childhood intervention on educational achievement and juvenile arrest: A 15-year follow-up of low-income children in public schools. *Journal of the American Medical Association,* 285(18), 2339-2346.

Rheingold, H. L. (1956). The modification of social responses of institutional babies. *Monograph of the Society for Research in Child Development,* 21(2, Serial No. 63, 5-48).

Ribeiro, J., Guerra, S., Pinto, A., Oliveira, J., Duarte, J., & Mota, J. (2003). Overweight and obesity in children and adolescents: Relationship with blood pressure and physical activity. *Annuals of Human Biology,* 30, 203-215.

Rickert, V. I. *et al.* (1996). The effects of peer ridicule on depression and self-image among adolescent females with Turner syndrome. *Journal of Adolescent Health,* 19, 34-39.

Riese, M. (2003), Newborn temperament and Sudden Infant Death Syndrome: A comparison of victims and their cotwins. *Applied Developmental Psychology,* 23, 643-653.

Righettin-Veltema, M., Bousquet, A., & Manzano, J. (2003). Impact of postpartum depressive symptoms on mother and her 18-month-old infant. *European Child and Adolescent Psychiatry,* 12, 75-83.

Riskind, J. H., Abreu, K., Strauss, M., & Holt, R. (1997). Looming vulnerability to spreading contamination in subclinical OCD. *Behavior Research and Therapy,* 35(5), 405-414.

Ristow, M., Moller-Wieland, D., Pfeiffer, A., Krone, W., & Kahn, C. R. (October 1, 1998). Obesity associated with a mutation in a genetic regulator of adipocyte differentiation. *New England Journal of Medicine,* 339, 953-959.

Ritchie, M. A. (February, 2001). Self-esteem and hopefulness in adolescents with cancer. *Journal of Pediatric Nursing,* 16(1), 35-42.

Ritz, B., Yu, F., Chapa, G., Fruin, S., Shaw, G., & Harris, J. (2002). Ambient air pollution and birth defects. *American Journal of Epidemiology,* 155, 17-25.

Robbins, J. (July 4, 2000). Virtual reality finds a real place as a medical aid. *New York Times.*

Roberts, D. F., Henriksen, L., & Foehr, V. G. (2004). Adolescents and the media. In R. Lerner & L. Steinberg (Eds.), *Handbook of Adolescent Psychology.* New York: Wiley.

Roberts, J., & Sutton-Smith, B. (1962). Child training and involvement. *Ethnology,* 1, 166-185.

Robertson, E. G. (1981). Adolescence, physiological maturity, and obstetric outcomes. In K. G. Scott, T. Field, & E. Robertson (Eds.), *Teenage Parents and Their Offspring.* New York: Grune & Stratton.

Robinson, T. N. (March 25, 1998). Does television cause obesity? *Journal of the American Medical Association, 279*(12), 959-960.

Robinson, T. N., & Killer, J. D. (1995). Ethnic and gender differences in the relationship between television viewing and obesity, physical activity and dietary fat intake. *Journal of Health Education,* 26, S91-S98.

Rodgers, D. B. (May, 1998). Supporting autonomy in young children. *Young Children,* 75-80.

Rodkin, P. C., Farmer, T. W., Pearl, R., & Van Acker, R. (2000). Heterogeneity of popular boys: Antisocial and prosocial configurations. *Developmental Psychology,* 36, 14-24.

Roijen, L. E. G., Postema, K., Limbeek, J., Kuppevelt, H. J. M. (2001). Development of bladder control in children and adolescents with cerebral palsy. *Developmental Medicine and Child Neurology,* 43, 103-107.

Rolls, E. T. (2000). Memory systems in the brain. *Annual Review of Psychology,* 51, 599-630.

Rome, E. S. (1995). Sports-related injuries among adolescents: When do they occur, and how can we prevent them? *Pediatrics in Review,* 16(5), 184-187.

Rosenthal, M. S. (1996). *Fertility Source Book.* Los Angeles: Lowell House.

Rosenthal, R., & Jacobson, L. (1968). *Pygmalian in the Classroom: Teacher Expectation and Pupils' Intellectual Development.* New York: Holt, Rinehart, & Winston.

Rosenzweig, M. (2000). Ethology. In A. Kazdin (Ed.), *Encyclopedia of Psychology*. Washington, D. C. & New York: American Psychological Association and Oxford University.

Rothbart, M. K., Ahadi, S. A., & Evans, D. E. (2000). Temperament and personality: Origins and outcome. *Journal of Personality and Social Psychology*, 78, 122-135.

Rothbart, M. K., Ahadi, S. A., Hershey, K., & Fisher, P. (2001). Investigations of temperament at three to seven years: The children's behavior questionnaire. *Child Development*, 72, 1394-1408.

Rothbart, M. K., & Putnam, S. B. (2002). Temperament and socialization. In L. Pullinen & A. Caspi (Eds.), *Paths to Successful Development*. New York: Cambridge University Press.

Rotherman-Boris, M.J., Walker, J.U., Ferns, M. (1996). Suicidal behavior among middle-class adolescents who seek clinical services. *Journal of Clinical Psychology,* 52, 137-143.

Rousseau, J. J. (1911). *Émile*. London: Dent.

Rovee-Collier, C. (2002). Infant learning and memory. In U. Goswami (Ed.), *Blackwell Handbook of Childhood Cognitive Development*. Malden, MA: Blackwell.

Rowe, D. C. (July/August, 1990). As the twig is bent? The myth of child-rearing influences on personality development. *Journal of Counseling and Development*, 68, 606-611.

Rubenstein, R. (November, 1990). The power of touch. *Child*, 86-89, 91, 120.

Rubin, K., & Balow, B. (1979). Measure of infant development and socio-economic status on predictors of later intelligence and school achievement. *Developmental Psychology*, 15(2), 225-227.

Ruble, D. N. (2000). Gender constancy. In A. Kazdin (Ed.), *Encyclopedia of Psychology*. Washington, DC & New York: American Psychological Association and Oxford University Press.

Ruble, D., Alvarez, J., Bachman, M., Cameron, J., Fuligni, A., Coll, C. G., *et al.* (2004). The development of a sense of "we:" The Emergence and implications of children's collective identity. In M. Bennett & F. Sani (Eds.), *The Development of the Social Self.* Hove, East Sussex, England: Psychology Press.

Rudloff, L. M., & Feldmann, E. F. (April, 1999). Childhood obesity: Addressing the issue. *Journal of the American Osteopathic Association,* 99(4), S1-S6.

Rugh, R., & Shettles, L. G. (1971). *From Conception to Birth*. New York: Harper & Row.

Rumberger, R. W., & Thomas, S. L. (2000). The distribution of dropout and turnover rates among urban and suburban high schools. *Sociology of Education*, 73, 39-67.

Runeson, B. (1990). Psychoactive substance use disorder in youth suicide. *Alcohol and Alcoholism,* 25(5), 561-568.

Rusell, C. (September, 1990). 25 particle markets for the 1990s. *American Demographics, Special News Supplement*, 10.

Russell, L. B., & Russell, W. L. (1952). Radiation hazards to the embryo and fetus. *Radiology*, 58, 369-376.

Rutter, M. (2002). Nature, nurture, and development. From evangelism through science toward policy and practice. *Child Development,*73, 1-21.

Ryan, A. M. (July/August, 2001). The peer group as a context for the development of young adolescent motivation and achievement. *Child Development*, 72(4), 1135-1150.

Rycek, R. F., Stuhr, S., McDermott, J. H., Benker, J., & Swarts, M. D. (Winter, 1998). Adolescent egocentrism and cognitive functioning during late adolescence. *Adolescence,* 33(133), 746-749.

Rymer, R. (1993). *Genie*. New York: Harper Collins.

Sallis, J. F. (1993). Promoting healthful diet and physical activity. In S. G. Millstein, A. C. Petersen, & E. O. Nightingale (Eds.), *Promoting the Health of Adolescents: New Directions for the Twenty-First Century*. New York: Oxford University Press.

Salk, L. (1973). The role of the heartbeat in the relationship between mother and infant. *Scientific American*, 228(3) 24-29.

Salkind, N. J. (2004). *An introduction to Theories of Human Development*. Thousand Oaks, CA: Sage.

Sampaio, R. C., & Truwit, C. L. (2001). Myelination in the developing human brain. In Charles A. Nelson & Monica Luciana (Eds.), *Handbook of Developmental Cognitive Neuroscience*. Cambridge, MA: Harvard University Press.

Sampson, R. J. (2000). A neighborhood perspective on social change and the social control of adolescent delinquency. In L. J. Crockett, & Y. R. K. Silbereisen (Eds.), *Negotiating Adolescence in Times of Social Change*. New York: Cambridge University Press.

Sandoval, C., Davis, A., & Jayabose, S. J. (March, 2005). Eyelid mass as the presenting finding in a child with down syndrome and acute megakaryoblastic leukemia. *Pediatrics*, 115(3), 810-811.

Sandstrom, M. J., & Coie, J. D. (August, 1999). A developmental perspective on peer rejection: Mechanisms, stability and change. *Child Development,* 70(4), 955-966.

Santiago-Delefosse, M. J., & Delefosse, J. M. O. (2002). Three positions on child thought and language. *Theory and Psychology*, 12, 723-747.

Santora, M. (January 30, 2005). U.S. is close to eliminating AIDS in infants, officials say. *New York Times,* A1.

Santrock, J. W. (2005). *Children* (8th ed.). Boston: McGraw-Hill.

Sattler, Jerome M. (2008). *Assessment of children: cognitive foundations* (San Diego: J.M. Sattler).

Sawin, K. J., Cox, A. W., & Metzger, S. G. (2000). Transitions to adulthood. In P. L. Jackson & J. A. Vessey (Eds.), *Primary Care of the Child with a Chronic Condition*. St. Louis, MO: Mosby.

Saylor, C. F., Boyce, G. C., Peagler, S. M., & Callahan, S. A. (2000). Brief report: Cautions against using the Stanford-Binet-IV to classify high-risk preschoolers. *Society of Pediatric Psychology*, 25(3), 129-183.

Scarr, S. (1993). Biological and cultural diversity: The legacy of Darwin for development. *Child Development*, 64, 1333-1353.

Scarr, S., & Eisenberg, M. (1993). Child care research issues, perspectives, and results. *Annual Review of Psychology*, 44, 613-644.

Scarr, S., & Weinberg, R. A. (1976). IQ performance of black children adopted by white families. *American Psychologist*, 31, 726-739.

_____ (1983). The Minnesota adoption studies: Genetic differences and malleability. *Child Development*, 54, 260-267.

Schaeffer, E. R. (1973). The onset of fear of strangers and the incongruity hypothesis. In L. B. Stone, H. T. Smith, & L. B. Murphy (Eds.), *The Competent Infant, Research and Commentary*. New York: Basic Books.

Schickedanz, J. A., Schickedanz, D. J., Forsyth, P. D., & Forsyth, G. A. (2000). *Understanding Children and Adolescents*. Boston: Allyn & Bacon.

Schifter, J., & Madrigal Pana, J. (2000). *The Sexual Construction of Latino Youth: Implications for the Spread of HIV/AIDS*. New York: Haworth Hispanic/Latino Press.

Schmitt, B. B. (June, 1997). Nocturnal enuresis. *Pediatrics in Review*, 18(6), 183-190.

Schmidt, Louis A. and Segalowitz, Sidney J. (2008) *Developmental psychophysiology: theory, systems, and methods* (New York: Cambridge University Press).

Schoendorf, K. C., & Kiley, J. L. (1992). Relationship of sudden infant death syndrome to maternal smoking during and after pregnancy. *Pediatrics,* 90, 905-908.

Schultz, D. P., & Schultz, S. E. (2001). *Theories of Personality*. Pacific Grove, CA: Brooks/Cole.

Schwartz, I. L. (June, 1990). Low-birth-weight effects of demographic and socioeconomic variables and prenatal care in Pima County. *The Western Journal of Medicine*, 152(6), 725-728.

Schwartz, R. H. (1994). Your healthy pregnancy. *American Baby,* 18, 32, 34.

Schweinhart, L. J., Weikart, D., & Larner, M. B. (1986). A report on the High/Scope preschool curriculum models through age 15. *Early Childhood Research Quarterly*, 1, 15-45.

Schwimmer, J.B., Burkinkle, J. W., & Varni, J. W. (April 9, 2003). Health-related quality of life of severly obese children and adolescents. *Journal of the American Medical Association*, 289(14), 1813-1819.

Sear, W., & Sears, M. (November, 1997). Reading to babies. *American Baby*, 76-78.

Searight, H. R., Nahlik, J. N., & Campbell, D. C. (March, 1995). Attention/hyperactivity disorder: Assessment, diagnosis, and management. *The Journal of Family Practice*, 40(3), 270279.

Sears, W. (1995). *SIDS: A Parent's Guide to Understanding and Preventing Sudden Infant Death Syndrome*. Boston: Little, Brown.

Seibel, M. M. (1997). *Infertility: A Comprehensive Approach* (2nd ed.). Appleton & Lange.

Seifer. R. *et al.* (1994). Infant temperament measured by multiple observations and mother reports. *Child Development, 65,* 1478-1490.

_____ (2004). Attachment status in children prenatally exposed to cocaine and other substances. *Child Development, 75,* 850-868.

Seifer, R., LaGasse, L. L., Lester, B., Bauer, C. R., Shankaran, S., Bada, H. S., *et al.* (2004). Attachment status in children exposed to cocaine and other substances. *Child Development, 75,* 850-868.

Selman, R. L. (1976). Social-cognitive understanding: A guide to educational and clinical practice. In T. Lickona (Ed.). *Moral Development and Behavior: Theory, Research, and Moral Issues.* New York: Holt, Rinehart & Winston.

_____ (1980). *The Growth of Interpersonal Understanding.* New York: Academic Press.

_____ (1981). The child as a friendship philosopher. In S. R. Asher & J. M. Gettman (Eds.), *The Development of Friendships.* New York: Cambridge University Press.

Senechal, A, Thomas, E., & Monder, J. (1995). Individual differences in 4-year-old children's acquisition of vocabulary during storybook reading. *Journal of Educational Psychology*, 87, 218-229.

Shaffer, D. R. (2000). *Social and Personality Development* (4th ed.). Belmont, CA: Wadsworth/Thompson Learning.

Shah, M. A. (2002). Professional visions...contemporaty realities. Presidential address delivered at the 47th Annual Meeting of the American College of Nurse-Midwives, Atlanta, Georgia. www.acnm.org.

Shaughnessy, J. J., Zechmeister, E. B., & Zechmeister, J. S. (2003). *Research Methods in Psychology* (6th ed.). New York: McGraw-Hill.

Shaw, G. (2001). Adverse human reproductive outcomes and electromagnetic fields. *Bioelectromagnetics*, 5(Suppl.). S5-S18.

Shaw, G. M., Schaeffer, D., Velie, E. M., Morland, K., & Harris, J. A. (1995). Periconceptual vitamin use, dietary folate, and occurrence of neural tube defects. *Epidemiology*, 6, 219-226.

Shepard, T. H., & Smith, D. W. (1977). Prenatal life. In D. W. Smith (Ed.), *Introduction to Clinical Pediatrics* (2nd ed.). Philadelphia: Saunders.

Sheldon, W. (1942). *The Varieties of Temperament: A Psychology of Constitutional Differences.* New York: Harper.

Shettles, L. B., & Rorvik, D. M. (1997). *How to Choose the Sex of Your Baby.* New York: Doubleday.

Shibley, J. S., & DeLamater, J. D. (1997). *Understanding Human Sexuality* (6th ed.). New York: McGraw-Hill.

Shiffrin, R. M. (1993). Short-term memory: A brief commentary. *Memory and Cognition, 21,* 193-197.

Shiono, P. H., Klebanoff, M. A., Nugent, R. P., Cotch, M. F., Wilkins, D. G., Rollins, D. E., *et al.* (1995). The impact of cocaine and marijuana use on low birth weight and preterm birth: A multicenter study. *American Journal of Obstetrics and Gynecology*, 172, 19-25.

Shonkoff, J., & Phillips, D. (Eds.), (2000). *From Neurons to Neighborhoods.* Washington, DC: National Academy Press.

Short, R. J., & Talley, R. C. (1997). Rethinking psychology and the schools: Implications of recent policy. *American Psychologist*, 52, 234-240.

Shulman, Brian B. and Capone, Nina C. editors (2010). *Language development: foundations, processes, and clinical applications* (Sudbury: Jones and Bartlett Publishers).

Shute, N. (November 10, 1997). No more hard labor. *U.S. News & World Report*, 92-95.

Sibai, B. H. (1998). Prevention of preeclampsia: A big disappointment. *Journal of Obstetrics and Gynecology*, 179, 1275-1278.

Siegler, R. S. (1981). Developmental sequences within and between concepts. *Monographs of the Society for Research in Child Development*, 46(2), Serial No. 189.

_____ (1991). *Children's Thinking.* (2nd ed.). Englewood Cliffs, NJ: Prentice-Hall.

_____ (1998). *Children's Thinking* (3rd ed.). Upper Saddle River, NJ: Erlbaum.

Siegler, R. S., & Booth, J. L. (2004). Development of numerical estimation in young children. *Child Development, 75*, 48-444.

Siervogel, R. M., Maynard, L. M., Wisemandle, W. A., Roche, A. F., Guo, S. S., Chumlea, W. C., & Towne, B. (2000). Annual changes in total body fat and fat-free mass in children from 8 to 18 years in relation to changes in body mass index: The Fels Longitudinal Study. *Annals of the New York Academy of Sciences*, 904, 420-423.

Silverman, W. K., & Dick-Niederhauser, A. (2004). Separation anxiety disorder. In T. L. Morris & J. S. March (Eds.), *Anxiety Disorders in Children and adolescents* (2nd ed.). New York: Guilford Press.

Silverstein, L., & Auerbach, C. F. (June, 1999). Deconstructing the essential father. *American Psychologist, 54*(6), 397-407.

Sim, T. N. (2000). Adolescent psychosocial competence: The importance and role of regard for parents. *Journal of Research on Adolescence*, 10, 49-64.

Simmons, B. J., Stalsworth, K., & Wentzel, H. (1999). Television violence and its effects on children. *Early Childhood Education Journal*, 26(3), 149-153.

Simpson, R. L. (1962). Parental influence, anticipatory socialization, and social mobility. *American Sociological Review*, 27, 517-522.

Singer, D. G., & Singer, J. L. (2005). *Imagination and Play in the Electronic Age.* Cambridge, MA: Harvard University Press.

Singer, J. D., Fuller, B., Kelley, M. K., & Wolf, A. (1998). Early child-care selection: Variation by geographic location, maternal characteristics, and family structure. *Developmental Psychology*, 34, 1129-1144.

Singnore, C. (2001). Rubella. Primary care update. *Obstetrics and Gynecology*, 8, 133-127.

Sinkkonen, J. (1994). *Hearing impairment, communication and personality development.* Helsinki: Department of Child Psychiatry, University of Helsinki.

Sirover, M. A. (December, 1999). Gene therapy: A new frontier in the treatment of disease. *Pharmacy Times, 68-76.*

Skeels, H. M. (1966). Adult status of children with contrasting early life experience. *Monographs of the Society for Research in Child Development*, 31(3), 5.

Skinner, B. F. (1948). *Walden Two.* New York: Macmillan.

_____ (1957). *Verbal Behavior.* New York: Prentice-Hall.

_____ (1971). *Beyond Freedom and Dignity.* New York: Knopf.

Skolnick, A. (May 16, 1990). CDC expands dental disease prevention role. *The Journal of the American Medical Association*, 263(19), 2609.

Slaby, R. G., Rodell, W. C., Arezzo, D., & Hendrix, K. (1995). *Early Violence Prevention.* Washington, DC: National Association for the Education of Young Children.

Slater, A., Field, T., & Hernandez-Reif, M. (2002). The development of the senses. In A. Slater & M. Lewis (Eds.), *Infant Development.* New York: Oxford University Press.

Smith, D. (2004). *Introduction to Special Education* (5th ed.). Boston: Allyn & Bacon.

Smith, J. E., & Brook-Gunn, J. (August, 1997). Correlates and consequences of harsh discipline for young children. *Archives of Pediatrics and Adolescent Medicine*, 777-786.

Smith, L. M, Chang, L., Yonekura, M. L., Gilbride, K., Kuo, J., Poland, R. E., Walot, I., & Ernst, T. (2001). Brain proton magnetic resonance spectroscopy and imaging in children exposed to cocaine in utero. *Pediatrics*, 107, 227.

Smith, M. G., & fong, R. (2004). *The Children of Neglect: When No One Cares.* New York: Brunner-Routledge.

Smith, M. L., Klim. P., & Hanley, W. R. (2000). Executive function in school-aged children with phenylketonuria. *Journal of Developmental and Physical Disabilities,* 12, 317-332.

Smith, W. E. (1975). *Minamata.* New York: Holt, Rinehart.

Smyth, C. M., & Bremmer, W. J. (June 22, 1998). Klinefelter syndrome. *Archives of Internal Medicine,* 158(2), 1309-1314.

Smithey, M., & Ramirez, I. L. (2004). Suspicion of sudden infant death syndrome & injuries to infants: The effects of death certifier, training, and economics. *Deviant Behavior,* 25, 415-482.

Smolak, Linda and Thompson, J. Kevin editors (2009). *Body image, eating disorders, and obesity in youth : assessment, prevention, and treatment* (Washington: American Psychological Association).

Snow, D. S. (2000). The emotional basis of linguistic and nonlinguistic intonation: Implications for hemispheric specialization. *Developmental Neuropsychology,* 17, 331-392.

Snyder, J. J. (1977). Reinforcement analysis of interaction in problem and nonproblem families. *Journal of Abnormal Psychology,* 86, 528-535.

Solomon, R., & Liefeld, C. P. (1998) Effectiveness of a family support center approach to adolescent mothers: Repeat pregnancies and school drop-out rates. *Family Relations,* 47, 139-144.

Solowij, J., Stephens, R. S., Roffman, R. A., Babor, T., Kadden, R., Miller, M., Christiansen, K., McKee, B., & Vendetti, J. for Marijuana Treatment Research Group. (2002). Cognitive functioning of long-term heavy cannabis users seeking treatment. *Journal of the American Medical Association.* 287, 1123-1131.

Sondike, S. B., Copperman, N. M., & Jacobson, M. S. (May, 2000). Bringing a formidable opponent down to size. *Contemporary Pediatrics,* 133-157.

Sorenson, R. C. (1973). *Adolescent Sexuality in Contemporary America.* New York: World.

Sorenson, S. B., & Vittes, K. A. (2004). Adolescents and firearms: A California statewide survey. *American Journal of Public Health,* 94, 852-959.

Sowchock, F. S., Gibas, I., & Jackson, L. G. (1993). Chromosomal errors as a cause of obstetric history. *Fertility and Sterility,* 59, 1011-1014.

Soby, Jeanette M. (2006). Prenatal exposure to drugs/alcohol : characteristics and educational implications of fetal alcohol syndrome and cocaine/polydrug effects (Springfield, Ill.: Charles C Thomas).

Speece, M. W., & Brent, S. B. (1992). The acquisition of a mature understanding of the three components of the concept of death. *Death Studies,* 16, 211-229.

Spencer, J. M., *et al.* (2002). Self-esteem as a predictor of initiation of coitus in early adolescents. *Pediatrics,* 109, 581-584.

Spitz, R. (1945). Hospitalism: An inquiry into the genesis of psychiatric conditions in early childhood. *Psychoanalytic Studies of the Child,* 1, 53-74.

_____ (1946). Anaclitic depression. *Psychoanalytic Study of the Child.* 2, 313-342.

Spitzer, Alan R. and White, Robert D. editors (2008). *Neuroprotection in the newborn* (Philadelphia: Saunders).

Spitzer, S., Cupp, R., & Parke, R. D. (1995). School entrance age, social acceptance, and self-perceptions in kindergarten and first grade. *Early Childhood Research Quarterly,* 10, 433-450.

Springer, K. (June, 1990). In defense of theories. *Cognition,* 35, 293-298.

Squire, L. R., & Kandel, E. R. (1999). *Memory: From Mind to Molecules.* New York: Scientific American Library.

Sroufe, L. A. (1982). Attachment at the roots of competence. In H. E. Fitzgerald & T. H. Carr (Eds.), *Human Development: Annual Editions.* Guildford, CA: Dushkin.

Stagno, S., & Cloud, G. A. (1994). Working Parents: The impact of day care and breast-feeding on cytomegalovirus infections in offspring. *Proceedings of the National Academy of Science, USA,* 91, 2384-2389.

Stallard, Paul (2009). *Anxiety: cognitive behaviour therapy with children and young people* (London: Routledge).

Stanley, L. (April, 2000). The Language of Babies. *American Baby,* 18-20.

Steen, F., & Owens, S. A. (March, 2000). Implicit pedagogy: From chase play to collaborative world making. Paper presented at the Evolution Social Mind Speaker Series. University of California at Santa Barbara.

Stegler, R. S. (1998). *Children's Thinking* (3rd ed.). Upper Saddle River, NJ: Prentice-Hall.

Stein, M. T., Kennell, J. H., & Fulcher, J. (2003). Benefits of a doula present at the birth of a child. *Journal of Developmental and Behavioral Pediatrics,* 24, 195-198.

Steinberg, L. (1996). *Adolescence* (4th ed.). New York: McGraw-Hill.

Steinberg, L. D. (1986). Latchkey children and susceptibility to peer pressure: An ecological analysis. *Developmental Psychology*, 433-439.

Steinberg, L., Darling, N., & Fletcher, A., with Brown, B. B., & Dornbusch, S. M. (1995). Authoritative parenting and adolescent adjustment: An ecological journey. In P. Moen, G. Elder, Jr., & K. Luscher (Eds.), *Examining Lives in Context: Perspectives on the Ecology of Human Development*. Washington D. C.: American Psychological Association.

Steiner, M. S., Morton, R. A., & Walsh, P. C. (1991). Impact of radical prostatectomy on urinary continence. *Journal of Urology*, 145, 512-515.

Steinmetz, G. (February, 1992). The preventable tragedy: Fetal alcohol syndrome.*National Geographic*, 181, 36-39.

Stephenson, J. (October 15, 1997). Health agencies update. *Journal of the American Medical Association*, 1227.

Sternberg, R. J. (2000). Patterns of giftedness: A triarchic analysis. *Roeper Review*, 22, 231-235.

_____ (2004). Individual differences in cognitive development. In P. Smith & C. Hart (Eds.), *Blackwell Handbook of Cognitive Development*. Malden, MA: Blackwell.

Sternberg, R. J., Wagner, R. K., Williams, W. M., & Horvath, J. A. (1995). Testing common sense. *American Psychologist,* 50, 912-1127.

Stetsenko, A., Little, T. D., Gordeeva, T., Grasshof, M., & Oettingen, G. (2000). Gender effects in children's beliefs about school performance. *Child Development*, 21, 517-527.

Stevens-Simon, C., & White, M. M. (1991). Adolescent pregnancy. *Pediatric Annals*, 20, 322-331.

Stevenson, H. W., & Lee, S. (1990). Contexts of achievement. *Monographs of the Society for Research in Child Development.* 55.(1-2, Serial No. 221).

Stevenson, R. D. (2001). Health status of children with moderate to severe cerebral palsy. *Developmental Medicine and Child Neurology,* 43, 364-370.

Stewart, L., & Pascual-Leone (1992). Mental capacity constraints and the development of moral reasoning. *Journal of Experimental Child Psychology*, 54, 251-287.

Stewart, S. D., Manning, W. D., & Smock, P. J. (2003). Union formation among men in the U. S.: Does having prior children matter? *Journal of Marriage and the Family,* 65, 90-104.

Stinnett, T. A., Harvey, J. M., & Oehler-Stinnett, J. (1994). Current test usage by practicing school psychologist: A national survey. *Journal of Psychoeducational Assessment, 12,* 331-350.

Stith, S. M., & Davis, A. J. (1984). Employed mothers and family day-care substitute caregivers: A comparative analysis of infant care. *Child Development*, 55, 1340-1348.

Stoppard, M. (1993). *Conception, Pregnancy, and Birth.* New York: Viking.

Stormshak, E. A., Bierman, K. L., McMahon, R. J., Lengua, L. J., and the Conduct Problems Prevention Research Group. (2000). Parenting practices and child disruptive behavior. *Child Psychology*, 29, 17-29.

Strauss, N. A. (September/October, 2001). New evidence for the benefits of never spanking. *Society*, 52-60.

Strober, M., Freeman, R., Lampert, C., Diamond, J., & Kaye, W. (2000). Controlled family stuffy of anorexia and bulimia nervosa: Evidence of shared disability and transmission of partial syndromes. *American Journal of Psychiatry*, 157, 393-401.

Strong, T. H. Jr. (2000). *Expecting Trouble. The Myth of Prenatal Care in America.* New York: New York University Press.

Stunkard, A. J., Harris, J. R., Pedersen, N. L; & McLearn, G. E. (1990). The body mass of twins who have been reared apart. *New England Journal of Medicine*, 322, 1483.

Substance Abuse and Mental Health Services Administration. (1998). *Cocaine Use.* Washington, DC: Government Printing Office.

Sue, D. W., & Sue, D. (2002). *Counseling the Culturally Diverse: Theory and Practice* (4th ed.). New York: Wiley.

Sullivan, J. L. (2003). Prevention of mother-to-child transmission of HIV--what next? *Journal of Acquired Immune Deficiency Syndrome*, 34 (Suppl. 1), S67-S72.

Sullivan, K., & Winner, E. (1993). Three-year-olds' understanding of mental states: The influence of trickery. *Journal of Experimental Child Psychology,* 56, 135-148.

Sullivan, L. (September 26, 1990). An opportunity to oppose: Physician's role in the campaign against tobacco. *Journal of the American Medical Association,* 250(22), 3059-3062.

_____ (May 5, 1991). U.S. Secretary urges TV to restrict irresponsible sex and reckless violence. *Boston Globe,* p. A1.

Summers, T., Kates, J., & Murphy, G. (2002). *The Tip of the Iceberg: The Global Impact of HIV/AIDS on Youth.* Menlo Park, CA: Henry J. Kaiser Family Foundation.

Super, C. M., Herrera, M. G., & Mora, J. O. (1990). Long-term effects of food supplementation and psychosocial intervention on the physical growth of Colombian infants at risk of malnutrition. *Child Development,* 61, 29-49.

Surkan, P. J., *et al.* (2004). Previous preterm and small-for-gestational-age births and subsequent risks of stillbirth. *New England Journal of Medicine,* 350, 777-785.

Susman, E. J., Dorn, L. J., & Schiefelbein, V. L. (2003). Puberty, sexuality, and health. In R. M. Lerner, M. A. Easterbrooks, & J. Mistry (Eds.), *Comprehensive handbook of psychology.* Vol. 6. *Developmental Psychology.* New York: Wiley.

Suter, P. M., Schutz, Y., & Jequier, E. (1992). The effect of ethanol on fat storage in health subjects. *New England Journal of Medicine,* 326, 983-987.

Sutherland, G.R., Haan, E.A., Kremer, E., Lynch, M., Pritchard, M., Yu, S., & Richards, R.I. (August 3, 1991). Hereditary unstable DNA: a new explanation for some old genetic questions? *The Lancet,* 338(8762), 289-291.

Suzuki, L. A., Meller, P. J., & Ponterotto, J. G. (2000). *Handbook of Multicultural Assessment: Clinical, Psychological, and Educational Applications* (2nd ed.). New York: Jossey-Bass.

Sware, J. A., Hansen, B. B., & Molsted-Pedersen, L. (2001). Perinatal complications in women with gestational diabetes mellitus: Significance of a diagnosis early in pregnancy. *Acta Obstetricia et Gynecologica Scandinavica,* 80, 899-904.

Taft, C.H., Mickalide, C.H., & Taft, A.R. (February, 1999). *Child Passengers at Risk in America: A National Study of Car Seat Misuse.* Washington, DC: National SAFE KIDS Campaign, 19.

Tager-Flusberg, H. (2000). Putting words together: Morphology and syntax in the preschool years. In J. B. Gleason (Ed.), *The Development of Language,* Boston: Allyn and Bacon.

Taipale, P., & Hilesmaa, V. (1998, Dec.). Sonagraphic measurement of uterine cervix at 18-22 weeks' gestation and the risk of preterm delivery. *Obstetrics and Gynecology,* 92(6), 902-907.

Takano, K., Hizuka, N., Asakawa, K., Sukegawa, R., & Shizume, K. (1990). Effects of short-term growth hormone therapy in short children without growth hormone deficiency. *Acta Paudiatrica,* 366, 14-22.

Tan, L. (1985). Laterality and motor skills in four-year-olds. *Child Development,* 56, 119-124.

Tanner, J. M. (1990). *Foetus into Man* (2nd ed.). Cambridge, MA: Harvard University Press.

_____ Tanner, J. M. (1963). *Growth at Adolescence.* London: Blackwell Scientific Publications.

_____ (1970). Physical growth. In P. H. Hussen (Ed.), *Carmichael's Manual of Child Psychology.* Vol. 1. (3rd. ed.). New York: Wiley.

_____ (1981). *A History of the Study of Human Growth.* Cambridge, MA: Harvard University Press.

Tenenbaum, H. R., & Leaper, C. (2003). Parent-child conversations about science. The socializations of gender iniquities? *Developmental Psychology,* 39, 34-47.

Teplin, S. W. (1995). Visual impairment in infants and young children. *Infants and Young Children,* 8, 18-51.

Terman, L. (1925). *Mental and Physical Traits of a Thousand Gifted Children. Genetic Studies of Genius.* Vol. 1. Stanford, CA: Stanford University Press.

Terry, W. S. (2003). *Learning and Memory* (2nd ed.). Boston: Allyn & Bacon.

Thapar, A. (1997). Anxiety and depression symptoms in childhood. A genetic study of comorbidity. *Journal of Child Psychiatry and Psychology.* 38(6), 651-656.

Thiedke, C. C. (2001) Sleep disorders and sleep problems in childhood. *American Family Physician,* 63, 277-284.

Thomas, A., & Chess, S. (1977). *Temperament and Development*. New York: Brunner/Mazel.

_____ (1984). Genesis and evaluation of behavioral disorders: From infancy to early adult life. *American Journal of Psychiatry*, 41, 1-9.

Thomas, A., Chess, S., Birch, H. G., Hertzig, M. E., & Korn, S. (1963). *Behavioral Individuality in Early Childhood*. New York: New York University.

Thomas, K. M., & Casey, B. J. (2003). Methods for imaging the developing brain. In M. DeHaan & M. H. Johnson (Eds.), *The Cognitive Neuroscience of Development*. New York: Psychology Press.

Thomas, R. Murray (2009). *Sex and the American teenage: seeing through the myths and confronting the issues* (Lanham: Rowman & Littlefield Education).

Thomas, R. M. (1996). *Comparing Theories of Child Development* (4th ed.). Pacific Grove; CA: Brooks/Cole.

_____ (2000). *Human Development Theories: Windows on Culture,* Thousand Oaks, CA: Sage Publications, Inc.

Thompson, R. A. (2000). Early experience and socialization. In A. Kazdin (Ed.), *Encyclopedia of Psychology*. Washington, DC, & New York: American Psychological Association and Oxford University Press.

Thornberry, T. P., Smith, C. A., & Howard, G. J. (August, 1997). Teenage fatherhood. *Journal of Marriage and the Family*, 51, 505-522.

Tirozzi, G. N, & Uro, G. (March, 1997). Education reform in the United States: National policy in support of local efforts for school improvement, *American Psychologist*, 241-249.

Thornton, A., & Camburn, D. (1989). Religious participation and adolescent sexual behavior. *Journal of Marriage and the Family*, 51, 641-654.

Tizard, S., & Rees, J. (1974). A comparison of the effects of adoption, restoration to the natural mother, and continued institutionalization on the cognitive development of four-year-old children. *Child Development*, 45(1), 91-99.

Tolmie, J. L. (1997). Down syndrome and other autosomal trisomies. In D. J. Rimoin, J. M. Connor, & R. E. Pyeritz (Eds.), *Emery and Rimoin's Principles and Practices of Medical Genetics*. Vol. 1. (3rd ed.). New York: Churchill Livingstone.

Treiman, R., Tinkoff, R., Rodriguez, K., Mouzaki, A., & Francis, D. J. (1998). The foundations of literacy: Learning the sounds of letters. *Child Development,* 8, 213-223.

Treboux, D., & Busch-Rossnagel, N. A. (1990). Social network influence on adolescent sexual attitudes and behaviors. *Journal of Adolescent Research*, 5, 175-189.

Trickett, R. K. (1993). Maladaptive development of school-aged, physically abused children: Relationships with the child rearing context. *Journal of Family Psychology*, 7(1), 134-147.

Trinklein, N. D., Aldred, S. F., Hartman, S. J., Schroeder, D. L., Otillar, D. I., & Myers, R. M. (2004). An abundance of bidirectional promoters in the human genome. *Genome Research,* 14, 62-66.

Tripician, R. J. (January/February, 2000). Confessions of a (former) psychologist. *Skeptical Inquirer*, 44-47.

Troster, H., & Bramberg, M. (1992). Early motor development in blind infants. *Journal of Applied Developmental Psychology*, 14, 83-106.

Tudge, J., & Scrimsher, S. (2003). Lev S. Vygotsky on education: A cultural-historical, interpersonal, and individual approach to development. In B. J. Zimmerman & D. H. Schund (Eds.), *Educational Psychology: A Century of Contributions*. Mahwah, NJ: Erlbaum.

Truglio, R. (April, 2000). Research guides: Sesame Street. Public lecture presented as part of the Consider the Children's Program, Illinois State University, Normal, IL.

Trute, B., Adkins, E., & MacDonald, G. (1996). *Professional Attitudes Regarding Treatment and Punishment of Incest: Comparing Police, Child Welfare, and Community Mental Health*. New York: Plenum Publishing Corporation.

Tsai, M., & Wagner, N. (1979). Incest and molestation: Problems of childhood sexuality. *Resident and Staff Physician*, 129-136.

Twedell, S. *et al.* (1996). Twenty-year experience with repair of complete atrioventricula. *Annals of Thoracic Surgery,* 62(2), 419-424.

UNAIDS (December, 2002). *AIDS Epidemic Update.* http://www.unaids.org (3)

U.S. Bureau of the Census. (2004). *Statistical Abstract of the United States: 2004-2005: The National Data Book.* (124th ed.). Washington, DC: U.S. Government Printing Office.

_____ (1996). *Statistical Abstraction of the United States, 1996* (116th ed.). Washington, DC: Department of Commerce.

_____ (1997). *Statistical Abstract of the United States*: 1986-1997. Washington, DC: U.S. Government Printing Office.

_____ (2000). *Statistical Abstract of the United States* (120th ed.). Washington, DC: U.S. Government Printing Office.

_____ (2002). *Statistical Abstract of the United States* (122nd ed.). Washington, DC: U.S. Government Printing Office.

U.S. Centers for Disease Control. (2000). *Sexually Transmitted Disease Surveillance, 1990.* Atlanta: Author.

U.S. Department of Education (USDE)(2000) *Digest of Educational Statistics 1999.* Washington, DC: U.S. Government Printing Office.

_____(2000) *Digest of Educational Statistics 2000.* Washington, DC: U.S. Government Printing Office.

U.S. Department of Health and Human Services. (2000a). *The Childhood Immunization Initiative.* www.hhs.gov/news/press/2000.

_____ (2000b). *Promoting Better Health for Young People Through Physical Activity and Sports.* Washington, DC: U.S. Government Printing Office.

_____ (2000d). *United States 1999-2000 Health and Injury Chartbook.* Washington, DC: U.S. Government Printing Office.

U.S. Department of Justice. (2000). *Crime in the United States.* Washington, DC: U.S. Government Printing Office.

U.S. Surgeon General. (1994). *Preventing Tobacco Use among Young People: A Report of the Surgeon General.* Washington, DC: U.S. Government Printing Office.

Underwood, L.E. (March/April, 1991). Normal adolescent growth and development, *Nutrition Today*, 11-16.

United Nations Children's Fund (UNICEF). (1994). *The State of the World's Children.* New York: Oxford University Press.

Valencia, R. (1983). Stability of the McCarthy Scales of children's abilities over a one-year period for Mexican-American children. *Psychology in the Schools*, 20-29-34.

Vancouver, J. (2005). The depth of history and explanation or benefit or bane for psychological control theories. *Journal of Applied Psychology*, 90(1), 38-52.

Van Galen, G. P. (1993). Handwriting: A developmental perspective. In A. F. Kalverboer, B. Hopkins, & R. Geuze (Eds.), *Motor Development in Early and Later Childhood: Longitudinal Approaches.* Cambridge: Cambridge University Press.

Van den Boom, D. C. (August, 1997). Sensitivity and attachment: Next step for developmentalists. *Child Development*, 64(4), 592-594.

Van Os, J., & Selton, J. P. (1998). Prenatal exposure to maternal stress and subsequent schizophrenia: The 1940 invasion of the Netherlands. *British Journal of Psychiatry,* 172, 324-326.

Venn, J. J. (Ed.). (2004). *Assessing Children with Special Needs* (3rd ed.). Upper Saddle River, NJ: Pearson.

Venter, J. C., Adams, M. D., Myers, E. W., Li, P. W., Mural, R. J., Sutton, G. G., *et al.* (2001). The sequence of the human genome. *Science*, 291, 1304-1351.

Ventura, S. J. (October-December, 1994). Recent trends in childbearing in the United States. *Statistical Bulletin*, 10-17.

Vinovskis, Maris A. (2005). *The birth of Head Start: preschool education policies in the Kennedy and Johnson administrations* (Chicago: University of Chicago Press).

Vitaro, F., Tremblay, R. E., & Gagnon, C. (1992). Peer rejection from kindergarten to grade 2: Outcomes, correlates, and prediction. *Merrill-Palmer Quarterly,* 38, 382-400.

Vitz, P. (June, 1990). The use of stories in moral development: New psychological reasons for an old education method. *American Psychologist*, 45(6), 709-720.

Von Hofsten, C., & Ronnqvist, L. (1993). The Structuring of neonatal arm movements. *Child Development*, 64, 1046-1057.

Voyer, D., Voyer, S., & Bryden, M. P. (1995). Magnitude of sex differences in spatial abilities: Ameta-analysis and consideration of critical variable. *Psychological Bulletin*, 117, 250-270.

Vygotsky, L. S. (1934). *Thought and Language*. Cambridge, MA: MIT Press.

_____ (1962). *Thought and language*. Cambridge, MA: MIT Press.

_____ (1967). *Vaobraszeniye i Tyorchestyo v Deskom Voraste* (Imagination and Creativity in Childhood). Moscow: (Originally published in 1930).

_____ (1978). *Thought and language*. Cambridge, MA: MIT Press.

_____ (1993). The fundamentals of defectology. In R. W. Rieber & A. S. Carton (Eds.), *The Collected Works of L. S. Vygotsky*, Vol. 2. New York: Plenum. (Original work published 1925).

Wachsler-Felder, J. L., & Golden, C. J. (2002). Neuropsychological consequences of HIV in children: A review of current literature. *Clinical Psychology Review*, 22(13), 411-462.

Wagner, H. M. (1997). *Family Risk Factors for Child and Adolescent Suicidal Behavior*. Washington, DC: American Psychological Association.

Wahlsten, D. (1994). The intelligence of heritability. *Canadian Psychology,* 35, 244-259.

Walden, T. (1991). Infant social referencing. In J. Garber & E. Dodge (Eds.), *The Development of Emotional Regulation and Dysregulation*. New York: Cambridge University Press.

Walden, T, & Garber, J. (1994). Emotional development. In M. Rutter & D. Hay (Eds.), *Development Through Life Span: A Handbook for Clinicians,* Oxford: Blackwell.

Walker, H. M., Severson, H. H., Feil, E. G., Stiller, B., & Golly, A. (July, 1998). First step to success intervening at the point of school entry to prevent antisocial behavior patterns. *Psychology in the Schools*, 15(3), 259-269.

Wallerstein, J. S. (1984). Children of divorce: Preliminary report of a ten-year follow-up study of young children. *American Journal of Orthopsychiatry*, 54, 444-458.

_____ (1984a). Parent-child relations following divorce. In J. Anthony & C. Chiland (Eds.), *Clinical Parenthood*. Vol. 8, *The Yearbook of the International Association of Child and Adolescent Psychiatry*. New York: Wiley.

_____ (1985). Children of divorce: Preliminary report of a ten-year follow-up of older children and adolescents. *Journal of the American Academy of Child Psychiatry*, 24, 545-553.

_____ (1987). Children of divorce: Report of a ten-year follow-up of early latency-age children. *American Journal of Orthopsychiatry*, 57(2), 191-211.

Wallerstein, J. S., & Blakeslee, S. (1989). *Second Chances: Men, Women, and Children a Decade After Divorce*. New York: Ticknor & Field.

Wallerstein, J., Lewis, J.M., & Blakeslee, (2000). *The Unexpected Legacy of Divorce,* New York: Hyperion.

Walters, J., Roberts, A. R., & Morgen, K. (1997). High risk pregnancies: Teenagers, poverty, and drug abuse. *Journal of Drug Issues*, 27(3), 541-562.

Wardle, F. (2003). *Introduction to Special Education*. Boston: Allyn & Bacon.

Waters, E., *et al.* (2000). Attachment security in infancy and early adulthood: A twenty-year longitudinal study. *Child Development,* 71, 684-689.

Watson, J. B. (1930). *Behaviorism*. Chicago: Chicago University Press.

Watson, J. B., & Rayner, R. (1930). Conditioned emotional reactions. *Journal of Experimental Psychology*, 3, 1-4.

Watson, J. L. (1995). *Improving Communication between Regular Students and a Physically Impaired Nonverbal Child Using Alternative Communication Systems in the Kindergarten Classroom.* Nova University, Abraham S. Fischler Center for the Advancement of Education. Solana Beach, CA: Mayer-Johnson Co. (ERIC Document Reproduction Service No. ED 393 256).

Webster, W. S., & Freeman, J. A. (2003). Prescription drugs and pregnancy. *Expert Opinions in Pharmacotherapy*, 4, 949-961.

Wechsler, D. (1944). *The Measurement of Adult Intelligence* (3rd. ed.) Baltimore: Williams & Wilkins.

_____ (1992). *The Wechsler Preschool and Primary Scales of Intelligence-Revised,* San Antonio, TX: Psychological Corporation.

_____ (1994). *The Wechsler Intelligence Scale for Children.*(3rd ed.). San Antonio, TX: Psychological Corporation.

_____ (2003). *The Wechsler Intelligence Scale for Children.*(4th ed.). San Antonio, TX: Psychological Corporation.

Wehman, P. (1997). *Exceptional Individuals in School, Community and Work.* Austin, TX: Pro-Ed.

Weil, A., Director (January, 1999). *Snapshots of America's Families: Assessing the New Federalism.* Washington, DC: The Urban Institute press.

Weinstock, H., Berman, S., & Cates, Jr., W. (2004). Sexually transmitted diseases among American youth: Incidence and prevalence estimates, 2000. *Perspectives on Sexual and Reproductive Health, 36,* 6010.

Weiss, G. (November 15, 1990). Hyperactivity in childhood, *The New England Journal of Medicine,* 20, 1413-1415.

Werker, J. F. (April, 1987). Infants prefer parentese. Paper presented at the Biennial Meeting of the Society for Research in Child Development, Baltimore.

Werner, H. (1948). *Comparative Psychology of Mental Development.* Chicago: Follett.

Westinghouse Corporation and Ohio University (1973). The impact of Head Start: An evaluation of the effects of Head Start on children's cognitive development. In J. L. Frost (Ed.), *Revisiting Early Childhood Education.* New York: Holt, Rinehart & Winston.

Wheeler, Derek S.; Wong, Hector R. and Shanley, Thomas P. editors (2007). *Pediatric critical care medicine: basic science and clinical evidence* (London: Springer).

Whitaker, R. C., Wright, J. A., Pepe, M. S., Seidel, K. D., & Dietz, W. H. (1997). Predicting obesity in young adulthood from childhood and parental obesity. *New England Journal of Medicine,* 327, 860-872.

Whitehurst, G. J., & Lonigan, C. J. (1998). Child development and emergent literacy. *Child Development,* 68, 848-872.

Whitehurst, G. J., Zevenbergen, A. A., Crone, D. A., Schultz, M. D., Velting, O. N., & Fischel, J. E. (1999). Outcomes of an emergent literacy intervention for Head Start through second grade. *Journal of Educational Psychology,* 91(2), 261-272.

Whitley, Jr., B. E. (1996). *Principles of Research in Behavioral Science.* Mountain View, CA: Mayfield.

_____(2002). *Principles of Research in Behavioral Science* (2nd ed.). New York: McGraw-Hill.

Wicks-Nelson, R., & Israel, A. C. (1991). *Behavior Disorder of Children* (2nd ed.). Englewood Cliffs, NJ: Prentice-Hall.

Wickelgren, I. (1997). Getting a grasp on working memory. *Science,* 275, 1580-1582.

Widdowson, E. M. (1951). Mental contentment and physical growth. *The Lancet,* 1, 1316-1318.

Wierson, M., Long, P. J., Forehand, R. L. (1993). Toward a new understanding of early menarche: The role of environmental stress in pubertal timing. *Adolescence,* 28, 13-24.

Wigfield, A., & Eccles, J. S. (1994). Children's competency beliefs, achievement values, and general self-esteem: Changes across elementary and middle school. *Journal of Early Adolescence,* 14, 107-138.

Wilfond, B.S. (May, 1999). Genetic testing in children: Ethical issues of research and practice. Paper presented at the meeting of the Society for Pediatric Research, San Francisco.

Williams, C. L., & Bollela, M. (1993). Treatment of childhood obesity in practice. *Annals of New York Academy of Sciences,* 699, 207-219.

Williams, S. R. (1989). *Nutrition and Diet Therapy* (6th. ed). St. Louis: Mosby.

Williams, W., & Evans, J. W. (September, 1969). Evaluation: The care of Head Start, *Annals of the American Academy Political and Social Sciences,* 385-122.

Wine, J. (1971). Test anxiety and direction of attention. *Psychological Bulletin,* 76, 92-104.

Winer, G. A. (1982). A review and analysis of children's fearful behavior in dental settings. *Child Development,* 53, 1111-1133.

Winik, M., Brazel, J., & Rosso, P. (1972). *Nutrition and Development.* New York: Wiley.

Wisotsky W., & Swencionis, C. (2003). Cognitive-behavioral approaches to the management of obesity. *Adolescent Medicine*, 14, 37-48.

Wolfe, D. A. (1999). *Child Abuse: Implications for Child Development and Psychopatholgy* (2nd ed.). Thousand Oaks, CA: Sage Publications, Inc.

Wolfe, S. M. *et al.* (2005). *Worst Pills: Best Pills.* New York: Pocket Books.

Wolff, H. (1966). The causes, controls, and organizations of behaviors in the newborn. *Psychological Issues*, 5(1, Whole No. 17) 1-105.

Wolff, P. H. (1969). The natural history of crying and other vocalizations in early infancy. In B. M. Foss (Ed.), *Determinants of Infant Behavior.* Vol. 4. London: Methuen.

_____ (1996). The causes, controls and organization of behavior in the newborn. *Psychological Issues,* 5, 1-105.

Wolk, S. I., & Weissman, M. M. (June 1, 1996). Suicidal behavior in depressed children grown up: Preliminary results of a longitudinal study. *Psychiatric Annals,* 331-333.

Wolpe, J. (1958). *Psychotherapy by Reciprocal Inhibition.* Stanford, CA: Stanford University Press.

Wong, D. L., Hockenberry-Eaton, M., Wilson, D., Winkelstein, M. L., & Schwartz, P. (2001). *Wong's Essentials of Pediatric Nursing* (6th ed.). St. Louis.

Wong, D. L., Hockenberry, M. J., Wilson, D., Winkelstein, M. L., & Kline, N. E. (2003). *Whaler & Wong's Nursing Care of Infants and Children.* St. Louis: Mosby.

Wong, E. Y., Gohlke, J., Griffith, W. C., Farrow, S., & Faustman, E. M. (2004). Assessing the health benefits of air pollution reduction in children. *Environmental Health Perspectives,* 112, 226-232.

Woodward, A. L., & Markman, E.M. (1998). Early Word Learning. In W. Damon (Ed.), *Handbook of Child Psychology.* Vol. 2. New York: Wiley.

Woodward, L., Taylor, E., & Dowdey, L. (1998). The Parenting and Family Functioning of Children with Hyperactivity. *Journal of Child Psychoanalysis and Psychiatry,* 141-169.

Woodward, S. A., *et al. (2001).* Infant temperament and the brainstem auditory evoked response in later childhood. *Developmental Psychology,* 17, 533-538.

World Health Organization. (2005). *Sexually Transmitted Infections among Adolescents: Issues in Adolescent Health and Development.* Geneva, Switzerland: Author.

Wray, H. (June, 1982). The evolution of child abuse. *Science News,* 24-26.

Wright, V. C., *et al.* (2003). Assisted reproductive technology surveillance — United States, 2000. Division of Reproductive Health, National Center for Chronic Disease Prevention and Health Promotion (Online). Available at http// www.cdc.gov/record.

Yablonsky, L. (2000). *Juvenile Delinquency into the 21st Century.* Belmont, CA: Wadsworth Thompson Learning.

Yang, Q., Rasmussen, A. A., & Friedman, J. M. (March 23, 2002). Mortality associated with Down's syndrome in the USA from 1983 to 1997; A population-based study. *The Lancet,* 350, 1019-1025.

Yanovski, J. A., & Yanovski, S. Z. (October 27, 1999). Recent advances in basic obesity research. *Journal of the American Medical Association,* 282(16), 1504-1506.

Yoon, Paula, W. *et al.* (1996). *Advanced Maternal Age and the Risk of Down Syndrome Characterized by the Meiotic Stage of the Chromosomal Error: A Population-Based Study.* Atlanta, GA: The American Society of Human Genetics.

Young, S. (November, 1990). In the pink: A parents' manual of baby body basics. *Child,* 76-80.

Young, W. C., Goy, R. W., & Phoenix, C. H. (1964). Hormones and Sexual Behavior. *Science,* 143, 212-218.

Zigler, E., & Gilman, E. (1998). The Legacy of Jean Piaget. In G. A. Kimble, M. Wertheimer, *et al.* (Eds.), *Portraits of Pioneers in Psychology.* Vol. 3. Mahwah, NJ: Erlbaum.

Zimmerman, B. J., & Schunk, D. H. (2004). Self-regulating intellectual processes and outcomes: A social cognitive perspective. In D. Y. Dai & R. J. Sternberg (Eds.), *Motivation, Emotion, and Cognition.* Mahwah, NJ: Erlbaum.

INDEX